D1163609

TIDEWATER'S NAVY

Ships of the Great White Fleet steam out of Hampton Roads for Thimble Shoals Channel at the start of their record-setting, world-circling cruise in December 1907. *U.S. Naval Institute*

TIDEWATER'S NAVY

AN ILLUSTRATED HISTORY

Bruce Linder

NAVAL INSTITUTE PRESS
Annapolis, Maryland

Naval Institute Press
291 Wood Road
Annapolis, MD 21402

Library of Congress Cataloging-in-Publication Data
Linder, Bruce, 1949–
Tidewater's navy: an illustrated history / Bruce Linder.
p. cm.
Includes bibliographical reference and index.
ISBN 1-59114-465-5 (alk. paper)
1. Navy–yards and naval stations—Virginia—Tidewater (Region)
2. Tidewater (Va.: Region)—History, Naval. I. Title.
VA70.T5356 2005
359.7′09755′521022--dc22
2005019790

Printed in the United States of America on acid-free paper ∞

12 11 10 09 08 07 06 05 9 8 7 6 5 4 3 2
First Printing

To Deb—my inspiration.

CONTENTS

LOGBOOK. Ship-of-the-line *Delaware*.

Saturday, 16 January 1830 at anchor in Hampton Roads:

12 noon (Meridian): Strong gales from the South and heavy rainy weather.
At 2, sent down Topgallant yards.
At 3, called all hands. Weighed anchor and made sail standing up for Norfolk.
At 3.30, passed Craney Island.
At 4, aground 2 miles south of Craney Island, took in sail.
At 5.30, took a kedge out astern waiting for tide.
From 4 to 6, heavy gales and, from 6 to 8, the same with constant rain.
From 8 to midnight, blowing hard from NNE with rain.
From Midnight to 4 A.M., fresh breezes from the NNE and cloudy.
At 2.30, the ship went off, slipped the stern hauser, hoisted the jib.
At 3 A.M., came to off Town Point with the starboard anchor in 6 fathoms water veered to 30 fathoms cable.
From 4 to 8 A.M., moderate breezes from the North.
From 8 to Meridian, moderate breezes from the North and pleasant weather.
At 9, fired a salute of 13 guns which was returned from the Navy Yard.
At 10, moored ship 30 fathoms on each cable. Received on board 1,000 pounds fresh beef with vegetables for the crew. Lighters from the Navy Yard alongside for the powder.

. . . . A simple page torn from a leather-bound logbook of yesteryear, each word carefully inked by quill and bottled ink

. . . but one that would be as clear to a naval officer today as it was two hundred years ago

. . . a consummate and timeless picture of Tidewater's Navy.

FOREWORD

The history of the Navy in Hampton Roads and the lower Chesapeake—that gate to the Atlantic that swings on the hinges of Cape Charles and Cape Henry—is very nearly the history of the United States Navy itself. And conjointly, as compatible as the stars and stripes on the American flag, the story of Tidewater Virginia's relations with the Navy is very nearly the history of Tidewater itself.

Like certain other sea-penetrated regions of the world—the Hellespont, the English Channel, the Strait of Hormuz—the unique geography, hydrography, culture, and commerce of the Tidewater have left their mark on each page of the Navy's history here. And the Navy, in turn, has left its footprint on nearly every part of this sandy, sea-girt land.

I myself was wearing a uniform when I first saw the Tidewater. I've sailed, explored, and written about its beaches and bays and rivers for nearly forty years now, both on duty and for pleasure; and today I make it my home. Hearing the roar of jet engines overhead or admiring the rake of a gray superstructure cutting past the Hampton Roads bridge-tunnel or the jaunty saunter of a Marine out on the town, no visitor or resident can possibly forget even for a day that this area hosts the greatest fleet concentration in the world.

But this was not always so—though for almost two hundred years Virginia was an important port of call for the Royal Navy.

The first English settlers recognized the fertile, forested lands bounding the lower Bay as potentially profitable. But with ownership came the necessity of vigilance. The Jamestown settlers posted coast-watchers at Old Point Comfort to sound the alarm if a hostile sail rose into view. For four hundred years now, that watch has been kept in the Tidewater.

Norfolk's history began in 1680, when Charles II ordered towns be created to act as ports for seaborne trade. Tobacco out, English-made goods in, was the foundation of commerce then.

On New Year's Day, 1776, four Royal Navy ships drew up to the wharf and opened with their guns. What was left of the waterfront, the British set fire to.

This attack was part of an internecine war as brutal as anything in the Middle East today. Tories and Revolutionaries executed each other. Loyalist guerrillas called Picaroons raided farms and villages on orders from the last royal governor. One citizen who objected to the confiscation of his livestock was nailed to his own barn door. It took fifty years for this zealous conflict to end.

Norfolk was quickly rebuilt. One of the first Continental Navy yards began supporting the U.S. fleet in Portsmouth, beginning a tradition that still continues.

The momentous years of 1861 through 1865 saw the abandonment, burning, and capture of the Navy Yard, the fitting out of southern raiders, and, most famously, the battle of the great ironclads, whose names will forever be linked to Hampton Roads. Union power, based in Fort Monroe, barred the Confederacy's door to the outer world, until Appomattox brought down the curtain on the bloodiest war in our history.

The next great attack on this linchpin of American sea power came not quite halfway through the twentieth century. German U-boats descended on the unprepared Chesapeake approaches beginning in January 1942. They targeted ships silhouetted against the lights of Virginia Beach, and waterfront residents watched the night sky flame as tankers burned. But gradually this enemy too was pushed back and finally defeated.

The yearned-for peace after 1945 yielded to a new threat. For almost forty years the naval forces built, repaired, and based here deterred Soviet aggression around the world. But even as the Cold War ebbed, a new adversary was emerging. On September 11, 2001, our leaders, intelligence services, and armed forces were surprised again by a determined enemy.

History is the record of change. But one constant remains: over and over, the Navy and Marine Corps have been the linchpin of our defense. And over and over, so has southeastern Virginia.

The Roads and the Chesapeake have always been the most direct thoroughfare to the heart of America. This was true when the Colonies huddled along the sea; it is no less so now, as our population migrates back to the coastlines. The mountains of containers passing through Norfolk, Newport News, and Portsmouth testify that the maritime commerce that built our area in the 1600s is no less vital today. It has always made eminent military sense to our enemies that to strike at the United States, one strikes here first. If we wish to defend our country, we must do so from this watery foothold as well.

Just as fascinating as the movement and countermovement of fleets and armies is the story of how Navy men and women have interacted with their civilian hosts. Not every local resident welcomed the huge military influxes of World War I and II. The relationship is much warmer today. Many enlisted men and women now have families and interact with the community much more than the bachelor sailor used to. Retirees settle here. Business and civic leaders now recognize and celebrate their role in the country's defense, courting the Navy to boost the region's economy. And why not? The most modern armed forces on the planet give Tidewater unparalleled access to new technologies and intellectual trends.

This volume records all these stories and more. Bruce Linder, author of the critically acclaimed *San Diego's Navy*, has done it again. With over 300 pages, 225 photos (over half of them never published before, from deep in archives and repositories), copious footnotes, and groundbreaking research, it is the most detailed, comprehensive, and robust narrative of the Navy in Tidewater Virginia ever compiled. I will keep it in a convenient place on my reference shelf, and I recommend it without reservation for yours.

With cordial best wishes,
Dave Poyer

PREFACE

The Shakespearean adage that "what's past is prologue" speaks volumes about the U.S. Navy's uncommon relationship with the Virginia Tidewater, for its storied past has shaped its present and portends its future. Just as relevant in defining the distinctive relationship between Tidewater and its Navy is a sign at the Hampton Roads Naval Museum and battleship *Wisconsin* that declares simply that Norfolk is the "Homeport of Navy History."

Between these two maxims lies the premise of this book.

The chop of the sea, an invigorating tang to the air, a limitless horizon, a far-off darkening and squally sky are as they have been for thousands of years. Aboard a warship approaching Hampton Roads from sea, it is possible, in a sense, to take a step away from the present and be touched by the past. This is not the history of dog-eared textbooks or dusty museum cases. Naval history in Tidewater is alive and exhilarating and can be felt in the sway of a ship, the damp of a gunwale, or a breeze on the cheek.

The waters off the Virginia Capes can ignite the soul like no others. Feel the fresh dew on a morning deck, spy a dazzling wake curving away in a churning arc, or hear gulls soaring in pursuit of your stern. Each of these would have been equally apparent to Stephen Decatur conning frigate *United States* on a larboard tack, Robney Evans forming the Great White Fleet into steaming divisions, or Bull Halsey ordering carrier *Yorktown* into the wind. Ships approaching the Chesapeake today from the northeast trace the same course as *Monitor*, from due east spy Cape Henry just as a German U-boat commander would, and from the southeast share the water with the ghosts of the Battle of the Virginia Capes. At sea, within this captivating vortex of time, history, and circumstance, 2005 feels much like 1776 or 1898 or 1941.

You cannot say the Navy's presence in Tidewater is an accident, nor can its story be drawn with a straightedge and pencil across a nautical chart. It is a story of zigs and zags, of sudden rushes and lengthy doldrums, of tempests in the night, and of careful sculling around exposed hazards and unknown shoals. It is the story of the bounty of Virginia's soil, of the mind of a Swedish inventor, of a meteor from deepest space, of the California Gold Rush, of small children standing pierside, and of bubble gum and bailing wire.

Naval history is as alive, as tangible, and as stirring in this region as anywhere else in the nation. The cities clustered around Hampton Roads owe their current cachet to that history, and how the people of the great Virginia Tidewater think of themselves springs in large part from the maritime traditions and culture of a score of generations. The Navy is a portal through which Norfolk views the world, and through which the world views Norfolk.

As its story is retold a thousand times, the naval history of Tidewater has the power to invoke vivid memories—for much of its setting and its connection with the enduring sea remain as genuine today as they would have been to any American bluejacket two hundred years ago. Every sailor worth his salt can be stirred by the thought of a sailing frigate in a topgallant breeze, every line taut, every snow-white sail drawing, every spar scraping the sky, with the Stars and Stripes flickering at the mizzen halyard. Every engineer can readily identify with the hiss and rush of steam, a shower of soot drifting to windward, the thumping of machinery, the clank of chain cable, or the touch of white at the stern.

Across Virginia's Tidewater, the Navy's past has shaped what we see today on every waterfront; it is the prologue to that shining future just over the cloud-flecked horizon.

Tidewater's Navy is the history of this incomparable region as seen through the lens of a quarterdeck long-glass. Its perspective may be relatively narrow, but its breadth is exhilarating and expansive.

ACKNOWLEDGMENTS

One cannot go far in any history with a regional focus without the enthusiastic support of many people who specialize in the flavor, the culture, and the feel of the land, the sky, and the water—the *essence* of a specific locale. In many cases their insight, guidance, and sensitivity go much further than simply guiding the historian—they add the most important of all ingredients to a successful endeavor, they add *perspective*. I was blessed with the help of many who fit this mold and were willing to help, including Joe Mosier of the Jean Outland Chrysler Library; Alice Hanes, curator of history at the Naval Shipyard Museum in Portsmouth; Dr. William Andrews, professor emeritus at Eastern Virginia Medical School and past president of the Norfolk Navy League; and Joe M. Law, former public affairs officer and historian of Norfolk Naval Shipyard. Although we never met, I count historian and prolific writer Alan Flanders in this list; I have kept close track of his periodic historical column in the Portsmouth *Currents*.

Of primary assistance in understanding the naval imprint on Hampton Roads were the insightful professionals of the internationally recognized Hampton Roads Naval Museum at the Nauticus National Maritime Center. Their collection of naval memorabilia, their impressive displays, and their infectious enthusiasm for all things Navy across Hampton Roads spurred me from my first minute of research. Of particular note was assistance from the museum's director, Becky Poulliot, curator Joe Judge, and editor of the incomparable *Daybook,* Gordon Calhoun. They are the conscience of the history of this important corner of the Navy, and there is no one who is better qualified to speak on these matters. Their willingness to go to any length to protect this incredible story for the present and future generations is an eloquent editorial on the importance of history to the Virginia Tidewater.

Norfolk Naval Shipyard, which describes itself as the U.S. Navy's oldest, is a natural lodestone for the naval historian, and public affairs officer Steve Milner proved to be the perfect navigator through those venerable brick buildings and granite structures. His enthusiasm for the value of the historic record was a tremendous boon for my research, and his introduction to Susan Fleming, Mel Gipson, and Bill Black of the shipyard's photo lab allowed me to tap a golden resource of dusty negatives, antique glass plate photos, and exciting panoramas.

Rear Adm. Stephen Turcotte of Navy Region, Mid-Atlantic, lent his support and ideas to my planning, as did Navy public affairs officer Lt. Cdr. Ron Hill. Roger Clapp, force historian of the Naval Special Warfare Command, helped with details of UDT and SEAL history. Jack Hornbeck of the Hampton Roads Chamber of Commerce helped me understand the interaction between the Navy and his organization. Congressman G. William Whitehurst graciously allowed me to interrupt a lunch and then chatted eloquently about the intricacies of the Navy–Hampton Roads interface.

Special thanks to my dear friend and colleague Miriam Browning, who contributed original material about Little Creek from her father, Lt. Harold Freeman, USNR (Ret.), to David Ridgway for his seagoing insight and pictures of LSM training drawn literally from his attic, and to Lt. (jg) Courtenay Smith of the guided missile frigate *Elrod,* who reeducated me on the particulars of Thimble Shoals Channel.

The assistance, advice, and long-lost remembrances from the following individuals formed the backbone of my efforts to get a host of details right: Capt. Bud Reynolds, Rear Adm. Christopher Cole, Capt. Ray Boucree, Capt. Dana Roberts, Capt. Mike Duncan, Capt. Gerry Nifontoff, Robert E. DeVary, Capt. Steve Laabs, and Jeff Kibben.

Librarian Robert Hitchings of the Sargeant Memorial Room of the Norfolk Public Library knows more about local history than I can fit into twenty volumes. He helped me make the most of my rushed hours as a guest in his venerable domain. I owe thanks as well to Glenn E. Helm, head of reference at the Navy Department Library in Washington, DC, the enthusiastic photographic staff of the Naval Historical Foundation, Mac MacDonald and Theo Elbert of the National Museum of Naval Aviation in Pensacola, Sarah Tapper and Cynthia Malinick of the Stephen Decatur House Museum in Washington, DC, Charles Johnson at the National Archives in Washington, DC, John V. Quarstein of the Virginia War Museum, Tom Twomey for his unmatched photographic sense, and the excellent and patient staff of the Mariner's Museum Library in Newport News.

The Naval Institute Press provided an inspiring level of support for this project at every turn and set high standards for perfection. I am particularly thankful to my good friends Paul Stillwell, Fred Rainbow, Donna Doyle, Susan Artigiani, Brian Walker, Tom Cutler, and Linda O'Doughda, who all assisted. David Stebbing generously helped with editing and proofing.

Some of my first memories of the Navy are of a wardroom dinner aboard *Pocono* at the NOB waterfront when I was but nine years of age and a television broadcast of an Army-Navy game at a hangar ready room at Breezy Point, compliments of my dad, Rear Adm. Sam Linder. This is rivaled only by an early remembrance of my mom patiently coaching me through a childhood sketch of the battleship *Iowa* at those same piers. It was a thoughtful introduction to Norfolk and its Navy, and it helped me even from that early age to begin to develop that all-important *perspective*.

TIDEWATER'S NAVY

PROLOGUE

To a sailor, a "roads" is a place of safety, a sanctuary from evil tempests, a protected harbor. The nuances associated with a "roads" are doubly satisfying, as they suggest both a pleasurable and longed-for respite after a long and dangerous cruise and an anchorage full of optimism and promise where vessels are carefully prepared for voyages of profit and discovery. The finest nautical roads are icons of commerce, concentration points for profitable trade, and magnets for the rich and influential. Along their shores generations of mariners are nurtured and eclectic cottage industries for shipwrights, sailmakers, and maritime engineers are spawned. The world's preeminent nautical roads are frequently economic prizes, coveted by others, giving rise to the ready presence of a nation's warships poised for their defense.

Hampton Roads has been all of this and much more. Named for the English Earl of Southampton (a financial supporter of Jamestown's Virginia Company), Hampton Roads stands as a great expanse of protected water surrounded by gentle shores. It generates its own mystique, set as it is at the convergence of the sparkle of Virginia's rivers, the lively essence of the Chesapeake, and the salt and spindrift of the untamed Atlantic. The wealth of nations touches its shores; the mettle of mariners opens its treasures. This navigational waypoint known the world over, this subject of chanteys and lore, this trading megaport owes its distinction foremost to geography.

The Hampton Roads we know today is heir to millions of years of sculpting by titanic natural forces, from the cataclysmic to the subtle. Deep in the primordial past, between 65 and 200 million years ago, the tectonic forces of continental drift began to widen the early Atlantic Ocean, and streams draining the ancestral Appalachian Mountains began to cut deep basins for what would become the modern Susquehanna, Potomac, and James rivers. As years passed, the eastward flowing rivers of Virginia became well established, and river sediment began forming today's distinctive flat coastal plain, where the newborn James probably formed a broad river delta near current Albemarle Sound.[1]

This natural progression was savagely disrupted in the literal blink of an eye 35 million years ago when a meteor or comet streaked across the eastern seaboard and plunged into the water near Cape Charles. Its fiery passage penetrated water, sediment, and deep into the bedrock, and its cataclysmic shockwave formed an impact crater 1.2 miles deep and 50 miles across, with a southern rim of high-packed debris sweeping from Newport News to northern Norfolk, Virginia Beach, and Cape Henry.[2]

River drainage from the Susquehanna to the James began to converge on the crater. The crater's southern wall bisected the James River's flow and turned its course sharply northeastward to capture the outflow of both the Nansemond and Elizabeth rivers and draw them into a single large bight—the Hampton Roads of today.[3] The rushing flow of the Susquehanna River turned southward to gouge a pathway toward the impact crater that would form the long axis of what would become Chesapeake Bay.

Over the last million years, alternating glacial (lasting about one hundred thousand years) and interglacial (about ten thousand years) periods caused ocean water levels to rise and fall, the bay to fill and drain, and soft coastal plain sediments to build with each cycle. During the most recent cycle the Chesapeake Bay has filled with water to its present size, drowning its river basins.[4] Formed by tidal water, the mud of Hampton Roads contains mud drawn from the clay of the Chesapeake's western cliffs, sand from the Eastern Shore, and silt from inland rivers. This inhospitable carpet of mud, which challenges the unwary mariner daily, has been given such colorful names as Thimble Shoals, Tail of the Horseshoe, and Middle Ground.

The product of millions of years of evolution, the Virginia Tidewater, pristine and welcoming, opened its arms to its first European visitors with the dawn of the sixteenth century. Those first visitors would be mariners, armed to the teeth against adversity, and drawn to a land of storied riches and destiny.

The French under Verrazzano and the Spanish under Estevan Gomes sailed past the Chesapeake in 1524, and Spaniard Pedro de Quejo first mapped the entrance to the bay that he called Bahía de Santa Maria. Englishman John Rut followed in 1527, another French ship called in 1546, and, in 1561, Pedro Menéndez de Avilés sailed *Santa Catalina* from Havana to chart the bay for its first settlement, a short-lived Spanish Jesuit mission on the shores of the York River in 1570.[5]

By the time Capt. Christopher Newport's three small ships of the Virginia Company sighted what he would call Cape Henry on 26 April 1607, Englishmen already had read much about the promising shores of Virginia. After short excursions around Cape Henry and then across Hampton Roads to a site that gave them "good comfort" (named "Cape Comfort" or Point Comfort), the colonists ventured farther up the James River to land at Jamestown Island by 14 May.[6]

With settlements came crops and with crops came the lucrative promise of trade, with the Virginia Tidewater uniquely advantaged for trade by its abundant natural waterways. Tidewater planters profited handsomely in the trade of tobacco, lumber, wheat, and corn delivered along oceanic pathways to England or the West Indies. But with prosperity also came the threat of attacks from nations at war or privateers lurking off the Chesapeake coast, and thus defense became a key priority of the colonial government.

In 1667 the Virginia Council petitioned the Royal Navy to assign a permanent guard ship in the Chesapeake to protect trade and defend the countryside against marauders. Frigate *Elizabeth* of 46 guns became the first of many British warships sent sporadically to the "Virginia Station," but she fell victim to a five-ship Dutch squadron. Although defensive forts would be constructed, it quickly became apparent that only patrolling warships could properly protect the great expanse of the Bay. In 1684, the Royal Navy assigned the ketch *Quaker* and then other small vessels to Virginia's defense. The frigate *Shoreham* of 28 guns arrived in 1700, and frigate *Southampton* of 48 guns, a year later.[7] Soon, "hired ships" armed by colonial decree joined vessels carrying the red and white naval banner of His Britannic Majesty in patrols that allowed the Tidewater maritime community to mature and prosper.

The Tidewater landowner in the best position to profit by improved safety and maritime commerce was Capt. Thomas Willoughby, who owned extensive holdings along the Elizabeth River and Hampton Roads during the seventeenth century. Willoughby had arrived in Virginia in 1610 at age nine as a passenger on *Prosperous* and across his life volunteered for the militia, rose to be justice of Elizabeth City, and served as a colonial burgess and councilor.[8] He built his manor house on Willoughby Point and counted within his sweeping land the current sites of the Norfolk waterfront, the Naval Hospital, and the Naval Air Station.[9]

Willoughby's neighbor during this time was Henry Seawell, who settled in Elizabeth City County by 1629. According to a record made shortly after December 1633, Seawell did "cleare, seate, build and plant" on 150 acres of the tract later known by his name, Seawell's Pointe (now Sewell's Point) at the mouth of the Elizabeth River. Seawell married Willoughby's daughter Alice and prospered in the tobacco trade.[10]

After Dutch raids across the lower Chesapeake during the mid-1600s, the Virginia Assembly authorized construction of a fort south of Sewell's Point at Four Farthing Point in lower Norfolk County. The presence of the fort attracted ships, which anchored in its shadow for safety, as well as the Crown's guardships, which could refit or careen in security along the river. At the same time, the Virginia Assembly passed an act providing for a town in "Lower Norfolk County on . . . land on the Eastern Branch of the Elizabeth River at the entrance of the Branch." John Ferebee formally surveyed the site chosen for "Norfolk Towne," and on 16 August 1682, Lt. Col. Anthony Lawson and Captain William Robinson, acting on behalf of the county court, bought the town site for ten thousand pounds of tobacco in casks.[11]

As fertile as the colonial Tidewater proved to be for its planters and plantation owners, its true prosperity depended on the vitality of its trading links. Norfolk Towne grew rapidly, the beneficiary of rapidly expanding trade, and the people across Tidewater were soon speaking with a personality distinct from Richmond, Alexandria, Carolina, or Baltimore—a blend of a planter's savvy, a trader's intensity, and a sailor's braggadocio, seasoned with a wide worldview and a flinty pragmatism.

By 1728, Col. William Byrd II described Norfolk as having

> more the air of a town of any in Virginia. There were then near twenty brigantines and sloops riding at the wharves, and oftentimes they have more. . . . The town is built on a level spot of ground along the Elizabeth River, the banks whereof are neither high as to make the landing of goods troublesome or so low as to be in danger of overflowing. The streets are straight and adorned with several good houses, which increase every day. Its inhabitants consist of merchants, ship carpenters, and other useful artisans, with sailors enough to manage their navigation. . . . The two cardinal virtues that make a place thrive, industry and frugality, are seen here in perfection.[12]

The livelihood of everyone in Tidewater, it seemed, depended on the viability of maritime commerce, and its protection became a constant concern. As privateers, pirates, and enemy navies periodically menaced the coast, "the course of events in the seventeenth and eighteenth centuries demonstrated that the Chesapeake could be defended only by a naval force and not by troops, batteries, or forts," according to historian Arthur Pierce Middleton. "The maintenance of an adequate squadron of warships was quite beyond the financial resources of the tobacco colonies. Because of the Bay, then, the Chesapeake colonists were even more dependent upon Great Britain for their defense than were the other continental colonies.[13]

Prosperity, trade, livelihood, defense, the Navy—all would blur together in a natural alliance to shape the Virginia Tidewater across more than three centuries.

1776

New Year's Day 1776 dawned steely cold and gray—anything but joyous—along the shores of a bleak Elizabeth River. For days, an unbroken file of wagons and carriages had carried Norfolk residents slowly away from the city in a sad exodus driven by revolution and civil convulsion. Few walked the deserted streets; the once-teaming waterfront lacked its normal forest of masts and spars. Small groups of Virginia militia gathered around thin curls of smoke rising from cooking fires.

Tory and Patriot forces faced each other in a tenuous standoff in southeastern Virginia. The Royal Governor of Virginia, Lord Dunmore, controlled the water with the power of the Royal Navy behind him; he had built up a sanctuary of brigantines, sloops, and schooners at anchor in Hampton Roads for hundreds of Loyalists and their families. Patriot Virginians, fresh from routing Dunmore's British regulars at Great Bridge, held sway over Norfolk, Portsmouth, and surrounding communities.

John Murray, fourth Earl of Dunmore, was clearly the focus of Patriot ire. Few colonials harbored a neutral view of his authority, which was symbolic of the strength and omnipotence of the Crown. As revolutionary fervor rose throughout Virginia during the spring of 1775, Lord Dunmore was not conciliatory. He ordered powder removed from the magazine in Williamsburg, issued proclamations urging all to "repair to my assistance," and threatened the destruction of those who opposed him. By the end of April 1775, Dunmore had declared Virginia to be in rebellion. Lady Dunmore fled with her children to HMS *Fowey* (20)* and HM schooner *Magdalen* at Yorktown, and Dunmore joined them aboard the *Fowey* after midnight on 7 June. In the face of escalating sedition, Dunmore crafted a scheme to extinguish the rebellion, with the Royal Navy and the communities of Hampton Roads forming two poles of his strategy. The Royal Navy possessed the strength and discipline he would need to prevail and the mobility required to penetrate deep into the Virginia countryside along its numerous rivers and watercourses. Dunmore considered the Tory element to be strong in Norfolk, buoyed by the support of many Scottish merchants whose fortunes depended on trade with Great Britain.[1]

There was significant logic to Dunmore's strategy of turning Norfolk into a Loyalist stronghold and base for his efforts to retake Virginia. It was a bustling and growing seaport and one of the largest towns in Virginia, with a prosperous merchant class with strong ties to English and European trading markets. The region's abundant access to the sea would also promise Dunmore both the heavy guns of the Royal Navy and a ready flow of troops from English commanders.

On 15 July 1775, Dunmore placed his plan in motion by boarding HM sloop *Otter* (16) and ordering her to sail to the Elizabeth River to join the 14th Regiment of British regulars and HMS *Mercury* of 20 guns. Dunmore took over several

** The number in parentheses indicates a sailing warship's rating, roughly equivalent to the number of guns she was rated to carry. Typically, a ship-of-the-line might have been rated as a 64 or 74; a frigate 36, 44, or 50; and a sloop 18 or 20.*

merchant vessels—converting and renaming one *Dunmore* as his seagoing headquarters—and ordered raids into the surrounding country, seeking hidden rebel supplies and threatening those who opposed him.[2]

Loyalist Andrew Sprowle's large shipyard at Gosport on the Elizabeth River helped to fit out Dunmore's expanding fleet. The Elizabeth River's natural protection from weather, ready access to the sea, abundant supplies of timber, and relatively deep water had attracted a concentration of shipbuilding almost from the time of the first Virginia settlements.

The third son of John Sprowle of Milton in the Galloway area of Scotland, Andrew Sprowle emigrated to America as a young man before 1733. With marked canniness, Sprowle purchased sixteen riverside acres on the southern branch of the Elizabeth, where the water was deep and where Royal Navy commanders traditionally careened and repaired their warships. On 1 November 1767, he formally established a small shipyard there, across what was known as Crab Creek, south of Portsmouth. To catch the attention of British skippers, Sprowle named it "Gosport" (derived from "God's Port" and the well-known Royal dockyard at Portsmouth, England).[3]

With the shipyard as his foundation, Sprowle prospered, building an expanding business realm that included trading ships, privateers, two plantations, major buildings, fine merchandise, slaves, wharves, and cattle. Reflective of his respected position in society, he was appointed British Navy Agent, elected Chairman of Trade in Virginia, and made a trustee of the town of Portsmouth.[4]

By the time of the Revolution, "the place named Gosport, in Virginia, of which Mr. Sprowle was sole Proprietor," was described as "situated on the south branch of Elizabeth River, and separated from the town of Portsmouth by a small creek, from which it extends along the river, about half a mile, in all which space the river, near the shore, is deep, and being well sheltered from winds, forms on the whole a most excellent harbor for ships of great burthen, either for careening, sheathing, repairing or loading." Buildings at the yard included an imposing five-story marine warehouse built of stone, three smaller warehouses, a blacksmith's shop, a large iron crane, and a counting house. Sprowle's own home, a three-story "large, well finished Dwelling House situated upon the River," with a large gallery with broad steps leading up from "a large garden enclosed in the best manner," stood across Crab Creek in Portsmouth.[5]

Dunmore and Sprowle were close, and the governor visited Sprowle many times in Norfolk. In all likelihood, however, Sprowle's first allegiance was to his ledger books (as argued by historian Joe Law), and in the turbulent months of 1775 he sought to walk a fine line between Loyalist and Patriot identities. When Dunmore quartered British regulars in a Gosport shipyard warehouse, Sprowle was careful to point out to the Committee of Public Safety that he, as a mere businessman, had no choice in the matter and that he "was as much attached to the American cause as anyone but more moderate than many."[6]

But, as tensions rose, nearby British military power shaped Sprowle's destiny, because it provided the only chance of protecting his investments, and he threw in his lot with Dunmore. He wrote to a friend: "The people in Norfolk and Portsmouth have been struck with such a panic, all removing into the Country [with] their effects . . . The Virginians (are) all against the Scot men, threatening to extirpate them. While the Soldiery remains at Gosport I am safe."[7]

A series of British raids across Tidewater led the Virginia Committee of Safety to order militia to Norfolk under the command of Col. William Woodford to root out Dunmore before he became entrenched. Woodford marched from Williamsburg on 24 October 1775, thwarted British plans to burn buildings in Hampton, but fell back after an engagement with red-coated regulars at Kemp's Landing. Following the battle, Woodford's militia reformed and built a breastwork on the southern end of the Great Bridge causeway, blocking an important road network into Norfolk. Intent on opening the road, Dunmore ordered his British regulars, sailors from the *Otter,* and Tory volunteers to march from Norfolk on 8 December to attack the American breastwork. In a battle that lasted merely half an hour, the British were soundly defeated and driven back. Five days later Woodford occupied the borough, from which most of the inhabitants (including all of the leading Tory families) had fled, many seeking refuge aboard Dunmore's already crowded ships in the harbor. Col. Robert Howe's North Carolina provincial troops arrived shortly thereafter, and Howe assumed control of all colonial forces in Norfolk. Suspicious of Dunmore's scheme to create a "nest of Tories" in Norfolk under the protection of British arms, some American commanders were willing to destroy the town to prevent its use as a British base of operations.[8]

Dunmore's position afloat quickly became desperate as stores of food and water for the men, women, and children crowding the holds were exhausted. Many became ill as American sharpshooters peppered Dunmore's ships from concealed positions ashore. A desperate Dunmore threatened to bombard the Norfolk waterfront to coerce cooperation.

By mid-afternoon of New Year's Day 1776, frigate *Liverpool* (28), sloop *Otter,* sloop *Kingfisher* (16), and ship *Dunmore* (8) had anchored between Town Point and the upper wharf on the eastern branch. The dark ships, with worn and tattered sails, had an undisguised air of impending doom. At 1515, on signal from the flagship, the thunder of heavy guns sounded across the water as British broadsides fell among waterfront warehouses and buildings. The firing was brief, intended only to disperse the rebel militia and to cover small groups of British who rowed ashore to scavenge for supplies and set torches to the wharves. Wide destruction was not Dunmore's intent, because he still hoped for a Loyalist foothold in the region.[9]

Intended or not, the fires spread rapidly in the ensuing chaos and terror. Militia fired the homes of known Loyalists, and destruction multiplied as many ashore became drunk and unruly. Gangs went house to house to plunder and burn. Already convinced that destruction of the borough held certain advantages for the American cause (particularly because blame for the destruction could readily be attributed to Dunmore's bombardment), Woodford and Howe were slow to rein in their troops. By the time they acted on the third day, two-thirds of Norfolk lay in ashes. A month later, the Virginia Convention ordered four hundred more houses destroyed to deny their use to Tories. By the end of this onslaught, more than thirteen hundred buildings lay in smoldering ruins.[10]

Maj. Gen. Charles Lee took command of colonial forces in March 1776 and continued the pointed eradication of Tory influence. He forced the evacuation of Portsmouth, destroyed the prominent homes of leading Tories (including that of Andrew Sprowle), and confiscated the Gosport shipyard for the Commonwealth. By May, Lee had surrounded the small remaining Loyalist breastworks at Tucker's Point (Hospital Point) and threatened the Tory fleet, forcing Dunmore to withdraw his ninety ships to Gwynn's Island in the Chesapeake Bay. There, disease and malnutrition took their continuing toll; among the victims was Andrew Sprowle, who died miserable and penniless. Dunmore ultimately sailed for England that August.[11]

Beginning in 1775, brothers James and Richard Barron armed two pilot boat schooners, manned them with local seaman, and set out to counter Dunmore's waterborne raids in Hampton Roads. The brothers were merchant marine masters of Hampton, and James was a local militia commander. During the month of December 1775, the *Patriot* and *Liberty* took ten suspected Loyalist vessels, earning an official letter of gratitude from the Virginia Convention. Taking its cue from this success, the Convention passed a decree on 11 January 1776 empowering the Committee of Safety to provide armed vessels "for the protection of the several rivers in the colony," setting the stage for the Virginia State Navy.

Virginia naval forces were initially authorized by river area; the Potomac flotilla was the largest, with fourteen vessels at one point. Two vessels were obtained for the James River, brig *Hope* (renamed *Raleigh*) and schooner *Peggy* (renamed *Mosquito*), with two row galleys (*Norfolk Revenge* and *Hero*) that had been built locally. The merchant brig *Liberty* and two galleys, *Henry* and *Manley,* patrolled the York, and three armed vessels and two row galleys were planned for the Rappahannock. Shipyards were established at Gosport, Fredericksburg, Frazer's Ferry on the Mattapony River, and near the site of present-day Toano on the Chickahominy.[12]

On 6 May 1776, five new naval commissioners (two of whom, John Hutchings and Thomas Newton Jr., were Norfolk men) established the Virginia Navy Board to "superintend and direct all matters and things to the navy relating." Their first action was to combine the different river defense forces into a single unit, the Virginia State Navy, with Capt. John Boucher as its commodore. By late 1776, the Virginia Navy had sixteen armed ships and seven trading vessels (used to elude British patrols as they transported gunpowder and military supplies from the West Indies). Privateers with Virginia letters of marque augmented this small force.[13]

Although many served in the Virginia State Navy, the brilliant legacy of the Barrons of Hampton is best remembered throughout the communities of Hampton Roads. For more than a century and through five generations, the Barrons represented Virginia's most distinguished family of naval officers. The progenitor of this extraordinary naval lineage was Capt. Samuel Barron, who emigrated from Bristol, England, to Petersburg and then to upper Mill Creek, just outside Hampton. Samuel Barron was a merchant and a captain of the provincial forces and served as Commandant of Fort George on Old Point Comfort. The fort had been completed, with its guns mounted, by 1740 but was largely destroyed in 1749 by a violent hurricane.[14]

Captain Barron had five sons, including James (born at Old Point Comfort in October 1740), Richard, and William. James first went to sea at age ten in the merchant trade and by age twenty had command of a small ship. By thirty years of age, James had risen to be a prosperous shipmaster and one of the most prominent citizens of Hampton. In 1778, William was serving as first lieutenant of the Continental Navy's frigate

Boston when he was tragically killed in a gun explosion. Before William's death, John Adams had described him as exactly the kind of officer "much wanted in our infant navy."[15]

James and Richard Barron, both destined to be captains in the Virginia State Navy, were at the center of one of the first significant victories for that navy on 21 June 1776. Posing as pilots for hire off the capes of Virginia, they hailed the British transport *Oxford,* which was inbound from Glasgow, carrying 220 Scottish Highlanders. That night, with the help of Americans being held on board, the Barrons overpowered the crew and sailed *Oxford* triumphantly into Hampton Roads to deliver their prisoners. Later, to great public acclaim, the Highlanders were marched through the streets of Williamsburg in their kilts.[16]

The Barrons' schooner *Liberty* was engaged in more than twenty sharp actions during the war, the most memorable of which occurred in the spring of 1779. With James Barron in command and brother Richard as part of a crew of sixteen, *Liberty* gave chase to *Fortunatus,* an armed schooner tender of the English frigate *Emerald,* and caught her five miles inside Cape Henry. Barron repeatedly raked the *Fortunatus* with bags of musket balls fired from cannon, which decimated her exposed crew and forced her surrender without taking a single American loss.[17]

James Barron was appointed as one of five Virginia State Navy commissioners and then, on 3 July 1780, was elevated to the post of commodore, a position he retained until his death in 1787. James's son Samuel Barron (born 25 September 1765 in Hampton) joined the Virginia State Navy and served in *Dragon* when he was just fourteen. He distinguished himself in actions around Newport News, helped capture a Tory sloop, and later became acting captain of the pilot boat *Patriot.* James's second son, also named James, was born on 15 September 1768 in Hampton and joined the Virginia State Navy in 1781 at age twelve.[18]

To aid American merchantmen, a lookout post with a fifty-foot staff was erected on Cape Henry and manned with state navy volunteers. A large red-and-white-striped flag was flown from the staff when enemy ships were sighted, and a lantern was hoisted at night when the capes were clear.[19]

The Virginia State Navy existed as a form of floating militia, and although successful in its primary duties of dissuading Tory privateers and British raiders, it suffered losses in action and budgetary cuts that decimated its numbers as the war wore on. By 1781, little was left to oppose the British at Yorktown, and by war's end the Virginia State Navy consisted merely of the small *Nicholson* (used to carry messages and supplies) and the resolute schooner *Liberty,* which had been sunk in a shallow creek bed in 1779 to save her from capture.[20]

On 15 October 1775, the American Continental Congress approved the purchase of two vessels for a national Navy to be armed and dispatched in search of enemy supply vessels. In the weeks that followed, a total of eight other vessels were authorized, and on 13 December 1775, congressional delegates authorized the construction of thirteen frigates within three months. Although only a paltry force in comparison with the force sailing under the red ensign of the Royal Navy, the British would squander its many advantages.

The Royal Navy was in a position to dominate American naval opposition, to lay waste to every American population center of note, and to strangle American seaborne commerce—the lifeblood of the revolt. It did none of these. Poorly served by its leadership, poorly supplied from the homeland, and poorly aimed by clumsy strategists, the Royal Navy frittered away its advantages, wasted opportunities, and then, perhaps fittingly, lost the climactic battle that ultimately ensured American independence.

Historian Wade Dudley argues that the Royal Navy's failure to establish a comprehensive blockade supported by a seized American dockyard (for upkeep, repairs, naval stores, provisions, without the requirement to return to Halifax or England) during the first two years of the Revolution was a clear strategic mistake. In the face of a dominant Royal Navy blockade, "perhaps nine-tenths of George Washington's powder would not have arrived from overseas sources through 1777, and the war would have ended without overt European involvement."[21]

Virginia was the largest and richest of the American colonies, and maritime trade from Virginia and Maryland through the Virginia capes to Europe and the West Indies was the most prosperous the colonies knew. Virginia should have been the first target of British naval power, but Royal Navy strength was haphazardly applied. Early in the war, operations in the lower Chesapeake involved only a handful of small ships (none in excess of 28 guns) grudgingly provided to support the Royal Governor.

The newly built two-decker frigate HMS *Roebuck* (44) did reach Hampton Roads early in 1776, but for the most part early British fleet operations amounted to little more than a few patrols, although they generated an abundance of colorful stories of British cruisers lurking unseen in Virginia waters. The British commodore, William Hotham, was ordered in December to "repair . . . to Chesepeak [*sic*] Bay . . . to establish . . . a Chief Station," and he arrived at the capes on

20 January 1777 with *Phoenix* (44), *Preston* (50), and *Brune* (20) to join *Emerald* (38). Although he captured a ship loaded with tobacco on his first day, he captured *Betsey* returning to Petersburg with a cargo of salt on his second day, and he had sixteen American prizes within two months, the need for repairs and supplies limited Hotham's effectiveness and the length of his stay.[22]

Blockade difficulties notwithstanding, the English showed their seagoing muscle on 14 August 1777, when Capt. Francis Bright of the Virginia State Navy's lookout brig *Northampton* reported a fleet of two hundred sail standing directly into the capes; these were invasion forces destined for Brandywine and Philadelphia at the northern end of the Chesapeake Bay. The Americans could do little to stop the British fleet, and Virginia State Navy vessels *Norfolk Revenge, Hero,* and *Henry,* based at Hampton, and *Manley* in the York River scrambled for safety.[23]

The leaky British blockade made its biggest capture in April 1778, when the newly built Continental Navy frigate *Virginia* (28) fell unexpectedly into British hands. Authorized by the Continental Congress in December 1775 and built in Baltimore, *Virginia* was on her maiden voyage with the Navy's most senior officer, Capt. James Nicholson, in command when she accidentally grounded on Middle Ground while making her way to sea through the capes. With British frigates *Emerald* and *Conqueror* quickly approaching, Nicholson reportedly fled in his nightshirt, leaving 1st Lt. Joshua Barney in charge. Before Barney could mount a defense, his crew had broken into the liquor stores, and the ship surrendered without a shot.[24]

What Tidewater lacked in Royal Navy attention it more than made up for in privateers that spanned an astonishing spectrum, from Loyalist to Patriot, fishing boat to frigate, licensed ship to pirate. The numbers of privateers clearly surprised the British, throwing their uninspired plans further into a cocked hat. State governors issued letters of marque with a fluidity that challenged Chesapeake shipyards to keep up with demand. Under this guise of authority, enterprising masters fought for the American cause and sought their riches with equal enthusiasm.

Prosperous Loyalist mercantile and shipping families, like that of John Goodrich from Norfolk-Portsmouth, turned their merchant fleets into flotillas of warships to pummel Patriot trade. Moving up the creeks, other Loyalist privateers raided rebel property owners, looting, burning, and carrying away cattle, slaves, and possessions. Hampton was set ablaze during one such raid, ostensibly because of its rebel sympathies.

Experienced Tidewater seamen gravitated toward privateers with promises of riches many times more than service in a state or national navy could ever provide. Newspapers in Virginia's maritime centers carried frequent reports of captured prizes and the results of admiralty prize courts. It was not uncommon for some ships in the merchant service to be captured, recaptured, and captured again on the same voyage.[25]

Historian Marshall Booker estimates that some four hundred Patriot privateers manned by ten thousand men from the Chesapeake were operated during the war, much more maritime power than either the Continental Navy or state navies could have mustered. Patriot privateers helped inflate London insurance rates, increase English opposition to the war, and tie down Royal Navy warships in convoying. Prize cargoes sent in by privateers, especially gunpowder, salt, munitions, and clothing, were critical for sustaining the war effort and helped to maintain trade in the face of Tory or British privateers.[26] Time and again, swift Chesapeake-designed clipper-schooners performed well, guaranteeing privateer owners and speculators handsome returns on investment.

Beginning in 1778, the stance of the Royal Navy in America changed radically when France and its powerful fleet joined the fray. Unable to thwart American independence when it held all the advantages, the Royal Navy now faced a determined, professional, deep-water foe, and planning shifted from lethargic blockade to preparation for full fleet actions.

Between 1778 and 1782, British and French fleets in the Atlantic would engage seven different times in battles that featured twenty or more heavily armed warships arranged, in the tactics of the day, in long, ponderous battle lines.[27]

Beginning in the summer of 1778, the French Navy sailed squadrons to American waters to duel with the British for advantage. A dozen French ships-of-the-line under Charles Hector, Comte d'Estaing, nearly caught the British North American squadron under Lord Howe in Delaware Bay and then helped capture Rhode Island. The importance of these new strategic dynamics was not lost on American leaders.

French and British naval forces in the Atlantic were well matched. At times the Royal Navy would display advantages in individual verve, training, and gunnery, but just as often the French would excel in these very points. The French fleet was well trained, and its professional officer corps was proficient in tactics. Worldwide, the Royal Navy was larger, but French forces would prove time and again that they could concentrate rapidly for decisive advantage, vastly complicating Britain's strategy and its unquestioned command of the seas in America.

With the French Navy in play, Royal Navy deployments to the Americas surged and British cruisers stepped up their seaward patrols. The British commander in North America, Gen. Sir Henry Clinton, and the senior naval officer, Adm. Sir George Collier, suddenly felt a greater urgency for action. New plans were devised for blockade and invasion, plans that would include, in Collier's words, "cutting off the resources by which the enemy could continue war, these being principally drawn from Virginia, and principally tobacco."[28]

In early May 1779, Collier (with Maj. Gen. Edward Mathew commanding troops) gathered the flagship *Raisonable* (64), *Rainbow* (44), *Solebay* (28), *Otter* (16), *Diligent* (8), *Haarlem* (14), *Cornwallis* (8), twenty-eight transports, and twenty-five hundred troops at Sandy Hook. Collier wrote to Clinton:

> After leaving New York the 5th instant [5 May 1779] with the men of war and transports under my command, I proceeded towards the place of our destination with the most propitious winds, and on the 4th day made the capes of Virginia. The fleet anchored that night between the sands near Willoughby's point, which they had hardly done, when the most terrible flurry of thunder and lightning, wind and rain came on that I ever recollect; its continuance however was not more than half an hour, and the ships were all so fortunate as to escape driving on shore. At sunrise we saw some rebel ships and vessels in Hampton road, with their sails loose, who, as soon as the tide admitted of it, got under weigh and ran up Elizabeth and James rivers; our fleet also weighed and the *Raisonable* anchored shortly after in Hampton road, her great draught of water not admitting her going farther with convenience.[29]

The few ships of the Virginia State Navy fled in advance of the British fleet, and, in their wake, the sole remaining defense was Fort Nelson, erected only months before on the western shore of the Elizabeth above Portsmouth.[30] Collier transferred his flag to the shallower-draft frigate *Rainbow* and loaded troops into flatboats to advance against the fort, "covered by the *Cornwallis* galley and two boats." With troops and artillery outflanking the fort and with the *Rainbow* moving into position, the Virginia militiamen fled.

Collier moved up the Elizabeth River, now unopposed, and reported: "The town of Portsmouth within one half-mile of the fort was taken possession of at the same time Norfolk on the opposite shore and Gosport where the rebels had established a very capable marine yard for building ships . . . the enemy previous to their flight set fire to a fine ship of war of twenty guns ready for launching . . . many vessels of war were taken on the stocks."[31]

That "fine ship of war" that Collier found burning at Gosport was the Continental Navy frigate *Virginia,* which was being constructed under the watchful eye of its prospective commander, Capt. James Barron. After Virginia had taken full possession of the Gosport yard in 1776 (later purchased in 1780 as Loyalist property sold at public auction), two new frigates (each planned for 36 guns) were authorized by the Continental Congress, with Richard Henry Lee of the Marine Committee of Congress stipulating that they be built at Gosport. James Maxwell was appointed to superintend Virginia State Navy construction at the yard, assisted by Paul Loyall, former mayor of Norfolk. A contract for the two ships was issued in February 1777, but persistent funding problems delayed progress, and by October 1778, it was decided to finish only the frigate closest to completion and reduce her armament to 28 guns.[32]

Once in possession of Portsmouth and Gosport, Collier dispatched the *Cornwallis* galley, two gunboats, and flatboats with troops to capture ships that had fled up the Elizabeth. He ordered the *Otter* to patrol the Chesapeake. Suffolk was seized and military supplies were destroyed; Tory privateers engaged in several reported incidents of pillage. "The enemy was much harassed and distressed," Collier concluded in his report. "The *Raisonable,* remained before the town of Hampton with some armed tenders, blocks up that port, and the navigation of James river; Elizabeth river is already taken effectual care of, and [*Otter's*] squadron renders the ingress and regress of the Chesapeak [*sic*] impracticable for the rebel vessels without their being taken."[33]

Collier pressed Clinton to spare the Gosport yard and turn it into a permanent British base:

> Permit me however as a sea officer, to observe that this port of Portsmouth, is an exceeding safe and secure asylum for ships against an enemy, and is not to be forced even by great superiority, the marine yard is large and extremely convenient, having a considerable stock of seasoned timber, besides great quantities of other stores; from these considerations joined to many others, I am firmly of opinion that it is a measure most essentially necessary for his Majesty's service that this post should remain in our hands, since it appears to be of more real consequence and advantage, than any other the Crown now possesses in America, for by securing this, the

whole trade of the Chesapeak [*sic*] is at an end, and consequently the sinews of the rebellion destroyed.[34]

Collier had finally articulated what should have been the British strategy since the opening days of the Revolution. A British base in Portsmouth could logistically support an effective British blockade, help create a Loyalist enclave in southern Virginia (Dunmore's old dream), and arrest the rich trade in Virginian farming products, so important to the Patriot cause.

Ultimately, Collier was forced to abandon this idea, and he withdrew on 25 May, putting Gosport to the torch and destroying Fort Nelson. Collier described the scene vividly: "The conflagration in the night [24 May] appeared grand beyond description, though the night was a melancholy one; five thousand loads of fine seasoned oak knees for ship building, an infinite quantity of plank, masts cordage and numbers of beautiful ships of war on the stocks were all at one time a blaze and totally consumed not a vestige remaining but the iron work that such things had been!" Collier went on to report, "the whole number [of ships] taken, burnt and destroyed [during the expedition] . . . amounted to 137 sail of vessels!"[35]

The raid proved anew that, for the British, the geographical imperative of Hampton Roads held an uncommon attraction. Command of its waters offered the British a dependable anchorage astraddle an American trade route where they could reap its largess while denying the same to the hard-pressed Americans. And as the Royal Navy was drawn to its waters as if by strong cords, so too came massive torments inflicted by war. No other American region would suffer as much.

British redcoats returned to Hampton Roads in October 1780 with a small naval squadron under Commo. George Gayton and twenty-five hundred troops under Maj. Gen. Alexander Leslie to disrupt supplies to American forces in Virginia and the Carolinas. The Virginia *Gazette* reported that: "On the 20th instant [20 October 1780], arrived in Chesapeake Bay a British fleet of 54 ships, 25 of which are large, the residue small. On the 23rd they landed 1000 infantry and 100 horse at Newport News, who immediately proceeded to Hampton, of which they took possession." Leslie secured Hampton and Suffolk relatively easily, comfortably fortified a post at Portsmouth, and then sent couriers to Charles, Lord Cornwallis, in the Carolinas to coordinate actions. As before, he met little American opposition in Tidewater. The only Virginia State warship in the area, galley *Henry,* was captured without a fight, and Patriot trading vessels scattered to the four winds. Leslie's invasion could have been even more decisive had he not received unexpected orders to decamp from Portsmouth on 22 November and sail for Charleston to provide reinforcements for Cornwallis.[36]

Clinton was quick to order a new British invading force to the Chesapeake. On 30 December a new squadron, led by Captain Symonds in HMS *Charon* (44) with a detachment of sixteen hundred troops under Brig. Gen. Benedict Arnold, arrived in Hampton Roads.[37] Arnold's instructions were similar to those given Leslie and, earlier, proved by Collier: fortify a position near deep water for continued contact with the Virginia State Navy; harass the enemy and disrupt commerce; interdict agricultural supplies flowing to American forces; and support Lord Cornwallis's objectives in his campaigns through the Carolinas.

Arnold wasted no time in aggressively carrying out his orders. A day after arriving he brashly advanced up the James River in an amphibious raid covered by HM warships *Hope, Swift,* and *Bonetta*.[38] After destroying military supplies and tobacco stores, taking Richmond, and destroying Virginia's major foundry at Westham, Arnold returned down the James, finally reaching the fortifications in Portsmouth on 20 January. While Arnold raided up the James, Symonds's ships created havoc in the bay, taking many ships filled with tobacco and other stores.

News of the damaging raid, especially the vexing knowledge that it was led by that most infamous of traitors, so incensed Governor Thomas Jefferson and Congress that they demanded all available resources to counter it. By the end of January, Continental troops were readied to march to Virginia, and American dispatches flew to Narragansett Bay, where a French naval squadron lay at anchor under the command of Charles-René-Dominique Sochet, Chevalier des Touches.

The British were well aware of Arnold's exposed position in Portsmouth and his dependence on the Royal Navy for communications with the sea. When British spies spotted the preparations being made by the French to sail from Newport, the British commander of the North American squadron, Vice Adm. Marriot Arbuthnot, rushed to sea from New York to block the French advance. A sudden and fierce nor'easter delayed the French sortie but hit the British with full force, causing the loss of ship-of-the-line *Culloden* and damage to others. Unsure of the location of the superior British squadron, des Touches canceled his sortie but ordered Marquis de Tilly in ship-of-the-line *L'Eveille* (64) to the Chesapeake with two frigates, *Gentile* (40) and *Surveillante* (32). De Tilly arrived there on 15 February 1781 but could not reach Arnold and his screen of support ships at Portsmouth, causing Jefferson to write: "they are equal to the destruction of the British vessels, could they get at them, but these are drawn up into Elizabeth river into which the 64 cannot enter." Fearful of being bottled up in the Chesapeake Bay by Arbuthnot's arrival, de Tilly withdrew to Newport after just four days, capturing half a dozen privateers and the British frigate *Romulus* (44), inbound to Portsmouth to support Arnold from a station off Charleston.[39]

L'Eveille's return to Newport was temporary; des Touches, confident that he now held superiority over the British, ordered his squadron to sea on the morning of 8 March, bound for the Virginia Capes.[40] When this news reached Arbuthnot, he followed at once, departing New York on 10 March in a squadron numbering seven ships-of-the-line and four frigates. Arbuthnot maintained his flag in *Royal Oak* (74), with Rear Adm. Thomas Graves in *London* (98). Favored by better wind, Arbuthnot outstripped the French, and at 0600 on 16 March, the French were spotted astern the British some forty miles east northeast of Cape Henry.

The British admiral went about at once, making the signal for line of battle. The French were of equal strength, with seven ships-of-the-line, led by *Neptune* (84), *Burgoyne* (84), and *Conquerant* (84), the recently captured British *Romulus,* and four frigates. Soon both lines were maneuvering for the weather gauge.[41]

The preeminent naval fighting machine of the period was the line-of-battle ship. By 1781, the workhorse of the battle line was the standard 74-gun ship, with two gundecks of 56 cannon (32- and 24-pounders) and 18 more 9-pound guns on an upper deck. Tactically, these imposing behemoths were best employed as a file of ships in a tight bowsprit-to-stern formation where broadside fire could be concentrated, where no single ship would be exposed, and where an admiral could effectively maneuver his fleet as a single unit. With line-of-battle tactics favoring side-by-side gunnery, the "weight" of the broadside was a crucial factor, and the arrangement of ships within a battle line was carefully planned.

Ships were routinely stationed a cable's length apart (720 feet), so that a battle line of twenty ships would stretch three and a half nautical miles. The rear of the line was its most vulnerable point, and fleets with a superiority of even a few ships could maneuver to swing around the end of the line, doubling the gunpower against ships of the rear and, theoretically, causing a cascading collapse of the entire opposing fleet. The squadron to windward held the advantage of controlling the engagement's tempo because it could run down upon the other line at will, timing the impact of first salvos.

Lines of battle were notoriously difficult to form, and their success depended on effective signaling, made more difficult by distance or the smoke of battle. Because the individual captains did not enjoy the larger strategic picture of the admiral, they were frequently conservative, knowing that individual intrepidity could disrupt the line and spell ruin for the fleet.

Off Cape Henry on 16 March 1781, the French admiral won the initial advantage as he maneuvered his tightly packed battle line with precision in order to capture the windward gauge. Veering wind, thickening haze, and slowly increasing seas caused both admirals to order a series of circling course changes and wearing maneuvers as they fenced for position through the morning and into the early afternoon. Tacking and wearing, sheeting new canvas into place or luffing to stay in formation, each captain fixed on following the flag's lead, while gun crews stood nearby their guns, slow matches in hand. Shouted orders would be repeated from lieutenant to midshipman, salt spray would wet the sloping decks, and the great oaken timbers would grind and creak in the seaway. Each captain could occasionally glimpse his counterpart in the enemy line, just as meticulously concentrating on his own maneuvers. French and English naval commanders were well known to one another, since many of the ships on each side were deployed for months (even years) to American waters.

Shortly after 1400, the French gained a momentary advantage by choosing a tack whereby the heel of the ships prevented the parallel British line from opening its lower gunports in the high seas, while the French had full use of theirs. Des Touches quickly opened with thundering broadsides, raking the British van with a crippling fire. The center of the British line sagged briefly, and several French vessels were damaged, but the large three-decker *London* could not bring her full broadside to bear against the elusive French. Firing became intermittent as a fickle wind unsettled both sides' tactics. Smoke and haze dominated; signals became confused. Des Touches ordered the French line to wear away, again raking the British vanguard ships as he turned. Arbuthnot did not respond, and the forces broke off action in the haze. Arbuthnot re-formed his force, carefully staying between the French and the Chesapeake. He cautiously withdrew to anchor at Lynnhaven Bay; des Touches returned to Newport.

The battle proved an inconsequential tactical draw, but it was a strategic win for the Royal Navy. The British absorbed more damage than the French but successfully controlled the entrance to the Chesapeake, protected Arnold, and guaranteed his access to vital reinforcements.[42]

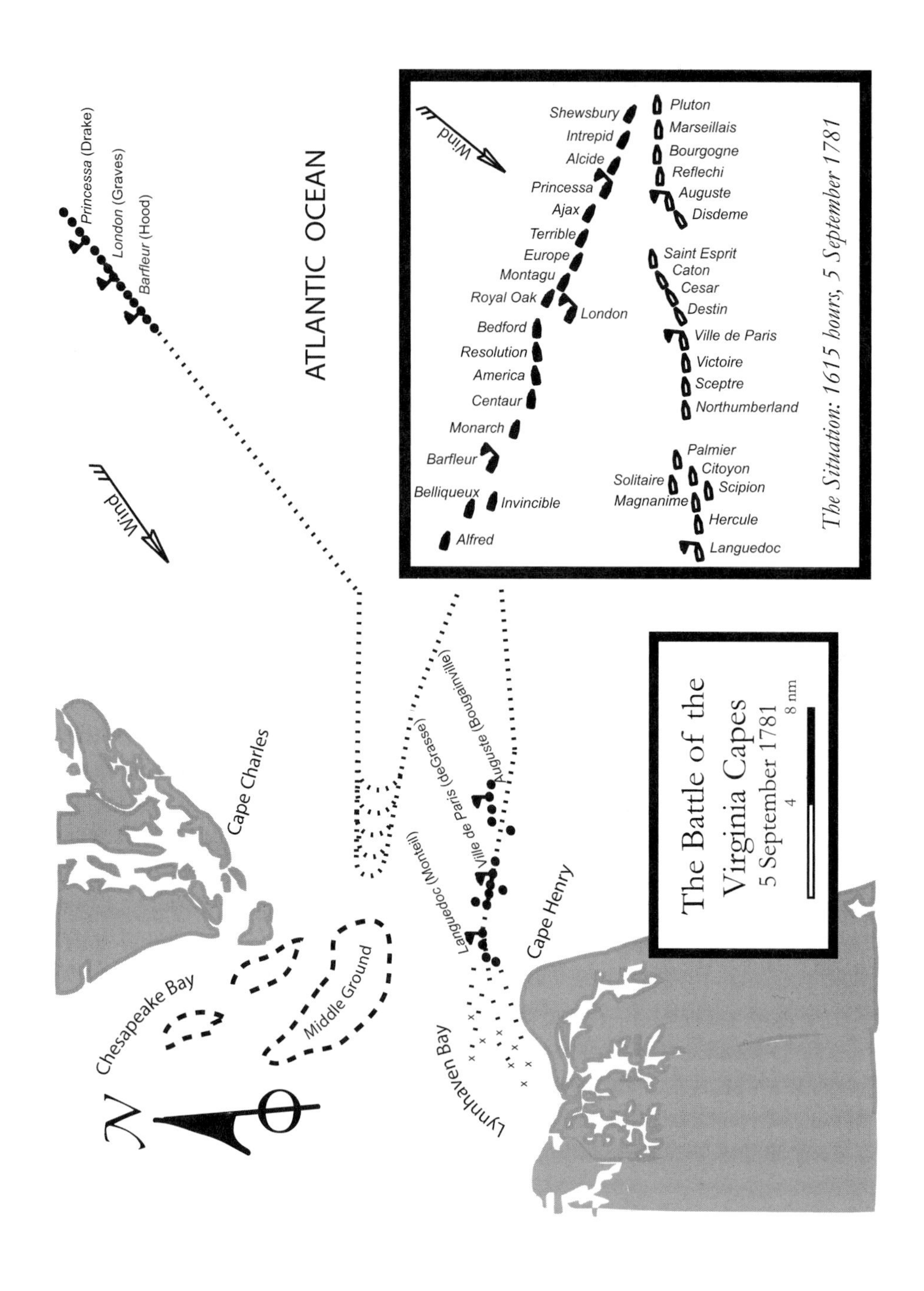
The Battle of the
Virginia Capes
5 September 1781
4
8 nm
The Situation: 1615 hours, 5 September 1781
Wind
Shewsbury
Intrepid
Alcide
Princessa
Ajax
Terrible
Europe
Montagu
Royal Oak
London
Bedford
Resolution
America
Centaur
Monarch
Barfleur
Belliqueux
Invincible
Alfred
Pluton
Marseillais
Bourgogne
Reflechi
Auguste
Disdeme
Saint Esprit
Caton
Cesar
Destin
Ville de Paris
Victoire
Sceptre
Northumberland
Palmier
Citoyon
Solitaire
Scipion
Magnanime
Hercule
Languedoc
ATLANTIC OCEAN
Princessa (Drake)
London (Graves)
Barfleur (Hood)
Wind
Cape Charles
Chesapeake Bay
Middle Ground
Lynnhaven Bay
Cape Henry
Languedoc (Monteil)
Ville de Paris (deGrasse)
Auguste (Bougainville)
N

The Battle of Cape Henry was not an isolated skirmish; rather, it was one event in a continuum of crisscrossing American, British, and French strategies that, in 1781, increasingly intersected near the Chesapeake Bay. During this period, the British Army in America had become divided; one force, commanded by General Clinton, was situated near New York City; a second force, led by Lord Cornwallis, was in the Carolinas. The only link between the two (and their only chance for supply, reinforcement, and mutual support) was the Royal Navy. Conversely, the best chance for an American victory would be to discover a means to disrupt these communications, isolate a portion of the British Army, and defeat it piecemeal. The small British raiding force at Portsmouth, commanded first by Leslie and then Arnold, shared a similar dependence on the ability of the Royal Navy to protect its lifeline to either Clinton or Cornwallis.

All of the military commanders in the American theater, English, American, and French, were well aware of the equations of success or failure and the importance of sea power in realizing ultimate victory. By 1781, those commanders also recognized that the only way to checkmate the Royal Navy would be through concentration of French fleet forces at a decisive point along the American coastline. John Paul Jones had written the American diplomatic commissioners in Paris in February 1778, outlining his belief that the French fleet could pin British land forces in place, where they could be destroyed by the Continentals—a "single blow," he called it, that could ensure the Revolution. Thomas Jefferson mentioned a similar strategy in October 1780 to American Gen. Horatio Gates, pressing him to surround Leslie in Hampton Roads and "to notify the French Admiral that his enemies are in net, if he has leisure to close the mouth of it." George Washington and Marquis de Lafayette discussed this design as well in their correspondence.[43]

Because large navies were so crucial in the last stages of the American Revolution, English and French commanders maneuvered their ships knowing there was much to lose in the event of an error or misstep. Any single victory at sea would be valuable, but neither party's commander would hazard his fleet for a mere tactical advantage if the risks were high, as was shown during the Battle of Cape Henry. The English had parried the French thrust at Cape Henry; for the French, it was much better to break off contact and wait for a future advantage.

With the Chesapeake in control, Clinton quickly dispatched two thousand fresh reinforcements to Arnold from New York. Commanded by Gen. William Phillips, the transports arrived at Lynnhaven Bay on 26 March. Phillips quickly solidified defensive positions in Portsmouth and launched a new set of raids up the James, capturing the Virginia State Navy schooner *Patriot*. The British burned stores and vessels at that navy's Chickahominy yard and forced their opponents into a last brave stand at Osborne's Wharf on the James.[44]

Arnold's forces approached cautiously.

> Finding the enemy had a very considerable force in ships four miles above Osborn's drawn up in a line to oppose us, I sent a flag to the Commodore proposing to treat with him for the surrender of his fleet, which he refused, with the answer that he was determined to defend it to the last extremity. I immediately ordered two 6 and two 3-pounder brass field pieces to a bank of the river, nearly level with the water, and within one hundred yards of the *Tempest,* a twenty gun State ship, which began immediately to fire upon us, as did the *Renown* of 26 guns, the *Jefferson,* a State-brigantine of 14 guns and several other armed ships and brigantines . . . the fire of [our] artillery . . . took such place that the ships were soon obliged to strike their colors and the [Virginia] militia drove from the opposite shore.[45]

Arnold further reported that twelve craft were captured, "many with tobacco cargoes," and nine ships plus some smaller craft were sunk or destroyed. "We had not a man killed or wounded."[46]

By late May 1781 Lord Cornwallis's northward march had brought him to Petersburg and a link with Arnold. Harried and shadowed by American forces, some led by the Marquis de Lafayette, Cornwallis received orders from Clinton to take defensive positions in southeastern Virginia to await the end of the hurricane season and the availability of more British ships.[47] After surveying Old Point Comfort, and considering the already garrisoned British position at Portsmouth, Cornwallis decided on Yorktown and Gloucester as the best defendable sites with ready access to deep water. The fortifications at Portsmouth were evacuated, and those troops concentrated at Yorktown by 22 August.

At the same time, a thousand nautical miles distant in the West Indies, strong squadrons of the British and French fleets were forming to depart the tropics with the arrival of the hurricane season. On 5 July a British frigate sighted the main French squadron of twenty-seven ships of the line withdrawing to Cap Français (now Cap Haitien in Haiti), where the final seasonal homeward-bound merchant convoy of nearly two hundred French ships was preparing to sail. The British fleet commander, Adm. Sir George Rodney, fearful for the safety of his own ships and seeing the French withdraw, ordered Rear Adm. Samuel Hood to sail for the safety of New York with the majority of the British West Indies squadron.

Adm. François Joseph Paul de Grasse-Rouville, granted the title Comte de Grasse, led the French fleet in the West Indies. Commanding in stature, standing six feet, two inches, Admiral de Grasse was wealthy and well known within the French court. Within the French Navy his reputation was that of a capable and gallant leader in battle against the British.[48]

De Grasse arrived at Cap Français on 16 July to find urgent letters from George Washington and French Gen. Jean-Baptiste Donatien de Vineur, Comte de Rochambeau, carried by the French frigate *Concorde*. They told of Cornwallis's position in Virginia, Washington's desire for a coordinated American-French attack at New York, the desirability of a campaign in the Chesapeake to help Lafayette, and a request to bring additional troops from the West Indies. Stirred by these letters, de Grasse replied on 28 July (again carried by *Concorde*) that he planned to sail for the Chesapeake at once with his entire force, twenty-six ships-of-the-line, including flagship *Ville de Paris* of 104 guns. He did not say in his confident reply to Washington that such a move, advantageous as it would be for the American cause, held some decided risk and would leave the French homeward convoy dangerously unprotected. De Grasse loaded three French regiments of infantry, artillerymen, and one hundred dragoons aboard fleet ships and transports on 3 August and sailed two days later.[49]

François Joseph Paul, Comte de Grasse, commanding French Navy squadrons in the West Indies, boldly snatched the strategic initiative from the British in the last great campaign of the Revolutionary War. By brilliantly blocking the British from Chesapeake Bay at the Battle of the Virginia Capes, he sealed the fate of Lord Cornwallis and forced the capitulation of the British Army at Yorktown. *U.S. Naval Institute*

In the West Indies on 3 August, Hood read remarkably accurate dispatches from Clinton and the English naval commander, Rear Adm. Thomas Graves (who had taken over for the ailing Admiral Arbuthnot), indicating their opinion that "de Grasse may be expected on this coast in the hurricane season, if not before, with all the sea and land forces he can assemble." They expected de Grasse to first proceed to Rhode Island (with its French squadron of eight ships-of-the-line, now under Adm. Count Louis de Barras) and then sail against New York. But Hood felt, as did Graves, that de Grasse's force would be small because they expected the French to divert warships to guard the seasonal convoy. Hood sailed for New York with fourteen ships-of-the-line on 10 August, comfortable in the knowledge that he would outnumber any French squadron.[50]

Hood sailed past Cape Henry on 25 August, detected no enemy ships, and sailed on to New York, arriving on 28 August. As Hood dropped anchor at Sandy Hook, Graves told him to prepare for an immediate sailing, reporting, "We have as yet no certain intelligence of De Grasse, the accounts say that he was gone to Havana to join the Spaniards and [they are] expected together upon this coast. A little time will show us." Two days later, in a dispatch to the Admiralty, Graves continued: "The *Richmond* came in on the 29th from the Chesapeake in four days where everything is quiet. . . . Whether the French intend a junction [de Grasse joining de Barras at Newport] or whether they have left the coast is only to be guessed at."[51]

While the British puzzled, the coordinated American-French strategy for the Chesapeake was taking shape. By 14 August, de Grasse had sailed through the difficult and little-used Bahama Channel to just north of Havana and headed into the Florida Straits with his entire squadron. The American and French allied armies hastened south from New York to Virginia.[52] They knew that Cornwallis had finally reached Yorktown and that de Grasse was moving toward the Chesapeake. A dispatch from Lafayette had said, in part, "Should a French fleet now come to Hampton Roads, the British army would, I think, be ours." French Admiral de Barras, strongly pushed by Washington and Rochambeau to join de Grasse, sortied from Newport on 25 August with eight ships of the line, en route to the Chesapeake.

Late in the afternoon of 29 August, American lookouts at Cape Henry pointed to a set of distant topgallants, the only white on a clear horizon of blue. Then, astern the first set of sails there was a second; frigates, they supposed. Then, there was a third and a fourth. Within hours the entire distant vista was filled with billows of sails rapidly approaching from the southeast. That evening, de Grasse, with twenty-eight ships-of-the-line and three thousand troops, anchored on the banks outside the Virginia Capes. The next day he moved the bulk of the fleet to anchorage in Lynnhaven Bay. The British lookout sloop *Loyalist* (14) was captured, while HMS *Guadaloupe* (28) escaped to Yorktown to join *Charon,* two smaller frigates, and six armed sloops in the York River. In smoothly orchestrated operations, de Grasse sent *Vaillant, Triton,* and *Glorieux* to block the York and *Experiment, Andromaque,* and *Diligente* to the James. He further ordered all of the fleet's boats readied to ferry troops ashore.[53] American personnel from the decimated Virginia State Navy helped by providing river pilots, lookout boats, and provisions.

In an exact replay of their operations in March, word reached the British that the French had sailed from Newport, and Graves concluded that their destination would again be the Chesapeake in order to threaten the British Army. Following this practiced script to the letter, Graves weighed anchor in New York, added five ships-of-the-line to Hood's squadron, and turned south. Graves had little inkling of the plans of Washington and Rochambeau and, at least at first, considered Cornwallis safe in his defended positions. He was comfortable with his generous advantage in firepower over de Barras's force (or the combined force of de Barras and the small number of ships from the French West Indies, if they ever arrived).[54]

Thomas Graves, rear admiral of the red, had achieved command of the British North American station just two months previous, but he had served in the Royal Navy his entire life, starting as a boy on a ship commanded by his father and achieving lieutenant rank at age eighteen in 1743. He had been captain of *Conqueror* (74) in 1778 and was made rear admiral of the blue in 1779. He was widely seen as "courteous, kindly, and rather dull, though by no means lacking in courage." Others commented that he was "fitted to command a squadron which was comfortably superior to the enemy. But he was not the man for a crisis."[55]

Graves pressed on sail and made rapid progress south; dawn on 5 September found Cape Charles low on his horizon. At 0800 the French lookout frigate *Aigrette* reported the approaching fleet to de Grasse, who had twenty-four of his twenty-seven ships-of-the-line at anchor. At first de Grasse thought that the report referred to de Barras's squadron. At 1000, the British frigate *Solebay* signaled the presence of the anchored French force to Graves, who likewise assumed that it was de Barras, but by 1100 the full French anchorage was in view and the adversary well estimated.

The weather was fair. "Enemy in sight" signals snapped from British mastheads in a brisk northeast breeze, and all ships cleared for action. Graves rapidly approached the French under foresails and topgallants on a leading wind, the most favorable condition for attack in the battle-line tactics of the day. Hood, commanding the van, pressed forward. De Grasse, on the other hand, was at a tremendous and unexpected disadvantage. To meet the English battle line with any chance of success, he had to first align his own fleet, steering to sea against wind and an inflowing tide that could potentially pin him against the lee shore of Cape Henry.

A flurry of signals raced up the halyards of the *Ville de Paris*. All captains had been waiting for the signal, and instantly masts and yards broke out in tall white pyramids of sail. One French participant remembers: "At half-past eleven, orders were given to slip our cables, leave [the anchor] at the buoy; at noon, to clear decks and to form in order of speed."[56] The French headed offshore on the larboard tack, ships backing and filling as captains vied for the most auspicious positions of honor in the ragged battle line. Maneuvering was clumsy, and there were several near collisions. Captains cursed that parts of their crews were still away operating boats for the troops as the ships fought for sea room. Most were forced to take multiple tacks to round Cape Henry.

The British were inferior in numbers by five and in aggregate firepower by an important five hundred cannon, and several of their ships were in doubtful condition. HMS *Terrible,* for instance, had all of her pumps running even before the battle commenced. Arguably, de Grasse might have won simply by staying at anchor, where his numerical superiority would have blocked Graves, guaranteeing Cornwallis's destruction. But once de Grasse committed to battle, it was suddenly the British who held the tactical upper hand. As one English naval historian commented: "Graves was in a position beyond the wildest dreams of a sea commander. His whole fleet was running down before the wind, and his enemy was before him, working slowly out of harbor. He had only to fall upon their van with full force and the day was his."[57]

Graves's well-ordered line was in a remarkable position of advantage and could have descended upon the confused French line with victory almost totally guaranteed. Only by steering a perilous course to open sea and surviving long enough to get his disconcerted line in shape could de Grasse take advantage of his numerical superiority.[58]

Rather than ordering his line to overwhelm the disorganized French, Graves changed course to due west, slowed to keep his line tightly packed, and waited. By 1400, still slow to act, Graves had run out of sea room as he approached the shallows of the Chesapeake Middle Ground. He ordered the entire British line to "wear together" (all ships turning simultaneously 180 degrees, keeping their place in line) to head to the east. Rear Adm. Samuel Drake now held the responsibility for the British van, Hood the rear. The French fleet was in line about three miles to leeward with its van opposite the British center, heading eastward.

It must have been a noble spectacle: forty-three imposing two- and three-decker ships maneuvering in close proximity with every detail of every ship fully visible from the quarterdecks of all others in the clear midday air. It was a sight not witnessed before and or after along the American coast. Cautious as they were, the commanders could not ignore the fact that they sailed at an intersection of history. The courses of two empires hung in the balance, as did the future of a struggling young nation.

Drake's British van included *Terrible* (74), *Ajax* (74), *Princessa* (70), *Alcide* (74), *Intrepid* (64), and *Shrewsbury* (74). Hood's rear included *Alfred* (74), *Belliqueux* (64), *Invincible* (74), *Barfleur* (90), *Monarch* (74), and *Centaur* (74). The English center (with Graves aboard flagship *London*) included *America* (64), *Resoiution* (74), *Bedford, Royal Oak* (74), *Montagu* (74), and *Europe* (64). Commo. Louis-Antoine de Bougainville commanded the French van with *Pluton* (74), *Marseillais* (74), *Bourgogne* (74), *Reflechi* (74), *Auguste* (80), *Disdeme* (74), *Saint-Esprit* (80), and *Canton* (74). The *arriere-garde* (or rear) was commanded by Commo. François-Aymar, Baron de Monteil with *Citoyen* (74), *Scipion* (74), *Magnanime* (74), *Hercule* (74), *Languedoc* (80), *Zele* (74), *Hector* (74), and *Souverain* (74). The *corps de bataille,* or center, was led by de Grasse aboard three-decker *Ville de Paris* (104), one of the most powerful ships of her day, and included *Cesar* (74), *Destin* (74), *Victoire* (74), *Sceptre* (80), *Northumberland* (74), *Palmier* (74), and *Solitaire* (64).

After the British wearing maneuver, their line had surged slightly ahead of that of the French on parallel courses, a point of tactical disadvantage, as the French could "double" the British rear, bringing extra fire to bear on straggling British ships. But de Bougainville had pressed the French van forward, disconnecting it from the French center, and the rear was poorly formed.[59] Again, another tactical advantage was lost to Graves as he concentrated on slowing his force to better match the lines, giving the French even more time to compose their line.

Finally, at about 1600 (more than six hours since sighting one another), Graves raised the signal to "bear down and engage" but confused his captains when he did not order the lowering of the signal that had been flying for "line ahead." Flagship *London* turned and surged toward the French, but the rest of the line fell into disarray; some ships struggled to follow the flagship, and others turned independently toward the French. The British rear did not respond at all.[60]

As the lines came within musket range, the French could concentrate diagonal fire on the British van while receiving replies principally from only British bow guns. In this mismatch, the lead French ship, *Pluton,* raked her counterpart in the line, HMS *Shrewsbury,* with a murderous fire that took off the leg of the British captain. The French *Marseillais* pounded *Intrepid,* which was reported to have sixty-five shot holes in her hull. *Alcide, Ajax,* and *Princessa,* next in the British line, suffered damage in their rigging. Commodore de Bougainville, in *Auguste,* closed on *Princessa* and then poured her fire into *Terrible,* the weakest ship in the British line.[61] The British van wobbled under the onslaught; the momentum of its rush toward the French was broken.

The British center had closed within range, and its first two ships, *Europe* and *Montagu,* were the next ships to absorb the full weight of French shot. The British rear still hung back, disengaged. Hood would say later, unconvincingly, that Graves's signals were confusing. After an hour of engagement, diminishing winds turned the battle into a slowly moving drama, keeping the ships in the van fully engaged and the rear separated and depriving the British of any chance to concentrate firepower to overcome their numerical disadvantage. By 1830, half an hour before sunset, the exhausted vans had ceased firing, and the French line soon disengaged.[62]

Dawn brought a silent sea and sky and a wind grown eerily calm. Ominously, both fleets were still in full view as the horizon sharpened in the light, and both Graves and de Grasse signaled to renew the engagement. De Grasse had reformed his line to seaward during the night, but the British line straggled. HMS *Shrewsbury, Intrepid, Princessa, Montagu, Terrible,* and *Ajax* all reported that "they were in no condition to renew the action," and Graves weighed one report that the French "had not the appearance of near so much damage as we had sustained."[63]

With the weather gauge in the English favor, Hood pushed Graves to head to the Chesapeake—Arbuthnot's tactic at the Battle of Cape Henry and a chance to link with Cornwallis—but Graves balked, for fear of being pinned in the Chesapeake by a superior force and perhaps losing his entire force. By the afternoon of 6 September, British repairs lagged and it became even more apparent that Graves's force was in no condition to reengage. British losses were a relatively low 90 killed and 246 wounded (against French casualties of 209), but their real loss—the death knell of line-of-battle tactics—was in speed and maneuverability.

On 7 and 8 September de Grasse gained the weather position with a shift in wind but did not seek action because he was uncertain of the strength of his opponent. On the ninth, de Grasse broke contact and sailed for the Chesapeake, and sighted de Barras's eight warships anchored under Cape Henry by 1100 on the tenth. De Grasse also captured the English frigates *Iris* (32) (formerly the Continental Navy frigate *Hancock*) and *Richmond* (32), which had been caught on a fool's errand cutting the French anchor buoys adrift at their former anchorage.

Graves shadowed de Grasse on the eleventh and sent frigate *Medea* ahead to reconnoiter. When *Medea* reported de Grasse at anchor with de Barras's squadron now joined—bringing the French an unassailable advantage of thirty-six ships-of-the-line—the battle's final judgment was clear to all. After burning the floundering *Terrible,* Graves withdrew toward New York, with Hood concluding that it was "a truly lamentable state we have brought ourself." The French were left in sole possession of the waters of the Chesapeake, and the Americans in possession of the initiative.[64]

Washington and Rochambeau joined Lafayette on 14 September at Williamsburg, and, shortly thereafter, de Grasse sent the captured British ship *Queen Charlotte* to convey them to Cape Henry, where, resplendent in his royal blue and scarlet dress uniform, de Grasse welcomed all to the great cabin of *Ville de Paris* to study the final details of the cam-

Fortune shone on the fleurs-de-lis in action off the Virginia Capes on 5 September 1781 in what Yale historian Jonathan R. Dull called "the most important naval victory of the 18th century." *Hampton Roads Naval Museum*

paign. The American and French armies were streaming toward Yorktown, many transported on ships down the Chesapeake Bay. James Thatcher, an American Army surgeon, recorded in his diary: "20th [September], Passed Hampton road, and entered James river . . . [with] a distant view of the grand French fleet . . . This is the most noble and majestic spectacle I ever witnessed, and we viewed it with inexpressible pleasure and the warmest gratitude . . . towards our great ally." Within days, allied American and French forces laid siege to Yorktown.[65]

Graves anchored at Sandy Hook on 19 September, and Clinton readied nearly his entire force of six thousand men to embark for Cornwallis's relief. However, extensive repairs to damaged ships held Graves back until 19 October, when he sortied with twenty-five sail. Arriving off the Chesapeake five days later, he found de Grasse anchored in a crescent between the capes, a nearly impenetrable barrier. Regardless of the tactical situation at sea, Graves had arrived too late to aid Cornwallis. French and American allied forces had begun their siege bombardment of the final British Army positions on 9 October, and by the next day the four remaining British warships trapped on the York (*Charon, Guadaloupe, Fowey,* and *Vulcan*) had been sunk by French artillery. Allied troops carried Cornwallis's principal redoubts on the fourteenth and received Cornwallis's final surrender of seventy-six hundred troops on 19 October.[66]

George Washington would say later that success at Yorktown exemplified naval rather than military power. In battlefield terms, the Battle of the Virginia Capes was little more than a skirmish. After a mere three hours of broadsides, British losses amounted to merely a single ship, with relatively inconsequential damage to five others; the French reported noteworthy damage to only two of their own. But the brilliance (and significance) of the battle was at the strategic level, a classic concentration of the right military force at the decisive point. Only tactical brilliance on the part of British naval commanders could have righted the situation—and British naval leadership on 5 September 1781 was far from brilliant. The Battle of the Virginia Capes was at one time a stirring spectacle and a plodding bore. The extraordinary repercussions of the battle stand as the key to its importance. The impact of the battle could not have been realized at any other point on the globe, and its influence (never fully appreciated by its participants at the time of the battle) was a thousandfold more significant than the two and a half hours of cannoning that signaled the battle's peak. At a moment of infinite importance, the Royal Navy had failed at the most dramatic point of need, and American victory was ensured.[67]

English naval historian W. M. James's conclusion was perhaps most apt: "Yorktown has often been described as one of the decisive battles of the world, but it was the naval skirmish off the Chesapeake that was decisive."[68] The Battle of the Virginia Capes, much of it within distant sight and sound of those ashore, ultimately became one of the great culminating battles of the era of giant sailing battleships, shaped the fate of nations, and signaled the exact moment of ultimate triumph of our Revolution.

1800

Norfolk emerged from the Revolution barely breathing, a scene of total ruin where only rows of chimneys marked where the course of lanes and alleyways had been. The town had been ravaged by fire and neglect; its population had scattered and most of its prosperous Tory merchant class had been evicted. In no corner of America had the havoc visited by war been as great. In 1781 one visitor described the town as "mere heaps of rubbish," another in 1783, "there were not yet twelve houses rebuilt."[1]

Norfolk's rebuilding would be uneven, plagued by crazy-quilt planning, yellow fever spurred by swamps and squalor, and not infrequent fires. "It is one of the ugliest, most irregular, and filthy towns that can any-where be found," recorded one visitor. Historian Thomas Parramore summarized the situation simply: "Norfolk had earned a reputation of altogether legendary proportions for ugliness and nastiness."[2]

Tidewater's destiny had always rested with the sea, and it was in that direction that most gazed during the struggle to recover from the Revolution's devastation. Old trading relationships were gradually restored, new commerce routes forged, shipbuilding restarted. The dynamism of maritime trade slowly primed the pump of recovery, and each month seemed to bring a few more weather-beaten traders from across the world's oceans to the wharves of Norfolk, Portsmouth, and Hampton. By 1790, Virginia had again clawed its way to the forefront, leading all other states in import duties and agricultural exports (primarily tobacco).[3]

The recovery of shipbuilding along the James and Elizabeth rivers was slow to begin, but with shipping inexorably drawn to Hampton Roads, timber sheds, smiths' forges, and ropewalks were soon in bustling operation. The city of Portsmouth annexed Sprowle's old Gosport yard in 1784, and shipbuilding resumed there in 1794 and 1795.

All Continental Navy ships had been sold or discarded at the end of the Revolution, but by 1793, threats to American trade by French privateers in the West Indies and Barbary corsairs in the Mediterranean led to renewed calls for a national navy. Virginia merchants were among the most vociferous in demanding action, and, on 27 March 1794, Congress passed an an Act to Provide a Naval Armament, formally founding the Navy of the United States and authorizing the construction of six frigates, four planned for 44 guns and two for 36.[4] President Washington signed the commissions of six captains, providing an officer to oversee the construction of each ship.

Secretary of War Henry Knox named Philadelphia shipbuilder Joshua Humphreys to prepare the designs for the ships (with Josiah Fox, a young shipbuilder from England, and Philadelphian William Doughty collaborating). The resulting frigate designs were large for their rating (twenty feet longer than comparable British designs); they were built with fast lines and a flush upper deck that accommodated two full gun decks, conferring a decided advantage in broadside weight against similar Royal Navy frigates. The four 44's, *United States, Constitution, President,* and an unnamed ship (which would later be christened *Chesapeake),* were to be built at Philadelphia, Boston, New York, and Norfolk, respectively. The 36's, *Congress* and *Constellation,* would be built at Portsmouth, New

The sleek, 38-gun frigate *Constellation* was launched in Baltimore on 7 September 1797 and quickly became a mainstay in the Navy's actions during the Quasi-war with France and in the Mediterranean. She was pinned in Norfolk in the opening days of the War of 1812 by British blockade and contributed to Hampton Roads defenses throughout the war. She was broken up at Gosport in 1854. *U.S. Naval Institute*

Hampshire, and Baltimore. Although Secretary Knox had first recommended that one of the 36's be built at Norfolk and the fourth 44 at Baltimore, President Washington switched those two provisions for political reasons.[5]

Already well known in Tidewater, Revolutionary War hero Capt. Richard Dale (fifth in seniority of the six captains) was selected to command the frigate at Norfolk and to oversee her construction. Born 6 November 1756, the oldest of five children of shipwright Winfield Dale and Ann Dale of Norfolk County, Richard Dale had made his first transatlantic voyage at the age of twelve in a ship commanded by his uncle.[6]

In 1776, Dale was appointed a lieutenant in the Virginia State Navy but was captured by a tender of the British frigate *Liverpool*. While confined aboard a Tory ship of Dunmore's fleet at Norfolk, he was persuaded to join the Loyalist cause by an old schoolmate, but when he was captured by Capt. John Barry of the Continental Navy brig *Lexington* (14), he reversed direction and agreed to sign aboard as a midshipman. Later, when British cutter *Alert* (10) captured *Lexington,* Dale and other officers were sent to prison near Plymouth, England. Ultimately Dale escaped, disguised as a British naval officer, and made his way to France, where he joined John Paul Jones as master's mate and later first lieutenant of the frigate *Bonhomme Richard.* He fought with distinction in Jones's desperate engagement with HMS *Serapis* (44) on 23 September 1779 off Flamborough Head on the Yorkshire coast of England. Importantly, Dale's account of that historic battle first brought to public attention Jones's acclaimed declaration, "I have not yet begun to fight." Jones's biographer Evan Thomas described Dale as universally well liked aboard *Bonhomme Richard* and as professional but calm, a refreshing contrast to Jones's intense, demanding reputation.[7]

Later in the war, Dale joined Capt. James Nicholson aboard frigate *Trumbull* (28) but fell wounded in an engagement off Delaware Bay with British frigate *Iris* (36) and sloop-of-war *Monk* (18). Taken to New York, yet again as a British prisoner, Dale was paroled and later served aboard an armed merchantman. After the war, he continued in the merchant trade.[8]

There were no public shipyards to build Joshua Humphreys's frigates, so steps were taken to lease the necessary facilities and assign Navy agents and yard clerks at each site. With the strong support of Moses Myers, ship captain and merchant William Pennock of Norfolk was appointed Navy agent for Gosport in July 1794 to manage all of its naval activities. Under direction from the secretary of the Navy, Pennock arranged supplies for ships, both under construction and preparing for sea, recruited crewmen, appointed shipmasters, organized stowage of material, furnished quarters, and transferred messages to ship captains from the secretary. The secretary's instructions to Pennock read, in part, "whenever a Vessel of War arrives at Norfolk you are to supply the Capt. with whatever he specifies to be necessary in a written return, signed by himself, a Copy of which you will immediately transmit to me."[9]

Josiah Fox arrived in Gosport in 1795 to serve as master builder of the Virginia frigate, but delays in fencing the yard and getting timber (especially the tough and durable live oak preferred by Humphreys) postponed keel laying until that December. Dale collaborated with Fox on some design details but was otherwise rarely involved in construction plans. Fox ceased work after only three months with news of peace in the Mediterranean and was ordered to sell off some of the materials prepared for the frigate. A disappointed Dale went to Philadelphia and sailed for China as captain of the merchantman *Ganges*. The yard at Portsmouth was demoted to caretaker status, with only minimal appropriations for its upkeep approved by Congress.[10]

On 30 April 1798, as tensions with France steadily mounted (referred to by historians as the "Quasi-war") and with American merchant ships again at risk on the open seas, Congress approved legislation to establish the United States Navy as a separate department. As the young nation struggled to rapidly increase its naval forces, several merchantmen were purchased and converted to armed cruisers, ships of the revenue cutter service were transferred to Navy control, and the Navy accepted several small warships sponsored by private citizens through "subscription" campaigns. At Dale's urging, one of the first merchantmen purchased, on 3 May 1798, was *Ganges* (which carried 26 9-pounder guns), and Dale's commission as a Navy captain was restored. On 23 May, Dale went to sea on an anti-privateer patrol between New York and Cape Henry.[11]

With its "fleet" expanding, the Navy needed a central operating base. Although still only under lease from the Commonwealth, Gosport responded immediately to the Navy's sudden surge in activity. With an experienced naval agent in place and with a location convenient to ships sailing to and from the West Indies, Gosport soon assumed the charge as the Navy's first full-service naval base. Literally, the entire Navy (including frigates *United States, Constitution, Constellation, Congress,*

Richard Dale was born in Norfolk County, Virginia, on 6 November 1756, served with John Paul Jones as first lieutenant in *Bon Homme Richard,* and later was named as one of the first six captains of the U.S. Navy in 1794. *U.S. Naval Institute*

Chesapeake, and *Insurgente*) would routinely use Gosport and would rely upon William Pennock for its supply and repair during the Quasi-war. Seagoing ships constantly plied the Elizabeth River, making Gosport, at times, the largest industrial enterprise in Virginia.[12]

With the sudden surge in Navy work at Gosport came a bevy of supporting industries. Local mills shaped and trimmed strakes, smoke curled skyward from local ironwork forges, and a Portsmouth mold loft became nationally known for its excellent patterns for ship frames. Gosport Distillery opened in the late-eighteenth century just outside the shipyard gates and soon reached a top production of more than 400 gallons of rum (grog) per day for the Navy. When *Constitution* sailed from Gosport in July 1798, listed on her manifest of stores were 48,600 gallons of water, 7,400 cannonshot, 11,600 pounds of black powder, and 79,400 gallons of rum.[13]

In June 1798, frigate *Constellation* (Capt. Thomas Truxtun) anchored at Hampton Roads, fresh from her Baltimore building yards. With help from Pennock, Truxtun gathered final

After his appointment as one of the first captains in the U.S. Navy in 1794, Thomas Truxtun (1755–1822) operated primarily from Hampton Roads. He commanded the frigate *Constellation* in the Quasi-war with France where his victory over the French frigate *L'Insurgente* made him one of the first nationally known naval heroes. *U.S. Naval Institute*

supplies and a crew (120 men recruited from Norfolk) and sailed later that month on a shakedown cruise through the capes, escorting a dozen merchantmen. Although Truxtun hailed from Long Island and New Jersey, Norfolk became his second home, and he quickly became known along the Portsmouth and Norfolk waterfronts. More importantly, both he and Dale, two of the Navy's most senior voices, became strong advocates of the advantages of Hampton Roads.[14]

In July, a two hundred-ton brig built by the Nash and Herbert shipyard of Portsmouth was purchased by the government, named *Norfolk,* and ordered to Gosport for fitting out. That same month, Capt. Thomas Williams was ordered to Gosport to command *Norfolk* and to superintend final preparations for sea. *Norfolk* carried 18 6-pounders on a flush deck and was known as a good sailer, fast and well suited for the West Indies. Williams's stay at Gosport lasted only a few months, and his naval career was equally brief, since Commo. John Barry cashiered him on his first cruise for operational lapses. Schooner *Virginia* (14), a revenue cutter built at Hampton and transferred to naval service, was also fitted out at Gosport and sailed to the Caribbean under Capt. Francis Bright.[15]

By August, Navy Secretary Benjamin Stoddert ordered Agent Pennock to clear the ways at Gosport and recommence building of the uncompleted Virginia frigate that was soon to be named *Chesapeake*. Josiah Fox hurried to Portsmouth to resume the role of naval constructor, and on 10 December 1798 the ship's new keel was set in place. For economy, the plans were redrawn, and *Chesapeake* would become the smallest of the six frigates, rated for 36 guns.

During the summer of 1798, a committee of five prominent Norfolk citizens (Robert Barraud Taylor, William Pennock, Moses Myers, Thomas Willock, and Warren Ashley) began a subscription drive among leading citizens and merchants of Norfolk, Richmond, and Petersburg to provide an armed Navy ship to help protect trade. The campaign went well—an early indication of Tidewater's vibrant interest in the Navy—and the committee soon wrote Stoddert, offering the services of any of four ships nearing completion in Norfolk. Stoddert replied that "either of the Brigs . . . will be acceptable" and suggested the choice be left to Samuel Barron of Hampton, who would receive a captain's commission and command of the ship. Barron picked *Augusta* (a ship being built by Norfolk merchant Moses Myers, bearing the name of his daughter), which the Navy valued at $27,896.87 and renamed *Richmond*. She was fitted out during the fall at Gosport and was rated at 16 guns.[16]

Samuel Barron's connection with this subscription ship was hardly an accident. Well known and respected in Tidewater, Barron had already commanded several ships for Myers after leaving the Virginia State Navy in 1788. By the time of the subscription campaign, Barron was lobbying vigorously for a naval commission and had paid several visits on Secretary Stoddert, carrying endorsements from the Norfolk congressman, Myers, and other leading citizens.[17]

Constellation was back in Hampton Roads by November 1798 to refit for a deployment to the West Indies. Just before sailing, Truxtun enjoyed a Christmas dinner with British Adm. George Vandeput, whose squadron lay at anchor in Hampton Roads; a relatively constant Royal Navy presence accumulated in Norfolk and at Lynnhaven Roads during the decade 1798–1807, which had begun as escorts for American merchant ships doing trade with the British Isles. Truxtun suggested an exchange of salutes between the two highest-ranking officers of their respective services when *Constellation* sailed, a common politeness between naval officers. Although not intending to offend, Vandeput agreed, adding a postscript that his return salute would be with two fewer guns, appropriate for an admiral answering the salute of a captain and ignoring the fact that Truxtun was acting as the senior naval officer in the American Navy. Proud, and probably a bit put out with the implication of second-class status, Truxtun sailed on New Year's Eve but refused to fire the salute, writing later: "It was impossible for me to acquiesce, without degrading the Flag of the United States."[18]

When Truxtun sailed, Samuel Barron's *Richmond* and a convoy of four merchant ships accompanied him. Once in the Caribbean, *Constellation* joined a growing American naval squadron—including the new frigate *United States* (44) and brig *Norfolk*—that protected American merchant ships from French privateers and warships. In February 1799, the U.S. Navy recorded its first significant trial by fire when Truxtun engaged and captured the French frigate *L'Insurgente* (40). Three months later Truxtun returned triumphantly to Hampton Roads with *Constellation* leading her prize with the tricolor of France fluttering beneath the American ensign on her mizzen gaff. Truxtun was feted with abandon by adoring Norfolk society and became the borough's first widely acclaimed naval hero. Parades were held in his honor, speeches and balls crowded his calendar, and many rowed out to visit *Constellation* and her prize in the harbor.

Good fortune also shined on Samuel Barron, who had been shifted from *Richmond* to the larger brig *Baltimore* (20) while in the West Indies. Arriving back in Norfolk about 16 July 1799, Barron received new orders releasing him from *Baltimore* to "superintend the equipment of the Frigate building at Norfolk with a view to command her." During this same time, with a head full of sudden fame, Truxtun toyed with resigning his commission. Samuel Barron, available for command, was ordered to succeed him aboard *Constellation* and left Gosport for New York. But the dashing Truxtun had second thoughts and, as Barron sailed *Constellation* into Hampton Roads, a suddenly contrite Truxtun rushed to recoup both his commission and command. Barron returned to *Chesapeake* just before Fox had her ready to launch.

View of Norfolk from Smiths Point 1796 by Benjamin Henry Latrobe. Latrobe became the country's first professional architect and engineer with a practice that began in Virginia that same year. In 1798 he was sent to survey Norfolk's defenses for the War Department and later was appointed Architect of the Capitol Building in Washington, D.C. *Sargeant Memorial Room, Norfolk Public Library*

On 1 December 1799, the *Chesapeake* stood proudly on her building blocks at river's edge; her freshly painted sides were black with a wide stripe of white denoting her gundeck, and her coppered bottom shone dully in the light. Despite a bitterly cold morning, the Gosport yard swarmed with spectators, and many small boats floated nearby in the Elizabeth. Naval officers, including Commodore Truxtun and Captain Barron, were resplendent in full-dress uniforms and navy greatcoats. At the intended hour, the order was given to the two hundred workmen to start hammering wedges under the ship to raise her from the blocks. The last stanchion was knocked away and, as the Norfolk *Herald* reported, "the tallow on her ways being frozen and the weather extremely cold . . . (after) the blocks (were) removed from under her, she started and went only a few feet but slowly." The crowd waited, their cheers frozen in midair, but *Chesapeake* refused to budge another inch on her launching ways. After directing her safely back onto her blocks, Fox ordered a delay until 1300 on the following [warmer] day, and the *Herald* ultimately reported success: "at half past one o'clock, in the presence of a great concourse of people was safely launched into her element the United States frigate *Chesapeake,* of 44 guns [*sic*], commanded by Samuel Barron, Esquire."[19]

Truxtun sailed *Constellation* out through the Virginia Capes on Christmas Eve 1799 on a second cruise to the West Indies and again earned laurels by battling another superior French frigate, *La Vengeance* (44), to a heroic standstill. Gosport, again, was Truxtun's return destination, and the public's acclaim mounted to an even higher crescendo than the year before.

Even at this early stage in American history, Hampton Roads was more aware of the importance of *naval* success than any other corner of the nation, and Truxtun's return (with a crew of many fathers and sons from Tidewater families) was welcomed with unrestrained enthusiasm. Truxtun's two Quasi-war cruises signaled a point of transformation for Tidewater communities by moving Hampton Roads to a leading position in the nation's practice of foreign affairs. Long comfortable with their international prominence, achieved through commerce and trade, the people of Tidewater now considered themselves leaders in the application of *naval* power to the shaping of world events. Thomas Truxtun, through word and deed, brought that new perspective to Hampton Roads—a legacy that lives to this day.

Acting as the senior naval officer in Hampton Roads (where the greatest concentration of the Navy lay), Truxtun began to act, quite logically, much as an operational fleet commander would today, many times issuing orders at variance with the plans of the secretary of the Navy. It was an audacious step, not seen before in the Navy and, from a modern perspective, not entirely wrong. In one instance, the newly built 36-gun frigate *Congress* limped into Hampton Roads during the spring of 1800, having been demasted during a storm on her maiden voyage. Primarily for cost-saving reasons, Sec-retary Stoddert had ordered Pennock to transfer masts and yards reserved for *Chesapeake's* construction and *Chesapeake* workmen to *Congress* to hasten her repair. Truxtun, acting on his own and convinced that he could get *Chesapeake* to sea faster to face the French, restored priority work to *Chesapeake* and transferred half of *Congress*'s crew to the ship. Proving Truxtun correct, *Chesapeake* left Hampton Roads on 24 May 1800 for her first extended cruise to the West Indies.[20]

Recognizing the increasing importance of the Gosport Navy Yard to the Navy, Stoddert moved to formally buy the property from Virginia. In a letter dated 20 January 1800 addressed to James Monroe, governor of Virginia, Stoddert wrote:

> Sir, the United States have heretofore occupied for Navy purposes a piece of ground at Gosport, belonging to the Commonwealth of Virginia—it is supposed to contain about ten acres—the ground is considered to be very well situated for a permanent Navy Yard, and if it should be so appropriated, it will be desirable to commence imm. some buildings for the accommodation of workers and the security of timber. Permit me therefore by order of the President to solicit the favor of your Excellency to communicate to the Legislature of Virginia the desire of the Government of the United States to obtain this property either by purchase or in some other way as the Legislature shall deem proper.[21]

An assessment of the property was ordered, and a report dated 8 May 1800 concluded: "Thomas Newton (for the State of Virginia) and William Pennock (Naval Agent) jointly measured and assessed the Yard at Gosport to be about 16 acres and value of $12,000." True to form, Commodore Truxtun, not worried at all about costs, rushed to endorse the assessment and pressed for the immediate construction of specific capabilities including: "A mast house with a sail loft above . . . a joiners shop two stories high . . . a rigging loft 180 × 40 feet . . . a blacksmith shop . . . a storehouse three stories high . . . a spacious coppers shop and shed . . . a bason [*sic*] for the deposit of timber." Stoddert, thinking the $800 per acre price outrageous, but pushed into a corner by Truxtun, begrudgingly wrote Pennock on 7 August 1800, approving the purchase: "although I think the state should have charged nothing for the Navy Yard at Gosport, yet that property must be taken at the valuation." Thomas Mathews, of Norfolk, pushed a bill through the Virginia Assembly authorizing the sale for $12,000 with a deed dated 15 June 1801.[22]

Cleverly, Stoddert had not sought authority from Congress to purchase the Gosport land (or the five other Navy yards). These first six Navy "shore bases" resulted from Stoddert's nimble use of funds voted on 25 February 1799 for six ships-of-the-line and six sloops on the grounds that the six yards were needed for their construction.[23]

Both the new administration and the new Congress ordered investigations into Stoddert's use of ship funds to acquire bases without "express provision made by Congress for establishing navy yards." Working quickly, Stoddert authorized the purchase of substantial lumber for ship construction and stored it at Gosport and the other yards and then quietly circulated word that if the Navy yard purchases were reversed, the Navy would have to dispose of an even greater value of lumber. Stoddert's shrewd gambit worked, and the Jefferson administration (no friend to the Navy at the time) took no action to surrender Gosport or the other yards.[24]

It had taken the undeclared war with France for American naval power to begin to acquire respectability throughout the world, and it had taken the same war to prove the value of the Gosport yard throughout the Navy. Before the war, the Navy had few ships, no recognized commanders, and no central base to concentrate and victual its ships. After the war, the Navy fully owned what Truxtun described as "the most complete Navy Yard in the United States. Plenty of water, no ice in winter, a good harbour, and choice masts and other timber."

After the Quasi-war, the thirty-odd ships in the Navy would be reduced to the thirteen largest, with only six of those considered operational, but Gosport's importance continued to increase. The Navy's first squadron to oppose the Barbary States in the Mediterranean was organized in Hampton Roads during May 1801 under Commo. Richard Dale. With his broad pennant flying from frigate *President* (44) (Capt. James Barron), Dale's squadron also included the new frigate *Philadelphia* (36) (Capt. Samuel Barron) and frigate *Essex* (32) (where a young Lt. Stephen Decatur sailed as first lieutenant). A second Mediterranean Squadron was readied for sailing from Gosport in April 1802, composed of frigates *Chesapeake, Adams,* and *Constellation* and sloop *Enterprise*. Gosport's work to ready *Chesapeake* was particularly noteworthy, as she was in poor shape after over a year in unsupervised ordinary.[25]

On 26 April 1802 Daniel Bedinger replaced William Pennock as Navy agent. Pennock had done an immense amount of work over eight years to help establish the Navy at the Gosport yard and was considered by Secretary Stoddert to be "an active man—an excellent quality in an Agent." Constantly pressured by the cost-conscious secretary to economize, Pennock had rapidly learned his job and was a careful and conscientious administrator of public funds. It was said later that he was replaced when it had been "found necessary to reward partizans [*sic*] at the expense of merit and he [Pennock] was removed without a complaint against him."[26]

But not everyone agreed that Pennock was doing a good job. Vice President Aaron Burr had pressed to get Norfolk businessman Luke Wheeler the job; he said of Pennock: "on all hands it is agreed that your [Navy] Agent [Pennock] is a bad one."[27] Although Pennock might have been cashiered for *Chesapeake's* poor material condition, he was probably simply the victim of a general housecleaning of Federalist office hold-

Commo. James Barron (1769–1851) of Hampton came from one of the first great Virginia families of naval heritage but is primarily remembered, infamously, for the *Chesapeake-Leopard* affair of 1807 and his fatal duel with Stephen Decatur in 1820. *U.S. Naval Institute*

ers by the new Jefferson administration. Whatever the cause for Pennock's departure, his steady hand overseeing Gosport operations helped guarantee the viability of a Hampton Roads naval base. William Pennock returned to business as a shipowner and merchant but did poorly during the economic downturns of the next ten years. He died in Norfolk at age sixty-four on 8 May 1816.

A two-story brick structure that was to be known as the Commodore's House was one of several structures in the first phase of federal construction at the Gosport yard beginning in 1803. As there was no "commodore" assigned to Gosport in 1803, it was said that the first occupant of the house was an eccentric old sea captain named Thomas Dulton who acted as a storekeeper or clerk of the yard. According to legend, Dulton thought of himself as the most important person within the yard, mustered all employees daily, and attended to the ringing of the yard bell at regular times. Prior to 1810, the chief administrator of the yard, by practice, was the appointed Navy agent, a position held by Pennock, Bedinger, and Theordorick Armistead (beginning 10 February 1808). At times, a commissioned Navy captain would also be present at the yard to superintend the construction of a warship or a senior naval officer would be present in the area (as Truxtun was between his war cruises). In those instances, the senior officer present would have the authority to direct the activities of the Navy agent, but, by practice, this oversight was disjointed and inconsistent.

By 1810, the Department of the Navy, after experiencing considerable difficulty with civilian naval agents operating Navy yards (all of whom had outside commercial interests), established the new position of Commandant for each yard and ordered active-duty naval officers to that position. The first formal Commandant of the Gosport Navy Yard was Capt. Samuel Barron, who assumed the position on 7 July 1810. By this time, however, Barron was in poor health with an unknown and lingering fever, one that had caused him to surrender his command of the Mediterranean Squadron in 1805 and had kept him from consistent service. News of his appointment cheered the Barron family, as it was felt his recuperation could be hastened by the care of family and friends. This was not to be the case, however, and Samuel died suddenly on 29 October 1810 at the early age of 45 while visiting his brother James in Hampton. At Gosport, the duties of his office fell temporarily to Lt. Robert Henley until he was relieved by Capt. Samuel Evans on 1 May 1811.[28]

The first Marine Guard was ordered to the Gosport yard in October 1803, and a wooden shop building was assigned to them for barracks. The guard was reassigned briefly between 1804 and 1807 to the Washington Navy Yard but then returned and remained continuously on station until September 1978, the second oldest corps post when it finally closed.

In December 1803, a naval courier delivered new Navy Department orders to the Hampton home of Captain James Barron:

> The President having determined to build two Gun-Boats, I have to request that you will undertake the superintendency of one to be built at the Navy Yard at Gosport, or at Portsmouth, or Norfolk, whichever may be found the most convenient. We conceive the Gun-Boats can be employed with great effect in the protection in times of war of our Sea-Port Towns. We have determined to build two . . . as models . . . we leave you to be funded entirely by your own judgment, We will only observe that she must be constructed to carry 1 long 32 pdr Cannon . . . Money will be deposited with D. Bedinger Esq. subject to your orders.[29]

The orders signaled a new dimension of duty for James Barron, who had risen, along with his brother Samuel, through a series of shipboard assignments, including commands of brig *Warren* and frigates *United States, Essex, President,* and *New York*. The Barrons' service to the Navy had been consistent and stalwart, and the two brothers from Hampton had moved steadily ahead in seniority in the young Navy.

The orders also signaled an unusual new phase for the American Navy, one, again, that would be witnessed first in Hampton Roads. Many in the Jefferson administration wanted to avoid the expense of a seagoing fleet and, instead, favored the construction of small gunboats to defend the American coast. The inexpensive gunboats were quick to build, and theory at the time had it that gunboats operating in swarms with 32-pounder guns could overpower British ships. The Jefferson administration planned for as many as two hundred of the craft to be built in many small shipyards.[30]

James Barron was one of the very few naval officers who did not regard the gunboats with disdain. He supported them as "the proper kind of vessels to afford the most effectual means of defence and annoyance within the bays and rivers of the United States . . . (twenty of them) in Hampton Roads would be sufficient to repel any attack in that quarter and be very formidable to a larger force." Jefferson would allocate sixty gunboats to Norfolk.[31]

The first two gunboat prototypes tested different designs, with *Gunboat No. 1* built at Washington and *No. 2* in Hampton Roads (by George Hope of Hampton). Both boats entered service during the summer of 1804. Barron enjoyed the new challenge and meticulously oversaw every detail of the construction of *Gunboat No. 2,* sending pages of correspondence arguing for the proper armament and equipment. Once the boat was in the water, Barron continued to test and tinker, perfecting design details and examining new tactics. His design for *Gunboat No. 2* (featuring a single lateen sail, bowsprit, and jib; armed with a single 32-pounder in the bow; and manned by twenty-three men) was slightly smaller than *Gunboat No. 1* and became the standard for the next phase of building that included twelve gunboats built in Hampton, Portsmouth, and Mathews County in 1806. Ten more gunboats were planned for construction in Norfolk between 1806 and 1809. Later, Barron worked closely with Constructor Hope in Hampton to develop plans for a new, smaller class of gunboats for "narrow rivers where the water is smooth" and "intended to act as a Defensive Force in the Rivers, Hampton Roads & occasionally in the Bay or on the Coast."[32] When the 1806 phase of gunboat construction began in Hampton Roads, a rising star in Tidewater's Navy, Lt. Arthur Sinclair, was placed in charge of construction.[33]

In September 1805, the frigate *Congress* (Capt. Stephen Decatur) sailed through the capes and anchored in Hampton Roads after a rapid transit across the Atlantic from duty in the Mediterranean. Young Decatur stood as an unquestioned naval war hero, the toast of the nation that had been thrilled by stories of his valiant exploits in the Barbary Wars. In what had been called the "most bold and daring act of the age" by Adm. Horatio Nelson, Decatur had led an intrepid night raid deep into Tripoli harbor to liberate and burn the former U.S. frigate *Philadelphia,* which had been captured after running aground. Months later, he had also led his men in hand-to-hand fighting while boarding and capturing an enemy gunboat near Tripoli.

Decatur's stop in Hampton Roads was to be brief, as he had still to formally deliver the new Tunisian ambassador and his entourage to Washington. During his short stay, Decatur was invited for dinner and a ball honoring the ambassador at the Granby Street residence of noted businessman and mayor Luke Wheeler of Norfolk. Striking in his blue and gold uniform, handsome and urbane, the dashing naval hero would surely have taken more than one breath away from the formally gowned ladies present. But Decatur's attention immediately fastened on the mayor's stunning daughter, Susan. The chance meeting rapidly bloomed into a dizzying infatuation that quickly became the talk of both proper society and the naval officer corps.

Miss Wheeler, three years Decatur's senior, was one of the most dazzling lights in the elite circles of Norfolk and Washington society. Beautiful, intelligent, charming, and well read, she had many distinguished admirers. As the daughter of a leading politician, Susan also sparked controversy and gossip, and her origins were said to be suspect—in a day when strong family lineage was everything, nothing specific was known of her mother. It was common knowledge that she was close to the powerful Carroll family of Maryland. Jerome Bonaparte (brother of Napoleon) had visited Norfolk in June 1803 and had brazenly courted Susan until she steered clear of entanglement.[34] She was well acquainted with Vice President Aaron Burr and Secretary of the Navy Robert Smith. Truxtun cavalierly mentioned "the lovely Susan" in his Norfolk correspondence.

After escorting the Tunisian ambassador safely to Washington and placing the *Congress* in ordinary, Decatur journeyed to Philadelphia to visit his parents, retrieve the gift of a ceremonial sword presented by Congress, and break off a longstanding romantic arrangement with a Philadelphia belle—so taken had he been with his magical evening in Norfolk.

By early December, Decatur was back in Washington and chanced upon a close friend, Master Commandant Isaac Chauncey, captain of the newly commissioned Navy brig *Hornet* (18). *Hornet* was due to stop briefly in Norfolk before sailing for South America, and Decatur talked Chauncey into calling upon Susan to deliver a gift. After departing Norfolk, Chauncey penned a personal letter back to Decatur:

> She blushingly received the Music and with looks that experessed [*sic*] the feelings of her Soul thanked me as the Bearer but more particularly, the Donor for not forgetting her—She asked me to call the following day, I did so, and found the little packet had wrought mericles [*sic*], it indeed had been Music to her Soul, for Joy beemed [*sic*] in her Eyes and her every gesture was heavenly . . . She cou'd not help saying that she had heard that you was to be married on your arrival in Philadelphia, that the Sword presented to you by a voat [*sic*] of Congress, had been sent to Miss _____ of that place for safe keeping, that you wou'd be obliged to Marry the Lady to save the Sword, I told her that . . . that

> report had been premature in that particular for I did not believe you had an Idea of marrying any person in Philadelphia, that I knew as far as related to the Sword was not true, for to my knowledge it was forwarded to your father.[35]

Decatur reappeared in Norfolk early in January, bent on formally proposing. At that same time, an oft-repeated tale surfaced in which it was said that James Barron happened upon Decatur and a male friend on a Norfolk street. Barron and Decatur were close acquaintances (Decatur served as Barron's first lieutenant aboard frigate *New York,* and Barron had been third lieutenant aboard frigate *United States* on Decatur's first voyage as a midshipman), and during introductions, jest was made, tying Decatur's swift return to Norfolk with the presence of a certain lady. Decatur's long Philadelphia engagement was common knowledge in the Navy, and Barron voiced his opinion that a dalliance in Norfolk would be inappropriate. Decatur, doubly offended both at Barron's meddling and by the implication that his Norfolk amour was not as discreet as he had intended, roundly scolded his friend. His sense of honor pricked, Decatur then traded heated words with Barron before the two men finally went their own ways. Barron's biographer quotes Barron as saying, "from that day Decatur was an altered man to me," and others have pointed to this chance meeting as the beginning of bad blood between these two well-known commodores.[36]

On 8 March 1806 the couple was married in the Presbyterian Church with an announcement appearing in the next issue of the Norfolk *Gazette & Publick Ledger*: "Married—On Saturday last by the Rev. Mr. Grigsby, the gallant Captain Stephen Decatur, jun. of the United States' Navy to the accomplished and much admired Miss Susan Wheeler, only daughter of Luke Wheeler, Esq., Mayor of this Borough."[37]

At first, the Decaturs lived in a home built by Luke Wheeler, referred to as "Summer House," on Tripoli Street (named in honor of Decatur's heroics). Decatur purchased several properties in Norfolk between 1810 and 1812. On one tract near the water on Union Street (purchased 26 March 1810), Decatur built an impressive house that would be known for its grand ballroom and two large crystal chandeliers. Merritt Moore Robinson Todd, who had moved to Norfolk from Bermuda, subsequently bought the house. A daughter, Maria Louisa Todd, married Dr. Armistead Thompson Mason Cooke, who inherited the house. One of their daughters later married Henry Aston Ramsey, chief engineer of the ironclad CSS *Virginia.* Sadly, Richard Dickson Cooke, later a mayor of Norfolk, tore the house down about 1921.[38]

In November 1806, Decatur was ordered to command the growing Tidewater gunboat flotilla and to superintend the next phases of construction. He reported his arrival to the secretary of the Navy on 2 January 1807 but soon reported that the gunboats were in much worse condition than expected. "The fact is," he wrote, "that the stores have been broken open three times, three-fourths of the articles delivered from the boats [including muskets, cutlasses, pistols] have been stolen, of the things left many have been rendered useless in consequence of having had no care taken of them." Decatur had little faith in the theory of gunboats, once commenting to a fellow naval officer, "What would be the real national loss if all the gunboats were sunk in 100 fathoms of water?" He would use his time in Norfolk to study designs and suggest improvements.[39]

Decatur had reason to be concerned, for, by 1805, Europe had again exploded into war. Trade blockades constrained American trade, and ships from Hampton Roads had been boarded on the high seas or captured by privateers. Particularly galling for those in Norfolk was the Royal Navy practice of impressing seamen from American ships. Royal Navy ships hovered within sight of the American coast, and, as British ships typically were undermanned, captains felt they had the legal right and the operational need to impress "Englishmen" from neutral ships to augment their crews. English law did not recognize naturalization; anyone born in England was the king's subject and was eligible for service. Royal Navy impressments of American sailors steadily increased between 1802 and 1812, with almost a thousand men per year conscripted off American merchant ships by the end of the decade.[40]

In February 1807, three seamen fled British frigate *Melampus* (36) and had appeared at Lieutenant Sinclair's Norfolk "rendezvous" for the recruiting of sailors for *Chesapeake*. The British protested first to Decatur in Norfolk (who refused to act, as Lieutenant Sinclair was not under his orders) and then to the American secretary of state. Commo. James Barron was asked to investigate, and he found that all three were American citizens (two from Maryland and one from Massachusetts) who had been illegally impressed.[41]

At about the same time, on 7 March, five seamen deserted the British sloop-of-war *Halifax* by overwhelming a midshipman and rowing a jollyboat to Sewell's Point. All of the deserters appeared at Sinclair's rendezvous and were also enlisted into American service. *Halifax's* first lieutenant discovered the five in Norfolk, and, later, two of the five publicly insulted *Halifax's* captain. Formal English protests were again made to Lieutenant Sinclair and the mayor of Norfolk, again to no avail. Vice Adm. George Berkeley, commander of the British North American station in Halifax, was said to have been furious at the public insult and the stubborn refusal to surrender men he considered to be British sailors.[42]

Tidewater's relations with the British were not helped when, during the summer of 1806, a British squadron anchored *inside* American waters in Lynnhaven Bay to blockade two French warships that were undergoing storm repairs in Annapolis and Norfolk. On 14 September 1806, British ships-of-the-line *Belleisle* (74) and *Bellona* (74) and frigate *Melampus* were some thirty-five miles off Cape Henry when the French line-of-battle ship *Impetueux* (74), under jury masts, was sighted heading for the Chesapeake. After a desperate chase, the French warship grounded inside the capes, and the British took off the crew and set fire to her.[43]

The morning of 22 June 1807 dawned with a blue sky, the promise of summer heat, and breezes from the southwest—the first favorable wind in several days in Hampton Roads. *Chesapeake* lay at anchor, where she had been for more than two weeks while provisioning at Gosport in preparation to relieve frigate *Constitution* as flagship of the American Mediterranean Squadron. *Chesapeake* flew the broad pennant of Commodore Barron, who had embarked aboard *Chesapeake* only the day before. On Barron's writing desk lay sailing orders from the secretary of the Navy and a letter written by Thomas Jefferson, asking him to arrange the safe transport home from Malta of a pipe of good Madeira and wishing him a pleasant voyage. Master Commandant Charles Gordon commanded the frigate. "At ¼ past 7," read the ship's log, "weighed anchor, made sail with a pleasant Breeze from WSW . . . and stood out for sea."[44]

Aboard *Chesapeake* were 339 men and boys (many newly signed on from recruiting sweeps along the Norfolk water-

The 36-gun frigate *Chesapeake* was launched 2 December 1799 at the Gosport Navy Yard, one of the first six frigates of the U.S. Navy. She served ably in the Quasi-war with France and in actions against the Barbary pirates, but was fired upon and disgraced by HMS *Leopard* in 1807 off Cape Henry and ultimately fell victim to HMS *Shannon* in fierce battle during the War of 1812, remembered widely for the valiant words of her mortally wounded captain, James Lawrence: "Don't Give Up the Ship." *Chesapeake* was taken into the Royal Navy and broken up in 1820. *Naval Historical Center*

front) and a marine contingent of fifty-two. Dr. John Bullus, the new U.S. Navy agent in the Mediterranean, his wife Charlotte, their three children, a maidservant, and a boy were aboard as passengers, as was the young wife of the *Chesapeake's* marine captain, John Hall, and a dozen or more Sicilian musicians with their instruments and families. Although Gordon had reported the ship ready for sailing, many of the stores and pieces of furniture and passengers' baggage had not yet been stowed below. Sick men had hung their hammocks on the relatively cooler spar deck, and cables were laid out along the gundeck. It had been the practice of American warships to stow materials in the first few days of a long voyage, so nothing was necessarily out of the ordinary.[45]

British blockaders *Melampus* and *Bellona* were anchored in Lynnhaven Bay, and a third ship-of-the line, *Triumph* (74), lay at anchor just north of Cape Henry. A fourth British warship, 50-gun frigate *Leopard,* commanded by Capt. Salusbury Pryce Humphreys, had arrived the day before, bearing dispatches from Halifax. She had anchored briefly in Lynnhaven Bay and then weighed and made sail at 0400 that morning, reanchoring in company with the *Triumph.*

Unknown to Commodore Barron, Captain Gordon, or other American naval officers in Norfolk on this pleasant summer morning, a sensational drama was slowly emerging that would culminate within the next eight hours in one of the most ignoble episodes in American naval history. It was a drama that had been months and years in the making, one that would overpower one of Tidewater's favorite sons and would radiate outward from Hampton Roads to affect the great navies of the Atlantic.

Before she arrived in Hampton Roads, *Chesapeake* had been rapidly refitted at the Washington Navy Yard after many months in ordinary and was barely fit for sea (when sailing past Mount Vernon, she had been unable to even fire the traditional gun salute to the late president). Nearly all of that blame rested on the shoulders of Gordon, who had just risen to his first command as the Navy's most junior master commandant and had put little emphasis on the ship's condition or the crew's training. Barron, never an overbearing commander, was appalled at the ship's condition but pointedly took no action to worsen an already strained relationship with Gordon, only meekly apologizing to the secretary of the Navy: "I am sorry that the *Chesapeake* has arrived here [Norfolk] in want of anything that may [cause] delay."[46]

Barron considered Gordon (who had served under Barron aboard frigate *New York*) to be undependable and foppish and "an officer too much addicted to pleasure and parade to bend his mind to business."[47] Gordon, aware of Barron's distrust of his abilities, viewed the commodore with some apprehension, as he would hold a key to Gordon's continued advancement. When Barron had first learned of Gordon's orders to *Chesapeake,* he had requested Navy Secretary Robert Smith to intercede; now, faced with a lengthy cruise, he chose to avoid confrontation.

The two were nearly professional opposites. At thirty-eight years of age, James Barron had risen in seniority through steadiness and the avoidance of risk. He was tall and rotund, with a grave smile and flinty eyes. In the service it was said that he did not delight in the prospect of physical combat but was also known as a competent mariner. His lack of boldness was balanced by a well-meaning countenance and a flair for the academic, including an interest in inventions.[48]

Aboard *Chesapeake* that morning the early breeze shifted, and it took two hours for the ship to pass Lynnhaven Bay. As the American ship slowly sailed past, *Bellona* sent a signal to the *Leopard* to weigh anchor and reconnoiter southeast by east. *Chesapeake* glided out past Cape Henry around 1400, tacked back toward shore briefly to drop off her pilot, and then made sail to the east.[49] The midday meal was called, and, as it was the first meal of the voyage, the commodore invited all of the ship's guests to join him in his cabin. All, including Gordon, accepted this invitation, except Mrs. Hall, who was ill with first-day seasickness. Through the open porthole on the starboard side one could see *Leopard* to the south, also standing east.

Among the dispatches that Captain Humphreys had delivered from Halifax was an ominous order signed by Admiral Berkeley dated 1 June 1807: "The captains and commanders of his Majesty's ships and vessels under my command, are . . . required and directed, in case of meeting the American frigate the *Chesapeake,* at sea, and without the limits of the United States, to show to the captain of her this order and to require to search his ship for deserters . . . and if a similar demand shall be made by the American, he is to be permitted to search for any deserters from their service, according to the custom and usage of civilized nations, on terms of peace and amity with each other."[50]

Captain Humphreys was no unknowing captain on a distant station. He held a respected reputation within His Britannic Majesty's service, was in Halifax when the reports of deserters being recruited at the *Chesapeake* rendezvous had been received, was serving as Berkeley's flag captain (so was, conceivably, included in the ensuing discussions), and had been handpicked to carry the commander in chief's order to Hampton Roads. He was in an envied position for someone in command, for he not only knew what the order was intended to accomplish but also how far he could proceed in enforcing the order without fear of censure.

About an hour after *Chesapeake* had dropped off her pilot, about three leagues east of Cape Henry, *Leopard* wore round and headed in the direction of the American, taking position on her windward quarter. It was customary when a ship hailed another that the approaching ship did so from leeward, but British ships invariably approached American ships from windward, a discourtesy and an implied threat of tactical advantage. *Chesapeake* backed her main topsail.[51]

By now it was just before 1600 and *Leopard* hailed that the captain had dispatches for the American. Barron replied, "We will heave to and you can send your boat." With due formality a British lieutenant named Meade was met at the *Chesapeake's* gangway by an American lieutenant, who took him to Master Commandant Gordon, who then escorted him below to the commodore. Barron was handed a copy of the British admiral's search order and an accompanying note from Humphreys: "The captain of the *Leopard* will not presume to say anything in addition to what the commander-in-chief has stated, more than to express a hope that every circumstance respecting them may be adjusted in a manner that the harmony subsisting between the two countries may remain undisturbed."[52]

Startled by the menacing implication, Barron immediately called for Doctor Bullus as a witness and for Gordon to ask if the men Humphreys sought appeared on *Chesapeake's* rolls. Gordon replied that he did not know. Barron sat to write his reply to Humphreys, fully aware that no American captain would yield to such an outrageous search, clearly one that violated national sovereignty and the self-respect of the young American Navy: "I know of no such men as you describe. The officers that were on the recruiting service for this ship were particularly instructed by the Government, through me, not to enter any deserters from his Britannic Majesty's ships, nor do I know of any being here. I am also instructed never to permit the crew of any ship that I command to be mustered by any but their own officers. It is my disposition to preserve harmony, and I hope this answer to your dispatch will prove satisfactory."[53]

Barron fully realized that *Chesapeake's* decks were in disarray and it would take valuable time to ready her for battle and to distribute arms and powder to the crew. Noting that *Leopard* had already cleared for action and had run her guns out, Barron decided to play for time by delaying the departure of the English lieutenant with his reply, but when Humphreys impatiently ordered his boat recalled, Barron tepidly allowed Meade to leave, fearing to ignite an immediate response. Now agitated with indecision, Barron confusingly ordered Gordon to clear the gundeck for action, but not to sound the drums or show the men running to station.

Motivated by what he later described, defensively, as an "ardent desire to prevent bloodshed," Humphreys hailed *Chesapeake* for clarification once he had received Barron's reply. Barron delayed as best he could as he watched his crew clumsily stumble toward their stations, answering Humphreys: "I do not hear what you say, sir." The feint was transparent; Humphreys' reply: "Captain Barron, you must be aware of the necessity I am under of complying with orders." Barron's response was, as before, that he could not hear.[54]

Resolving "no longer to be trifled with, and observing on board the American frigate indications of intended resistance," *Leopard* discharged a shot across the *Chesapeake's* forefoot, then a second and possibly a third. Now at 1630, "with no further response coming from *Chesapeake*," Humphreys ordered a full broadside from a distance of less than seventy yards.[55]

Shrapnel hit Barron as he stood fully exposed on the quarterdeck. Below decks, none of the *Chesapeake's* guns were ready for action; no slow matches or firing irons were on station. Hoping to halt the deadly fire, Barron hailed that he would send a boat, and Humphreys ordered a cease-fire. But "as the *Chesapeake* was now clearly making preparations to return the fire, the thing was considered to be an artifice to gain time," Humphreys recalled, and *Leopard* renewed her fire with a second and a third full broadside (some reports refer to a fourth broadside).[56]

Barron, painfully injured, stood helplessly amid the confusion and carnage. Leery of Gordon's leadership and unfamiliar with his officers, Barron was heard to cry, "For God's sake, gentlemen, will nobody do his duty." In agony, he turned to Captain Hall of the Marines and ordered: "Go down to the gun deck and ask them for God's sake to fire one gun for the honor of the flag. I mean to strike." Lt. William H. Allen, in charge of a division of guns, finally fired a gun with a red-hot coal that he had brought from the galley in his bare hands.[57]

With that single impotent shot Barron ordered *Chesapeake's* flag struck in humiliating surrender. *Leopard* had fired for fifteen minutes, holing *Chesapeake's* hull and damaging masts and rigging. Three *Chesapeake* seamen were killed and eighteen wounded. Barron sharply addressed his flag captain: "We ought to have been better prepared for it." Gordon defensively replied, "Certainly all has been done that could be."[58]

In his cabin and in severe pain from his wounds, Barron sent a note to Humphreys by ship's gig: "Sir, I consider the frigate *Chesapeake* your prize and am ready to deliver her to an officer authorized to receive her."[59]

At 1700, three British lieutenants and several petty officers boarded *Chesapeake* and requested a crew's muster. Disgraced and humiliated, Gordon refused to surrender his muster roll, and it was Barron who finally ordered all hands assembled on deck, a sight so offensive to Gordon that he left the deck to sit in his cabin. Only one of the five *Halifax* men, Jenkin Radford (or Ratford), was found and dragged out from below decks. The three deserters from *Melampus* were also seized and a dozen others questioned. Radford was subsequently hanged, one seaman died in captivity, and the other two were pardoned and returned to *Chesapeake*.[60]

By sundown the British officers had departed with their prisoners and Humphreys signaled: "Having, to the utmost of my power, fulfilled the instructions of my commander-in-chief, I have nothing more to desire, and must in consequence proceed to join the remainder of the squadron; repeating, that I am ready to give you every assistance in my power, and do most sincerely deplore that any lives should have been lost in the execution of a service which might have been adjusted more amicably not only with respect to ourselves but the nations to which we respectively belong." *Leopard* made sail and withdrew toward Lynnhaven Bay without acknowledging Barron's offer of *Chesapeake* as a prize. With jury-rigged masts, *Chesapeake* inched back to Hampton Roads, dropping anchor at 1230 the next day in a cheerless drizzle.[61]

Barron immediately dispatched Doctor Bullus and Gordon to Washington by pilot boat with a formal report. Gordon also carried a private letter from the ship's lieutenants and sailing master critical of Barron and claiming *Chesapeake* could have resisted further. The lieutenant's letter was leaked quickly to the press, but not Barron's official report of the attack.[62]

Reaction in Hampton Roads was immediate and fanned the flames of public outrage that quickly spread from Virginia, to Washington, and finally throughout the country. When eleven *Chesapeake* wounded landed in Norfolk on 23 June, the *Publick Ledger* described the reverberations as "a degree of agitation beyond anything we ever witnessed or can attempt to describe" and later described the incident as a "most unexampled outrage" with "the honour and independence of our nation insulted beyond the possibility of further forbearance."[63]

The next day, mass meetings voted boycotts of supplies, water, and pilots to British men-of-war, "until ample justice is obtained by our Executive," and ships in the Chesapeake were alerted to watch for further signs of hostile intent. On 27 June, Robert MacDonald, one of *Chesapeake's* wounded, died at the Marine Hospital, and a funeral procession from Market Square to Church Street with four thousand mourners touched off even greater signs of outrage.[64]

Tensions mounted daily. At Hampton, revengeful citizens smashed two hundred water casks bound for *Melampus*. When the British schooner *Hope* anchored near Fort Norfolk to deliver dispatches to the British consul, her boat was intercepted and an officer threatened. In Norfolk, the local militia was mobilized and Fort Nelson readied for action. Navy Agent Bedinger accelerated the construction of ten more gunboats at the Navy Yard.[65]

Decatur quickly had four gunboats ready for Norfolk's defense, with an additional twelve nearing completion, but all lacked trained crews. On 28 June, a public committee in Hampton delivered a resolution to Decatur, calling on him "as the commander of the naval force in Hampton to equip and resist with the gunboats the threatened invasion by the British." Decatur characteristically vowed his undying support but also pleaded for additional volunteers, for, despite the furor, "only eleven men had been found for the gunboats, needing 430."[66]

For their part, the British held firm. Captain Humphreys provided a full report and was told, "you have conducted yourself most properly." British Commo. John E. Douglas moved *Bellona, Leopard, Triumph,* and *Melampus* threateningly into Hampton Roads and demanded civil order or he would "obstruct the whole trade of the Chesapeake."[67]

With rumors of an imminent declaration of war, Decatur moved vigorously to improve defenses and wrote to the Navy secretary on 29 June that "the British commander has threatened that he will again take possession of the *Chesapeake* . . . under the impression that they will do as they say, I feel satisfied preparing to act on the defensive will meet the approbation of the President and yourself. If, however, it should be thought I have been precipitate, I beg it may be attributed to my extreme desire not to omit any service I might render my country."[68]

On 2 July, President Jefferson issued a proclamation forbidding British men-of-war from entering American harbors and recalled the *Constitution* from the Mediterranean. By the Fourth of July, anti-British rhetoric had reached a crescendo, and a parade in Richmond was replete with anti-British banners. Speeches, formal dinner toasts, and editorials denounced

British aggression, and many urged economic sanctions or even a declaration of war.[69]

Decatur updated the secretary late on 4 July: "[British] movements are extremely suspicious . . . they have been at anchor inside the Capes and have brought to by firing at every vessel that has passed in or out of the Capes. They have sent many insolent and menacing messages to Norfolk. Such as if the people do not supply them with articles they might want, they would come up and retake the *Chesapeake* and cut out the French Frigate *Sybele* [*sic*]."[70]

Hearing this, President Jefferson ordered Secretary of War Henry Dearborn to review the plans for the defense of American ports, including Norfolk and New York, as "the British commanders have their foot on the threshold of war. They have begun the blockade of Norfolk." A day later, Decatur reported that Fort Norfolk boasted eight guns and that *Chesapeake* and *Cybelle* were moored across the Elizabeth channel, supported by four gunboats.[71]

But as Decatur wrote, cooler heads were beginning to prevail. Norfolk attorney Littleton Tazewell visited Douglas aboard *Bellona* on 5 July and was told that British actions had been "misapprehended" and that "no menace" had been intended. British ships soon pulled back from Hampton Roads and patrolled beyond sight of land, and *Leopard* was discreetly ordered to Bermuda. Ultimately, the British Admiralty disavowed searches of ships "in another nation's service," promised suitable reparations, and recalled (but did not punish) Admiral Berkeley.[72]

In the wake of the *Chesapeake* incident, Navy Secretary Smith dispatched three letters to Norfolk: one to Decatur ordering him to assume command of the frigate and restore the ship to seaworthy condition, another to Barron relieving him of command and ordering him to "remain at Hampton until you shall hear from me," and a third to Gordon ordering him to remain on board.[73]

At noon on 1 July, Decatur boarded the *Chesapeake* and took command of the disoriented and disheveled crew. Three days later he reported to Secretary Smith:

> On receipt of your order of the 26 ultimate, I repaired on board the *Chesapeake* and relieved Commodore Barron in his command . . . On an examination of the damage sustained by the Ship, I find it to be as follows: the hull has received fourteen shot which can be repaired in four days by ship carpenters. The main mast three and the mizzen mast one shot, which has irreparably injured them. The fore mast one shot, it can be repaired, the bowsprit one shot, the sails many of them injured but all capable of repair, seven of the fore and main shrouds together with the main and spring stays cut, capable of repair. The mizzen rigging very old, much cut and incapable of repair. Those, sir, are the only damages of any consequence . . . all of which I feel confident we shall be able to repair in three weeks . . . the *Chesapeake* when I took command of her had been brought up into the bite of Craney Island in consequence of threats of the British.[74]

Naval constructor Josiah Fox supervised the restoration; by 17 July Decatur was able to report that repairs were nearly finished, and on 27 July the *Publick Ledger* echoed him with an article headlined "The *Chesapeake* Restored" and reporting: "Today we have the satisfaction to perceive [the *Chesapeake*] completely ready for sea. Great credit is due to Commodore Decatur and his officers for the activity which he and they have used in preparing this ship for sea in so short a time . . . this circumstance ought to prove to the navy department the superior advantages of this place over Washington for naval equipment."[75]

In Hampton Roads and across the Navy, there was strong consensus that Barron had disgraced the service and the nation with a premature surrender, especially when it became known how rapidly the ship had been repaired. Calls for his censure were made, and none of his fellow officers visited him in his sickbed. In their letter, *Chesapeake's* five lieutenants had talked of "the disgrace which must be attached to the late premature surrender" and had pressed for a court of inquiry. On 5 October a court was convened in Norfolk, which was chaired by Capt. Alexander Murray, with Capt. Isaac Hull and Capt. Isaac Chauncey as members. None of the three were considered friendly to Barron. The court deliberated until 4 November, but Barron attended for only the first week and was represented thereafter by Robert Barraud Taylor, a Norfolk attorney of considerable repute. The court's final report blistered Barron, citing the ship's poor readiness and the dishonor of surrender without a fight.[76]

On 7 December Secretary Smith ordered a general court-martial to try Barron, Gordon, Gunner William Hook, and Captain Hall of the Marines. Members of this court included thirteen officers—six captains, three master commandants, and four lieutenants—including Capt. William Bainbridge (who had once been exonerated at a court-martial over which Barron presided for the loss of the frigate *Philadelphia*), Decatur,

Lt. Joseph Tarbell (who would distinguish himself in the defense of Norfolk during the War of 1812), Lt. James Lawrence, and Lt. Charles Ludlow (who would die heroically aboard *Chesapeake* during her later disastrous battle with *Shannon*). Commo. John Rodgers presided as senior member despite the well-known fact that he disliked Barron and had once agreed to meet Barron in a duel. Barron's brother Samuel was frequently in the audience.[77]

As soon as the court was announced, Decatur had written to Secretary Smith, asking to be disqualified. "I formed and expressed an opinion that Commodore Barron had not done his duty," wrote Decatur. "It is probable that I am prejudiced against Commodore Barron and view his conduct in this case with more severity than it deserves." Smith refused to remove Decatur, and, in fairness, Decatur forwarded a copy of his correspondence to Barron's counsel.[78]

On 4 January 1808, with the threat of ice and snow in the gray clouds, a single quarterdeck gun solemnly signaled the opening of the court, held in *Chesapeake's* great cabin while she swung at anchor in Hampton Roads. The officers of the court, formally attired in dress blue uniforms with ample trimmings of gold, sat behind a long covered table with the great cabin windows at their backs. Littleton Tazewell, a future governor of Virginia, served as judge advocate, and Robert Barraud Taylor continued in the defense. Barron was tried on four charges: negligently performing the duty assigned him; neglecting, on the probability of an engagement, to clear his ship for action; failing to encourage in his own person his inferior officers and men to fight courageously; and not doing his utmost to take or destroy the *Leopard,* which it had been his duty to encounter.[79]

The trial lasted for twenty-seven days, and after several days of deliberations, verdicts were ready on 8 February. The court found Barron innocent on nearly all charges but guilty on a single charge of "neglecting to clear his ship for action," citing Barron's error in judgment, despite Barron's testimony that it would have been provocative to the British to clear for action while their officer was still on board. Despite the narrow findings, Barron was sentenced "to be suspended from all command in the navy . . . without any pay or official emoluments of any kind for the period and term of five years." Gordon and Hall were also found guilty of "negligently performing the duty assigned" but were sentenced to only a "private reprimand." William Hook was also found guilty of the same charge and was discharged from the Navy.[80]

The *Chesapeake* court-martial was the most watched and contentious naval trial of its era, with Norfolk and Hampton Roads sitting at center stage. Despite the relatively benign sentence, James Barron was thoroughly discredited and broken in spirit. With no naval commission, Barron returned to merchant service, spending long periods in Europe. His friends in Hampton never left his side, and he always felt that a prejudiced court had damned him, a conclusion with some weight, as the minutes of the proceedings remained purposely unpublished for fourteen years.

By the time of the *Chesapeake* incident, Norfolk and Portsmouth handled three-quarters of Virginia's exports and an even larger share of its imports. "From some downtown areas one could not see the waterfront, so crowded together were the warehouses . . . with log wharves stretching in every direction of obliquity," read one description. But by the winter of 1807, the renewed war in Europe precipitated attacks against American shipping, and Jefferson instituted flawed trade embargoes in 1807 and 1809 that all but ruined Norfolk. Warehouses closed, shipyards fell silent, and unemployed seamen and shipwrights appeared everywhere. The Navy shouldered the distasteful duty of enforcing this unfortunate law at sea. Norfolk gunboats patrolled the Chesapeake Bay, and Decatur took the *Chesapeake* on enforcement patrols along the New England coast between June and November 1808.[81]

The Embargo Acts ended in 1810, and a new secretary of the Navy, Paul Hamilton, reorganized the Navy to better protect American commerce. Two divisions of ships were formed, a northern division based in New York, commanded by Commodore Rodgers, and a southern division based in Norfolk, commanded by Decatur, with smaller flotillas operating from Charleston and New Orleans. Decatur flew his broad pennant from frigate *United States* and began patrols from Cape Henry to Florida. Rodgers assumed command of his flagship *President* on 17 June 1810 in Hampton Roads and, three days later, satisfying Hamilton's planning, seized the French privateer *Revanche du Cerf,* which had been lurking off the Virginia coast.[82]

On 1 May 1811, HMS *Guerriere* (38) stopped the American merchant brig *Spitfire* near Sandy Hook and impressed yet another American sailor. *President* and brig *Argus* (18) responded, and on 16 May, about forty-five miles northeast of Cape Charles, Rodgers spotted a ship hull on the horizon that he hoped would be *Guerriere*. The ship was HMS *Little Belt* (20), a sloop-of-war of Danish design sailing under orders to avoid any Americans because of the tensions between the two nations. *Little Belt* tacked away from *President,* and it was not until dusk that Rodgers closed the distance. Rodgers later reported that *Little Belt* fired a single shot (possibly an accidental discharge), which was answered by a single American cannon, quickly followed by a ragged broadside from the British ship. A general action of forty-five minutes ensued in which *Little Belt* was badly damaged and lost thirteen killed. It was a sign of the times in Norfolk that Rodgers's action was widely applauded, with many pointing to the engagement as revenge for the *Chesapeake–Leopard* affair. Rodgers wrote to great acclaim that he acted, determined not "to suffer the Flag of my Country to be insulted with impunity."[83]

Just as the Quasi-war with France had put Hampton Roads at the forefront of official naval thinking for the first time, the *Chesapeake* debacle and its ensuing widely publicized court-martial again made Hampton Roads and the young Navy synonymous. By 1808, the people of Hampton Roads, steeped in national pride, embraced their Navy with renewed fervor.

Incipient themes that would dominate Tidewater's Navy for two hundred years had their beginnings during the dozen years between 1796 and 1808. The Navy would value the safe, comforting confines of Hampton Roads, would look to Gosport as its largest yard, and would actively plan defenses around Hampton Roads to protect it from enemy attack. The people of Norfolk and Tidewater would grow comfortable with the expanding presence of naval officers in its societal affairs and naval dollars in its economy. They viewed the Navy as a protector of prosperous trade and began to relish the opportunity to be at center stage in the play of national and world events. It was a marriage of common benefit with surprising strength and verve brought to fruition during these first years of a tempestuous century.

1812

By 1812, American independence was but thirty-six years old. Most who had fought in the Revolution were in their fifties and sixties. Most who were ready to fight the British again knew war only through fireside tales of Saratoga, Valley Forge, and Yorktown. Tidewater's first generation of naval leaders had passed from the stage—Richard Dale and Thomas Truxtun had resigned their commissions, James Barron was in virtual exile in Europe, and Samuel Barron had died. Its next generation had yet to be revealed.

By 1812, Tidewater's mood was one of fervent nationalism, calls to honor, and patriotism, whipped to frenzy by a virulent press, shrill politicians, and "war hawks." National leaders eased the nation toward war fueled by expansionist designs on Florida, Canada, and the American West. Tidewater merchants, nearly clubbed into the ground by unceasing years of maritime blockades, embargoes, foreign privateers, and rampant impressments, viewed the drift toward hostilities with equal amounts of resignation and unease.

By 1812, Hampton Roads was clearly on the Navy's map. It had taken an undeclared war with France and continuing aggression against American trade in the Mediterranean to define its importance, and it had taken the strong personalities of several distinguished naval leaders to maintain that focus. As events began to lumber again toward war, the same dynamics that had first drawn the Navy to southeastern Virginia would begin to propel Hampton Roads and the Navy toward an even closer and more substantive relationship.

Of all those in the Navy, it was Stephen Decatur who had the keenest sense of the importance of Hampton Roads. Instantly recognizable on Norfolk streets or in Norfolk society, Decatur radiated an attractive blend of personal honor, confidence, and swashbuckling national optimism that Norfolk easily identified with. Despite strong family ties with Philadelphia, for ten years beginning in 1806, Decatur clearly represented the Navy to the people of Tidewater. He helped establish Hampton Roads as the main operating nexus for the Navy, and, as war approached, he commanded a strong American squadron centered on the frigate *United States* (44) from its portals.

In February 1812, HMS *Macedonian,* a British frigate of 38 guns with a reputation as one of England's best, dropped anchor in Hampton Roads, bearing diplomatic dispatches. Visits by British warships to Virginia had been a rarity since the *Chesapeake* incident, and *Macedonian's* call on the port generated much attention within Tidewater society. During the visit, Littleton Tazewell played the correct host and introduced Decatur (as the senior American officer in port, since the *United States* was being recoppered at Gosport) to *Macedonian's* captain, John Surman Carden. Over the fortnight of *Macedonian's* visit, the two captains became close professional acquaintances, undoubtedly agreeing on many of virtues of their seagoing calling while disagreeing on the relative merits of their respective services. At *Macedonian's* sailing, both captains made the good-natured and customary reference to meeting at sea again as enemies. Carden was reputed to have

By the time of the War of 1812, the daring and charismatic Stephen Decatur was the best known naval officer in America and the most vocal proponent of Hampton Roads as the site for the Navy's primary support base. Decatur died from a gunshot suffered in a duel with Commo. James Barron in 1820. *U.S. Naval Institute*

politely implied that *Macedonian* could best any American. His counterpart's reply was classic Decatur, unflinching and direct, and would have hung in the air for the Englishman to ponder: "The conflict will undoubtedly be a severe one, for the flag of my country will never be struck while there is a hull for it to wave from."[1] The American Navy of 1812 was a breed different from that which the British had seen before.

War was declared in June 1812, and the attention of the nation immediately turned toward the U.S. Navy. American naval captains itched to get under way, primed for revenge against their British nemesis and impatient to prove their worth. American naval power was concentrated within two primary squadrons, led by Commo. Stephen Decatur and Commo. John Rodgers, and both commodores pressed to get to sea quickly to slash British commerce, as most thought the war was going to be short. Decatur sailed from Hampton Roads with frigates *United States* and *Congress* and brig *Argus* to join forces with Rodgers in New York; then the two squadrons put to sea together.

The British Navy, large as it was, was committed worldwide against France and had assigned "only" five ships-of-the-line, nineteen frigates, forty-one brigs, and sixteen schooners to its North American station. As the war began, the U.S. Navy boasted six frigates, three sloops-of-war, and seven smaller ships in service. In the Chesapeake, twenty-four American gunboats were assigned—ten in Baltimore, four in Washington, and ten in Norfolk—but few were operational.[2]

The Norfolk privateer *Dash* recorded the first naval success of the war, capturing the Royal Navy packet *Whiting* (4) in Hampton Roads in July.[3] Frigate *Constitution* (Capt. Isaac Hull) sailed from Alexandria, resupplied in Annapolis, and sailed for New York, clearing the capes by 12 June. Unfortunately for Hull, a full British squadron appeared on the horizon to intercept her. A chase of over sixty hours ensued, one of the most dramatic in American naval annals, as Hull tried every trick of seamanship he knew, with winds nearly in a flat calm, to extract the frigate from the English trap and escape, ultimately, to Boston.

America's chosen naval strategy favored operations by its frigates against British mercantile trade far from American shores. To defend the American coast, the Navy depended on its gunboats. In Norfolk, Capt. Samuel Evans, commandant at Gosport, quickly built up his gunboat force to twenty-one ships. With manning limited, he assigned eight regular navy men to each and sought volunteers and militia to fill out each gunboat's complement of about forty.[4]

Within months it was clear that American strategy was producing dividends. Early American patrols far at sea had produced a series of victories that stung the British: *Constitution* defeated *Guerriere* and sank *Java* (38), *Hornet* sank *Peacock* (18), *Wasp* (18) bagged *Frolic* (18), and Norfolk's master commandant, Arthur Sinclair II, captured six prizes while commanding brig *Argus*. Closer to home, the coastal defense appeared to be holding, with no British threats.

At dawn on 25 October 1812, on one of those exquisite mid-ocean mornings of blue sky, sparkling airs, and early warmth, Decatur's *United States* was at sea patrolling for British prizes. *United States* was south of the Azores and west of the Canary Islands on a latitude equal to that of northern Florida when the lookout detected a distant dot of white on a horizon as sharp as a ruler's edge. When it became apparent that the unknown quarry was an English warship, Decatur cleared for action and steered for advantage. *United States* began the engagement at long range, where it held best advantage, and American shot was soon falling close aboard the

British ship. In a twist of history, Decatur's first lieutenant was William H. Allen, who had been serving aboard *Chesapeake* at the time of its distasteful surrender to *Leopard* five years previously, and he exhorted the American gun crews with extra fervor. Decatur's well-practiced gunners quickly gained the range, decimating the enemy's masts and rigging and pounding the once proud English frigate into a helpless hulk. At last, with the English colors struck, Decatur hailed across the water for her identity, and the answer was as surprising to Decatur as the rapidity of the engagement: "His Britannic Majesty's Frigate *Macedonian,* Captain Carden."[5]

Charles Stewart (1778–1869) was commissioned a Navy lieutenant in March 1798 and won recognition in both the Quasi-war with France and fighting in Tripoli. With the outbreak of war in 1812, Stewart commanded *Argus, Hornet,* and then *Constellation*, which became closely blockaded in Norfolk. He took command of *Constitution* in 1813 and made two brilliant cruises capturing HMS *Cyane* and HMS *Levant.* He later commanded squadrons in both the Mediterranean and the Pacific and rose to become the Navy's senior flag officer and was promoted to rear admiral on the retired list in 1862. *U.S. Naval Institute*

British naval strategy finally began to exert itself late in 1812 with its most compelling element, blockade, aimed directly at Hampton Roads. In December 1812, Adm. Sir John B. Warren, commander in chief of "His Majesty's squadron on the Halifax and West Indies stations," received orders from the Admiralty to "establish the most complete and vigorous Blockade of the Ports and Harbours of the Bay of the Chesapeake and of the River Delaware." The British recognized (as they had failed to do during the Revolution) that sealing the Chesapeake would thwart American commerce and stifle any attempt by the American Navy to use its large naval shipyard at Gosport.[6]

Formidable Royal Navy ships, including several ships-of-the-line, began establishing Chesapeake blockade stations in February 1813, and a complete blockade of the entire American coast from Long Island to Charleston was in place by May. Warren placed his Chesapeake blockaders near the capes or in Lynnhaven Bay, and once they were in place, commerce effectively ceased. Across Tidewater, buildings were shuttered, warehouses were abandoned, and normally bustling waterfronts lay quiet, choked with inactive ships. The American Navy was powerless to resist, as its frigates were inferior to British ships-of-the-line and its gunboats had never been designed to break a blockade. The American defensive naval strategy was best suited for a short war; a blockade was a "long war" tactic. Within the first month of the British blockade, thirty-six American trading ships were lost in the Chesapeake.[7]

On 1 February 1813, ice forced the frigate *Constellation* (Capt. Charles Stewart) from her anchorage off Annapolis, and Stewart sailed south to Hampton Roads to obtain supplies for a wartime cruise, arriving on 2 or 3 February.[8] On the morning of 4 February, Stewart spotted ships of a newly arrived British squadron sailing through the capes. Although he reported "two sail of the Line, three Frigates, a Brig and Schooner of the enemy working up between the Middle ground and Horse Shoe for the Roads," indications are that what he spotted was a four-frigate squadron led by HMS *Maidstone* (36). Whether ships-of-the-line or frigates, Stewart was clearly outmatched, and he turned to sail deeper into Hampton Roads for safety but ran aground on Willoughby Spit Shoal in a calm wind. Although Stewart later made light of the incident in a letter to the secretary of the Navy ("It being calm we hove up and kedged the Ship up to the flats where the tide having fallen the Ship took the ground.") the fact was that *Constellation* was in serious jeopardy of ignominious capture and was saved only by the lack of a British response.

A rising tide refloated *Constellation* at dusk, and she proceeded slowly toward safety down a channel lit by volunteers in small boats and anchored between Forts Norfolk and Nelson. Despite his good fortune in avoiding capture, swinging at anchor in the Elizabeth was the height of disappointment for Stewart, who had received a report just two days before that the capes were free of the British. Although in safety, *Constellation*

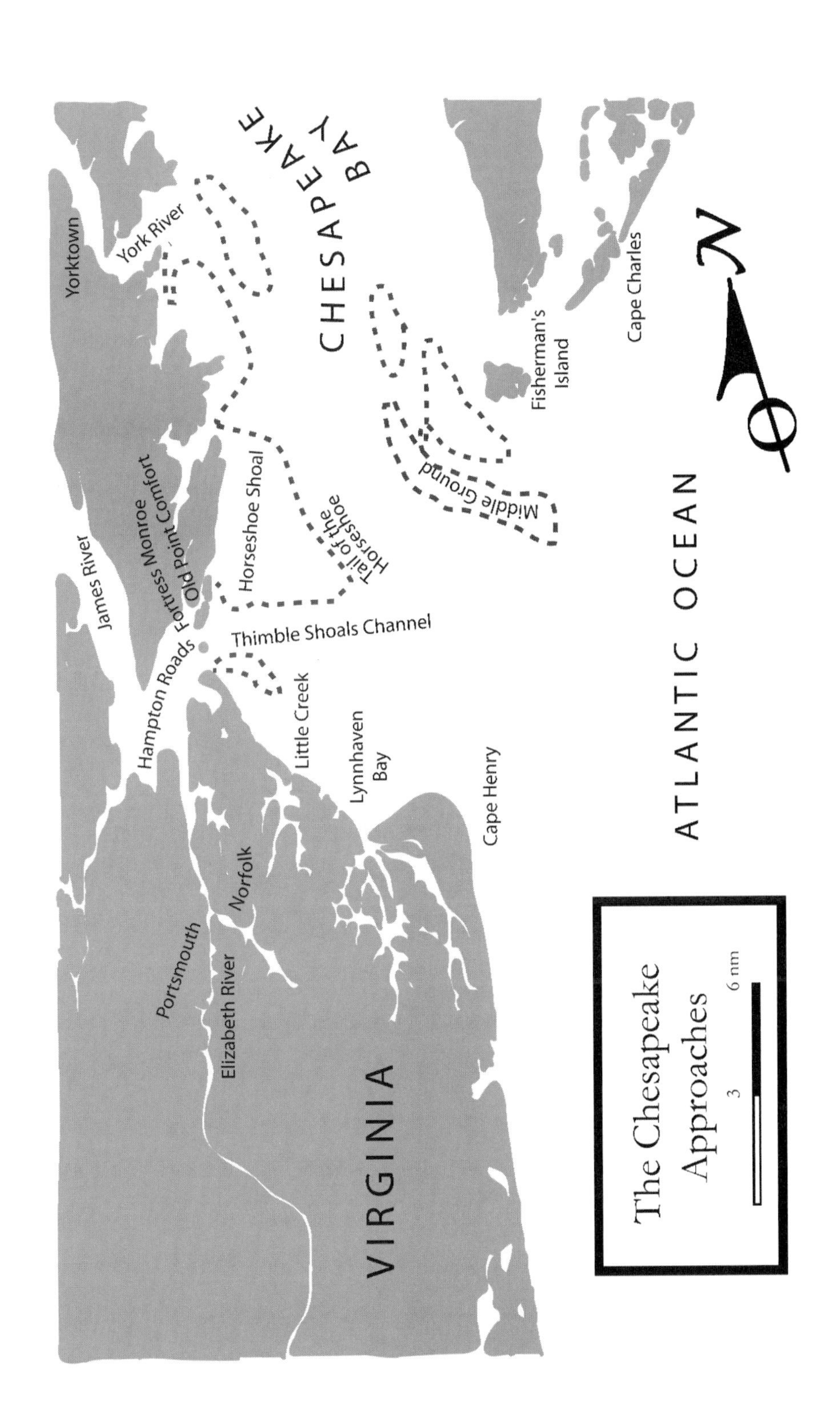
The Chesapeake Approaches
3
6 nm
Yorktown
York River
CHESAPEAKE BAY
Cape Charles
Fisherman's Island
Middle Ground
Tail of the Horseshoe
Horseshoe Shoal
Fortress Monroe
Old Point Comfort
James River
Hampton Roads
Thimble Shoals Channel
Little Creek
Lynnhaven Bay
Cape Henry
Norfolk
Portsmouth
Elizabeth River
VIRGINIA
ATLANTIC OCEAN

was penned in at Norfolk with little chance of catching the British by surprise: "our chance of getting to sea [from Norfolk] would be rendered difficult, as the Enemy possesses, no doubt, the earliest information from their Agents."[9]

Three days later, on 8 February, in another indication that the British had clamped down, the privateer schooner *Lottery* (Capt. John Southcomb) was set upon by British boats in Lynnhaven Bay as she vainly tried to make for the open sea. The violent struggle was witnessed by many ashore and ultimately claimed the life of Southcomb, and many of his men and British sailors were wounded. Capt. Richard Byron of the Royal Navy, in deference to the American's bravery and skill, sent Southcomb's body ashore to Captain Stewart with every mark of respect. That same day, the Norfolk *Herald* reported: "This port is now effectively blockaded by the enemy's squadron under Admiral Warren. Not a vessel can pass from Hampton Roads either up or down the Bay, without being intercepted."[10]

It suddenly became apparent to all in Norfolk that the calm of the war's first half-year was behind them. The British Navy, an ominous and intimidating force, was present in strength and within sight. Tidewater merchants were in an uproar, many meeting in coffeehouses and taverns to trade rumor and strategy, and the fear of an imminent invasion was on everyone's minds. Governor John Barbour inspected Norfolk defenses and activated the local militia under Brig. Gen. Robert Barraud Taylor (of Barron court-martial fame). All of the prewar promises of how gunboats would stoutly defend the coast now appeared as so much blather.[11]

In March 1794, Congress had authorized the building of fortifications to protect all major seaports. At the recommendation of French-born engineer John Jacob Ulrich Rivardi, land was purchased in 1795 at a site that would be developed as Fort Norfolk just downriver from Norfolk on the eastern side of the Elizabeth. At the same time, Fort Nelson (on the west bank across from the Norfolk wharves) was rebuilt from its Revolutionary War configuration.[12]

Fort Norfolk lay abandoned for a time, beginning in 1802, but by the start of the War of 1812 it boasted 30 guns, complementing Fort Nelson's 39 cannon. Breastworks and a small blockhouse were hurriedly prepared on the southeastern point of Craney Island (mounting two 24-pounders and one 18-pounder), and plans were advanced for booms and chains to be thrown across the Elizabeth between the island and Lambert's Point.[13]

On 3 March 1813 Capt. Sir George Cockburn arrived in Lynnhaven Bay aboard his flagship HMS *Marlborough* (74) to assume command of the Chesapeake squadron, which, by that time, consisted of four ships-of-the-line, *Poictiers* (74), *Victorious* (74), *Dragon* (74), and *Marlborough;* four frigates, *Maidstone, Junon* (38), *Belvidera* (36), and *Statira* (38); and seven smaller ships. His orders were specific: "To blockade . . . in the most strict and rigorous manner according to the usages of war acknowledged and allowed in similar cases. To capture and destroy trade and shipping off Baltimore and particularly in the Potomac, York, Rappahannock and James Rivers. To obtain intelligence of the numbers of gunboats and state of the enemy's ships operating in the Chesapeake and elsewhere . . . To ascertain the situation affecting the frigate *Constellation* and the best means of capturing her; also the defenses and troops in the vicinity of [Norfolk]."[14]

Cockburn's mission was both to blockade and to threaten. In a broad, strategic sense it was hoped that such a large and obvious British force so close to Washington, Baltimore, and Norfolk would force the Americans to withdraw from the Canadian border to protect their capital. Tactically, Cockburn moved to capture prizes, seal off sources of marauding privateers, and tie down American forces.

The naval forces in Norfolk faced a formidable foe in Cockburn. Having once served as Nelson's flag captain, Cockburn was a seasoned, war-hardened commander with years of combat experience against the French and Spanish. Theodore Roosevelt once described Cockburn as a "capable, brave, energetic man, hating his foes and enjoying his work."[15]

Once in place, Cockburn quickly started to carry out his orders. On the night of 20 March, Cockburn ordered a cutting-out expedition on *Constellation. Marlborough's* first lieutenant, George Westphal, led several barges of sailors and marines up the Elizabeth, but contrary winds and tides ultimately forced the barges to turn back. Ironically, this might have robbed the Americans of an early victory, as Stewart had prepared his defenses well and *Constellation* was surrounded by booms and rigged with netting to prevent boarders. Seven Norfolk gunboats patrolled nearby, manned by *Constellation* sailors, and Stewart had ordered four hulks sunk off Lambert's Point to thwart British frigates and ships-of-the-line.[16] Navy yard defenses were also in good shape under the command of Capt. John Cassin, who had relieved Samuel Evans on 10 August 1812. Cassin also commanded the Norfolk gunboat flotilla.

By 13 March 1813, Admiral Warren arrived in Lynnhaven Bay in *San Domingo* (74) to join Cockburn. Within ten days, Cockburn had written an elaborate situation plan, detailing each element of the formidable American Norfolk–Portsmouth defense line. To breach this line, capture Norfolk, burn the

Gosport yard, and capture *Constellation,* in his estimate, would require a coordinated assault with both Army and Navy elements.[17]

On 1 April, Cockburn was promoted to rear admiral, and he and Warren opened raiding campaigns up the Virginia rivers ranging as far north as the head of the Chesapeake Bay. On 3 April, the British squadron captured four large schooners (*Arab, Lynx, Racer,* and *Dolphin*) near New Point Comfort, and the devious Cockburn then used these ships (flying American colors) in a ruse to intercept other unsuspecting Chesapeake craft, with great success.[18]

With Warren operating northward in the bay, Stewart reported only a few enemy ships remaining near Hampton Roads, causing Secretary of the Navy William Jones to reply, mistakenly, that "I do not believe it his [Warren's] intention to attack [Norfolk], or the force in its waters." Convinced that Norfolk was safe for the time being (and knowing *Constellation* had been stripped of supplies), Jones ordered Stewart, on 7 May, to leave immediately for Washington and Boston to take command of *Constitution.* Jones also ordered Master Commandant Joseph Tarbell—who had been stationed in Norfolk since March, relieving Cassin of command of the gunboat flotilla—to temporary command of *Constellation.*[19]

Warren and Cockburn returned to Lynnhaven Bay by 13 May, and Warren left four days later for Halifax with forty prizes, a sign of their success in disrupting Chesapeake commerce. Cockburn continued sporadic raiding into June, capturing revenue cutter *Surveyor* in the York River, among other successes.

Warren reappeared in Lynnhaven Bay on 19 June with reinforcements, including two battalions of Royal Marines, three hundred infantry of the 102nd regiment, and three hundred troops designated "Canadian Chasseurs" (a controversial corps that was not Canadian, but was made up of French prisoners of war who preferred fighting for the British rather than sitting in English prisons) under Col. Sir Thomas Sydney Beckwith. The sudden concentration of force in Hampton Roads, something Navy Secretary Jones had not foreseen, was alarming. Warren's warships totaled seventy percent of the entire British fleet in America (eight ships-of-the-line, twelve frigates, eight smaller warships, and six transports). Beckwith's force numbered 2,650 troops.[20]

British activity was intense and was clearly aimed at Norfolk's defenses. Cockburn ordered detailed soundings of the waters of Hampton Roads, buoyed the major channels, and gathered intelligence on American positions. Beckwith favored landing the major portion of British troops west of Norfolk on the Nansemond River and then marching on Portsmouth and the Gosport Navy Yard. Cockburn developed an alternative plan to attack Norfolk from the east and overrun the city. The two plans shared the need to neutralize the American defenses on Craney Island to open navigation on the Elizabeth to the big guns of the Royal Navy.[21]

Warren choose Beckwith's proposed flanking attack on Portsmouth's rear, combined with an assault on Craney Island, and assigned Capt. Samuel J. Pechell of *San Domingo* to coordinate the attack. Cockburn transferred his flag from *Marlborough* to frigate *Barrosa* (36) to lead the expected naval bombardment of the Craney Island defenses.[22]

American defenses had been strengthened all spring, with fortifications toughened on the outskirts of both Norfolk and Portsmouth. The center axis and strongest point of these defenses was along the Elizabeth River, to prevent the British from sailing their big guns directly down upon Portsmouth and Norfolk as they had done during the Revolution. Forts Nelson and Norfolk would secure this defensive line, with the *Constellation* anchored in mid-channel as a formidable floating battery supported by the flotilla of Navy gunboats arrayed in an arc across the river. On the "point" of this defensive line stood meager Craney Island on the western edge of the Elizabeth approaches. In 1813, Craney Island was a mere fifty acres of scrub pines, sand, and underbrush tucked behind belts of mudflats and was separated from the shore by two small creeks.

The strategic importance of Craney Island was obvious to both sides, and the overall commander of the American defense, Brigadier General Taylor, had pressed to complete a small blockhouse and redoubt on the island's southeastern shore. While planning to assign additional troops in its defense, he wrote Secretary of War John Armstrong Jr., "should the enemy . . . attack Craney Island, it must fall unless we throw the greater part of our forces there."[23]

Under the gaze of Warren's intimidating fleet, Taylor, Tarbell, and Cassin rushed forces into place to meet the expected British assault. One hundred fifty sailors and Marines from *Constellation* and thirty regulars from Fort Norfolk were dispatched to Craney Island, where a new breastwork was hastily thrown up along the northwest shore. Gunboats were hurried forward, many rapidly augmented by sailors from both *Constellation* and the Navy yard.[24] Even with these preparations, Craney Island defenders numbered only 767 men.

British frigate *Junon* anchored near Newport News on 18 June to reconnoiter the mouth of the James with its boats. Separated as she was from the main British squadron, *Junon* made an inviting target, and Cassin ordered Tarbell to attack *Junon* on the night of 19 June with fifteen gunboats manned by *Constellation* sailors and Craney Island riflemen. At 2300 that night, Tarbell's gunboats moved down the river under cover of darkness, and by 0400 had closed within gunshot of the frigate. For forty-five minutes the two forces exchanged a spirited gunfire until a freshening breeze allowed *Junon* to maneuver away from the boats and brought two nearby British warships, *Narcissus* (32) and *Barrosa,* into the action. *Junon* reported one Royal Marine killed and three seamen wounded in the skirmish. On board *Gunboat No. 139,* Master's Mate Thomas Allison of *Constellation* was killed and two others were wounded. The engagement was largely inconsequential but gave the American defenders a rousing burst of enthusiasm.[25]

A day later, on 21 June, the British invasion swung into motion. In the complex two-pronged amphibious assault, the bulk of Beckwith's seasoned regulars were to land by barge on the Nansemond River and advance on Craney Island from the west and rear while a second group of boats would directly assault the island, covered by naval bombardment. After subduing Craney Island, British forces would then come together to march on Fort Nelson and Portsmouth.

"At half past 1 p.m. of Monday [21 June] the enemy's ships were in motion," the *Publick Ledger* reported, "one ship off the mouth of the Nansemond River, two at the mouth of the James River and boats passing from ship-to-ship apparently filled with men." Shortly after dawn on 22 June, with mist shrouding the British advance, an American cavalryman on picket duty galloped across the Thoroughfare (a small, shallow creek separating Craney Island from the mainland) to report that the British were landing at Hoffler's Creek, two and a half miles west. The British commander later reported that his troops had entered boats at midnight, "pulled on shore by moonlight, and landed in tolerable confusion at daybreak without opposition."[26]

As the morning haze slowly lifted, those on Craney Island could finally see the British invasion barges unloading hundreds of red-coated infantrymen. Sgt. William P. Young of the Virginia militia on Craney Island reported:

> We saw by the movement of the enemy's boats in passing and repassing from their ships to the shore that they were landing troops, so that a fight was expected to come off, and we went to work . . . the three cannons from the fort and four six-pounders belonging to the Artillery were taken to the west side of the island . . . Early in the morning we were joined by . . . Lieuts Niele [*sic*], Shubrick and Sanders, with about 150 sailors. Every arrangement being made to defend the fort, we waited the approach of the enemy . . . As we had no flagstaffs, a long pole was got, to which the "Star Spangled Banner" was nailed . . . We could distinctly see [the British] marching and countermarching on the beach and after forming into columns, they took up the line of march. But such was the dense growth of trees and underwood between us that they were soon lost to our view. We knew not but their intention was to march to the town of Portsmouth, get possession of that place and Gosport, and destroy the Navy Yard. We were, however, soon undeceived.[27]

The British troops, divided into two brigades, marched toward the island, aiming to wade across the Thoroughfare. Redcoats mixed with the green uniforms of the Canadian Chaussers as they approached, and bright sunlight glinted off bayonets and muskets. By the time they made the creek, the tide had made the Thoroughfare too deep to ford and artillery fire was ordered while they waited. American artillery responded and accurately dropped shot within the concentration of British troops, immediately killing or wounding ten marines.[28]

The American fire was led by an 18-pounder worked by *Constellation* seamen under Lt. Benedict I. Neale of *Gunboat No. 152* and two other cannon largely manned by naval ratings. Capt. Arthur Emmerson of Portsmouth commanded one company of light artillery from the Virginia militia under the overall command of Maj. James Faulkner. Two members of Neale's gun force that morning, Midn. Charles S. McCauley and Midn. Josiah Tattnall, would return to Norfolk to write important pages of the city's naval heritage: McCauley as the Gosport commandant who would burn the yard in the opening hours of the Civil War, and Tattnall as a flag officer in the Confederate Navy, who would serve as ironclad *Virginia's* final commander.[29]

The steadfast Americans stood their ground in the exchange of artillery. The olive drab uniforms of the militia mingled with the blue and red of the regulars and the blue and gold of the naval officers. American batteries continued to hammer at the concentrated troops. With American shot falling among the British troops, with no chance to ford the Thoroughfare, and out of range to employ the superior weight of British musketry, Beckwith finally ordered his troops to fall back.[30]

With the artillery barrage reaching its peak on the western side of the island, the second phase of the assault struck the island's north and east. Fifty armed boats of Captain Pechell's force (with fifteen hundred sailors and Canadian Chasseurs) divided into two columns and rowed steadily toward the island. One column of barges, led by Capt. John M. Hanchett of the *Diadem* (an illegitimate son of King George III), headed toward the rear of the island to work up the creek. Hanchett stood boldly at the stern of the *Centipede,* Warren's personal 52-foot-long green barge, propelled by twenty-four oars and armed with a brass 3-pounder in the bow.

The American batteries remained silent until the barges had drawn close to the island and Captain Emmerson was reputed to have ordered: "Now my brave boys, are you ready? Fire!" In the withering fire, one round crashed into the *Centipede,* wounding several Frenchmen and striking Hanchett in the thigh. Within a few short minutes, three of the largest barges had been disabled and others were grounded in mud. The second column approached from the north but struck mud three or four feet thick over two hundred yards from the beach, making landing impossible. The remaining barges quickly scattered back toward the British squadron in disorder. Several groups of American sailors waded out to capture the stranded barges and their crews, including the handsome *Centipede,* which was taken to the Navy yard in triumph. The gunboats, although relatively close by, did not engage—only *Gunboat No. 67* fired on enemy troops approaching the Thoroughfare, without apparent effect.[31]

The battle lasted only a few hours, but its impact on Norfolk was dramatic. While hundreds of citizens watched from Town Point and Lambert's Point, Taylor's plan of rapidly assigning defenders at the point of greatest need proved to be the strategic difference that helped turn back the overwhelming British numerical superiority.

Warren, in his official report to the Admiralty, downplayed the defeat: "I am happy to say the Loss . . . has not been considerable." The naval losses were limited, he said, to "only two Boats sunk . . . 1 officer [Hanchett] severely, but not Dangerously wounded, 7 sailors wounded and 10 missing." He concluded: "The Officers and Men behaved with much Bravery, and if it had been possible to have got at the Enemy, I am persuaded we would soon have gained the place." Beckwith filed a report showing that among the marines and soldiers under his command, their losses were three dead, eight wounded, and fifty-two missing. Some historians, however, have estimated British losses at about two hundred. No casualities were recorded on the American side.[32]

General Taylor's final report summarized the impact well: "The courage and constancy with which this inferior force in the face of a formidable naval armament, not only sustained a position in which nothing was complete, but repelled the enemy with considerable loss, cannot fail to command the approbation of the government and the applause of their country."[33]

Repulsed at Craney Island, Warren quickly regrouped for an assault on Hampton three days later. Under Cockburn's overall command, British troops landed two miles west of town and marched toward the camp of Maj. Stapleton Crutchfield's Hampton militia of 436 men. After minor resistance, Crutchfield surrendered the field to the British (who numbered twenty-four hundred troops landing in thirty to forty boats) and retreated toward Yorktown. In the wake of the battle, two companies of Frenchmen stormed through town, pillaging and terrifying the citizenry in alleged retaliation for losses and "atrocities" suffered at Craney Island.[34]

On 28 June thirteen British ships moved up the James River, causing widespread panic, and on 29 June six British ships-of-the-line and four frigates moved to the mouth of the Elizabeth, compelling Cassin and Taylor, once again, to man defenses. By early July, however, much of the British force had withdrawn from Hampton Roads, while a strong blockade station was maintained in Lynnhaven Bay and between the capes. Although American naval defenders in Norfolk never let down their guard and thwarted any direct attack, they were powerless to take the offensive against the remaining British squadrons.[35]

Frustrating as the naval situation was to Americans in Tidewater, Hampton Roads provided an ideal test site for the development of an unusual new naval weapon, the underwater mine, or, as it was called in the nineteenth century, the "torpedo."

Beginning in the first decade of the 1800s, inventor Robert Fulton had experimented with underwater waterproof canisters crammed with explosives and detonated either by a timer or "on command" from a nearby boat. Spurned by European navies, Fulton approached the American secretary of war, Henry Dearborn, to propose "torpedoes" to defend the ports of Norfolk and New York against British ships in the wake of the *Chesapeake* incident. "Fulton . . . is very desirous of being permitted to blow up some of the [British] Ships that have given us so much trouble near Norfolk," Knox wrote. "He ascertains no doubts of complete success . . . If he could blow up one of their . . . Ships, I doubt whether any others would trouble us again."[36]

Interest in Fulton's work subsided as the war scare of 1807 waned. Although he published "Torpedo War and Submarine Explosions" in 1810 and earned a small appropriation from Congress to continue experiments, most in the Navy felt that ships could be protected with nets and booms and the use of Fulton's torpedoes would be "dishonorable." It was not until March 1813 that Congress passed the so-called Torpedo Act authorizing Americans to use "torpedoes, submarines, instruments, or any other destructive machine," and promising payment of half its value for any British ship destroyed.[37]

A young sailor from Baltimore named Elijah Mix volunteered to experiment with some Fulton torpedoes left in storage in Washington. During April and May 1813, he worked closely with Capt. Charles Gordon (of *Chesapeake* infamy), then in charge of the naval defenses and gunboats of Baltimore, to test the theory. When the British departed the upper bay for Lynnhaven Bay in May, Mix followed them. He made at least one attempt to snare the anchor line of ship-of-the-line *Victorious* with a floating torpedo off Old Point Comfort. Cockburn reported to Warren that boats had picked up a "Powder Machine" drifting with the ebb tide on 5 June, "made to explode under Water and thereby cause immediate destruction to whatever it may come in contact with."[38] The *Victorious* weapon consisted of six barrels of gunpowder floating about twelve feet below the surface and triggered by a line reaching to a boat.

In the dark of the night of 18 July, Mix (accompanied by a local sea captain named Bowman and a Midshipman McGowan) targeted the 74-gun ship-of-the-line *Plantagenet,* anchored near Cape Henry. Rowing to within eighty yards of the enemy, the Americans were hailed before they could complete their timer settings and hastily withdrew. Two nights later they approached to within twelve yards of the bow, but again, a sentry spotted them and fired a musket as a warning. Although *Plantagenet* shifted anchorages and placed a guardboat in the water, the persistent Mix tried again on 24 July, this time placing the torpedo gently into a current that would draw it down upon the British warship. Again, misfortune dogged Mix's venture and the weapon exploded prematurely, producing only a large column of water that rained down upon the British and ruining what might have been a major milestone in naval history.[39]

Although unsuccessful, this was not the end of torpedoes in Norfolk's defense. In late 1814, eight torpedoes were anchored in the narrows of the Elizabeth in an experiment to see if mines could be used as effectively as sunken hulks to prevent an enemy transit up the river.[40]

Captain Gordon was ordered from Baltimore to take command of *Constellation* in Norfolk on 15 September 1813. Recovered in spirit from the fallout of the *Chesapeake* affair and the discomfiture of the "private reprimand" issued by his court-martial, he was not totally unscathed. In a duel undertaken with a relation of James Barron after the trial, he had suffered a debilitating wound to the stomach from which he would never fully recover. Family connections and discerning social grace had helped his resuscitation in a Navy that bestowed promotion and command based upon longevity rather than accomplishment.[41]

Gordon arrived in Norfolk itching for glory. Although locked inside a tight British blockade, Gordon knew that the nation still warmed to stories of the American Navy's successful frigate actions early in the war, and he visualized himself continuing this tradition from the decks of the famous *Constellation.* To his dismay he discovered a ship not only unready for sea, but lacking great amounts of materiel and supplies. *Constellation's* crew had been scattered to the gunboat flotilla, and all of the ship's voyage provisions had to be removed. The disarray was so widespread that Gordon even found that the captain's cabin furniture was mysteriously missing. "I found the Ship without order or arrangement," wrote Gordon to Secretary Jones, "in any degree owing to her Crew being so long absent & indeed had become almost strangers to the Ship, to their stations & every thing like system & regularity."[42]

Both Captains Stewart and Tarbell were queried about the reason for the disarray, but neither facts nor culpability emerged. Gordon openly blamed Tarbell and his inexperience, an interesting juxtaposition with Gordon's own difficulties in preparing *Chesapeake* for sea in 1807. Tarbell, who had been promoted to captain on 24 July 1813 in the wake of success at Craney Island, had seen his own dreams of commanding *Constellation* at sea dashed with Gordon's arrival and resented both Gordon's arrogance and insinuation.

Gordon was the senior of the three Navy captains in Norfolk but was pointedly not named as the overall commander of the defenses until well into 1814. This led to constant carping between Gordon, Tarbell, and Cassin, as each assiduously guarded his own command dominions (*Constellation,* the gunboat flotilla, and the Navy yard, respectively), and any opportunity for tactical success against the British enemy was made that more difficult. In large measure, Norfolk's most significant contribution to the historic archives of the final years of the war was the steady flow of quibbling correspondence to the secretary of the Navy from this triumvirate of naval leadership.

In the first week of December 1813, Tarbell took nine gunboats and two schooners up the bay to attack two British brigs and two tenders reported to be at the mouth of the East

River. The venture came to naught when a patrolling frigate spotted Tarbell, and he was lucky to catch a favorable wind to run back to Norfolk unscathed. Gordon was openly critical of the enterprise, saying the citizens of Norfolk feared that the gunboats (key to their defense) would be lost. Later, Tarbell planned a second Chesapeake patrol with his gunboats, but Gordon nixed the plan, telling Tarbell that he needed the gunboats to help *Constellation* break out. Tarbell complained to Secretary Jones that Gordon was depleting his flotilla of qualified tars; Gordon groused that Tarbell and Cassin were not giving him sufficient support in getting *Constellation* to sea.[43]

For their part, the British were comfortably in control. The Chesapeake Bay was, in large part, an English lake, and from September to December 1813 the British squadron captured or destroyed seventy-two merchantmen. With their spies reporting negligible action in Norfolk, British commanders were little worried about *Constellation* or the offensive potential of the gunboats. Admiral Warren wrote instructions to Capt. Robert Barrie (who had relieved Cockburn as commander of the British Chesapeake squadron) in January 1814, implying that a simple schooner could match Gordon: "As to the *Constellation,* I suppose She will not easily trust herself out of Hampton Roads if she should Creep there. I suppose if you have something off Cape Charles with the [schooner] *St Lawrence* you must obstruct that passage." Not all American losses came from the tight British blockade. *Gunboat No. 164* sank in a severe squall in the Chesapeake Bay on 16 September 1813, with the loss of twenty drowned.[44]

By September 1814, Gordon's naval defenses at Norfolk were little changed from earlier in the war. His force consisted of *Constellation* and seventeen gunboats (six of which were permanently moored as floating batteries to protect Fort Nelson and Portsmouth) with booms and obstructions in the Elizabeth to prevent a British assault. Gordon still yearned for the chance for a blue-water cruise that would bring him the glory he felt he deserved, and when the British concentrated to the north during the fall of 1814 for attacks on Washington and Baltimore, Gordon proposed a sortie. Secretary Jones wisely disapproved Gordon's undistinguished plan, as even with a depleted force the British were too much for the Americans.[45]

If Gordon needed any proof that the Royal Navy was still to be feared, validation came quickly on 26 October when the *Publick Ledger* reported:

> On Saturday afternoon five barges from the enemy's ships in Lynnhaven Bay, came into Hampton Roads, as high as Sewell's Point. They captured a small vessel from Richmond to Hampton, with whiskey and butter, and a small sloop in ballast; also the Hampton packet boats *Huntress* and *Margaret*. The former was run on shore by the crew, who made their escape. Captain Gordon, having received intimation of this movement, dispatched a tender and two barges, at whose approach the enemy's barges retired, having burnt the *Huntress* and run the *Margaret* on shore.[46]

On 6 November, the British audaciously captured one of *Constellation's* tenders, schooner *Franklin,* off Old Point Comfort.

Serious British campaigning in the Chesapeake ended with their repulse at Baltimore in September 1814. Various major fleet units continued to operate in the bay until mid-December, when all British ships-of-the-line departed the Chesapeake for operations off Georgia and Florida, leaving only a few frigates and sloops to maintain patrols.[47]

The war came to an end with the Treaty of Ghent, signed on Christmas Eve 1814, although word did not reach Norfolk until February. On 9 March 1815, Cassin was ordered to "dismantle all the Gun boats and Barges on the Norfolk Station, except two of the best Gun Boats, that you will retain for occasional service, with crews sufficient to navigate them . . . the Gun Boats will be laid up in ordinary at the Navy Yard, in the most convenient and suitable place for their preservation."[48]

Gordon received orders to (finally) put the *Constellation* to sea. The *Publick Ledger* reported on 16 March 1815, "On Monday last, the United States frigate *Constellation,* Captain Gordon, sailed from Hampton Roads for New York . . . to her gallant commander, her officers and crew, it was a mortifying circumstance to be blockaded by a superior force for two years, but,

> to the publick [*sic*] and to Norfolk in particular, it was highly beneficial. To the *Constellation,* the citizens of Norfolk have looked with confidence as a part of their defense in case of attack."[49]

Gordon thought differently, complaining one last time to the secretary of the Navy: "During this war it has been my misfortune to be deprived of all opportunity of performing my part in common with my Brother officers."[50]

American privateers from Tidewater played a significant role in confronting British interests, especially in light of the limited effectiveness of American naval ships. For instance, during the U.S. Navy's most successful year of operations,

1812, its ships captured six Royal Navy warships and twenty-eight merchantmen. In contrast, around three hundred privateers sailed from American ports during 1812, capturing somewhere between three hundred and five hundred of the enemy.[51]

In Tidewater, privateers presented a golden opportunity for merchant owners and investors to recoup past losses incurred during the embargo and to stay profitable during the British blockade. Historian Joe Mosier captured the sense of optimism that swirled around privateering during the first heady months of the war when he unearthed this editorial from the Norfolk *Herald,* dated 17 July 1812:

> Privateering—This species of marine warfare is likely to become a means of considerable annoyance to our enemy. From the expedition already used in fitting out privateers in all our ports, we may calculate, that in less than two months, we shall have a *private* navy equal, at least in numbers [if not so in strength] to that of Britain. Since the declaration of war three schooners have been converted into privateers in this port manned and equipped; one of them has sailed on a cruise, and the other two will probably sail this day. A number of other vessels, we understand, are in a state of forwardness, and will be got ready for sea with all speed.[52]

By the end of the War of 1812, the U.S. Navy had more ships, personnel, and combat experience than at any other time in its young history. The number of captains had increased from 13 to 30, masters commandant from 9 to 17, and lieutenants from 70 to 146.[53] One important legacy from the war was a growing appreciation of the strategic significance of Hampton Roads and its importance to the entire fabric of an expanding naval service. The success the British enjoyed in threatening the United States through control of the entrance of the Chesapeake Bay was not lost on American Army and Navy planners, nor was the proven ability of Hampton Roads to support a large contingent of naval forces. In the years immediately following the war, the Navy would look anew on how best to increase its infrastructure in Norfolk and to defend the Chesapeake.

The end of the war also brought the need for a renewed naval presence in the Mediterranean. The Barbary States, using the disruptions of the War of 1812 to their advantage, were again preying on American shipping, and President Madison was of a mind to use the improved size and strength of the Navy to stifle the pirates once and for all. Plans were immediately drawn for the sailing of two strong squadrons to the Mediterranean. The first squadron sailed from New York on 20 May 1815, led by Commodore Decatur, with the new frigate *Guerriere* (44), *Constellation* from Norfolk, and eight other ships.

Constellation posted a successful record, joining in on the capture of the Algerian flagship frigate *Meshuda* (44) and a smaller Algerian brig. Within weeks of his arrival in the Mediterranean, Decatur had exacted new treaties of peace with Algiers, Tunis, and Tripoli, ending the payment of tribute and wresting full payment for injuries to American commerce. *Constellation* remained with the squadron to enforce the new treaties, returning to Hampton Roads only in December 1817. Charles Gordon would not return with his ship, finally dying of medical complications from the stomach wound he had suffered in his old duel.

Decatur's return from the Mediterranean marked the zenith of his eminent naval career. At a dinner in his honor in Norfolk on 4 April 1816 (attended by 120 Army and Navy officers from Hampton Roads and all of the distinguished citizens of the borough), a series of patriotic toasts peppered the proceedings. When it came Decatur's turn to speak to his many friends from Norfolk, he responded with what was to become his most famous words. Decatur raised his glass to still the tightly packed Norfolk ballroom and then sent them into a patriotic frenzy with the toast: "Our Country! In her intercourse with foreign nations, may she always be in the right, but our country right or wrong."[54]

1830

The Elizabeth River has never had the attractiveness of the Shenandoah or the James or the drama of the Hudson or the St. Lawrence; it has always been a river of commerce and industry. It has served and nurtured generations of businessmen, shipwrights, tradesmen, and watermen who have earned their living directly from its shores. It has been the draw that has kept the Navy close to Tidewater's bosom, and Tidewater's Navy owes its character and longevity to the Elizabeth.

Rising out of the Dismal Swamp's dark juniper water, the river has a workaday blue-collar personality: rough, muddy, and dependable. Its colors usually favor gray, yellow, and silver, with the sparkle of aquamarine ready to surprise. Its value over the years has been unmistakable, with repair yards, ship breakers, industrial plants, marine terminals, and loading piers fighting for preeminence along every linear inch of its run.

It was immediately after the War of 1812 that the Navy began to recognize the tantalizing value of the Elizabeth. It was a time of newfound vigor in the Navy as it moved during a lengthy peace to prove itself on a worldwide stage. For the Navy, the tone was long term, the theme was for careful and measured growth, helped by congressional approval of nine new ships-of-the-line and nine frigates. The Navy would need a new administrative structure to manage its expansion and the Elizabeth River to nurture its maturation. To Norfolk's benefit, these imperatives emerged at exactly the same time.

In 1815, a Board of Navy Commissioners was formed from the most distinguished and senior officers of the Navy to help direct the administration of an expanding Navy. Initial board members included Commo. John Rodgers as president, Commo. Isaac Hull, Commo. David Porter, and Norfolk's Littleton Tazewell, who served as secretary. Hull soon left the board, and, to no one's surprise, Stephen Decatur was named in his stead. Plans to fashion the fleet would cross board members' desks daily, as would invoices for naval supplies, timber, and food and arrangements for an escalating naval infrastructure.[1]

In 1815, the board faced the question of establishing shore stations and Navy yards to support the new fleet. Before Decatur arrived on the board, Rodgers, Hull, and Porter favored a Navy yard somewhere on the Chesapeake but were opposed to continuing the yard at Gosport. "The yard at Norfolk is objectionable," read the board's first opinion. "The navigation is too shoal for line of battle ships and the passage difficult for vessels of every class. Ships can at no time get to sea with the same wind with which they leave the yard—neither can they get to sea at all while an enemy of superior force shall be in possession of Hampton Roads, as was demonstrated by the detention of the *Constellation* during the whole of our late war."[2] At this critical juncture, Gosport's standing had fallen to a historic low. The official Navy List of 2 January 1816 listed forty-eight oceangoing naval vessels in inventory, with ten at sea, fifteen assigned to New York, seven in Boston, five to Philadelphia, four in New Orleans, and only two—the small ketch *Spitfire* and the schooner *Nonsuch* (14)—laying in ordinary at Gosport.

The board ordered an extensive survey, led by Capt. Arthur Sinclair and Hydrographer D. P. Adams, to seek locations as

After the War of 1812, the new ships at Gosport were being built to be superior to European designs of the same rating (as powerful in weight of broadside as British warships of 120 guns). These ships-of-the-line, such as *Delaware* here, would also introduce the practice into the American Navy of naming first-class combat ships after states. *U.S. Naval Institute*

alternatives to Portsmouth. Four locations were considered: Clay Banks on the York River, St. Mary's harbor on the Potomac (seven miles from Point Lookout), Tangier Island, or Gosport. Sinclair's direction was to evaluate locations for a Navy yard, a full-service support base, a Navy depot for supplies, and a naval "rendezvous" (anchorage), all (it was hoped) at the same location for efficiency's sake. With the War of 1812 fresh in their minds, the commissioners demanded that the site be defendable from both land and sea attack.[3]

By November 1815 (before Decatur's arrival), Rodgers and Porter had all but decided on the York River as the future site of a naval base. We "are engaged in surveying York River in Virginia which is believed to possess the greatest advantages for a naval depot of any place on our southern coast," they wrote the Navy Secretary. "The commissioners are of the opinion that an important establishment upon York River . . . would infer many advantages."[4]

The Board of Navy Commissioners operated best by consensus, and Rodgers convened meetings throughout 1816 to converge on an acceptable solution. Decatur had, by far, the greatest appreciation of the importance of Hampton Roads to the Navy and began to speak out against plans to abandon Gosport. Tangier Island rapidly fell from consideration because of its small size and its distance from a labor force. St. Mary's was a favored naval anchorage for wintering from the ice that frequently clogged the Potomac and the Washington Navy Yard. In July 1816, Rodgers and Porter conducted their own personal survey of the site (Decatur declined the invitation, his mind made up), and both subsequently referred to St. Mary's in glowing terms.

By December, the call was made for a final resolution, but despite Rodgers' strong urging, no accord could be reached for a specific site. In extreme frustration, Rodgers finally agreed to do what the board absolutely never did, to forward to the secretary of the Navy not a consensus recommendation but a report from each commissioner of findings and opinions; it was assumed that the secretary would make the final decision.

Commodore Rodgers struck first in a report dated 23 December that was highly critical of the difficult navigation of the Elizabeth River and its hazards to large warships. He spoke well of St. Mary's, concerned only with vulnerability to attack, but saved his most glowing adjectives for the York River site (above Yorktown at Clay Banks), calling it "the key to the Chesapeake."[5]

Commodore Porter weighed in four days later. "I have always considered a strong objection to Norfolk as a great naval depot," he pressed, citing, "a want of sufficient depth of water at all times for the easy ingress and egress of the largest ships." He, too, emphasized the advantages found at Clay Banks but concluded that his vote was for St. Mary's.[6]

Decatur waited until 2 January 1817 to file his report with the secretary. Rather than take the approach of grading each site against fixed criteria as had his fellow commissioners (no doubt fearing the inevitable result), Decatur concentrated on two major themes: economy and defensibility. His arguments were masterful and compelling. First, he pointed out that $200,000 had already been spent developing the Gosport yard. Then he showed the great efficiencies to be gained by collocating the depot with the fleet's anchorage and emphasized that Hampton Roads was the best naval rendezvous in the Chesapeake—"it furnishes excellent anchorage and has sufficient room for a fleet to maneuver in under sail"—and would be used by the Navy regardless of where the depot was finally located.[7]

Then he devoted his most telling analysis to the defensibility of the site. Referring to studies already under way on how best to defend the Chesapeake from seaborne attack, he noted that measures would have to be taken to protect Hampton Roads, regardless of what the Navy did, because of its population and commercial importance (studies pointed to establishing a major fortification at Old Point Comfort, with batteries at Rip Rap shoal). If the Navy chose to place its depot at any other site farther up the bay, the government would have to build and then man additional fortifications; if the Navy chose, however, to concentrate in Hampton Roads it could leverage the investment in defenses at Old Point Comfort while, at the same time, adding to them by use of Navy ships and floating batteries. Placing the Navy in Hampton Roads would afford a synergy that could not be ignored: "by raising the fortifications [at Old Point Comfort and Rip Raps shoal] and placing the Depot near the ocean, the Chesapeake, at present the most vulnerable point of the coast, would be-come one of the strongest."[8]

Finally, Decatur tackled the costs of defending the naval depot from land attack. Pointing out the vulnerabilities of Clay Banks and St. Mary's and describing the fortifications and garrisons that would have to be provided by the Army, he then explained that land defenses at Norfolk and Portsmouth were already in place from the last war, and "all the approaches to Norfolk and the Navy Yard by land, are interrupted by water courses and lead through swamps . . . and are insulated by creeks." Decatur concluded: "having weighed all the advantages and disadvantages of these several positions, it is my decided opinion that the present Navy Yard at Norfolk—independent of the protection it would afford the Chesapeake—is in all respects incomparably the best place for a naval depot, if Hampton Roads be properly fortified."[9]

Compelling as Decatur's case for Gosport was, the Navy never did make a final decision, and a year later, President James Monroe visited Norfolk, "to decide the fittest place for the naval depot," according to Moses Myers, who added, "his opinion cannot of course be known but mine is that . . . the Navy Yard here cannot be surpassed."[10] Decatur's sponsorship of Gosport did have the effect of deterring any efforts to close it in favor of other sites, developments that became increasingly less likely in the tight economic conditions of the early 1820s. Efforts did proceed with new Hampton Roads defenses at Old Point Comfort (Fortress Monroe) and at Rip Raps shoal (which would later become known as Fort Calhoun). As with many bureaucratic decisions, it became easier (and more politically sound) to slowly enhance existing bases during times of peace than to construct expensive new ones.

In December 1818, Commo. James Barron returned to Virginia from Europe, where he had been since before the War of 1812. Barron, now that the mandated five years of his sentence had been satisfied, appealed to the secretary of the Navy for full reinstatement to service. Although he quickly received the support of Virginia congressmen in his quest, nearly every senior member of the Navy's officer corps objected. Many cited the stain of his dishonorable loss of *Chesapeake,* and others pointed to rumors that he had snubbed the United States and even captained a merchantman under British license during the war.[11]

Decatur was outspoken in his opposition to Barron's reinstatement. Decatur disliked Barron, the two officers held opposing political views, and Decatur felt that Barron was unworthy of a position of seniority in the new and vastly different Navy that arose after the War of 1812. In many ways Decatur became the spokesman for a generation of naval officers tested in the crucible of combat and who had led the Navy back from dishonor to the height of public admiration. Barron did not fit their mold, they would say; let him not taint our honor again.

In a particular moment of heat after hearing from acquaintances in Norfolk that Decatur had insulted him publicly, Barron initiated a series of polite but dissonant letters between the two. This remarkable dialogue of correspondence survives to this day, a collection of vindictive quarreling, high-browed posturing, and faux decorum. Barron, oversensitive to exemplars of personal honor, and theoretically senior to Decatur in the rigid seniority system of the time, fought for a return to respectability. Decatur, while conscious of the need for social politeness, had a lot on his plate and at times considered Barron a time-consuming, pompous irritant.

At first, neither party directly challenged the other to a physical confrontation, and there was little zeal in their accusations carried through correspondence. It is evident, however, that with each letter, both Decatur and Barron became inextricably boxed into corners of honor and position that could only be satisfied on the field of honor.

As Barron continued to poke at Decatur's honor, Decatur sought advice from his fellow commissioners and other captains in the Navy. To a man, they advised Decatur to avoid Barron, and all refused to act as Decatur's second if mere confrontation was to be elevated to the status of a duel. It appeared for a time as if a meeting on the field of honor could be avoided, much to the satisfaction of the Navy and Hampton Roads.

Onto the stage now stepped two other officers, Commo. William Bainbridge (then flying his pennant from ship-of-the-line *Columbus*) and Capt. Jesse Elliot, who began to "advise" their "friends," Decatur and Barron. In short order, the tone of the Decatur–Barron correspondence hardened. Events began clumsily spiraling out of control. Elliot persuaded Barron that he must stand by his honor and challenge Decatur to do likewise. Decatur felt he had a reputation to protect. Barron called Decatur to the field. Decatur responded: "Sir, I have received your communication of the 16th [January 1820] . . . if you intended it as a challenge, I accept it."

The particulars arranged by the two "seconds" specified that pistols would be employed at eight paces, a surprisingly short range, apparently out of consideration for Barron's poor vision. Also unusual was the agreement of first carefully aiming and then firing on a specific count, at variance with the normal practice of a rushed fire from weapons held at one's side that promised some degree of wildness. Together these factors would almost guarantee tragedy.

On the cold, overcast morning of 22 March 1820, Decatur and Barron met at Bladensburg, outside Washington. Neither Barron's wife nor Susan Decatur was aware of the planned confrontation. The two duelists stood ready, both attired in Navy greatcoats. As Bainbridge prepared to call them to present arms, Barron unexpectedly declared: "I hope, Commodore Decatur, that when we meet in another world, we shall be better friends than we have been in this." Decatur replied flatly: "I have never been your enemy, sir."

To witnesses this unexpected concession satisfied the strict *code duello* without further bloodshed, but both Bainbridge and Elliot allowed this accommodation to pass unnoticed.

"Gentlemen, your places."

"Present!"

The two men aimed at each other's hips—normally a relatively safe shot. Decatur had declared before the match that he would make no attempt to kill Barron, and that he might even discharge his pistol into the air.

The count began: "One, two, . . ."

Two shots rang out simultaneously.

Barron spun around with the force of the hit and fell to the ground, cavalierly commenting: "You must excuse my quitting the ground." Decatur, hit as well, remained standing, then was eased to the ground by Bainbridge, saying: "Oh, lord, I am a dead man."[12]

Doctors and several bystanders (including Commodores Rodgers and Porter, who had been secretly observing from the woods) rushed to the side of the duelists. Elliot, suddenly fearful that he could be charged in the death of either man, rushed for a nearby carriage and dashed away. Porter, seeing this disgraceful act, raced after him on horseback to shame him into returning. Doctors found Barron's wound to be serious but not life threatening. Decatur's wound, on the other hand, involved a severed artery, and nothing could be done to stem his bleeding. Both contestants were sadly lifted into carriages for the long trip back to Washington. Rodgers rode with Decatur, comforting him as he could. Decatur, gritting his teeth against the waves of pain, said quietly that he would have preferred to die on the quarterdeck.

Stephen Decatur, a brilliant and romantic figure, the nation's greatest hero of the era and Norfolk's brightest advocate, died at his home on President's Square in Washington at 2230 that night after a dozen hours of extreme suffering. Susan Decatur laid the blame for her husband's death solely on the shoulders of the two seconds and not Barron.

James Barron returned to Hampton and months of recuperation. Inwardly assured that his confrontation with Decatur had restored his honor and, in the words of Elliot, "convinced the world that he was not the man represented to be," Barron renewed his fight for reinstatement to his former rank of captain. The secretary of the Navy ordered a court of inquiry in 1821 to resolve Barron's request, and Caesar A. Rodney, a respected Delaware attorney, represented Barron during the proceedings, serving without pay. The court found for Barron, who regained both his naval commission and seniority on the Navy List. The court's decision cheered the Tidewater community, where Barron was still well respected, and the citizens of Norfolk and Portsmouth commissioned a silver urn for presentation to Rodney, with an inscription that said: "To Caesar A. Rodney, jurist outstanding as much in capacity as in knowledge, who, when he had seen his fellow citizen, James Barron, distinguished commander in the American Navy, threatened with a cruel fate, could not endure the sight of an occurrence so unworthy, but to the glory of his name, rushed to his aid, protected him, and wrestled him from danger. This token of regard the citizenry of Norfolk gives and dedicates with a grateful heart."[13]

On 24 July 1824, sixteen years after his suspension from service, orders were finally issued to Capt. James Barron to command the Philadelphia Navy Yard. A year later, a second set of orders returned Barron to the familiar locale of the Norfolk Navy Yard as its commandant. Barron's biographer records an even more significant set of orders in November 1828, ordering Barron to command of the Pacific Squadron. For the proud Barron, this represented the pinnacle of a complex career, a chance to again raise his broad pennant aboard ship and another important signal of his full restoration of status. Barron ultimately declined the Pacific assignment for reasons of age and family responsibility and remained at Gosport until 1831. Later he was ordered again to Philadelphia for six years, returned to Norfolk, and in 1842, at age seventy-four, headed the Naval Asylum (an old sailor's home) in Philadelphia for two years.[14]

Courtly, broad-shouldered, and with his confidence returned, Barron rose to rank as one of Tidewater's leading citizens. On the death of Commo. John Rodgers in 1838, Barron became the ranking captain in the Navy. He died at age eighty-three on 21 April 1851 and is buried in the Trinity Churchyard in Portsmouth.[15]

Throughout his life, Barron prided himself on his inventions, including a ship's ventilator and an improved anchor windless, which were adopted by the Navy, and his innovative design for a floating dry dock, using principals that are still in use today. His most interesting and historically controversial invention was an invulnerable, steam-propelled warship, armed with a bow ram and protected by slanting, iron-covered sides. Henry A. Wise, a congressman from Virginia and a member of the House Naval Committee, recalled that Barron approached the committee in the late 1830s to build such a craft and to test its invulnerability under the guns of Fortress Monroe. "The (iron-covered) form," Wise later recounted, "would be a terrapin-back at a very acute angle . . . so that the shot would be deflected upwards and could never perforate the sides or upper works." Although Congress took no action on Barron's proposal, the Barron model found its way to Wise's home. "The model of Barron came to our mind," said Wise in 1861 as the Confederacy struggled with the challenge of defending Virginia harbors. "We immediately, by letter, described it to General Lee," an act that would link the Barron legacy to Tidewater's most revered naval icon, the ironclad *Virginia*.[16]

The Barron family naval heritage continued in Tidewater well after James Barron. Before he died in 1810, Commo. Samuel Barron had a son, also named Samuel, born 28 November 1809. On 1 January 1812, as a tribute to his father, young Samuel—barely two years old—was appointed a naval midshipman, and, four years later, the Navy ordered the six-year-old lad to report for duty at Gosport, making him the youngest person ever to receive such orders. At age ten, Midshipman Barron sailed to the Mediterranean, probably aboard *Constitution,* and by age eighteen had risen to lieutenant. Samuel later commanded the brig *Perry* (10), built at the Norfolk Navy Yard in 1843, with service in the Pacific during the Mexican War. Samuel Barron was promoted to captain in 1855 and ordered to command of the naval station at the Norfolk Navy Yard. In 1858 he was named to command the steam frigate *Wabash,* one of the top assignments in the Navy at the time. *Wabash* served as flagship of the Mediterranean Squadron with, interestingly, Midn. (later admiral of the Navy) George Dewey serving onboard.[17]

James Barron Hope, namesake and grandson of James Barron, was born on 23 March 1829 at the Gosport Navy Yard while his grandfather was commandant. He served as a civilian secretary to his uncle, Capt. Samuel Barron, first aboard ship-of-the-line *Pennsylvania* (tied up at Gosport as a receiving ship) and then in sloop-of-war *Cyane* in the West Indies. In 1856, Hope was named Commonwealth's attorney and quickly volunteered for the Confederate cause to serve as secretary to Capt. French Forrest, Confederate commandant of the Gosport yard. Later, Hope would rise to captain in the Army and was with Gen. Joseph E. Johnston at the time of his surrender in North Carolina. After the war, he returned to Norfolk to become one of the borough's most distinguished citizens as editor of the Norfolk *Day-Book* and the Norfolk *Virginian* and later founded the Norfolk *Landmark.* Interestingly, in April 1849, using the pistol from his grandfather's infamous duel, Hope fought his own duel on the beach near Fort Monroe with J. Pembroke Jones, an ensign in the Navy.[18]

By 1820 the face of the Norfolk Navy Yard included: "A brick wall around the Yard. A comfortable dwelling for the Commandant. A large convenient smith of brick. Two large brick warehouses. A few frame buildings used as joiners shops, coopers shops, etc. Very convenient houses and quarters for the marines. A building slip. A substantial ship house. A pair of mast shears."[19] The British sloop-of-war *Alert,* captured by frigate *Essex* (36) on 13 August 1812, served as the yard's first receiving ship—or "guardo" in sailor vernacular. At about this time, the Navy established a second commanding officer post at the Navy yard. This position (variously referred to as Norfolk Naval Station or Norfolk Station) was subor-dinate to the commandant of the yard and concentrated on waterfront operations, preparing ships for sea, and the assigned receiving ship. The first commander with this title was long-time Norfolk figure Capt. (later Commodore) Arthur Sinclair.[20]

Two of the largest ships yet built for the Navy were on Gosport's building ways in 1820, ships-of-the-line *Delaware* and *New York,* being built under the careful supervision of Francis Grice, who had been appointed naval constructor at Norfolk in May 1817. The new American ships-of-the-line represented the Navy's boldest step in matching the world's major naval powers. Others, including ship-of-the-line *Columbus* (74), also called at Gosport's docks for refitting.

Delaware was launched on 21 October 1820 in front of a crowd estimated at twenty thousand, with "the streets approaching the river almost impassable." She would lie in ordinary at Gosport for some years after completion and was not fitted out for sea until 1828. Another member of the class, *North Carolina,* was launched in Philadelphia but completed at Gosport in 1824. *New York* was framed but remained unfinished on her stocks.[21]

Frigate *Guerriere* (44) was placed in ordinary at Gosport in November 1820 but—far from being inactive—became the site of the first formal training classes for midshipmen in the American Navy. For seven years commencing in August 1821 (predating by many years the establishment of the Naval Academy), the school helped midshipmen prepare for lieutenant examinations, emphasizing mathematics and navigation. As Navy chaplains at the time were assigned teaching duties, Chaplain David P. Adams led instruction aboard *Guerriere.* Moses B. Chase, studying theology in Norfolk, assisted with an appointment as an acting chaplain.[22]

One of Adams's first students was Midn. David Glasgow Farragut—destined to be the first full admiral in the American Navy—who had failed his first attempt at lieutenant exams in

By 1826 two substantial ship houses containing building ways had risen at Gosport. Large enough to construct American ships-of-the-line, they became easily recognizable landmarks in Norfolk. Both were burned with the Federal evacuation of the yard in March 1861. *Harpers Weekly lithograph from Naval Historical Foundation*

David Glasgow Farragut, the Navy's first rear admiral, was a central member of the Hampton Roads naval community across nearly forty years leading up to the Civil War. Despite strong family connections and personal inclinations for the South, he threw his lot with the Union and would ultimately triumph in two decisive victories at New Orleans and Mobile Bay. *U.S. Naval Institute*

1820 and had been assigned to the yard specifically to prepare for a second try. The son of sailing master George Farragut, who had served in the Revolutionary South Carolina Navy, Farragut had been raised by Capt. David Porter after his mother had died. Midshipman Farragut entered the Navy's rolls on 17 December 1810, six months shy of ten years.[23]

In August 1811, Porter and Farragut arrived in Norfolk to join frigate *Essex*—the first glimpse that Farragut would have of the city that would serve as his home for nearly sixty years. On 9 August, Porter sent a note to the ship's first lieutenant, announcing his arrival in Norfolk and stating: "I have sent Mr. Farragut and David Fittimary on board and beg you to take them under your particular care. When the wherry is perfectly dry, I will thank you to send her over to me every morning at ½ past 9, under charge of Mr. Farragut."[24]

One morning during their stay, Farragut had drawn the gig up to a Norfolk dock to await the arrival of Porter from business ashore when several old salts on the pier began to make fun of the ten-year-old midshipman. A scuffle quickly ensued, with Farragut's boat crew chasing the offenders toward Norfolk's Market Square, where the local constable quelled the fight and arrested the lot. Porter was delighted with the story and reportedly told his officers that Farragut was composed of "three pounds of uniform and seventy pounds of fight."[25]

Once described by his biographer as having "coal-black hair, dark eyes, dark shaggy eyebrows, a handsome face bronzed by sea winds and sunshine, an open countenance befitting a sailor and a look of firmness and resolution and a touch of imperiousness," Farragut was a dashing figure in the 1820s, attracting much attention from the ladies of Norfolk. During his studies for lieutenant exams, Farragut met and courted Susan Caroline Marchant, the third daughter of Jordan and Fanny Marchant of Norfolk. On an ensuing voyage Farragut contracted yellow fever and, while recuperating in Washington, continued his courtship. Farragut and Susan were married at Trinity Church in Portsmouth on 2 September 1824.[26]

When Farragut returned from a voyage to the Mediterranean in frigate *Brandywine* (44) in 1826, he discovered that his young wife was suffering painfully from neuralgia (severe arthritis). Farragut requested detachment and for four months traveled to specialists to help to arrest the disease. When Susan did not immediately improve, Farragut sought shore duty orders in Norfolk, where he was assigned to the receiving ship *Alert* and received permission to bring his wife aboard so that he could care for her.

During this time, Farragut was tasked by the commander of the naval station to establish a school for boys (apprentice seamen) aboard *Alert* in what may have been the first example of apprentice training ashore in the Navy. He came to the attention of Commo. James Barron, who made the school a point of special interest in official tours of the Navy yard.

After two years on the Brazil station aboard sloop-of-war *Vandalia* (18), Farragut again requested special consideration. With the encouragement of Commodore Barron, he was assigned to the Norfolk receiving ships *Congress* and *Java* and was again was allowed to keep his invalid wife with him. By this time, Susan was restricted to a bed and a wheelchair, and Farragut's biographer records that his "patience and understanding with his wife brought him an almost sainted reputation among the ladies of the Navy Yard."[27]

Between 1834 and 1838, Farragut lived in Norfolk on half pay, "awaiting orders." Despite Farragut's attentions, Susan's illness worsened, and she finally died on 27 December 1839. Later, from 1841 to 1844, Farragut served aboard three different Norfolk ships, first as executive officer of ship-of-the-line *Delaware* (Capt. Charles S. McCauley), then command of sloop *Decatur* (16) and executive officer of ship-of-the-line *Pennsylvania* (120). On 26 December 1843, Farragut was married for the second time, in Norfolk's Christ Church, to Virginia Dorcas Loyall, the oldest daughter of William Loyall, a prominent citizen of Norfolk.[28]

Farragut then was ordered ashore briefly as second in command of the Norfolk Navy Yard under Capt. Jesse Wilkinson and then assumed command of sloop-of-war *Saratoga* (22) during action in the Mexican War. In 1848 he returned to duty at the Norfolk Navy Yard, requested to relieve Cdr. Samuel Barron as commander of the naval station, but was, instead, assigned as ordnance officer at the yard. His Norfolk luck continued in 1859 with command of the powerful new steam sloop *Brooklyn* (18).[29]

In a major study of the time, Congress asked the secretary of war to outline plans to build defensive works to protect the most important harbors in the United States. In February of 1821, that report, codifying the government's future military preparedness plans, defined Hampton Roads and Boston (Massachusetts) Roads as the two "great rendezvous" of the Navy and further proposed two primary "naval arsenals" to be built to support these naval concentration areas, one in Burwell's Bay on the James River and the second at Charlestown, Massachusetts.[30]

This Boston–Norfolk axis was further reinforced six years later when Congress passed An Act for the Gradual Improvement of the Navy of the United States, which provided the Navy a half-million dollars for each of six years to upgrade its shore facilities. The lion's share of that appropriation went to the design and construction of two large dry docks—the first of their kind in the United States—to be constructed at Gosport and the Boston Navy Yard.

Without dry docks, the usual practice of repairing ship hulls involved careening the ship on mud flats at low tide. Although Gosport foreman Charles D. Brodie had developed an experimental wooden diving bell in 1824 to allow workmen to descend eighteen feet into the river to repair a ship's copper bottom, underwater repair was a time-consuming and expensive process.[31]

Loammi Baldwin Jr., one of America's first civil engineers, was appointed engineer in charge of construction of the two great dry docks at Gosport and Boston in early 1827, building the two on identical plans. William P. S. Sanger assumed duties as Baldwin's principal assistant at Gosport. Only seventeen years of age when construction began, Sanger would later become the first naval civil engineer.[32]

The chosen dry dock site at Gosport projected 150 feet into the Elizabeth River and about 150 feet inland from the shoreline. A cofferdam was built to protect the site from the river, and excavated mud was used to extend the nearby shoreline behind stone quay walls. Large blocks of Massachusetts granite were placed to form a dock 40 feet deep, 340 feet long, and 100 feet wide. Construction of an engine house for steam-powered pumps and a system of piping and inner and outer gates completed the dry dock, whose final cost was $974,365. The granite walls of the dock were 7 feet thick at the top and 35 feet thick at the bottom and were so well dressed that less than $100 was spent altering the stone after its arrival at Gosport.[33]

The new dry dock was flooded and its huge gates were opened for the first time on the morning of 17 June 1833 to admit ship-of-the-line *Delaware*—the first dry-docking in North America. "The huge floating castle was accurately adjusted in the centre of the Dock," recorded a reporter from the *Herald,* "presenting a great spectacle to the thousands of spectators who surrounded her . . . the noble ship settled down till her keel rested on the blocks, props were applied to either side to preserve her level and successive rows of these were affixed as the water was drawn off until at last she was left 'high and dry' standing fast and upright in the positioning which it was intended to place her."[34] In only two weeks' time, *Delaware* was out of dock with a newly coppered bottom, proving the dock's worth.[35]

The construction of the Gosport dry dock spurred other expansion at the yard, including new buildings, a new perimeter wall, river dredging, and reclamation of swampy areas. By 1829 an additional forty-three town lots south of the facility were purchased for a cost of $23,600. Between 1828 and 1840 five timber sheds and the third of three imposing boathouses were completed, as were a mast shop; a capstan and rudder shop; shops for blacksmiths, coopers, coppersmiths, and tinsmiths; stables; new officer's quarters; and a watch house.[36]

Navy Agent Bedinger's original 1803 commandant's house had fared poorly over the years. When Capt. John Cassin reported to the shipyard in 1812, he immediately complained to the Navy secretary: "I caught a violent cold in the river followed up by going into the house which is too Small entirely for my family and on the first night we had 18 inches water in the cellar." Although two new wings and a kitchen were added with Cassin's urging, the house soon slipped further into disrepair, and a new Quarters A was constructed in 1837. This

Dry Dock No. 1, inaugurated on 17 June 1833 with the successful docking of ship-of-the-line *Delaware,* was the first dry dock constructed in the Western Hemisphere. The dock was added to the National Register of Historic Places in 1970 and is still in use today. *U.S. Naval*

commandant's house, still standing today, is a two-story example of Greek Revival architecture built of Flemish-bond brick; it was added to the National Register of Historic Landmarks in 1974.[37]

The Marquis de Lafayette visited the Navy yard on 2 October 1824 during his celebrated return tour of the United States and embarked on a special Navy barge for a visit to Yorktown. During July 1829, President Andrew Jackson visited Norfolk; a local reporter wrote: "As the [steamboat] *Potomac* glided in majestic style up our river, the wharves and shipping became crowded with a multitude of spectators . . . The President and suite were waited upon by Navy and Marine officers of the station and those attached to the Yard, who were severally introduced by Commodore Barron and the Hon. Secretary of the Navy to the President. A national salute was fired from the battery in the Yard—the yards of the frigate *Constellation* and sloop of war *Erie* were also manned in beautiful style, affording one of the finest displays we have for a long time witnessed."[38] In 1833, Chief Black Hawk, war chief of the Sauk people who had resisted white settlement on tribal lands in Illinois and Iowa, was taken through the industrial buildings of the Navy yard in an undisguised effort to impress him with the might of U.S. forces.

The mid-1820s also saw Gosport settle into a steady regimen of shipbuilding that was to continue unabated until the Civil War. Frigate *St. Lawrence* (44) was laid down in 1826, quickly followed by sloop *Natchez* (20) in 1827, brig *Pioneer* (6) in 1836, sloop *Yorktown* (16) in 1838, brig *Truxtun* (10) in 1842, storeship *Southampton* (4) in 1842, brig *Perry* (10) in 1843, sloop *Jamestown* (20) in 1843, and steam bark *Powhatan* (9) in 1847.[39] With its increasing capability to maintain steam-powered ships, the yard was chosen to build two powerful steam frigates, *Roanoke* in 1857 and *Colorado* in 1858. These ships, along with sisters that included *Merrimack* and *Minnesota,* served as the center of the American battle line and were the match of any ship in the world.

Beginning in 1827, Gosport was also at the center of the unusual naval practice of "administratively rebuilding" ships. To meet an urgent need for ships, but with few appropriations available for their construction, the Navy turned to the concept of using repair funds to "rebuild" ships—ostensibly repairing older ships but, in fact, building brand-new ships and then transferring the persona of the old ship to the new. The rotting old frigate *John Adams* (28) was in such dire conditions at Gosport that she was ordered broken up while a "rebuilt" sloop of the same name, but with 18 guns, was laid down next to her and constructed in 1830. The old captured frigate *Macedonian* (38) was in such poor shape that she had been dragged onto the mudflats of the Elizabeth to prevent her from sinking. The keel for a "rebuilt" *Macedonian* was laid in February 1833, and for a time there were two *Macedonians* at the shipyard with some parts of the old ship—such as the British figurehead of Alexander the Great—cross-decked onto the new ship. *Congress* was the extreme example of rebuilding: she was broken up at Gosport in 1836, and the "rebuilt" sister constructed nine hundred miles away in Portsmouth, New Hampshire.[40]

A disputed final example of "rebuilding" involved Thomas Truxtun's old frigate *Constellation,* which was dismantled at Gosport beginning in February 1853. The new sloop-of-war *Constellation* (22), designed by Chief Constructor John Lenthall, was launched on 26 August 1854, also at Gosport, with the distinction of being the last all sail–powered warship designed for the U.S. Navy.

By the 1840s, the advent of steam technology was also making its impact on the Navy yard. New shops slowly evolved, new construction techniques were tested, and new trades were introduced into the yard community. The first successful ocean-going steam propulsion designs featured large side-mounted paddlewheels. Although offering improved maneuverability, such designs (with their highly exposed and vulnerable paddlewheels and steam rooms) proved ill-suited for warships. Inventor John Ericsson's ideas for a revolutionary new screw propeller caught the Navy's attention, but so, too, did a design offered by Lt. William W. Hunter of the Gosport yard, who proposed submerging a ship's paddle wheels below the waterline and mounting them horizontally so that they would rotate merry-go-round style within the lower hull. With these "Hunter wheels" below the waterline and with steam machinery now low inside the hull, it was thought the resulting ship would be less susceptible to enemy fire.

With the Navy's backing, a privately funded, experimental steamer was built at Gosport in 1841 to test Hunter's ideas. Named *Germ* (for the "germ" of a new idea), the small craft was the first steam-powered boat built by the yard. *Germ* could make five knots in Hampton Roads and made enough believers within the Navy Department that three additional craft were constructed with Hunter wheels, one of which, *Union* (4), was constructed at Gosport in 1842. Hunter would later join the Confederate cause and assisted naval constructor John L. Porter in designing the screw propeller for ironclad *Virginia.*[41]

All naval activity in Tidewater centered on the Navy yard for the first half of the nineteenth century. In October 1818, frigate *Macedonian* sailed from Norfolk for a two-year cruise that established the first American naval cruising station in the Pacific. Frigate *Congress* (Capt. J. D. Henley) sailed from Hampton Roads on 16 May 1820 to become the first U.S. warship to gain important trade concessions in China. In 1823, Commodore Porter combated Caribbean pirates with sloop-of-war *Peacock* and eight Chesapeake Bay schooners, with Franklin Buchanan, Josiah Tattnall, and David Farragut among the officers of his force.[42]

On 18 August 1838 the U.S. Exploring Expedition under the command of Lt. Charles Wilkes cleared Hampton Roads on a four-year cruise to survey and chart areas in the Pacific Ocean and the South Seas. Although the expedition—composed of sloop-of-war *Vincennes* (18), sloop *Peacock* (18), storeship *Relief,* brig *Porpoise* (10), and schooners *Flying Fish* (2) and *Sea Gull* (2)—had been authorized under a special act of Congress, its chosen commander quickly fell into disfavor among the tight Tidewater naval officer corps for his brazen pomposity, pettiness, and questionable lack of command and seamanship skills. When President Martin Van Buren visited Norfolk a month before Wilkes's sailing, Commo. Lewis Warrington, who had relieved James Barron at the Navy Yard, would not even attend a presidential reception in Wilkes's honor.[43]

Upon its return in 1842, the Exploring Expedition could claim the naming of Antarctica and had charted fifteen hundred miles of its shore, discovered South Sea islands, surveyed the Columbia River, and collected thousands of specimens that eventually would become the foundation of the Smithsonian's scientific collections. But Wilkes's legacy was much more complex. Rather than being hailed a hero, Wilkes was court-martialed and reprimanded.[44]

The venerable frigate *Constitution* would enjoy much more worthy public acclaim when she set out on what would be her only circumnavigation of the world in 1844. After recaulking and recoppering in dock at Gosport, *Constitution* set sail on a foggy 12 April and had cleared the capes by the seventeenth. Under the command of Capt. John "Mad Jack" Percival, she would sail some fifty-three thousand nautical miles, including stops in Rio de Janeiro, Mexico, Hawaii, China, Borneo, Southeast Asia, Muscat, and Mozambique before returning to the United States in 1846.[45]

On 24 November 1852, Commo. Matthew Calbraith Perry sailed from Norfolk in the paddle frigate *Mississippi* (20), commanded by Capt. Sydney Smith Lee, to take command of the East India Squadron and to lead the "black ships" that would open Japan to trade with the West. Other members of Perry's historic squadron included *Mississippi's* sister *Susquehanna,* which sailed from Norfolk in June 1851, and Norfolk steam frigate *Powhatan.*[46]

Hampton Roads would also repay the favor and welcome the first Japanese delegation to the United States. Directly following from Perry's efforts, this special delegation from the Japanese emperor sailed across the Pacific in *Powhatan* and then in screw frigate *Roanoke* from Panama. *Roanoke* arrived in Hampton Roads on 12 May 1860. One reporter wrote: "The sun-light glistened on the bright uniforms which filled the deck. Every window porthole, or opening of any kind in the *Roanoke,* was filled with anxious faces. The Japanese flag waved from the fore-mast, and a Japanese artist stood on the poop-deck sketching the scene . . . a Marine band struck up an air as the sails were furled and tops manned."[47] Amid great fanfare and curiosity, Capt. Samuel Francis DuPont met the Japanese delegation, who were outfitted in their traditional court finery, formally welcomed them to the United States, and escorted them by steamer to the Washington Navy Yard, where they were further escorted by Captains David Farragut and Sydney Smith Lee.

These years also saw the slow expansion and refinement of the Navy yard. On 26 August 1846, land across the river, "admirably located for the storage of guns and shot, and for a coal depot," was purchased and added to the yard. Commandant Capt. Jesse Wilkinson had actually privately purchased this land, known as St. Helena, in advance—the government reimbursed his purchase price plus interest of $2,403.50 for the 9.9 acres. The St. Helena tract was first used as an ordnance center, and the state finally ceded jurisdiction on 22 March 1847. By 1849, St. Helena housed a coal house, a gun park, and a landing wharf, and the lot adjacent to the gun depot was used as a testing range, where new Dahlgren and Parrot guns were fired across the river toward open land and marsh. Improvements within the Navy yard included a foundry, boiler shop, and new engineering equipment, all connected by an internal rail system. The largest set of shears in the United States was installed in 1856 along the yard's quay.[48]

In 1848 the Navy's Bureau of Yards and Docks asked that Fort Norfolk be transferred to the Navy for construction of a powder magazine. Both Forts Nelson and Norfolk had been abandoned since 1824 in favor of garrisoning Fortress Monroe and new artillery positions on Rip Raps Shoal. On 14 September 1849 Fort Norfolk became Navy property, and work began in 1851 on two barracks and several additional structures, including a 55 × 136-foot powder magazine with walls more than 4 feet thick.[49]

In the years before the Civil War the Navy established new "Naval Rendezvous" commands at Boston, Baltimore, New York, Philadelphia, and Norfolk to act as combined recruiting and personnel stations. The staff of the Norfolk Naval Rendezvous evaluated personnel desiring to enlist, determined initial assignments, and ensured that height, health, and age requirements were maintained. By directive, the recruiting officer could not enlist any boy younger than thirteen years or shorter than four feet, nine inches in height, and no one under the age of twenty-one without parental consent. No one could be named an "ordinary seaman" unless they could demonstrate

View of the Elizabeth River and the Naval Hospital from a lithograph published in 1851. *Norfolk Naval Shipyard*

two years' experience at sea. The recruiting officer could not enlist "free colored persons" under twenty-one or any slaves or convicted felons. Once signed into naval service, the recruit's first stop was the Navy yard's receiving ship, for accommodation and instruction until ordered to sea.[50]

In 1826, commissioners of the Navy Department's Naval Hospital Fund began to look for a hospital site in Norfolk, and surgeons Thomas Harris and Thomas Williamson investigated promising sites at Fort Norfolk, Fort Nelson, Old Point Comfort, and Craney Island. A site on the western end of Craney Island was initially favored, but the land title was easier to obtain at Fort Nelson, and the latter site ultimately was selected. The secretary of the Navy and the commissioners of the Navy Board visited the site in March 1827 to formally approve its selection.[51]

The Virginia Legislature had first provided for the medical care of Tidewater's mariners in 1787 when they authorized the establishment of a Marine Hospital in Berkley. That hospital was transferred to Federal control under Surgeon George Balfour in 1801 as the first U.S. Marine Hospital in the United States. The Berkley Marine Hospital continued in operation until Confederate forces took it over and used it as a barracks in 1861.[52]

Historian Joe Law writes that the sick of the Navy in Hampton Roads were first cared for in an "ancient Dutch-roofed house just across Second Street" in Portsmouth in 1803, with a Doctor Hultz as the first surgeon assigned. A small house, known as the Galt house, served as a makeshift dispensary within the Navy yard as early as 1811. Navy yard medical staff moved into a formal marine hospital as early as 1813, which was described by Captain Cassin: "The marine hospital stands in the center of the Yard, two stories high and was formally occupied as boatswains and gunners storerooms, built of wood, the center of which is occupied as a hospital, the garret as a rigging loft and the lower part gunners stores, storekeeper's office, purser's issuing room and office." In 1818 this building was torn down, and a small frame building, located near the bridge leading over the Southern Branch to St. Helena, was used as a hospital until 1829.[53]

The Fort Nelson site that had caught the attention of the Navy was originally a part of the 1636 land grant provided to Capt. Thomas Willoughby. When Fort Nelson was built, it was on private land, 18 acres of which was acquired by the government in 1799 for five hundred pounds sterling. The government purchased an additional 61 acres at the site in 1827 for $9,000 and by 1830 held title to a total of 102 ½ acres.[54]

Beginning in 1827, hospital architect John Haviland ordered the dismantling of the old fort and discovered that he could use much of the original brick "for the purpose of employing, when cleaned, the old materials in the new buildings . . . and save several thousand dollars in the expenditure of the new hospital." Even with these efficiencies—amounting to the reuse of an estimated 570,000 bricks—construction was halted for a time in 1829 for lack of funds. Surgeon Thomas Williamson (from the Navy yard) acted as the first senior medical officer for the new hospital and admitted his first patients in July 1830, when the first wing and the Doric colonnade of the new hospital were completed (Haviland would finally complete full construction in 1836). Surgeon W. P. C. Barton took over for Williamson in 1830 and later rose to be the first surgeon-general of the Navy between 1842 and 1844.[55]

The hospital had its first real test in 1855, when a yellow fever epidemic of overwhelming proportions swept through Norfolk and Portsmouth. On 7 June of that year, the merchant

William P. C. Barton (1786–1856) was an eminent writer, botanist, and noted surgeon who assumed duties as senior medical officer at Portsmouth Naval Hospital in the year it opened, 1830, and served there for nine years. He wrote on a variety of topics having to do with the embryonic science of health care aboard ships at sea and was named as the first chief of the Navy's Bureau of Medicine and Surgery in 1842. *U.S. Navy*

ship *Ben Franklin* arrived in Hampton Roads from the tropics and was placed in quarantine, but the ship apparently disobeyed quarantine rules and opened her holds or discharged her bilges into the Elizabeth. A shipyard machinist named Carter was diagnosed with the disease on 5 July and died three days later. Then a woman who lived within sight of the ship's anchorage also became ill and died. Panic suddenly gripped Tidewater as the epidemic quickly spread, with more infections reported daily. Many abandoned their homes, and yard work came to a standstill. Before the epidemic subsided with the first frosts of autumn, about 2,000 in Norfolk and another 1,050 in Portsmouth had died, including the wife and daughter of Cdr. Samuel Barron.[56]

During the epidemic, the naval hospital labored at full capacity, treating 587 cases between 25 July and 10 November and recording 208 deaths. Dr. Randolph Harrison, one of six surgeons at the naval hospital, recorded: "No one who had never witnessed anything of the kind could form any idea of the utter desolation of the two cities [Norfolk and Portsmouth]; no hotel nor store open, the very drug shops kept by the doctors themselves, as the apothecaries had all fled, in fact, everything was given up to the physicians and the undertakers." In deep gratitude for the heroic service of the hospital staff in fighting the disease, Portsmouth publicly thanked the Navy and had six gold medals struck and presented to the hospital's surgeons.[57]

During the many years between the end of the War of 1812 and the approach of the Civil War, the Navy in Tidewater went about its business in peace. Warships of every description, from ships-of-the-line to steam-powered side-wheelers, had swept down the Elizabeth with the tide, surged through the whitecaps of the Chesapeake, and proceeded past Cape Henry light out to sea. Bound for the Mediterranean, African, Pacific, and East Indian stations, they would mount exploring expeditions, protect American commerce, and show the flag in the ocean's far corners.

Norfolk, too, benefited from the years of peace and relative prosperity. Local trade converged on the lower Chesapeake, and Norfolk merchants, as they had done for generations, profited from the many thousand sail that called Tidewater home. "The City of Norfolk," described in 1853, "presents to the eye a picture, which, though not as exciting as some of her sister cities, is one of considerable interest and beauty; producing in the mind very pleasurable emotions. An appearance of neatness, cleanliness and thriftiness is very perceptible."[58]

And always there was the fine harbor of the Elizabeth and, beyond it, Hampton Roads.

> The waterfront is spacious, well sheltered from the northern and eastern winds in winter and open to the southerly and southwesterly breezes in summer. The navigation is not obstructed by ice for a single day once in half a century. The great ship *Pennsylvania,* the largest vessel in the world, is now riding at her moorings, within a stone's throw of the shore and, if equipped for service abroad, could be at sea in a few hours without the aid of steam. The eastern and southern branches of the Elizabeth River, in uniting, form the harbour of Norfolk—a basin some four miles in circumference . . . the outlet is sufficiently capacious and yet the harbour, in sailors' phrase, is so 'land-locked' as to afford entire security to vessels of every class, from the small oyster boat to the ship of the line. The bottom is composed of stiff mud to hold the anchor, and is free from rocks and all other obstructions. A fine anchorage extends from the basin down to the roads, distant seven miles; indeed, the harbour of Norfolk may be said to terminate only at the point where Hampton Roads is merged into the Chesapeake, where the fleets of the world could lie in perfect security in all kinds of wind and weather.[59]

Security, safety, neatness—a scene of tranquility and peace that was on the verge of extinction . . .

1861

There was, perhaps, no other place in the nation quite like the public houses and taverns along Norfolk's Duke and Wolfe streets in early 1861. Topics of war and secession, so distant just months before, now swirled between the naval officers, merchants, and prosperous shipowners who would gather daily to gauge the tenor of the news. Across Tidewater, the secessionist mood grew by the day, but with the region's economic lifelines so firmly tied to northern port cities and with most of the American merchant marine owned by northerners, the buzz along the streets took a much more subdued and pragmatic tack.

Norfolk's initial inclination was probably to oppose splintering the Union, but as news from the South, especially from Charleston, became increasingly tense, so, too, did conversation in the taverns. Among those most engaged was Tidewater's large population of naval officers assigned to the Gosport yard, attached to ships recently arrived from distant stations or residing in Norfolk "awaiting orders," a common practice in which naval officers between assignments were retained at half pay but were not assigned duties. Many awaiting orders settled near Norfolk to be readily available for assignment. There was hardly a respected family in town that did not have a son in the naval service or a daughter married to a naval officer.

This concentration of naval officers provided a unique dynamic to the Norfolk scene that was unmatched in other locales across the country. With railroad and carriage travel difficult across the country, longtime family association or local bias likely fostered regional consensus for secession or union. But in Norfolk society, the influential naval officer corps hailed from all states of the Union. Many were native-born Virginians, but it was just as likely to find others from the Deep South, the expanding West, or industrial New England. All held sectional or family loyalties, to be sure, but all also had been exposed to wider worldviews and were influenced by their tightly knit professional society. Although some sea officers would inevitably favor southern secession and others would be ardently opposed to it, as a group they spoke largely from the center and urged caution and discretion. Many who had served the flag for all of their professional lives in all the corners of the globe hesitated at the thought of national dissolution and its likely international repercussions.

Capt. David Glasgow Farragut was a perfect example. of this officer corps, caught between opposing forces of history. Living on Duke Street, "awaiting orders" since his detachment from command of the steam sloop *Brooklyn,* he walked to the middle of town every morning to join friends from the Navy to weigh the daily headlines. Although he had married into a prominent Norfolk family, had been born in Tennessee, and had long considered Norfolk his adopted residence, Farragut steadfastly opposed secession. If the Confederacy could make a peaceable break with the Union, his plans were to settle down in retirement in Norfolk, but if civil war came, he would stay loyal to the Navy and fight on the northern side.[1]

March 1861 turned into April, and there was plenty for Farragut to absorb as he huddled with friends for his daily discourse. As President Abraham Lincoln promised to "preserve, protect and defend" the Union, Fort Sumter lay within a circle of Confederate guns, and a naval relief expedition readied to sail to Charleston. By 12 April, the first cannon shot had arced over Sumter's walls, and three days later Lincoln called for seventy-five thousand military volunteers.

Across Tidewater, secessionist banners fluttered above downtown buildings and over Craney Island, and parades and music greeted the news of Sumter's fall. While attending church, Farragut heard a troubling rumor that the customary prayer for the president of the United States was to be omitted from the service. In a moment of heat, Farragut grimly decided to walk out of the church if the rumor proved to be true. The service was conducted as usual, but his biographer points to this as the event that finally crystallized his plans to support the Union.[2]

The day after news of Virginia's vote of secession reached Norfolk, Farragut shared with his wife his decision to stand for the Union: "This act of mine may cause years of separation from your family, so you must decide quickly whether you will go north or remain here." She was unflinching in her decision. On 19 April, after tearful good-byes at the Loyall home on Granby Street, the family booked passage on a Baltimore steamer—Farragut, his wife and son, Mrs. Farragut's sister, her two small children, and the old family servant woman Sinah.[3]

Farragut had carefully avoided contact with the Navy Department when he was in Norfolk, fearing last-minute orders to the Navy yard, where he could face the unpalatable chore of fighting against comrades or neighbors. Finally safely north after two weeks of travel, Farragut wrote: "I have the honor to inform the Department of my change in residence to this place [Hastings-on-Hudson, just north of New York City]. On the afternoon of the 19th ultimate I left Norfolk . . . I hurried my departure. Perceiving that things were fast culminating to a crisis, by which . . . my position as a United States officer, would be rendered uncomfortable."[4] He did not mention the more personal cost of his rushed departure: the loss of most of his personal belongings, which were left behind in his pleasant Norfolk home.

Most of the officers then stationed at the Navy yard, including Commanders Robert G. Robb, Thomas Rootes, and Richard Page; Lieutenants Charles F. M. Spotswood, William Sharp, and George Sinclair; and Surgeon R. F. Mason, were southern in their sympathies. Between three and four hundred naval officers would ultimately submit resignations to join the Confederacy. In Washington, Capt. Samuel Barron had been serving as a member of the Lighthouse Board after leaving command of steam frigate *Wabash* a year earlier. Although he opposed secession, he felt bound by Virginia's sovereign decision to leave the Union, and he quickly organized his household for the trek south. His son Samuel (born about 1836) made immediate arrangements to return to Virginia from California when the war began. He traveled by ship to New York and eventually to Richmond with his friend (later major general) George E. Pickett. Son Samuel accepted a Virginia State Navy appointment as acting master and then lieutenant in the Confederate Navy aboard the armed sidewheel steamer *Jamestown* in Hampton Roads.[5]

Union Flag Officer Garrett J. Pendergrast, commander of the Home Squadron, arrived in Hampton Roads in the razee sloop *Cumberland,* on 23 March 1861; few on board imagined that in less than a year's time this proud ship would be sitting at the bottom of these same roads. *Cumberland* stopped briefly at Gosport for repairs and proceeded to anchor in the Elizabeth on 31 March within sight of the Norfolk wharves—a purposeful move, after which anyone in town could look out on the dignified and imposing vessel with her long line of white-painted gunports, an explicit reminder of the power she could unleash on the town.[6]

Cumberland was one of the most beautiful and striking ship-rigged sailing vessels in the Navy, with a direct design lineage reaching back to *Constitution* and the other powerful American frigates of the War of 1812. Laid down in Boston in 1825, she was not finished until 1843, with a rating as a first-class frigate of 44 guns. Later her spar deck was cut away, making her a magnificent "razee" sloop-of-war of twenty-two 9-inch Dahlgren guns, a 10-inch pivot gun near the bow, and an after rifled 70-pound pivot gun, her most powerful weapon. One of the last sailing warships in an era of rapid development of steam propulsion, she was, nonetheless, a prized command among naval officers of her era.[7]

Cumberland was the only warship fully in commission at Gosport, but the naval presence at the yard was impressive nonetheless. A stately row of ships, all in ordinary, lay moored in the river opposite the yard, headed by the receiving ship *Pennsylvania* and including ships-of-the-line *Columbus* and *Delaware*; frigates *United States, Columbia,* and *Raritan*; brig *Dolphin*; and sloop-of-war *Plymouth.*

Sloop-of-war *Germantown* lay at the seawall between ship-houses A and B, taking on guns, ammunition, and stores with the help of the yard's giant shears. She had returned from a stint in the Far East eight months before, and she had not yet been assigned a crew. On the building ways of Shiphouse A stood ship-of-the-line *New York,* still incomplete from her

Cumberland, a handsome 1,726-ton sailing frigate, was built between 1825 and 1843 at the Boston Navy Yard and operated with the Home Squadron and Mediterranean Squadron and in operations during the Mexican War. In 1855–56, she was converted to a sloop-of-war, allowing her to carry a battery of heavier, though fewer, guns (in 1861: twenty-two 9-inch Dahlgren guns, one 10-inch pivot gun, and a rifled 70-pounder at the stern). Artifacts from the ship are on display at the Hampton Roads Naval Museum. *U.S. Naval Institute photo of a Currier and Ives lithograph*

1818 keel laying. The powerful steam frigate *Merrimack* lay pierside, undergoing engineering repairs. The dry dock was empty, its gate closed.[8]

It was obvious to all that Gosport—the most important naval base in the United States and the largest federal facility in Virginia, with its dry dock, machine shops, and ordnance stores—would be a fine prize to secessionists. "The public buildings and other structures [at Gosport] . . . are with few exceptions, of the first class," read one contemporary account. "Many of them, particularly those recently erected, are splendid structures. Among these may be mentioned the foundry, boiler house, power magazine, ordnance building and provision store. No expense has been spared in their construction." Of special value were the yard's ordnance facilities at Fort Norfolk and St. Helena, the largest in the Navy, with an arsenal of three hundred Dahlgren smoothbore cannon of the newest design and fifty-two potent 9-inch guns.[9]

Added to the value of the Navy yard was the nearby naval hospital, the largest and best equipped in the Navy and "located at the most beautiful and healthy point in the harbor. It is built of free stone and granite and is capable of accommodating six hundred patients. It is provided with every convenience and appliance needed for the objects for what it was designed. All the necessary dependencies for a first class hospital—a surgeon's dwelling, keepers house, cemetery, stables, etc. are provided; and the grounds are covered with a growth of shade trees."[10]

The officer in charge of the Navy yard was Commo. Charles Stewart McCauley, sixty-eight years old and near the top of the seniority list, with fifty-two years of commissioned service. His career had won him an excellent service reputation and had included command of the Washington Navy Yard and the Home Squadron, where President Franklin Pierce personally commended him in 1855 for helping to protect American interests in Cuba.[11]

Dependable, unobtrusive, and comfortable with order and routine, Commodore McCauley fit well within a Navy that at the beginning of 1861 was largely inactive. Of the ninety ships on the Navy's roles, only forty-two were in commission; the with the others had been dismantled or placed "in ordinary." Seventeen ships were on foreign service, and in January 1861, when a relief expedition to Fort Sumter was organized, only steam sloop *Brooklyn* was available, which McCauley capably outfitted at Gosport.[12] For the performance of such peacetime duties, McCauley compared well with other contemporary Navy yard commanders, including Commo. Samuel Francis DuPont (Philadelphia), Commo. A. H. Foote (New York),

By 1861, Commo. Charles Stewart McCauley, Commandant of the Gosport Navy Yard, was sixty-eight years old and had served in the Navy for fifty-two years including time aboard frigate *Constellation* in Norfolk during the War of 1812 and participation in the Battle of Craney Island. Unable to cope with the rapidly changing circumstances that swirled around him in the opening hours of the Civil War, he ordered the abandonment and firing of the Gosport yard and thus awarded Virginia and the Confederacy a priceless early advantage. He was placed on the retired list on 21 December 1861 and died in Washington, D.C. on 21 May 1869. *Hampton Roads Naval Museum*

Commo. Silas Stringham (Boston), and Commo. Franklin Buchanan (Washington), all of whom would assume senior war-fighting roles in the months to come.

McCauley had few troops or Marines at Gosport and so few sailors that he could not man a single ship. There had been talk of reinforcements for Gosport, but the new Lincoln administration, aware of Virginia's sensibilities, feared that such a deployment would be provocative and had rejected such plans. Without a garrison or defensive earthworks, the yard would be largely indefensible.

McCauley was also responsible for ships assigned to the yard but, guided by long tradition, acted only on orders from the secretary of the Navy. Knowing that Gosport's older ships (without crews and in poor material condition) could be activated only with great effort, Secretary of the Navy Gideon Welles had ordered McCauley to concentrate the yard's resources on brig *Dolphin,* sloops *Germantown* and *Plymouth,* and, of course, the powerful steam frigate *Merrimack.* In each case, McCauley acted to bring these ships to a condition where they could be either removed from the yard or could assist in the yard's defense. By 25 March, *Germantown* was completely ready for sea and fully armed, but lacked officers and crew. *Plymouth* and *Dolphin* were also relatively ready for sea, but McCauley's chief engineer had reported that it would take a month to repair *Merrimack.*

But as April began, secessionist fervor swirled around Gosport, throwing McCauley out of his comfortable peacetime routine. "The civil population about Norfolk," commented one observer at the Navy yard, "were very much excited and the more radical among them organized a vigilante committee and made active preparations for hostilities." McCauley faced desertions of his workforce and daily resignations from officers with southern sympathies, including Norfolk-born Cdr. John R. Tucker, who was in command of *Pennsylvania.* Instructions from Washington—many seemingly contradictory—bombarded an increasingly confused McCauley. He was to "exercise his own judgment" in protecting shipping and stores, said one order, but "there should be no steps taken to give needless alarm," said another. McCauley and Pendergrast caucused continually, and *Cumberland* anchored closer to the yard to help with its defense. Orders arrived in Gosport on 11 April to "have the *Merrimack* prepared in as short a time as possible," and, a day later, McCauley was further pressed with orders that "the department desires to have the *Merrimack* removed from the Norfolk to the Philadelphia navy yard with utmost dispatch." Engineer-in-chief Benjamin Isherwood, who had reported to Welles that he could get *Merrimack* ready in a week's time, rushed to Norfolk with Cdr. John Alden, who would assume *Merrimack's* command.[13]

Arriving on 14 April, Isherwood and Alden hired local repairmen and coal heavers and immediately launched round-the-clock repairs. Two days later, McCauley reported to Welles that the *Merrimack* "may now be taken and used for temporary service . . . [and] all that is required to be done . . . will be completed by tomorrow evening."

After a shipyard commander had reported a ship's readiness, normal procedure was then for him to await specific sailing orders. Commo. Hiram Paulding arrived from Washington the same day with Welles's orders: "It may not be necessary that [*Merrimack*] should leave [on the 17th], unless there is immediate danger pending . . . it is not anticipated that any sudden demonstration can be made which will endanger either [*Merrimack*] or stores. The *Plymouth* and *Dolphin* should be placed beyond danger of immediate assault at once, if possible. The *Germantown* can . . . be towed out by the *Merrimack* if an assault is threatened." Paulding conferred with McCauley and Pendergrast but provided no further direction beyond what McCauley already held in his hand. With no sailors available to him to place on *any* ship and with sailing orders for *Merrimack* apparently held in abeyance, McCauley stood pat.[14]

With the news of Virginia's vote of secession on the seventeenth came a barrage of new information for McCauley to unravel. A militia was rumored to be gathering, new earthen fortifications and artillery were reported in Portsmouth, a lightship was said to have been captured on the James River, and then word came of three lightships that had been sunk in the channel off Craney Island to obstruct access to the Navy yard. In the midst of this sudden turmoil, Isherwood reported in person to McCauley that he was ready to light fires in *Merrimack's* boilers. With Welles's latest instructions in mind, McCauley told Isherwood to wait until the following morning. Isherwood dutifully reported early the next morning, telling McCauley that *Merrimack's* "steam was up and the engines [were] working at the wharf." McCauley, hesitant to act without sailing orders and paralyzed by indecision, again deferred, telling Isherwood that he was uncertain of reports of obstructions and had decided to retain *Merrimack.*[15]

Paulding returned to Washington on 18 April and optimistically reported to Welles that the situation in Norfolk was under control, but Isherwood and Alden painted a conflicting picture of irresolution, confusion, and disloyalty. Welles swung into action, ordering Marines from the Washington Navy Yard and the steam sloop-of-war *Pawnee* (Cdr. Stephen Rowan) to rush to Norfolk under the overall command of Commodore Paulding. Urgent telegrams were also fired off to other naval commanders to send all available sailors directly to Norfolk to man the ships.[16] But in his rush to action, Welles unaccountably failed to alert McCauley to these impending measures. This second major communications lapse between Welles and McCauley in two days was especially damaging, because it became clear, based on the events of the next twenty-four hours, that McCauley would have stood firm at Norfolk if he had known relief was imminent.

By the morning of 19 April, McCauley estimated that his command had been reduced to 3 loyal officers, 60 Marines, 60 sailors aboard receiving ship *Pennsylvania,* and the 350-man crew of *Cumberland*—a total of 470 defenders against what he estimated to be thousands of insurgents. McCauley's mathematics were further skewed by clever stratagems by the sur-

Screw sloop *Pawnee* of 10 guns was commissioned 11 June 1860 and, under the command of Cdr. Stephen C. Rowan, saw immediate service in the aborted attempt to relieve Fort Sumter. Upon returning to Washington she embarked troops and stores and sailed to relieve the Gosport Navy Yard, only to arrive too late to do anything other than assist in the destruction of the yard. *Pawnee* then was ordered to patrol the Potomac River where she captured Alexandria, convoyed Union ships, and bombarded Confederate shore batteries. She survived in Navy service until 1882. *U.S. Navy*

rounding Virginians. As militia arrived from Richmond and Petersburg, their commanders would shuttle the same troops into and out of town on railcars, cheering as they arrived and hiding on the outbound trip, successfully giving the impression of a much larger force.

All day on the eighteenth and again on the nineteenth McCauley waited anxiously for instructions. All he received were continuing reports of nearby troop movements and river obstructions and a disturbing account that Virginians had captured twenty-eight hundred barrels of gunpowder stored at Fort Norfolk.[17] Late on 20 April, seemingly cut off from outside support, at the end of a long river blockaded by obstructions and with even his watchmen deserting him, McCauley turned in the only direction he felt open to him, the destruction of the yard. Orders were issued to individual crews about 1800 that evening to start scuttling all of the ships. Aboard *Merrimack,* sea valves were opened and machinery was disabled, and she slowly settled next to her berth until water had risen to the level of her gundeck. Across the yard, shop machinery and the great shears were destroyed, and cannon were either spiked or thrown into the river.

During McCauley's excruciating periods of self-doubt and despondency, help was, in fact, sailing rapidly in his direction. Commander Rowan had anchored *Pawnee* off the Washington Navy Yard early on the nineteenth, fresh from an aborted attempt to provide naval support for Fort Sumter. Like clockwork, ninety-nine Marines, supplies, and combustibles arrived onboard, closely followed by Commodore Paulding and several officers of unquestioned loyalty, including Capt. Charles Wilkes (assigned to take over *Merrimack*) and Cdr. John Rodgers (detailed to *Plymouth*). Paulding's orders from Welles were clear: "On no account should the arms and munitions be permitted to fall into the hands of the insurrectionists, or those who would wrest them from the custody of the government; and should it finally become necessary, you will, in order to prevent that result, destroy the property."[18]

Pawnee was under way down the Potomac at 1930 that evening and had reached Fortress Monroe by 1430 on the twentieth. In short order, she embarked 350 troops of the Third Massachusetts Regiment and sailed for the Navy yard by 1845. In the gathering dark, Rowan skillfully passed the obstructions in the river, with the crew at stations and guns run out. Cheers from *Pennsylvania* and *Cumberland* greeted *Pawnee* at 2000 when she arrived alongside a Gosport wharf, but Paulding was stunned to also hear that all of the ships had been ordered scuttled only two hours before. After a too-hasty investigation in the gloom of early evening (and believing the rumors of a large Virginia force), Paulding decided to finish

Steam frigate *Merrimack* was one of the most powerful ships in the world in the pre-ironclad era before the Civil War. She was a close sister to *Minnesota, Roanoke*, and *Wabash,* who saw considerable time in Hampton Roads during the war. *U.S. Naval Institute*

the job that McCauley had started. Crews with turpentine, explosives, and sledge hammers spread out throughout the yard to prepare for its demolition. "Commodore Paulding considered it urgent that the evacuation begin at once," remembered Lt. Thomas Selfridge, "to minimize the risk of the *Cumberland* and *Pawnee* being blocked by obstruction of the lower channel, and he gave the orders to apply the torch to the large buildings ashore and to all ships that might be of value to the enemy."[19]

By 0145 that night all was in final readiness to light the fuses that would destroy the yard. Every ship was crammed with combustibles except the venerable frigate *United States* ("we could not bear to destroy such an embodiment of naval tradition") and the ship-of-the-line *Delaware,* which was too distant to be reached.[20] At this critical juncture, with all in readiness for the first sparks, Commodore McCauley unaccountably refused to abandon Quarters A (at least one report had him overcome by drink, another suggested a breakdown), and Paulding had him placed bodily aboard *Pawnee* as she finally stood off the pier to take *Cumberland* in tow. In the glow of the premature firing of the Marine Barracks, Commander Rodgers and Capt. Horatio G. Wright of the Army Engineers led a party of forty army engineers and *Pawnee* sailors ashore to prepare Gosport's dry dock for destruction. Two thousand pounds of powder, fused by four separate slow matches, was placed in the vulnerable pumping gallery.

By 0415 *Pawnee* and steam tug *Yankee* had hauled *Cumberland* down the Elizabeth, and at 0420, with the firing of a signal rocket from *Pawnee,* fuses and combustibles were lit ashore. "The *Merrimack* lay close astern of the *Germantown,*" Captain Wilkes wrote,

> . . . and the fire soon reached her rigging and spars . . . [along the wharves] the conflagration was rapid, in vast sheets of flames, and dense smoke which enveloped us from the *Merrimack* . . . then the mast and spars of the *Germantown* were on fire and portions of her hull enveloped in the flames from the *Merrimack.* I directed the boats pull out, the large flakes of fire falling around us. We had scarcely got beyond the ship *Pennsylvania,* which was [moored first in line closest to Norfolk], when the flames from the lower ship house reached her sides, and shortly after she was enveloped in flames.

Wilkes reached *Cumberland* off Craney Island, missing only Rodgers and Wright who, after lighting fuses at the dry dock, had found their way blocked by fire and surrendered to Virginia troops. After being given their parole, they were sent to Richmond and then, with the hospitality of Governor Letcher, on to Washington.[21]

Although witnesses heard several explosions, Rodgers's explosives at the huge graving dock failed to ignite. One account, provided in a 1927 history of the yard, states that in an act of humanity, a sailor broke the powder train so that falling stones and jagged iron would not injure the innocent in Portsmouth.[22] At dawn, Lt. C. F. M. Spotswood discovered the charges and partially flooded the dock to ensure safety.

From the two towering shiphouses along the shore to the ropewalks and foundries inland, the yard burned furiously. The deep thunder of heavy guns discharging aboard the burning *Pennsylvania* resounded along the Elizabeth. The conflagration could be seen for thirty miles, bringing nearly all in Norfolk to witness the disaster across the fire-lit Elizabeth. With the opposite shore standing out in bold relief and with tendrils of smoke rising everywhere, "the scene was indescribably magnificent," read one account, "all the buildings being in a blaze and explosions here and there, scattering the cinders in all directions."[23] "The scene was most impressive," wrote Lieutenant Selfridge later from his station on *Cumberland's* weather decks. "The great conflagration made it as light as day. Norfolk was in the hands of an armed mob, which lined the shores, angry at the destruction that was taking place. As the *Cumberland* passed, both batteries were well manned, prepared at the first fire from shore to pour in her broadsides."[24]

Near daybreak, in smoke and haze, *Cumberland* snagged a channel obstruction off Sewell's Point and had to be dragged free by *Yankee* and steamer *Keystone State.* As *Pawnee* proceeded back to Washington, *Cumberland* anchored under the guns of Fortress Monroe to become the nucleus for the blockade of Hampton Roads that would shortly be initiated.[25]

Spectacular as the blaze had been, damage at Gosport turned out to be largely superficial, thanks in part to Portsmouth citizens and militiamen who had rushed into the yard to extinguish the flames. "The important graving dock lay unharmed," according to one report, "and the ordnance building, smiths' shops and sheds, timber shops, brazing shops, foundries and machine shops were relatively undamaged."[26] George T. Sinclair sent a hurried telegram to Secretary of the Confederate Navy Stephen Russell Mallory on 22 April: "Destruction less than might be expected. The two lower ship-houses burned, with *New York,* line-of-battle ship on the stocks. Also the rigging loft, sail loft and gun carriage depot with all the pivot gun carriages and many others. No other buildings burned."[27] A more complete report was made later by surveyor William H. Peters:

> The total destruction of every ship in ordinary at this station, except the frigate *United States,* was attempted and in part accomplished. The line of battle ship *Pennsylvania,* the frigate *Columbia* and the brig *Dolphin* were burned to their floor heads. The lower bottom timbers and keels only remain and are visible at low water. The frigate *Raritan* has disappeared altogether. Whatever is left of her is out of sight in the deep-water channel. The steam frigate *Merrimack* was sunk and burned to her copper line and down through her berth deck, which, with her spar and gun decks were also burned. The sloop of war *Germantown* was sunk and burned to her bulwarks on the port side. The sloop of war *Plymouth* was scuttled and sunk. The old line of battle ships *Delaware* and *Columbus* were scuttled and sunk at their moorings. The frigate *United States,* a very old ship . . . was in no way molested. Many heavy cannon were spiked and for the time rendered useless, but they have since been restored.[28]

Governor Letcher sent an appointment letter to former Navy Lt. Robert B. Pegram on 16 April 1861, naming him a captain in the Virginia State Navy, with orders to "proceed to Norfolk and there assume control of the naval station with authority to organize naval defenses." Several former U.S. Navy lieutenants were hurriedly commissioned as "captains" in the Virginia State Navy (a reference, perhaps, to the Army rank of captain, equivalent to the Navy rank of lieutenant), only to revert to their former rank of lieutenant in the Confederate States Navy. It is unlikely that Pegram ever commanded at Gosport. Capt. French Forrest, the Confederacy's third-ranking naval officer, captured the yard and immediately assumed command as its commandant on 21 or 22 April.[29]

Forrest had been born in St. Mary's County, Maryland, and had served in the U.S. Navy since 1811. He had commanded frigate *Cumberland* and the successful landing operations at Vera Cruz and had headed the Washington Navy Yard from 1855 to 1856. Tall and dignified with wavy white hair, he was sixty-five at the outbreak of war.[30]

The Confederates raised *Germantown* in June 1861 and fitted her out as a floating battery to serve near Craney Island, then sank her as a river obstruction shortly before evacuating Norfolk in May 1862. *Plymouth* was raised and outfitted for

Engraving from "Harper's Weekly" showing the burning of the Navy Yard as Confederate forces withdrew in May 1862. *Naval Historical Foundation*

the James River Squadron but was also scuttled at Gosport. The *United States* was commissioned into the Confederate Navy (it is sometimes referred to as CSS *Confederate States*) as Gosport's receiving ship and was provided a battery of nineteen guns for harbor defense.[31] The Confederates also seized the schooner-rigged U.S. revenue cutter *William J. Duane* at Norfolk.

Several scholars have suggested that the events of April 1861 could have had much different consequences if Paulding had stood firm and organized a defense of the Gosport yard. Paulding, in fact, had carefully planned for such a defense, expecting to use the yard's ships as a floating wall of batteries to defend Gosport and threaten the destruction of both Norfolk and Portsmouth. Even without the ships, Paulding could have assembled almost a thousand troops in short order and could have repulsed the disorganized insurgents, probably holding southeastern Virginia for the war's duration.[32] But so focused was he on the need for shipboard guns, that when a wrinkle to his plans appeared, he rushed to the conclusion that he must destroy the yard.

The yard proved a treasure trove for the Confederate cause. The cache was huge: the largest dry dock in America, millions of dollars of industrial infrastructure, large quantities of stores and munitions, and over a thousand pieces of heavy ordnance to be used in fortifications around Norfolk and the South at a time when the Confederacy had virtually no facilities to produce cannon. "There is no place in the Southern Confederacy that the Yankees so much desire as the Gosport Navy Yard," wrote the *Virginia Daily Transcript,* "and the loss of which would cause us so much injury. Its spacious storehouses are filled with materials for building and equipping ships that could not be procured by this country at this time at any cost."[33]

No such sense of euphoria existed in Lincoln's Navy Department, which now grappled with the immense task of planning for a naval blockade of the Confederacy. With the stroke of a pen on 30 April 1861, a naval blockade of Norfolk was established with official proclamation:

> To all whom it may concern, I hereby call attention to the proclamation of his Excellency Abraham Lincoln, President of the U. States under date of April 27th 1861 for an efficient Blockade of the Ports of Virginia and N. Carolina and warn all personnel interested that I have a sufficient naval force here for the purpose of carrying out that proclamation. All vessels passing the Capes of Virginia, coming from a distance and ignorant of the proclamation will be warned off, and those passing Fortress Monroe will be required to anchor under the guns of the Fort and suffer themselves to an examination. //s//G. J. Pendergrast, Commanding Home Squadron.[34]

Pendergrast, in fact, did not possess "a sufficient naval force" at all, with only the *Cumberland* and steam gunboat *Monticello* anchored in the roads and the armed steamer *Quaker City* detailed to stand by the capes to intercept all inbound vessels. Few Union warships could come to Pendergrast's aid. The core of Union naval strength at the beginning of the war lay with its six powerful stream frigates (*Niagara, Roanoke, Colorado, Merrimack, Minnesota,* and *Wabash*), but they were poorly suited to blockade duty. Secretary Welles launched an aggressive plan to purchase or charter a wide variety of merchant steamers, of which shallow-draft steamers and ferryboats were especially prized for operations in the Virginia Tidewater. During the war, the service would acquire and arm over five hundred vessels, the majority powered by steam.[35]

Crowds gather as the Gosport yard goes up in flames with the Federal withdrawal in April 1861. *Naval Historical Foundation*

On 1 May, the Navy officially established the Atlantic Coast Blockading Squadron (or the Atlantic Blockading Squadron) under Flag Officer Silas H. Stringham. The squadron was intended to establish a conspicuous blockade presence on the front doorstep of the Confederacy at Hampton Roads. Stringham had been appointed midshipman at age eleven, had served in the War of 1812 and the Mexican War, and had commanded the Navy yards at both Gosport (1851–52) and Boston. Within a week, Stringham's flagship, *Minnesota,* sailed into Hampton Roads, becoming the fourth vessel of the Union force. The next day, five tobacco schooners from Richmond sailed through the roads, assuming they could slip through the leaky Federal cordon; all were captured.[36]

Hampton Roads soon became a watery buffer zone between North and South. A semicircle of Confederate defense positions ringed the southern and eastern edges of the roads—at Sewell's Point (30–40 guns), Lambert's Point, Bush Bluff, Pinner's Point, Fort Norfolk, Pig's Point (16–18 guns), and Craney Island (18 guns). The Third Virginia Regiment held hospital point and the naval hospital with two 8-inch shell guns and eight 32-pounder cannon in a battery referred to, again, as Fort Nelson. Cdr. Charles F. McIntosh commanded the battery, and Surgeon George Blacknell, who had been in charge of the institution from 1839 to 1842, directed the hospital.[37]

To the north and west of Hampton Roads lay Union defenses anchored by Fortress Monroe at Old Point Comfort. On 27 May, twenty-five hundred men from Fort Monroe landed at Newport News from *Quaker City* and *Monticello* and revenue cutter *Harriet Lane* to establish a battery of four 8-inch Columbiads that closed the James to Confederate traffic. By September, Fort Calhoun (later Fort Wool) on Rip Raps Shoal boasted a 24-pounder on the wharf, seven 8-inch Columbiads, and two rifled 42-pounders awaiting carriages.[38]

Opposing forces spied each other every day, but naval actions were rare. After steam tug *Yankee* had probed the new Confederate batteries at Sewell's Point and Craney Island, *Monticello* was ordered to "reconnoiter in the vicinity of Sewell's Point and procure all information that may be useful and necessary." On the afternoon of 18 May, she crossed the channel and fired a shot toward an uncompleted Confederate breastwork, throwing sand high into the air but otherwise causing no damage. Responding to what amounted to only an affront to honor, Confederate artillerists rushed three 32-pounder cannon and two rifled guns to the site, and the next day the two sides traded boisterous but largely ineffective volleys in the first reputed Civil War engagement in Virginia.[39]

In the midst of this North–South standoff, history's first waterborne ascent by observation balloon was made by John La Mountain on 3 August 1861 when the armed transport

This 18-pound English-made cannon was one of many pieces of ordnance captured by Confederate forces when Gosport fell. This cannon found its way to Confederate defenses around Vicksburg and was recaptured by Union forces in July 1863. *Norfolk Naval Shipyard*

Fanny towed his balloon barge toward Sewell's Point, where he ascended to two thousand feet in the balloon's wicker basket to draw sketches of Confederate batteries. On 30 August, Confederate steam tug *Harmony* fired on frigate *Savannah,* damaging the mainmast and rigging. On 13 September, Confederate armed sidewheel steamer *Patrick Henry* also skirmished with *Savannah,* and on 2 December *Patrick Henry* came down the James in a brief hit-and-run raid described by a newspaper as "a roar of artillery that shook the windows in Norfolk and roused the people . . . at a most inconvenient hour."[40]

The importance of the blockade was so vital to the North and the challenge so daunting (thirty-five hundred miles of southern shoreline, much of it a double coastline with inner sounds and outer shores) that Secretary Welles created the Blockade Strategy Board in July 1861 to study the situation and "arrange a programme of blockade." The resulting blockade, with Hampton Roads as its key early focal point, proved to be one of the Union's most important naval strategies of the war, enabling the North to control the seas, reduce overseas aid for the industrially deficient South, and deter foreign intervention in the war.[41]

To better administer the blockade, the Blockade Strategy Board recommended that two Atlantic blockade jurisdictions be created: a North Atlantic Blockading Squadron (patrolling from Hampton Roads to the North Carolina–South Carolina border) and a South Atlantic Blockading Squadron (continuing southward to Key West). Flag Officer Louis M. Goldsborough was to command the North Atlantic Squadron (replacing Stringham), and Flag Officer Samuel Francis DuPont was detailed to the South Atlantic Squadron.[42]

Immediately recognizable in Hampton Roads for his great size, rotund belly, and sailor's nickname of "Old Guts," Goldsborough exerted iron control over local naval operations and became known as a vocal champion of the Navy in its give-and-take with the Army. Goldsborough's fifty years of service included an assignment as superintendent of the Naval Academy, command of ship-of-the line *Ohio,* and command of the Brazil Squadron. His father had served for years as the powerful chief clerk of the Navy Department. Paymaster William Keeler of *Monitor* was less complimentary, describing him as "course, rough, vulgar & profane in his speech, fawning & obsequious to his superiors—supercilious, tyrannical & brutal to his inferiors . . . he is monstrous in size, a huge mass of inert animal matter."[43]

During the fall of 1861, Hampton Roads functioned as a support base for both the North and South Atlantic Blockading squadrons; ships traveled to and from station assignments and Flag Officers Stringham, Goldsborough, and DuPont organized major expeditions against the Confederate coast. Old Point Comfort became a ship repair center with a small naval machine ship, carpentry shop, and storehouse, and the old frigate *Brandywine,* moored at Fortress Monroe, became the squadron's primary supply, repair, and receiving ship.[44]

In mid-August, a naval expedition was assembled in Hampton Roads to attack the Confederate positions at Hatteras Inlet, North Carolina. *Minnesota, Wabash, Cumberland, Susquehanna, Monticello, Pawnee,* and *Harriet Lane* sailed with three troop carriers and nine hundred troops on what was to be the Union's first major amphibious assault of the war. Despite a telegraphed alert of the expedition's departure by Confederate spies, Forts Hatteras and Clark were surprised by troops who landed by surfboats supported by a naval bombardment. Confederate Flag Officer Samuel Barron, in command of all Virginia and North Carolina sea defenses, surrendered the forts, 670 men, and numerous guns originally from Gosport.[45]

Two months later, Hampton Roads again filled with Union vessels; this was the largest assemblage of warships ever commanded by an American officer. Steam frigate *Wabash* flew Flag Officer DuPont's flag at the head of fifty sail gathered for the assault on Port Royal, South Carolina. Any northerner who watched the armada sail was filled with a new warmth of optimism, for despite Union setbacks in other theaters it was clear that the South could not long hold out against the rapidly improved naval power that was now arrayed against it. Many in the Navy agreed with what Goldsborough wrote after Dupont's overwhelming victory at Port Royal: "The Navy must end the war! The Army cannot do it."[46]

Confederate Navy Secretary Mallory's response to DuPont's immense fleet was that the South would have to emphasize untraditional naval answers—like the idea of an invulnerable warship encased in armor—if it ever hoped to overcome Union might. The concept itself was not new—the French had sheathed three floating batteries with iron during the Crimean War, and France and Britain had designs for armored-side warships—but an ironclad vessel was untried in America, and naval architects had no clear idea of how best to design, build, and field such a radically new craft.

It could not have been lost on Mallory that any Confederate naval initiative would inevitably be countered by the overwhelming industry of the North. Time would be of the essence. An ironclad force would have to be constructed quickly and be thrown at the Federals without the slightest restraint, and must

Ironclad *Virginia* in Gosport's Dry Dock No. 1. *U.S. Naval Institute*

make such an overwhelming impact that the Union blockade would collapse for an interval sufficiently long for the South's foreign allies to turn the tide.

Knowing that every day was important, Secretary Mallory pressed the Confederate Congress with his bold, even addictive, vision and pleaded that "not a moment should be lost" in building an ironclad. Later, in a letter to the Naval Committee, Mallory reemphasized just how important an ironclad warship could be: "I regard the possession of an iron-armored ship as a matter of the first necessity. Such a vessel at this time could traverse the entire coast of the United States, prevent all blockade, and encounter with a fair prospect of success, their entire navy."[47]

Despite the fact that no such craft had ever been constructed in America, there would be no time for prototypes, no time for engineering tests, no time for float and trim tests. Civilian Naval Constructor John Luke Porter of Portsmouth (who claimed a 1846 ironclad design and who had produced a model for a "flat-bottomed, light-draught propeller, casemated battery with inclined iron sides and ends") was contacted, as was former congressman Henry Wise, who still held James Barron's model of a slope-sided ironclad ram.

On 10 June, the head of the Confederate Navy ordnance branch, Lt. John Mercer Brooke (inventor of the gun that bore his name), was directed to frame specifications for an ironclad warship, and William P. Williamson (the Gosport chief engineer) and Porter were ordered to Richmond to collaborate, arriving there on 23 June. As the drawings were being finalized, Williamson suggested the use of *Merrimack's* hull and engines to save time. The concept quickly gelled, and the design team was able to write Mallory that "we have carefully examined and considered the various plans and propositions for constructing a shot-proof steam-battery and respectfully report that in our opinion the steam-frigate *Merrimac* [which had been brought into Gosport's granite dry dock in late May] . . . can be made an efficient vessel of that character, mounting 10 heavy guns, 2 pivot and 8 broadside guns of her original battery, and . . . this is our only chance to get a suitable vessel in a short time."[48]

On 11 July Mallory approved the concept and sent instructions to the Gosport yard: "You will proceed with all practicable dispatch to make changes in the form of the *Merrimack,* and to build, equip and fit her in all respects according to the design and plans of the constructor and engineers, Messrs.

Porter and Williamson." Returning immediately to Norfolk, Porter concentrated on ship construction, Williamson on the repair of *Merrimack's* engines. Brooke arranged for the ship's guns and the necessary iron from the Tredegar Ironworks near Richmond. He and young Lt. Catesby ap Roger Jones secretly tested ordnance against different thicknesses of iron at Jamestown Island, which would be continued later at Fort Nelson and Craney Island. Jones had been a well-known ordnance expert in the U.S. Navy, had assisted John Dahlgren, and had sailed on *Merrimack's* maiden voyage to test her cannon.[49]

Despite limited industrial capacity and a lack of skilled mechanics, foundries, rolling mills, and arsenals, southern planning proceeded smoothly; all involved believed in the critical importance of their work to smash the Yankee blockade. The final Porter design called for four inches of iron overlaying twenty-four inches of oak and pine framing, with a protective casemate slanted at 35 degrees to allow shot to glance off its sides.[50]

As *Merrimack's* conversion began in July, the Union Navy began to receive its first regular reports of her design from spies and newspaper articles. But the energy level in Washington was decidedly less than that in Richmond, and it would take a month for Congress to approve Navy Secretary Welles's request for an Ironclad Board to study the situation and a week longer still to advertise for proposals for "iron-clad steam vessels of war."[51]

The Ironclad Board included Commo. Joseph Smith, Commo. Hiram Paulding, and Cdr. Charles H. Davis, all long-serving naval officers but ironclad novices. Their task was not just to find a design to counter Confederate ironclads, but to meet two other major strategic objectives: protected floating batteries that could spearhead Federal attacks against southern harbor defenses, and craft to counter any threat of foreign naval intervention in the war. After laboriously reviewing seventeen different proposals (many of them ridiculously unrealistic), the board gave its endorsement to three designs, an iron-plated gunboat (to be named *Galena*) proposed by New Haven businessman and lobbyist Cornelius S. Bushnell, a fully-rigged, iron-sided frigate with a broadside battery that followed European designs (named *New Ironsides*) proposed by the Philadelphia firm of Merrick & Sons, and a novel design for a single-turret, low-freeboard vessel proposed by inventor John Ericsson and advocated by Bushnell. Although Ericsson's design posed significant technological risk, he made the cut by promising construction in a mere three months.[52]

Ericsson went immediately to work, trusting in only a verbal contract. *Monitor's* keel was laid at Greenpoint, New York, on 25 October 1861, and three months and five days later the ship slipped down the ways with Ericsson proudly standing on her decks. As built, the *Monitor's* novel design incorporated many never-before-seen innovations that sprang directly from Ericsson's inventive mind: five inches of iron plate protection; armored edges that overhung the lower hull, protecting it from shot or ramming; a 21-foot diameter rotating turret with two 11-inch Dahlgren cannon; one-of-a-kind gun carriages, complex recoil friction plates; a multibladed screw propeller; a horizontal side lever steam engine; removable smokestacks; and forced air ventilation—some forty patentable devices. *Monitor* even pioneered the introduction of flush toilets for a crew that lived *below* the waterline. As important as anything else, the revolutionary turret would change everything about how a captain would use his ship in a fight, providing the advantage of aiming gunfire without necessarily maneuvering the ship. *Monitor* was turned over to the Navy on 19 February and commissioned on 4 March 1862.[53]

The first day of March 1862 dawned quietly across a Hampton Roads still locked in the web of a military standoff. Several blockading warships lay at anchor between Newport News and Old Point Comfort, various transports lay under the guns of Fortress Monroe, dispatch steamers came and went from Baltimore and Washington destinations, and occasionally a ship cleared the harbor bound for the capes. The top priority was vigilance; lower on the list was battle readiness. Ships would air their daily laundry from halyards and stays; captains would leave for ship's business ashore. The Confederate enemy had not interrupted this routine in months.

Flag Officer Goldsborough had left the area to join action near Roanoke Island in North Carolina, leaving flagship *Minnesota* off Newport News and passing command responsibilities in Hampton Roads to Capt. John Marston of steam frigate *Roanoke*. As the first morning of March broke, both Goldsborough and Marston undoubtedly woke to yet another intelligence report of the "monster" ironclad *Virginia,* which nearly everyone still called the *Merrimack.* Goldsborough had been reading "reliable information" about *Virginia's* "imminent" sortie since 17 October. Most men in the squadron paid little attention to these reports, believing the prevalent gossip that engine troubles and shoddy construction would keep *Virginia* forever in the yard or, at best, it would remain a stationary floating defense battery.

With a tight blockade in Hampton Roads and with the Confederates seemingly at bay, Goldsborough was less concerned about *Virginia* than he was with developing a grand strategy. On 1 March, Goldsborough penned a lengthy letter to Assistant Secretary Gustavus V. Fox: "I have been thinking a great deal of late of an attack upon Norfolk from this quarter [Roanoke Island] and the more I think of it the more I am persuaded that it can be done successfully." The plan, he explained, would involve a two-pronged assault of forty thousand to fifty thousand troops, some landing at Cape Henry and advancing on Norfolk from the northeast, others transported through the Carolina sounds to approach from the south to "take all [Norfolk's] present defences in reverse; Richmond, of course, would go to the devil at once and . . . both Virginia and North Carolina would sue for mercy . . . that dockyard at Norfolk is an infernally sore thing to us, and have it we must!!"[54]

Any threat from the Confederate "monster" in Hampton Roads was far down on the Navy's list in Washington as well, certainly much lower in importance than either the impending move of Maj. Gen. George McClellan's enormous Army of the Potomac to Hampton or the planned attack on New Orleans by Flag Officer Farragut. Indeed, the Navy Department had already moved ahead with plans to strip its primary sail warships from Hampton Roads (frigates *Congress* and *St. Lawrence* and sloop *Cumberland*) and send them to escort McClellan down the Potomac River and to assign Ericsson's *Monitor* to Farragut, whenever she was finished.[55]

Franklin Buchanan (1800–1874) was born in Baltimore, entered the service as a midshipman in 1815. He rose to command steam frigate *Susquehanna* and to serve as the first superintendent of the Naval Academy. After commanding ironclad *Virginia* in Hampton Roads he was named an admiral in the Confederate Navy and led forces at the Battle of Mobile Bay. *U.S. Naval Institute*

On this same first day in March, *Virginia* lay two weeks out of dry dock and aside the quay at Gosport, the object of intense interest. Although *Virginia's* conversion had begun with a huge head start over her northern counterpart, construction had been plagued by slow delivery of the more than eight hundred tons of iron, and the final shipment of plating from Tredegar had arrived at Gosport only two weeks before. Her testy new commanding officer, Flag Officer Franklin Buchanan, had just arrived in Gosport and was pressing for results. Newly reenergized yard workers scrambled everywhere to finish the thousand details necessary for sailing, powder and stores were readied for loading, and armored shutters were hurriedly fitted over gunports.

More than four hundred men would serve aboard *Virginia* during her brief career. The officers would prove outstanding; nearly all of them had extensive experience. Lt. John Taylor Wood had served on *Cumberland* and had taught gunnery at the U.S. Naval Academy; Henry Ashton Ramsey had served as assistant engineer on board *Merrimack* under Engineer A. C. Stimers (the engineer aboard *Monitor*); and Portsmouth native Walter R. Butt was serving as a midshipman aboard *Congress* at the beginning of the war. Aides to the commodore aboard *Virginia* would include Arthur Sinclair IV and Douglas F. Forrest (son of Flag Officer French Forrest), and the crew included many volunteers from Norfolk's United Artillery Company of the 41st Virginia.

Arthur Sinclair IV had been born in Norfolk and was the grandson of Commo. Arthur Sinclair of War of 1812 fame and the son of Capt. Arthur Sinclair III, who had commanded one of Commodore Perry's ships, *Supply,* in the expedition to Japan and had commanded Confederate gunboat *Winslow.* Arthur Sinclair IV had served as a clerk to his father aboard both *Supply* and *Winslow* and later told the story that, "on the night of Friday, March 7th, a group of officers gathered at the house of my father on Washington Street to discuss the grave question as to the capacity of the *Merrimac* . . . I came forward into the circle of light about the table, 'Take me with you tomorrow, Captain Buchanan,' I begged. Captain Buchanan smiled slowly and turned to my mother. I recall that he did not consult my father. 'How about that, Lelia?' he asked quietly . . . 'my boy's service is sworn to his country, Captain," she answered. My father nodded his head with satisfaction."[56]

On that first day of March 1862, while Union blockaders snoozed, Goldsborough strategized, and Buchanan chafed, John Ericsson was wrestling with last-minute repairs aboard *Monitor* four hundred miles to the north along the East River in New York. Like *Virginia, Monitor* lay pierside, amidst a furious emergency fix to correct a rudder deficiency that had caused her to steer down the river on sea trials "like a drunken man." Her new commanding officer, Cdr. John Worden, likewise labored with a myriad of problems, not the least of which was familiarizing the crew with her singular features.[57]

Worden and Buchanan had been well chosen for their respective assignments, and each, as history would tell, was capable of rapidly and skillfully adjusting to a completely new style of warfare. Flag Officer Buchanan, white-haired and patrician, with the sailor's nickname "Old Buck," had served in the Navy for nearly fifty years with notable assignments, such as command of steam frigate *Susquehanna* in Commodore Perry's historic expedition to Japan and first superintendent of the new Naval Academy at Annapolis. Commander Worden, a lean, serious, and polite man twenty years Buchanan's junior, with a long graying beard, had commanded the sloop *Levant* and had had the rather dubious distinction of being the first Federal officer captured by the Confederacy (returning from the Navy yard at Pensacola at the start of the war).

On March fourth, a day after *Monitor* had completed her final sea trial in the East River, Worden was given sailing orders to "proceed with the *Monitor* under your command to Hampton Roads and on your arrival report to the senior naval officer there." Departure was so rushed that Worden had not been
able to test his guns with anything more than blank charges. That same day, Buchanan wrote Secretary Mallory: "Today I assumed command & hoisted my flag on board this ship [*Virginia*]. The honor conferred upon me, and the confidence reposed in me, by the Department I fully appreciate." At the same time, he ordered armed sidewheel steamers *Patrick Henry* and *Jamestown* and armed steam tug *Teaser* to be placed under his squadron command with instructions: "it is my intention . . . to appear before the enemy off Newport News at daylight on Friday morning next [7 March 1862] . . . my object is first to destroy the frigates *Congress* and *Cumberland* and then turn my attention to the destruction of the battery on shore and the gunboats . . . much is expected of this ship and I expect and hope that our acts will prove our desire to do our duty, to reflect credit upon the country and the navy . . . No. 1 signal hoisted

The first sea battle of a new era. *Courtesy William R. McGrath*

under my pennant indicates 'Sink before you surrender.' "[58]

After waiting a day for a storm to pass, Worden had *Monitor* under tow of sidewheel tug *Seth Low* and passed Sandy Hook in New York harbor by 1600 on the sixth, reporting favorable weather and flat seas. *Seth Low,* accompanied by gunboats *Sachem* and *Currituck,* headed due south and then south by southwest, guided by the lighthouses of the New Jersey coast. That same afternoon in Portsmouth, Buchanan ordered lights lit along the Elizabeth River and *Virginia*'s ironsides covered in grease (with the thought of improving the chance of projectiles glancing off her slanted sides). When the pilots hesitated at navigating the channel in the dark, Buchanan delayed departure for a day to ride out poor weather.

By sunrise on the morning of 7 March, the same weather that delayed *Virginia*'s sailing had closed in around *Monitor,* and the mounting seas soon swept across the ironclad's low freeboard and sloshed around the turret's base. Before long, water was reported leaking through the hawse on the bow and from under the turret. Forward progress slowed as the waves rose further. By 1600, alarmed engineering officers detected water cascading down the stack and the blower inlets. Drive belts on the engine room's blowers, wetted by seawater, first slipped and then parted. With no fresh ventilation, the interior filled with exhaust gases, and the engines and pumps stopped.

For over an hour *Monitor* teetered on the edge of disaster as her engineers worked frantically to restore systems. As a precaution, Worden ordered *Seth Low* toward the beach, but by 1900 that evening, engine power had been restored and the seas abated. *Monitor* passed Chincoteague Island on the Maryland coast by dawn of 8 March, but the crew took little comfort in the respite. Tossed by contrary seas, chilled by unceasing leaks, and bedeviled by cranky equipment, many had not slept in forty-eight hours.

After the storm passed at Hampton Roads, the morning opened bright and clear, with a light breeze and mild temperatures. Although nearly sixty ships were spread across the roadstead, the primary strength of the Union blockade lay with only five ships: *Congress* and *Cumberland* blocking access to the James near Newport News and steam frigates *Minnesota* and *Roanoke* and sailing frigate *St. Lawrence* near Fortress Monroe defending the approach to the Chesapeake Bay. *Minnesota* and *Roanoke* (near-sisters to *Merrimack*) were the most powerful of the bunch, each featuring a gundeck of twenty-four to twenty-eight new 9-inch Dahlgren smoothbore shell guns and an upper deck with 8-inch shell guns in broadside and a 10-inch Dahlgren pivot gun on the forecastle. *Roanoke's* engineering plant, however, was disabled, and her shaft had been removed for repairs. *Congress,* the last sailing frigate built by the Navy in 1842, featured a formidable armament of forty-eight guns. *St. Lawrence* (which had arrived only two days previously) carried fifty guns and a crew seasoned by blockade duties off the Georgia and Carolina coasts.

By mid-morning at the Navy yard, *Virginia*'s crew stood ready for what supposed was to be at most an underway trial, as the ironclad had not even test-fired her guns. "Nothing was known of our destination," wrote Acting Chief Engineer H. Ashton Ramsey. "All we knew was that we were off at last. Then Buchanan sent for me . . . 'Ramsey,' he said, 'I am going to ram the *Cumberland.* I'm told she had the new rifled guns, the only ones in the whole fleet we have cause to fear. The moment we are in the Roads I'm going to make right for her and ram her.' "[59]

At 1100, *Virginia*'s lines were cast off and she moved ponderously into the river, accompanied by the small gunboat *Raleigh* and armed tug *Beaufort.* The Confederate ensign fluttered from her after staff, Buchanan's red pennant from the fore.

As would quickly become clear and as Buchanan was already well aware, the whims of tide would set the inexorable agenda of battle. Then at half flood, the tide would be at full

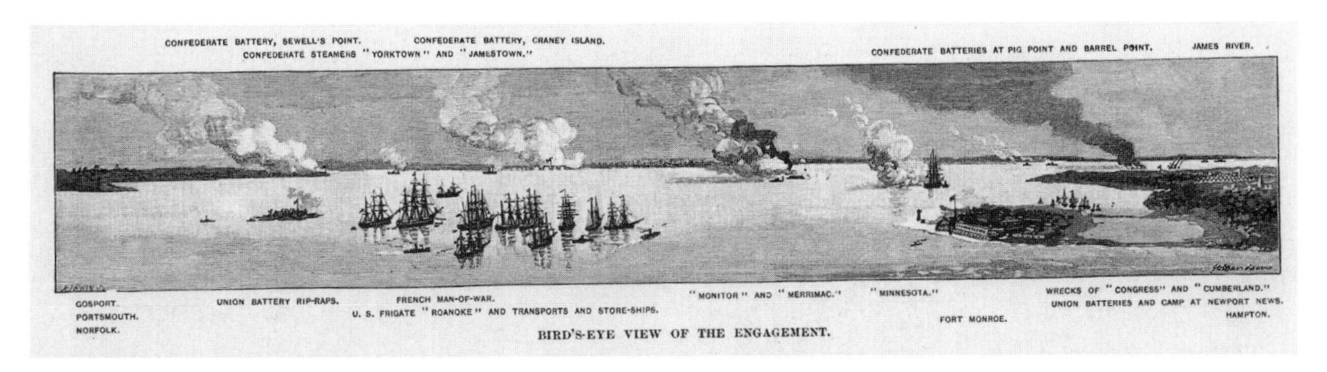

Monitor-Virginia engagement sketch. *Naval Historical Foundation*

Although an inaccurate portrayal of the types of guns used aboard ironclad *Virginia* and the uniforms of the crew, this picture does give some sense of the tight, noisy, and smoke-filled conditions within *Virginia's* casemate during battle. *U.S. Naval Institute*

height by 1400, but then would cycle dangerously low again by sunset.[60]

As *Virginia* moved slowly down the Elizabeth, citizens of Norfolk and Portsmouth hurried to Sewell's Point and Craney Island to watch the impending battle; "women, children, men on horseback and on foot were running down towards the river from every conceivable direction shouting, 'the *Merrimac* is going down,'" wrote Private James Keenan of the 2nd Georgia Infantry.[61] Small craft crammed with spectators shadowed the black bulk of the ironclad leviathan, her greased sides shiny in the bright sunlight. Although some cheered from the batteries, most simply waved caps and handkerchiefs while "a great stillness came over the land." Aboard *Virginia,* William Drake would write: "The men were standing at their guns, a bright sun overhead; all quiet save an occasional order and the throbbing of the machinery below; passing between the two cities we beheld what seemed to be the entire population, and from the wharves, balconies, windows and even housetops ten thousand waving handkerchiefs told us that in their hearts they were bidding us Godspeed!"

By 1240, *Virginia* and her two consorts passed Sewell's Point and turned to port to make the south channel for Newport News. Buchanan was a man in a hurry; *Virginia*'s engineering "trial" would take place as he crossed the width of Hampton Roads heading for battle.[62]

The Yankee signal station at Newport News Point spotted the telltale smudges of *Virginia'*s smoke coming down the Elizabeth and sounded the alert. Aboard the Union warships, crews hurried to their stations. The commander of the French man-of-war *Gassendi,* anchored nearby, described the approaching Confederate craft as "a mass, having the appearance of a barrack's roof surmounted by a large funnel."[63] No formal war plan was in place to react to the *Virginia,* but all captains understood they were to converge on the enemy. *Minnesota,* steam already to her boilers, slipped her chain and steered toward Newport News; *Congress* and *Cumberland* shook out their topsails and cleared their decks. Lt. Thomas Selfridge viewed the *Cumberland* from her quarterdeck: "The *Cumberland* presented an inspiring sight; a splendid type of an old-time frigate; towering masts, long yards, neat and trim man-of-war appearance, with her crew standing at their guns for the last time; cool, grim, silent and determined Yankee seamen."[64]

Faithful to Buchanan's orders, *Patrick Henry, Jamestown,* and *Teaser* formed in line ahead on the James River and headed downriver, clearly visible to those aboard *Cumberland.* North of Craney Island, *Virginia* lumbered into a sweeping larboard turn and steadied on a course directly toward *Cumberland.* Buchanan gathered most of his crew on the gundeck. "Men," he began, his voice resonant, penetrating, every word clearly enunciated, "the eyes of your country are upon you. You are fighting for your rights—your liberties—your wives and children. You must not be content with only doing your duty, but do more than your duty! Those ships [pointing to the Union fleet] must be taken and you shall not complain that I do not take you close enough. Go to your guns!"[65]

Congress, closest to the surging ironclad, fired a ranging shot and then a full lethal broadside in "a tremendous roar," but observers reported that the shots glanced off *Virginia*'s sides "like India-rubber balls." Buchanan ordered *Virginia's* first shot from the 7-inch Brooke rifle on the bow aimed at the *Cumberland;* it hit at the starboard rail, sending a hail of splinters across the sloop's deck.[66] Two withering broadsides from *Virginia*'s heavy guns, some with heated shot, were quickly fired at *Congress,* decimating her gundeck and setting fires in a dozen locations. *Beaufort* and *Raleigh* added their own salvos. Lt. Joseph B. Smith—who had reported as *Congress*'s captain just two days previous—ordered her anchor slipped and the tug *Zouave* to guide the helpless frigate away from the ironclad and toward shallow water.

But as he pummeled *Congress,* Buchanan never wavered from his prime objective and kept the "splendid" *Cumberland* squarely in his sights. As *Virginia* inexorably bore down on *Cumberland,* the sloop's executive officer, Lt. George U. Morris (her commanding officer was ashore on court-martial duty) tried unsuccessfully to bring his guns to bear by twisting the ship against the tide with spring lines. It would have made little difference. Within moments, *Virginia* was turning to rake the defenseless sloop with a rippling broadside. "The carnage was frightful," wrote Selfridge. "Great splinters torn from the ship's side and decks caused more casualties than the enemy's shell. Every first and second captain of the guns of the first division was killed or wounded, and with a box of cannon primers in my pocket, I went from gun to gun firing them as fast as the decimated crews could load."[67]

A depiction of *Cumberland's* demise as *Virginia* drives her ram deep within the sloop's starboard bow during the first day's action. For several minutes the ships were locked together, the *Cumberland* sagging against her attacker and breaking the ram before *Virginia* was able to back her engines to extract. *Cumberland* continued to fire broadsides into *Virginia* as she slowly sunk into the shallow waters of Hampton Roads, and when hailed by *Virginia* asking for surrender, *Cumberland's* acting captain, Lt. George U. Morris, was said to respond: "Never! We will sink with our colors flying." *U.S. Naval Institute*

In exquisite slow motion, *Virginia* swung around and "struck the *Cumberland* upon the starboard bow, the ram penetrating the side under the berth deck, and for a few minutes holding the two ships together."[68] With bow and stern held in place with spring lines, *Cumberland*'s hull sagged heavily against the ironclad's ram, pushing it underwater and bringing the Confederate's forward gunports dangerously close to swamping. "The ram was broken off in *Cumberland*'s side by the combined strain of the *Cumberland*'s sinking and the swinging of the *Merrimac* under the influence of the tide," wrote Selfridge. "The current brought [*Virginia*] up broadside to us and there she lay for some moments without moving." *Cumberland* fired three heroic but ineffective broadsides into *Virginia,* and Lieutenant Morris hailed Buchanan, "We will sink with our colors flying."[69]

"I could hardly believe my senses when I saw the masts of the *Cumberland* begin to sway wildly," recorded one eyewitness. "After one or two lurches, her hull disappeared beneath the water guns firing to the last moment. Most of her brave crew went down with their ship, but not with their colors for the Union flag still floated defiantly from the masts."[70] More than 120 of her crew of 376 would perish in the first bloody hour of battle, including the first Navy chaplain to die in combat, John T. Lenhart.

After ramming *Cumberland, Virginia* backed off and turned in a wide circle until her guns could again bear on *Congress* that had succeeded in grounding, safe from *Virginia*'s ram but not her guns. Despite the obvious destruction, *Minnesota* and *St. Lawrence* defiantly closed the scene (*St. Lawrence* under tow), and *Roanoke* had been towed under the guns of Fort Monroe. After exchanging brief fire with the Confederate batteries at Sewell's Point, *Minnesota* swung toward the west in the direction of *Virginia.* In a moment of haste in the rush to engage, her captain lost his bearings and grounded in the mud of Middle Ground shoal, instantly transforming this worthy adversary into a helpless victim.[71]

Virginia slowed to a stop and pounded *Congress* from safe range and deep water, aided by rounds from Confederate gunboats. Union casualties mounted aboard the helpless frigate. Shortly after *Congress*'s gallant young commander fell, she struck. Ships of the Confederate flotilla closed upon *Congress* to secure the surrendered ship and evacuate wounded but attracted a constant peppering of shot from nearby Yankee shore batteries. Buchanan, standing on *Virginia*'s top decking, was felled by a sharpshooter's round and was carried below, with *Virginia*'s exec, Lieutenant Jones, assuming command.

It was now near 1700, with the bright sun low on the horizon and the tide fast ebbing. Although *Minnesota* stood at *Virginia*'s mercy (*St. Lawrence* had grounded as well, close to *Minnesota*), Jones followed the advice of his pilots and directed the ironclad's return toward Sewell's Point. "The late afternoon sun shone upon the glancing waters," remembered one commentator observing from Ragged Island across from Newport News.

> The fortifications of Newport News were seen swarming with soldiers, now idle spectators of a conflict far beyond the range of their batteries, and flames were bursting from the abandoned *Congress.* The stranded *Minnesota* seemed a huge monster at bay, surrounded by the *Merrimac* and the gun-boats. The entire horizon was lighted up by the continual flashes of the artillery of these combatants, the broadsides of the *Roanoke* and *St. Lawrence* and the Sewell's Point batteries; clouds of white smoke rose in spiral columns to the skies, illumined by the evening sunlight, while land and water seemed to tremble under the thunders of the cannonade.[72]

Virginia had suffered two dead, twenty wounded (greater casualties had been suffered aboard the gunboats), had lost her ram and several guns, many of her plates were loose, her stack was riddled, and, of course, her commander was severely wounded—a trifling loss in comparison to that of her enemy. Triumphant, invincible, and confident, the *Virginia* turned until the warmth of the setting sun was broad on her starboard quarter. Gun crews stood down and slumped to rest by their cannon, jaunty seamen raced forward to prepare the anchor; engineers paused to stroke the warm metal of faithful machinery. To Jones, perhaps, came the thought that Mallory was right and that a single ship could eclipse an entire fleet, lift a blockade, and spread panic and confusion to an enemy. Jones's focus was on temporarily withdrawing, to return the next day to complete the destruction. As the sun slowly lowered, Jones stood at a pinnacle that few men in uniform ever witness; on this one afternoon, the Confederate States Navy ruled the seas.

During all of Saturday, 8 March, *Monitor* continued coasting southward, still in tow. Although the weather was bright and clear and the temperature warm, the ironclad still rolled prodigiously and Worden kept the crew below, who for the most part were tired and chilled to the bone. Cape Charles slowly rose above the horizon about noon, and by 1500 Cape Henry Light was recorded in the log. "At 4 p.m. we passed Cape

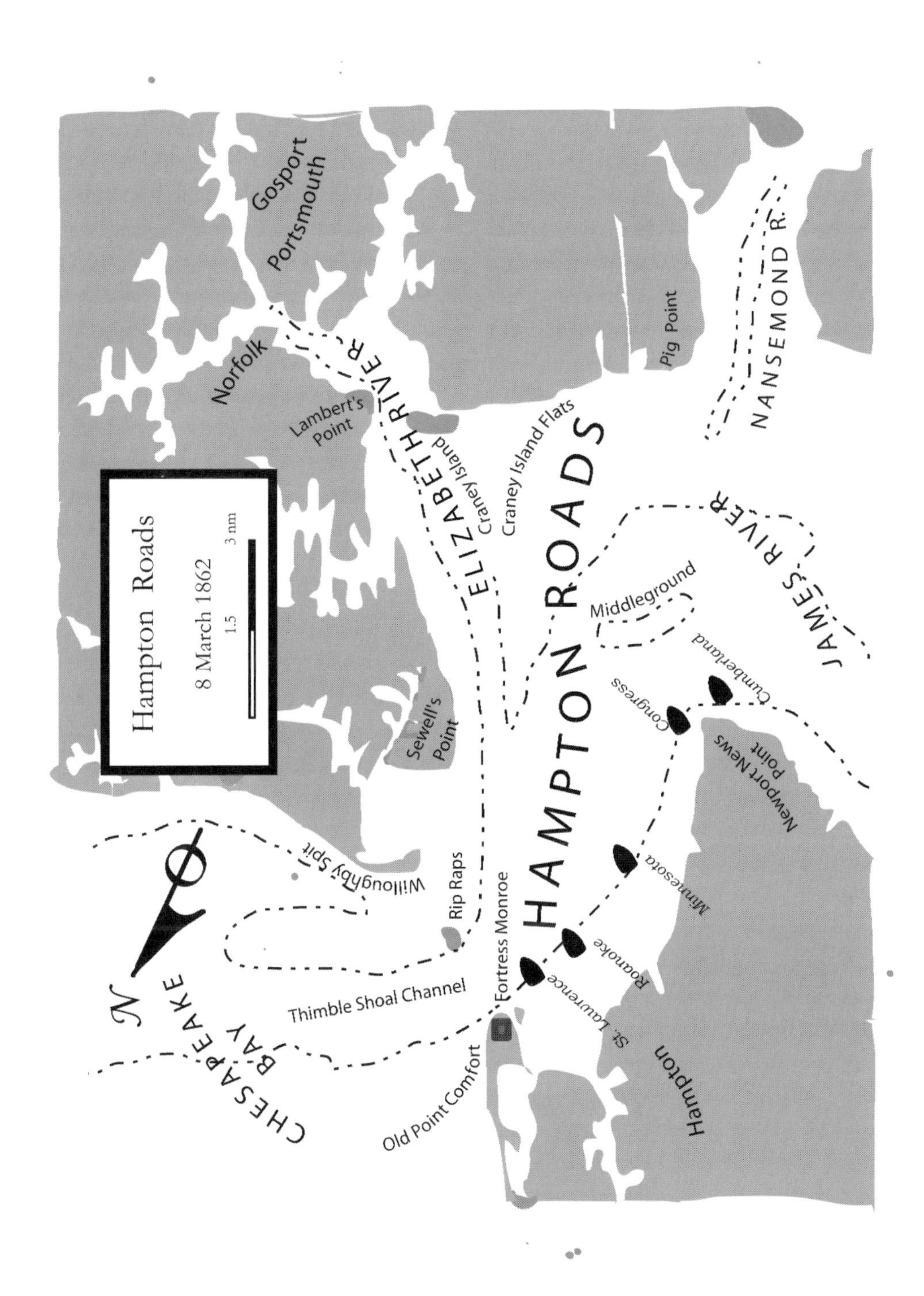
Hampton Roads
8 March 1862
1.5
3 nm
Gosport
Portsmouth
Norfolk
Lambert's Point
ELIZABETH RIVER
Craney Island
Craney Island Flats
Pig Point
NANSEMOND R.
HAMPTON ROADS
JAMES RIVER
Middleground
Cumberland
Congress
Newport News Point
Sewell's Point
Willoughby Spit
Rip Raps
Fortress Monroe
Minnesota
Roanoke
St. Lawrence
Hampton
Thimble Shoal Channel
Old Point Comfort
CHESAPEAKE BAY
N

Henry and heard heavy firing in the direction of Fortress Monroe," recounted Lt. Samuel Dana Greene, *Monitor's* exec. "As we approached it increased and we immediately cleared ship for action. When about half-way between Fortress Monroe and Cape Henry, we spoke a pilot boat. He told us the *Cumberland* was sunk, and the *Congress* was on fire and surrendered to the *Merrimac.* We did not credit it at first, but as we approached Hampton Roads we could see the fine old *Congress* burning brightly and we knew then it must be so."[73]

Monitor anchored briefly at the Horseshoe and then approached *Roanoke,* where Captain Marston ordered *Monitor* to *Minnesota's* aid. Worden left a short dispatch for Secretary Welles: "Sir, I have the honor to report that I arrived at this anchorage at 9 o'clock this evening, and am ordered to proceed immediately to the assistance of the *Minnesota,* aground near Newport News."[74] By 0100, *Monitor* anchored alongside the helpless *Minnesota.* The crew stood at quarters all night; no one slept. One observer wrote that night:

> The moon in her second quarter was just rising over the waters, but her silvery light was soon paled by the conflagration of the *Congress* whose glare was reflected in the river. The burning frigate four miles away seemed much nearer. As the flames crept up the rigging, every mast, spar and rope glittered against the dark sky in dazzling lines of fire. The hull, aground upon the shoal, was plainly visible, and upon its black surface each porthole seemed the mouth of a fiery furnace. At irregular intervals, loaded guns and shells, exploding as the fire reached them, sent forth their deep reverberations. The masts and rigging were still standing, apparently almost intact, when, about 2 o'clock in the morning, a monstrous sheaf of flame rose from the vessel to an immense height. A deep report announced the explosion of the ship's powder magazine. It continued to burn until the brightness of its blaze was effaced by the morning sun.[75]

Worden hardly stirred from his perch atop *Monitor's* turret throughout the short night. As the first light of dawn colored the waters of the roads a pale aquamarine, Worden cautiously picked out the distant inky black silhouette of *Virginia* to the south-southeast through patches of low morning haze.

Likewise, *Monitor's* presence quickly became known across the roadstead in the early light of a magical morning. Aboard *Virginia,* Lieutenant Wood commented: "At daybreak we discovered, lying between us and the *Minnesota,* a strange-looking craft, which we knew at once to be Ericsson's *Monitor,* which had long been expected in Hampton Roads and which, from different sources, we had a good idea. She could not possibly have made her appearance at a more inopportune time for us, changing our plans, which were to destroy the *Minnesota,* and then the remainder of the fleet below Fort Monroe. She appeared but a pigmy compared with the lofty frigate which she guarded."[76] And from Lt. James H. Rochelle aboard *Patrick Henry*:

> At the first peep of dawn on the 9th of March, the Confederate squadron was underway . . . as the daylight increased . . . the *Minnesota* was not the only thing to attract attention; close alongside of her lay such a craft as the eyes of a seaman does not delight in; an immense shingle floating on the water with a gigantic cheese box rising from its center; no sails, no wheels, no smokestack, no guns, at least none that could be seen . . . some thought it a water tank sent to supply the *Minnesota* with water, others that it was a floating magazine replenishing her exhausted stock of ammunition, but a few were of the opinion that it was the *Monitor* which the Northern papers had been boasting about a long time.[77]

Lieutenant Jones had *Virginia's* crew ready early, and the dawn brought the smells of a hearty breakfast wafting through the casement. *Virginia's* surgeon landed Captain Buchanan and the seriously wounded at Sewell's Point for travel to the naval hospital, and as soon as he returned, Jones ordered the anchor raised. Just before 0800, with her engine steadily thumping, *Virginia* steadied on course directly toward *Minnesota,* followed by *Patrick Henry, Jamestown, Teaser,* and gunboat *Raleigh.* Few fully understood *Monitor's* potential, and nearly all observers voiced the same opinion as Dr. Edward Shippen, late of the *Congress,* "she seemed so small and trifling that we feared she would only constitute additional prey for the leviathan."[78]

When *Virginia* had closed to about a mile, she opened the engagement with two shots fixed at *Minnesota,* striking the frigate's side in a hail of splinters. Unruffled, Worden calmly ordered all below to their stations. Capt. Gershom Jacques Van Brunt of *Minnesota* wrote: "[I] made signal to the *Monitor* to attack the enemy. She immediately ran down in my wake right within the range of the *Merrimac,* completely covering my ship, as far as was possible with her diminutive dimensions, and, much to my astonishment, laid herself right alongside of the *Merrimac,* and the contrast was that of a pigmy to a giant."[79]

Worden stood in the ironclad's pilothouse, low in the hull near the bow, where he could see out through the slits of a small armored port. With him were a pilot and quartermaster. Executive Officer Greene commanded the turret accompanied by the master and "sixteen brawny men" to handle shot (which could weight 170 pounds each). "As the *Merrimac* came down," Greene recounted, "the Captain passed the word to commence firing; I triced up the [gun]port, ran out the gun and fired, thus began the great battle between the *Merrimac* and *Monitor.*"[80]

Monitor's course placed her on *Virginia's* starboard bow at right angles to the Confederate. Worden ordered the rudder hard to port to turn *Monitor* to a parallel and opposite course from *Virginia,* then ordered engines stopped; firing commenced. *Monitor's* first shot struck at *Virginia's* waterline and *Virginia* adjusted course slightly and unleashed a full broadside in return. Greene wrote: "The turret and other parts of the ship were heavily struck, but the shots did not penetrate; the tower was intact, and it continued to revolve. A look of confidence passed over the men's faces, and we believed the *Merrimac* would not repeat the work she had accomplished the day before."[81]

The two captains fenced for position as broadside matched broadside. *Monitor,* by far the more maneuverable, took position for a moment where no *Virginia* gun could reach her. Jones responded with musketry aimed at *Monitor's* small pilothouse. Greene's guns belched round after round. *Minnesota* added her own weight of shot to the duel. Thick, prodigious clouds of smoke, accented within by sharp stabs of red and yellow, frequently hid the participants from outside view but did nothing to muffle the thunderous cannonade.

Virginia's engineering officer, H. Ashton Ramsay, wrote: "We hovered about each other in spirals, gradually contracting the circuits until we were within point-blank range, but our shell glanced from *Monitor's* turret just as hers did from our sloping sides . . . On our gun deck all was bustle, smoke, grimy figures and stern commands, while down in the engine and boiler rooms the sixteen furnaces were belching out fire and smoke."[82]

Still the shots came, roughly in eight-minute intervals, as sweating, tired gun crews toiled in a world of unrelenting noise and semidarkness. Greene had tremendous difficulty in aiming: "the effect upon one shut up in a revolving drum is perplexing, and it is not a simple matter to keep the bearings . . . when a gun was ready for firing, the turret would be started on its revolving journey in search of the target, and when found it was taken 'on the fly,' because the turret could not be accurately controlled."[83]

At one point, *Virginia* ran aground and extracted herself only by jacking the boilers to their highest possible pressures to back her off the ever-present harbor mud. At another, Worden tried to clip *Virginia's* stern to damage her rudder or propeller but missed by two feet. Jones tried ramming his nimble opponent but could reach her with only a glancing blow.[84]

At around noon, *Monitor* again maneuvered close to *Virginia's* stern, but a shot from *Virginia's* heavy stern gun slammed into *Monitor's* low conning tower. Powder and debris immediately blinded Worden, and the concussion stunned all in the pilothouse. Worden was helped below, replaced by Greene. By now, however, the epic battle had reached its final stages, with both ships' crews utterly exhausted, many senseless from the roar of cannon and concussions of impact, and ammunition and coal running low. For the second straight day, Jones took the initiative to quit the battle. "I'm going to haul off under the guns of Sewell's Point," he told Engineer Ramsey, "and renew the attack on the rise of the tide. Bank your fires."

After four vivid hours, the *Monitor* had seemingly accomplished the impossible—she had fought the impregnable *Virginia* to a standstill and prevented the destruction of the Union fleet. *Virginia* withdrew slowly toward the Elizabeth River; *Monitor* fell off to a position near *Minnesota.* Greene looked up at *Minnesota's* quarterdeck from the turret to see Assistant Secretary Fox, who had hurried to the scene the night before from Washington. "Secretary Fox hailed us," he later wrote, "and told us we had fought the greatest naval battle on record, and behaved as gallantly as men could."[85] Fox's wire to Welles that night was reassuring but pragmatic: "These two ironclad vessels fought part of the time touching each other, from 8 a.m. to noon, when the *Merrimack* retired. Whether she is injured or not it is impossible to say . . . the *Monitor* is uninjured and ready at any moment to repel another attack."[86]

The clatter of Fox's words resounding in the closed space of a Washington telegraph office sounded the end of Confederate Secretary Mallory's vision of ending the war by breaking the Union's blockade. His bold gambit had come tantalizingly close to success. If Ericsson's aggressive construction schedule had slipped by a mere month or if *Monitor* had foundered in mid-ocean on the transit south (a significant possibility, as later events would prove), the Confederacy would have had sufficient time to sweep the Federals from the Virginia Capes and probably would have gained the vote of foreign powers seeking an excuse to intervene. If *Virginia* had carried armor-piercing bolts or even solid round shot for her cannon (in

Harper's Weekly engraving of both Union ships at anchor in the Elizabeth River supporting the occupation of Norfolk in 1862 and a bird's-eye view of the Gosport yard during that same year. *Hampton Roads Naval Museum*

anticipation of engaging only wooded ships, she had loaded explosive shells, hot shot, and canister), the odds of disabling *Monitor* would have increased greatly, and with *Monitor* out of action, the Union would have had no ironclad to match *Virginia* until September 1862.

Lt. Jones's decision to retire was tactically correct, as no means lay at his immediate disposal to break the stalemate, and *Virginia* had grown increasingly vulnerable to shot as she grew lighter and higher in the water during the engagement. But *Virginia* would be unable to immediately renew combat, as he had hoped (as yard constructors would capture her for repairs and improvements), and it was there that the battle would ultimately be decided. Although not fully appreciated at the time, Union strength and defensive tactics would improve (relative to *Virginia*'s strength) with each passing day, inexorably diminishing any chance the southern ironclad would have for victory in a renewed clash.

With his crew dropping from exhaustion and the ship's pumps working full time, Jones sailed *Virginia* directly to dry dock for repairs. Ninety-seven shot marks were counted, with twenty of which were estimated to be from the 10-inch guns of *Monitor* (*Monitor* withstood twenty-three hits). Six shielding plates were broken, but the hull and the wood casement framing were remarkably untouched. Porter and the Gosport engineers generated a broad series of improvements, including underwater hull plating, new gunport shutters, replacement rifled guns, and a heavier new ram. Intricate plans were also created to overcome *Monitor* through boarding, blinding her pilothouse, or sending inflammables down her air intakes.[87]

Flag Officer Goldsborough rushed back to Hampton Roads, fearing the worst but finding *Monitor* ready for immediate battle. "We'll make [the situation] good before long," he wrote his wife. "Keep cool and quiet, Buchanan is badly wounded, by a minie ball through his thigh." In his writings to Assistant Secretary Fox, Goldsborough displayed a more cautious tone: "On a careful scrutiny of the *Monitor,* it will not do, in my judgment, to count too largely on her prowess. She is scarcely enough for the *Merrimac.* It should be remembered that the latter was injured when the *Monitor* engaged her."[88]

Without other ironclads between *Virginia* and Washington, Lincoln, too, was concerned with *Monitor*'s safety, especially after learning from Lieutenant Worden of *Monitor*'s vulnerability to boarding parties and hearing other rumors of rebel plans to use chloroform to produce insensibility on board *Monitor.* Fox's ensuing order to *Monitor* was specific: "It is directed by the President that the *Monitor* be not too much exposed; that in no event shall any attempt be made to proceed

Known in the Union Navy for his expansive girth as well as his blasphemous, combative and no-nonsense personality, Commo. (later rear admiral) Louis M. Goldsborough was named to command of the North Atlantic Blockading Squadron in Hampton Roads in October 1861 and, to his credit, quickly built a dominant Union naval position while directing operations in Hampton Roads, the James River, and the Carolina sounds. *U.S. Naval Institute*

with her unattended to Norfolk." Not only would *Monitor* be employed conservatively, which fit the inclination of her new commander, Lt. William N. Jeffers, but she would be accompanied by consorts to sweep her decks of any Confederate boarders. Goldsborough: "The salvation of McClellan's army . . . greatly depends upon my holding the *Merrimac* steadily and securely in check . . . my game therefore is to remain firmly on the defensive unless I can fight on my own terms."[89]

With a conservative mind-set and with the president's restrictions on his freedom of action, Goldsborough pressed for more ships to counter *Virginia:* "I am satisfied that I could easily capture the *Merrimac* by running her down with one or more [large, fast steamers] at any time she might make her appearance. No arms need be put on board of them. Upon their immense momentum alone I should rely, and, in my judgment success could be certain."[90]

Secretary Welles immediately responded, ordering several large steamers with their civilian crews to Hampton Roads, including *Vanderbilt,* the former flagship of Commo. Cornelius Vanderbilt's North Atlantic Mail Steamship Line. Goldsborough's orders to the chartered side steamer *Illinois* were typical: "It is advisable that [*Illinois*] should be made to strike [*Merrimac*], with the greatest possible velocity, at right angles to her side or stern, or . . . a severe blow, somewhat slanting delivered on either her side or stern, [to] disable her so as to ensure at least her capture . . .you will perform this duty to the best of your ability and thus destroy the *Merrimac* if possible."[91]

Goldsborough's untried tactics were met with little enthusiasm among the civilian crews, and he soon complained to Welles that "the conduct of the captain of the *Illinois* has been anything but what I expected and his whole crew is demoralized and unwilling to run down the *Merrimac* . . . in chartering steamers, it would, I think, be infinitely better for the government to officer and man them entirely."[92]

By the last week of March, Goldsborough's optimism was on the rebound, with the arrival in Hampton Roads of nearly four hundred transports carrying the 120,000 troops of McClellan's Army of the Potomac, "one of the spectacular sights of the Civil War." Goldsborough was downright effusive with confidence in a letter to his wife: "I am gloriously well, and, as the saying is, spoiling for a fight with the *Merrimac.* The sooner she comes, the better; and in my humble judgment, the sooner she will be sent to destruction. I expect to sink her in ten minutes from the time I put at her . . . I am well prepared for her iron carcass, I can slice it to atoms as easily as either of you can break an egg for breakfast."[93]

With *Merrimack's* name on every tongue of the Blockading Squadron, *Virginia* undocked on 4 April and was under way the next day for trials, anchoring near Craney Island. Aboard was her new commander, the veteran Commo. Josiah Tattnall, one of the most experienced seamen on the southern side. On 11 April she sortied in company with *Patrick Henry, Jamestown,* and four smaller vessels, all with trained boarding parties. Union transports scattered for safety. *Virginia* maneuvered for most of the day near Newport News, trying to draw *Monitor* away from Fortress Monroe's guns. While all eyes were on *Virginia, Patrick Henry* alertly captured two brigs and a schooner off Hampton. At 1600, with *Monitor* not taking the bait, *Virginia* fired three final shots toward *Monitor* and retired behind Sewell's Point.[94]

Goldsborough was satisfied with his cautious strategy to deny the Confederates the chance for a breakout victory: "Had the *Merrimac* engaged the *Monitor,* which she might have done, I was quite prepared with several vessels to avail of a favorable moment and run her down. This experiment must not be made too rashly or until the right opportunity presents itself as to fail in it would be to enable the *Merrimac* to [escape and] place herself before Yorktown."[95]

Even more confident the next day with no sign of *Virginia,* Goldsborough wrote his wife: "The *Merrimac* and consorts are still keeping quiet . . . My determined defensive tactics, the others say, completely disconcerted him, and has put him at a loss to know what is not best to do. He may, and probably will, attempt something desperate before long, but desperation is at all times a very uncertain remedy against disaster."[96]

While Tattnall waited for the best opportunity to harry the Union Navy, activity at Gosport proceeded around the clock; Secretary Mallory ordered that women be employed to hold lanterns so that workmen could see. First in priority at Gosport was the new ironclad *Richmond*—designed by John L. Porter and aided by Virginia citizens who collected both money and scrap iron for her construction—and a new series of gunboats designed by Cdr. Matthew Fontaine Maury.[97]

Maury's gunboats were to be mass-produced, steam-powered craft; more than a hundred were originally planned for construction (but under a dozen were actually built). Each measured about 179 tons, was 21 feet in length, and mounted a 9-inch rifled pivot gun forward and a 32-pounder aft. Their design called for attacks in groups or squadrons, just as the "Jeffersonian gunboat" designs did sixty years earlier. Four were laid down at Gosport, and a few others at other nearby yards.[98]

McClellan's Army of the Potomac stalled before the Confederate defenses across the peninsula, anchored at Yorktown. Navy gunboats on the York and James rivers were to protect the Army's flanks and provide an assured line of logistics, but the rivers were blocked by the *Virginia* in Hampton Roads and by Confederate batteries at Yorktown and Gloucester Point. Goldsborough half-heartedly sent seven wooden gunboats (*Marblehead, Wachusett, Penobscot, Currituck, Sebago, Corwin,* and *Chocura*) to the York in early April under Cdr. John S. Missroon to reduce the Confederate emplacements, but little progress was made. Although *Virginia* had not broken the blockade, her mere presence had forced McClellan to modify his campaign plan and had bought important time to improve the defenses of Richmond.[99]

Consensus among Confederate commanders held that Norfolk should be held as long as the Confederate line at Yorktown held, but if the Confederate Army were to fall back upon Richmond, Norfolk would be vulnerable. As early as 14 April, Confederate Gen. Joseph E. Johnston—commanding the Yorktown line—recommended that Yorktown be abandoned and Norfolk evacuated. Although he was overruled, plans proceeded at Gosport to evacuate naval stores to Charlotte and to scuttle the hulks of *Delaware* and *Columbus* and floating battery *Germantown* near Sewell's Point to impede any Union advance.[100] In mid-April, Flag Officer Forrest was ordered to Richmond to become chief of the Bureau of Orders and Detail, leaving Gosport under the command of Capt. Sydney Smith Lee, a former U.S. Navy officer and a brother of Gen. Robert E. Lee.[101]

On 1 May, with positions at Yorktown untenable, General Johnston alerted Tattnall:

> Finding it necessary to abandon this position, and regarding the evacuation of Norfolk as a consequence of that measure, I have directed Major-General Huger to withdraw his troops from the place and remove to Richmond. I have also desired Captain Lee to abandon the navy yard and report to the Secretary of the Navy, in Richmond, after saving as much as possible of the public property and destroying, if practicable, what he cannot save. I beg that the *Virginia* may cover these operations . . . the disposal of the *Virginia,* after she has performed all the service that can be required of her, can be trusted more safely to no one than yourself. The enemy will never have possession of her.[102]

Beginning on 3 May, the Confederate Army fell back from Yorktown. Two days later, Union gunboats (now commanded by Cdr. William Smith) punched past abandoned Confederate batteries on the York and landed troops near West Point, an important rail terminus.

On 2 May, Goldsborough wired Assistant Secretary Fox: "[*Merrimack*] has been lying for the last three days at the buoy off the Naval Hospital, with her steam up . . . Today four of the enemy's steamers, which I take to be the new gun boats, are lying off Craney Island. If I can only get a fair crack at the *Merrimac,* I feel certain of crushing her." Two days later, *Virginia* moved to an advanced anchoring position near Sewell's Point for a time, but steamed back to Craney Island, lying to with steam up.[103]

On the evening of 6 May, President Lincoln arrived at Fortress Monroe to assess the Peninsula Campaign, stopping first aboard *Minnesota,* as Goldsborough recounted to his wife: "Last night at 10 o'clock I was visited by the President, Mr. Chase, Mr. Stanton, Gen Wool and various other small fry and they remained until midnight . . . they took me completely by surprise."[104] On that same evening, *Patrick Henry* and *Jamestown* slipped past Union patrols in Hampton Roads, towing the uncompleted ironclad *Richmond* and gunboat

Hampton up the James River toward Richmond.

On the morning of the eighth, after receiving detailed tours of *Monitor* and the newly arrived ironclad *Galena* and continuing to press for naval action, Lincoln watched as *Galena* and the steam gunboats *Aroostook* and *Port Royal* departed Hampton Roads (under the command of Commander Rodgers of *Galena)* to test Confederate resistance up the James River. Rodgers immediately intercepted *Patrick Henry* and *Jamestown* returning down the James and forced them upriver while also engaging southern batteries at Day's Point and Harden's Bluff.

Also on the eighth, infused with new ardor (undoubtedly ignited by Lincoln's presence), six Federal ships, including *Monitor,* shelled Confederate positions at Sewell's Point. With *Monitor* away from the protective guns of Fortress Monroe, Tattnall responded immediately. "We stood directly for the *Monitor,*" wrote *Virginia*'s Lieutenant Wood, "but as we approached they all ceased firing and retreated below the forts. We followed close down to the Rip-Raps, whose shot passed over us . . . We remained for some hours in the roads, and finally the commodore, in a tone of deepest disgust, gave the order: 'Mr. Jones, fire a gun to windward, and take the ship back to her buoy [near Craney Island].' "[105] Goldsborough confirmed the cautious strategy: "*Merrimac* came out, and had a fair chance to engage the *Monitor,* but [*Virginia*] was extremely cautious, and took good care not to expose herself to even half a chance in the way of a dash by this ship [*Minnesota*] and the merchant rams to run her down. After remaining outside of the Point for a little while, she returned and anchored under Sewall's Point, and there she lies."[106]

On the morning of 10 May, with Lincoln as an eyewitness, six thousand Union troops landed at Ocean View against no resistance. By early evening Tattnall had been told of the Confederate Army's evacuation of the city. "Sharp and quick work was necessary," remembered Lieutenant Wood, as Tattnall called for the crew to lighten ship to pass the shallows of the James River, "for to be successful, the ship must be lightened five feet, and we must pass the batteries at Newport News and the fleet below before daylight next morning. The crew gave three cheers, and went to work with a will, throwing overboard the ballast from the fan-tails, as well as that below,—all spare stores, water, indeed everything but our powder and shot."[107]

On the same day, Captain Lee ordered the Navy yard set ablaze and the dry dock mined for destruction. For the second time in thirteen months, local citizens witnessed a surreal red glow reflected off the clouds above Portsmouth and flames licking upward from the industrial center of the yard. Again the dry dock escaped destruction as Confederate charges exploded, but water in the dock prevented substantial damage.[108]

Shortly after 0100 that morning, *Virginia* had been lightened but the pilots now claimed that they could not proceed beyond Jamestown Flats on the James River, an area controlled by the Union. Tattnall reported: "I had no time to lose. The ship was not in a condition for battle even with an enemy of equal force and their force was overwhelming. I therefore determined, with the concurrence of the first and flag lieutenants, to save the crew for future service by landing them on Craney Island, the only road for retreat open to us, and to destroy the ship to prevent her falling into the hands of the enemy."[109]

Lieutenant Wood wrote: "She was run aground near Craney Island and the crew landed with their small-arms and two days' provisions. Lieutenant Catesby Jones and myself were the last to leave. Setting her on fire fore and aft [about 0300], she was soon in a blaze, and by the light of our burning ship we pulled for the shore, landing at daybreak. We marched 22 miles to Suffolk and took the [railway] cars for Richmond." Midn. Hardin Littlepage spied the *Virginia*'s colors on deck as he disembarked the ship. Taking his own clothes out of his pack, he retrieved the colors and packed them safely away for the march. *Virginia* burned for an hour on the mud flats of Craney Island and exploded around 0500 in a violent display that many remembered vividly.[110]

The next morning, President Lincoln and his party embarked aboard the Navy's armed side-wheel steamer *Baltimore* to view Norfolk inner harbor and the still-smoldering Navy yard in the distance. Armed steamers *Susquehanna* and *Seminole* and other ships of the Blockading Squadron were already anchored off Norfolk and Portsmouth. For Lincoln's immediate staff it had been an exhilarating week, and they were fully ready to attribute the breaking of the stalemate in Norfolk to the president's enthusiasm. In the words of Secretary Chase, "so ended a brilliant week's campaign by the President."[111]

Goldsborough's aide, Lt. Thomas Selfridge, reported that only five brick houses, the foundry, a boiler shop, and a wooden timber shed stood at Gosport.[112] Goldsborough wrote to his wife that "the Navy Yard is still burning in hundreds of places. It is, literally, a complete wreck; and, for one, I am glad of it. Not one stone should be allowed to stand upon another in that spot hereafter. This is my decided opinion."[113]

On the southern side there was nothing but despair. "The abandonment of Norfolk stripped us not only of a vast amount of valuable property and building material," lamented Secretary Mallory, "but deprived us of our only drydock and of tools which are not found and cannot be replaced in the Confederacy."[114] Ironclads, however, had proved their worth, and although Mallory had lost the South's largest Navy yard, he pressed for ships of increasing sophistication for his navy—ironclads constructed in southern yards for harbor and river defense and foreign-built ironclad ships to strike at the blockade.

With Norfolk's fall, civility between the Union Army and Navy deteriorated rapidly. Goldsborough's ire had been raised when the Army took public credit for both Norfolk's capture and *Virginia's* destruction with hardly a compliment for the Navy. With no attempt to hide his outrage, he had labeled Gen. John E. Wool of the Army a scoundrel and dashed off a letter of grievance to Welles: "The Secretary of War has certainly acted very strangely in claiming the destruction of the *Merrimac* as one of the successes of the Army . . . our Army, unfortunately, is too much given to claim for itself every thing, and rob the Navy of every credit . . . had it not been for the Navy in these roads, Norfolk would not have surrendered, nor would the *Merrimac* have been blown up at all, Messrs. Wool and Stanton to the contrary notwithstanding!!!"[115]

Fort Norfolk became the next battlefield. Before the war, the fort had been Navy property, its primary ordnance magazine and shellhouse. Now with "our Ordnance stores at Fort Monroe piled up out of doors, & exposed to injury," Goldsborough pressed to have Fort Norfolk restored to the Navy. The Army refused—and used the fort as a prison. Again Goldsborough fired off a heated missive to Welles: "The Navy has expended a great deal of money upon [Fort Norfolk], & made it a place of great convenience for the supply of our ships with Ordnance. It is of no earthly use to the Army, & is of great use to us."[116]

The Navy hospital also played prominently in the growing Army-Navy feud. When Portsmouth was taken, the Army assumed control of the facility and, for a time, used it for its own sick and wounded to the exclusion of sailors. The hospital was finally restored to Navy control in 1863. Ens. Robley D. Evans, who would later head the Great White Fleet in Hampton Roads, recuperated in the hospital after being wounded painfully in both legs during fighting at Wilmington's Fort Fisher. It was said that a naval hospital doctor recommended amputation of Evans's leg, and upon hearing this, Evans drew a pistol from under his pillow.[117]

The Navy had also operated several transports as temporary hospital ships in the James River (*Wilson Small, Ocean Queen,* and *Daniel Webster*) and equipped the ordnance supply ship *Ben Morgan* as a hospital ship in the charge of Surgeon James H. Macomber and stationed her off Hampton and Old Point Comfort until 1865.[118]

The primary focus of naval operations in Tidewater now turned to the James River—brownish yellow and placid—as the days of 1862 moved from spring toward summer. With the York River entirely in Union hands and with the mouth of the James now open, the Union Navy could do for McClellan what had been planned all along: cover the flanks of the Army of the Potomac and provide the Army mobility, firepower, and unfettered lines of logistics.

With the scuttling of *Virginia* and the sudden collapse of Confederate forces in southeast Virginia, a dazzling new opportunity seemed to magically appear within Goldsborough's reach. If he acted quickly and boldly, he could force open the James River and attack the capital of the Confederacy. While the Army plodded up the peninsula, the Navy could vault their positions, bombard Richmond, and claim all the honors that Goldsborough knew were its due. Barely holding his excitement in check, Goldsborough dashed off orders to *Monitor* and Revenue Service steamer *Naugatuck* to join Rodgers and "reduce all the works of the enemy . . . and then get up to Richmond with the least possible delay, and shell the city to a surrender."[119] By early morning of 15 May 1862, the combined Union squadron arrived in front of Confederate earthworks at Drewry's Bluff, within sight of the spires of Richmond only eight miles distant, and the city's last line of defense.

A mixed force of Confederate soldiers, sailors, and Marines stood in readiness at their positions on the bluff about two hundred feet above a narrow bend in the James River as Navy Cdr. Ebenezer Farrand finally spotted the Union ironclad *Galena* leading the single-file Union squadron through the haze of early morning. Within Farrand's force stood the gun crews from the late *Virginia* led by Lieutenant Catesby Jones and fighting beneath *Virginia's* colors thanks to Midshipman Littlepage. The river was obstructed with a collection of pilings, chains, boulders, and sunken hulks. It would turn out to be their "last meeting" with the *Monitor.*

Galena anchored six hundred yards from the Confederate batteries, and *Monitor* anchored just behind her with the other wooden ships at a safer distance, all harassed by skirmishers along the shoreline. At 0745 *Galena* opened fire and the rebel batteries replied, reputedly striking *Galena* with their first shot. Just before 0900, Lieutenant Jeffers moved *Monitor* ahead of *Galena* but could not elevate his guns sufficiently to hit the bluff and dropped back. After several Confederate rounds had penetrated *Galena's* thin armor, Rodgers broke off the fight and withdrew from what would be the Navy's high-water mark of the war, with the Confederate Navy rightfully claiming that they had saved Richmond. Rodgers reported twelve men killed and twenty-four wounded; notably, Cpl. John F. Mackie of the *Galena* was decorated with the Marine Corps' first Medal of Honor for heroism during the fight.[120]

Although Goldsborough's gusto had been dashed and the Union Navy repelled at Drewry's Bluff, the Union gunboats were clearly making a difference. By late June 1862, the Navy was supporting McClellan's right with armed steamers *Jacob Bell* and *Delaware* on the Chickahominy River and *Galena, Monitor, Aroostook,* and *Mahaska* on the James to protect the left. Gunboats *Port Royal* and *Maratanza* stood off City Point with armed ferryboat *Southfield* to guard the supply ships there.

On 30 June, the *Galena, Mahaska,* and *Aroostook* shelled southern troops near Malvern Hill as McClellan withdrew toward Harrison's Landing. Try as he might, Confederate Gen. Robert E. Lee could neither advance against the Navy's gunfire nor find a way to neutralize it. "As far as I can now see there is no way to attack him [McClellan] to advantage; nor do I wish to expose the men to the destructive missiles of his gunboats," wrote Lee to Jefferson Davis. "I fear he is too secure under cover of his boats to be driven from his position."[121]

McClellan would stay at Harrison's Landing, his campaign in tatters, until 15 August, supported by Navy gunboats that prevented what could have been a deathblow to the encircled Army of the Potomac. When a withdrawal was finally ordered, *Galena, Port Royal,* and armed steamer *Satellite* covered McClellan's rear guard as the Army retired across the Chickahominy on its march back toward Yorktown, where transports waited to return the troops to Washington.

Lurking on the James at the same time was a strange new naval craft, the U.S. Navy's first submarine, the submersible *Alligator.* Designed by Brutus de Villeroi (originally of France but living in Philadelphia), the "submarine propeller" *Alligator* featured an air-scrubbing system, a diver's airlock, onboard air compressors, and a crew of fourteen; she was driven manually by underwater oars. *Alligator* would "attack" by approaching her foe under water and passing a diver through her airlock to plant explosives on an enemy's hull.

On 23 June 1862, *Alligator,* painted a dark shade of green, arrived in Hampton Roads and was ordered to join Commodore Rodgers off City Point and attack a key railroad bridge over the Appomattox River. When the river proved too shallow for *Alligator* to submerge, the attack was canceled and *Alligator* returned to Hampton Roads, to prevent the Confederates from capturing her. "This machine is so terrible an engine if employed against us," Rodgers reported to Goldsborough, "that if I retain her I must keep a strong force to guard her."[122]

Lieutenant Selfridge was briefly named as *Alligator*'s commander, and the craft was sent to the Washington Navy Yard for replacement of her oars by a manually driven screw propeller. On 2 April 1863, while en route to Charleston under tow, she foundered off Cape Hatteras.[123]

Ruins of the Norfolk Navy Yard after the Confederate withdrawal in 1862. *Naval Historical Center*

Union officers aboard *Monitor* on the James River in July 1862. *U.S. Naval Institute*

With the bad taste of the failed Peninsula Campaign in Union mouths, Navy Secretary Welles's confidence in Flag Officer Goldsborough slowly waned, which was not helped at all by Goldsborough's difficult relations with the northern press and the Army. Despite pleading his case in a cascade of letters in June 1862 ("You say that the public does not appreciate my services in watching the Army of the Potomac . . . There is not an officer in this squadron that I know of who does not approve of all I did," read one particularly poignant plea), Welles broke the James River Flotilla away from Goldsborough on 6 July and established it as a separate command, naming Capt. Charles Wilkes as its commodore.[124]

Goldsborough submitted his resignation in September, allowing Welles to appoint Capt. S. Phillips Lee to the post with the rank of acting rear admiral. Phil Lee, a cousin of Robert E. Lee, had been born in Virginia and had joined the Navy at age thirteen. Early in his career he had been a lieutenant aboard *Peacock* in Wilkes's Exploring Expedition and had commanded sloop-of-war *Vandalia* (22) in the East Indies when the war broke out (sailing her back to the United States without waiting for orders to ensure the crew's loyalty). His marriage into the politically powerful Blair family of Washington, DC, and his widely regarded command of sloop *Oneida* (18) under Farragut at New Orleans established Lee as a Welles favorite. Lee hoisted his pennant in *Minnesota* on 4 September 1862.[125]

During the Peninsula Campaign, the Navy was rarely, if ever, consulted, and coordination with the Navy was more assumed than planned for. Army officers viewed the Navy's role as a subordinate one and took no interest in understanding that naval support frequently was influenced by daylight, tides, river conditions, and competing missions. Frequently during battle, they gave illogical and impetuous demands for attacks and rarely moved to follow-up Navy assaults with coordinated advances. A case typical of the give-and-take between Army and Navy occurred on 17 August, as Wilkes watched the Army withdraw from Harrison Landing and disappear to the south with no further communications. When Wilkes, viewing the silent shores of the James around him, asked Secretary Welles for instructions, it was clear that Welles, likewise, had not been advised of McClellan's intent and could only reply to Wilkes with a rather lame: "Your telegram is received. I have no new instructions to give. Keep your force in position. Will communicate more fully by mail. /s/Gideon Welles."[126]

After their repulse of McClellan, Confederate naval forces remained in strong defensive positions on the river approaches to Richmond, supported from the Rocketts Navy Yard. The Confederate James River Squadron remained an important element of the defense until the last days of the war and generally consisted of *Patrick Henry;* armed tugs *Beaufort* and *Raleigh*; gunboats *Nansemond, Hampton,* and *Drewry;* and ironclads *Richmond, Virginia II,* and *Fredericksburg.* Capt. Sydney Smith Lee and, later, Capt. John R. Tucker commanded the shore naval defenses on the upper James.[127]

The James River Squadron became the most successful of the South's naval squadrons and furthered a host of innovative naval tactics. Efforts to perfect the "torpedo" (mine)—weapons so despised by Union naval officers that they dubbed them barbaric "infernal machines"—were orchestrated by Matthew Fontaine Maury, universally acclaimed for his revolutionary work in oceanography and hydrography as first superintendent of the U.S. Naval Observatory in Washington, DC. At the beginning of the war, Maury was commissioned as a commander in the Confederate States Navy and began to experiment with underwater tanks of powder that could be exploded with various triggers; these were used against blockaders *Cumberland* and *Roanoke* in Hampton Roads during July 1861 and ships off Newport News in October.[128]

Activity along the James intensified during the summer of 1862, and minefields were planted at Chapin's Bluff and at various other points along the river. On 9 April 1864, the small Confederate torpedo boat *Squib* attacked frigate *Minnesota* near Newport News with a single torpedo mounted on a sixteen-foot oak boom that nearly caused the frigate to sink. On 6 May 1864, a 2,000-pound rebel torpedo detonated under the armed steamer *Commodore Jones* in the vicinity of Four Mile Creek, killing sixty-nine people. The discovery and removal of torpedoes became a major task of the Union flotilla, and small boats would sweep the river while naval patrols on the riverbank would search for the galvanic batteries that were needed to activate the exploders.[129]

By the fall of 1864, James River naval operations were locked in a stalemate, but the Union Navy still rotated their newest ironclads into duty there to keep Confederate squadrons bottled up and the stranglehold on Richmond and Petersburg intact. Here, Union naval officers pose on board the newly commissioned *Canonicus*-class monitor *Mahopac* as she first arrives on the James. *National Archives*

Heralding a mission that would also come many years later, Yorktown served as a key Union logistics base and transshipment point for both Army and Navy supplies during the Peninsula Campaign in 1862. *U.S. Naval Institute*

Similarly innovative, explosives engineer William Cheeney designed a two-man submersible in Richmond during the summer of 1861 with the help of the Tredeger Ironworks. The craft employed the same "attack" technique as *Alligator,* approaching a target submerged and then employing a diver to attach an underwater charge to the target. Tested on the James, the craft was used in an attack on *Minnesota* in Hampton Roads in October 1861 but failed when the craft ran afoul of protective antitorpedo netting.[130]

On 27 February 1862, Secretary Mallory recommended the establishment of a Confederate States Naval Academy aboard frigate *United States.* With Norfolk's fall, *Patrick Henry* of the James River Squadron was converted to a school ship and accepted her initial class of fifty-two midshipmen in late 1863. Those midshipmen saw service in raids in North Carolina, onboard ironclads of the James River squadron, in James River batteries, and in the defense of Richmond in the final days of the war. Lt. William H. Parker, former commander of the tug *Beaufort,* was assigned as the school's superintendent, and Benjamin Pollard Loyall of Norfolk served as the commandant of midshipmen in 1863.[131]

On 5 May 1864, seven Union wooden gunboats steamed up the James to drag for torpedoes in advance of ironclads *Tecumseh, Canonicus, Onondaga,* and *Saugus* and the captured Confederate *Atlanta,* which escorted transports with thirty-nine thousand troops for an attack at Bermuda Hundred between the James and Appomattox rivers. Although little progress was made by the Army, opposing naval forces stayed in close proximity, and on 23 January 1865, Flag Officer John K. Mitchell of the Confederate James River Squadron was

Crew of the screw gunboat *Mendota,* a 970 ton side-wheel steamer taken into naval service in May 1864, armed with two 100-pounder, four 9-inch, two 24-pounder (seen at the stern) and two 20-pounder naval guns operating near Four Mile Creek in the James River. A good study of the demographics of naval crews of the day. *Hampton Roads Naval Museum*

ordered to attack the Union supply base at City Point. Mitchell sortied with ironclads *Richmond, Virginia II,* and *Fredericksburg*; gunboat *Drewry*; torpedo boat *Torpedo;* and the torpedo launches *Scorpion, Hornet,* and *Wasp,* with only the double-turreted Union ironclad *Onondaga* and Union shore batteries to counter them. In the ensuing melee, *Drewry* was blown up, *Scorpion* was abandoned, and *Virginia II* and *Wasp* were damaged before Mitchell withdrew. The sortie was an inauspicious final sting by the Confederate Navy, with Navy Secretary Mallory replacing the ineffective Mitchell with Rear Adm. Raphael Semmes. Although *Onondaga's* powerful guns had proved more than a match for Confederate armor, *Atlanta* and *New Ironsides* soon reinforced the squadron.[132]

During the final half of the war, the Navy looked to Norfolk and Hampton Roads as an increasingly important coaling station, staging anchorage, and support area for its entire blockading force. After Commo. John W. Livingston assumed charge of the Norfolk Navy Yard in May 1862, he set crews to restore its shops, survey the hulks in the river, and repair the dry dock. The first Union ship arrived for repairs in the fall of 1862, and others soon made the long trip up the Elizabeth with regularity. Conditions were stark, as remembered by John Grattan, who joined a ship of the blockading squadron in Gosport:

> After passing Craney Island the scenery would have been beautiful were it not for the ruin and desolation constantly before my eyes. On either bank of the river broken chimneys and charred timbers marked the spot where before the war had been elegant mansions. The fields and meadows were disfigured with abandoned earthworks and batteries without guns. In the river, buoys marked the locality of sunken vessels and one in particular denoted the position of the ram *Merrimack* which had caused such terrible destruction and loss of life. These silent monuments of ruin and devastation on the banks of the Elizabeth made everyone realize to a certain extent the effects resulting from the bloody war.[133]

The dual-turreted monitor *Onondaga* at anchor at Aiken's Landing along the James River in 1864. *Onondaga's* advanced 15-inch guns firing solid shot proved decisive against the six-inch armor plate used aboard Confederate ironclads. *National Archives*

The yard's work force grew steadily, as many in Norfolk and Portsmouth sought a steady wage in times that already spoke of depression. To ensure their loyalty, workers were only appointed upon recommendations of the local postmaster and political leaders. Although Flag Officer Goldsborough had ardently opposed restoration of the Navy yard, Admiral Lee felt just as strongly that Gosport should be rapidly pressed into service. "I hope you . . . have the facilities for repairing the vessels of this Squadron promptly supplied at [Norfolk]," he said as he pressed Assistant Secretary Fox. "You know the crowded state of the Northern Yards, the consequent delays & backset to this blockade. I only ask to have our Machine Shops at Gosport sufficiently extended for our purposes."[134]

Frigate *Brandywine* became a floating repair and receiving ship at the Navy yard, soon joined by *St. Lawrence* in the same capacity.[135] Frigate *Sabine* arrived at the yard in August 1864 as a training ship for navy apprentices and landsmen, and a steady stream of Union ships called at the yard for both supplies and small repairs. Late in December 1864, Capt. John Rodgers returned to the Norfolk Navy Yard as captain of the powerful new monitor *Dictator.* While *Dictator* was undergoing repairs, Rodgers happened upon the hulk of the old frigate *United States,* newly refloated and alongside the quay. Laying his hand along timbers so stout that they had resisted all efforts to scuttle her, Rodgers was taken by the legacy and tradition she represented (extending back to his father and to Stephen Decatur) and sent a letter to Secretary Welles, begging that she be saved from the breakers. For a time, Welles was persuaded, but the gallant ship finally met her ultimate fate shortly after the war ended.[136]

Under Admiral Lee's capable administration, the day-to-day operation of the blockade improved but not, to no one's surprise, the Navy's relations with the Army. Lee felt strongly that the blockade was in place, in part, to prevent the smuggling of goods across the Chesapeake into the Confederacy, and he ordered the destruction of 250-plus Tidewater craft suspected of engaging in this trade. When the Army pressed for open trade status for Norfolk (similar to the status enjoyed by New Orleans), Lee resisted, ordered every ship searched, and

The drama of *Monitor's* last minutes off Cape Hatteras as she founders in high seas with her support ship *Rhode Island* nearby. *U.S. Naval Institute*

uncovered an illegal trade in Army trade licenses obtained through graft.[137]

At daybreak on 13 December 1864, eighty ships under the command of Rear Adm. David Dixon Porter—the last great naval assemblage of the war—lay anchored in Hampton Roads before sailing for Fort Fisher, North Carolina. "The flagship fired a gun and hoisted the general signal 'prepare to get underway,' " read one account. "It was answered by every vessel and in a few moments the fleet began to move. The transports loaded with troops . . . were the first to leave Hampton Roads. The powder boats soon followed and at 8:00 a.m. the monitors with their convoys and the frigates, sloops of war and gunboats started for sea. As the vessels fell into line, the sight was magnificent and cheer after cheer greeted their departure by the great throng of spectators who lined the shores and filled the wharf at Fortress Monroe."[138]

As the Civil War finally plodded to an end at Fort Fisher, Richmond, and Appomattox, the scars of war were everywhere evident but so, too, were stories of honor and sacrifice, survival, and conquest. Tidewater's mighty engine of maritime trade—given a head start during northern occupation—again promised to ignite regional recovery, and soon, forests of masts and the sounds of ships' whistles and stevedore chants filled the waterfront. Across Hampton Roads there was not a single family that had not been deeply affected by war, but also across Tidewater there was a sense of optimism and renewal that could not be found elsewhere in the South.

After he left Norfolk at the onset of the war, Rear Adm. David Glasgow Farragut's first orders were to proceed to Hampton Roads and take command of the squadron he would lead at the Battle of New Orleans. He joined flagship *Hartford* at anchor in the roads and undoubtedly viewed with mixed emotions the familiar surroundings and the sight of Norfolk in the distance. At the end of the war, Farragut was among the first senior Union officers to visit Richmond and then his old home in Norfolk. Although snubbed by most of the first families of the Norfolk, he attended several receptions during his brief visit but was never to return. In 1866, Congress created the grade of admiral for the Navy and awarded that rank to Farragut. The following year he was appointed to command

The last glimpse of the *Monitor* before her loss in the dark, storm-tossed waters of Cape Hatteras was of her red lantern that hung from the pennant staff above the turret. This same lantern, recovered from the *Monitor,* is now on display at the Mariner's Museum in Newport News. *BRL Pictures*

the European Squadron. David Glasgow Farragut passed away on 14 August 1870.[139]

After the war, Flag Officer Samuel Barron returned to Norfolk from his final posting as the Confederacy's senior naval officer in Europe, where he helped arrange the widely successful attempt to build and purchase Confederate raiders and blockade runners from European yards. He retired to a farm in Essex County and died at age seventy-eight in 1888.[140]

Son Samuel Barron fought in the Battle of Hampton Roads as a lieutenant aboard *Jamestown* and later at Drewry's Bluff and aboard gunboats *Beaufort* and CSS *Roanoke.* In February 1864, he was assigned to commerce raider *Florida* but avoided capture when *Florida* was surprised by Union gunboat *Wachusett* while in a neutral Brazilian harbor. Lieutenant Barron joined his father on duty in Europe and was posted to the seagoing ironclad ram *Stonewall* when the war ended. He lived in Mexico and, later, at a farm in Richmond County. Samuel Barron died on 29 November 1892 in Norfolk.[141]

Of all the ships to visit Hampton Roads during the Civil War, three would become cornerstones of Tidewater's naval legacy. *Virginia* and *Cumberland* would not survive the titanic naval battles that swirled around Norfolk in 1862. The *Monitor* would fail to survive a much different battle—that against the elements.

On 24 December 1862 orders were issued for monitors *Monitor* and *Passaic* to be towed south to join Union forces concentrating in Beaufort, North Carolina. Weather delayed the ships' departure from Hampton Roads, but on the afternoon of 29 December supply ships *Rhode Island* (towing *Monitor*) and *State of Georgia* (with *Passaic* in tow) departed Newport News and by 1800 that evening were passing Cape Henry for what should have been a routine three-day transit along the Carolina coast. The following morning dawned clear and calm, but any good omen that may have been in the air quickly vanished with the onset of a stiff southwest wind that steadily increased throughout the afternoon, hauling to the south. By 1900 on the night of 30 December, with Hatteras light in view, wind and seas had picked up considerably and water was breaking across *Monitor's* low-freeboard deck. In rain and squalls, one of the two towing hawsers to *Rhode Island* parted, increasing *Monitor's* motion. As the navigator estimated that *Monitor* lay off Diamond Shoal, fifteen miles south of Cape Hatteras, the alarming report came that seawater was cascading into the ship and that the pumps could not keep up. The captain of *Passaic,* in similar distress, reported that the seas had partially separated the forward armor hull plating, allowing water to flow directly into the interior, a condition that *Monitor's* executive officer, Lt. Dana Greene, also suspected aboard *Monitor.*[142] *Passaic* turned north to go downwind and sea, an action that reduced her violent motions and allowed her pumps to regain their edge over the sea—an action that might have saved *Monitor.*[143]

As they headed into the mounting seas, "the sea rolled over us as if our vessel were a rock in the ocean," related one survivor. *Rhode Island* could do little to stabilize the tow and *Monitor* wallowed heavily, caught in the trough of rising waves. By 2230, with pumps unable to keep up with the seven-plus inches of water already in the engine room, Cdr. John P. Bankhead on *Monitor* ordered the distress signal raised, which was a red lantern on the top of the turret, and the crew prepared to abandon ship. A launch and cutter were rapidly lowered from *Rhode Island* as Bankhead ordered the final tow line cut. Minutes later Lieutenant Greene gathered as many men as he could and hurried a party to the *Monitor's* open decks to board the boats. As waves broke over the huddled crew members, several were swept over the side and, in the drama of the moment, *Rhode Island* momentarily lost propulsion and drifted down almost on top of *Monitor*. Both cutter and launch made the side of *Rhode Island* with the first batch of shivering survivors, but only the cutter could return to the stricken ironclad. By the time the cutter returned, *Monitor*'s engines and pumps had failed and the ship was rapidly filling. Twenty-five to thirty men remained aboard, and Bankhead held the cutter's sea painter until the last moment, while several men, stupefied with terror, refused to come out on the storm-tossed deck. A final rescue attempt was launched from *Rhode Island* about 0130. The rescue cutter steered directly for *Monitor*'s red turret light, but when it arrived at the spot where *Monitor* should have been, there was nothing to be found.[144]

1898

In the first frantic hours of the Civil War in Tidewater, Cdr. Stephen C. Rowan of steam sloop-of-war *Pawnee* had played a conspicuous role in the burning of the Gosport yard. Five years later, on 4 September 1866, he returned, this time as a rear admiral and as Norfolk Navy Yard's new commandant. Ambitious, tireless, resourceful, and with a heroic war record behind him, Rowan proved to be the right tonic at the right time for a naval base with an uncertain future.

Admiral Rowan could easily have rested on his laurels, planned a well-deserved retirement, or acted as a mere caretaker for the smallest, most disused, and most ramshackle of the Navy's shipyards at a time when even the most important navy bases were being reduced in size or closed. But he did not. In a sterling career that had seen duty in the Ordnance Department at Gosport during the late 1850s, combat service in California during the Mexican War, participation in the first naval engagement of the Civil War (Aquia Creek), fighting in the sounds of North Carolina, and command of three ships, including ironclad *New Ironsides,* Rowan had always been associated with action and triumph—a style he brought to the Norfolk yard.

Rowan started fast on an uphill battle to wrangle every dollar he could from a lethargic and demobilizing Navy Department. He reversed momentum to close the base and successfully argued that the yard would be useful—indeed strategic—for future operations in the Caribbean.

At the yard, Rowan bolstered repair work inside the shops, ensured that *New Hampshire* (the last American ship-of-the-line) was outfitted to serve as the yard's receiving ship, and encouraged relations with those in Portsmouth, helped in no small measure by the fact that he had married a Norfolk belle before the war. On 4 September 1866, Rowan began one of the yard's most esteemed traditions, the regular firing of the 9 o'clock evening gun, first from the decks of *New Hampshire.*[1] Rowan's energetic efforts were commended by the Navy Department, and upon his detachment he was ordered as commander in chief of the American Asiatic Squadron in the Orient and promoted to vice admiral.

At the close of the Civil War the U.S. Navy was the largest and most modern in the world, but in a matter of months, at a zenith of power and prestige, it deteriorated to just a few dozen warships. The blockade fleet was the first to go, when more than four hundred ships were auctioned or broken up for scrap within nine months of Lee's surrender. With the remarkable monitors ill-suited for transoceanic operations and with most suffering from rushed wartime construction, the staunch old wooden ships of prewar vintage again became the core of the Navy's operations.

With the onset of peace and with the nation focused exclusively on reconstruction, few resources were available to the Norfolk Navy Yard. Navy Secretary Welles, an advocate for the yard's reconstruction, pressed for funding in 1866: "The yards at Norfolk and Pensacola are as essential to the Navy and the country as either of the yards to the north, and in the event of a foreign war we could better dispense with one of the yards north of the Chesapeake than with either of these. The rebellion has passed away, the States are parts of the Union,

The first ships of the New Steel Navy shown at anchor together in the so-called Squadron of Evolution. Cruisers *Chicago, Boston*, and *Atlanta* are present, as is gunboat *Yorktown*, in the distance. *Naval Historical Foundation*

and the establishments which are to be renovated are national in their character, and of general interests to all." Welles would reiterate his appeal to renovate the yard in 1867 and 1868, but his suggestions went largely ignored. The hospital was awarded a paltry $20,000 for repairs in 1866, and in the gloom of the times, this was considered a major victory. The funds were used judiciously, and soon people in Norfolk were again pointing out that "there was not more delightful place about Norfolk or Portsmouth than the Hospital grounds with beautiful white oyster-shell roads meandering about among the tall pine trees in the woods behind the Hospital or along the beach in front down about the Hospital Point."[2]

By early 1869, it was reported to President Ulysses S. Grant that not a single Navy ship was ready for sea, and it would take five months for one to be ready for an overseas cruise. Hoping to attract congressional attention to the Navy's plight, Rear Adm. S. H. Stringham prepared a general review of all navy yards. He praised the strategic location of Norfolk Navy Yard on a great bay and its ability to service ships from any part of the East Coast. He also highlighted, interestingly, a new advantage the Navy could realize in Norfolk: "The Dismal Swamp will afford, at small cost, fresh water for a great basin, in which scores of iron-clads may be kept without rusting, ventilated, ready for sudden service, especially for the defense of our great sea-board cities." Admiral Stringham concluded forcefully: "We earnestly recommend the immediate purchase for naval purposes of both banks of the Elizabeth River, from the navy yard to the locks of the Dismal Swamp Canal for the breadth of one mile from the middle of the river. This important site, worthy of defense, and on good lines by sea and land, may be got for the low price of farm land in that region." Alternatively, Stringham recommended purchasing thirty acres adjacent to St. Helena. Congress was swayed by neither recommendation.[3]

With its buildings and shops largely in disrepair and its workforce melting away, the Norfolk Navy Yard needed a means to dramatize its importance. As would be seen so many times in its future, it needed a national crisis. Just such a tailor-made crisis arrived on Norfolk's doorstep in 1873—the *Virginius* Affair.

Second-class battleship *Texas* was completed in 1895, the first battleship ever built at Norfolk Navy Yard. All four warships of the modern American Navy named *Texas* have been constructed in Hampton Roads. *U.S. Naval Institute*

The *Virginius,* a former Confederate sidewheel steamer and blockade-runner—was being used by Cuban rebels and their American collaborators as a gunrunner, supporting the fight for Cuban independence from Spain. On 30 October 1873, *Virginius* was intercepted near Guantanamo Bay by the Spanish corvette *Tornado. Tornado* hauled ship and crew to internment at Santiago and, after a slapdash military trial, a score of captives (including American and British citizens) were executed by firing squad. Although the United States was officially neutral, American sympathies were clearly on the side of the rebels, and war hysteria quickly gripped the nation. Orders were cabled to the Norfolk Navy Yard to mobilize a naval squadron, the most action the yard had seen since 1862. Monitor *Mahopac* and steamer *Mayflower* were prepared for recommissioning, sloops-of-war *Macedonian* and *Constellation* were surveyed for reactivation, and the steamer *Dispatch* was hurriedly loaded with supplies and ammunition for Key West.

Diplomacy, ultimately, quelled the ardor for war (an eminently sensible conclusion, since the Spanish navy was many times superior to anything the American Navy could have fielded), and naval activity returned to low ebb. But the crisis had made its mark on Navy planning, and the importance of Hampton Roads was discussed once again in Washington.[4]

By 1876, new timber sheds had risen at the yard, and a new coal-gas lighting system was installed, but a hurricane in August 1878 destroyed much of this work, choking off any momentum for improvement. Beginning in the 1870s, Norfolk Navy Yard served as the main support base for the North Atlantic Squadron, which in 1873 consisted of eight wooden steamers, two ironclads, and five reserve ironclads. But on 24 November 1877, steam sloop-of-war *Huron* was lost at sea with all hands (despite hurricane warnings flown by Cape Henry Light), and by 1881 squadron numbers had deteriorated to only six wooden steamers and no ironclads. Conditions at the yard were not aided by charges of inefficiency, political patronage, and official corruption during the mid-1870s. Congressional investigations specifically targeted rumored improprieties at Norfolk Navy Yard, but in the end, findings were inconclusive.[5]

In the 1880s, plans were again drawn up for a special freshwater naval basin to lay up decommissioned ships and moni-

Cruiser *Raleigh* (C-8) represented the second of the ships of the New Steel Navy to be constructed at Norfolk Navy Yard, with her keel laid on this building way adjacent to Trophy Park on 19 December 1889. *Raleigh* would later fight with Dewey at Manila Bay. The entrance to the Navy Yard featured a handsome portico at right. *Norfolk Naval Shipyard*

tors—a plan of some urgency after it was discovered that much of the Navy's ironclad force had deteriorated in the brackish water near Bulls Bay on the James River. Again, like many other renovation proposals, the project was never funded.[6]

One priority of the yard during this period was the reclamation of ships that had been scuttled or sunk during the war. On 13 January 1870, the venerable ship-of-the-line *Delaware* was admitted to Dry Dock No.1 for breaking up, thirty-seven years after she had entered the dock to such international acclaim. The hulk of ironclad *Virginia* was raised and brought into her building dock in 1875 (two of *Virginia*'s boilers had been recovered in 1867). Most of the wreck was sold for scrap, and the anchor, wheel, drive shaft, and a few iron plate sections were presented to museums. Some iron and wood sections of the hull were recast into souvenirs that attracted special attention throughout the South.[7]

Although the navy yard was in the doldrums, the Navy in the 1880s was beginning a rebound. At the end of 1879, the North Atlantic Squadron and the Navy's School Squadron held an impressive naval review in Hampton Roads that was officiated by the secretary of the Navy. Following that, the secretary endorsed the Norfolk Navy Yard in his 1881 annual report as "one of the most important on the Atlantic Coast" and one that "should be built up to the full extent of capacity."[8] This was echoed by a major review of navy shipyards in 1883 that strongly endorsed Norfolk's value, its strategic location, its strong defenses, and, newly important to the Industrial Age, "its water and rail connections with the iron and coal regions."[9]

Congress approved plans in 1883 to reinvigorate the Navy by building three steel cruisers and one steel dispatch boat for a "New Steel Navy." One cruiser would be a respectable forty-five hundred tons with four 8-inch, eight 6-inch, and two 5-inch guns, and the remaining two cruisers would be two thousand tons. They came to be called the "ABCD ships," from their names, *Atlanta, Boston, Chicago,* and *Dolphin,* and operated in a so-called Squadron of Evolution.

Conditions now combined to finally smile on Norfolk's naval community. With congressional interest in building ships of the New Steel Navy in public yards, the contract for the first American battleship was awarded to Norfolk Navy

Norfolk Navy Yard's second dry dock (the Simpson Dry Dock) was completed in 1889 to handle new steel warships for the Navy and to provide the Navy the opportunity to build them (it was thought more efficiently) in public yards. Here cruiser *Olympia* of Battle of Manila Bay fame refits. *Norfolk Naval Shipyard*

Yard in the spring of 1887. The yard's second dry dock (the Simpson Dock) was completed in 1889 to support these endeavors. The keel of the sixty-three-hundred-ton second-class battleship *Texas* was laid on 11 June 1889; she was launched on 28 June 1892 and commissioned on 15 August 1895. Six months after the keel for *Texas* was laid, the keel for the cruiser *Raleigh* (C-8) was laid on an adjacent slip—representing, together, the first warships of the New Steel Navy completely built by public yards. *Raleigh* would later fight with Dewey at Manila Bay.[10]

A yard producing steel ships is not the same as one producing wooden ships—the people, the apprenticeship, the materials, and the shops are all dramatically different. Where once a yard would welcome sailmakers, caulkers, carvers, carpenters, and master builders, now the need was for ironworkers, torchmen, and riveters. Historically, few private yards would make the epic transition from wood to steel. Few could afford to retool, and during the years of transition, fewer still could maintain a crew of craftsmen devoted to both specialties. The enduring exception was the publicly funded Navy yard that was organized less for profit than to support a Navy both of wood and steel. Across the history of hundreds of American shipyards, only two or three can claim the distinction of a heritage balanced by both wood and steel, sail and steam—and Norfolk Navy Yard stands at the pinnacle of that elite group.

Employment at the Navy yard surged, and a new sense of optimism began to permeate the Navy in Hampton Roads, spurred in no small measure by the yard's commandant, Commo. Aaron Ward Weaver. Weaver's long-term association with the Navy yard was legend. His father, William Augustus Weaver, had been assigned to frigate *Chesapeake* during its building at the Gosport yard, and Aaron Weaver would serve in three different capacities at the yard: equipment officer, captain of the yard, and, finally, commandant. In witnessing the worst of the yard's fortunes over the years, Weaver was also in a position to propel its resurgence to meet the demands of the New Steel Navy.

Day-shift machine shop workers at Norfolk Navy Yard circa 1910. *Norfolk Naval Shipyard*

The rekindling of American naval pride was on dramatic display during the International Columbian Naval Rendezvous held in Tidewater to celebrate the four-hundredth anniversary of the discovery of America. Congress invited all nations to send naval representation to America for a naval rendezvous in Hampton Roads on 17–24 April 1893. Fourteen of the most modern American warships—commanded by Rear Adm. Bancroft Gherardi—headed the festivities. The American ships were moored in neat rows near Old Point Comfort, and ships from Russia, France, Germany, Netherlands, Brazil, Argentina, England, Spain, and Italy were arrayed nearby.[11]

The naval rendezvous reemphasized the standing of Hampton Roads in the world as the premiere gathering ground for the resurgent American Navy. Just as important, businessmen across Hampton Roads benefited handsomely from the Navy while hosting the estimated fifty thousand visitors who poured into Tidewater for the festivities. A Naval Rendezvous Association, headed by Col. George W. Johnston and former Norfolk mayor Barton Myers, decorated downtown buildings with bunting and coordinated parades, fireworks, concerts, and an International Naval Ball. Historian Joe Mosier mentions that the *Norfolk Virginian* devoted two full columns to the description of the ball, where "Norfolk's beautiful daughters [who] never looked lovelier or appeared to greater advantage."[12] Replicas of the *Pinta, Niña,* and *Santa Maria* were on display as part of a Columbian theme. But the presentations that caught people's eye were those that underscored modern naval technologies and one naval communications test where two carrier pigeons were released from *Dolphin* at 0700 one morning off Fort Monroe and arrived in a loft in Washington five hours later. The messages were hurried to the White House, where the President "expressed his surprise at the speed of the service."[13]

At the completion of the naval rendezvous, many hundreds of spectators packed excursion steamers, and many thousands more watched from Sewell's Point and Ocean View as the American ships formed into a single line, "well closed up, full speed—eight knots—south to Newport News Middle Ground and then countermarched to pass between the visiting squadrons and Old Point Comfort." The visiting squadron then got under way to steam in parallel, and the joint formation then stood out for the capes.[14]

The advent of new steel warships in the 1880s and 1890s brought its own new challenges with steel fabrication, steam engineering, and armor protection. Shipbuilding sites that once needed only a sloped piece of land, navigable water, and nearby timber now required ready access to iron and steel, good transportation, and inexpensive industrial power—elements that were all beneficially present in Hampton Roads.

At the center of this surprising nexus of Industrial Age economics in Hampton Roads stood millionaire tycoon Collis

A rusty naval auxiliary and battleship *Iowa*—hero of the Battle of Santiago—crowd the Navy Yard's docks in October 1908. *Norfolk Naval Shipyard*

Potter Huntington. Huntington, who had made his fortune during the California Gold Rush (not with gold, but by selling supplies to miners) and then owned both the Central Pacific and Southern Pacific railroads, gained control of the Chesapeake and Ohio Railway and its eastern terminus at Newport News in 1869. Huntington astutely expanded rail links from Ohio Valley coalfields to the Virginia coast and opened a new coal port at Newport News in May 1882. To attract coal ships to Newport News and to diversify his business base, Huntington also arranged to offer ship repair services at a newly planned shipyard.[15]

Huntington's ship repair yard incorporated as the Chesapeake Dry Dock and Construction Company on 28 January 1886, and work began on a six-hundred-foot dry dock in June 1887. The repair yard opened for business in April 1889 with a contract to build a railroad tug for New York harbor. The Navy awarded its first repair contract to Huntington in 1889 for the overhaul of monitor *Puritan,* a contract that was purposely underbid to catch the Navy's attention.[16]

On 17 February 1890 the name of Huntington's company—extending four blocks around two shipways—was changed to Newport News Shipbuilding and Dry Dock Company. Pay for the yard's two hundred employees averaged twenty-five cents an hour for a ten-hour day, six days a week.[17] Although Huntington generally favored commercial work over Navy contracts, recession in the early 1890s compelled him to bid for the construction of battleship *Iowa* and armored cruiser *Brooklyn.* Although Huntington failed with these proposals, Newport News's first Navy contracts soon followed in 1892 for gunboats *Nashville* (PG-7), *Wilmington* (PG-8), and *Helena* (PG-9).[18]

Now convinced that it could prosper with Navy work, Newport News won contracts for its first two capital ships, battleships *Kearsarge* (BB-5) and *Kentucky* (BB-6), in 1896. Both were well-conceived members of the expanding battle line and boasted four 13-inch and four 8-inch guns, a huge broadside of fourteen 5-inch rapid-fire guns, and new electrical machinery.[19]

Battleship *Kearsarge* towers over launch-day crowds at Newport News Shipbuilding with her twin, *Kentucky,* partially visible to the right. With patriotic fervor high in the days leading up to the Spanish-American War, more than twenty thousand streamed to Newport News on 24 March 1898 to watch the dramatic launching of the first capital ships to be built by the Newport News yard. *The Mariner's Museum*

By the time of launching, the nation was feeling the tensions leading up to the Spanish-American War, and patriotic excitement ran high. In a masterful display of business savvy, Huntington heavily advertised the launchings, and on 24 March 1898, more than twenty thousand spectators crammed the Newport News shorefront to watch a spectacle heavily spiced with patriotic fervor and local pride. An on-scene reporter captured the scene:

> An immense crowd gathered this morning to witness the launching of the *Kentucky* and *Kearsarge.* At 10:02 the *Kearsarge* glided gracefully down the ways into the historic James River. Mrs. Winslow christened her with sparkling champagne as the straining timbers which held her in place were heard to crack and she immediately floated down the ways. An hour later the programme was repeated when the *Kentucky* went through the same formality . . . Amidst storms of applause, the blowing of whistles, firing of guns and waving of flags the boats were towed to the docks where thousands thronged beside them. . . . The dual event of the two ships of such magnitude being launched on the same day marks an era in the history of our new navy, while each ship in itself will be the heaviest mass of the kind ever moved from keel-blocks to water in this country.[20]

With the momentum of the *Kearsarge* and *Kentucky* success at its back, the Newport News yard quickly won additional contracts, especially for capital ships that would help establish its reputation. On 5 April 1904, the fifteen-thousand-ton battleship *Virginia* was launched on a day that was declared a state holiday to allow crowds from all over the state to attend.[21]

From the early 1880s the Norfolk and Western Railway matched Huntington's railroad plans and made Norfolk one of the greatest coal ports in the world at a time when coal was the energy king. The presence of cheap coal gave the city a sizable maritime shipping advantage over other Atlantic ports, and many steamers stopped in Hampton Roads simply to refill their bunkers before voyages. By 1904, the coal trade was proceeding so rapidly that a new rail line, the Virginian, was constructed to feed a new thousand-foot coal-loading pier at Sewell's Point.[22]

The captain's cabin of battleship *Kentucky* offers an interesting study of one dimension of the Navy in Hampton Roads at the turn of the twentieth century. *U.S. Naval Institute*

This concentration of relatively inexpensive coal spilling through Hampton Roads was not lost on the Navy. As historian John D. Alden once noted: "The New Steel Navy was essentially a navy of coal." Every stage of naval operations depended on a reliable source of coal, and there could be no stronger magnet bringing modern naval warships to Hampton Roads than the promise of nearly limitless quantities of coal for their scuttles and bunkers. By the early 1890s, if there was any lingering doubt of the importance of Hampton Roads to the Navy, it was ended by the logistical realities of keeping the fleet in coal.[23]

By 1897, American sympathies, fanned by jingoism and the yellow journalism of the day, were focused anew on the plight of the native Cuban insurrection against long-time Spanish rule. On 11 December 1897, battleship *Maine* stood out from Hampton Roads, bound for Key West and Cuba, and arrived in Havana on 24 January 1898. Three weeks later, as she swung lazily at her buoy in Havana harbor, two mighty explosions staggered the battleship. Excitement for war skyrocketed, and the march toward hostilities gained further momentum when the blast aboard *Maine* was "confirmed" by a naval court of inquiry to have been caused by the external explosion of a submarine mine. President McKinley led the charge to "free Cuba," and the Navy quickly divided its Atlantic forces into three squadrons to meet the crisis.

The first of these squadrons was the Northern Patrol Squadron, composed of small auxiliary boats, old monitors, and gunboats to protect the coast from Delaware to Maine against any possibility of a Spanish raid. A much stronger "Flying Squadron," commanded by Commo. Winfield Scott Schley, anchored in Hampton Roads; it consisted of armored cruiser *Brooklyn* (ACR-3), cruiser *Columbia* (C-12), battleships *Massachusetts* (BB-2) and *Texas,* and cruiser *Minneapolis* (C-13). *Texas* assumed duties as primary guardship of Hampton Roads and was ordered to a defensive anchorage off Fortress Monroe. The strongest American battle line lay with the main body of the North Atlantic Squadron, commanded by Rear Adm. William T. Sampson and assigned to Key West to impose a blockade of Cuba.[24]

Dry Dock No. 3 under construction in December 1905 with the Shipfitters Shop behind it. This image was captured by glass plate. As standard photographic film was made of cellulose nitrate and could be explosive, its use was discouraged in naval shipyards until safety film was introduced in the late 1930s. *Norfolk Naval Shipyard*

In the first weeks of the war, Commodore Schley later recalled:

> Time was taken to organize the squadron and put it upon a war footing. Pickets and patrols were thrown out towards the capes of Virginia; lights were masked; officers were required to be on board at sundown; leaves of absence beyond signal distance were withdrawn; sea watches were ordered and surveillance maintained day and night. Gun practice with the sub-caliber guns was ordered and was maintained every day regardless of the weather, leading up to very great precision and skill as attested later in action. A short cruise of a few days off the capes was made to exercise the squadron in technical maneuvers, to inculcate alertness, quick signaling and to hold their places in battle order near each other for mutual support or attack.[25]

As an additional defensive measure for Hampton Roads, an electrically controlled field of 108 mines was laid between Fortress Monroe and Fort Wool, and the naval militia manned small guard boats to guide harbor traffic through the defenses. The south wing of the naval hospital, long disused, was quickly renovated, and ninety new beds were set up. Six volunteer nurses and five sisters of charity from Norfolk and local physicians assisted the staff.[26]

The Flying Squadron's presence at Hampton Roads allowed Schley the flexibility to sail either north or south to protect the American coast. When the strongest Spanish squadron of six cruisers under Adm. Pasqual Cervera was confirmed to be in the Caribbean on 13 May 1898, the Flying Squadron sailed to Cuban waters to join the large North Atlantic Squadron.[27]

Direct naval hostilities during the Spanish-American War were over in short order, and Sampson and Schley cornered Cervera and orchestrated a decisive victory over the Spanish

The Navy Yard's third dry dock (completed in 1908) with battleship *North Carolina* (shown here in December 1908) as its first customer. Dry Dock No. 3 was extended from 550 feet to 723 feet in 1911. At the same time, a higher caisson and side walls were added to allow "superflooding"—raising water in the dock higher than the water level of the river. *Norfolk Naval Shipyard*

squadron off Santiago on 3 July. With no further organized Spanish resistance, American ships largely redeployed back to their East Coast bases. Admiral Cervera and many senior Spanish officers were detained at the Naval Academy in Annapolis, and forty-eight Spanish sailors were brought by the hospital ship *Solace* and admitted to the naval hospital in Portsmouth. Cervera made two visits to the hospital to ensure the health of his men; however, three Spanish sailors died at the hospital (one of disease and two of their wounds) and were buried at the hospital's cemetery.[28]

In the last years of the nineteenth century, the training of Navy enlisted men was conducted almost exclusively aboard ship and in training squadrons. These training squadrons were abolished by 1905, and shore-based training stations were established at Newport and San Francisco. In 1902, the Navy expanded its holdings at St. Helena by annexing the former Cedar Grove plantation in Berkley and established a "training station" to be used when Newport became overcrowded or was shuttered by quarantine. Also in 1902, an "artificers school" for the training of woodworkers, plumbers, blacksmiths, painters, and shipfitters opened at Norfolk, and specialized training for masters-at-arms, musicians, ships' cooks, and yeomen soon followed.[29]

A 1906 description of the St. Helena mentioned that

> The Training Station is located on the opposite side of the river from the Navy Yard proper. The receiving ships *Franklin* and *Richmond* are moored at wharves there and trained men for general service are received at all times and transferred to the different ships of war. Three converted yachts, the *Hornet, Restless* and *Siren* are attached to the station and recruits are frequently put aboard them and taken out to sea for practice. On these trips the men are required to take the helm, heave the lead, etc and are instructed in getting under way . . . the course of training for a recruit is limited to four months, after which he is examined and if found qualified, is rated as an ordinary seaman and transferred to a regular cruising ship where his training is naturally expanded . . .

During May 1899, the mangled Spanish cruiser *Reina Mercedes* was raised from Santiago harbor and towed to Hampton Roads to be triumphantly paraded down the Elizabeth River. Thousands of cheering spectators lined the shoreline to see the Spanish prize and small vessels covered with red, white, and blue bunting loudly sounded steam whistles. *Reina Mercedes* would stay in dry dock for eighteen months and she later served for many years as the station ship at the Naval Academy where midshipman tradition anointed her with the rubric the "fastest ship in the Navy," for always being tied fast to the pier. *Hampton Roads Naval Museum*

> adjoining the training station on the south is the Reserve Torpedo Flotilla Station. A number of wharves and slips have been constructed for torpedo boats and submarines. A torpedo storage building, machine ship, etc. have recently been erected.[30]

At first, the St. Helena Training Station did not enjoy formal status, and Congress rejected a specific appropriation for its maintenance. Capt. Albert C. Dillingham, the commanding officer of *Franklin* and, by extension, the "commander" of the training station, complained in 1907 that "the training station at Norfolk seems to be still without an official status," and thus, "there are not the proper facilities for caring for the command that should exist."[31]

By 1910, however, conditions were improved at the station. An article in the Naval Institute *Proceedings* commented:

> Within the past few years there has grown up at St. Helena one of the most successful and efficient training stations for apprentice seamen that the navy possesses. This development has been without recognition by Congress and is largely due to the energy and efficiency of the officers in command who have had direct charge of this training station . . . the apprentice seamen are accommodated in temporary buildings and tent houses, with the result that they become strong and hardy and are not spoiled by undue luxury for the life they must soon take up on board ship . . . the proximity of the navy yard and frequent visits of ships of war familiarize and educate the apprentice seamen with the life before them.[32]

A study at the Norfolk Training Station in 1908 investigated the spread of contagious diseases among recruits and recommended that separate "detention camps" be established at all navy training stations to quarantine newly reported recruits for up to three weeks. At St. Helena, this camp was established on land formally occupied by the Reserve Torpedo Flotilla. These camps were temporarily suspended during

By 1906, the St. Helena Training Station was in full operation although it acted at times more as a "annex" to a larger Navy Training Station at Newport, Rhode Island. By 1914, three independent camps existed at the site, each with its own administration and facilities. *Naval Historical Center*

World War I to improve recruit throughput, resulting in a sudden dramatic increase in diseases transmitted to the fleet.[33]

Congress passed the first appropriation that recognized the existence of the St. Helena Training Station in 1914, and permanent barracks and instructional buildings were quickly raised. Three independent camps were established within the station (Lawrence, Perry, and Farragut), each with separate barracks, mess halls, and infirmaries. As World War I approached, Lawrence took on the extra duty of training armed guard crews for the merchant marine.

On the afternoon of 8 November 1906, President and Mrs. Theodore Roosevelt boarded the presidential yacht *Mayflower* for what would be the first of several history-making cruises through the Chesapeake to Hampton Roads during his presidency. Roosevelt's support of the Navy was legend, and during his first term alone, thirty-one new warships (ten of them powerful new battleships) were added to the Navy, making it the third largest among the world's fleets.

At St. Mary's, Maryland, the presidential party embarked aboard the new battleship *Louisiana* (BB-19) (built at Newport News Shipbuilding) for a voyage, escorted by two cruisers, to inspect the Panama Canal. It was the first time that a serving American president had traveled outside the United States while in office, and from the Navy's standpoint, it served as an excellent opportunity to showcase the near-perfection of the spit and polish of the *Louisiana.* On his first day at sea, the president wrote his seventeen-year-old son, Kermit, "it is a beautiful sight, these three great warships standing southward in close column."[34]

The president would be back in Hampton Roads five months later to help open Norfolk's Jamestown Exposition, which ran from 26 April to 1 December 1907 at an expansive 340-acre fairground at Sewell's Point to commemorate the three-hundredth anniversary of the Jamestown Settlement. The first day of the exposition began with an early morning fog, which lifted slowly like an opening curtain to unveil a spectacular view of an international naval fleet swinging impressively at anchor in the nearby roads. The sight was magnificent: battleships, cruisers, and smaller ships arrayed in rigid rows, pennants and flags flying, saluting batteries at the ready. By opening day, sixteen American battleships, five cruisers, and an assortment of torpedo-boat destroyers, torpedo boats, and auxiliary ships stood ready, joined by warships from Argentina, Austro-Hungary, Brazil, Chile, Germany, and Britain.[35]

President Roosevelt reviewed the anchored warships from the *Mayflower,* calling them "an inspiring sight." Roosevelt then officially opened the exposition grounds from a crowded platform busy with bunting. "Governors, congressmen, senators,

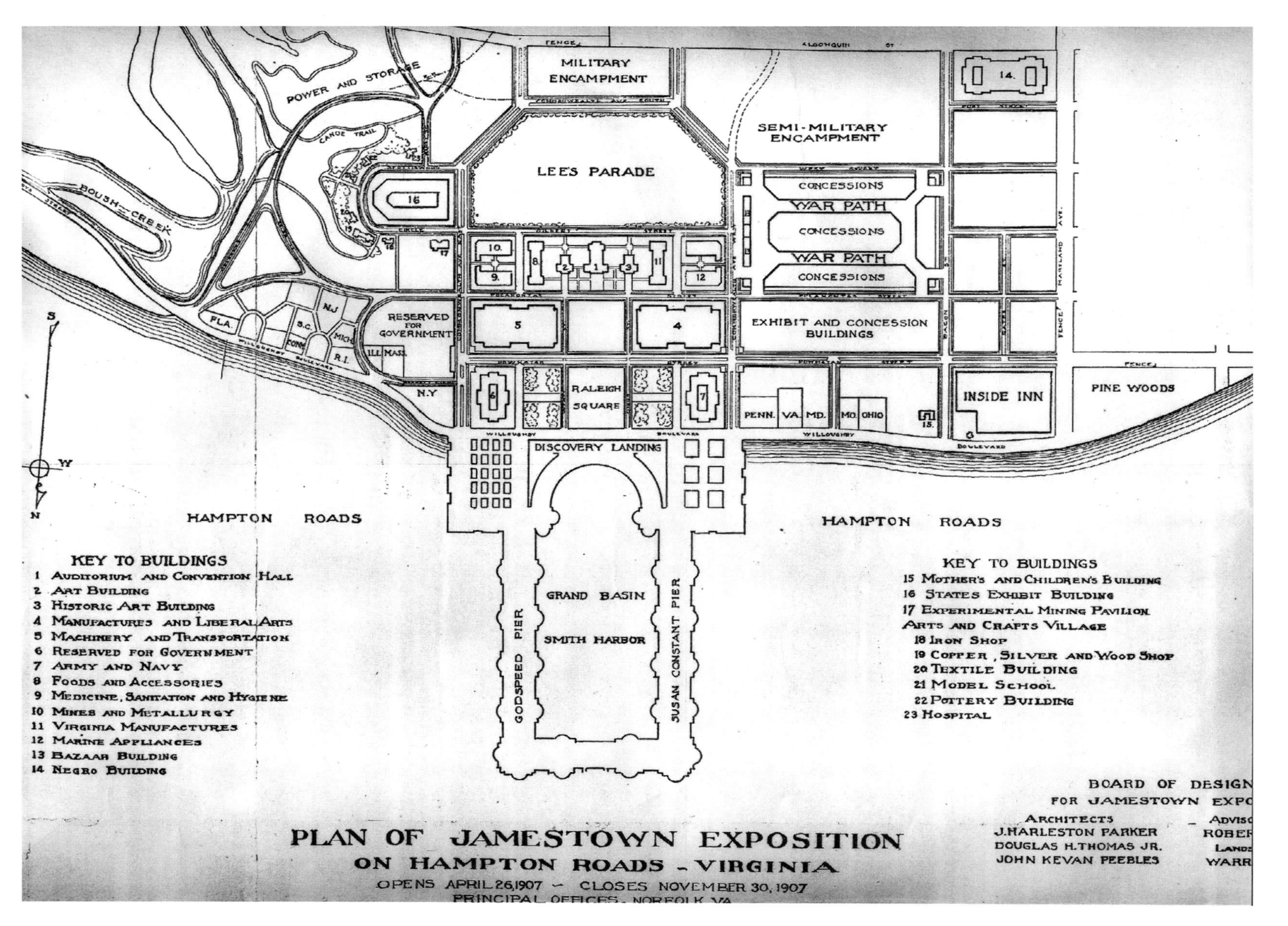

Final design plan for the Jamestown Exposition site as approved by Norfolk city officials. *Sargeant Memorial Room, Norfolk Public Library.*

Battleship *Georgia* maneuvers into place alongside a Norfolk Navy Yard quay in January 1907 following her shakedown cruise as many spectators aboard *Virginia* (foreground) watch. Both ships would attend the Jamestown Exposition during the summer and sail with the Great White Fleet in December 1907. *Norfolk Naval Shipyard*

diplomatic delegations from at least 21 foreign nations and a crowd that official estimates placed at over 40,000 swelled the Exposition site at Sewell's Point just outside Norfolk," read one eyewitness account. "They came by trolley, boat and horseback. A fortunate few who owned them came by automobile."[36]

The exposition itself featured an eclectic series of attractions and concessions, including a wild animal show, a Wild West show, an exotic Middle Eastern bazaar, a haunted house, a huge relief of the new Panama Canal, and—its most successful attraction—a reenactment of the "Battle of the Merrimac and Monitor." A central group of exhibition buildings held displays of art, machinery, food, medicine, and transportation in a "world's fair" format. Along the shore sat the iconic buildings sponsored by individual states, including several that were Americana replicas, such as a two-thirds-size copy of Independence Hall that became "Pennsylvania House" and the Old State House of Massachusetts. These buildings rose with a flair and attractiveness that remain even to this day as an eloquent legacy of this singular event.

As important as anything else, the exposition drew Navy officials and Tidewater leaders together as never before. Navy ships at anchor provided a pleasing backdrop for exposition sightseers, and not a day would pass without the Navy present: there were Marines at the exposition military camp, bluejackets strolling on shore leave, sailors on parade, rowing contests, Navy band concerts, or naval displays in the exhibit halls. Three times during the exposition, ships at anchor provided stunning nighttime searchlight shows. Armored cruiser *Brooklyn* and battleship *Texas* (veterans of the Battle of Santiago) and monitor *Canonicus* (the last surviving monitor of the original Ericsson design) served as visit ships during the entire run. "The vessels were visited by great numbers of citizens, and it was a common remark of the visitors that an inspection of the ships was worth the time and cost of a trip to the Exposition."[37]

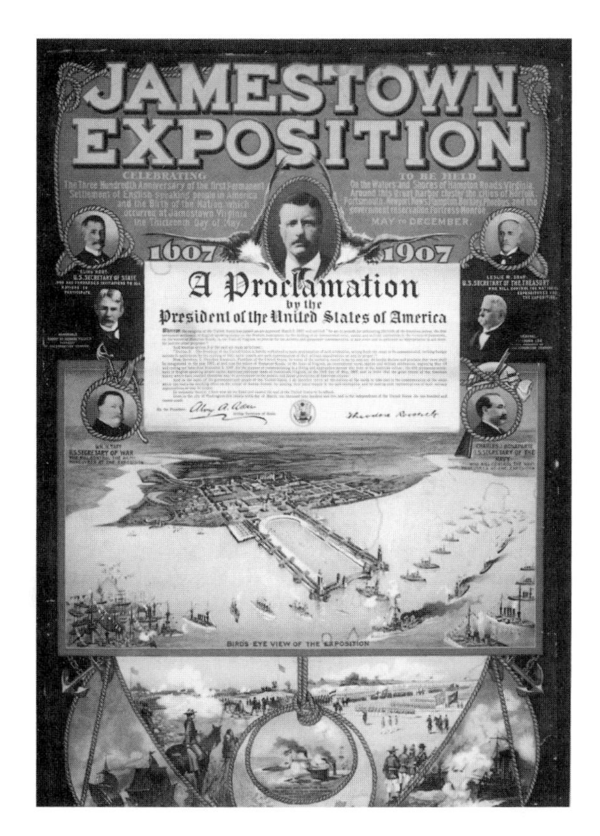

Although the Jamestown Exposition was largely viewed as a financial bust and one that fell decidedly short of the expectations of its promoters, most in Tidewater were proud of the exposition's beauty and international renown. As Norfolk Historian Thomas J. Wertenbaker concluded, "The dignified buildings, the thousands of lights, the avenues set with trees and bushes, the waving pennants, all set off by the broad expanse of Hampton Roads, presented a picture of rare beauty." *Hampton Roads Naval Museum*

The large, vocal, and enthusiastic naval presence at the Jamestown Exposition created great expectations throughout Tidewater that the Navy would immediately act as advocate for improvements at Sewell's Point for a new naval base or training station. Local promoters, politicians, and members of the Exposition Board—who were hoping for the sale of exposition buildings and lands for over $2 million to satisfy debts—did not discourage these stories.

Typical of these "authoritative" reports was this article in the *Virginian-Pilot:* "The announcement from Washington yesterday that the government was considering the acquisition of the Exposition site for a larger naval training station than that at St. Helena created much interest at the Exposition. It had been known for some time that the disposition of the Exposition grounds has been considered. Last August, a number of government engineers visited the Exposition on the quiet and made a careful survey of the site for a naval training station as well as a revenue cutter training school."[38]

The Navy was fully aware of the talk associated with converting the Exposition into a base, but in 1907 it had no immediate need for such a base in Hampton Roads (no matter how attractively situated). Any new base would require funding for both land and improvements (the Navy Department cringed at the rumored $2 million price tag, thinking it wildly inflated) at a time when money was needed for dreadnought battleships. Moreover, the Navy was happy with what it already had in Hampton Roads: a topflight Navy yard and naval station at Portsmouth, a superb man-o-war anchorage in the Roads, a respected naval hospital, and a newly acquired training station at Berkley/St. Helena. A Sewell's Point site would either duplicate existing facilities or force the Navy to close one site to open another—neither was an attractive option.

Although the Navy carefully explained its position to local authorities, no one was listening, least of all the financially strapped exposition bondholders, who were desperate for a bailout. When Rear Adm. Willard H. Brownson of the Bureau of Navigation inspected the St. Helena Training Station in

President Theodore Roosevelt reviews the fleet at the Jamestown Exposition from Presidential yacht *Mayflower* in April 1907 as gun salutes ring out from the fourteen assembled American battleships and a second line of foreign warships. *Hampton Roads Naval Museum*

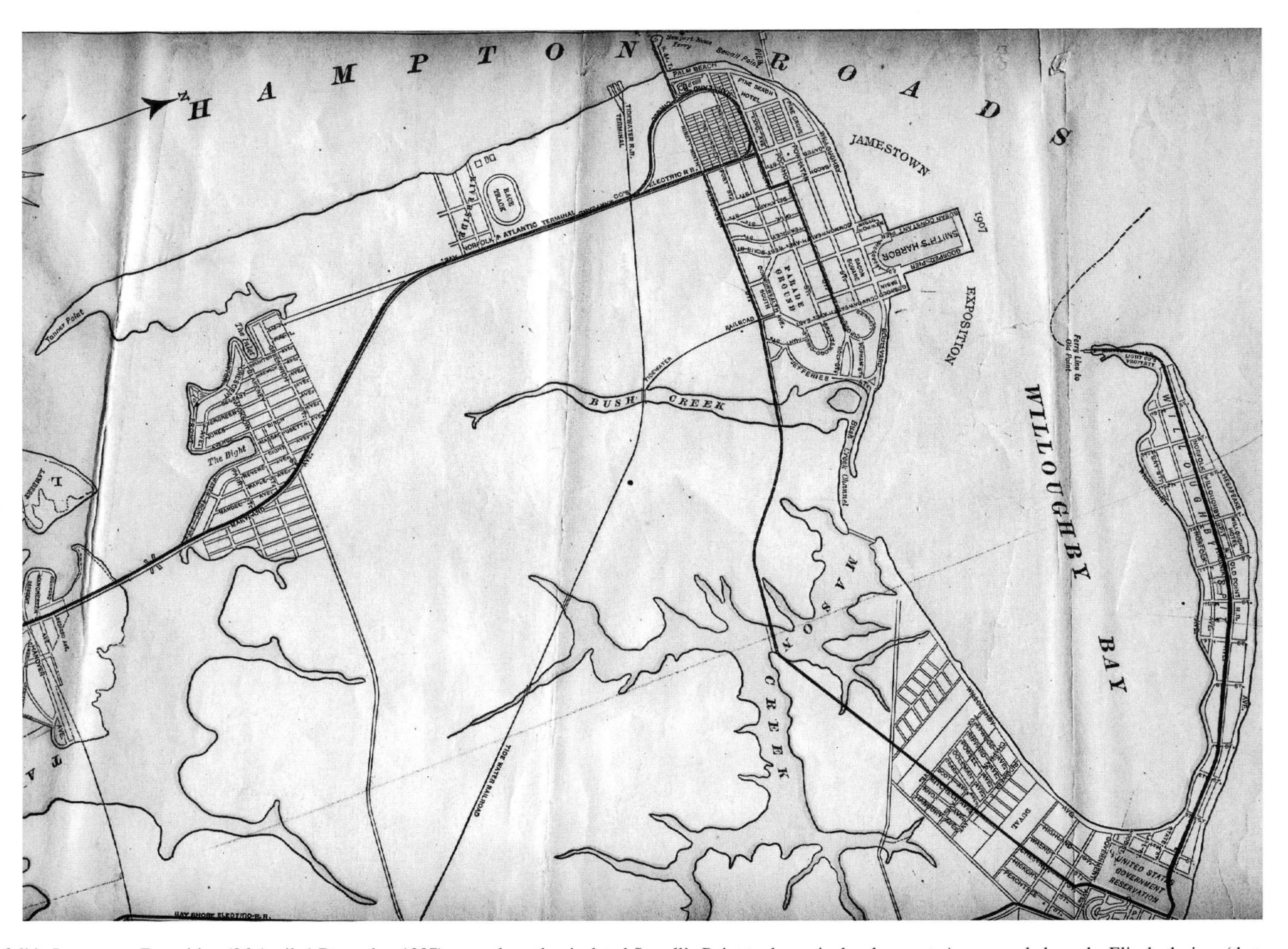

Norfolk's Jamestown Exposition (26 April–1 December 1907) opened a rather isolated Sewell's Point to dramatic development. A new road along the Elizabeth river (that would later be called Hampton Boulevard) was built to connect the city to the Exposition and trolley lines were extended to handle the expected throngs. New streets, sidewalks, and water, telephone and power lines turned what was once simply vacant fields, scrub pines and marshlands into a small city. *Sargeant Memorial Room, Norfolk Public Library.*

Visitors with parasols and top hats stroll outside one of the Jamestown Exposition exhibit buildings while a street vendor provides convenient fare. *Hampton Roads Naval Museum*

November 1907 (where about a thousand recruits were quartered in tents and temporary wooden barracks), the *Virginian-Pilot* reported that local officials "suggested that the government take over the permanent buildings on the Jamestown Exposition grounds for this purpose." Brownson, on the other hand, brushed aside such suggestions and was quoted as saying that he "felt that the government should provide permanent buildings only at [Berkley]."[39]

The "Grand Basin" at Discovery Landing of the Jamestown Exposition was later turned into a seaplane operating site for the Hampton Roads Naval Air Station. *Hampton Roads Naval Museum*

Although it slowly dawned on Norfolk promoters that the Navy did not intend to act with any speed, the exposition had made a lasting impression that few from the Navy could forget. As the Norfolk *Landmark* described: "The beauty of the location is beyond description. Here in Tidewater, Virginia we have grown so used to the magnificence of Hampton Roads that we do not fully appreciate it. To the visitor looking upon the majestic marine roadstead for the first time, the impression of grandeur is overwhelming. There is no other such site in the world."[40]

During the early years of the twentieth century, the vast bulk of the American battle fleet operated in the Atlantic. Among naval officers, the primary focus was eastward toward Europe, especially Germany, with its expanding high seas fleet. In addition to this Atlantic focus, there was concern about potential threats from the Pacific and Japan. Adm. George Dewey was known to be in favor of a cruise to the Orient by the battle fleet, and the Navy had written up various plans for a "practice cruise," but no consensus existed among senior naval officers. Many were said to be concerned with the thought of the American East Coast lying undefended.[41]

President Roosevelt pressed for a decision that would showcase "his" Navy, send a signal to the Japanese, and impress the American public. He convened meetings during the summer of 1907 to discuss Dewey's recommendations and as a result of these discussions ordered the Navy to dispatch the battle fleet to the Pacific, but only as far as the West Coast. He further stipulated that as many battleships as possible should go.[42]

In August 1907, the first official statement was made announcing that sixteen battleships of the American fleet (forever after known to history as the "Great White Fleet") would make a voyage via the Magellan Straits to San Francisco. The announcement caused a flurry of negative reaction from East Coast newspapers and politicians flapping about the threat of attack and the loss of naval revenue. When the chairman of the Senate Naval Affairs Committee mused that funds would not be appropriated for the cruise, Roosevelt replied that he already had enough money to send the fleet to the West Coast, and if Congress refused the money to bring them back, they could stay there.[43]

All sixteen battleships had entered Hampton Roads by 12 December 1907 and anchored in two neat rows immediately off Fort Monroe. Thousands of well-wishers flooded into Tidewater, and officers and crew surged ashore to meet them. Hotels were packed with friends and family who had come to bid farewell before a voyage that promised to last, perhaps, for years. Many others flooded in from surrounding Tidewater communities to watch the spectacle. There was a gala at-

The sailing of the Great White Fleet from Hampton Roads in December 1907 was a masterstroke. As it sailed from Virginia's shores, diplomatic cables circled the globe announcing to the world that the United States was a world-class naval power. The ensuing voyage would prove to be a superb technical achievement, as the fleet visited twenty-six foreign countries and expended 435,000 tons of coal while suffering no serious accident or breakdown. *U.S. Naval Institute*

mosphere, and during the Friday evening before the final sail, high society from Norfolk and Washington gathered at the Chamberlin Hotel's grand ballroom, decorated with flags and bunting, to wish the Navy well. Resting at anchor, the fleet looked powerful and beautiful.[44]

Aboard the ships, the pace was more frantic. Last-minute supplies were carefully loaded aboard, ranging from coal and ammunition to lavish foods for diplomatic receptions and five dozen pianos.[45] Seamen touched up the shields, eagles, and fancy curlicues that adorned the ship's prows and polished hardwood decks and the elegant brass and walnut trim of the bridges.

Monday, 16 December, dawned clear after a day of heavy rain, and the fleet's crews were awakened at 0500 by bugle, boatswain's pipe, and the traditional "all hands, up all hammocks, roust out, lash and carry." The battle line lay resplendent in sparkling white and buff, and every Navy man looked with keen anticipation across the roads, where presidential yacht *Mayflower* was expected at any moment. The fourteen thousand men of the fleet and many thousands ashore had had this date circled on their calendars for months. Now as clocks approached eight bells, it was clear that the day would be like no other in Tidewater's long and storied maritime history.

The sixteen leviathans of the battle line represented a unique study in the speed of technological growth. Seven were battleships of the "first class": flagship *Connecticut* (BB-18), *Louisiana* (BB-19), *Vermont* (BB-20), *Kansas* (BB-21), *Minnesota* (BB-22), *New Jersey* (BB-16), and *Rhode Island* (BB-17). The remaining nine were the "coast" battleships: *Kearsarge* (BB-5), *Kentucky* (BB-6), *Illinois* (BB-7), *Alabama* (BB-8), *Maine* (BB-10), *Missouri* (BB-11), *Ohio* (BB-12), *Virginia* (BB-13), *Georgia* (BB-14). The two oldest, *Kearsarge* and *Kentucky,* were but seven years older than the very newest ship, *Kansas,* fresh from the builder's yards. But design improvements had proceeded so rapidly that the speed, cruising range, armor protection, and mixed battery of 7-, 8-, and 12-inch breech-loading guns of *Kansas* were so superior to those of older battleships that a gunnery duel would have been over in minutes. Local pride was very much in evidence, since seven ships of the fleet were from Newport News builder's ways.[46]

Rear Adm. Robley D. Evans had earned the popular fleet nickname "Fighting Bob" for his determined conduct while commanding gunboat *Yorktown* and protecting American interests during the Chilean revolution of 1891–92. He later commanded battleship *Iowa* during the Battle of Santiago and the Asiatic Fleet from 1902–4. Evans was named as the first commander in chief of the Atlantic Fleet on 1 January 1906 and organized the Great White Fleet for its historic cruise. *U.S. Naval Institute*

Rear Adm. Robley D. Evans commanded the newly reclassified United States Battle Fleet. Advance forces had already sailed with armored cruisers *Tennessee* (ACR-10) and *Washington* (ACR-11), leaving Hampton Roads on 12 October, and a flotilla of black-painted torpedo boat destroyers—*Whipple* (DD-15), *Lawrence* (DD-8), *Hopkins* (DD-6), *Stewart* (DD-13), *Truxtun* (DD-14), and *Hull* (DD-7)—departed Lynnhaven Bay on 2 December.[47]

A colorful, stubborn, and gifted commander, Evans was the nation's best-known naval officer aside from George Dewey and enjoyed the popular fleet nickname "Fighting Bob." It was well known that Evans had a gouty left foot and that doctors advised him not to make the cruise, but Evans characteristically brushed off such advice and carried on.[48]

Immediately after morning colors, the Fort Monroe saluting battery announced the arrival of *Mayflower,* carrying Roosevelt and Navy Secretary Victor H. Metcalf. The naval yacht "steamed slowly down the avenue flanked by the battleships," with signal flags flying gaily from each warship in up-and-over decoration. *Mayflower* received a twenty-one-gun salute from the fleet and came to anchor to receive the flag officers, staffs, and battleship captains.[49]

Dramatic panorama of the Norfolk Navy Yard on 13 May 1908 taken by an enterprising photographer high atop a smokestack and catching detail during a time when the Great White Fleet was circling the globe. Visible (from left to right) are the Norfolk/Portsmouth ferry at the far left, battleship *Iowa,* ancient receiving ships *Franklin* and *Richmond,* torpedo boats moored across the river at the St. Helena piers, a monitor (probably *Arkansas)* and a new armored cruiser (most likely *Montana,* preparing for her July commissioning) in the wet basin, cruiser *Olympia* preparing for a summer midshipman training cruise, and even several small skipjack workboats on the river. *Norfolk Naval Shipyard*

Once the officers returned to their ships, *Mayflower* steamed to a point about ten miles from Fort Monroe off the Tail of the Horseshoe, where she anchored to give the president an opportunity to review the fleet as it passed. Evans had *Connecticut* under way crisply with engine bells clanging, and signal flags soon broke from the flagship's halyards, ordering each division to follow in succession. "The ebb tide had swung the ships so as to head them into the harbor," wrote one contemporary account, "and a neat piece of engineering and navigation was executed from the bridges of the battleships as they swung in obedience to their helms . . . the churning of the huge propellers lashed the whole harbor to a foam and black smoke rolled in dense volume in the northwest wind."[50] The fleet formed a vast white wall three miles long as throngs of onlookers ashore cheered and waved.

As the fleet flagship swung close to *Mayflower,* all hands presented a salute to the president, who all could see clearly on *Mayflower's* bridge. "The scene aroused the martial spirit in the nation's executive, and as the *Connecticut* was broad off the beam of the *Mayflower,* moved by the impulse, President Roosevelt, took off his hat and voiced three cheers, which were followed by all the members of the Presidential party."[51] Following at intervals of four hundred yards at a steady ten knots, each ship passed close to the *Mayflower,* giving a presidential salute in passing. It was an intoxicating experience for the president: the loom of impeccable white sides and polished gun barrels; the controlled silence on deck, tinged with the sounds of boatswain's pipes and ventilator fans; the sensation of one fifteen-thousand-ton battleship after another surging through the water close aboard. "By George!" Roosevelt bubbled to his Navy secretary. "Did you ever see such a fleet and such a day?"[52]

Once out past the capes, course was altered to 150 degrees in a gentle swell. "A stiff northwest wind seized hold of the great streamers of smoke that poured over the tops of the smoke pipes," read an account from a reporter on board, "and as these streamers frayed themselves out against the blue sky and the bright sun, the breeze seemed to lift them toward the southeastern heavens, where some power wove them together to pull the ships along and give them a fine sendoff."[53] Evans ordered the fleet into an open order cruising formation, in which ships paired off to port and starboard and maneuvered into two parallel lines, guided by the flagship. Roosevelt had finally confirmed to Evans that the fleet would not just cruise to the West Coast, but would sail around the world, and Evans passed that word to his captains once they were under way. On every ship the band played good-bye medleys composed of "Home, Sweet Home," "The Girl I Left Behind Me," and "Auld Lang Syne." Once in clear water, the starboard section assumed the first underway watch for a deployment that, for even the saltiest crew member, would be the longest at-sea cruise of their lives.

Although the cruise, which would circle the globe and visit twenty-six foreign countries, proved a diplomatic tour de force

and a powerful instrument of international politics, its most important role for the Navy was probably its significant contribution to fleet training. This was to be a working cruise from its first day, and as mile after mile disappeared in the fleet's wake, the officers and crews were slowly molded into tightly knit, well-trained organizations.

The wardrooms of the Great White Fleet included a stunning collection of future four- and five-star admirals, Medal of Honor recipients, and naval aviation pioneers; leaders of the great battle fleets of World War II would take from this experience a lasting taste of professionalism and naval expertise. Ens. William "Bull" Halsey served as gunnery officer on *Kansas;* others included Lt. Harry E. Yarnell and Ens. Royal Ingersoll (*Connecticut*); Lt. Henry Mustin, Lt. J. K. Taussig, and Lt. E. C. Kalbfus (*Kansas*); Ens. H. R. Stark and Midn. Raymond Spruance (*Minnesota*); Ens. Husband Kimmel

President Theodore Roosevelt stands aboard battleship *Connecticut* in February 1909 to welcome Great White Fleet sailors back to Hampton Roads. *U.S. Naval Institute*

Officers and men of battleship *Virginia,* shortly after returning from their round-the-world cruise with the Great White Fleet. *U.S. Naval Institute*

(*Georgia*); Midn. R. S. Edwards (*Stewart*); Midn. John Towers (*Kentucky*); Ens. D. W. Bagley and Midn. W. H. Lee (*Rhode Island*); Ens. D. I. Selfridge (*Virginia*); Lt. F. J. Horne (*Illinois*); Midn. Thomas Kinkaid (*Nebraska*); Midn. H. K. Hewitt (*Missouri*); Lt. Cdr. E. W. Eberle (*Louisiana*); and Midn. Isaac Kidd (*New Jersey*).[54]

On the night of 21 February 1909—434 days after last spotting the Chesapeake capes—the Great White Fleet dropped anchor off Cape Henry. Scaffolds were lowered over the sides, and crews worked all night applying fresh coats of brilliant white paint. Although some had urged the fleet to steam to either New York or New Orleans for their triumphant return, the Navy Department finally ordered them to Hampton Roads, "out of consideration for the men."[55]

Early the following morning, Washington's Birthday, the fleet entered the Chesapeake Bay in triumph, as the first battle fleet to have ever circumnavigated the world. The weather was not as inviting as it had been for the departure, with gray overcast skies and drizzle, but hundreds of small craft still crowded the roads, with blaring whistles and foghorns. Ashore sixty thousand men, women, and children waited, with, as in 1907, hotels across Tidewater filled to capacity.

Mayflower was again on hand with Roosevelt on board, as was President-elect William Howard Taft, who was somewhat lost in the exuberance. Roosevelt exalted in the spectacle; ships' bands struck up the "Star-Spangled Banner," puffs of white smoke marked thunderous gun salutes, and thousands of bluejackets stood in disciplined ranks to salute the president in his last official duty aboard *Mayflower.*

The president immediately bounded up *Connecticut's* ladder to congratulate Rear Adm. Charles S. Sperry (who had replaced Evans midway through the cruise) and pound him briskly on the back. The crew assembled on the foredeck, and the president energetically climbed up the barbette of the forward turret. Halfway up, he slipped and fell backward, saved only from inopportune injury by several quick-thinking sailors who caught him. Unfazed, he regained his improvised dais and delivered a classic, rousing Rooseveltian speech: "Other nations may do as you have done, but they'll have to follow you."[56] It was, in short, bully.

Hampton Roads glowed in the light of the fleet's success but most instinctively realized that the return of the Great White Fleet also represented an end to one era and the beginning of another. Within weeks, Norfolk Navy Yard workers descended on the battle line to remove the gilded scrollwork on the bows, and white sides would turn to purposeful battleship gray.

The distressing truth was that by the time of its return, the Great White Fleet was obsolete, eclipsed by the revolutionary "all-big-gun," high-speed, armored dreadnought battleship—a design transformation so radical that the proud ships of Roosevelt's fleet would henceforth be carelessly disparaged as simply "pre-dreadnoughts." More ironic still was the fact that the gray-painted harbingers of this new dramatic era in naval history already stood at Newport News Shipbuilding within sight of the man-o-war anchorage at Hampton Roads. There, new American dreadnought battleship designs were taking shape in the form of *Delaware* (BB-28), which had been launched on 6 February 1909, just sixteen days before the fleet's return.

But not lost to history was the clear fact that it had been the "New Steel Navy" era that had propelled the United States Navy from a position of impotence on the world's stage to a new pinnacle befitting a world power. And it had been the Great White Fleet of Hampton Roads that stood as the embodiment and exemplar of that era.

1914

By 1500 on the blustery afternoon of 14 November 1910, aviator Eugene Ely had waited long enough. He had been standing for hours on the open bridge of the light cruiser *Birmingham* (CL-2), dressed in a heavyweight flying suit, leather helmet, and goggles, trying to stay warm in the wind and drizzle of a stormy afternoon on Hampton Roads. Much to his distress, a world of misty gray surrounded *Birmingham*'s unsteady anchorage off Old Point Comfort. Wintry squalls raced across the nearby Chesapeake, gusty whitecaps dotted the harbor, and drizzly veils frequently obscured the cheerless battlements of nearby Fort Monroe.

Ely's *Hudson Flyer* sat immediately in front of the bridge, tied down securely to a temporary wooden flight deck hurriedly constructed over the cruiser's foredeck. Ely had always considered "Hudson Flyer" a rather jolly name for a rickety biplane that, ungraciously, displayed all the flight dynamics of a winged bicycle. Although the charmed "aeroplane" had once won inventor Glenn Curtiss a $10,000 purse for a nonstop flight from Albany to New York City, today it looked all too frail and spiritless as it was buffeted by the gusts and wet of Hampton Roads.

Since sailing from the Navy yard, little had gone according to plan aboard *Birmingham.* It was to be a daring and history-making flight; the details had been carefully coordinated between Ely, a twenty-four-year-old Curtiss-trained civilian flyer, and Capt. Washington Irving Chambers, the first officer in the Navy Department to direct aeronautic activities. The plan called for the lucky Hudson Flyer to launch from *Birmingham*'s deck while the ship steamed into the breeze near the mouth of the Elizabeth River and then fly back down the river (in full view of hundreds, perhaps thousands, of spectators) to land at the Navy yard parade ground. The intrepid attempt, the first of its kind in history from any ship, had been optimistically advertised in the local papers, and a division of destroyers had been positioned along the Elizabeth to aid the pilot's navigation or (more likely, some said) to rescue him from drowning. Captain Chambers had carefully scripted the attempt to match the Navy's "vision" of the future, even to the point of encouraging Ely to plug a tagline that said "the aeroplane is the best thing for Navy scout work and dispatch carrying." Few others saw any immediate value of planes flying from ships, and the crowds that were forecast were not coming for the practical but for the dramatic.[1]

But weather—or luck—had not cooperated, and Ely's big day had dawned cloudy with rain. By 1130, as *Birmingham* left her pier to proceed downriver for the attempt, conditions had deteriorated still further, and Chambers delayed the launch and ordered *Birmingham* to anchor. All then waited together—pilot, engineers, crewmen, supporting destroyers, photographers, watchstanders, Navy officials—for any improvement in the elements. Spectators along the Elizabeth slowly melted away, preferring the warmth of the hearth to the dampness of the riverfront.

Then, with the day closer to sunset than to noon, Ely abruptly announced that the clouds were lifting—optimism questioned by others on the cruiser's bridge. Before anyone had a chance to check the barometer or examine the logic of the only trained aerialist aboard, Ely sharply ordered his two

The Hudson Flyer aboard *Birmingham* at Norfolk Navy Yard on 13 November 1910. The aircraft and its engine had been separately hoisted on board, and Eugene Ely and his mechanics had spent several hours reassembling the pair. Although well-respected naval architect William McEntree had designed the temporary deck on *Birmingham,* none of his calculations could boast the comfort of experimental confirmation. In fact, the two most critical dimensions of the 83 × 24 foot deck—its length and its downward slope—were driven not by aeronautical insight but simply by the distance and height from the ship's open bridge to her prow. *Hampton Roads Naval Museum*

Curtiss mechanics into place; the schedule of an exhibition pilot in 1910 was tight, and he could not afford another lost day aboard a dank and drafty warship.

By 1515, Ely had awkwardly positioned himself at the aeroplane's controls and had coaxed the four-cylinder, fifty-horsepower pusher engine behind him into motion. The engine's sputtering soon smoothed with manual adjustments to the throttle and choke, and Ely carefully added more power to test the engine's strength. Although his motions were practiced and routine, there was little around him that could have been reassuring to the pilot. In front of him, Ely would have seen only the aeroplane's tiny forward stabilizer, gangly struts perched above a small front wheel, and fifty-seven feet of wooden deck abruptly ending in the nothingness of a thirty-four-foot drop to frigid gray water. Ely could not even depend on the sanctity of dry land and level ground for his spring into history. The temporary deck was pitched downward at 5 degrees, and once the pilot started his forward roll, he would be losing height with every foot of run, diving *toward* the water. All this would be disconcerting under the best of circumstances, but it was especially daunting to a young pilot whose ability to swim was in doubt.[2]

As Ely continued to tinker with the Hudson Flyer's settings, the biplane pulled against a single restraining line tied to its rear, itching to start the attempt. With raindrops spattering his goggles and the engine clattering in his ears, Ely was finally satisfied with the power and thrust, and he waved his arm to signal his crew. Suddenly released, the craft jerked forward, jouncing across uneven planks. Ely's total concentration focused on the necessity for a straight run to the bow—any other path would lead to immediate disaster—while trusting to engine power and gravity for sufficient speed for lift.

Within seconds, the aeroplane had reached the end of the deck, and its front wheel dropped awkwardly toward the water,

Eugene B. Ely was born in Davenport, Iowa, on 21 October 1886 and taught himself to fly on a refurbished Curtiss aircraft in early 1910. He joined the Curtiss commercial flying team and traveled extensively through the eastern United States entertaining audiences with aerial exploits. Capt. Washington I. Chambers was introduced to Ely at an international air meet at Belmont Park, New York, and convinced the flyer to participate in two pioneering acts of flying, the first flight from cruiser *Birmingham* and the first landing aboard armored cruiser *Pennsylvania.* Ely was killed in a plane crash on 19 October 1911 at Macon, Georgia. In 1933 Eugene B. Ely's historic achievements were posthumously recognized by the award of the Distinguished Flying Cross. *Hampton Roads Naval Museum*

pitching the pilot further forward in his seat. Instinctively, Ely struggled with the controls to raise the Flyer's nose, but his predominant direction of flight was still downward. On *Birmingham's* open bridge, Captain Chambers watched the craft vault from the front edge of the flight deck, hesitate in flight for a split second, and then dip alarmingly toward the water. Fighting for lift, Ely kept his wings level, his engine at full throttle.

Those on the foredeck of destroyer *Roe,* anchored nearby, saw Ely reassuringly adjust the craft's attitude upward, but its weight continued to pull the unsteady biplane toward the water. The Flyer's wheels grazed the water's surface, and spray blasted against the tips of his pusher propeller, but Ely, gratefully, was finally level and, a moment later, climbing. Clawing his way to a height of about fifty feet, Ely turned to look upriver. As he dipped his starboard wing to turn, the *Flyer* began to vibrate violently, which was caused, as Ely later discovered, by the splintered tips of his propeller. He aimed for the only dry land within reach, Willoughby Spit, and landed on hard sand five minutes later, sooner than expected but well within Chambers's criteria for a declaration of success.

Birmingham's understated log entry was hardly the stuff of history: "[time] 3:17, Aeroplane left ship and made flight to Willoughby Spit."[3] The *Virginian-Pilot* was more effusive: "With a broken propeller and in weather conditions unfavorable for flying, the daring birdman, shortly after 3 o'clock yesterday afternoon, glided from the platform erected on the front of the big black cruiser *Birmingham,* swooped down like an immense bird of prey until he touched the water, then rose rapidly into the misty air of the lower bay and was off in the direction of the broad Atlantic. Four minutes after having taken his sudden farewell of the *Birmingham* he was a lost speck on the eastern horizon and an instant later had landed on Willoughby Spit."[4]

The U.S. Navy had accomplished what no other had attempted. Although Chambers had shown that it was possible to operate aircraft from ships, the Navy showed little immediate interest in tactics, training, aircraft design, or ship modifications. And as Ely stood on a damp, cold beach that afternoon, inspecting his damaged propeller, a dark gray, big-gun battleship steamed slowly down the channel for sea without even noticing.[5]

In the years before World War I, Hampton Roads had also become a center of another quiet revolution in naval warfare, the rise of the submarine. During the 1890s fleet buildup, the Navy had advertised an open competition for undersea craft designs. The effort was purely exploratory, inasmuch as no submarines existed in any of the world's navies. American inventors John Holland and Simon Lake responded, each building experimental craft (Simon Lake's *Argonaut* and Holland's *Plunger*); *Argonaut* was tested in trials and experiments in Hampton Roads by 1898. Lake designed *Argonaut* with an interest in the profit to be made in locating cables or wrecks and tried to convince officials at Fort Monroe to use *Argonaut* to inspect the defensive minefield that had been laid to protect Hampton Roads during the Spanish-American War.[6]

The Navy awarded its first submarine contracts to Holland, even rejecting Lake's improved *Protector* in 1902 (with its patented "omniscope," a predecessor of the submarine peri-

Historic photo of Ely's first moments airborne from *Birmingham* in Hampton Roads on 14 November 1910. Dramatic as this photo was, Ely's success was very much in doubt at this point as he struggled for airspeed and lift. His rear wheels and propeller would strike the water briefly before he could gain aeronautic control, and the damage to his propeller blades would force him to land at the closest point of land, Willoughby Point. *Hampton Roads Naval Museum*

scope). Lake's first naval contract did not come until 1908, and the keel for *Seal* was laid on 2 February 1909 at Newport News Shipbuilding. Renamed *G-1* before her commissioning on 28 October 1912, the craft of four hundred tons was built with wheels for lying on the bottom.[7]

Lt. Theodore "Spuds" Ellyson, who headed a submarine division based at Norfolk Navy Yard and had previously commanded the Holland submarines *Shark* and *Tarantula,* was named to command *Seal.* The quick-witted and resourceful Ellyson had a thorough appreciation of engineering and, to Lake's displeasure, frequently questioned several of the craft's design details. When another opportunity for "experimental" Navy duty surfaced, Ellyson volunteered for flying instruction, which led to his designation as "Naval Aviator No. 1."[8]

During trials, *G-1* dove to 256 feet, a record at the time. Interestingly, the ship was designated "SS-19 ½," the story being that the Navy had mistakenly numbered a pair of other submarines under construction as SS-19 and SS-20. Lake joked that he had provided the Navy half a submarine whose performance was better than anything else the Navy had at the moment. *G-1* conducted training dives and mock attacks in the Chesapeake Bay in 1915 and acted as an experimental test ship for the rest of her career. With the success of *G-1,* Lake won a follow-on contract for *Tuna* (later *G-2*) (SS-27), also built at Newport News.[9]

Norfolk naval officers were also intensely interested in the arrival of the large German merchant submarine *Deutschland* on 9 July 1916. Evading British and French patrols in the Atlantic, *Deutschland* anchored at Baltimore with a cargo of dyes, mail, and diplomatic mischief. When three Allied cruisers arrived off the capes (one violating wartime neutrality by sailing into the bay), the Navy dispatched the Norfolk-based armored cruiser *North Carolina* and three destroyers to Cape Henry. *Deutschland* eluded Allied patrols and returned to Germany.[10]

The Navy's first submarine, *Holland* (SS-1), was based at the Norfolk Navy Yard between 1905 and 1910 and is shown here on a repair way at the yard. *Norfolk Naval Shipyard*

After Hampton Roads's prominence in the Spanish-American War, a pro-Navy clamor grew among businessmen looking to the federal government to help stimulate industrial expansion in Tidewater. Several communities across the country sought Army or Navy installations to spur economic improvement by substituting federal investment for despoiling industrialization. Norfolk's approach emphasized the opposite, clearly aiming at attracting military investment as a means to stimulate manufacturing and industrial expansion.[11]

Interest in building a large naval base at the Jamestown Exposition site became especially intense when Exposition shareholders began to descend into financial distress. Theodore J. Wool, a Norfolk lawyer and developer who had helped promote the Jamestown Exposition, became the leading voice in the campaign to attract the Navy's attention to the property. Wool lobbied members of the Virginia congressional delegation and prevailed upon well-regarded Rear Adm. Purnell F. Harrington (Ret.) to press the site's advantages, seeking $2 million for the property to recoup losses.[12]

Wool and other Norfolk boosters were gladdened when a bill was finally introduced in the Senate in 1908 for a $1 million appropriation to purchase the exposition site. The bill lost steam, however, when a committee chairman was reputed to have told the assistant secretary of the Navy that he could have either the new base in Norfolk or a new collier for his $1 million, but not both—to which the Navy responded by choosing the collier as the higher priority. As much as anything, this was another indication that the Navy was generally satisfied with what it had in Hampton Roads. Given a good deal, the Navy would have considered expansion onto Sewell's Point, but a new naval base in Norfolk was not a priority.[13]

Failing in their quest for a Navy bailout, the Jamestown Exposition Company went into receivership in 1908, and the lands were sold to the newly incorporated Fidelity Land and Investment Corporation (organized by Theodore J. Wool and others) for a bid of a mere $235,000.[14]

Rather than end speculation in the property, Wool (who assumed the office of secretary and general counsel of Fidelity) and his fellow investors intensified their game and began a persistent, multiyear effort to keep the matter in play. This venture accelerated with the change in administrations in 1913, when Woodrow Wilson named North Carolina newspaper edi-

Submarine *G-1* (originally named *Seal)* was built by Newport News Shipbuilding in 1911–12 and christened with the unusual designation of SS-19 1/2. *G-1* was Lake's first submarine for the U.S. Navy and introduced the even keel and other innovations into submarine design. *U.S. Naval Institute*

tor and southern populist Josephus Daniels to be his new secretary of the Navy. Norfolk boosters clearly considered Daniels a friend in court. When the Navy secretary and members of Wilson's cabinet visited Norfolk in April 1913 to observe battleship gunnery practice and to inspect the St. Helena Training Station and the Navy yard (where Daniels became the first secretary of the Navy to submerge in a submarine, at a pier), Norfolk business leaders tried to charm the secretary at every opportunity. Daniels later said that he had found "much to interest and impress him."[15] To remind everyone anew that the Jamestown Exposition site was still available, Wool circulated a ten-page booklet around Washington titled *Reasons* that plugged Hampton Roads's many advantages, such as safe anchorage, climate, open land, and good rail and shipping links. In addition, according to historian Gordon Calhoun, "possibly to appeal to [Daniels's] deeply held Christian beliefs and his philosophy of clean living, Wool made the case that the base [at Sewell's Point] would be near the city but not so close that sailors would be tempted by sinful things like alcohol, prostitution and gambling."[16]

In 1913, the Norfolk Chamber of Commerce, headed by longtime Norfolk politician and businessman Barton Myers, urged Daniels to schedule a naval rendezvous in Hampton Roads for 1915, which he heartily endorsed. Virginia senators and the Norfolk congressman were also growing in seniority in the new Democratic administration, and in 1915 the Norfolk Chamber of Commerce established "a Special Committee to Cooperate with Congressman Holland [Congressman E. E. Holland, Norfolk member of Congress 1911–1921] in matters pertaining to important improvements in the Navy Yard, Harbor Channel and Cape Henry fortifications, which need early attention."[17] A Joint Committee on Naval Affairs soon followed to help spread Tidewater's influence, with members from the Norfolk Chamber of Commerce, the Board

Beginning in 1904, Theodore J. Wool, a Norfolk lawyer and developer, became one of the leading voices in the Norfolk business community urging the Navy to establish new bases in Hampton Roads. He helped promote the Jamestown Exposition and lobbied members of the Virginia congressional delegation, even the secretary of the Navy himself. After the Exposition, Wool continued to dangle the idea of a large new naval base in front of Washington decision makers and helped establish the Fidelity Land and Investment Corporation which acted as a holding company for Sewell's Point land. *Hampton Roads Naval Museum*

Tall, educated, and articulate, with long experience in Norfolk, Rear Adm. Albert C. Dillingham was the perfect choice to lead the effort of establishing the Naval Operating Base beginning in 1917. *U.S. Naval Institute*

of Trade, and the Portsmouth Businessmen's Association, chaired by Gordon Hatton of Portsmouth. Early in 1916, the Norfolk Chamber of Commerce hosted members of the House Committee on Naval Affairs on a visit to the Navy yard and Cape Henry, discussed the need for a new Navy training camp, and feted them with an old-fashioned Chesapeake oyster roast.[18]

Through these political and business links, Hampton Roads began to sharpen its message to Washington at the same time that the Navy began to grapple with the realities of a world war that by 1914 and 1915 were dominating every newspaper headline. The loss of the American tanker *Gulflight* and the Cunard liner *Lusitania* in May 1915 to German U-boats accelerated the Navy's preparations for war and, again, increased its interest in Tidewater.

The Navy's renewed interest in Hampton Roads was grounded in the strategies of the day, which required super-dreadnought battleships and relatively large numbers of destroyers and submarines. Furthermore, British, French, and German experience was proving that "modern" navies needed access to levels of industrial production, repair, and logistics that had never been seen before. To support modern navies properly, existing naval stations had to be expanded or new bases created. Although the Navy had been satisfied with the ability of the Norfolk Navy Yard and nearby Hampton Roads anchorages to support the fleet just a few years before, the accelerating support demands of destroyers, submarines, aircraft, and ordnance and supply were clearly beyond what the Navy had in Tidewater.

An Atlantic Fleet study in September 1915 explicitly proposed that "the property in the vicinity of Sewall Point [sic], which was used for the Jamestown Exposition . . . be acquired for the purpose of establishing a base for the use of destroyers and submarines," and included recommendations for piers on the northern shore of Sewell's Point, dredging to twenty-

The state houses and the nearby shoreline of Willoughby Bay as they appeared in 1917 when the Navy first began construction on Sewell's Point land. *Hampton Roads Naval Museum*

five feet, and, interestingly, construction of a seawall from Fort Wool to Willoughby Spit.[19]

In early 1916, naval expansion in Hampton Roads suddenly gained momentum with congressional approval of Navy yard improvements and Norfolk lobbying for battleship construction and a new armor plant in Tidewater. Also buried in the Navy secretary's annual report for 1916 was the first official signal of Daniels's interest in Sewell's Point: "The work of major importance that should be undertaken immediately is the development of Norfolk as one of the main naval bases, which includes not only the development of the yard itself but the acquisition of a site or sites in the vicinity, bordering on Hampton Roads, for training station, submarine and aviation bases, fuel-oil storage and transfer depot for supplies."[20]

Other factors also began to influence the debate. In late 1915, Assistant Secretary of the Navy Franklin D. Roosevelt chaired a review of the Navy's training stations. Roosevelt's report recommended that St. Helena be "abandoned as a training station as being inadequate and unsatisfactory in every way even for present conditions and numbers. Purchase a new site . . . either on Hampton Roads where, in addition, to serving as a training station, it could be used for recreation grounds for the fleet . . . or on the James River . . . or on the York River in the vicinity of Yorktown." The report caused only passing interest in 1915 but, within a year, would frame the primary argument for building a new Norfolk training site.[21]

In the fall of 1916, the Commission on Navy Yards and Naval Stations, headed by Rear Adm. James M. Helm, launched into a comprehensive review of all Navy yards, naval stations, submarine bases, and airfields to find the best base locations to support preparations for war. Interest in expanding at Hampton Roads intensified, especially for naval aviation. Rear Adm. Frederick R. Harris urged that an airbase for "experimental" naval aircraft be built "near Washington," and the Bureau of Construction and Repair specifically recommended the Jamestown Exposition site for this "experimental station." Similarly, the director of naval aeronautics, Capt. Mark L. Bristol, pressed for Cape Henry or Lynnhaven Inlet or "some other place near Chesapeake Bay" as a priority site for a naval air base.[22]

Naval Operating Base (NOB) during the spring of 1918, with seaplanes operating from four hangars at the tip of the exposition boat basin and the results of Admiral Dillingham's massive construction efforts to build barracks and classroom buildings for the training station clearly visible. *Hampton Roads Naval Museum*

In only two years, the formula defining the naval presence in Hampton Roads had changed dramatically. The status quo at Norfolk (which the Navy appeared so satisfied with in 1908) could no longer meet accelerating naval requirements. Although the Norfolk Navy Yard could be modernized to increase repairs and shipbuilding, additional bases were needed for training, for destroyers and submarines, and for basing the Navy's new air arm. Furthermore, such bases had to be centrally located near the fleet and, for efficiency, near each other, a solution that looked remarkably like Norfolk's Jamestown site!

Navy Secretary Daniels was fully aware of these developments, but his first inclination was to bargain for best value. On 10 October 1916 he wrote Virginia Senator Claude Swanson: "The previous estimates of cost of purchase of the [Jamestown Exposition] site as submitted by Mr. T. J. Wool amounted to, roughly, $1,500,000, is, in the opinion of the Department, excessive, and it is requested that this gentleman be advised to submit new estimates which will represent absolutely minimum purchase prices, so that the Department may submit estimates which will meet the approval of the Congress."[23]

Wool replied on 27 November 1916, inviting Daniels to Norfolk and astutely updating his well-known list of Norfolk's advantages to include "facilities for training" and land "for aeroplanes and ample room on the water for the launching, rising and lighting of hydroaeroplanes, a fuel station, supply station and a submarine base." He artfully quoted a lower price of $943,950, glossing over the fact that it was for a smaller parcel than originally estimated.[24]

In January 1917, Daniels received Virginia Senators Thomas Martin and Claude Swanson, Norfolk Congressman Holland, Theodore Wool, and James V. Trehy to discuss acquisition of the Jamestown property. The group reiterated their original offer of $1,450,000, but Daniels played the huckster, saying first that the site was "very desirable for the Navy," but ending by saying that he did not need it. Unknown to Norfolk's delegation at the time, Daniels would ask his staff for a detailed scheme for the base and would visit the site later that winter.[25]

Recruits gather into formation outside barracks at the NOB's training station circa 1918. *Hampton Roads Naval Museum*

On 7 April 1917, the day after war was declared, Barton Myers of the Chamber sent a letter to Daniels reemphasizing Norfolk's desire to sell "the Pine Beach and Exposition site for . . . storage, training, aviation, submarine base, etc," but his push was hardly needed. On that same day, Daniels began to play his hand. Hoping for the best deal, he first called Wool and told him that the Navy wished to "lease" the property but finally agreed to a sale after he had already approved staff recommendations for site layout and budget. Daniels shepherded funding bills through both the House and the Senate and met several times with Norfolk representatives concerning the details of what he referred to as the "Jamestown Base." On 3 May he testified at length, carefully describing the base's advantages for training sailors, supplying the fleet, and providing mooring sites for the fleet's largest ships.[26]

At a Cabinet meeting on 8 June, Daniels discussed the "Jamestown Exposition matter" with the president, who directed that he move forward. When Daniels talked with members of the House Naval Affairs Committee the next day, sentiment was strongly in favor of purchasing the tract. Daniels said: "Ours is the only Navy in the world that lacks an important naval base and nature seems to have fixed this as the proper site for what is now the greatest shore need of the Navy, and it is in the most strategic place on the Atlantic." On 11 June, Daniels testified one final time and on the next day President Wilson sent a letter to Congress placing his own weight behind the proposal. "It seems to me," he wrote, "that a naval base and training station should be established, and established at the earliest possible day, at Hampton Roads. I have considered this matter from a great many points of view and am more and more impressed with the immediate necessity for such a training station. If it cannot be had, and had promptly, the most serious embarrassments will ensue."[27]

The bill was passed that same day, after a brief debate involving alternative sites on the York River and at Pigs Point on the Nansemond River. On 15 June 1917, the president signed the bill into law for "Naval Operating Base, Hampton Roads, Virginia," saying, "The President is hereby authorized and empowered to take over for the United States the immediate possession and title . . . of the tract of land known as the

Recruits at St. Helena about 1915 train and exercise with pulling boats. Steel-hulled sailing bark *Cumberland*, in the background, served as a receiving ship at the training station from 1914–1919. In April 1917, the St. Helena Training Station had a population of 9,642 but closed as a training station on 20 May 1919, with all land returning to Navy Yard authority a month later. Receiving ship *Richmond,* the last of the Navy Yard's receiving ships at St. Helena, was stricken from the Navy's rolls on 30 June 1919. *Hampton Roads Naval Museum*

Jamestown Exposition site, Hampton Roads, Virginia." It was the first time that the term "Naval Operating Base" (NOB) had been used for the Sewell's Point station, terminology chosen to differentiate it from Navy repair yards. The government took possession on 28 June within boundaries defined by "Hampton Roads and Willoughby Bay on the north and west, Boush Creek on the east; and Ninety-ninth and Algonquin Streets on the south," and notified all civilians to vacate by 1 August.[28]

Appropriations of $2.8 million were approved for the 474-acre site, $1.2 million as payment for the property and an additional $1.6 million for development of facilities. The land was condemned, with final resolution of compensation to Fidelity, the Pine Beach Hotel Corporation (which had title to a nearby resort), and other private landowners thrown to the courts, where final awards amounted to $1.4 million. The Fidelity bondholders received $494,000, substantially less than they hoped, but nearly twice their investment.[29]

Local papers greeted the announcement of the Navy's action with headlines that boomed: "Hampton Roads Destined to Be the Most Important Center of Activity for United States Navy Hereafter"; "Immense Task That Must Be Rushed to Completion, Calls Forth Army of Workers and Millions of Dollars"; "Building Greatest Base for the Navy: Transforming Playground of 1907 into Grim War Depot for Uncle Sam's Seagoing Fighters in 1917." Articles lauded local politicians and boosters, and at one point the Navy boasted that its total investment for the development of a naval training, aviation, and recreation station could reach $10 million.[30]

For his part, Secretary Daniels called the new base at Hampton Roads "the most ideal naval operating base in the world" in his 1917 annual report and continued, "we are making the Hampton Roads naval operating base not only a great operating base, but an educational naval center embracing every character of instruction and training . . . in fact, every

The winter of 1917–18 was one of the coldest on record. Portions of Hampton Roads were frozen over; Navy battleships and cruisers (such as *Cleveland* [C-19] shown here) were used as icebreakers to open paths to shipping terminals and to assist in the delivery of construction materials to Sewell's Point. *Naval Historical Center*

need of the Navy except ship construction and repair, will be provided at this chief naval base."[31]

Immediately after assuming title to the land, the Navy called Rear Adm. Albert C. Dillingham from duties in the Dominican Republic to build the base. Well thought of throughout the Navy, Dillingham was a tough, no-nonsense, mercurial administrator who disliked idle chitchat. His widely read article on the development of training stations, written in 1910, specifically named Norfolk as "a locality with almost ideal conditions for a training station" and then listed in detail all of the planning, architectural, and building requirements for classrooms, barracks, gymnasiums, and drill halls necessary for recruits.[32]

Construction of the training camp began on Independence Day 1917, and within a month it was reported that the government had two thousand men working, with the workforce projected to swell to between twelve thousand and fifteen thousand. Within the first thirty days of construction, housing and mess for seventy-five hundred men had been completed. Over the next six months work slowly spread throughout the site, including the establishment of a Fifth Naval District headquarters, refurbishment of exposition buildings for the training station, clearing of parade grounds, and preparing for the air station and submarine station. The exposition's History building served as the installation's headquarters, and Pennsylvania House became an officers club. The old exposition entrance was adopted as the base's main gate, and the old Pine Beach Hotel became a bachelor officers quarters.[33]

Many of the buildings named for various states were turned into homes for officers and their families, and today all of the surviving exposition state houses are listed on the National Register of Historic Places. West of the intersection of Farragut and Dillingham, the Georgia, Maryland, Missouri, North Dakota, Ohio, Pennsylvania, Virginia, and West Virginia houses have remained on their original sites. All of the state houses to the east (Delaware, Connecticut, New Hampshire, Michigan, North Carolina, Rhode Island, and Vermont houses) were moved to their present locations beginning in April 1932.

By 12 October 1917, Dillingham had completed enough facilities (including a multitude of new permanent wooden barracks) so that the new training station could be commissioned and the transfer of training functions from St. Helena to the exposition site could begin. A reporter from the *Virginian-Pilot* was at the ceremony: "At 11 o'clock yesterday morning, with appropriate ceremonies, the training station at the naval base on the site of the Jamestown Exposition was turned over to the government as ready for use, and was immediately occupied by a regiment of apprentice seamen." Fourteen hun-

The old Pine Beach Hotel, constructed in 1902, was reopened in 1917 as NOB's Bachelor Officers Quarters and was subsequently used as Marine barracks until torn down in 1942. *Hampton Roads Naval Museum*

dred sailors marched through Norfolk, moving from St. Helena to Sewell's Point, headed by a drum and bugle corps and a band. The marching sailors "swung out upon the parade ground where, awaiting them, were drawn up the ship's company, stationed at the base and reviewing officers of the Navy, standing before the flag pole."[34] Dillingham provided a brief ceremonial speech, but his chance to be remembered in history for stirring commemorative words escaped him, and he was quoted as saying merely that "the Base has begun to function" as he officially handed over the training station to Capt. John H. Dayton, who had been the commanding officer of both the St. Helena Training Station and the receiving ship *Richmond* since October 1916. As commander of the training station at the NOB, he also effectively commanded what would later be known as the Naval Station.[35]

During the first six months of operation, 17,132 men were received, outfitted, and trained at the NOB. The station opened with the radio and signal schools both in full operation. Within a month, a school for hospital corpsmen opened, and six other schools opened in December.[36]

The first winter at Sewell's Point would have been difficult in any circumstance, since many facilities were incomplete or poorly heated, but as chance would have it, the winter was one of the coldest on record. Portions of Hampton Roads froze and ambitious schedules inevitably slipped. Worse, outbreaks of scarlet fever and spinal meningitis occurred among the tightly packed recruits in training, forcing many sailors into quarantine. Training station recruits drilled despite the weather, in ankle-deep in mud on milder days and slippery ice when it was colder. Subsequently, two seventy-two-thousand–square-foot drill halls were built, to everyone's relief.[37]

By April 1918, 125 buildings were in operation at the training station. The electrical school was established by May 1918, and its "signature" land-battleship, USS *Electrician,* rose alongside the drill field in 1919 to instruct students with shipboard electrical apparatus. An officers candidate school began operating from Pennsylvania House in 1918, a musicians school started in 1919, and a buglers school a year later. The peak of training activity was reached in November 1918 with fourteen thousand officers and men at the training station.[38]

Recruits practice semaphore signaling on a training station field at the NOB during World War I. *Hampton Roads Naval Museum*

The unprecedented wartime demand for manpower for new mass-produced ships soon outstripped even Admiral Dillingham's herculean efforts, and ways were sought to train still more sailors to meet requirements. Two proposals soon surfaced to either expand NOB to the east across Boush Creek or relocate the entire training station to a new site near Yorktown.

Washington favored the move to Yorktown, pointing to cheaper land prices, greater expansion room, and persistent water shortages at Sewell's Point. The comment most heard was that "Norfolk has more than it can handle now."[39]

Norfolk was taken aback, and the threatened loss of the training station relit a flame under the business community. Barton Myers rose in indignation: "If we lose this training station it will mean the loss of ten million dollars annually to the merchants."[40] Many others pointed to "the extreme folly" of extra construction costs at Yorktown (including the need to build a branch railroad line). The chamber weighed in and offered to negotiate with the "public-spirited citizens" east of NOB to lower property prices for expansion and finally broke the impasse. The threat of a "Yorktown solution" soon receded, and the Navy moved to acquire land across Boush Creek that would be called "East Camp."[41]

With the training station in operation, attention quickly shifted to the development of piers for submarines and destroyers, an airfield, a supply warehouse, and a Fifth Naval District headquarters. Dredging deepened the water near Sewell's Point to 35 feet and produced 8 million yards of mud and sand that was placed behind a bulkhead stretching 22,150 linear feet, increasing the original NOB tract from 474 acres to more than 800. This work was primarily undertaken during the record-breaking winter of 1917–1918, winning private contractors considerable praise from Dillingham for their mettle. The Elizabeth River was also deepened to 40 feet as far as the Navy Yard, giving Norfolk "the deepest and widest channel of any port on the Atlantic coast with the exception of New York," according to the *Ledger-Dispatch.*[42]

As early as 1916, the Norfolk Chamber of Commerce and Congressman Holland pressed the Navy to build a submarine base at Lynnhaven Inlet. The submarine station was completed in 1919 and included an enclosed mooring basin of two bulkheads and a pier at the northwestern corner of the base. The

Tying knots at the training station, circa 1920. *Hampton Roads Naval Museum*

mooring basin could handle as many as thirty-one submarines, protected from wave action by the enclosing bulkheads. A torpedo storage warehouse, administration building, battery storage warehouse, machine shop, boiler house, and an air compressor station were also built. Submarine Division Five arrived at the sparkling new facility in May 1919, and Submarine Division Nine overhauled in Norfolk before sailing for the Pacific in 1920.[43]

The genesis of a new naval air station at Sewell's Point began with the passage of the August 1916 Naval Appropriations Bill, which created a Reserve Flying Corps and funded naval aviation facilities and aircraft. With war in the offing and the threat of U-boats on everyone's mind, the chief of naval operations asked in a letter of 5 February 1917 for the "immediate establishment" of coastal air patrols by dirigibles and seaplanes at eight locations along the eastern seaboard (including Hampton Roads). The Joint Army and Navy Board on Aeronautic Cognizance rapidly agreed and established panels for in-depth study. The Atlantic Coast Panel (headed by an Army flyer and including Navy Lieutenants E. F. Johnson, John H. Towers, and Patrick N. L. Bellinger) recommended ten sites for development for Navy airships, and Hampton Roads would be shouldering additional responsibilities for Navy patrol aircraft and training.[44]

Rather than wait for the new airfields before starting the time-consuming task of aviator training, Reserve Flying Corps funds were used to bring eight private airfields under naval jurisdiction for training. One of these fields, the Curtiss Atlantic Coast Aeronautical Station at Newport News, was opened for reserve naval aviator training by the Curtiss Exhibition Company by 4 May.[45]

On 19 May 1917, fifteen naval reservists (primarily from Harvard) and two ensigns under the command of Lt. Henry B. Cecil arrived at Newport News to be trained by Curtiss civilian instructors. After ground courses, flying instruction began on 23 June with F-boat-type seaplanes and JN-4 land planes. Three N-9 seaplanes and one further F-boat were received and assembled by the students. Several of the students already had flying hours under their belts, and between flying lessons Lieutenant Cecil had the group help with preparations at the airfield under construction at Sewell's Point. Ensigns C. S. Reid and K. MacLeish

Instructors of the signal school at the training station June 1918. *Hampton Roads Naval Museum*

were added as instructors in August, and Cecil led the unit to their new base at Sewell's Point on 28 August.[46]

In October, Lt. Edward O. McDonnell replaced Cecil, and the nucleus of five officers, eighteen students, and twenty mechanics was formally designated as a naval air detachment. The detachment staked seven sea planes in the man-made exposition lagoon and erected six canvas hangars for maintenance. Later that month, additional personnel transferred from the naval air station at Squantum, Massachusetts, practically doubling the size of the command. Two days after forty-two aviation midshipmen from the Massachusetts Institute of Technology reported for advanced training on 28 November, Lt. Patrick N. L. Bellinger reported to head the Norfolk naval air detachment.[47] At the time, the detachment included thirty officers, ninety students, and several hundred enlisted personnel, and the base consisted of a machine shop, enlisted barracks, storage buildings, four small boats, three seaplane hangars, eleven tent hangars, twenty-one seaplanes, and a two-hundred-foot runway.[48]

The first class of student aviators trained during the severe winter of 1917–18, and Bellinger, brimming with initiative, found it a demanding time of stress and hard work. Seaplane operations were frequently curtailed because of ice in Willoughby Bay, and flying conditions in open cockpits and maintenance in the open demanded the most from the small band of motivated airmen. A normal student aviator syllabus included five to ten hours in the air with an instructor and from twenty-five to forty hours of solo flying before the student became eligible for a commission.[49]

In January 1918, Bellinger began a school for aviation mechanics, and in that same month, the Navy relocated the Experimental and Test Department from Pensacola to Hampton Roads. With the use of R-9 and R-6 seaplanes, aerial experiments were conducted with bombs, landing lights, wireless radio, seaplane hull forms, and machine guns. Although the naval aviation experimental mission was later transferred to Anacostia and then Patuxent, a small experimental division continued at Hampton Roads through the 1920s, where tests of aircraft carrier landing systems, deck lighting, radio, and aircraft for aircraft carrier operations were carried out.[50]

Naval Air Station Hampton Roads was officially commissioned on 27 August 1918 with Bellinger (now a lieutenant commander) in command. Bellinger reveled in his newfound freedom of action and attacked his assignment with energy and verve. Many of the first improvements at the base bore his mark, including the removal of the archway over the lagoon's entrance (to eliminate the hazard to the wingtips of taxiing seaplanes) and the creation of the new main airfield on reclaimed land immediately east of the lagoon, which he named Chambers Field, for Capt. Washington Irving Chambers.

Bellinger took a hands-on approach to planning schedules and priorities for each of the three missions assigned to the air station (experimental testing, aviation training, and wartime antisubmarine patrols), and much of the air station staff would be engaged in all three missions. Preliminary and advanced instruction was given to pilots in seaplanes, dirigibles, and kite balloons, and by war's end, 668 aviators (including thirty-two lighter-than-air pilots) and several thousand mechanics had been trained at Norfolk. By 11 November 1918 the base's complement had reached 167 officers, 1,227 men, and sixty-five seaplanes.[51]

Anti-U-boat patrols flown from Norfolk extended far along the coast, using rest and refueling sites at Chincoteague Island, Roanoke Island, and Morehead City. An experimental radio station was established at Fisherman's Island near Cape Charles to support these patrols.[52]

Patrick N. L. Bellinger (Naval Aviator No. 8) reported to head the Norfolk naval air detachment in November 1917 and assumed duty as the first commanding officer of Hampton Roads Naval Air Station in 1918. He returned to command the station again in 1938, and was named Commander, Naval Air Force, Atlantic (COMNAVAIRLANT) in Norfolk as a rear admiral in 1943. *Hampton Roads Naval Museum*

Naval aviation's outstanding technical product of the war was the long-distance flying boat. Two primary designs saw extensive service at Norfolk: the Curtiss HS-2 (biplane flying boat with a single pusher propeller and crew of three), and the Curtiss F5L (twin-engine flying boat with a crew of four). The larger Curtiss NC-type flying boat joined the station by war's end.

A typical day of patrolling consisted of three missions. Two HS–2 seaplanes would depart a few minutes before dawn for a four-hour patrol north to Chincoteague, and two would fly south to Morehead City, where they would receive gas and oil and return in the afternoon to Hampton Roads. At about 1000, two F5L seaplanes would depart on distant patrol, returning about 1500 in the afternoon. If daylight remained, two HS-2s patrolled until dark. Position reports were radioed every ten minutes to Fisherman's Island.[53]

On 16 November 1918, regular aerial mail service between Hampton Roads and Naval Air Station, Anacostia, became an important new mission for the naval air station. Every day one plane flew each way; one-way service averaged two and a half hours.[54] Although this service generally ran smoothly and provided excellent flying experience for young pilots, some days inevitably proved more challenging than others, as reported in this citation from the director of naval aviation's weekly report of 12 February 1919:

> Ensign A. W. Gorton flying a seaplane and mail arrived at the mouth of the Potomac River when the throttle rod running to the gravity tank broke. After attempting several remedies . . . the pilot ascended to the upper wind of the seaplane and laid on the top, manipulating the throttle control with one hand. At one time, his foot became fouled with the radio generator propeller, injuring his foot quite severely, and another time he was forced to clutch at the radiator cap, which gave way, spraying his face with hot water. The second pilot flew all the way to Washington DC with Ensign Gorton on the top of the plane although forced to land several times because of his releasing his hold on the throttle to save himself.[55]

The naval air station grew steadily, with the addition of new facilities (including a large dirigible hangar) and personnel, which by June 1919 had increased to more than a thousand men. An area southeast of the flying field was filled in, and several hangars and buildings were constructed for the industrial and aviation repair section of the station. In August 1921 a new high-technology AGA beacon began operations, with six thousand candlepower, eighteen flashes per minute, and a previously unheard optical range of twenty miles.[56]

NAS Hampton Roads saw several "firsts" during this period, partly because of its experimental mission. On 7 March 1919, Lt. (jg) F. M. Johnson launched an N-9 land plane from the deck of a motorboat doing almost fifty knots to test the feasibility of using U.S. Navy attack planes against German submarine pens. On 26 April 1919 a world flying endurance record of twenty hours and nineteen minutes and 1,250 miles was set by a F5L flying boat. A year later, the first successful test of a gyrostabilized automatic pilot system was conducted with another F5L seaplane, and on 6 July 1920, an F5L was used to test a new radio compass on a record-setting 190-mile round-trip flight to the battleship *Ohio* (BB 12) at sea.[57]

In March 1919, Commander Bellinger detached from Norfolk to participate in a historic transatlantic flight by a squadron of Navy NC flying boats. This first-ever crossing

Curtiss HS-2L patrol seaplane operating in the air station boat basin, circa 1918. *Naval Historical Foundation*

was made by flying boat *NC-4* in May 1919 with airborne radio compasses developed at NAS Hampton Roads. Bellinger piloted sister ship *NC-1,* but was forced down in mid-ocean and never completed the attempt. Bellinger later returned to command the Norfolk Naval Air Station in June 1938 after commanding aircraft carriers *Ranger* and *Langley.*[58]

In 1902, the Navy established a "naval district" concept to regionally administer Navy yards and stations and named three naval districts for the Atlantic, Gulf, and Pacific coasts. On 7 May 1903, the secretary of the Navy rewrote this structure and established thirteen naval districts; the new Fifth Naval District included southeastern Virginia. This new naval district designation was of little real significance in Hampton Roads because the Norfolk Navy Yard commandant performed naval district duties without additional staff. In time of war, however, it was planned that the posts of district commandant and yard commandant would separate, and as war approached, Rear Adm. Walter McLean, commandant of the Navy yard, formally reported to the chief of naval operations for additional duty as "Commandant, Fifth Naval District." In his letter to the CNO dated 8 January 1917, Admiral McLean listed the Navy yard, the naval ammunition depot at St. Julien's Creek, the naval hospital at Portsmouth, and the naval training station at St. Helena as commands within the naval district.[59]

J. H. McCuen, McLean's chief clerk, went to Washington to align funding for district offices and subsequently rented four rooms on the seventh floor of the Citizens National Bank Building in downtown Norfolk to accommodate the commandant, his staff, and clerks. The district headquarters opened on 1 February 1917 with a staff of two officers and a single chief clerk. Within two months, five more officers had been added.

The two posts of Navy yard commandant and naval district commandant were not formally divided until January 1918, when Navy Secretary Daniels established the new Naval Operating Base, Hampton Roads. McLean was relieved of his Navy yard duties by Rear Adm. Augustus F. Fechteler, but he continued as commandant of the Fifth Naval District and assumed concurrent duties as commandant of the new Naval Operating Base, Hampton Roads, as directed by Daniels. "[NOB] shall consist of the naval training station," according to General Order No. 363, "the naval air station, the naval submarine station, the naval supply station, the naval hospital, and such other naval activities as may be established there." The Fifth Naval District headquarters moved to NOB from downtown Norfolk on 15 June 1918.[60]

The intertwined nature of the relationship between the commands of the Fifth Naval District and NOB was unique among naval districts. General Order No. 363 described "the same general relations between the commandant of the naval operating base and the various organizations contained in his commands that exist between a division commander afloat and the vessels of his division," but, as the later history of the Fifth Naval District recounts, "due to the fact that the Naval Operating Base was nothing more than a series of separate commands in geographic proximity to each other, an urgent need never arose for a separate commander for the Base."[61]

Admiral Fechteler, in turn, left command of the Navy yard and relieved Admiral McLean in April 1919. Fechteler wanted to stay active and convinced his aide to frequently play tennis with him. Tragically, following one of those exercise periods on a humid summer day, he suffered a stroke and died on 26 May 1921.[62]

The final piece of the puzzle for Dillingham, as he capstoned his NOB construction efforts in 1919, was the construction of new supply warehouses. Large fleet warehouses were planned for the west end of the base on reclaimed land, and work was phased to start only after the land was ready.

Beginning in 1818, a Navy purser was assigned to the Gosport yard to assume the supply, victualing, and warehousing functions from the naval agent. In 1870, a separate U.S. Navy Pay Corps was established, and in 1913, Pay Director Thomas H. Hicks designed the first standard Navy stock catalog for ordering efficiency, and then he pioneered the matching of storehouse organization with the same sequencing found in the supply catalog at the Norfolk Navy Yard. Later, as a rear admiral, Hicks became a strong voice for moving the supply warehousing for Norfolk that traditionally had been at the Navy yard to large modern fleet warehouses at Sewell's Point that would have ready access to rail-serviced piers.[63]

Led by Pay Director Ramsey, a Fifth Naval District Supply Department was opened in 1917 to coordinate warehousing matters in Hampton Roads, and the first large Navy warehouse (sixty thousand square feet) and a wharf were leased on Front Street in Norfolk on 14 April 1917. By December 1918, Dillingham had completed the first permanent storehouse at NOB, and on 1 March 1919 the naval supply station was formally commissioned, with Cdr. E. H. Van Patten designated as officer in charge. Ten major supply storage buildings were planned, including two matching six-story warehouses of 360,000 square feet with rail connections to two covered piers (1,400 feet in length and 125 feet in width). By its first anniversary, the station could boast 1,896,000 square feet of warehouse space.[64]

Before the war, fueling and coaling were accomplished from bunker facilities at the Naval Fuel Depot, Yorktown. During the war, the naval supply station at Hampton Roads took control of additional government-owned fuel depots on Craney Island and gradually shifted primary fleet fueling there, although some gasoline and kerosene fueling came from St. Helena wharves.[65] During the war, the naval supply station employed twenty-five hundred employees, who serviced an average of seven ships per day, with thirty-nine troop transports and several hundred other Naval Overseas Transportation Service (NOTS) vessels based in Hampton Roads. Many remember that the doughboys were sent off with great fanfare at Newport News with bands, banners, and piers teaming with cheering family members. Coordinated by the NOTS office in Norfolk, convoys of twenty to forty-two ships were sent out of Hampton Roads every eight days for Europe.[66]

The explosive wartime surge in the federal and military presence in Hampton Roads brought with it immense difficulties for communities that were not at all ready to cope. In quick order, Hampton Roads was faced with innumerable challenges to its comfortable lifestyle, brought on by rapid spikes in demands for labor, transportation, and utilities.

With many entering military service and with many more already lured from Hampton Roads to work for northern war industries, Tidewater faced both immediate labor problems and wartime burdens. The Navy's demands for construction and shipyard work increased the region's employment requirements and attracted a great influx of labor from distant locales. Norfolk's population shot from an estimated one hundred two thousand in 1916 to one hundred fifty thousand by 1918, a statistic even more impressive when compared with Norfolk's 1910 official population of sixty-seven thousand. With this doubling of population in eight years, Norfolk faced extraordinary housing problems, strained local supply sources, smothered public utilities, and overwhelmed transportation, police, fire, and school infrastructure.[67] Multiple families crowded together in older homes, and others sought shelter in abandoned trolleys, in makeshift camps, or on distant farms. Although the federal government belatedly financed new housing developments like Cradock and Truxtun near Portsmouth and Glenwood near the NOB, Norfolk saw little immediate relief during the war years.[68]

Fearing that continued strains on Norfolk's infrastructure could negatively affect the war effort, the Navy tried to proactively consult on transportation improvements, utilities sharing, and water usage. Admiral Dillingham, desperate to keep construction flowing at NOB, had the Virginian freight line add passenger trains from Norfolk to NOB and pressed the

Norfolk and Portsmouth Ferry Company to institute a steamer line from Norfolk to the base.[69]

Already beset by severe strains on its economy, Norfolk was struck by one of the worst fires in its history on New Year's Day 1918, which destroyed four major buildings along Granby Street. "Never in the history of Norfolk has a fire presented such serious possibilities or been so heroically fought," said the fire chief. The Navy plunged in to assist, and the newspapers were filled with wire photos of many sailors aiding hard-pressed firefighters.[70]

Tidewater's social framework was also under severe stress as it sought a sense of equilibrium in the shadow of massive wartime expansion. The strain of war, the deficiencies in transportation, the lack of ready entertainment venues, and the profiteering by some merchants at the expense of navy personnel placed Tidewater in the worst possible light for legions of officers and sailors. Many long-term Tidewater residents looked upon the huge influx of bluejackets with suspicion, and it was easy to blame the sailor for the broad deterioration in local lifestyle. Although many prospered with increased federal spending, most citizens were also faced with a higher cost of living, a rising crime rate, widespread shortages, and general havoc.

Evidence of civic stress could be seen everywhere. Poor sailor-civilian relationships in Norfolk helped Halloween celebrations in 1918 to degenerate into a series of downtown disorders in which a policeman was killed. Two months later on New Year's Eve, downtown rioting resulted in smashed store windows and the death of a sailor. Policing was strengthened, and the Navy established a shore patrol for the first time in its history to patrol downtown Norfolk streets.[71]

Many across Tidewater actively sought means to support service members, mostly in the name of patriotism and national service. The War Camp Community Service, the Red Cross, and the YMCA all raised funds and provided consistent entertainment for sailors and Marines. The Liberty and Red Circle theaters opened exclusively as military movie houses, and many Hampton Roads families welcomed navymen into their homes. Recruits from the new training station at NOB kept spirits high by performing weekly parades to encourage recruiting.[72]

Although Tidewater would inevitably weather nearly all of the extreme difficulties brought on by wartime necessity, the Navy's priorities would profoundly reshape the region and forever alter its way of life. The war provided an impetus for

Industrial production at Newport News Shipbuilding and Dry Dock Company proceeded at an energetic clip in the years around World War I. Battleships were launched regularly including *Delaware* (1909), *Texas* (1912), *Pennsylvania* (1915), *Mississippi* (1917), *Maryland* (1920) (shown here), and *West Virginia* (1921); twenty-five destroyers were also constructed. *Naval Historical Center*

civic reorganization and revitalization that no mere planning cycle could have orchestrated.

The nation's first thoughts as it plunged into the Great War during the spring of 1917 were of U-boats. With the war locked in the morass of trench warfare and the German High Seas Fleet blockaded in its ports by the Royal Navy, Germany saw U-boats as its only means of tipping the war in its favor. Beginning on 1 February 1917, the declaration of unrestricted German submarine warfare would nearly bring England to its knees, and 1917 would see more than 4 million tons of Allied shipping sunk by U-boats.[73]

In America, the unrestricted U-boat campaign had been the final straw that had turned Wilson's impassioned neutrality into a declaration of war. The threat of U-boats was on Cdr. Joseph K. Taussig's mind as he began antisubmarine patrols in the Chesapeake Bay and Hampton Roads about 2 April 1917. Taussig's Destroyer Division Eight operated from "Base 2," a fleet anchorage on the York River protected by a net screen across the river at Carmine's Wharf, but almost immediately was ordered to the European theater. Sailing at daybreak on 14 April with destroyers *Wadsworth* (DD-60), *Wainwright* (DD-62), *Davis* (DD-65), *Porter* (DD-69), *Conyngham* (DD-58), and *McDougal* (DD-54), Taussig's division would be the first American naval force to enter the war when it arrived at Queenstown, Ireland, on 4 May. Asked when he would be ready for duty after a difficult, storm-tossed transit, Taussig replied with the now famous words, "We are ready now, sir." Thirty-four American destroyers would ultimately be sent to Queenstown, and Taussig would be awarded a Distinguished Service Medal for his World War I service.[74]

Hampton Roads's first efforts for defense were aimed at U-boats. An antisubmarine net, installed in February 1917 between Fort Monroe and Fort Wool, closed the harbor from dusk to dawn and was guarded by a small patrol boat at a gate five hundred feet wide. A second line of nets ran from Cape Henry to Fisherman's Island to seal the entrance to the Chesapeake Bay. This net was in place by April 1917 but was prone to damage from fishing boats and currents, and a second net was strung from Fisherman's Island to the Tail of the Horseshoe Shoal and then to Lynnhaven Beach by September 1918.[75]

Under Fifth Naval District coordination, sea patrols were established to monitor the Chesapeake entrance. One boat patrolled outside Cape Henry, a second patrolled along the Chesapeake net, and a third guard boat patrolled inside the net line. These boats challenged and boarded all neutral vessels (in bad weather this inspection was held at Lynnhaven Roads, a frequent cause of complaint). A naval section base was set up at Cape Charles to support Naval Local Defense Forces that consisted of 170 torpedo boats, submarine chasers, state fisheries boats, converted yachts, and pleasure craft. Fifteen hundred naval mines were available for defense and held in storage at the NOB but were never planted. By the beginning of 1918, a small detachment of older submarines began regular defensive ASW patrols from Hampton Roads.[76]

After British successes with the defense of their great Scapa Flow base, pioneering experiments were performed with new magnetic loops and galvanometers that could be used in a shipping channel to alert defense forces to the approach of a submarine. Cape Henry was the scene of some of the first naval underwater hydrophone experiments in 1918, which attempted to triangulate the position of approaching submarines from propeller sounds picked up by multiple hydrophones on underwater tripods secured to the ocean bottom.[77]

Hampton Roads was already teaming with wartime shipping by the time of America's entry into the war. Shipping tonnage from Hampton Roads had doubled in 1915 and doubled again in 1916. To better control the heavier demands on shipping in Hampton Roads, the Navy created the post of Captain of the Port in 1917 and assigned Capt. J. G. Ballinger to those responsibilities. Ballinger coordinated all naval and commercial traffic, even to the point of synchronizing arrivals and departures with other ports along the East Coast.[78]

The Fifth Naval District established a communications department in April 1917, and five radio compass stations for offshore navigation were established at Hog Island, Virginia; Virginia Beach; Poplar Branch, North Carolina; Cape Hatteras; and Cape Lookout. The communications department also worked with the Department of Justice in "dismantling all unauthorized and amateur radio stations and the sealing of the apparatus," and taking over the Marconi Radio Station in Virginia Beach. Long-distance trunk telephone lines appeared from district headquarters to Washington, Fort Monroe, Cape Henry, and the coal piers, and a wartime telegraph office opened, with wires to Washington, the Western Union office in Norfolk, Radio Station Virginia Beach, the Weather Bureau at Cape Henry, and the Coast Guard.[79]

No German U-boat penetrated the Chesapeake defenses during the war, but in mid-1918, German U-boats deployed a total of fifty-seven mines between Fire Island, New York, and North Carolina in groups of six or seven, including a concentration of mines at the Chesapeake entrance laid by *U-151*. Interestingly, *U-151* intercepted the Norwegian freighter

Vindeggen off Cape Hatteras and substituted her cargo of copper ingots—in short supply in Germany—for the submarine's own iron ballast before sailing home, being careful not to harm any passengers.[80]

Despite the urging of the Royal Navy, elements of the main American battle fleet did not immediately deploy to Europe but lay anchored in Hampton Roads, New York, and Boston during the first months of the war. There was considerable debate concerning the fleet's best use; the chief of naval operations favored a plan to keep the battle line concentrated on the East Coast for defense in the event of a British collapse. Navy concerns might have been valid, as proved by a secret German plan discovered after the war. According to historian Robert Massie, if the Germans had been successful in forcing Britain out of the war, the German navy planned to cross the Atlantic, defeat the inferior American fleet off the East Coast, and then attack and occupy Norfolk, Hampton Roads, and Newport News as a springboard for further attacks up the Atlantic seaboard until America was forced to terms.[81]

When plans were eventually approved to send American battleships forward, it was the U-boat, not the German battle line, that finally forced America's hand. By the summer of 1917, the Royal Navy was desperately short of manpower for its many new destroyers built to counter U-boats and proposed that four American dreadnoughts sail to join the British Grand Fleet, allowing the transfer of the crews of five older British battleships to destroyers.

On 25 November 1917, Battleship Division Nine of the U.S. Atlantic Fleet—*New York* (BB-34), *Wyoming* (BB-32), *Florida* (BB-30), and *Delaware* (BB-28) —weighed anchor in Hampton Roads, bound for Scapa Flow under the command of frequent Norfolk resident Rear Adm. Hugh Rodman. Battle flags snapped from every halyard, and clouds of black smoke belched from the stacks of these massive, broad-beamed dreadnoughts as they passed slowly in column to take their departure. Hundreds somberly viewed the battleships, silent and dark gray against the late-day sun as they maneuvered out toward Thimble Shoal. They were, as Winston Churchill descriptively wrote of the distinctive, powerful dreadnoughts of World War I: "gigantic castles of steel wending their way across the misty, shining sea, like giants bowed in anxious thought . . . and bearing with them . . . the safeguard of considerable affairs."[82]

The *New York* boasted the fleet's largest guns (14-inch) and thickest armor, but *Delaware* was remembered fondly throughout Tidewater as a Newport News–built battleship. The American battle line contributed little, however, to Allied efforts because the Americans fared poorly at gunnery and readiness in comparison with crack British crews. On 14 July 1918, *Arkansas* (BB-33), a member of Battleship Division Seven in Hampton Roads, sailed to relieve *Delaware,* while *Nevada* (BB-36) joined the Hampton Roads battleships *Oklahoma* (BB-37) and *Utah* (BB-31) to protect American troop convoys in European waters.[83]

On 1 January 1917 the St. Julien's Creek naval magazine was redesignated as a naval ammunition depot and on 1 July 1918 was named an independent command. "St. J's" had its start in 1895 when Congress appropriated $75,000 to remove ammunition stored on Craney Island and Fort Norfolk and move it to a forty-eight-acre site, purchased from Edward M. Watts, at the mouth of St. Julien's Creek, four miles south of the Navy yard. By 1897, the site boasted five magazines, two wharf houses, and two hundred-foot loading wharfs.[84]

The St. Julien's Creek naval magazine was formally established in 1898 as a department of the Navy yard. The magazine began to stockpile projectiles in 1907, and in 1909, a bag plant was opened to produce powder charge bags for large naval guns. Ordnance was moved around the site on man-powered rail carts. By 1918, the magazine had expanded to a total of 250 acres and held a population of six officers and six hundred civilians at the main depot and three officers and twelve hundred civilians and sailors at a new mine plant.[85]

Between October 1917 and November 1918 about one hundred thousand Mark VI naval mines were constructed at St. Julien's Creek (sometimes at the rate of a thousand per day) in one of the most celebrated World War I stories of Tidewater. A twenty-two-building assembly line was needed to construct the mines, which consisted of black ball casings about three feet in diameter atop a two-foot-square anchor box with a glass float suspended above the mine, holding a thin copper wire trigger. High explosive was first melted in steam kettles to about the consistency of hasty pudding, and this was drawn off and poured into waiting mine spheres, amounting to about three hundred pounds of TNT for each mine. A mechanical conveyor then slowly carried the mines to the end of a nearby pier, by which time they would be cool enough to load onto a fleet of twenty-four Great Lakes steamers used as mine transports. Beginning in February 1918, two or three of these ships sailed each week for Scotland. There, Capt. Reginald G. Belknap (Commander, Mine Squadron One) transferred the mines onto the vintage cruisers *San Francisco* and *Baltimore* and eight other ships that had been converted into minelayers. Their destination was the open ocean gap between Scotland

Beginning in June 1918, a combined U.S. Navy and Royal Navy force laid the extensive "North Sea Mine Barrage" to help block German U-boats from the Atlantic Ocean. Taking up stations line abreast in the stormy North Sea, the combined force of minelayers deployed a mine every 11.5 seconds for a total of 4,000 mines in the first run. Thirteen excursions for the American squadron and eleven missions by the British by October 1918 seeded a total of 70,117 mines (56,571 by the American squadron); the great majority had been manufactured in Hampton Roads. *Hampton Roads Naval Museum*

and Norway, where a 240-mile-long by 35-mile-wide minefield was to be planted to stop U-boats from escaping into the Atlantic Ocean.[86]

Across thirteen months of intense operations at the mine plant, St. Julien sailors handled 25 million pounds of explosives without a single significant accident. The threat of an accidental explosion was so great, however, that the operation was moved to a more rural location with the establishment of the Yorktown Navy Mine Depot in April 1918.[87]

As it had done for decades, the Norfolk Navy Yard rapidly escalated its industrial output to match wartime requirements. Anticipating the need, congressional appropriations in 1916 included extra funds to construct many new shops, rail facilities, wharves, and power plants and to begin the construction of dry docks. Later, between 1917 and 1920, seventy-five new structures were added to the yard. Much of this expansion was concentrated within in the "Schmoele Tract," directly south of Dry Dock No. 3 and where the Navy also prototyped a new "standard" navy yard layout to streamline the expansion of shipyards nationwide to meet wartime needs.[88]

Work on Dry Dock No. 4 was begun in January 1917 and completed on 1 April 1919 (King Albert and Queen Elizabeth of Belgium were on hand for the christening and the battleship *Wisconsin* was the first ship docked on 5 May 1919). The dock, which was 1,011 feet long, was the largest in the country and was specifically designed to handle the Navy's largest battleships. Dry Dock Nos. 6 and 7 (each 465 feet in length) were constructed with funds provided by the Fleet Emergency Corporation of the U.S. Shipping Board and completed on 31 October 1919.[89]

The yard was quick to ramp up to full production with the onset of war. Employment reached a peak in February 1919, with 11,234 workers (compared with 2,718 workers in June

Norfolk Navy Yard's brand-new Dry Dock No. 4 is shown to the right with battleship *Wisconsin* in May 1919. Battleship *Nevada* is to the left in Dry Dock No. 3. *Norfolk Naval Shipyard*

1914). For the first time, the yard hired women in large numbers to fill clerical positions. In parallel, the Navy opened its ranks to women for the first time in March 1917, creating the rating of Yeoman (F), or "Yeomanettes," and training women to serve as typists, radio electricians, stenographers, bookkeepers, storekeepers, and drivers. More than eight hundred Yeomanettes reported to the Navy yard, some to be trained for duty at NOB, some to cover the yard's three shifts. When the war ended, many continued at the yard as part of the civilian workforce.[90]

The Navy's crucial need for ASW escorts drove the first wartime ship construction orders received by the yard. In July 1917, Secretary Daniels approved a robust building program to bring the Navy's destroyer total to 273, augmented with hundreds of additional submarine chasers. The first of the yard's twenty-one wooden submarine chasers (SC-116/136) was rapidly commissioned on 4 October 1917; four destroyers were also built: *Craven* (DD-70), which became HMS *Lewes* in 1940, *Hulbert* (DD-342), *Noa* (DD-343), and *William B. Preston* (DD-344). Many of the wildest camouflage designs seen during the war had their source at the Navy yard, where detailed experiments were held to find the best designs of camouflage that would disorient German U-boat targeting by distorting appearance or disguising range, course, and speed. With its new dry docks in place, Norfolk Navy Yard also won a construction contract for battleship *North Carolina* (BB-52), whose keel was laid in January 1920.[91]

In 1915, before the United States entered the war, the yard became the reluctant host of *Kronprinz Wilhelm* and *Prinz Eitel Friedrich,* two German liners that had been converted into commerce raiders. Although they had come to Hampton Roads for repairs and coal, when units of the Royal Navy appeared off the capes, the German captains wisely avoided battle by choosing internment for the war's duration. The Germans became affable "neighbors" of the yard's workforce before war was declared and fostered a cooperative air by using scrap materials to construct a typical German village (named "Eitel Wilhelm") that attracted many visitors. Three

The Navy established the Yeoman (F) rating for women in 1917 to bring women into active service for the first time. These "Yeomanettes," posing in front of the shipyard wall in Portsmouth, were among the first to be assigned clerical, supply, and other administrative jobs, working in all three shifts at the yard. *Norfolk Naval Shipyard*

similarly interned German merchant vessels—the *Bulgaria, Rhein,* and *Neckar*—were converted at the yard to transport American forces to Europe in 1917.[92]

During World War I, the naval hospital in Portsmouth expanded to fill wartime needs by erecting many temporary wooden buildings across the site. First to be built were eight new pavilion wards of forty beds built in a circle at the rear of the hospital. Six semipermanent bungalows of twenty-four beds came next, and then twenty bungalows at the northwest corner of the grounds as a contagious unit. The hospital had undergone extensive remodeling between 1907 and 1910, in which new wings were added and the main building of the old hospital was renovated.[93]

The Navy's first formal course of instruction for the Hospital Corps was opened at the naval hospital in August 1902. The school's three-month studies covered nursing, military requirements, anatomy, bandaging, first aid, elementary hygiene, clerical skills, and pharmacy. In 1917, the school moved to the NOB training station but returned to the hospital in 1921.[94]

Although the hospital had expanded to handle expected war casualties and the huge wartime influx of military personnel in Norfolk, nothing would fully prepare it for the so-called Spanish flu, or influenza, that swept the country beginning in August 1918. By the time it had run its course, the pandemic would claim an appalling six hundred thousand lives across America.

The ravaging epidemic was aided in its spread by the great number of people drawn into military service, who generally lived in confined spaces and were frequently transported across national boundaries. As early as January 1918, signs of flu surfaced aboard Navy ships; cruiser *Minneapolis* reported an outbreak while moored in Philadelphia. Within a month, the Bureau of Medicine and Surgery received its first flu reports from ships and bases in Hampton Roads. After subsiding during the summer months, new reports surfaced in August of up to sixty sailors sick in Boston. Shortly afterward, on 13 September 1918, influenza appeared at the NOB training station and three days later at the St. Helena receiving ship.[95]

By October, the naval hospital was caught in the grip of an overwhelming influx of admissions, taxing a staff of sixty

Unusual as it is in the Virginia Tidewater, snow brings its own hush to a normally vibrant waterfront. *U.S. Navy*

The guided missile destroyer *Ramage* as she pulls pierside in Norfolk in 2002 following a deployment in support of Operation Enduring Freedom in the Indian Ocean. *U.S. Navy*

The "Tophatters" of VF-14 in Oceana can trace their history to biplane fighters that flew from carriers *Langley* (CV-1), *Saratoga* (CV-3), and *Ranger* (CV-4). Here, an F-14 flown by VF-14 trains near North Bay. *Courtesy Tom Toomey*

The nuclear-powered aircraft carrier *George Washington* steams seaward past Cape Henry light. *U.S. Navy*

Norfolk-based guided missile destroyer *Donald Cook* launches a Tomahawk Land Attack Missile toward Iraq during the initial stages of Operation Iraqi Freedom on 21 March 2003. *U.S. Navy*

The view seaward from Virginia Beach. *U.S. Navy*

The Norfolk-based guided missile cruiser *Vella Gulf* maneuvering at sea. *U.S. Navy*

Norfolk has been the home to helicopter squadrons since 1952. Here, eight MH-60S Nighthawk helicopters assigned to the "Chargers" of Helicopter Combat Support Squadron Six (HC-6) line up in formation to land at the Naval Station in 2004. *U.S. Navy*

Nuclear-powered aircraft carrier *George Washington* returns from a deployment to the Middle East in 2002 to an appreciative and heartfelt Hampton Roads welcome. *U.S. Navy*

An F/A-18 Hornet assigned to Carrier Air Wing Seven launches from the flight deck of nuclear-powered aircraft carrier *George Washington* in operations off the Virginia Capes in 2003. *U.S. Navy*

Battleship *Iowa* suffered a catastrophic explosion in the center gun of number two turret on 19 April 1989 causing the death of forty-seven crew members. Across Norfolk there was a great outpouring of public sympathy for *Iowa* sailors and their families, and Iowa Point was designated at the naval base as a site of remembrance that today also serves as a memorial site for other Hampton Roads sailors who have died in the service of their country, such as those aboard destroyer *Cole*. *BRL pictures*

The transom over the entranceway to the Mariner's Museum in Newport News reflects the distinctive naval influence that percolates through the Virginia Tidewater. *BRL pictures*

Friends and family bid farewell to those aboard guided missile destroyer *Oscar Austin* in December 2002 as she sails for a six-month overseas deployment. *U.S. Navy*

The nuclear-powered aircraft carrier *Ronald Reagan* outbound in Thimble Shoals Channel during a late afternoon in September 2003. *U.S. Navy*

From the days of sail, the voyage up the Elizabeth River to Norfolk Naval Shipyard has challenged the best captains, masters, and navigators. The transit today is no less ticklish as nuclear-powered aircraft carrier *Harry S Truman* demonstrates in 2003. *U.S. Navy*

Newport News Shipbuilding has built all of the nuclear-powered aircraft carriers for the Navy including *Harry S Truman* shown departing from the Naval Station's Pier 14 with her crew ringing the deck. The shipyard has long had a saying, reputed to have been said by its founder, Collis Potter Huntington: "We shall build good ships here; at a profit if we can, at a loss if we must: but always good ships." *U.S. Navy*

Much of the Navy's work in Tidewater actually takes place in the extensive naval operating areas off the Virginia Capes where warfare skills and operating procedures are tested and honed. Here, the guided missile cruiser *Vella Gulf* escorts nuclear aircraft carrier *George Washington*. *U.S. Navy*

F/A-18 Hornets of Strike Fighter Squadron 81 approach the Virginia Beach ocean front in formation in December 2002. *U.S. Navy*

The breathtaking sight of battleship *Wisconsin,* looming majestically between buildings along Plume Street, surprises many a visitor to Norfolk's downtown. *BRL pictures*

The Comte de Grasse could have viewed the majestic battle lines of French and British warships as they formed for the climactic Battle of the Virginia Capes from this lookout near Cape Henry, just as this commemorative statue of the great French Navy admiral portrays. *BRL pictures*

An F-14 fighter in the "break" over NAS Oceana. *Courtesy Tom Toomey*

An E-2C Hawkeye assigned to the "Bluetails" of Carrier Airborne Early Warning Squadron 121 positions for launch from the flight deck of nuclear-powered aircraft carrier *George Washington. U.S. Navy*

Norfolk-based Aegis destroyer *Winston S. Churchill* at high speed exemplifies for many the excitement and esprit de corps of the modern naval service. *U.S. Navy*

SEALs practice fast-roping from an MH-53 “Pave Low” helicopter during a Maritime Interception Operation (MIO) training exercise. *U.S. Navy*

On the ship's mess decks aboard guided missile destroyer *Cole* there are stars engraved into the deck in a "Hall of Heroes" where each star represents a fallen sailor and shipmate killed in the 12 October 2000 terrorist attack on the ship in the port city of Aden, Yemen. *U.S. Navy*

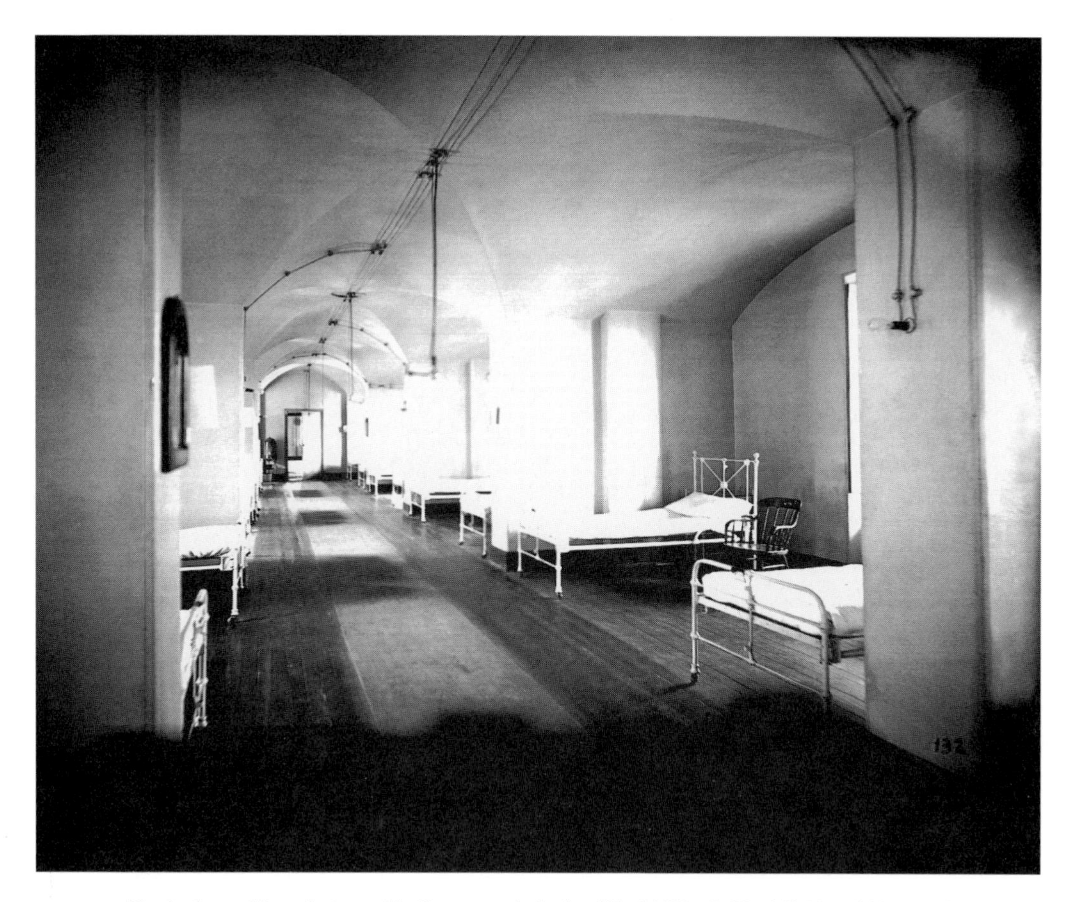

Typical naval hospital ward in Portsmouth during World War I. *Norfolk Naval Shipyard*

officers and eighty nurses that had already been depleted by overseas deployments. A total of 2,257 navy men would be admitted to the hospital that month, the most patients ever seen by the hospital. Every bed was full, and more people crowded in. The disease typically would start with a worsening cough and then deteriorate into pneumonia, with raging fevers and delirium. No medicine or vaccine could combat it, and although most people in Tidewater would wear white protective masks, there was little that could be done to protect against infection.[96]

Rear Adm. Kent Melhorn, Medical Corps, relates a story that the commanding officer of the naval hospital in Portsmouth, Capt. Leckinski Spratling, received a telephone call from the commandant of the Navy yard. "What's the most important thing we can do to be prepared for this epidemic?" Captain Spratling's reply was, "Build coffins."[97]

Fortuitously, in December 1917 a new hospital had been completed at NOB in a grove of tall loblolly pines near the Pine Beach Hotel. It consisted of an administration building and a surgical pavilion with adjoining wards, quarters, barracks, and a capacity of 250 beds. But it, too, quickly became overcome with the sick and reached a daily peak of 880 cases by mid-October.

By early November 1918, the pandemic began to miraculously slip away as rapidly and mysteriously as it had come, and daily routine began anew. By the time the pandemic was over, the disease had inflicted an estimated forty percent of the Navy. The naval hospital reported a final toll of 244 dead and more than four thousand admitted; 175 more died at NOB.[98]

When the armistice was signed to end World War I, the fourteen thousand people of the NOB already exceeded the populations of several nearby cities. But its city-sized infrastructure of everything from buildings and houses to water lines and parks had come as no mere accident of civic growth; it ws through the consistent stewardship of one man, Admiral Dillingham. So great was the impact of the new NOB that it was said, "nothing of greater importance had come into the life of Norfolk since it was established as a town 230 years earlier." Admiral Dillingham was awarded the Navy Cross for his

Temporary hospital buildings with wooden floors and canvas tenting were established on the naval hospital grounds to increase hospital capacity during World War I. This photo was dated 26 September 1918. *Norfolk Naval Shipyard*

efforts and, after his retirement from naval service, he was quickly named Norfolk's Director of Public Safety, a capacity in which he oversaw policing and firefighting. Dillingham was an active director, frequently explaining policies and plans in the local press while he continued to be a trusted liaison with the Navy, easing the burdens as Norfolk adjusted to the now-larger naval presence.[99]

When the war began, Norfolk still broadly considered itself a small southern town with what historian Thomas Parrimore described as a "lingering river-town perspective"—and there lay the seeds for the increasingly strained relations between navy men and Tidewater citizens that would last for generations. The *Ledger-Dispatch* ran an editorial in 1918 that said, "We hear on all sides that enlisted men in particular dislike Norfolk . . . the cause most frequently given is discrimination against men in uniform . . . but if the men will analyze their feelings they will find that they 'dislike Norfolk' simply because there is not enough for them to do, not enough amusement, not enough excitement of various sorts . . . neither Norfolk nor any other community of like size can attempt or pretend to compete as an amusement center with the larger cities."[100]

In short, neither Tidewater's infrastructure nor its day-to-day sentiments were prepared for the huge Navy influx during the war. The region would be torn by the strains of complex outside forces, buried in tidal waves of unsought war workers and navy men, and thrown off balance by conflicting views of national service, patriotism, and local pride. As with all of the wars in which Norfolk participated, World War I was a defining milestone in shaping the region and its subsequent development. But no other war determined the character of Norfolk's future as assuredly as World War I.

In a sense, World War I marked the beginning of modern Norfolk. From a historic retrospective of almost a hundred years, the transformation was impressive, and it was similarly recognized at the time as an important milestone in the region's history, proved by the frequent use of the phrase "the New Norfolk" in the early 1920s. Tidewater's metamorpho-

Nurses at the naval hospital in Portsmouth circa 1914. *Naval Historical Foundation*

sis would produce a military-commercial center of national importance in which its long-time relationship with the Navy would become ever more prominent. The region would realize its dream of both attracting the Navy and using federal investment to boost industrialism (especially coal, oil, metals, and shipbuilding) and trade, and the Navy would grow to see Norfolk and Hampton Roads as not just one port of many, but as its premier concentration point on the Atlantic coast.

1925

As World War I ended, it left behind an unsettled, agitated relationship between Hampton Roads and the Navy. On one hand, the region was economically robust, stimulated by wartime investment and energy. On the other hand, all recognized that Norfolk would never return with complete satisfaction to the traditions and tempo of the pre-war years. The Navy had cleaved open the seams of Tidewater's daily life; had changed the alignment of streets and trolley lines; had overwhelmed local utilities; had forced its way into schools, public meetings, and newspaper editorials; and had spurred economic growth in various sectors, many of which were not self-sustaining.

Whipsawed by tremendous economic and social strains driven by wartime needs, Tidewater now faced a clouded and uncertain future guided neither by chart nor by comfort of prior experience. To prosper and grow, Tidewater's harmony with the Navy would have to find a new foundation amid widespread uncertainty about what this new naval array really meant.

There was only one certainty: Tidewater's relations with the Navy after World War I would never return to what they had been before, nor would they be the same as that experienced in the heat of wartime. Both Tidewater and the Navy would have to find a new and equitable fit for both parties, and all suspected that that would not happen overnight. Few realized, however, that finding that new "even keel" between the city and the Navy would take not months, but decades.

Tidewater approached the immediate postwar period brimming with optimism. The *Virginian-Pilot* began 1919 by editorializing the obvious, that the Navy was the link to the region's welfare: "1919 offers the chance of realizing our greatest dream, the winning of a proper share of the world's commerce. Military activities have already brought to this harbor a larger share of the world's traffic . . . the new year places continued prosperity within the reach of the city. . . ."[1] Unseen and unforecast, however, by those charting such a rosy future was the fact that the Navy would soon enter its own dramatic cycle of change. As Tidewater looked confidently down a wide road ahead in 1919, the Navy was turning left.

The 1919 Navy was vastly different from what it had been before the war and would change still further in the lively years of the 1920s. American submarines and mass-produced destroyers were on the rise, dreadnoughts were in decline, and a new capital warship, the aircraft carrier, was on Norfolk's building ways.[2]

The first jarring surprise to Hampton Roads's postwar glow was the Navy's sudden decision to reorganize its fleet. On 10 January 1919, Navy Secretary Josephus Daniels redesignated the Atlantic Fleet as the "United States Fleet" but continued to concentrate it in the Atlantic for maximum effectiveness. Within five months, however, the secretary reversed that decision (citing Japanese expansion and political pull from the West Coast) and established separate Atlantic and Pacific fleets of roughly equal size. Daniels tried to cushion the blow, calling Hampton Roads "the chief and only operating base on the Atlantic Coast and . . . we contemplate making it the very heart of the Navy."[3]

"Admiral's Row" and the State Houses along Dillingham Avenue in 1925. *Hampton Roads Naval Museum*

The destroyers and submarines for the new Pacific Fleet began to sail from Hampton Roads during the summer of 1919, and the most modern, oil-fired battleships left several months later (because of the relatively larger supplies of coal on the East Coast and oil on the West, only older, coal-driven battleships stayed behind). Caught off-guard, Hampton Roads could do little but watch with growing economic angst as each ship departed.[4]

Daniels's successor, Edwin Denby, would ultimately reverse policy and reestablish the United States Fleet with General Order 94 of 6 December 1922—the fleet was to be "stationed in both oceans but anchored in neither." But Denby's decision would come too late for Hampton Roads to recoup its ships. The fleet consisted of four major and permanent commands: the Battle Fleet (the main battle-line and front-line ships), the Scouting Fleet (smaller, faster vessels, and, potentially, aircraft carriers), the Control Force (light forces, older cruisers, and destroyers to hold advance bases and provide convoy escort), and the Fleet Base Force (the fleet train and logistics ships). The Battle Fleet and Base Force were designated for the Pacific, with only the Scouting Fleet (with six older battleships) and (smallest of all) Control Force assigned to the Atlantic.

The trend was unsettling for Tidewater. Before 1919, the great preponderance of the fleet was stationed comfortably in the Atlantic. Between 1919 and 1922, about half of the Navy sailed for the Pacific. From 1922 on the Pacific's share grew still greater: in 1930 the Control Force would be disestablished, and in 1932 even the Scouting Force would be sent westward.[5]

All planning forecasts were thrown out the window. West Coast homeports struggled to meet the Navy's skyrocketing demand for piers, anchorages, and supply centers, while Hampton Roads sat with an awkward overcapacity for a proportionally smaller force. Just when most Norfolk businessmen had expected naval expansion to ignite continuous commercial prosperity, the region began to economically retrench. The Navy backed away from East Camp (the second naval training station planned between Boush and Mason creeks), the Army abandoned its Lafayette River terminal, and large portions of

The marshland southeast of Chambers Field was reclaimed beginning in 1921, and several hangars and industrial shops of the station's Assembly and Repair Department were erected. *National Museum of Naval Aviation*

the NOB and St. Helena fell to neglect and weeds.[6]

The single bright spot, almost lost in the gloom, was the growing importance of Hampton Roads in the world of military aviation. Post-war plans had concentrated Navy aircraft on the East Coast at Hampton Roads. Activity at the naval air station grew by the month, and Norfolk aviators were delighted by the Navy's decision to build its first aircraft carrier at Norfolk Navy Yard. But the world's attention would first be centered on another signature event in the history of the Navy, of aviation, and of Hampton Roads—Brig. Gen. Billy Mitchell's much-ballyhooed aerial bombing tests of 1921.

Shortly after the highly decorated William L. "Billy" Mitchell assumed the reins of the Army's Air Service, he approached the Navy's General Board to propose aerial bombing experiments with ships in the Chesapeake Bay. The idea was not a new one; Navy Lt. Cdr. H. T. Bartlett had already suggested exploding bombs near captured German warships to test ship designs. The decommissioned battleship *Indiana* survived only fourteen detonations in Bartlett's tests before she ran aground in the Chesapeake Bay in 1920.[7]

Mitchell's fierce advocacy of strategic air power needed a more spectacular stage than simple static ordnance tests. Speaking before a House committee in February 1920, Mitchell suggested that an air force could assume the Navy's traditional role as the country's first line of defense, bluntly charged that surface fleets could not stand up to air attack, and offered to "take the members of your committee down to Chesapeake Bay and show you these things from the air, so that you can judge for yourselves."[8]

Navy Secretary Daniels launched a verbal counteroffensive, questioning the ability of aircraft to find ships at sea, fight through antiaircraft fire, and hit ships maneuvering at high speed. "[Mitchell] will soon discover, if he ever tries laying bombs on the deck of a naval vessel, that he will be blown to atoms long before he is near enough to drop salt upon the tail of the Navy," said Daniels. Momentarily ahead in this heady contest of wit and counterthrust, Daniels unwittingly opened just the door that Mitchell desired, saying: "I am so confident that neither Army or Navy aviators can hit the *Iowa* [a decommissioned battleship used as a target vessel, radio controlled] when she is underway that I would be perfectly willing to be on board when they bomb her."[9]

With no escape after statements like that, Daniels approved

a series of limited aerial bombing tests against captured German ships with both Army and Navy fliers. The Army ordered a thousand men and 250 planes to Hampton's Langley Field and established the First Provisional Air Brigade. Mitchell also developed new large 2,000- and 4,000-pound bombs, accelerated the delivery of new Martin bombers to carry them, and practiced against the grounded wreck of the *Indiana.*[10]

The much-anticipated tests (now universally touted as a demonstration of aerial power or naval vulnerability, much to Mitchell's delight) opened on 21 June 1921. Although no warship had ever been sunk from the air, the odds for these tests had been stacked in the Army's favor. At the Army's request, destroyers would guide the bombers to the target seventy miles east of Cape Charles; Navy compasses would be supplied for Army aircraft; target wind conditions would be radioed to pilots; and all ships would be anchored (no maneuvering *Iowa* for Army fliers and no "salt upon the tail"). As Army film cameras began to roll and notables from Washington assembled nearby, Mitchell began to stage an extravaganza that would best fit his plans.[11]

The first planned target was the German submarine *U-117*—small, fragile to bombs, and unspectacular to the media. Mitchell kept his Army fliers away while Navy F5L flying boats quickly dispatched the submarine with 165-pound bombs. On 29 June, Navy aircraft with dummy bombs flew against the maneuvering *Iowa,* scoring only two hits. Again, Mitchell deftly stayed away and avoided the scrape.[12]

Two weeks later the German destroyer *G-102* was the target. This time the target was open purely to the Army. Eighteen pursuit planes attacked, followed by heavy bombers with 600-pound bombs. "In less time than it takes to tell," Mitchell told a salivating press corps, "[the ship] broke completely in two in the middle and sank out of sight." Five days later, the thinly armored light cruiser *Frankfurt* was the target; it held up to ten attack waves before succumbing and, by 20 July, only the elderly German battleship *Ostfriesland* remained for the climactic test of the series. Dignitaries (including observers from Britain, Japan, France, and Italy) observed nearby as Mitchell pressed an attack, breaking nearly all of the Navy's

The thinly armored ex-German light cruiser *Frankfurt* was the target for one phase of bombing tests by Billy Mitchell in July 1921. Ten waves of Army, Navy and Marine aircraft with 100-pound bombs, then 250-pounders and finally 600-pound bombs attacked the ship. Surviving nearly to the last, near misses with large bombs finally ruptured *Frankfurt's* hull sending her to the bottom. *Naval Historical Center*

rules to evaluate each hit. Army bombers scored three quick hits and two near misses.[13]

The next day, Army Martins returned with 1,000-pound bombs in nearly perfect flying conditions, arriving nearly an hour early to steal the stage. The bombers quickly scored a direct hit, ignored signals to halt for naval observers and dropped five more 1,000-pound bombs with three hits. A second Army wave was soon overhead, armed with huge experimental 2,000-pound bombs. Two near misses crumpled *Ostfriesland*'s side armor, a direct hit struck the forecastle, and two other near misses hit near the stern and amidships, lifting the ship the ship out of the water. *Ostfriesland* settled slowly by the stern, finally going over on her side.[14]

Although the Navy tried to explain away the results (citing the "sitting duck" nature of the ship and the fact that no damage control parties were aboard), Mitchell became an overnight hero. Simplistic and flawed, newspaper headlines that declared "Day of the Battleship Ended" nevertheless came breathtakingly close to the truth.[15]

Not everyone in the Navy saw the aerial bombing tests as a disaster. Rear Adm. William Moffett and Capt. Henry Mustin argued that the best way to defend battleships was with aircraft carriers and carrier-based fighters. Both had closely followed British carrier designs, and their support for an American carrier had helped win the argument to convert the collier *Jupiter* (AC-3) into the Navy's first carrier, *Langley* (CV-1). Despite avid opposition—Adm. Hugh Rodman, for one, protested that the conversion "would spoil a good collier to make an indifferent carrier"—*Jupiter* entered the Norfolk Navy Yard for conversion in March 1920.[16]

Langley proved to be a unique, awkward, plodding, yet mesmerizing vision for all naval aviators. She boasted an ungainly 540-foot flight deck cantilevered above the existing collier main deck, no hangar deck, a single elevator, and two cranes to lift float planes from the water. The former collier's bridge was retained in its original position and, with the flight deck above, provided poor visibility for conning and no visibility of flight operations. Her engineering plant—the first turbo-electric plant in the Navy—was rated at a mere fifteen knots (eight to ten knots was more likely). A single large funnel stood on the port side and swiveled down during flight operations.

Cdr. Kenneth Whiting was assigned to be *Langley*'s exec-

Shortly after her commissioning in the spring of 1922, *Langley* moored in the York River for practice aircraft landings. A system of mooring lines and anchors in the river kept her consistently pointed into the wind as aviators perfected their approaches. *U.S. Naval Institute*

Langley shown alongside Norfolk Navy Yard, probably during her summer 1924 refit. Carrier pilots refer to arresting wires as a "trap" and count their landings aboard carrier as "traps," all derived from the original *Langley* arresting wire arrangements at the aft end of the flight deck. Fore-and-aft wires about ten inches above the deck (modeled after a British design) were arranged on deck so that hooks on the plane's axle could engage them, preventing the plane from slewing from side to side as the aircraft slowed. Transverse wires were added to this design which could be snagged by a hook at the rear of the plane. *National Archives*

utive officer and acting commanding officer during conversion. Whiting had previously qualified in submarines; had commanded *Porpoise, Shark,* and *Tarpon*; and he had relieved Lt. Theodore Ellyson as captain of *Seal* while the submarine was under construction at Newport News. As with Ellyson, Whiting's interest turned to aviation. He had learned to fly under Orville Wright and was designated Naval Aviator No. 16 in 1914. During World War I he was awarded a Navy Cross while leading naval aviation units in England and France.[17]

On 20 March 1922, *Langley* was commissioned, with Capt. S. H. R. Doyle (not a naval aviator but previously in command of NAS Norfolk), to assume command. In planning the commissioning ceremony, Whiting discovered that the vessel had no mainmast (the masts were to telescope down into the flight deck during flight operations and the motors to raise them had not yet been installed). Key to the commissioning ceremony was the captain's order to "Break the colors and set the watches," for which a mast was required. Whiting, exasperated, told *Langley*'s flight officer (Lt. Cdr. Godfrey de C. Chevalier) to just make it happen. At the appointed time, responding to orders, *Langley*'s chief quartermaster appeared on the flight deck with the new commissioning pennant pinned on the end of a wooden swab handle and then nailed it upright to the side of the flight deck. After the ceremony, everyone gathered around the pennant drooping from the slightly askew swab handle, and Chevalier remarked, "That was about the most non-reg commissioning I have ever seen."[18]

Experiments had begun at NAS Hampton Roads during the summer of 1921 to perfect the carrier's arresting gear, and a large wooden revolving turntable had been built at the field to allow landings into the wind. Chiefly under the supervision of Lt. Alfred M. "Mel" Pride, experiments involving fore-and-aft wires and transverse wires were conducted, and early *Langley* pilots alternated their training among the turntable, the Army's Langley Field, and a decked-over barge on the

Potomac where they practiced touch-and-goes.[19]

After sea trials in the Chesapeake Bay, *Langley* anchored in the York River near the Yorktown Mine Depot. Five anchors were deployed in a circle about the ship to face her into the wind so that pilots could practice approaches up the stern. In this fashion, *Langley* fliers began to pioneer flight deck procedures that would be so important in efficient launch and recovery operations, including one important innovation that came quite by accident. "We were at anchor in the York River," related Lieutenant Pride. "This chap kept coming in high, then he'd give her the gun before he got to the deck, and go around again. This had happened several times, with executive officer Whiting observing from the nets. Whiting jumped up on the deck and grabbed the white hats from two sailors, and held them up to indicate that this character was too high. Then he put them down. He coached the fellow in . . . so from then on, an officer was stationed aft with flags to signal whether the plane was high or low or coming in too fast or too slow." The landing signal officer was born.[20]

After the Yorktown training period, the "Covered Wagon" sailed into the Chesapeake for underway operations. On 17 October 1922, just north of Tongue of the Horseshoe and seaward of the main channel, Lt. Virgil C. "Squash" Griffin made *Langley*'s first launch, flying a Vought VE-7. With no brakes, the VE-7's tail was held in place by a wire with a bomb release that was let go once the engine revved up. During the next two days, "Chevy" Chevalier practiced touch-and-goes while the ship was under way in the Chesapeake. Several days later, on 26 October, Chevalier rendezvoused with *Langley* in an Aeromarine 39-B. With a white flag replacing a red flag at the port quarter signaling readiness for landing, Chevalier brought the airplane carefully aboard, engaged both fore-and-aft and transverse landing wires, and, unceremoniously, nosed down as the aircraft came to a sudden halt, damaging the propeller. It took more than an hour to realign the landing wires and prepare the deck for the next landing.[21] Tragically, just seventeen days after his historic landing, the charismatic Chevalier, Naval Aviator No. 7, crashed while flying a Vought VE-7 from NAS Norfolk to Yorktown and died of his injuries at Portsmouth Naval Hospital on 14 November.

Again at anchorage on 18 November, another first was achieved aboard *Langley* when Capt. Whiting made the first

Naval aviators serving as department heads at NAS Norfolk gather in 1918. *Hampton Roads Naval Museum*

catapult launch in a twin-float PT seaplane, although not with untarnished results. The force of *Langley's* catapult shot ripped the plane's starboard pontoon free, and Whiting landed on the single remaining pontoon and coolly waited on the capsizing plane for a rescue boat. According to naval aviation lore, "Instrument Face" became the distinguishing feature of *Langley* pilots, who loosened teeth and flattened noses against their instrument panels while landing on the ship's small deck with its crude arresting gear.

The Navy did not assign specifically designed aircraft to *Langley,* but experimented with land planes with strengthened landing gear and arresting hooks. *Langley's* air detachment was built up and maintained at NAS Norfolk, growing from an initial composition of six Aeromarine 39-B's, four Vought VE-7's, four Moraine-Saulnier "parasols" (aircraft with high wings on a central support frame), and a Parnall Panther. Later, four TS-1 fighters were added for experiments.[22]

With the conversion of *Langley,* arresting gear trials, tests of new "carrier" aircraft, Army air operations near Hampton, and the nearness of aviation debates in Washington, Hampton Roads soon became the focus of naval aviation development, and the naval air station expanded in kind. During this time, two major Navy-wide studies helped solidify Norfolk's importance to naval aviation at a time of broad cutbacks elsewhere in the Navy. Both the Rodman Board of 1923 (named for senior member Rear Adm. Hugh Rodman, who was concurrently serving as commandant of the Fifth Naval District) and the Morrow Board of 1925 accentuated NAS Norfolk's importance as naval aviation entered an aggressive five-year expansion program.[23]

As early as May 1919, Norfolk-based F5F flying boats routinely conducted exercises with the Battle Fleet to hone joint operations. In 1919–20, Lts. Chevalier, T. S. Murphy, D. B. Murphy, and L. H. Lovelace successfully launched dummy and live torpedoes from R-6 aircraft and established Hampton Roads as a center of development for this new aerial weapon. In 1920, a squadron of new Martin MBT torpedo bombers split its time between Yorktown and Norfolk in tests and experiments. In 1922, PT-1 and Douglas DT torpedo

Boeing F3B aircraft from squadron VF3B of the carrier *Lexington* line up on the Norfolk NAS tarmac circa 1926. *Hampton Roads Naval Museum*

Beginning in 1917, Hampton Roads Naval Air Station assumed the duties as the Navy's designated site for experimental aviation. Although that mission would soon be transferred elsewhere, important experimental tests were conducted in Hampton Roads throughout the 1920s, especially involving carrier aircraft, carrier landing systems, seaplanes, and aerial weaponry. This Gallaudet D-series aircraft produced by the Gallaudet Engineering Co. in 1922 is seen on an air station ramp. Note the propeller in the mid-body of the aircraft aft of the pilot. *Hampton Roads Naval Museum*

bombers were introduced in Hampton Roads, but the development of torpedo attack from aircraft advanced only slowly, because of the fragile nature and heavy weight of the torpedoes of the day. Lieutenant Griffin landed the first torpedo bomber aboard *Langley* in March 1924.[24]

Griffin, who would become known for his experimental flying in Norfolk, flew the first aircraft from a submarine in Hampton Roads. In an experiment on 5 November 1923, a crew from *Langley* headed by Griffin disassembled a Martin MS-1 scout sea plane and stowed it aboard submarine *S-1*. After the submarine surfaced in Hampton Roads, the aircraft was reassembled on deck, *S-1* submerged under the plane, and Griffin took off and flew back to NAS.

One of the most important developments in naval aviation in the 1920s and 1930s was the development of dive-bombing as an effective attack tactic, a technique that was to define much of the punch of carrier aviation in World War II. The perfection of naval dive-bombing would involve a complex marriage of aircraft design, flying tactics, and experience. Most of the first dive-bombing work began with Battle Fleet squadrons in California during 1927, but Fighter Squadron Five (VF-5), based at NAS Norfolk, also played an important role, including tests on 4 May 1927 with seventy degree dives from eleven thousand feet, aimed at a painted target on the ground near Smithfield, Virginia. The squadron also began experiments that included dives against a towed, yellow-painted buoy pulled by destroyer *Putnam* (DD-287) off Cape Henry in October 1924. The bombing scores achieved by VF-5 were impressive (under some conditions reaching forty percent effectiveness) and resulted in several aircraft design improvements.[25]

In the days before radios, naval aviators took the subject of homing pigeons seriously, and the naval air station became the region's center for the Navy's use of pigeons. "Before you started on your flight," Lieutenant Pride recalled, "you went over to the pigeon loft and got your little box with four pigeons. You took them along with you. Then, if you had a forced land-

In December 1921, dirigible *C-7* was the first airship to use nonflammable helium in a flight from Hampton Roads to Washington, D.C. *C-7*'s demonstration flight was timely because on 20 February 1922 a major tragedy occurred when the Navy's experimental dirigible *Roma,* acquired from Italy and undergoing a test flight at nearby Langley Field, lost altitude, hit a high tension wire, exploded, and burned, with the loss of thirty-four lives. The loss of *Roma* and the near-simultaneous success of *C-7* spurred the use of safer helium instead of hydrogen in lighter-than-air craft. *Hampton Roads Naval Museum*

ing, of which we had quite a number, you wrote where you were on the piece of paper and stuck it in the capsule that was fastened to the pigeon's leg and let it go." In the director of naval aviation's weekly report of 5 February 1919 came the additional comment: "Within the past week five French Type Mobile pigeon lofts and eight hundred birds were received at [NAS Hampton Roads] from US Naval Air Stations in France . . . in one year they had delivered 10,995 messages, of which 219 were from planes that had landed . . . they are the best of French, English and Belgian blood and will produce wonderful youngsters for the future needs of the Navy."[26]

With this focus on pigeons, it surprised no one that *Langley* was built with a large pigeon loft on the fantail below the flight deck, although the birds never adapted well to the mobile conditions of a carrier at sea. As Lieutenant Pride remembers:

> We went into the Chesapeake Bay and anchored off Tangier Island. The pigeon quartermaster would let his pigeons out, one or two at a time for exercise, but one day he let all of them go and the flock flew back to the Norfolk Navy Yard. Pretty soon we got a dispatch from the Navy Yard, "Your pigeons are all back here and we haven't got any appropriation for pigeon feed." We put the quartermaster in a plane and flew him down to Norfolk where he retrieved them and took them to NAS. That's the last we ever saw of pigeons on *Langley.* They made the pigeon coop into the executive officer's cabin, a very nice one.[27]

The Naval Academy Preparatory School opened in a renovated building across from Chambers Field in 1919 and provided an immediate (and unexpected) impetus for naval aviation. All enlisted men from the fleet who wished admission to the Naval Academy had to complete prep school studies. Highly motivated—"They knew that to get out of the enlisted ranks and into the officer structure was something that was

Carriers *Saratoga* and *Lexington* at anchor in Lynnhaven Bay in mid-1934 viewed from Navy dirigible *Los Angeles* (whose tender, *Patoka,* is at bottom of picture). On 6 September 1934, *Saratoga, Lexington*, and *Langley* staged the largest naval air show ever in Tidewater, with more than three hundred planes taking part after being launched from the carriers off the Virginia Capes. *Hampton Roads Naval Museum*

very, very necessary," was how Adm. Gerald Miller put it—they absorbed the sights and sounds of Chambers Field with extra gusto. "That's what a good many of us wanted—aviation. So we used to sit in class, and look out the window at the airplanes coming and going."[28]

The Navy's first aviator, Lt. Theodore Ellyson, had not stayed with aviation; he returned to shipboard duty and in 1913 arrived in Hampton Roads as first lieutenant aboard battleship *South Carolina.* Although he visited the Curtiss School at Newport News in 1916 and flew an airplane for the first time in four years, he continued with duty aboard sub chasers and commanded four-stack destroyer *J. Fred Talbott* (DD-156). Later in 1920, while in command of destroyer *Brooks* (DD-232), Commander Whiting, Ellyson's Annapolis roommate, invited him to the navy yard to inspect *Langley* and prodded him back into aviation. Ellyson was posted as executive officer of the naval air station in January 1921 and, now considering Norfolk home, moved into one of the restored Jamestown Exposition houses fronting Willoughby Bay. He stayed for an enjoyable ten months before being ordered to Washington.[29] In June 1925, Ellyson wrangled a return to Norfolk in command of Torpedo Squadron One (VT-1), which operated from hangars along Willoughby Bay and from sea plane tender *Wright* (AV-1).

A provision of the Washington Naval Treaty of 1922 allowed the United States to convert two battle cruisers scheduled for scrapping, *Lexington* and *Saratoga,* into large aircraft carriers with thirty-six thousand ton displacements. As the twin ships neared completion, long-standing friends Whiting and Ellyson were assigned as the ships' executive officers, Ellyson to *Lexington* (CV-2) and Whiting to *Saratoga* (CV-3). Aviation detachments for both carriers stood up in June 1927 and were ordered to NAS Norfolk for training. New pilots were integrated with others who had been training aboard *Langley;* the outline of a carrier deck was whitewashed into the grass of Chambers Field to help pilots practice their landings.[30]

Saratoga was commissioned on 16 November 1927 and *Lexington* a month later, and both ships immediately generated a high-pitched competitive spirit, abetted by the enthusiasm of their two executive officers. *Saratoga* had orders to steam to San Pedro to join the Battle Fleet, and *Lexington*

Pilots of Fighting Squadron Six attached to carrier *Saratoga* on the tarmac at Chambers Field in 1934. *Naval Historical Center*

was slated for Hampton Roads and the Scouting Fleet, but *Lexington* was ordered at the last minute to also sail west.[31] Both ships anchored at Lynnhaven Roads in February 1928 to embark their air wings before sailing for the Panama Canal.

Ellyson was at Hampton Roads on 25 February 1928 when his wife wired from Annapolis that their eleven-year-old daughter faced immediate surgery for an alarming ear infection. Knowing that little time was left before *Lexington*'s departure, Ellyson arranged for the use of the only plane

The Navy Musician's School was one of many independent service schools maintained at the Naval Training Station, here on 24 June 1926. *Naval Historical Center*

Electrician, designed to look like a ship but built on dry land, assisted in the training of engineers in onboard equipment and would be a fixture at the training station until July 1933. *U.S. Naval Institute*

aboard that could land in water at Annapolis, a Loening OL-7. Ellyson sat as a passenger with two other *Lexington* pilots assigned to the mission, and the Loening was logged aloft from Willoughby Bay at 0200. The aircraft never arrived in Annapolis, and after an extensive search, wreckage was found near the Chesapeake's Middle Ground some days later. Sadly, six weeks after the crash, Ellyson's body washed up on Willoughby Spit, his wife's wire calling him to Annapolis still in his flight jacket pocket.[32]

As the 1920s waned, aviation activity at the naval air station quickened still further. Although *Langley, Lexington,* and *Saratoga* would operate primarily from West Coast ports, Chambers Field bustled as the central training and operational site for Scouting Fleet aircraft. Rear Adm. James F. Raby, Commander Aircraft, Scouting Fleet, established his headquarters at NAS Norfolk, the precursor of a later headquarters for the Commander, Air Force, Atlantic Fleet. Capt. Ernest J. King served temporarily as Commander, Aircraft, Scouting Fleet; commanded aircraft tender *Wright* in Norfolk; and would return as commanding officer of NAS Norfolk in May 1929. When the secretary of the Navy directed that, beginning with the class of 1926, all graduates of the Naval Academy be given twenty-five hours of flight instruction during their first year at sea, Hampton Roads was named as one of two sites to conduct this training.

Hampton Roads was also chosen as the site of the exciting Schneider Trophy air races of 1926. This series of dramatic, closely watched air races helped advance aeronautical engineering (especially that of high-performance military aircraft) and had been consistently supported by the Navy. The Navy's racing team had won the contest in 1925, giving it the right to choose Norfolk for its title defense. A fifty-kilometer, seven-lap course was laid out from the NAS to Thimble Shoals to Newport News and back to the NAS.

The Navy played the gracious host to the crush of spectators with pre-race aerobatics and band music. When the races began, "the astounding speed of the racers left the grandstand gasping and offering expressions of astonishment," commented one reporter. But from the start, bad luck, balky engines, and meager planning plagued the Navy's team, which experienced crashes in practice runs. In the final races, an Italian army team (dubbed "Mussolini's envoys of the air" in the press) took first and third places and the overall win.[33] Although NAS Norfolk underwent significant growth during

Sailors concentrate on Morse Code radio training at Hampton Roads circa 1920. *Naval Historical Center*

the 1920s, the same could not be said of the rest of the Fifth Naval District. The student population at the training station declined dramatically, at times numbering only five hundred recruits—one-third of capacity. With most of the Navy's ships in the Pacific, the operational tempo at the naval station and the supply station was also well below capacity. The new Yorktown Mine Depot operated at only modest levels, and the work force at the Navy Yard plummeted from 11,000 in 1919 to 2,538 five years later.[34]

It was in this environment of reduced operations that the role of naval district commandant acquired new dimensions. Always seen as the Navy's "face" in the community and as the self-styled "Navy mayor," the commandant now faced challenges more akin to those of a corporate CEO balancing the divisions within a complex conglomerate. Regional manpower, construction, logistics, and operations had to match tightening budget conditions of the 1920s, and the role of the commandant, by necessity, changed with the times.

The first commandant to fully recognize this shift and the first to formally integrate business management philosophies into the position was Rear Adm. Roger Welles, who took command on 31 August 1923. A battleship admiral who had commanded *Louisiana, Oklahoma,* and Battleship Division Four, Welles replaced the well-regarded Admiral Rodman, who had been absent from the district for long periods on special naval commissions.

Welles came to Norfolk with two years' experience as the Eleventh Naval District commandant, and he vigorously injected himself into the mainstream of Tidewater naval activities. Welles enjoyed traveling to Washington by airplane and pressed the powerful Navy bureau officers to visit Norfolk. Admiral Rodman left Welles an important legacy, the report of the Rodman Board, which provided recommendations for naval bases in budget-constrained times, and Welles wove these recommendations into his own plans for operating the district efficiently.

Welles looked first at the training station. Although the Station operated a dozen different service schools, its eleven-week recruit training course absorbed an inordinate amount of resources. From the "boot's" first days of detention camp near the old Pine Beach Hotel (for medical examinations, vaccinations, uniform issue, rudimentary drilling, and basic classroom instruction) to final graduation, a large portion of the station's staff and facilities was reserved for training, but were operating at only one-third of capacity. Welles slashed

The battleship modernization program awarded to Norfolk Navy Yard beginning in 1925 proved to be a huge economic boost to the community, helping to stave off the worst of the Great Depression. Six battleships were assigned one by one to the yard for major improvements to their superstructure, masts, propulsion plants, armor platting, and main battery. *Arizona* is shown here nearing the end of her refit in December 1930. Destroyer *Cole,* a unit of the Scouting Fleet, is in the background. *U.S. Naval Institute*

their budget and, as Rodman had recommended, pressed to have recruit training moved to Newport. In the end, Welles did not prevail (partly because retired Rear Adm. A. C. Dillingham, still a force to be reckoned with in Norfolk, loudly opposed the closure), and, fortunately for Hampton Roads, the training station stayed open. During the Depression, training sites at Great Lakes and Newport were closed, but San Diego and Norfolk remained open because of their proximity to large naval bases.[35]

Welles next focused on NOB's submarine station, which he thought too small to be operated efficiently. Again agreeing with Rodman, he recommended that all Norfolk submarines be transferred to Philadelphia, "where they can be cared for by yard workmen, relieving about 150 enlisted men for the benefit of the fleet."[36] Welles won this battle. All Norfolk submarines were transferred elsewhere, and the submarine station was shuttered on 20 November 1924.

At Yorktown, Welles found a brand-new base; it was the Navy's largest installation in the world, with land covering twenty square miles. The optimum naval ordnance facility requires open space for safety considerations, good transportation nodes for delicate explosives, and access to deep water for servicing of warships. Yorktown not only met all of these requirements, but also had been studied and coveted by the Navy since the days of Stephen Decatur.

The naval mine depot at Yorktown was originally estab-

With its workforce stabilized by the battleship modernization program, the Norfolk Navy Yard was further buoyed in 1933 with funds from the National Industry Recovery Act for two destroyers—*Tucker* (DD-374) and *Downes* (DD-375)—the first shipbuilding at the Navy Yard since World War I. *Norfolk Naval Shipyard*

lished in 1917 as a coal and oil depot, but was expanded by a significant 11,433 acres in August 1918 to accept all mining operations from St. Julien's Creek. Private landowners were ordered off the land within thirty days, with just compensation to be determined later.[37] The depot's primary mission included storing high explosives, servicing mines and depth charges, and overhauling and stocking ready torpedoes. In 1924, Welles, impressed with the depot's valuable status, reported that Yorktown had 14 million tons of TNT in storage and was reclaiming sixty mines per day.[38] During the 1920s, the Navy centralized shipboard ordnance functions at Yorktown for all Atlantic ships, and when new safety policies were adopted in 1928 that spaced magazines farther apart, the Yorktown depot was enlarged with the construction of seventy-seven new high-explosive magazines.[39]

Welles's view of the situation at Norfolk Navy Yard was less sanguine. The gloom of the shipbuilding "holiday" mandated by the 1922 Washington Naval Treaty blanketed Hampton Roads. More than $70 million in construction contracts had been lost (including battleship *North Carolina* at the Navy yard and battleship *Iowa* and new battle cruisers at Newport News), and with the fleet in the Pacific, repair and maintenance tasks declined. By 1924, the Navy yard's work force had declined to a level not seen since 1899.[40]

To take advantage of unused industrial capacity during this "disarmament depression," Welles vigorously lobbied for new

Beginning during World War I, the Navy consistently provided marching units and bands for civic celebrations and patriotic holidays. Many remember these displays as one sign of the Navy's impact on the future of Hampton Roads. Here, Navy recruits march through Norfolk on Memorial Day 1935. *Sargeant Memorial Room, Norfolk Public Library*

repair contracts for Hampton Roads. Knowing that West Coast yards were overwhelmed with routine ship repairs, Welles recommended that major battleship modernizations be performed on the East Coast to balance efforts.

The ensuing battleship modernization program that was awarded to the navy yard beginning in 1925 was a pivotal event in the yard's history. In all, six battleships were modernized at Norfolk Navy Yard: *Texas* (1925–1926), *New York* (1926–1927), *Nevada* (1927–1929), *Arizona* (1929–1931), *Mississippi* (1931–1933), and *Idaho* (1931–1934). This provided an important boost to the yard's workload. At the same time, Newport News won contracts to construct two cruisers, the well-respected *Houston* (CA-30) and *Augusta* (CA-31), the keels of which were laid in 1928.

The *Arizona* was typical. She entered Norfolk Navy Yard in mid-1929 for a $7 million overhaul, about half the cost of her original construction fifteen years earlier. Her entire superstructure was rebuilt, including the replacement of old cage masts with new tripod masts with massive three-level fire control tops. The bridge area was increased to hold a new flag bridge, additional armor was added to her deck and blisters to her side, and her turret guns were increased in elevation for extended range. Below decks, new boilers and turbines were installed and interior communications were enhanced.[41]

Immediately after modernization, *Arizona* was ordered to take President Herbert Hoover to the Caribbean. Shortly after 0700 19 March 1931, the president and his party boarded ship at anchor off Old Point Comfort. In addition to the normal measures of polishing, cleaning, and painting (the captain said, "Oh, we aren't doing anything except shining up the old brass knocker on the front door for the company."), the ship received the first motion picture projectors ever installed aboard a naval ship to show such "talkies" as *Charley's Aunt* and *The Grand Parade* for the president's pleasure. *Arizona* proceeded to sea surrounded by an entourage of small craft, airplanes, and blimps.[42] In his efforts to balance Navy resources across the district for greatest efficiency, Welles did

Hampton Roads has always been a favored place for inspiring naval reviews such as this attended by President Calvin Coolidge in 1927. *Hampton Roads Naval Museum*

not forget his duty to encourage a warm, supportive relationship with the communities of Tidewater. In 1923, Norfolk became even more closely entwined with the Navy when it extended its city limits across the Lafayette River to consume the NOB, Ocean View, and suburbs to the east and north, and Welles carefully praised community support while also challenging the city to do more for the Navy and its sailors. Typical of these exhortations was one letter he addressed to the Norfolk Chamber of Commerce: "There is no harbor on either coast of the United States which has so much to offer as Hampton Roads and . . . having been recently stationed in San Diego, I am able to state what that city did to attract the Navy to that port . . . the results of their generosity was that the Navy has spent millions of dollars in building permanent concrete and tile buildings and San Diego is assured of a large naval population for all time."[43]

When Welles departed in 1925, he garnered substantial congratulatory comments, including applause from the Norfolk City Council: "The sympathetic interest which you have ever manifested in this community has made us know and feel that we had a friend in the Commandant of the Fifth Naval District."[44] The Navy's "sympathetic interest" in Hampton Roads was also clearly on display as it assigned three of its most accomplished officers to the naval district during the 1920s: Admiral Rodman, the top naval commander during World War I and a former commander in chief of the Pacific Fleet; Admiral Welles, who would win a third star as commander of naval forces in Europe; and Adm. Coontz, who came to Norfolk after serving as chief of naval operations.

The Navy's emphasis on efficiency, the Navy yard's capture of lucrative battleship modernization contracts, the gain in civil service employment at naval installations, the Navy's increasing use of local goods and services, and the continuing expansion of naval aviation all helped Tidewater weather the difficult days of the Great Depression. Although many industries in the region were forced to curtail business, the vitality of the Navy actually improved, and its economic contributions to Tidewater stood out against a backdrop of unemployment and soup lines. In 1933, the Navy generated an infusion of $20 million into the region, and the Norfolk Navy Yard employed four thousand and NOB, two thousand.[45]

Despite the work of naval district commandants, the prodigious surge in naval presence had not fully been assimilated into the fabric of Tidewater life even late into the 1920s. Everyone knew there was an elephant in the room—the overwhelming economic contribution that the Navy brought to the region could not be ignored—yet many viewed such dependence with mistrust or, at best, as a forced marriage.

Many in Hampton Roads continued to frown on the pres-

The Charles W. Fox family in May 1934. *Sargeant Memorial Room, Norfolk Public Library*

ence of large numbers of sailors and habitually blamed them for the city's growing pains. By its nature, one historian wrote, "the presence of the Navy meant sailors on the streets, sometimes many of them and, the people of Norfolk did not have a very high opinion of sailors." But such conclusions did not extend to all, perhaps not even to a majority. Tidewater's new prosperity benefited many and protected nearly all from the economic depths of the Depression. The Navy also brought the region a fashionable sense of internationalism that was highly appreciated and dovetailed nicely with Hampton Roads's vision of itself as a worldwide market and shipping center.[46]

Although the naval officer corps and its leadership were nearly universally well received within society, most in Norfolk held Navy enlisted men in much lower esteem. Spurred, perhaps, by a lack of acceptance by the population, a sense of second-class status, a lack of entertainment venues, or the relatively long trip from the NOB to downtown, sailors grumbled the world over about the misfortune of landing liberty in Norfolk. With few enlisted men married and fewer still establishing homes ashore, their integration into the community was near zero.

Over the years, sailors established themselves along East Main Street from the ferry landings to Union Station—a sailor's territory and red-light district housing a bawdy cottage industry of dance halls, barrooms, penny arcades, uniform stores, tattoo parlors, flophouses, and locker clubs. The ensuing neon lights, dense cigarette smoke, and blaring jukeboxes might have been considered a haven to some, but to the community at large it helped to typecast sailors and segregate them in an inferior social level. Although mariners had long been a component of life in Tidewater, the easily recognizable U.S. Navy sailor did not invade the region in great numbers until after World War I. In large part, sailors and citizens chose to separate themselves; the shore patrol kept the peace and the community kept to itself.[47]

Entertainment alternatives for sailors did exist—the Navy's YMCA was perhaps the best known—but they were poorly financed, inconsistently attended and could never sway the public back to even a "neutral" opinion from its generally negative view of enlisted men. Civilian attitudes hardened from the 1920s to the 1930s, worsening the social divide; it was said

Until the advent of modern bridges, tunnels, and freeways, the Navy depended upon intricate local ferry systems to support the demands of its burgeoning workforce. It was a sign of the times that all public transportation, including this ferry, was segregated. *Sargeant Memorial Room, Norfolk Public Library*

that no "nice" girl was allowed to go out with a sailor. Across these two decades, Norfolk successfully kept in favorable standing with Navy leadership but was often embarrassed by the poor hospitality the city offered to the average navy man.[48]

Many, however, thoroughly enjoyed their Norfolk experiences. As a lieutenant, Adm. George W. Anderson was assigned to the Experimental Aircraft Division of the NAS in the early 1930s: "I had a . . . very, very pleasant time there at our Norfolk Naval Air Station. Prohibition was still in effect, but they had bootleggers in the area and we got Norfolk 'corn' at a reasonable price and good quality. The officers, I think, lived quite well. They had good respect from the community, good social life, interesting duty, interesting flying, good rapport with the Navy as a whole, and morale was generally high in spite of the Depression."[49]

The Navy, in turn, tried to do its part to encourage community relations. It periodically opened bases to public visits, conducted grand fleet reviews in 1921 and 1927 with Presidents Harding and Coolidge in attendance, contributed to community fund drives, provided bands and marching units for civic functions, and even helped with mosquito abatement campaigns.

In the end, however, the most important naval contribution to improved community relations centered on its people. Positive relations between the Navy and Hampton Roads could not be sustained purely through economic handouts or the appearance of bands. It would start with a better understanding from both sides of the unique attributes of the other and would be fostered by improved integration within the community. That teamwork would begin slowly in the 1920s, spurred by an increasing number of navy men leaving the service, liking what they had seen in the Virginia Tidewater, and choosing to stay and settle in the community.

Again in the 1930s, the activities of Norfolk's Naval Air Station were a bright spot in Tidewater's economy. In 1932, NAS encompassed 120 acres, and efforts were under way to purchase 540 acres of former East Camp property that had

Chambers Field in 1939. *U.S. Naval Institute*

been returned to private ownership. "The Naval Air Station, Norfolk, is the principal fleet air base on the east coast," explained Admiral Moffett. "But the congestion is very great . . . our plan at Norfolk . . . is to have a main field where the various squadrons of the fleet can operate, take off and then go to other fields in the neighborhood where they can drill and maneuver during the day and at night."[50] Although Congress agreed with the Navy's justification for expansion, appropriations for the East Camp site lagged. By late 1939, the NAS had expanded to only 236 acres by reclaiming Boush and Mason creeks, and it held two fields, Chambers and West Landing Field.

While Congress dithered in expanding the naval air station, aircraft were soon crowding the Navy's "principal fleet air base on the East Coast" because of the "Thousand-plane Program" of 1926. Government relief grants sponsored by the Works Progress Administration (WPA) and other organizations—described by one historian as "life-giving cloudbursts from beyond the Potomac"—helped fund base improvements and were another buttress against the worst of the Depression. From 1934 to 1938, Norfolk shore establishments received approximately $36 million for new facilities, and the NAS added an additional $519,000 from the WPA. Runways were extended; new floodlighting was installed; and larger hangars, better living quarters, and new industrial shops were added.[51]

As war clouds began to gather and the nation's support for naval disarmament waned, lucrative appropriations began to come Norfolk's way. The Vinson-Trammel legislation of 1934 set the tone by providing a boost of funding for destroyers, cruisers, submarines, and two aircraft carriers. Naval appropriations increased every year from 1934 to 1939.

In 1938, the Navy's Hepburn Board studied the needs for new shore bases to meet the needs of the rapidly increasing Navy. In reviewing Hampton Roads facilities, Hepburn found the NAS to be "entirely inadequate to serve the fleet in its peacetime operations or to take its pro rata of repair or overhaul work" and recommended expanding the station to operate two carrier groups (expanding to four), four patrol squadrons (possibly six), and two utility squadrons. For the NAS, these recommendations paralleled the Navy's number of authorized aircraft, which stood at forty-five hundred in May 1939, a month later at ten thousand and then at fifteen thousand in July 1940.[52]

In a move that was long anticipated, the Navy finally took by condemnation 1,034 acres of land stretching east from the

This aerial view of the NOB (taken probably in 1938 or early 1939) shows the still relatively remote nature of Navy development away from the city. The East Camp area in the bottom right of the photo would become the center of intense development in 1940–41. Boush and Mason creeks are still very much in evidence. The open field to the left of the former exposition boat basin was referred to as West Landing Field and was occasionally used for aircraft operations. *Hampton Roads Naval Museum*

NOB toward Granby Street on 11 July 1940. The largest construction contract in Norfolk history quickly followed. A total of 278 buildings, including two chapels, several storehouses, three bachelor officer's quarters, ten apartment houses for officers, three enlisted men's barracks, a radio-radar building, three aircraft hangars, three seaplane hangars with four adjacent ramps, seven large industrial overhaul and repair hangars, an engine test building, and a dispensary were hurriedly built, and the extension of all runways were extended. Mammoth dredges set to work, digging in Willoughby Bay, and pumped mud and sand into the final remnant of Boush Creek.[53]

On 6 June 1941, 227 additional acres that separated the station from Granby Street (including, appropriately, the old Norfolk airport) was added, fully drawing Breezy Point into the station. At the completion of this round of construction, the new East Field was said to have the capacity for 410 land planes, and Breezy Point's capacity was estimated at seventy-two sea planes.[54]

Operations at the NAS increased in fits and starts throughout the 1930s. Although the base suffered some reduction in activity when the Scouting Force was transferred to the Pacific in 1932, patrol, experimental, and industrial activities continued. On 7–8 September 1933, six Consolidated P2Y-1 "Ranger" flying boats of Patrol Squadron 5, under the command of Lt. Cdr. Donald Carpenter, flew nonstop to Coco Solo in Panama, a world formation flying record of 2,059 miles in twenty-five hours, nineteen minutes.

As long-range flying boats improved in the early 1930s, Hampton Roads became the center of testing of prototype craft, including the classic PBY-1 *Catalina* flying boat. Built by Consolidated Aircraft, the prototype plane underwent acceptance testing between March and May 1935 at NAS Norfolk and caught attention as a "mystery plane." A newspaper headline reported, "Secrecy Shrouds Flight of Plane at Air Station Here."[55]

The naval air station had trained enlisted aviation mechanics in motor construction, wing and fabric manufacture, aerial bomb releases, and armaments starting in 1917. In 1918 it

Newport News Shipbuilding launched carrier *Ranger* on 24 February 1933, the first American ship designed and built as an aircraft carrier from the keel up. *National Archives*

established a Construction and Repair Department with an Aviation Mechanics and Quartermasters School. During the war, more than 1,000 received training in the construction and maintenance of sea planes. In 1922, the Construction and Repair Department was renamed the Assembly and Repair Department and reorganized into assembly, structural, engine, and machinery sections. The work force was entirely active duty, but as industrial activity increased in 1930, civilian employees joined the department, including fifty mechanics from the Navy yard. During the 1930s, the department overhauled engines at the rate of 150 annually and by 1939 boasted a work force of 786 enlisted and civilian personnel.[56]

Beginning in 1933, Norfolk became the Navy's primary site for the training of new carrier air groups, nicely complementing nearby carrier construction. Newport News launched carrier *Ranger* (CV-4) on 24 February 1933, and contracts quickly followed for Newport News' largest ships to date; the keel for carrier *Yorktown* (CV-5) was laid on 21 May 1934 and that for *Enterprise* (CV-6) on 16 July of that same year.[57] The shipyard would establish itself as the leading American builder of aircraft carriers, winning contracts for *Hornet* (CV-8) (keel laid 25 September 1939) and *Essex* (CV-9) (28 April 1941). NAS Norfolk assumed training duties in navigation, gunnery, and aerial bombing as new air wings formed and training activity intensified as war approached. A formal fleet operational training program was established to standardize the training of replacement pilots before fleet assignment, and a fighter direction ground school was established. Interestingly, until about 1940, Chambers Field had no traffic control system for aircraft safety, except for a white placard inserted through a slot on a hangar roof to indicate the direction of the runway in use.

The Norfolk Supply Station was redesignated a naval supply depot in 1927 and by 1939 consisted of ten warehouses, two wooden piers, four fuel oil tanks, and six gasoline tanks. In December 1940, the Navy negotiated an agreement to take over the former Army base terminal located west of Hampton Boulevard and south of NOB, "with the assurance that the Norfolk Army Base would be made available to the Army upon 90 days' notice." In early 1941, the Navy assumed

Of all the Navy's carriers at the end of World War II, *Ranger* was the one that was most closely associated with Hampton Roads. Built in Newport News and commissioned at the Norfolk Navy Yard, she conducted her first flight operations off Cape Henry in August 1934. She was heavily engaged in Atlantic Fleet Neutrality Patrol operations 1939–41 and sailed into Norfolk on 8 December 1941 following one South Atlantic patrol. For most of the war, she was the only large American carrier assigned to combat operations in the Atlantic. *U.S. Naval Institute*

control of a million square feet of warehouse space and the south side of Pier 2 and designated the area as Naval Supply Depot, South Annex. Pier 4 was constructed at NOB, and the Navy further increased its storage space at South Annex to 1.6 million square feet by the end of the year. After the war began, all of the former Army land and all of Pier 2 were acquired, and twelve single-story warehouses were built.[58]

With its work force stabilized by the battleship modernization program, the Navy yard garnered additional funding from the Public Works Administration, the WPA, and other relief appropriations for new buildings, shops, streets, and rail lines. At the peak of the WPA program, more than fifteen hundred extra men were employed, providing badly needed unemployment relief for the community.[59] Contracts for destroyers *Bagley* (DD-386), *Blue* (DD-387), and *Helm* (DD-388) followed in 1934, with four more—*Rowan* (DD-405), *Stack* (DD-406), *Morris* (DD-417), and *Wainwright*—in 1935 and 1936. Newport News shared in this good fortune, with the keels of destroyers *Mustin* (DD-413) and *Russell* (DD-414) laid in December 1937 and cruisers *Boise* (CL-47), *St. Louis* (CL-49), *Birmingham* (CL-62), *Mobile* (CL-63), *Biloxi* (CL-80), and *Houston* (CL-81) constructed between 1935 and 1941. Tidewater's strong Navy presence and the influence of two prominent Norfolk politicians on the House Naval Affairs Committee (Colgate W. Darden Jr., and Norman R. Hamilton) helped bring about this sudden good fortune.[60]

When President Franklin D. Roosevelt asked Congress for a billion dollars in January 1938 for naval defense, "the effect on Norfolk was electric."[61] Employment at the Norfolk Navy Yard doubled in a year, with a construction order for battleship *Alabama* (BB-60), and Newport News received a like award for sister ship *Indiana* (BB-58).[62] In June 1940, the chief of naval operations called for a 70 percent increase in the fleet, and a month later the president signed the "Two Ocean Navy" bill, which led to even more shipbuilding.

By early 1941, activity at the Navy yard and Newport News had shifted to a virtual wartime routine, with work shifts stretching around the clock. Tidewater was aglow in new eco-

Destroyers *Blue* and *Helm* were authorized in 1934 and proved to be another bulwark against the Depression for those in Portsmouth. This joint launch was conducted on 27 May 1937. Both ships were in Pearl Harbor on 7 December 1941 and both got under way for sea during the attack *(Blue* with only four officers onboard, all ensigns). *Blue* was sunk by a Japanese torpedo in 1942; *Helm* participated in nearly all the large campaigns in the Pacific and survived the war. *Norfolk Naval Shipyard*

nomic affluence. It was a "war boom" without the war, painted with a haze gray naval hue.

Prosperity, however, mingled with equal portions of anxiety, as no one in America was closer to the tumult of war than Hampton Roads. War rumors matched the quickening pace of naval activity, and sailors appeared on every Norfolk street. In this volatile environment, the face of the Navy for an apprehensive populace was Rear Adm. Joseph K. Taussig, one of the most recognized naval officers in America and one with a long association with Tidewater.

Taussig had received nationwide acclaim when he led the first American warships to Europe in World War I and announced to the British, "We are ready now." His father, Rear Adm. Edward D. Taussig, had attended the Naval Academy during the Civil War, had claimed Wake Island for the United States while in command of gunboat *Bennington* in 1899, had commanded battleships *Massachusetts* and *Indiana,* and served jointly as commandant of the Norfolk Navy Yard and the Fifth Naval District from 1907 to 1909. Before assuming the reins of the same naval district that his father had commanded thirty years previously, Joseph Knefler Taussig had logged many years in Norfolk, beginning with duty aboard the Great White Fleet battleship *Kansas,* then an assignment at Norfolk Navy Yard, and, later, command of battleship *Maryland,* Battleship Division Three, and the cruisers of the Navy's Scouting Force. Married to a local woman, Taussig specifically requested the assignment to NOB because he said he had "a special liking for the place" and assumed the duties of naval district commandant in May 1938.[63]

The region's relations with the Navy were at a critical milestone. "The people of Norfolk wanted their city to grow," historian Thomas Wertenbaker said. "But they wanted growth to be gradual, to be the natural result of the advantages offered by their situation and their magnificent harbor. They did not want to repeat the experience of the First World War, with its explosive growth, so they watched with apprehension as the war clouds grew blacker."[64]

Tall and distinguished, with a dramatic nose and an open, understanding countenance, Taussig vigorously injected him-

The venerable frigate *Constitution* visited Norfolk in March 1932 to renew a link with the city that had been a frequent occurrence for more than sixty years beginning in 1798. This highly-publicized visit by "Old Ironsides" brought throngs of visitors to the foot of East Main Street to see her and helped raise funds for her continued restoration. *National Archives*

self into all manner of city planning to ensure that Navy bases could grow in a controlled manner. He fought for federal resources for housing, established himself as a trusted voice of the Navy, and tried hard to learn from the mistake-prone naval escalation of 1917. Taussig fought to bridge the social divide between Navy men and the people of Norfolk and once explained this to a reporter by saying: "The fascinating problem is how to bring to individual sailor boys and defense workers and their families, the decent, pleasant, and interesting life of the home town." Taussig's impact was so widely respected that the city renamed Kersloe Road (between Hampton Boulevard and Granby Street) Admiral Taussig Boulevard.[65] When the respected and dignified Taussig retired to Norfolk, he, like Dillingham before him, took a position in local government.[66]

With most of the fleet permanently concentrated in the Pacific, remaining Atlantic naval forces re-formed into the Atlantic Squadron of the U.S. Fleet on 6 September 1938. The fleets would periodically join for coordinated operations, and the Atlantic Squadron formed in Hampton Roads just before New Year's Day 1939 to prepare for upcoming exercises.[67] It was an eye-catching scene, especially with the twin carriers *Yorktown* and *Enterprise,* which had completed shakedown training just a month before. On 2 January 1939, the carriers and four destroyers sortied from Hampton Roads as Carrier Division Two bound for the Caribbean. In command of the force was long-time Norfolk hand, Rear Adm. William F. "Bull" Halsey.

Halsey had first come to Norfolk in 1904 to join battleship *Missouri* (BB-11) immediately after graduating from the Naval Academy. Two years later, he transferred to the *Don Juan de Austria,* a former Spanish gunboat under repair at Norfolk Navy Yard. The story is told that Halsey was aboard the *Don Juan* one afternoon, drilling his men on deck when something soft knocked off his cap. When he looked up, he noticed that he had been struck by a lady's muff, thrown by a stunning young woman, Fanny (Fan) Grandy of Norfolk, who had been aboard for tea at the invitation of the ship's executive officer and his wife. Fan's family had long been associated

Joseph K. Taussig was born 30 August 1877 in Dresden, Germany, and graduated from the Naval Academy in 1899. Taussig led Destroyer Division 8 to Europe at the beginning of World War I, the first group of American warships sent forward. After crossing the storm-filled Atlantic, Commander Taussig was asked by a Royal Navy admiral when he would be ready for sea. Taussig replied in the now famous words, "We are ready now, Sir." Taussig later commanded the Fifth Naval District in Hampton Roads. *U.S. Naval Institute*

with Norfolk society; her grandfather owned the distinguished home of Stephen Decatur in Norfolk, and Fan's uncle, H. Aston Ramsey, was engineer of the ironclad *Virginia.* Although Fan's cousins aided the ensuing courtship, the family was reportedly reluctant to fully embrace "a northerner," and Halsey's attentions advanced slowly.[68]

In 1907 Halsey transferred to the new battleship *Kansas,* which participated in the Jamestown Exposition and later joined the Great White Fleet, Fan attended the grand farewell ball at the Chamberlin Hotel on Old Point Comfort and watched the Fleet's dramatic departure from Hampton Roads. After his return, Halsey transferred to command torpedo boat *DuPont* (TB-7) in Charleston but again visited Norfolk in midsummer 1909. The couple was married on 1 December 1909 in Norfolk's Christ Church. After the honeymoon, Halsey returned to *DuPont* for a short time, leaving Fan in Norfolk.[69]

In April 1910, Halsey was ordered to Norfolk Navy Yard to take charge of the apprentice seaman training camp at St. Helena and moved with Fan to the only house at the site, a comfortable dwelling fronting the Elizabeth River. Their first child, Margaret, was born on 10 October 1910; two years later, Halsey was ordered to command destroyer *Flusser* (DD-20) and, a year later, *Jarvis* (DD-38), operating out of Norfolk. After the war, he organized his destroyer division in Hampton Roads before sailing to join the new Pacific Fleet.

When Halsey's Carrier Division Two joined other units of the U.S. Fleet in the Caribbean in 1939, Halsey reported for duty to Vice Adm. Ernest King, Commander, Aircraft, Battle Force. Already well known for his perfectionist, demanding, arrogant, and impatient demeanor—so flinty and tough that it was said he "shaved with a blow torch"—King lost little time in putting Halsey's carriers through their paces in a series of exhausting fleet exercises culminating in Fleet Problem XX.[70] The timing for such no-nonsense naval leaders as King and Halsey could not have been better; while the Navy exercised in the sunny Caribbean, Hitler was marching into Czechoslovakia and the Japanese into Shanghai.

Following their exercises, the entire U.S. Fleet, more than one hundred ships and four aircraft carriers, pulled into Hampton Roads for a brief stay before sailing again for the Pacific. With the fleet's departure, the Atlantic Squadron in Hampton Roads numbered only carrier *Ranger,* four old battleships, four heavy cruisers of Cruiser Division Seven, and four modern destroyers.[71]

Germany launched its blitzkrieg into Poland on 1 September 1939, and Britain and France declared war in short order. At first, reaction in Norfolk was muted; Admiral Taussig told the press that the war would have no immediate effect on the Navy. But on 6 September, President Roosevelt abruptly ordered the Navy to organize a Neutrality Patrol to prevent belligerents from threatening the Western Hemisphere. Thirty-six four-stacker destroyers were pulled from mothballs to join the Atlantic Squadron, and several were sent to the Navy yard for repairs. Many featured creaky and aged equipment, such as *Yarnall* (DD-143), which was safely anchored in Lynnhaven Roads in November when a rusted and weakened link in her anchor chair gave way, setting her for a time on the beach.[72]

Destroyer patrol areas were established along the Atlantic coast, and a ready reaction force of four old battleships, three heavy cruisers, and carrier *Ranger* was formed in Hampton Roads. Long-range Catalina patrol squadrons, including Norfolk-based VP-51 (to Puerto Rico), VP-52 (to Newfoundland and later Brazil), VP-53, and VP-54, deployed to perform air patrols throughout the western Atlantic.

On 21 October a six-hundred-mile Neutrality Zone was

The conditions facing Norfolk destroyers during Neutrality Patrol operations in the North Atlantic during 1940–41 were trying; a mixture of high tensions, 35-degree rolls, clammy fog, Force 9 gales, and towering seas (a convoy viewed from destroyer *Greer,* shown here). With Roosevelt's approval to "shoot on sight" any U-boat approaching defended convoys, the Atlantic Fleet entered wartime operations many weeks before any declaration of war. *Naval Historical Center*

declared along the Atlantic coast, and the Navy was ordered to identify and report any German warships or submarines. The patrols were arduous and wearying but served to put Norfolk's ships to sea, greatly enhancing the training and experience of officers and crew alike. In mid-1940, a destroyer-type command under Rear Adm. Ferdinand L. Reichmuth was established in Norfolk to help with neutrality patrol training.

President Roosevelt visited the Navy yard and the NOB on 29 July 1940, hosted by Taussig, Congressman Darden, and others. It was Roosevelt's first visit to Norfolk as president, and he gauged the fleet's readiness for himself while emphasizing the importance of Hampton Roads as a defense center. "Flying the Presidential Flag, the USS *Potomac* slipped into the wet basin at the Navy Yard this morning at exactly 9:45 o'clock," reported the Portsmouth *Star.* "Eight sideboys stood at rigid attention and two companies of Marines formed the guard of honor. Navy Yard employees hung from the windows of several buildings as many more gathered on the dock to catch a glimpse of the President. Opposite the *Potomac* as she drew near the pier were four vessels of the 'mosquito fleet' with their crews standing at attention."[73]

During the summer of 1939, the Atlantic Squadron numbered some fifty-six ships, but by 1 November 1940 it had grown to 125 ships and was renamed the Patrol Force, U. S. Fleet. On 18 December, in a ceremony aboard the battleship *Texas* at the Norfolk Navy Yard, Admiral Ernest King took command of the Patrol Force, and on 1 February 1941, the Patrol Force was redesignated the Atlantic Fleet, and King was promoted to four stars as its commander in chief.[74]

In mid-March 1941, the president directed that the Atlantic Fleet be brought to war readiness, and King was told, "This step is, in effect, a war mobilization." At the same time, intensive training in convoy operations and antisubmarine warfare began at Norfolk, with use of practice submarines. By April, the Atlantic Fleet had grown to 159 ships, including the carriers *Ranger* and *Wasp,* 3 battleships, 8 cruisers, 78 destroyers and 29 submarines. King arrayed his fleet into task forces: Striking Force of two carriers, two heavy cruisers, and four destroyers and the fleet's Service

President Roosevelt arrives at the Navy Yard aboard presidential yacht *Potomac* on 29 July 1940, one of twelve presidents to visit the yard. *Naval Historical Center*

Force, based in Hampton Roads.[75]

In May, the Atlantic Fleet was strengthened further with transfers of carrier *Yorktown,* three newer battleships (*Idaho, New Mexico,* and *Mississippi*), four light cruisers, and two squadrons of destroyers from the Pacific. Considerable secrecy veiled this transfer; crews were not told of their destination, ships transited the Panama Canal at night, and *Yorktown* wore *Wasp*'s hull number. By October, the Atlantic Fleet stood at 355 ships, all with relatively high morale, because Atlantic duty appeared to Navy bluejackets to be closer to the war.[76]

With neutrality patrols extending throughout the North and South Atlantic, the Caribbean, and the Gulf of Mexico, tension remained high. When King had first taken over the Patrol Force, he had commented to President Roosevelt that he was being given a big slice of bread with damn little butter. With the transfer of ships to the Atlantic, the president had deftly asked King how he liked the butter he was getting. King replied, reflecting on his increasing operational tempo, "The butter's fine, but you keep giving me more bread."[77]

On 11 September, Roosevelt called for "an active defense" of "waters which we deem necessary for our defense" and directed that the Atlantic Fleet relieve Royal Navy destroyers of convoy responsibilities between America and Iceland. Many naval officers in Norfolk were privately pleased, agreeing with Winston Churchill's conclusion that "Hitler will have to choose between losing the Battle of the Atlantic or coming into frequent collision with United States ships."[78] It was a dizzying escalation for the Atlantic Fleet, from formal neutrality to pro-British neutrality to intensifying operations to undeclared war, all in only nine months of 1941.

Atlantic Fleet destroyers formed into escort groups orchestrated by the fleet's newly designated Support Force. In the first six weeks of operation, Support Force destroyers escorted fourteen convoys of 675 ships across the North Atlantic. In this tension-filled environment on the edge of war, it would not be long before the Support Force suffered its first casualties. Seven weeks before the Japanese attack on Pearl Harbor, on 17 October, a German torpedo ripped into the fireroom of Norfolk destroyer *Kearny* (DD-432), killing seven. Two weeks later, *Reuben James* (DD-245) was sunk with the loss of nearly all hands. Norfolk's first war casualty was First Class Boatswain's Mate Leonard Frontakowsky, injured aboard *Kearny. Reuben James's* commanding officer, Lt. Cdr. H. L.

For as long as there have been Navy ships in Hampton Roads there have been scenes of poignant good-byes and enthusiastic welcomes, just as these women bade farewell to loved ones aboard destroyer *Leary* circa 1935. *Sargeant Memorial Room, Norfolk Public Library*

Edwards, was well known in Norfolk and men from Berkley and Ocean View were listed among the dead.[79]

With the world aflame and the United States moving toward war, most in Tidewater girded themselves for all of the problems they remembered from the war boom of 1917. Many optimistically believed that the city had learned important lessons from those trying years and was better prepared for what was to happen. Some even thought that the larger and now well-established Navy bases could operate more fluidly without great disruptions to the surrounding communities. None of these projections came true. Again, war was to visit Hampton Roads and again the region would be fundamentally transformed, with all the attendant heartaches accompanying precipitous change.

1941

As in conflicts past, the winds of war in 1941 converged on Hampton Roads from all points of the compass, with the Virginia Tidewater caught squarely in a turbulent vortex. The bedrock of success in modern global war is industrial production, nimbly planned, the fruits of which are placed in the hands of men and women intelligently trained. Norfolk would soon play a role in each of these levels of conflict, and by war's end, no corner of America would be more transformed.

More than any other single influence, it would be the Navy that would come to symbolize this regional transformation to the people of Tidewater. Everywhere one turned during the war years there were bluejackets in the streets or gray hulls with long guns anchored in the roadsteads. The old Norfolk would still be there—a mid-sized southern city with an easy gait and cultivated hospitality—but as each day of the war passed, it was a newer Norfolk that would dominate, an industrial juggernaut focused less on genteel manners than on the ledgers of production.

The evening of 6 December 1941 had brought a cold front and wintry airs to the Virginia Tidewater, but Sunday dawned brightly with ample, chilly sunshine. Capt. Marc "Pete" Mitscher, commanding officer of the newly commissioned carrier *Hornet* (CV-8)—moored starboard side to Pier 4, near carrier *Yorktown*—had taken the opportunity to play a Sunday round of golf on the course of the Norfolk Yacht Club. Already a naval aviation legend with flying experience predating World War I and a Navy Cross on his chest, Mitscher was a leathery, irascible fifty-four years of age and was well known for his affinity for his crew and the long-billed baseball cap he inevitably wore while at sea.

Warmly dressed in sweater and slacks, Mitscher had navigated the course well, shooting a steady game in the lower nineties. Shortly after 1400 he was sitting down for a late lunch when an ensign from *Hornet* rushed into the club, carrying an envelope from the ship's duty officer. Mitscher's face hardened as he scanned the note, and he turned to the table to somberly announce: "Pearl Harbor has been bombed; we're at war with Japan."[1]

The startling news of the Japanese attack swept Tidewater like wildfire. "The city was filled with bluejackets, Marines and soldiers from nearby posts," read the newspaper. "It did not take long for the news to reach into all places where the men were congregated and it spread quickly along the streets." Special news flashes dominated radio broadcasts, and phone requests for confirmation swamped the lone copy boy left on a Sunday afternoon at the *Virginian-Pilot* newsroom. All sailors were ordered back to base, and extra Marines appeared at naval base gates. A *Virginian-Pilot* extra appeared on street corners by 1800 that evening.[2]

Already living in the shadow of an Atlantic war, Norfolk was ready with several harbor defense contingencies. The harbor entry command post at the old Weather Service Building at Cape Henry received its first alert at 1700 from Fifth Naval District Headquarters that war plans were in effect. Two hours

Hornet, a product of Newport News Shipbuilding, is shown here in February 1942 just before sailing for the Pacific under the command of Capt. Marc "Pete" Mitscher. Many of the newly loaded aircraft on her decks would fight in the Battle of Midway four months later. Although many were impressed with the clean, new, high-waisted warship, one grizzly chief petty officer spit over the side and was heard to say: "She ain't nothin' more than a barn door laid over top of a bathtub." *National Archives*

later, a second call advised that dawn airborne patrols would begin the next morning, with six planes scouting the approaches to the bay.[3]

Upon hearing of the attack, Naval District Commandant Rear Adm. M. H. Simons called a meeting of his staff to discuss plans for underwater obstructions and pier patrols at NOB. Fearing sabotage at naval bases and defense industries (by foreign residents, raiders landing on the beach, or crews of Axis ships in the roadstead), Simons ordered that all officers "equip themselves with pistol, belt, holster and ammunition . . . at all times while in a duty status."[4] Axis ships were seized, and Norfolk's City Manager, Col. Charles B. Borland, ordered the arrest of alien Japanese, although the chief of police admitted that "he did not have any information from the Government concerning what should be done with the Japanese nationals."[5]

By 9 December, Army antiaircraft batteries of the Coast Artillery were in place around the city and at the Navy yard, and searchlights from Fort Story were placed at Plume Street; their beams swept the nearby skies each night. Power plants were sandbagged, and several buildings at the Navy yard were covered in dull gray-green camouflage paint. That week, the newspapers devoted entire pages to air raid instructions. The *Ledger-Dispatch* implored: "There is no longer anything perfunctory about the formation of civilian defense units. It is serious business and it becomes the duty of every person to cooperate to the limit of his ability."[6]

Three days after Pearl Harbor, *Yorktown* quietly cast off her lines and sailed for the Pacific. Activity swirled around *Hornet* at NOB and its air group at the Naval Air Station as preparations accelerated for departure. Mitscher had "Remember Pearl Harbor" painted in huge block letters on the *Hornet*'s stack, and at daybreak on 27 December she stood out to sea on a cold, windswept morning in company with the new battleships *North Carolina* and *Washington* to complete shakedown training. On 31 January 1942 she was back at NOB and on 2 February loaded two Army B-25 Mitchell bombers aboard. The Army pilots had practiced about thirty short take-

On 15 June 1942, within sight of the Cape Henry lighthouse, tanker *Robert C. Tuttle* was damaged by mines laid by *U-701*. *Tuttle* was salvaged and towed to Norfolk Navy Yard for repairs. *Naval Historical Center*

offs at a nearby Navy auxiliary field, and, once at sea, *Hornet* faced into forty-five knots of wind and, with Cdr. Apollo Soucek carefully guiding operations as *Hornet*'s air officer, launched both bombers successfully. It was a test whose significance was not appreciated at the time, but one that would lead to *Hornet*'s dramatic Doolittle raid on Tokyo two months later.[7]

With stories and pictures of the London blitz fresh in everyone's mind, air raid sirens sounded and lights went out at Navy reservations when ships off the coast spotted an "unidentified dirigible." The first citywide blackout was ordered for 13 December, with a second for the twenty-ninth of the month. Streetcars came to a halt; automobiles pulled over to the curb; streetlights, stores, and restaurants turned dark; and volunteer air raid wardens telephoned reports to an information center in the basement of the downtown post office building.[8]

The Army's Norfolk Region Anti-aircraft Command coordinated air defense, and the Army Fighter Control at Langley Field handled intercepts with both Army and Navy fighter planes. Antitorpedo nets were placed at the ends of piers at NOB to protect against aircraft torpedo attacks. Additionally, a Regional Defense Council, including representatives from the Army, Navy, Newport News Shipbuilding, and local municipalities, coordinated civilian defense services.[9]

Most thought enemy threats were real, saboteurs were expected, guards and patrols were on a hair trigger, and schoolchildren were even told to report any suspicious strangers. On 10 January 1942, two searchlights at Cape Henry spotted a shadowy boat approaching the beach. An Army reaction force with two machine guns raced to the dunes, along with soldiers rustled up by a young Army lieutenant at the Service Men's Club, armed, it was told, only with the hotdogs they held in their hands. The raiders were spotted carrying black bundles on their backs, and the machine gunners carefully squinted through their sights. Disaster was averted at the last moment when the "enemy saboteurs" turned out to be only a lost boat from *Alcor* (AR-10) with bags of the ship's guard mail from Little Creek.[10]

Rumored saboteurs and air raid drills captured everyone's attention, but it was the U-boat that would be the true face of war for most people in Tidewater. For those in the living

The Fifth Naval District port director was responsible for coastal shipping coordination, convoy routing, harbor movements, berthing, and the control of secret signals. By the end of the war, 609 convoys had been organized in Hampton Roads or Lynnhaven Bay. The port director's staff developed general instructions, order of departure, convoy diagrams, communications plans, sailing orders, routing plans, recognition signals, and sortie/rendezvous anchorage plans. *Hampton Roads Naval Museum*

rooms and on the front porches of Hampton Roads, the details of distant battles reported in the morning newspapers were one representation of war; far more poignant were the actual views of sinking tankers, forlorn survivors, and convoy ships waiting at anchor. Fought within view of those sitting on Virginia and North Carolina beaches, it would be the submarine war that would be the manifestation of combat that everyone in Tidewater would remember.

Three days before the formal declaration of war, Adm. Karl Dönitz of the German U-boat Command was ordered to commence unrestricted submarine operations against U.S. shipping. Employing five long-range Type IX U-boats (four of which invaded U.S. waters off Cape Hatteras), Admiral Dönitz's Operation Paukenschlag ("Drumbeat") began during the third week of December, with the quiet sailing of the first America-bound boats from the submarine pens at Lorient, France. Despite warnings from the British, there was little the inexperienced and unprepared Americans could do to avoid disaster—the attacks of the five were destined to claim a grisly 150,000 tons of shipping.[11]

Even as the menacing shadows of U-boats plodded slowly westward toward the Virginia Capes, American and British planners had assembled in Washington for the Arcadia Conference. Winston Churchill and his senior military staff sailed to Hampton Roads aboard the new British battleship *Duke of York,* arriving in great secrecy after a storm-tossed voyage on 22 December. "It had been intended that we should steam up the Potomac and motor to the White House," wrote Churchill, "but we were all impatient after ten days at sea. We therefore arranged to fly from Hampton Roads [NAS Norfolk] and landed after dark at the Washington airport. There was the President waiting in his car."[12]

By 12 January 1942, the first of the German invaders were within three hundred miles of Cape Cod, where *U-123* surfaced and calmly put two torpedoes into the British steamer *Cyclops.* The first Drumbeat kill would claim a hundred of the

Convoys anchored in Lynnhaven Bay awaiting departure were a common sight throughout World War II. *Hampton Roads Naval Museum*

181-man *Cyclops* crew.[13] Other losses quickly followed.

Six days later, *U-66*'s sharp bow knifed through the short chop of the Gulf Stream, 140 miles southeast of Cape Henry. The wind was blustery, the night dark, and *U-66* was but an inky black shadow. Her quarry, however, was fully lit. Her closest prey was a target favored above all others, a tanker, not zigzagging and unaware of immediate peril. In minutes, two torpedoes hissed toward Standard Oil tanker *Allan Jackson,* followed by two explosions that scissored the keel open near the bow and spewed flaming bunker cargo into the water. The crew was thrown into the sea, the lifeboats nearly useless.

The sun's first rays guided destroyer *Roe* (DD-418) to a scene of scattered flotsam in a noxious steel-gray sea, where she rescued only 13 survivors from a crew of 48 before returning to Norfolk. On 19 January off Cape Hatteras, *U-123* claimed freighters *Ciltvaria* and *City of Atlanta* and damaged tanker *Malay* (which was towed to Hampton Roads for repairs), and *U-66* sank passenger liner *Lady Hawkins,* with 250 killed. Between 19 and 23 January, *U-66* sank tanker *Empire Gem* and steamers *Norvana* and *Venore* off Nags Head, and *U-130* claimed tankers *Olympic* and *Francis E. Powell.* On 25 January, *U-125* torpedoes ripped into merchant *West Ivis* one hundred miles off the Virginia coast, and on 30 January, *Roe* landed 30 survivors from tanker *Rochester* after she had been sunk eighty-five miles east of the Chesapeake lightship by *U-106.*[14]

A *Virginian-Pilot* editorial that appeared after this first eruption of attacks proved much closer to the truth than either its editors or government censors thought possible: "These sinkings bring the war home, in a particularly tragic manner to ports like Norfolk where many of the dead and the survivors are known . . . even more important is the question of whether protective measures are near sufficient . . . perhaps the United States government itself has not had time to prepare."[15]

As the first wave of Drumbeat U-boats returned to France to replenish their torpedo loads, six fresh Type IX submarines reached American waters in late January to continue to press the attack. With the waters off the Chesapeake approaches and Cape Hatteras boiling with U-boats, there was little the inexperienced antisubmarine escorts could do except patrol for survivors. Aircraft and warships were scarce, and the American command structure was bloated and inefficient. The British Liberty ship *Ocean Venture* fell victim to two torpedoes from *U-108* sixty miles east of Cape Henry at 0400 on 8 February

Increasingly vigorous antisubmarine patrols (especially by Consolidated P4Y-2 Privateer patrol bombers such as this) beginning in the spring and summer of 1942 helped drive U-boats away from shallow coastal waters where they were most vulnerable to detection from the air allowing coastal convoys to sail close inshore for safety. *Hampton Roads Naval Museum*

during the *Ocean Venture*'s maiden voyage. The crew abandoned ship, and only fourteen survivors in one of three lifeboats reached safety. *U-432* quickly followed, claiming six ships for 27,900 tons during twelve days of mid-February between Hatteras and the Maryland Eastern Shore. "The U-boats ravaged American waters almost uncontrolled," a dispirited Winston Churchill wrote, "and almost brought us to the disaster of an indefinite prolongation of the war."[16]

Convoy plans were soon prescribed and coastal defenses were reconstituted as "Sea Frontiers" for better coordination, but few escorts were available for defense. During the week ending 21 March, fourteen ships were sunk in Fifth Naval District waters, and from January through April, a total of eighty-two sinkings were recorded across the Eastern Sea Frontier. Thick black oil from tankers and debris from sunken freighters fouled local beaches. U-boat captains jubilantly hailed their carnage as a "happy time," while panic gripped the Atlantic seaboard. In response, Churchill ordered a fleet of converted British trawlers and antisubmarine corvettes to the East Coast. The U-boats were achieving results far out of proportion to their small numbers.[17]

A protective convoy system was finally in place by April. Ships would zigzag in prescribed lanes, hugging the coast by day, and put into harbor or protected anchorages at night. Air patrols were increased, and the bulk of the few surface escorts were concentrated around Cape Hatteras. But destroyers were few, and only two or three consorts screened individual convoys—usually a ragtag collection of Coast Guard ships or small, outmoded auxiliaries.[18]

Key to the defense of the Chesapeake Bay against U-boats was a complex system of minefields and offshore patrols. By mandate, the Army held chief responsibility for harbor minefields and operated a submarine mine depot and submarine mine school at Fort Monroe. But the Chesapeake defense was so challenging that, eventually, both Army and Navy minefields were sewn.[19]

The Navy had experimented with underwater magnetic detection beginning in August 1918 at Cape Henry and installed its first wartime magnetic detection loop at that same location in May 1941. Although the system promised to detect the magnetic signature of a U-boat's steel hull, its effectiveness proved to be poor. At the same time, a grid of tethered sonobuoys was installed, but their operation also proved unsatisfactory.[20] "The tides," explained one officer, "twisted the buoys around and snapped their chains, and the duties of patrol vessels were like those of a cowpuncher, as they rode herd on the critters. The longest a sonobuoy ever stayed fixed in a position was three days." A second magnetic loop was laid in March 1942, and a third by the end of 1943, with a total of sixty-three miles of seafloor cable deployed across the approaches.[21]

An antimotorboat boom with an antitorpedo net was placed at the entrance to Hampton Roads by 23 January 1942 to augment the antisubmarine net that had been in place across the entrance to the roads near Fort Monroe since the first week of the war. In April 1942 the Army planted six groups of controlled mines just seaward of the net gate. A rarely used antitorpedo net was also installed across the mouth of the York River.[22]

The Army began laying its primary Chesapeake minefield the day after Pearl Harbor, in four lines northeast of Cape Henry. A Notice to Mariners dated 17 December 1941 announced the mined area and required all ships to employ commercial pilots. Distrustful of the Army minefield, the Underwater Defense Section of the Navy Staff in Washington planned for their own defensive field at the entrance to Chesapeake Bay, which was laid by three minelayers on 17 January 1942 and stood in place until the fall of 1943.[23] By the end of 1943, the Army maintained fifty-nine groups of mines between the capes and four groups in Thimble Shoals Channel.[24]

While the Army and Navy argued about the placement of each other's minefields, there was no argument that the Navy held overall responsibility for smooth traffic flow through the bottlenecked channels. An elaborate system of guard ships and signals was initiated, beginning with the "Jake" patrol boat twenty miles east of Cape Henry, which challenged inbound shipping and confirmed the challenge reply

Aircraft carrier *Wasp* was homeported in Hampton Roads after her commissioning in April 1940 and participated in operations with the Royal Navy in the Norwegian and Mediterranean seas during the opening days of the war. With the loss of carrier *Lexington* at the Battle of the Coral Sea, *Wasp* hurried back to Norfolk for a rushed refit at the Navy Yard and sailed (shown here) in June 1942 for the Pacific. She was sunk a bare three months after this photo was taken by a Japanese submarine off Guadalcanal. *Norfolk Naval Shipyard*

with the Harbor Entry Control Post at Cape Henry. An Outer Guard Vessel stood at the western end of the swept channel (about five miles WNW from the Cape Henry Lighthouse) to meter all inbound ships, and an Examination and an Inner Guard vessel each policed all traffic, boarded all fishing boats and smaller craft, and directed uncleared ships to Lynnhaven Roads for inspection. The lightship *Diamond Shoals* served as the Examination Vessel for two years, until she was accidentally rammed and sank. All outbound ships were required to clear at the Examination Vessel and then follow the swept channel.[25]

On 15 February 1942 freighter *E. H. Blum* blundered across the minefield in low visibility, took the blast of three friendly mines, and sank. To prevent other accidents and to tighten the security of traffic, additional patrol stations were established in October 1942. Four stations patrolled the northern half of the swept channel (named "Nail," "Neck," "Nice," and "Note") and four the southern half of the channel ("Sane," "Seat," "Sine," and "Sold"). Another outer patrol station was added outside the minefield ("Nude"), and the station at the far eastern entrance to the swept channel ("Fare") was strengthened to search for U-boats lurking off its entrance. Although this system worked well, the swept channel was still difficult to secure, and two notable collisions occurred. On 26 March 1943 *Cape Henlopen* and *Lillian Luckenback* collided, sinking *Lillian Luckenback;* on 1 June 1943, ammunition carrier *John Morgan* and *Montana* collided, causing the *Morgan* to explode and sink.[26]

Auxiliary sailing yachts were used as coastal pickets beginning in September 1942 to "report the approach of enemy submarines, surface and air forces and attack and destroy them." Nine picket stations were established at sea, 80–150 miles from Little Creek. Some pickets were equipped with underwater sound gear, and most were armed with small .30-calibre machine guns. Occasionally, carrier pigeons provided the most reliable means of ship-to-shore communications. Coastal picket duty was rugged, and although it boosted the morale of those stalwarts involved, the pickets did little to stop U-boats. The Navy and Coast Guard also set up a Coastal Lookout System at lifeboat stations, lighthouses, and radio direction finder stations.[27]

Augmenting its coastal pickets, the Navy also enlisted commercial offshore fishing boats into a network to spot enemy air and submarine contacts and report them by radiotelephone. At its height, 143 ships and boats were part of the plan. On 13 April 1942, trawler *Sea Roamer,* operating out of Hampton, radioed a submarine sighting twenty miles east of Bodie Island. Planes and ships saturated the area, and four-piper destroyer *Roper* (DD-147) scored the first U-boat kill of the war in American waters by sinking *U-85* the next day, thirty miles from *Sea Roamer's* contact.[28]

Virginia Beach and Outer Banks communities dimmed their shore lights in the belief that darkness made merchant shipping harder to spot by marauding U-boats. Dim-out regulations were enforced by late 1942, after which Norfolk storefront lighting was reduced to 10 percent of normal, night ball games were canceled, and exterior lights were hooded to reduce the amount of light produced.[29]

U-boat activity off the eastern seaboard peaked during April 1942 (with almost one sinking a day recorded). On 1 April 1942, the American tanker *Tiger* was torpedoed and sunk by *U-754* six miles southeast of the Outer Guard Station as she waited at dead stop for a pilot boat. A day earlier, the *Menominee* and three barges carrying coal to Boston had been boldly shelled and sunk by the same U-boat twenty miles north of the Virginia Capes. On 3 April, collier *David H. Atwater* was shelled and sunk by *U-552* ten miles east of Chincoteague Inlet.[30]

The *Cythera,* a large converted yacht commissioned as an antisubmarine patrol craft, had sailed from NOB on 1 May but was torpedoed a day later off South Carolina by *U-402.* Only Seamen James M. Brown and Charles Carter survived from the crew of seventy. They were picked up by the U-boat (despite Dönitz's strict orders to the contrary) and carried back to Europe, where they were interned for the duration as very unusual naval POWs.[31]

The first major East Coast convoys began in May 1942 along the Norfolk–Key West track, with 43 warships and numerous aircraft assigned to five escort groups. The first of these convoys, Convoy KS-500 (25 ships and seven escorts), sailed from Lynnhaven Roads on 14 May.[32] The new convoy system immediately proved effective, and only 4 merchant ships would be lost in the Eastern Sea Frontier in May. Hampton Roads and Lynnhaven Bay ranked as the second largest convoy center of the war, dispatching 609 convoys comprising 7,827 ships.[33]

U-701 left France on 19 May 1942 and arrived off the Chesapeake Bay after dark on 12 June. On a moonless night, the U-boat's captain used Chesapeake lighthouses to guide him into the main shipping channel, where he deployed fifteen delayed-action magnetic mines in thirty-six feet of water (despite the presence of a nearby patrol boat). On 15 June, inbound Convoy KN-109 arrived at the Chesapeake sea buoy, and shortly after 1700 a sudden explosion rocked the fifth ship in line, tanker *Robert C. Tuttle*. Damaged, she listed to starboard and fell out of column. In panic, tanker *Esso Augusta* broke out of column to avoid the suspected U-boat, hoisted zigzag signals, and ordered full speed, only to strike a second mine (she was towed to Norfolk later that night). A short time later, British antisubmarine trawler HMS *Kingston Ceylonite* (escorting the damaged freighter *Delisle*) suddenly exploded, the victim of yet another mine.[34]

The unfolding drama was in full view of those at Virginia Beach, "electrifying thousands of shore watchers," but like the *Virginian-Pilot,* everyone thought that the attack was from a lurking U-boat. Patrol aircraft from NAS, a blimp, and destroyer *Bainbridge* (DD-246) rushed to the scene, but when reporters wrote that they had seen "the underwater killer explode and disappear," it had only been *Bainbridge* depth charges setting off an additional mine that damaged the destroyer. The Chesapeake was closed to traffic for two days while minesweepers swept the channel, finding five German mines. When the channel was reopened, freighter *Santore* struck the last of *U-701*'s mines and sank, again in full view of Virginia Beach.[35] *U-701*'s mining proved such a remarkable success that the German U-boat sent *U-69* to reseed *U-701*'s original minefield on 10 September 1942 and directed *U-230* and *U-566* to plant twenty mines in the Chesapeake approaches between 26 and 30 July 1943.[36]

On the morning of 14 July 1942, Convoy KS 520—nineteen ships, escorts *Ellis* (DD-154), *McCormick* (DD-223), and five smaller craft—was a day out of Norfolk near Cape Hatteras when it was spotted by *U-576*. Maneuvering rapidly into attack position, the submarine fired four torpedoes in five minutes, hitting freighters *Chilore* and *Bluefields* and tanker *J. A. Mowinckel*. *Bluefields* quickly sank, but the other damaged ships turned to shallow water to beach. In the confusion of the attack, both ran into a defensive minefield, where *Chilore* sank and a tug responding to her distress exploded. *Mowinckel* made it back to Hampton Roads for repairs.[37]

Starting in September 1942, the main weight of the U-boat force was shifted from American waters back to the central North Atlantic, never to return in force. In the nine months of

A Vought OS2U-3 Kingfisher floatplane over Willoughby Spit. The Kingfisher was the Navy's primary catapult-launched monoplane observation floatplane used aboard battleships and cruisers. Both U.S. Navy and Royal Navy pilots received floatplane training at NAS Norfolk during the war. *Hampton Roads Naval Museum*

Operation Drumbeat, the Germans conducted 184 war patrols in American waters (averaging 20 sailings per month) and sank 609 ships (3.1 million tons, an average of 68 ships per month). To the credit of the American defense forces, their response to the U-boat attacks ultimately proved effective in blunting the U-boat's impact, but although shipping losses were substantial, they never proved to be decisive. By early 1943, the coastal convoy system had been strengthened still further, and by midyear, escort carrier hunter-killer groups operating in the mid-Atlantic were intercepting other America-bound U-boats before they could get to patrol positions near the Chesapeake Bay. During all of 1943, only 2 merchant ships and 1 Navy patrol craft were sunk in Fifth Naval District waters, compared with 67 sinkings during 1942.[38]

The Norfolk-based escort carrier *Guadalcanal* (CVE-60) and antisubmarine task group 21.12 contributed to this dominance as they operated in the mid-Atlantic, scouring the waters for U-boats. In early 1944, the task group sank *U-544, U-515,* and *U-68* and on 4 June 1944 forced *U-505* to the surface, where she was captured intact—a great boon for American intelligence.[39]

During April 1945, one final convulsion of U-boat activity was aimed at the Chesapeake, but American antisubmarine forces met the challenge. Between 14 and 23 April, *U-857* and *U-879* were credited with sinking freighter *Belgian Airman* and tanker *Swiftscout* and damaging tanker *Katy* while operating 150 miles off the Virginia Capes. So dominant was the American naval antisubmarine posture by the last two years of the war that no U-boat could hope to score any clean victories anywhere near the American coast. On 30 April one of the two U-boats was sunk by depth charges from *Natchez* (PF-2) and destroyers *Coffman* (DE-191), *Bostwick* (DE-103), and *Thomas* (DE-102), and the second U-boat never returned from patrol.[40]

In the first months of 1942, naval facilities in Hampton Roads quickly expanded to meet the demands of global war. In September 1939, the naval operating base and air station comprised a total of 945 acres with 472 buildings. By July 1945, the NOB, the air station, and the new south annex had burgeoned to more than 3,500 acres with 2,300 buildings.[41]

As war came to Hampton Roads, Norfolk Naval Air Station was already primed for rapid expansion. During the war years, the air station would become the largest naval air complex on the Atlantic coast, would host the operational headquarters for all naval air forces in the Atlantic Fleet, would serve as the chief aviation supply center in the Navy, and would develop into the Navy's largest aircraft overhaul and repair station. NAS Norfolk would grow from an average of 2,076 officers and men in December 1940 to 16,656 active-duty personnel three years later and, during the first six months of 1943, would handle an average of 21,073 flights per month.[42]

On 6 February 1942 the Navy condemned 508 acres of privately held land to the east of the NAS, adding that to 352 acres recovered from Willoughby Bay by dredging. New facilities mushroomed across the embryonic eastern portion of the base with the construction of three land plane hangars, two seaplane hangars, barracks and mess facilities, an operations building, aviation storage facilities, and aviation gasoline facilities. The three concrete runways of the new East Field were planned for 3,793 feet, 4,000 feet, and 4,325 feet.[43]

Fleet Air Wing Five was formed early in 1942 to coordinate all operational missions within the Fifth Naval District. Wing Five consisted of scouting squadrons, Kingfisher seaplanes, and PBY Catalina patrol planes of VP-83 and -84. Extensive antisubmarine air patrols dominated NAS operations in early 1942, and the air station commanding officer assumed additional duties as Commander, Air Facilities, Fifth Naval District, as air operations spread to a broad network of integrated airfields across Tidewater. By 12 October 1942, this concept, pioneered in Norfolk, would spread Navy wide with the establishment of naval air centers in fleet concentration areas to consolidate air stations, air facilities, and outlying fields under a central command. Continued expansion of naval air activities in Norfolk required the creation of the new position of Commander, Naval Air Bases, Fifth Naval District, on 2 August 1944.[44]

On 1 January 1943, the staffs of Carriers Atlantic, Carrier Replacement Squadrons Atlantic, and Fleet Air Wings Atlantic were combined to form a new major command, Naval Air Force, Atlantic Fleet, under the command of Rear Adm. Alva D. Bernhard, with headquarters at NAS Norfolk.[45] In March 1943, then–Rear Adm. P. N. L. Bellinger returned to Norfolk for yet another important tour of duty, assuming this command. In addition to logistics, maintenance, and training duties, COMNAVAIRLANT directed all Atlantic air combat operations against U-boats, including land-based patrols and carrier hunter-killer groups.

The dominant mission of Naval Air Center, Hampton Roads (and later Naval Air Bases, Fifth Naval District) was to furnish combat-ready carrier air groups, patrol squadrons, and battleship and cruiser aviation units to both the Atlantic and Pacific fleets. Nearly all Navy squadrons that fought in the war would train first in the Hampton Roads area. In 1944, Naval Air Force Atlantic deployed sixteen carriers, twenty carrier air groups, sixty-seven carrier-based squadrons, twenty-

The original Chambers Field is shown to the left in this aerial photo taken on 7 November 1941; the new East Field is to the right, with short runways but a tarmac filled with aircraft. The Breezy Point seaplane hangers are located across a still-robust Mason's Creek. *Hampton Roads Naval Museum*

one patrol squadrons, and eighteen aviation units to the Pacific. *Charger* (CVE-30) acted as a school ship for both squadrons in training and for flight deck personnel assigned to newly commissioned carriers.

Training activities at NAS Norfolk were widespread. The Aviation Service School offered courses in metalworking, engine repair, radio repair, and ordnance, and the Aviation Machinist's Mate "A" School provided classroom training and apprentice experience in aircraft repair shops. The Advanced Base Aviation Training Unit trained sailors destined for advanced air bases in combat theaters. Similarly, the Carrier Air Service Unit provided maintenance training for crews awaiting the commissioning of new carriers, and the Fighter Direction School taught fighter control techniques used in shipboard Combat Information Centers. The Aerial Free Gunnery Training Unit (an early version of "Topgun") moved from Breezy Point to Dam Neck in 1943.

NAS Norfolk also provided extensive training to British fighter and torpedo bomber squadrons and French and Russian PBY patrol squadrons. The station also provided training and maintenance facilities for British aircrew from visiting carriers HMS *Illustrious* and HMS *Formidable* and trained the float plane detachments aboard British battleships and cruisers.

As early as 1939, the commandant of the Fifth Naval District was asked by the Bureau of Aeronautics to forward recommendations for the establishment of outlying landing fields for NAS Norfolk. Eight sites were considered, and five (Pungo, Creeds, Oceana, Monogram, and Fentress) were immediately procured and ultimately designated as Naval Auxiliary Air Stations (NAAS) of the Naval Air Center, Hampton Roads. Although each was a distinct entity, all were relatively close to NAS Norfolk and all could be seen at the same time from an aircraft flying at ten thousand feet. On any day, the skies above Tidewater would fill with fighters, torpedo bombers, and dive-bombers—at one time, up to twenty different carrier air groups were present in Norfolk airspace—all completing complex training events and all, inevitably, dodging the flight patterns of others. Pilots would practice field "carrier" landings, aero-

At the beginning of World War II the air station's Assembly and Repair Department occupied four small hangars and employed 213 enlisted and 573 civilians in the overhaul of aircraft engines and fuselages. Within six months, the department operated on two ten-hour shifts, seven days a week, with a workforce of 1,600 enlisted and 3,500 civilians. Women, who had only been employed for sewing wing and fuselage fabric, began to take on regular duties in the machine shops. By 1943 civilian employment had increased to almost 6,000, and by war's end the workforce numbered 8,600 personnel. *Hampton Roads Naval Museum*

batics, formation flying, two-plane fighter section tactics, strafing, bombing, and instrument flying. For "graduation," coordinated strikes would be flown with an air group's fighter, torpedo, and dive-bomber squadrons. Training fatalities were well known. In one example, Fighting Fifteen lost two ensigns in training accidents in two months, and Bombing Fifteen lost six pilots during November 1943.[46]

By late 1943, planning estimates called for the basing of 64 carrier aircraft each at Oceana, Pungo, Fentress, and NAAS Manteo, North Carolina; 45 carrier aircraft each at Creeds and Monogram; forty-eight patrol aircraft each at Harvey Point and Elizabeth City, North Carolina; 24 patrol bombers at NAAS Chincoteague; with NAAS Franklin providing acceptance and transfer services for all.[47] By January 1944, Oceana had been authorized an increase to 180 carrier and 30 reconnaissance aircraft.

A swampy 329-acre tract near the crossroads of Oceana, Virginia, had been purchased in 1940 for an Outlying Landing Field (OLF) for NAS Norfolk and to meet the Army's requirement for a fighter base near Virginia Beach. Construction began in December 1940 on two 2,500-foot sand-asphalt runways, a single wooden building that served as an ambulance garage and caretaker's quarters, a modest tower, and several Quonset huts to accommodate 32 officers and 172 enlisted men. In 1942, Fighting Squadron Nine (commanded by Lt. Cdr. Jack Raby and equipped with F4F-3 Wildcats) was the first unit assigned to the field, and it was said that fighter pilots immediately liked Oceana, because it kept them away from the more stilted atmosphere at NAS Norfolk. VF-9 was formed as part of the *Essex* air group for duty in the Pacific but was redirected to *Ranger* for Operation Torch, the Allied invasion of North Africa.[48] When VF-9 returned to Oceana from Africa, it transitioned to the first F6F-3 Hellcats to be introduced.

The Oceana field closed in April 1943 to lengthen runways

Nearly all Navy squadrons that fought in the war would train first in the Hampton Roads area. The Carrier Qualifications Training Unit provided field carrier landing practice and qualification landings aboard carriers regularly operating in the Chesapeake Bay or occasionally off the Virginia Capes training sixteen carriers and sixty-seven carrier-based squadrons in 1944 alone. *U.S. Navy photo of a Lawrence Beall Smith work courtesy Milton L. Reynolds*

Naval Auxiliary Air Station Oceana 3 March 1948. *National Archives*

to six thousand feet and was reopened and commissioned as NAAS Oceana on 17 August 1943, with Lt. Jesse Harley as the first officer in charge. Carrier Air Group Thirteen moved to the field in January 1944, and Oceana's first commanding officer, Cdr. F. E. Dean, arrived on 9 March. Large PB4Y-1 Liberator patrol bombers (a navalized variant of the Army's B-24 bomber) moved to Chincoteague in December 1943 after encountering problems with weight on Oceana's runways. The station ultimately accommodated two carrier air groups of eight squadrons, and construction in 1945 included a steel arch hangar, personnel quarters, a new boiler house and administration building, a chapel, a gymnasium, a movie theater, a ship's service store, and a library.[49]

Construction began at NAAS Creeds in mid-1940, and the field was commissioned on 5 April 1943 with Quonset huts, hangars, and shops, and ready rooms and offices in a nearby existing "barnlike" building. Construction at NAAS Pungo began in February 1941, and the field was commissioned on 5 April 1943, but conditions were spartan. Pilots were quartered in long single-story temporary barracks, and ground school was conducted in unheated classrooms. During the war, twenty-four squadrons (primary composite squadrons) trained at the field. NAAS Fentress was commissioned on 15 April 1943 and, likewise, was home to a succession of composite squadrons. In March 1944, the field's population numbered 141 officers and 1,243 enlisted men.[50]

NAAS Franklin was commissioned on 8 May 1943, with Lt. William Lyons commanding. Franklin's primary duty was to transfer and receive fresh aircraft assigned to new squadrons and air groups. For most of the war, it maintained an inventory of about 300 aircraft, and, by war's end, 11,865 aircraft had been transferred. Franklin featured two three-thousand-foot runways that were extended and joined by a third forty-two-hundred-foot runway in the summer of 1945.[51]

NAAS Monogram, eighteen miles southwest of Norfolk in Driver, was originally leased in 1939 but was purchased outright in April 1941. Known first as Monogram Farm Field, it was designated a NAAS when it was commissioned on 15 May 1943. Monogram featured four sod and grass runways

Naval Auxiliary Air Station Pungo as it appeared in April 1944. Built to a runway plan similar to that used at Fentress, Creeds and Oceana, Pungo was the training home to a steady stream of Navy Composite squadrons composed of 9 Wildcat fighters and 12 Avenger torpedo bombers that served primarily aboard escort carriers. *National Archives*

Curtiss SB2C "Helldiver" Scout-bombers fly in formation over False Cape during training in 1943. *National Archives*

and was the designated landing field for aircraft with hung bombs or wheels-up landings. Because of its grass fields, rains would close the field about a third of the time. Naval Air Center, Hampton Roads, also used OLFs at Lively and Suffolk in Virginia and Edenton in North Carolina. A small, infrequently used site, referred to as Whitehurst Field, was built as a grassy OLF just north of the current Norfolk International Airport. In November 1942, NAAS Harvey Point seaplane base was provided with barracks for two thousand men, a timber hangar, and two sea-plane ramps; NAAS Chincoteague had quarters for four hundred men and a storehouse; and NAAS Manteo included barracks for three hundred men and a small wooden hangar.[52]

The Navy had maintained an outlying field at Chincoteague Island for many years, but in 1940, it expanded the site to two thousand acres and commissioned NAAS Chincoteague on 5 March 1942, with Lt. Frederick M. Smith commanding. Carrier fighter, torpedo, and composite squadrons used the base, as did PB4Y-1 Liberator patrol bombers and then the improved single-tail PB4Y-2 Privateer patrol bomber. Beginning in October 1943, the Bureau of Ordnance established an experimental unit at Chincoteague for secret tests and experiments in the latest aviation ordnance, and late in 1944, the Navy leased the airport at Salisbury as an outlying field for the station. In June 1946, the Navy transferred its East Coast guided missile testing activities to the redesignated Naval Aviation Ordnance Test Station (NAOTS) at Chincoteague.[53]

With aviation training operations concentrated at the network of NAAS fields, NAS Norfolk operated the majority of patrol missions and served as a concentration site for transient planes being ferried to distant theaters. VR-1, the first Naval Air Transport Service (NATS) squadron, was based at NAS beginning 9 March 1942. The station was heavily overloaded, and by mid-1944 it averaged 428 aircraft assigned, although it had an official capacity of 336.[54]

The most devastating war-related accident in Hampton Roads occurred on 17 September 1943 at the Naval Air Station. At 1100, an ordnance department truck pulling four trailers loaded with aerial depth charges turned onto the taxiway between Chambers Field and the NOB piers. Although designed for only four depth charges, each trailer was overloaded with six, with the topmost charges poorly chained down. As the truck rounded the turn, one of the charges fell under a trailer's wheels and started to smoke as it was dragged forward. The driver immediately ran to get help, and Assistant Fire Chief Gurney E. Edwards responded. As Chief

Note that rationing rules prohibited Norfolk residents from commuting by auto to work at the navy yard during the war. *Norfolk Naval Shipyard*

Edwards approached the scene with a fire extinguisher, the first depth charge exploded, killing him instantly. For the next several minutes the remaining charges exploded, shattering windows up to seven miles away. Forty died in the disaster (including Seaman 2nd Class Elizabeth Korensky, the first Navy WAVE to die in the line of duty), and another 426 people were injured. Eighteen buildings and thirty-five aircraft were destroyed, a loss of $1.8 million.[55]

The sting of war had been felt in Norfolk Navy Yard many months before Pearl Harbor when the damaged British aircraft carrier HMS *Illustrious* arrived on 12 May 1941 to undergo extensive battle damage repairs. *Illustrious* had suffered six bomb hits and three near misses from German dive-bombers off Malta, and with a Lend-Lease provision permitting the repair of British warships in American shipyards, she had sailed painfully around the Cape of Good Hope and up the Atlantic to Norfolk. Tidewater considered the ship's presence "secret," and yard workers and local media kept quiet. Although the carrier had sailed in plain view up the Elizabeth, British sailors thronged the streets, and *Illustrious* musicians played with the Norfolk Symphony, the Nazis claimed several times to have sunk the ship. "The whole town knew about *Illustrious,*" wrote one Norfolk historian, but no word about her appeared in newspaper type until August when Captain Lord Louis Mountbatten came to take command [accompanied by forty newsmen and photographers]. The British Ministry of Information itself announced that Mountbatten had arrived in the United States and would command *Illustrious,* "in an American shipyard undergoing repairs."[56]

One Royal Navy tale that made the rounds at the navy yard was not kept a secret. It was well known that British ships were notorious for their terrible food, and it was said that you could always recognize a British ship in the Elizabeth River because the seagulls circling in its wake did so with one wing folded under—because they had to carry their own rations.[57]

Before the war, St. Helena was used as housing for the crews of battleships undergoing modernization and other ships

In addition to aircraft carrier *Illustrious*, six other Royal Navy vessels put into Norfolk Navy Yard during 1941. During the war, another 140 British vessels received repairs in the yard, joined at times by other Allied vessels from Canada, the Netherlands, Russia, Australia, and France. Here British battleship *Royal Sovereign* is in the midst of a refit that lasted from September 1942 to September 1943. *Norfolk Naval Shipyard*

in refit after the gasoline and oil depot had been transferred to Craney Island. The Coast Guard operated facilities at the southern end of St. Helena, and the northern end was cleared for an aviation landing field that, ultimately, was never built. During the war, St. Helena was converted into a ship repair and fitting-out facility for destroyer escorts, tank-landing ships, minesweepers, and other small ships. Four new piers and fifteen new buildings (barracks, shops, and service buildings) were added.[58]

The Navy purchased a 62-acre parcel to the southwest of the Navy yard in 1942 to serve as a recreation center, naming it Scott Center, and on 5 June 1942 acquired a second parcel of 62.5 acres south of the yard (named Paradise Creek Annex) from the Norfolk Dredging Company (with an additional 25 acres added in 1946) for use as a disposal area. The yard also established the Southgate Annex on two parcels of 83 acres along the Elizabeth waterfront that were acquired in 1942 and 1944.[59]

During the war, the Navy yard doubled in size from 352 to 747 acres, including nearly 4.25 miles of water front. Berthing spaces increased from thirty-one to sixty-six, and Dry Dock No. 8—the yard's largest at 1,092 feet and able to accommodate the largest aircraft carriers—was opened in July 1942. More than four war housing projects comprising 16,487 family units were constructed in nearby communities. At war's end, the yard contained 413 permanent buildings.[60]

The yard's industrial activities during the war were split between new ship construction, ship modernizations, and battle damage repairs. A total of 6,850 naval ships (a combined weight of more than 27 million tons) were repaired, and 101 new ships and landing craft were built for the fleet, 44 of which were combatant ships.[61]

The yard's workforce had increased from thirty-five hundred to seventy-six hundred between 1938 and 1939, and by 1940 it was increasing at the rate of a thousand employees a month, reaching a peak of more than forty-two thousand in February

The yard's signature Hammerhead Crane (here supporting the 1941 refit of the Royal Navy carrier *Illustrious)* was constructed primarily for the purpose of outfitting destroyers with gun turrets. The crane reaches twenty stories high, houses three auxiliary cranes, and can lift 350 tons. Its uniqueness and significance to the Navy Yard mission has earned it a place on the National Register of Historic Places. *Norfolk Naval Shipyard*

1943. At its peak, still more employees were needed, but the manpower needs of the fighting forces and the severe shortage of houses in Norfolk and Portsmouth held down capacity. To stretch its workforce to the maximum, the yard operated two nine-hour shifts. Women, who had held only clerical positions in the previous war, now took on industrial jobs, and many were trained at National Youth Administration facilities.[62]

The Navy yard's largest project at the war's outset involved construction of the 44,500-ton battleship *Alabama,* the second battleship ever built by the yard and the sister to *Indiana,* built simultaneously at Newport News. The yard's efficiency was impressive; construction costs were $4 million less than for battleships built at commercial yards, and completion took thirty months instead of the planned fifty-five months because of collaboration with nearby Newport News.[63]

Battleship *Kentucky* (BB-66), sixth ship of the *Iowa* class, was laid down in March 1942 but was removed three months later when the Navy gave higher priority to the construction of landing craft. *Kentucky*'s incomplete hull bottom was moored for a time along the Elizabeth, with work continuing slowly until the ship was eventually scrapped at 73 percent. The yard also received a contract for the construction of *Louisiana* (BB-71), the most powerful battleship ever designed in the United States, with twelve 16-inch guns, but work was canceled with the end of the war, and no ships of the class were built.[64]

Three large aircraft carriers were built in the yard during the war: *Shangri-La* (CV-38), *Lake Champlain* (CV-39), and *Tarawa* (CV-40). After the celebrated Doolittle raid from the carrier *Hornet,* an exuberant President Roosevelt announced that the Army bombers had flown from a secret base at "Shangri-La," a reference to the mystical village of the James Hilton novel *Lost Horizon.* When *Hornet* was subsequently sunk and Americans learned that *Hornet* was "Shangri-La," a war bond drive netted $900 million to build a new carrier, to be named *Shangri-La,* at the Norfolk Navy Yard. On 24 February 1944, only thirteen months after her keel had been laid

Norfolk Navy Yard recruiters drove as far as West Virginia and Ohio to recruit tradesmen to help keep up the high pace of wartime construction. *Hampton Roads Naval Museum*

and with a crowd of a hundred thousand watching, Mrs. James H. Doolittle launched the ship with great fanfare. *Shangri-la* was commissioned on 15 September, and a month later she was under way on shakedown trials in the Chesapeake Bay before sailing for the Pacific.[65]

Two months after work began on *Shangri-La,* the yard laid the keel for carrier *Lake Champlain,* and for a year the two matching hulls rose slowly side by side. *Lake Champlain* was launched on 2 November 1944 and was commissioned on 3 June 1945. As soon as *Lake Champlain* was out of the way, the uncompleted hull section of *Kentucky* took her place; as soon as *Shangri-La* was moved from her building way, *Tarawa*'s keel was laid on 1 March 1944. The yard also refitted *Ranger* during May–July 1944, with the installation of new radars, a strengthened flight deck, and equipment for night fighter control.[66]

Battle damage repair inevitably created a buzz throughout the yard when battle-weary ships limped into port with stirring stories, high-priority repairs, and tight deadlines. Heavy cruiser *Chester* (CA-27) and light cruiser *Honolulu* (CL-48) both received extensive overhauls after torpedo damage, and several destroyers were repaired after kamikaze attacks. But the priority for twenty tank landing ships (LSTs) and fifty mechanized landing craft (LCM) proved to be one of the highest in the yard, crowding every available building way and dry dock. The yard also continued its destroyer construction line, begun in the 1930s, with the destroyers *Herndon* (DD-638) and *Shubrick* (DD-639) and fourteen destroyer escorts. The emphasis in destroyer construction was on speed, and *Shubrick* was launched just two months after keel laying.[67]

During the war, Newport News Shipbuilding delivered *Essex* (CV-9) on the last day of 1942, and then, in rapid succession, *Yorktown* (CV-10), *Intrepid* (CV-11), *Hornet* (CV-12), *Franklin* (CV-13), *Ticonderoga* (CV-14), *Randolph* (CV-15), and *Boxer* (CV-21)—a total of eight carriers in twenty-seven months, or an average of one every fifteen weeks. A ninth *Essex*-class carrier, *Leyte* (CV-32), was delivered in April 1946. *Franklin* was built in a record time of thir-

One of the top priorities at the Navy Yard (higher even than battleships and carriers) in the early part of the war was the construction of landing craft. Production occurred at every available open area on the yard and at many private sites throughout Tidewater contracted to government service. Here, LCM landing craft are under construction at the yard in early summer 1942. *Hampton Roads Naval Museum*

teen months, twenty-four days. The yard also built battleship *Indiana,* eight light cruisers (three others were on the ways and were canceled at the end of the war), and eleven dock landing ships (LSDs).[68]

At the onset of World War II, amphibious warfare was still in its infancy. Although warriors had attacked from the sea since the time of the Greeks, assault from the sea in modern warfare was unproved and was fraught with unknowns. The few twentieth-century examples of amphibious attack (such as at Gallipoli during World War I) had been awkward affairs, teetering on disaster. The U.S. Navy and its Marine Corps tested their unproved amphibious tactics in a series of exercises in the late 1930s, beginning with Fleet Landing Exercise Number One (FLEX-1) in Puerto Rico in March 1935. These nascent amphibious exercises were well intended but rarely a pretty sight. V-keeled utility boats foundered in high surf, heavy equipment was lost in the water, shore bombardment proved inaccurate, and boats could not land heavy equipment.

As Allied war planning advanced, it became abundantly clear that amphibious success would depend on refined tactics, newly designed specialty naval craft, and newly indoctrinated amphibious ratings with training in the ways of the "Gator Navy." To meet this daunting challenge, a humble boat basin in a Chesapeake tidal inlet called Little Creek would unexpectedly rise from obscurity to become a linchpin in complex Allied global war planning.

The Pennsylvania Railroad had first developed the swampy lowland area around Little Creek in 1928 as a railhead to load rail cars aboard barges for the brief transit across the bay to Cape Charles. The Navy obtained use of the property in January 1941 as a naval section base for its local defense forces protecting shipping in Lynnhaven Roads. Ground was broken in June 1941, and the base was commissioned on 2 September, with one finger pier and a bulkhead quay providing a total

Battleship *Alabama* was laid down on 1 February 1940 at Norfolk Navy Yard and commissioned (shown here) on 16 August 1942. Her nine 16-inch guns were used to advantage primarily in the Pacific theater during the war in operations against Tarawa, Truk, Saipan, Guam, Palau, Leyte, Okinawa, and the Japanese Home Islands. She is on display today in Mobile, Alabama. *Norfolk Naval Shipyard*

berthing space of eleven hundred feet.[69]

By early 1942, a series of small amphibious landing practices were arranged near Cape Henry and at Solomons Island on the Patuxent River, where a landing exercise center was built beginning in February 1942. Although a small landing party equipment depot had operated at NOB for a short time in August 1941, the first orders to establish an Atlantic Fleet Amphibious Force were not issued until 13 March 1942, when Rear Adm. Roland M. Brainard and a staff of eight were ordered to begin amphibious planning from Building 138 near Pier 7 at NOB.[70] Planning for amphibious assault was considered highly secret at the time, and it would be not until late 1943 that correspondents would be allowed to view amphibious training bases.

Training for Navy boat crew coxswains and diesel mechanics began at an ad hoc NOB drill hall in July 1942, and the first thousand in the classes did not receive their "diplomas" until they had completed a successful landing in the pounding surf at Fort Story. Space at Solomons was limited, and the Navy began searching for a central location on the Atlantic coast with varied beach conditions, proximity to the naval facilities, berthing for the new amphibious assault craft, and space for classrooms and barracks. Modest bean fields on the Whitehurst and Bradford farms east of the Little Creek Naval Sector Base met Navy requirements, and work began on 18 July 1942 on Camp Bradford, which was first designated a training base for the Navy's construction battalions (CBs, or "Seabees") and beach party battalions.[71]

Soon, a Beach Party School for the training of beach battalions was opened among the scrub pines and sand at Camp Bradford, and the camp quickly expanded into a training center for Army amphibious training while also hosting a Joint Communications School and a Naval Gunfire Support School. Between May 1943 and January 1944, more than one hundred thousand troops were trained at Bradford. The camp became the largest of Little Creek's amphibious training facilities, with fourteen hundred buildings and facilities for twenty-five thousand officers and enlisted men.[72]

Camp Shelton rose adjacent to Camp Bradford and was ini-

Norfolk Navy Yard built three large *Essex*-class carriers during World War II—*Tarawa, Lake Champlain*, and, most eye-catching of all, *Shangri-La* (shown here on 24 February 1944). Largely funded through nationwide bond drives, *Shangri-La*'s name comes from the mythical kingdom in the novel *Lost Horizon* that President Roosevelt quipped was the launch point for Doolittle's raid against Tokyo. *Norfolk Naval Shipyard*

Adm. Royal E. Ingersoll presents the Presidential Unit Citation to the officers and men of destroyers *Dallas, Cole*, and *Bernadou* on 4 May 1943 for their part in the invasion of North Africa. Destroyer *Dyson* (DD–572) and tender *Alcor* (AR10) are in background. *Hampton Roads Naval Museum*

tially used as a training center for bluejackets serving in gun crews for merchant ships. A third Little Creek compound, the Frontier Base, was constructed as a forwarding depot for personnel and supplies en route to the European theater. The area immediately surrounding the Little Creek boat basin was named the Amphibious Training Base (ATB) on 27 July 1942 and became the center of afloat training for sailors assigned to ungainly amphibious craft such as the LSM (landing ship medium), LCI (landing craft infantry), LCU (landing craft utility), LCM (landing craft mechanized), and LCVP (landing craft vehicle–personnel). The LSM was the largest and most complex of these craft, and the rigid LSM training program dominated all the activities of the ATB. By the end of the war, the ATB featured eight finger piers providing 5,650 feet of berthing space and a marine railway with a five-hundred-ton capacity for small boat repairs.[73]

The first LST in the Navy was laid down at Newport News Shipbuilding on 16 June 1942, launched on 28 September, and commissioned on 27 October. An awkward-looking but revolutionary warship, the LST was constructed with such high priority that, in at least one case, an aircraft carrier's keel was removed from a building way to make room for LSTs to be built in her stead. Despite the sobriquet "Large Slow Target," which was used by irreverent crew members, the versatile LSTs suffered few losses in proportion to their large numbers.[74]

During World War II, Little Creek pulsated with more activity than any Norfolk base. Rows of single-story clapboard barracks rose everywhere, with occasional Quonset huts scattered among them. Few roads were paved, and the camps turned into muddy quagmires with any hint of rain. Thousands woke to stern regimens of calisthenics, semaphore practice, and close-order drill. Construction crews labored over barracks, warehouses, roads, and classrooms. The boat basin resonated with the deep growl of small boat diesels and the shouted orders of coxswains. Offshore, landing craft practiced the complex choreography of beach assault.

"Upon arrival at Little Creek," explained the base comman-

This aerial photograph, taken in 1948, shows the extent of wartime development in the Little Creek area, with ATB at the top of the picture and Camps Shelton and Bradford in the foreground. The Norfolk Municipal Airport had been established at its present site at the upper left of the photo in 1938 after the Navy took over the existing city airport near Granby Street. During the war, the airport was operated by the Army but was returned to civic use in 1948. *National Archives*

der, "the new sailor is given classification tests by specially-trained men who dig into his background, determine his naval knowledge and ability to lead men. He's given voice tests, and an opportunity to express his desire of the type of work he'd like to do aboard ship. He is then sent to a receiving unit to await assignment to training where he gets training in military organization, berthing, drills and amphibious indoctrination. He sees movies, hears lectures, learns base regulations and, in two weeks time, is ready to start active schooling."[75]

Officers in training were required to be quartered in Quonset huts on base, shore leave was discouraged, and official base policy stated: "There is no regulation against wives and families accompanying officers, however, the extremely crowded living conditions in this entire area make it foolhardy to bring your family without first having living quarters for them assured." On 30 July 1945—after more than 200,000 naval personnel and 160,000 Army and Marine personnel had been trained during the war—the separate bases at Little Creek were combined to form what is now the Naval Amphibious Base.[76]

Although fourteen thousand men had passed through the portals of the naval training station at NOB during World War I, the ensuing twenty years had seen the station average only two to three thousand personnel in training. However, in 1938, anticipating an increase in recruiting to meet the demands of a rapidly expanding fleet, Congress approved $4 million to improve station facilities. Within a year, the station's training population had mushroomed to seven thousand recruits and fifteen hundred mess attendants, making Norfolk the largest of the Navy's four primary training stations.[77]

Basic training at the Norfolk Naval Training Station spanned eleven weeks and was dominated by drill, hygiene, medical processing, naval history and ceremony, physical fitness, and shipboard procedures. The day would start with mass exercises at 0530 on one of several "grinders" (drill fields), led in early 1941 by all-star Cleveland Indians pitcher Bob Feller.[78] "We spent a lot of time on drilling and a fair amount of time on weapons, boat training, pulling oars on long boats in the boat basin," said one recruit. "You also spent a good bit of time caring for your personal items, how to make up your

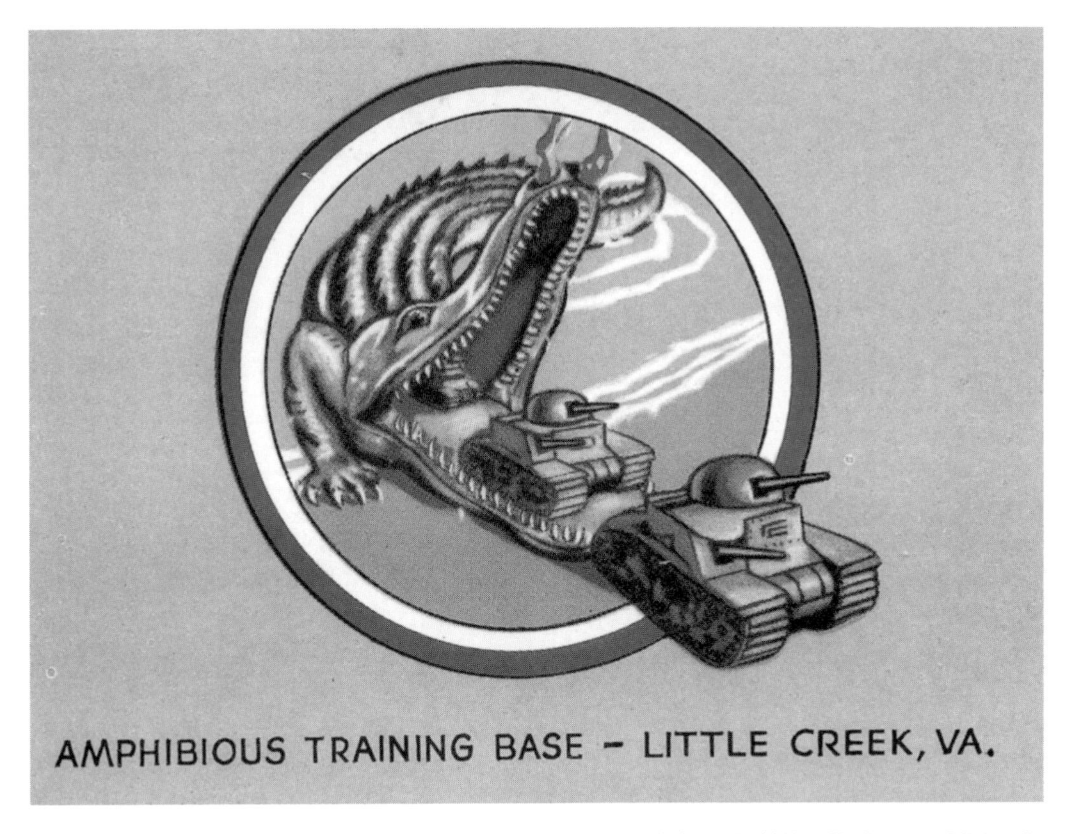

The apt "Gator Navy" logo of the Little Creek Amphibious Training Base during World War II. *Courtesy Miriam Browning*

The training of officers and men who would man the Amphibious Force's LSM groups was a major undertaking at Little Creek during the war. Here an LSM group practices beaching at Metomkin Island on the Eastern Shore in early 1944. *Courtesy David Ridgway*

Camp Bradford's beaches at Little Creek served as training sites for ship-to-shore movements and were equipped with foxholes, barbed-wire entanglements, and antitank obstructions. Beginning in early 1944, Camp Bradford began specializing in training for LSTs, the fleet's largest amphibious craft. *Naval Historical Center*

clothing, to roll it—we rolled clothing in those days—how to stow it, how to make up your hammock, how to lash your hammock and seabag in seagoing fashion."[79]

During the first months of the war, fleet service schools sprang up everywhere at the training station to provide advanced training for the huge influx of petty officers in such specialties as radarman, torpedoman, welder, firecontrolman, gunner's mate, machinist, cook, firefighter, and steward. When facilities became overcrowded at NOB, the Radar Operator's School was moved to the Cavalier Hotel in Virginia Beach.[80]

By late 1942, however, this master plan was overcome by other priorities, particularly the need to train thousands of sailors to man the flood of newly constructed ships, including mass-produced destroyer escorts (DEs) built to counter the

U. S. NAVAL AIR STATION

NORFOLK, VIRGINIA

PASS Harold Freeman, U.S.N.R.

ATTACHED TO Fighter Director School

TO THE SHIP'S SERVICE DEPARTMENT FACILITIES OF THIS STATION

EXPIRES
30 JUNE 43

DEPARTMENT HEAD OR SQUADRON COMMANDER

SIGNATURE OF BEARER

Somehow seeing the everyday paperwork that formed the framework of daily life aboard base brings the reality of the era just a little bit closer. *Courtesy Miriam Browning*

Development of the western end of the Little Creek complex in the vicinity of the amphibious training base, shown in 1948. The pier first used by the Pennsylvania Railroad to barge trains across the mouth of the Chesapeake can still be seen, a development that preceded the Navy's ownership of the base. *National Archives*

U-boat threat. Because this priority crew training had to be conducted at a fleet operating base, the decision was made in December 1942 to transfer all recruit training and fleet service schools from Norfolk to other bases, such as Bainbridge at Port Deposit, Maryland.[81]

Beginning on 14 March 1943, Rear Adm. Donald B. Beary, as commander of the Atlantic Fleet's new Fleet Operational Training Command (COTCLant), assumed the duties for training new destroyer escort crews in "shakedown training" and oversaw shore-based operational training. Later, his shakedown training responsibilities expanded to include all classes of ships. Beary used yacht *Williamsburg* for his flagship and battleship *Wyoming* as an afloat gunnery school.[82]

"Due to the size of the Escort Vessel Program [DE's]," wrote the commander in chief of the Atlantic Fleet to COTCLant, "I desire you to concentrate on perfecting your organization for the training of these new vessels." Each ship's crew was constituted several months before their ship was completed. Facilities at the naval training station were quickly converted to instruction in seamanship, lookout, supply, ordnance, and gunnery sections, and ship crews would be rotated through each. Several former recruit barracks and the immense recruit drill hall were converted into classrooms. "This is not a [Recruit] Training Station," the station's training officer, Capt. B. R. Harrison, pointed out. "It is a DD and DE Pre-com Tra Center where officers and men for these vital types of ships receive their combat training. It operates as a seagoing unit and is the last stop before officers and men go into actual combat."[83]

The first trickle of trainees for new construction DEs began to arrive in January 1943, and the number of recruits and service school trainees gradually fell off. The last class of recruits at the naval training station graduated in early March, and service schools closed by April, with only Class "C" Diesel School remaining. By July 1943, a tidal wave of almost four thousand DE trainees were in training, and between August 1943 and February 1944 an average of thirty-three DE crews were present each month.[84]

Admiral Beary's DE program worked so efficiently that it was expanded in September 1943 to include training for new larger destroyers, and a Destroyer Officer's School was established to provide similar training for officers. Soon this model would also be applied for patrol frigate (PF) crews, so that the training station's trainee population had risen to 11,450 by November 1943 and stood at 16,300 by February 1944. By the end of the war, COTCLant had trained 413 DE, 107 DD, 39 APD, and 60 PF crews at Norfolk Naval Training Station.[85] The Little Creek Minecraft Training Center was used in August 1943 for the shakedown training of Atlantic minesweepers.[86]

Facilities at the training station expanded to fit the need and soon included a seawall battery of 5-inch guns, Combat Information Center (CIC) mockups, a torpedo battery, a night convoy escort trainer (a destroyer bridge mockup on a rotating base called the "Merry-go-round" that turned in response to helm orders), a firefighting school, and engineering and damage control simulators.[87] An Anti-submarine Warfare Unit was moved to NOB in February 1944 to follow the British model of placing ASW instruction close to the operating forces. Acting as a gunnery training ship, *Wyoming* was used to instruct some thirty-five thousand officers and enlisted men. In March 1944 her old 12-inch guns were replaced by 5-inch/38 mounts for destroyer training. By 1945, the physical plant of the training station had expanded to include 445 buildings, 292 of which had been constructed since 1939.[88]

By late 1942, the need for additional pier space at NOB had skyrocketed. New destroyers and destroyer escorts were berthed and anchored everywhere; they were either on convoy duty or in shakedown training. After first reviewing the feasibility of expanding piers north of the submarine basin toward Willoughby Spit (disapproved for fear of fouling Willoughby Bay seaplane lanes), plans were approved for construction of three 50 × 750-foot piers (later lengthened to 1,000 feet) at an undeveloped waterfront area immediately south of the existing piers. Construction began in September 1943 for these "Convoy Escort Piers"; the first pier was completed by June 1944, and all three were finished by July. One pier was assigned to COTCLant and two for operating ships, and at one time, fifty-eight ships were berthed at these piers.[89]

In August 1943, COTCLant began to coordinate all CIC training for Atlantic ships. A CIC Group Training Center was opened at Little Creek on 1 November 1943, which was soon joined by new CIC schools at the NOB and the Navy yard and the former presidential yacht *Mayflower,* which was fitted with CIC spaces. Two CIC mockups for carrier and battleship/cruiser training and four mockups for destroyer training were set up in Little Creek Quonset huts.[90]

On 9 August 1943 the first WAVE officer reported to the training station, and for the rest of the war, WAVES played increasingly important roles, augmenting shore staffs. Their presence was especially important at the training station itself, where 250 WAVES were assigned by the end of the war.[91] At Hampton Roads's air stations, WAVES found work as parachute riggers, aircraft mechanics, and aerographers; at the supply station as storekeepers, yeomen, and mail clerks; and at navy hospitals as pharmacists and administrative specialists.

There was little need for at-sea "refresher training" early in the war, but by 1944, with ships regularly returning from battle zones for routine overhauls and battle damage repairs, the requirement for training increased. COTCLant sent training staffs to major East Coast Navy yards to organize this training. By August 1945 a total of 8,175 officers and 139,713 enlisted men had received precommissioning training at the Norfolk Naval Training Station. Seven French crews were trained in this manner, as was the African-American crew of *Mason* (DE-529).[92]

Brig. Gen. Samuel Chapman Armstrong had originally founded the Hampton Institute, historically a vocational college for African-American students, in Hampton soon after the Civil War. On 17 April 1942, Navy Secretary Frank Knox approved the use of facilities at Hampton Institute as an advanced training school for African-American recruits, recognizing the value that African-American servicemen would bring to the war effort but, in the temper of the times, keeping their training segregated from similar advanced training for whites.[93]

Norfolk had been the first site for the training of African-American sailors after the Navy began to allow them to enlist in 1932. Enlisted only as messmen, regardless of their intelligence and experience, these aspiring sailors were trained at Unit K of the training station. Good shop facilities at Hampton in 1942 offered a convenient place for the Navy to begin to train African-American sailors in seagoing trades while still maintaining separate training facilities for whites. Initially, the Navy established shops and courses of instruction devoted to training for the positions of machinist's mate, electrician, and metalsmith at Hampton.

"The men that went to Hampton had been selected out of boot camp to further advance in different areas, like machinist's mate and electrician's mate, metalsmith and that sort of thing," explained Frank E. Sublett, one of the original students

Although African-Americans had long been assigned to ships as stewards and messmen, the war brought an increasing number into naval service and into seagoing ratings. To receive training, in the still-segregated tenor of the times, the Navy established apprentice instruction for African-Americans at Hampton Institute. This program of training helped nurture the first generation of African-American navymen including many of the first African-American members of the Navy officer corps, an accolade that adds to the rich history of what is today Hampton University. *Naval Historical Center*

and one of the "Golden Thirteen," the first corps of African-American commissioned naval officers. "The attitude was definitely better there [than at the segregated boot camp at Naval Training Station, Great Lakes], because we had a different makeup of people. Some had been teachers; some worked for newspapers or publishers; some had been in the medical field or were getting into it. These were students who were better qualified than the others that did not pass [their classification tests]."[94]

Cdr. Edwin Hall Downes served as the respected commanding officer of the Navy school at Hampton. "Commander Downes was in charge of the whole thing," said Sublett. "And he was quite proud of what he was doing there. He was a real leader . . . he wanted to do well; he wanted all of us to do well. . . . he did want us to be successful. He pounded that time after time—to be good men. We were *men* of Hampton, and he wanted to make us realize that we were *men,* to be *good men* all the way through, no matter what we did. He was a real father actually."[95]

The Hampton Institute—specifically Downes—did much to move the Navy, still largely bound by the chains of strict segregation, toward a social transition to integration. In a sense, Hampton Institute was both an experiment and a symbol. It was a chance to recognize obvious talent; a means to teach many to be more productive, safe, and worthy; and an opportunity to prove something to those who doubted that African-American sailors could hold their own.

At the beginning of the war there was little impetus across the Navy to fully accept racial minorities (or women, for that matter) into its ranks, especially its officer corps. African-American sailors were blocked from most seagoing assignments and were given few opportunities to show their merit. "We would go over to Norfolk to see a real Navy base . . . and what Navy ships looked like," said one, "but never went aboard ships because we were black, you know. And they had steward's mates and cooks and all that sort of thing, but they didn't have any real integration."[96]

It was, perhaps, in cultivating the Golden Thirteen that the Hampton Institute had its greatest impact. Two of the recruits, Frank E. Sublett and John W. Regan, were singled out by

Downes for officers training at Great Lakes, saying, "We're sending you up to Great Lakes for a special class, and it's something that you'll like. It might lead to something that you never suspected." Regan said later, "I hadn't had any inkling that the Navy was going to commission any black officers. [Downes's] recommendation was undoubtedly a big factor in my being chosen for that first group."[97] Another of the Golden Thirteen, George Cooper, taught metalsmiths at Hampton and, after commissioning, returned as Hampton's personnel officer. He remembers that many members of the school's staff, largely white, refused to salute him.[98]

By the end of the war, largely because of the Hampton Institute's impact, the prospects available to African-Americans in the Navy had dramatically increased. By June 1945, recruit training was totally integrated, the Navy had sixty African-American officers (six of whom were women), restrictions on the assignment of African-American personnel to specific ships or shore duties had been lifted, and Navy housing had eliminated segregation.

Although the name "Dam Neck" had been associated with the beach area and dunes south of Virginia Beach since the seventeenth century, the name did not become firmly established until 1881, when it was given to a life-saving station. For a brief time beginning on 16 August 1917, the Navy had leased Dam Neck as a rifle range with sixty targets. The Coast Guard formally purchased the life-saving station in 1930 and used it as a radio signal station, and the Army leased the Virginia Military Reservation between Virginia Beach and Dam Neck in September 1940 and renamed it Camp Pendleton. Pendleton

The Dam Neck Gun Line was favored because of its relative remoteness from residential areas and its clear firing arcs to seaward. Surface targets could be positioned in the waters off the beach or aerial targets towed parallel to the surf. *U.S. Naval Institute*

provided a site for Coast Artillery training, including firing out into the ocean, and for the Navy's amphibious training.[99]

When the Navy introduced the Oerlikon 20-mm and Bofors 40-mm guns to provide antiaircraft protection for its ships, Dam Neck was identified as a suitable site for shipboard gun crew training. Begun with the construction of two small frame buildings, the new Anti-Aircraft Training and Test Center, Dam Neck, was completed on 29 November 1941, with an initial firing line of one 1.1/75-cal. quad mount and four 20-mm guns with a control tower and magazine. The staff consisted of nine men led by Lt. Phillip D. Gallery. Because there was no berthing on the site, the center's staff traveled daily from Little Creek.[100]

Although Lieutenant Gallery feared that he would have to wrangle for trainees for his relatively distant base, the attack on Pearl Harbor generated enormous interest in the center's antiaircraft capacity, and, by January 1942, 1,100-plus officers and enlisted men had already been trained. Dam Neck became the first of five similar AATCs built on the Atlantic coast, and it reached its training peak in May 1944 with 1,600 officers and 18,500 enlisted men trained during the month.[101]

On 4 April 1942, the activity was formally commissioned with now–Lieutenant Commander Gallery continuing as commanding officer. The first barracks, classrooms, and mess hall were completed, and the staff was increased to 2 officers and 40 men. The firing line added a 3-inch/50 dual-purpose gun and a Mark 52 gun director, and the Bureau of Ordnance established a second firing line specifically for the testing of new weapons and ammunition. By war's end, AATC Dam Neck had trained 448,900 personnel.[102]

Naval Supply Depot, Norfolk, grew from 1.9 million square feet of covered storage space at the beginning of the war to 7.2 million square feet at war's end.[103] Army Base Terminal (Norfolk Army Base) facilities were made available to the Navy beginning in 1941. Starting with three warehouses and a pier that had been built for the Army in 1917, the Navy quickly added fourteen storehouses at the site that became known as the Naval Supply Depot's South Annex. The Navy renovated Pier 2 at the Army Base Terminal and then shared the facility with the Army's Port of Embarkation command

Lt. Philip D. Gallery established the fledgling "Anti-Aircraft Range, Norfolk" at Dam Neck in 1941 and was named its first commanding officer when it was commissioned in April 1942. One of three brothers who would all rise to flag rank (including Daniel V. Gallery who would gain fame by capturing a German U-boat at sea), Gallery was awarded two Legions of Merit and two Bronze Stars during the war and later commanded Destroyer Division 72 and cruiser *Pittsburgh. Naval Historical Center*

Planes queue up along the road from NAS to the NOB piers to load aboard an escort carrier in 1943. *Hampton Roads Naval Museum*

throughout the war.[104]

During the 1920s the naval supply depot at the NOB had operated a small aviation annex. In September 1941, this annex was transferred to the naval air station. In 1943, the depot's south annex was transferred to the aviation supply annex, and the naval supply depot included a new supply annex on the peninsula between Williamsburg and Yorktown.[105]

This new supply center, Cheatham Annex, was created from the twenty-five-hundred-acre Penniman estate (a short distance from the Yorktown Mine Depot) in July 1942. In August, the Navy began construction on a supply pier on the York River, and in early September, work began on the construction of ten storehouses, an administration building, and other facilities. Cheatham Annex quickly developed as a wholesale and reserve warehousing facility offering decentralized storage and quick availability by rail and water. In the intense atmosphere of wartime logistics, it also offered hard-pressed supply officers the option of moving supplies between NSD Norfolk and Cheatham by barge, relieving congested rail traffic within the Norfolk area.[106]

Closely associated with the development of Cheatham Annex was the construction of Camp Peary, beginning during the summer of 1942. Seabee training at Little Creek's Camp Bradford was transferred to Camp Peary when the Construction Battalion Training Center was opened on 12 November 1942 under the command of Capt. J. G. Ware. The site was sized for a population of sixty thousand—about ten times the prewar size of nearby Williamsburg—and became the single largest military facility in Hampton Roads.[107] The nearby Williamsburg Inn and guest houses were reserved at reduced rates for U.S. Army and Navy officers and their families, and Williamsburg Lodge and the Tavern operated for enlisted members. On 12 April 1944, the base was redesignated as the Naval Training and Distribution Center, Camp Peary. A German prisoner-of-war camp was activated at Camp Peary on 8 January 1945, and up to seventeen hundred prisoners contributed to the construction of Camp Peary and Cheatham Annex.[108]

Hampton Roads operated as a key port of embarkation for the war, ranking third behind New York and San Francisco in total tonnage shipped overseas, and was a center for the

This photo of Craney Island taken in February 1948 bears little resemblance to the expanded Craney Island naval reservation of today—built on fill and thrusting well into Hampton Roads—but it provides a clue as to how Craney Island appeared in earlier years including its utility in harbor defense in the War of 1812 and the Civil War. *National Archives*

Naval Transportation Service. The tremendous expansion of military installations and shipping facilities in the Norfolk area during World War II stands as probably the single most important factor in the maturing of the city as an industrial seaport.[109]

The port of embarkation's biggest single day occurred on 24 October 1942, when the largest force of transports and warships ever assembled on American shores crowded Hampton Roads, preparing for the Allied landings in North Africa (Operation Torch). For a week preceding departure, military policemen had stood on every avenue leading to the waterfront, directing a steady stream of jeeps, trucks, and ambulances toward the piers at the Army base in Norfolk, NOB, and Newport News. Passenger and freight trains were sidetracked as other flat cars loaded with tanks were moved into position. Ship after ship was carefully loaded with supplies and troops and then shifted to anchorage in the roads to await departure. It was a sight remembered by many as Hampton Roads's most glowing contribution to the war effort.[110]

The Navy began to prepare for intensive combat mining campaigns as early as 1939; Yorktown was a key to those plans. Yorktown, fortuitously, had been expanding since 1928, and a new TNT reclamation plant and mine assembly building were constructed by 1940. A Mine Warfare School quickly followed by December 1940, and two new inert mine storage buildings and a deepwater pier were added in 1941.[111]

Wartime priorities accelerated Yorktown's expansion, and new production facilities and a loading plant for the new "torpex" explosive were erected in December 1942. Facilities for the new Mark 29 mine and new barricaded transfer buildings for assembled mines followed in 1943. In 1944, nitrate preparation and storage buildings and powdered-metal storehouses were built for "amatol" high explosive management, and a larger TNT reclamation plant was constructed to reclaim and purify older explosives for use in new mines.[112]

Yorktown enjoyed a sterling safety record during the war, marred only by a midnight explosion on 16 November 1943

During the summer of 1942 construction began on a new Navy supply center just north of the Yorktown Mine Depot on the York River. What would be referred to as Cheatham Annex would grow rapidly during the war aided by excellent rail and water connections to the warehouses at the site. This photo was taken in March 1948. *National Archives*

at High Explosives Plant 2, which caused seven deaths and twenty-five injuries. Yorktown Pier loading reached its peak during January 1943, when 13.2 million pounds of TNT was loaded aboard ships. At the end of the war, 148 officers, 1,314 enlisted men, and 1,592 civilians were assigned at Yorktown. Work continued at a high tempo immediately after war's end, with the need to continue to rework the Navy's extensive inventories of ordnance, and during 1946, 1.5 million pounds of TNT was processed at the site.[113]

The Naval Ammunition Depot, St. Julien's Creek, also contributed significantly to the war effort, specializing in the manufacture of shells (especially 20-mm antiaircraft ammunition) and powder bag charges and the loading of ammunition aboard Liberty ships. Wartime improvements at the site included construction of a new deepwater marginal wharf in 1942, the addition of eleven new magazines, and the inclusion of a forty-five-acre expansion in1944. At the end of the war, Norfolk Group, Atlantic Reserve Fleet, was established at St. Julien's Creek to accept decommissioning ships and to oversee the mothballing and maintenance of ships in reserve. This was redesignated as the Naval Inactive Ship Maintenance Facility in 1966 and is closely associated with the National Defense Reserve Fleet, James River Berthing Site.[114]

As the war began, the naval hospital in Portsmouth was already engaged in a expansion effort that would accelerate to include two four-story wings added to Building One, and a chapel, bachelor officers quarters, and improved occupational health and library facilities. A statistical snapshot of one day in August 1944 showed a patient load of 2,997, a bed capacity of 3,441, and a hospital staff of 3,055.[115]

A new major naval hospital was constructed at the annex south of the NOB, beginning in January 1942. The 750-bed hospital, which became Norfolk Naval Hospital, included six two-story wards, an administration building, a surgical laboratory, and X-ray and storehouse buildings.[116]

Hampton Roads ranked as the third largest port of embarkation in World War II behind only New York City and San Francisco. Hampton Roads dispatched 3,294 ships with 12.5 million tons of war materiel and 1.6 million troops. Here the North African invasion convoy sails eastward from Hampton Roads in 1942. *National Archives*

At the end of the war, the naval hospital in Portsmouth acted as a regional medical discharge board and helped conduct discharge physical examinations. During September 1945, based on "points" compiled for months in combat (1,228 hours of flying time, 126 carrier landings, 58 missions, and a Distinguished Flying Cross), a young naval aviator living in Virginia Beach, George H. W. Bush, received his physical examination and was discharged.[117]

"Norfolk was overwhelmed by construction of every kind, the shortage of nearly everything and waves of population that inundated the town," read one history of the tumultuous war years. "Nothing could stop the torrents of wartime development, and there was not much that local efforts or federal aid measures could do to keep development neat or orderly or clean or pretty or pure."[118]

One of the first victims of the explosion of wartime activity in Hampton Roads was the effort by many in business and government to define the best "equitable fit" of the Navy within the community. From the years before World War I, the Navy had represented (to many) the key to the region's prosperity by promising wealth through consistent economic or industrial growth. But the Navy also represented (to many more) rapacious development, a despoiling attitude toward local culture and environment, and the threat of destabilizing and uncontrolled expansion. To increase the positive while mitigating the negative had been a primary goal of city leaders during the 1920s and 1930s, with everyone focused on finding that "even keel" in city-Navy relationships to foster the economy while amiably absorbing the Navy within the region's culture, mores, and traditions.

No one wanted to repeat the wrenching civic tumult of the uncontrolled industrial buildup of 1917–19. But, as 1941 advanced toward 1942, it became increasingly clear to those who remembered 1917 that history was repeating itself. But it was to be 1917 on a much grander scale, with the Navy

The Naval Mine Warfare School and Naval Mine Depot, Yorktown on 4 September 1947. *National Archives*

again standing as the most visible culprit. The careful work that had been done during the two decades since World War I to enhance the city-Navy relationship toppled in the space of mere months.

Statistics tell part of the story of the impact of nationwide mobilization and wartime industrialization. Between April 1940 and May 1942 the civilian population of Hampton Roads grew by a staggering 122,525, or 37.9 percent. On some weekends, an additional sixty thousand military personnel "would roam the streets competing with civilians for scarce goods and services," read one post-war analysis, "even park benches." The normal population of Newport News stood around thirty-five thousand, but the war soon demanded that the shipyard alone employ over forty thousand. The 1950 Hampton Roads census recorded a whopping 54 percent population increase during the 1940s.[119]

Hampton Roads became a community in flux, and the sudden spike in population, swollen by new defense workers and military personnel, had an immediate and profound impact on the social structures of the region. Everything, it seemed, was overwhelmed at once—houses, water, schools, public transportation, traffic. The Norfolk Homes Registration Bureau found one apartment complex of 26 apartments with 58 families and a second of 208 residences with 306 families and numerous instances of people sleeping in cars.[120]

Tidewater's quality of life rapidly deteriorated as the war progressed, and the increase in daily stress was unrelenting. "In a sense," read one report, "the glue of the society began to give way."[121] National magazines called Norfolk "America's worst war town," and congressmen investigating Norfolk congestion heard tales of food shortages, social outrage, housing shortages, crowded streetcars, and limited recreation for young men.[122]

Many Tidewater citizens tried to withdraw from the pandemonium and to overlook, as best they could, the huge influx of sailors and defense workers. "All that the ordinary Norfolkian was doing was to continue the way of living which had preserved the local peace for many years," wrote historian Marvin W. Schlegel. "As before, he went about his business, completely ignoring the men in the bell-bottomed trousers. The Navy veteran was used to this attitude and had accepted it, but homesick youngsters inevitably were

A great many civic organizations, churches, the USO, and the YMCA were all notable in their recreational activities for servicemen during the war. *Hampton Roads Naval Museum*

rebuffed and found the city cool and arrogant . . . thousands of 'boots' at the Naval Training Station were being sent out to man the nation's ships with a hatred of Norfolk in their hearts."[123]

Civic attention frequently turned toward the subject of entertainment venues for servicemen and defense workers. Norfolk had clamped down on prostitution in early 1941, closing much of the red-light district on East Main Street, but municipal mandates did little to eliminate such practices, and prostitution and rabblerousing sprang up with rapidity outside the city's limits. East Main Street bars, locker clubs, pool halls, and tailor shops prospered, taking many a month's wage for their services. Along nearby Granby Street, the sidewalks were always packed with business for cafes, uniform shops, hotels, and the Loews and Norva theaters.

Providing entertainment alternatives proved challenging, but local organizations tried to keep up with the need. The downtown Navy YMCA on Brooke Avenue made itself a focus of sailor activities by providing a homelike environment with sleeping facilities, recreation rooms, a gymnasium, and lunch counters. The downtown YMCA traced its origins to 1902, with the opening of a special Navy "Y" to provide a wholesome atmosphere for young sailors, in a building that was expanded in 1907 with donations from John D. Rockefeller. During World War II, dances on Wednesday and Saturday nights, informal yet highly chaperoned, were always a hit. During its busiest days of the war, average monthly attendance at the "Y" was as high as 440,000, and it was said that, from its founding in 1909, five sets of stone steps at the front doors of the downtown YMCA had been worn away by visiting servicemen.[124]

A USO with a serviceman's recreation center was established in the old Norfolk city hall in 1940, a USO for women was opened across from the central YMCA, the Salvation Army set up a servicemen's recreation center at Granby and Plume Streets, the YMCA maintained a beach club at Ocean

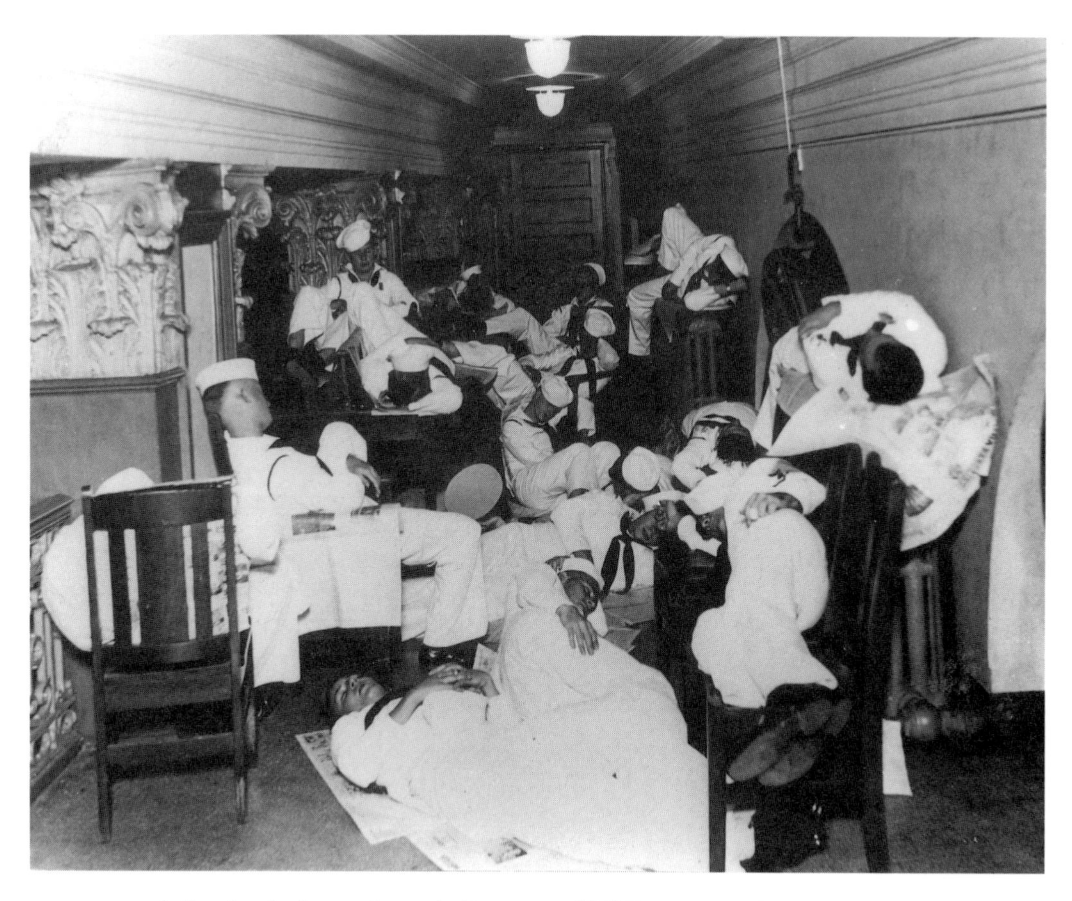

Sailors late in the evening at the Downtown "Y." *Hampton Roads Naval Museum*

View, and Lutheran and Catholic churches set up similar recreation centers. In 1943, a large Army-Navy USO auditorium and recreation center was erected in downtown Norfolk. Community concerts and the Norfolk Symphony provided entertainment, and the Navy added a forty-one-acre Fleet Recreation Park off Hampton Boulevard, new athletic fields, and beach clubs.[125]

Many in Tidewater recognized the need to be good hosts to the crush of Navy bluejackets, and as they contributed their talents to addressing this daunting task, entertainment gradually improved throughout the war. "Several years ago," observed a publication for sailors, "if you came to Norfolk all your friends gathered around to offer their condolences and you wondered what you had done to deserve such a horrible fate. Norfolk has long been notorious in the Navy as 'bad liberty' and 'bad duty.' But there've been changes made, and you men who have been away from Norfolk for a year of so are due for a pleasant surprise when you come this way again."[126]

Restrictive "Jim Crow" laws, which enforced strict levels of segregation, heavily influenced the recreational planning for the small but rapidly increasing number of African-American servicemen in Norfolk during the war. In general, African-Americans were barred from mainstream entertainment venues, a cruel reminder of their second-class status. However, spirited efforts surfaced to address these needs, including the opening of the Hunton Branch of the YMCA specifically for African-American servicemen. The Hunton "Y" included a dormitory with seventy beds and sponsored a wide variety of recreational activities, including Saturday dances at Booker T. Washington High School. A USO on Smith Street providing an impressive choice of recreational services was also opened for African-American servicemen, but its location in an admitted slum region of the city reduced its use. African-American married personnel also suffered, since most federal money allocated for the building of housing developments for white families in an era of segregation.[127]

With Navy community relations out of balance and nearly constantly in flux, it surprised no one that many who had shipped out from Hampton Roads carried with them a negative image of the region. It was in this light that the efforts of

Working with Norfolk public safety officials after riots between sailors and townspeople during New Year's of 1919, the Navy established an offbase Shore Patrol in downtown Norfolk that soon became a permanent downtown presence—a dubious distinction for Norfolk and a first for the Navy. These sailors patrol a downtown beat in 1950. *Sargeant Memorial Room, Norfolk Public Library*

Norfolk celebrates the end of the war. *Hampton Roads Naval Museum*

Hampton Roads sailors on VJ-Day. *Hampton Roads Naval Museum*

Ledger-Dispatch editor Tom Hanes were particular noteworthy. For one six-week period he rode a warship to speak with sailors, carefully accumulating data on what they thought of their time in Norfolk. When Hanes returned to Norfolk he explained to all "that the city's evil reputation, spread throughout the country would come back to haunt it in post-war years." In response, the Norfolk Kiwanis Club helped establish a Norfolk Citizen's Committee that provided reduced prices for servicemen.[128]

Just as in 1917, promised federal relief to the distressed Tidewater community was slow to arrive, and the summer of 1942 still found war workers routinely sharing rooms, even beds; rents soaring; and announcements of newly available homes rarely lasting a single day. With rationing in place, nearly everyone commuted by bus or streetcar. Crowding on the long trolley line along Hampton Boulevard to NOB was particularly intense, and many stories were told of long waits on street corners as bus after bus, jam-packed with war workers, would pass.[129]

Hampton Roads became a center of wartime volunteerism. Salvage drives for waste paper, scrap metal, tin cans, and rubber were heavily advertised in Norfolk. Rubber, for instance, was reclaimed for a penny a pound, and the Berkley branch of the Norfolk Boys Club donated more than a ton of old rubber collected from the Lafayette River. NOB captured headlines by donating five vintage cannon from its main gate as scrap. The peak of civic commitment to the war occurred between March and July 1943 with the successful fund-raising drive to pay for a new heavy cruiser to be named *Norfolk,* the keel of which was laid on 27 December 1944.[130]

On Monday morning, 7 May 1945, came the long-anticipated word that the Germans had surrendered in Europe. A sense of exhausted relief was reported by the papers, but there was at the same time a realization that the war was continuing in the Pacific and that it would involve many from Tidewater who would be repositioned from Europe to the Far East. Morale soared, however, when it was reported on 1 July that the Navy would return the Nansemond and Cavalier Hotels to their owners, an unquestioned symbolic sign of the end of hostilities. On the evening of 14 August, the president announced Japan's surrender over the radio, and excitement exploded throughout Tidewater. Celebrants leaned on car horns throughout the city, sailors tore telephone books into shreds and tossed confetti on the crowds below the USO, and shipboard searchlights arced across the sky. Everywhere Navy men received kisses from excited girls and joined into snake-dancing in and out among stalled cars on Granby Street.[131]

1961

Inevitably, the end of a great war brings with it economic adjustment. Powerful economic and social forces that fueled dizzying growth and naval expansion in Hampton Roads during wartime would turn on their unwary hosts during the postwar years to inflict equally dizzying dislocation, turmoil, and recession. Although consistent federal investment was good (cushioning peaks and valleys in Virginia Tidewater's economic health), rapid oscillations of wartime appropriations played havoc with local citizens and Navy bluejackets alike.

But the years after World War II proved to be an exception to this pattern. Rather than experiencing a rapid falloff of federal appropriations as happened after World War I, naval investment in the region first bottomed and then began to steadily grow. And rather than facing a period of prolonged peace as promised after past wars, Norfolk and the nation faced the beginning campaigns of the fifty-year-long Cold War. As the Navy faced this new challenge, the importance of Hampton Roads to national defense would grow in kind.

The Navy began to respond to the menace of Soviet power almost immediately after the conclusion of World War II. Despite broad cutbacks in a demobilizing Navy, reductions in Norfolk were relatively less severe than elsewhere, since the Navy concentrated much of its Atlantic strength and facilities in Hampton Roads. Norfolk's central location, desirable climate, versatile facilities, and strong congressional support quickly combined to make it the Navy's preferred home base along the Atlantic seaboard.

The Cold War would shape and perpetuate the Tidewater-Navy relationship like no prior epoch in the region's history. The people in Hampton Roads would not be idle bystanders or distant editorialists to the nationwide commitment to the Cold War. Naval investment would sustain two generations of Tidewater economic growth and would permanently remold Hampton Roads into America's most important center of naval power.

The Navy's priority in the late 1940s was consolidation. The auxiliary air stations at Franklin, Creeds, Monogram, Pungo, and Fentress were closed or placed in caretaker status; aircraft were moved to the redesignated NAS Oceana, which, by 1947, supported two carrier air groups and one fleet aircraft service squadron with 175 officers and 950 enlisted men.[1]

NAS Oceana and NAS Norfolk acted in tandem. Oceana hosted carrier-based aircraft, and NAS Norfolk patrol, seaplane, and support squadrons, while also serving as the Atlantic's aviation industrial hub, with a large aviation supply depot and a major rework plant. The Assembly and Repair Department of NAS Norfolk employed more than eighty-six hundred people in 1945 and still maintained a workforce of seventy-five hundred at the end of 1946.[2] NAS Norfolk continued as the operational headquarters for Fleet Air Atlantic and for Naval Air Bases, Fifth Naval District.[3]

At the naval shipyard, the workforce declined but not precipitously, buttressed by the requirement to decommission 538 ships. Many of these newly mothballed ships were sent into reserve either at the shipyard's South Fork Annex on the Elizabeth River or at anchor in the James River, and several

Midway was the first of a new class of large aircraft carriers designed with all the lessons of combat in the Pacific in mind. Built at Newport News Shipbuilding, she was commissioned 10 September 1945, and for the first years of the Cold War stood as the key representation of American naval strength overseas. Here she is under way in heavy seas in the Mediterranean in March 1949 with a deck full of Corsair and Avenger aircraft. *U.S. Naval Institute*

inactive carriers were sent to the largely unused piers at Sewell's Point. By March 1950, the shipyard's workforce had declined to 9,025.[4]

On 30 November 1945, the Naval Operating Base was redesignated Naval Station, Norfolk, and a new area command, naval base, Norfolk (COMNAVBASE), was established on 25 March 1946. The Naval Station, Naval Air Station, and other activities of the former NOB were made components of the new naval base command. The Fifth Naval District command remained, but, as in years past, the commandant of the district wore two hats, with additional concurrent duty as COMNAVBASE. Based on a recommendation of the Navy's inspector general, Naval Station, Norfolk, was dissolved as a separate command on 15 June 1948, and its duties were allocated to the Public Works Center, Receiving Station, and Port Director. This arrangement ultimately proved ineffective, and Naval Station, Norfolk, was reestablished on 1 January 1953 with the mission to "provide logistics support and inport services for the Operating Forces of the Navy, and for dependent activities as directed, including out-of-service, in-reserve craft and reserve fleet, when applicable."[5]

Other major command realignments also occurred. The four bases at Little Creek were consolidated to form Naval Amphibious Base, Little Creek, on 10 August 1945. The successful precommissioning and shakedown training program under the Atlantic Fleet's Operational Training Command was transferred to Newport, Rhode Island, in September 1945, and Norfolk's Naval Training Station was redesignated a Naval Training Center on 15 March 1946 and drew numerous fleet service schools back to Norfolk.[6]

The Yorktown Naval Mine Depot was redesignated a Naval Weapons Station on 7 August 1958.[7] By that time a large missile facility had been built on the site for the storage, static testing, and repairs of Terrier, Tartar, and Talos missiles, and three TNT pouring plans had been in place since the early 1950s for mines, torpedoes, and bombs. Yorktown managed a nuclear weapons storage facility at Skiff's Creek, and because of that it had one of the largest Marine barracks on the East Coast for security. Naval Ammunition Depot St. Julien's Creek became an annex of the Yorktown Naval Weapons Station on 1 January 1970, and its ordnance production, handling, and storage activities were transferred to Yorktown by 1975.

This aerial photograph of the NOB on 29 February 1948 gives the viewer a good appreciation of how the base built up around the coaling rail and pier concentrations of Sewell's Point. The D&S piers are choked with escort carriers in reserve, and the old Chambers Field has surrendered to the status of a parking area for reserve aircraft. *National Archives*

The Lee House weathered this flux of change at Yorktown much as it had done since 1650 as the home to nine generations of Lees. The bricks for the house came over from England as ballast in ships of the tobacco trade, and the house was originally constructed to withstand Indian raids, with thick walls and narrow slits for windows. The house burned in 1915 and was rebuilt on the original foundation; the nearby family burial ground is well preserved, and the Navy looks after its nearly four-hundred-year legacy.[8]

Postwar change also made Norfolk the centerpiece of a crucial realignment of worldwide military command mandated by the 1947 National Security Act. That act redefined the worldwide U.S. military command structure as a series of "unified" commands headed by senior commanders in chief who reported to the Joint Chiefs of Staff and made up of components from more than one branch of the service. One of these new unified commands held responsibility for the Atlantic region and the mission of guarding Atlantic sea-lanes. Because of the predominantly maritime nature of the new Atlantic Command, the decision was made to base it in Norfolk and to integrate it into the Navy's existing Atlantic Fleet structure.

From April 1941 to April 1948, Atlantic Fleet headquarters had stayed afloat aboard four different flagships: cruiser *Augusta* (CA 31), the historic sloop *Constellation,* patrol gunboat *Vixen* (PG 53), and amphibious command ship *Pocono* (AGC 16). On 5 April 1948, the headquarters moved ashore into the former Norfolk Naval Hospital compound off Hampton Boulevard, and Adm. William H. P. Blandy assumed concurrent duties as Commander in Chief, U.S. Atlantic Fleet, and the first Commander in Chief, U.S. Atlantic Command.[9]

With the establishment of the North Atlantic Treaty Organization (NATO) in April 1949, another new major command—Allied Command, Atlantic—was formed for the Allied defense of the North Atlantic. With a primarily naval mission, it, too, collocated with the U.S. Atlantic Command and the U.S. Atlantic Fleet to form a combined command with three

The Norfolk Naval Training Station color guard in 1945. *Sargeant Memorial Room, Norfolk Public Library*

separate staffs under a single American four-star admiral with headquarters in Norfolk. On 10 April 1952, Adm. Lynde D. McCormick, Commander in Chief, U.S. Atlantic Command and U.S. Atlantic Fleet, was the first to assume the title of Supreme Allied Commander, Atlantic (SACLANT).[10]

Norfolk became, in essence, the command center for the maritime defense of the entire North Atlantic—one of the most critical military responsibilities of the Cold War. Allied bases throughout the Atlantic basin all networked back to a single location, Norfolk, as the Atlantic Command countered Soviet efforts.

The outbreak of war in Korea in June 1950 unexpectedly provided the Navy with its first big test of the postwar era. The Pacific Fleet absorbed the first combat assignments of the war, but Atlantic Fleet ships were soon flowing westward to support Seventh Fleet operations. Carrier *Leyte* (CV-32) returned to Norfolk from the Mediterranean at high speed in late August 1950 and, after only two weeks, sailed for the Pacific. From 9 October through 19 January 1951, *Leyte* spent ninety-two days at sea and launched 3,933 sorties against North Korea. The Navy's first African-American aviator, Ens. Jesse L. Brown, was killed while flying a F4U Corsair fighter from *Leyte* in support of embattled U.S. Marines at Chosin Reservoir.[11]

Light carrier *Bataan* (CVL-29) was brought out of mothballs in Philadelphia, sailed to Norfolk, and then rushed to the Pacific while *Lake Champlain* (CV-39) was pulled from the reserve fleet in Norfolk, reactivated at Newport News Shipbuilding on 19 September 1952, and sailed for Korea in April

The establishment of SACLANT in Tidewater would not only bring its famous ring of Allied national flagpoles to Norfolk to stand outside the headquarters' entrance but would also introduce into the naval community of Hampton Roads a decided international air. *U.S. Naval Institute*

1953. Norfolk-based light cruiser *Worcester* (CL-144) sprinted through the Suez Canal, and battleship *Missouri* (BB-63) left Norfolk on 19 August 1950 to become the first American battleship to reach Korean waters. She soon began pounding shore targets, averaging nearly a thousand rounds of 16-inch fire per month on the gun line. *New Jersey* (BB-62) followed from Hampton Roads on 16 April 1951 for the first of her two tours of duty in Korean waters. *Wisconsin* (BB-64) was reactivated from the Norfolk reserve fleet on 3 March 1951 and sailed to Korea, where she contributed to the gun line for five months and frequently used her great speed to first handle tactical targets to the south and then, within a day, bombard troop staging areas and rail lines to the north.[12]

Tidewater's largest single loss during the Korean era came not from hostilities but from an accident. Norfolk-based destroyer *Hobson* (DD-464) was steaming as a plane guard for carrier *Wasp* on the night of 26 April 1952, seven hundred miles west of the Azores, when she became confused by *Wasp*'s maneuvers as the carrier turned into the wind. *Hobson* mistakenly crossed the carrier's bow and was struck amidships. The force of the collision rolled the destroyer over, breaking her in two. The ship and 176 of her crew were lost, including her commanding officer, Lt. Cdr. W. J. Tierney.

As crucial as battleship *Missouri* was in the naval war in Korea, she almost did not make the conflict at all. Five months before the war, in January 1950, she stood as an American icon, the last active battleship in service. It was well known that "Mighty Mo" was also a favorite of President Harry Truman, a fact that may have contributed to her continued service.

Missouri was under way at 0725 on 17 January 1950 from the Naval Station's Pier 7 for a week of shakedown training after completion of work on her engines and radar at Norfolk Naval Shipyard in December. As soon as tugs had nudged her safely away from the pier, *Missouri*'s new commander, Capt. William D. Brown, ordered a two-thirds bell and steadied the ship's long, majestic prow on a course toward the main channel near Old Point Comfort. Although the movement of Navy ships through Hampton Roads was an everyday occurrence, many still paused in their work to watch this embodiment of

Leyte was the first Atlantic fleet carrier to respond to the war in Korea in 1950, sprinting from the Mediterranean to Norfolk and then on to the western Pacific with this deckload of Cosair fighters and new Grumman F9F Panther jet fighters. *U.S. Naval Institute*

grace and power slowly pick up speed as she headed to sea. The morning was gray, and there was no traffic in the channel. Gulls soared in pursuit of the battlewagon, attracted by the churning white-brown wake from the ship's powerful engines.

Brown ordered the ship to run a new acoustic range along the eastern side of the channel. Five temporary spherical buoys were reported as identifying the range, but only the first two were in place. Almost immediately, the ship's unpracticed navigation team fell into confusion. The outbound Thimble Shoals Channel is challenging even on the best of days because of its lack of navigational landmarks, and now the nav team was distracted, looking for buoys that didn't exist. To make matters worse, the bridge was in turmoil with watch relief, the conn was shifting to the 04 level, and radar plotting from CIC was inconsistent.[13]

When two black-and-white spar buoys were reported ahead, Brown assumed they represented the remaining acoustic range markers, and *Missouri*'s bow fell off to the left to align with these new buoys (the new buoys actually marked the entrance to a small channel through Horseshoe Shoal). By now, proud *Missouri* was on the verge of disaster, plowing ahead at speed and angling toward rapidly shoaling mud. The navigator, not a paragon of strength in the unfolding drama, weakly recommended, "We should come right now." Brown, disoriented, disagreed: "We can't come right now or we'll spoil the run." Losing time but gaining nerve by rechecking the chart, the navigator repeated, "We *must* come right!" Vacillating and confused, Brown ordered a modest 10 degrees of right rudder but then countermanded that order, still fixed on requirements for the test. After further precious seconds had ticked by, Brown finally recognized his peril and yelled across the bridge for the helmsman to come right and then emphasized his order by ordering "hard right rudder," but forty thousand tons of steel and momentum still surged ahead, unstoppable. The next words heard were muffled reports from engineering that the condensers were losing their vacuum (with sand clogging the intakes). A host of rudder and backing orders was given, as if to will away the inevitable, but *Missouri* was no nimble destroyer, and the captain's urging was not enough to snatch safety from disaster. The men on deck felt only a small shudder as an eerie, watery murmur replaced the regular splash of bow waves and the gurgle and hiss of the wake. *Missouri* was mak-

Everywhere *Missouri* sailed she turned heads—instantly recognizable as a symbol of American naval strength and the pride of the Navy in Tidewater and a reputed "favorite" of President Truman—so it was doubly noteworthy when she ran aground off Old Point Comfort in a disastrous episode in January 1950. For more than two weeks she was pinned in the mud, with newspaper headlines declaring "Navy's Mighty Warship Caught Fast." *Naval Historical Center*

ing 12.4 knots when she grounded and plowed some twenty-five hundred feet into mud and sand, three full ship lengths, before coming to rest.[14]

Word of the incident traveled fast, and Rear Adm. Allan E. "Hoke" Smith, *Missouri*'s type commander, quickly mobilized salvage assets while saying to his surprised staff, "Gentlemen, the USS *Missouri* has just gone a half mile inland." Repair ships, tugs, a suction dredge borrowed from the Army, and small tankers to offload eight thousand tons of black oil raced to the scene, but nearly everyone underestimated the severity of the challenge. To add bad luck to misery, the highest high tide of the month had occurred just as *Missouri* grounded, and by the time the first tugs had arrived, the ship was already floating higher on an ebbing tide. *Missouri* soon commanded the headlines; the report by the *New York Times* was typical: "Navy's Mighty Warship Caught Fast." On the beach, sailor irreverence referred only to the "Muddy Mo."[15]

For the next two weeks salvors cut an escape channel from *Missouri*'s stern to open water and offloaded heavy objects like the anchors, but the ship still refused to budge an inch, raising concerns that sand, compacted with the ship's great weight, now acted as a kind of cement. Finally, Admiral Smith ordered one massive "Big Pull" by twenty-four vessels, including two salvage boats with beach gear, six tugs pulling astern, and three tugs on the bow to twist and surge. Beginning at 0545 on 1 February, the Big Pull began. All tugs slowly worked their way up to full power, and for fifteen minutes everything was caught in a maelstrom of churning white water. The first

Battleship *Wisconsin's* 18-inch guns fire against railway targets in North Korea in March 1952. *U.S. Naval Institute*

reports were disappointing; the bow had nudged just slightly to the right. Fifteen additional minutes passed—the bow was now definitely to the right, but by just 10 degrees after thirty minutes of maximum pull on the lines. Suddenly, like a cork being pulled from a bottle of champagne, the ship broke free, gaining rapid sternway back into the channel. At 0709, Smith triumphantly signaled: "*Missouri* reports for duty, 7 fathoms of water under her keel." To this day, there is a reminder of the *Missouri* on the maritime charts of Hampton Roads: a thin finger carved into the five-fathom line between Thimble Shoal and Old Point Comfort.[16]

At the ensuing court-martial, Captain Brown rightfully took full responsibility for the grounding and was punished by reassignment and reduction in seniority. Norfolk Naval Shipyard swiftly brought *Missouri* back to readiness, but the commander in chief of the Atlantic Fleet did not mince words in his final blunt editorial: "It is doubtful if a major unit of the United States Navy ever went aground under circumstances less excusable than in this case . . . a story of apathy, negligence and incompetence of both officers and enlisted personnel."[17]

Carrier-based jet aircraft also influenced planning for Norfolk's naval facilities during the Korean War. Traditionally, naval aviation bases had arisen near seaports where both seaplanes and landplanes operated. But by 1950, a new concept emerged: "Master Jet Complexes" that would support entire carrier air groups; NAS Oceana was tabbed as the first such base in the Atlantic. Oceana field was closed in September 1950 as runways were lengthened by two thousand feet for high-performance jets, and new fuel facilities, warehouses, barracks, and two new "Miramar" hangars were added. At the same time, a new jet runway was constructed at the abandoned Fentress field for carrier landing practice. Oceana opened for limited operations in September 1951 and was formally recommissioned on 1 April 1952 (Naval Air Landing Facility Fentress opened in July 1952) with the first of seven different air groups aboard.[18]

Beginning in 1960, basing concepts changed again. Entire carrier air groups would no longer be based together, as air stations began specializing in types of aircraft for the efficiencies of similar operations, supply, repair, and support. Oceana became the Atlantic Fleet home base for the new F-4 Phantom II fighter, the A-6 Intruder, and the A-4 Skyhawk attack aircraft.[19] The Phantom was the Navy's first operational fighter

Tidewater contributed many ships to the Korean War effort. Here destroyer *England,* flagship for Destroyer Division 161, returns to the NOB on 9 June 1951 after a seven-month deployment in Korean waters. *National Archives*

without guns; it carried instead a battery of Sparrow radar homing and Sidewinder infrared missiles and would set records for speed and altitude. The Intruder was a twin-engine, long-range, two-place attack aircraft designed for all-weather, low-level attacks. Both the Phantom and the Intruder would become common sights in the Oceana air traffic pattern, and by 1971 Oceana was home to nineteen fighter and attack squadrons.

With the introduction of the new F-14 Tomcat fighter, VF-14 and VF-32 from Oceana Fighter Country traded their Phantoms for Tomcats in 1974. The Tomcat was a two-place, variable-geometry, supersonic fighter with an advanced weapons system of Sparrow, Sidewinder, and Phoenix missiles. The fighter was well thought of; it was considered by many to be "ahead of its time," and in later years it would take on an additional air-to-ground attack role.

On 4 June 1977 the Oceana field was named in honor of Vice Adm. Apollo Soucek, a former chief of the Bureau of Aeronautics and commanding officer of *Franklin D. Roosevelt* (CVB-42). He was famous for setting world altitude records in both land planes and seaplanes in 1929 and 1930 and had piloted a Wright Apache land plane to 43,166 feet to test engines, oxygen apparatus, and high-altitude flying equipment.[20]

When Capt. Fitzhugh Lee assumed command of NAS Norfolk in 1952, the air station was the hub for most Atlantic Fleet aviation operations. It was the home to several squadrons, the chief supplier of aircraft parts and supplies in the Atlantic, and the home of the Navy's primary aviation rework plant. Captain Lee, who had commanded escort carrier *Manila Bay* (CVE-61) in "Taffy TWO" during the Battle of Leyte Gulf, was also closing the loop on a Tidewater Navy historic footnote: he was the great-grandson of Capt. Sydney Smith Lee, the brother of Robert E. Lee and the final Confederate commander of the Gosport Navy Yard. During the 1950s the annual payroll of the station's Overhaul and Repair Department came to nearly $45 million, and in April 1967, when the department was redesignated the Naval Air Rework Facility (NARF), it included 119 different buildings and employed six thousand people. By 1976, the NARF covered 174 acres, included 175 buildings, and was responsible for most of the Navy's frontline fighter and attack aircraft.[21]

In late September 1946, a Navy crew with Norfolk con-

Norfolk Naval Shipyard on 22 March 1948, with the carriers *Midway* and *Franklin D. Roosevelt*, battleship *Kentucky* (under construction), an *Iowa*-class battleship, and a large number of ships tied up in reserve. *National Archives*

nections set the world's record for nonstop unrefueled flight. Flying a P-2 Neptune patrol bomber (nicknamed the "Truculent Turtle"), a three-man crew and an Australian kangaroo flew 11,236 miles from Perth, Australia, to Columbus, Ohio. The "Turtle's" record held for nearly fifteen years, and the celebrated aircraft held a place of honor for many years at the corner of Granby Street and Taussig Boulevard.[22]

Long-range Neptunes were also used for experiments from NAS Norfolk in 1948 to prove the Navy's carrier-based nuclear strike capabilities. To compete with the Air Force, several Neptunes were converted to carry jet-assisted takeoff (JATO) rocket canisters for takeoff from carriers. Two Neptunes were launched by rocket booster from *Coral Sea* (CVB-43) off the Virginia Capes on 28 April 1948, during which the bombers' lengthy wingspans missed the carrier's island by just a few feet. Later, a Neptune was launched from a carrier off Norfolk, flew to the West Coast, dropped a dummy bomb, and returned to Patuxent, a mission of twenty-three hours and forty-five hundred miles.[23]

NAS Norfolk had served as the Atlantic Fleet's center for seaplane and floatplane operations since Lt. Henry Cecil brought the first detachment of N-9 seaplanes to Willoughby Bay in 1917. Seaplane operations were gradually shifted to Breezy Point, and Catalinas, Mariners, and Marlins operated from a square-shaped restricted seaplane landing area (12,300 feet east-west by 5,400 feet north-south) in Willoughby Bay, with an added landing lane extending into Hampton Roads. Seaplane operations were controlled by the Norfolk Navy Seaplane Tower located near the four seaplane ramps leading to the Breezy Point hangars.[24]

To bring the Navy's seaplane community into the jet age, several designs of jet-powered seaplanes were developed, including the experimental convair YF2Y-1 Sea Dart fighter and the Martin P6M SeaMaster patrol bomber. None of these concepts came to fruition, because the Navy selected different concepts for its long-range patrol, mining, and ASW missions. The SeaMaster had been built and tested in the Chesapeake Bay, and although there had been several SeaMaster flew into Breezy Point in 1958 during its test program, the cancellation of that program in 1959 sounded the death knell

An experimental P6M Seamaster jet-powered patrol bomber taking off from Chesapeake Bay in 1958. Originally intended to introduce jet propulsion to the Navy's large seaplane force to enhance ASW and minelaying missions, the Seamaster suffered crashes during flight tests and never was approved for serial production, ending almost fifty years of seaplanes in naval aviation. *U.S. Naval Institute*

for seaplane operations from Breezy Point. The end of an important era in aviation history occurred on the afternoon of 30 December 1963 when the last Navy seaplane to land on Willoughby Bay, a stately gull-winged Martin P5B Marlin, landed, inbound from Bermuda.[25]

In the years after the demise of the patrol seaplane, NAS Norfolk would host early-warning aircraft, helicopters, and cargo, support, and Naval Air Reserve squadrons. Early-

Still largely a rural site, the Naval Ammunition Depot St. Juliens Creek (just south of the Naval Shipyard) is photographed on 6 August 1947 with ammunition barges still crowding its lengthy quay. *National Archives*

warning aircraft had first been introduced aboard carriers with the radar-carrying TBM Avengers of World War II, followed by the "Guppy" version of the SD Skyraider and later the WF-2 (E-1B) Tracer, with its pancake-like radar above an S-2 Tracker airframe—all of which saw time at NAS Norfolk. But the dominant E-2 Hawkeye ultimately became the mainstay early-warning aircraft over a forty-year span; the first Hawkeye was delivered to Carrier Airborne Early Warning Squadron 120 at NAS Norfolk in July 1966.[26]

The first Atlantic Fleet helicopter squadron, Helicopter Utility Squadron Two (HU-2), was commissioned at NAS Lakehurst, New Jersey, in 1948. In 1952, HU-2 Detachment One came to NAS Norfolk with five officers and twenty enlisted men to provide utility and search and rescue services for Norfolk with the H-25 HUP and the H-43 HUK. Soon, the H-34 Seahorse and UH-2B Seasprite were added to the complement of aircraft operating from Norfolk, to be joined by the H-46 Sea Knight and RH-3A Sea King later. HU-2 Detachment One eventually became HC-4 Detachment Norfolk after utility squadrons were redesignated Combat Support (HC) squadrons in 1965, and in September 1967, HC-4 Detachment Norfolk was established as HC-6. By 1984, HC-6 had become so large that it was split into two squadrons, HC-6 and HC-8, and by 1987, into a third, HC-2. Minesweeping squadrons and heavy lift cargo squadrons, flying the MH/CH-53 helicopter, also called NAS Norfolk home.[27]

Helicopter Antisubmarine Squadron Seven (HS-7) was initially established in April 1956 at NAS Norfolk for ASW missions, including harbor defense. The squadron originally flew the HSS-1 Seabat helicopter, the first helicopter capable of both day and night ASW operations, until the early 1960s, when the SH-3 Sea King came into service. In 1973, the Atlantic Fleet's first Light Airborne Multipurpose System (LAMPS) helicopter squadron moved to NAS Norfolk, flying the SH-2D ASW variant of the Seasprite, to provide an over-the-horizon search and strike capability for antisubmarine destroyers.[28]

Tidewater's naval aviation legacy has always been bal-

In November 1944 the Navy began to look at its postwar needs for air stations. The first tentative list of stations in March 1945 called for the retention of only NAS Norfolk in full commission and NAAS Fentress in reduced commission. But based on later analysis of a greater need for aircraft and aviators, the CNO revised his list to include both Norfolk and Oceana to "continue indefinitely in full operation." Here, Oceana hosts an air show on 24 May 1953 after conversion to a master jet base. *National Archives*

anced by developments in both operational aircraft and aircraft carriers. When heavy, high-performance jet aircraft were on the drawing boards, there was concern that aircraft carrier design would not keep up with the challenge. But in the early 1950s, three major enhancements to carrier design—steam catapults, angled decks, and mirror landing systems—allowed carriers to operate heavier and faster jet aircraft safely. Each was originally a British innovation, but each would be developed, tested, and introduced at Hampton Roads.

In February 1952 the first evaluations of the powerful British steam catapult system were conducted aboard HMS *Perseus* in Norfolk when she launched three different types of American jets into the air while still alongside a naval base pier. The angled deck concept was first tested with a simulated angled deck painted on *Midway,* at sea off Norfolk, and the mirror landing system—which provides a visual cue to keep the pilot on the proper glide slope for landing—was taken through a trial run aboard *Bennington* (CVA-20) in 1955 off the Virginia Capes.[29]

From 1932 to 1947, Newport News Shipbuilding constructed fifteen carriers for the Navy, beginning with *Ranger* (CV-4). When supercarriers were introduced into the fleet beginning with *Forrestal* (CVA-59) in October 1955, Newport News became even more dominant, completing sixteen of the ensuing twenty carriers, including all of those with nuclear propulsion.[30]

Between 1947 and 1949 Newport News Shipbuilding unwittingly became the center of an explosive controversy between the Navy and the secretary of defense concerning the viability of aircraft carriers in the postwar, atomic-bomb era and "ownership" of the nation's long-range heavy (atomic) attack mission. It was a high-stakes competition, and the Navy's greatest fear was that the Air Force would be handed sole responsibility for nuclear attack, dooming any plans the Navy would have for the development of larger aircraft carriers and high-performance jet aircraft. The Air Force advanced a new intercontinental bomber, the B-36; the Navy proposed modifications to existing carriers to make them more compatible for heavy aircraft and began the design for a novel new aircraft carrier, the sixty-five-thousand-ton, flush-deck *United*

In 1946, a P2V Neptune patrol bomber named the "Truculent Turtle" flew nonstop from Perth, Australia (with a kangaroo on board), to Columbus, Ohio, a distance of 11,235 miles in fifty-five hours seventeen minutes—a record for the longest flight without refueling that stood for sixteen years. The "Turtle" stood for years as a landmark, first on Granby Street and then at the air station's main gate. It now is on display at the National Museum of Naval Aviation in Pensacola, Florida. *Hampton Roads Naval Museum*

States (CVA-58).

Although the Navy had experimented with JATO-launched Neptune patrol bombers as an interim step in heavy attack, it was interested in the AJ-1 Savage carrier-based, heavy-attack bomber for atomic weapons missions.[31] It was felt that a flush-deck carrier (without the traditional island) would allow larger aircraft with longer wingspans to operate from carriers.

President Truman's choice to replace Secretary of Defense James V. Forrestal was Louis A. Johnson, who arrived with a mandate for military cutbacks and who appeared to favor the Air Force in the debate over long-range attack. The Navy rushed ahead with its plans for *United States* and, with a minimum of ceremony (almost in secrecy), laid the keel of the huge new aircraft carrier in Newport News's Shipway 11 on 18 April 1949. Johnson, catching wind of the Navy's intentions, abruptly canceled construction five days later, without consulting the secretary of the Navy or the chief of naval operations. Furious, the secretary of the Navy resigned in protest, and in the subsequent brouhaha, the chief of naval operations also went by the wayside.[32] The "Revolt of the Admirals" created a shock wave that, in spreading out from Washington, affected Norfolk almost immediately. Aviation officer retention plummeted, and the future of naval aviation was a widely discussed topic in Tidewater's many officers clubs.

Spurred by the consequences of the Korean War, the Navy was ultimately able to obtain approval for a scaled-down version of the supercarrier, this time with the traditional island. *Forrestal* (CVA-59) was awarded to Newport News and was the first carrier to be built with an angled deck and the ability to operate jet aircraft. She also featured four catapults and four deck-edge elevators. *Forrestal* was proudly commissioned on 1 October 1955.

After completing carriers *Forrestal* and *Ranger* (CVA-61), Newport News turned to its most ambitious task in history, the construction of the world's first nuclear carrier, *Enterprise* (CVAN-65). The challenges were immense. *Enterprise* was the largest (and longest) ship ever built for the Navy. She was based on a complex and untested design, including a new flight deck layout and a host of novel innovations: slab-faced phased array radars, internal combustion catapults, and a newly introduced high-power reactor. Even more daunting,

Forrestal, here under way for sea trials from Newport News, represented the Navy's first carrier built with an angled deck and the first of the Navy's supercarriers of the Cold War era. *Hampton Roads Naval Museum*

The Navy experimented with jet-assisted takeoffs (JATO) of P2V Neptune patrol bombers from *Midway*-class carriers in order to provide the Navy with a long-range atomic attack capability in the opening years of the Cold War. Here, a P2V takes off from *Franklin D. Roosevelt* in 1949 off the Virginia Capes. *U.S. Naval Institute*

the Newport News yard was newly certified but completely unproven in the complexities of nuclear power construction, and Newport News management quickly fell under the scrutiny of the Naval Reactors Branch of the Bureau of Ships and the steely, unblinking gaze of Hyman G. Rickover.

Enterprise's keel was laid on 4 February 1958, and the ship was commissioned on 25 November 1961. Even though *Enterprise* was described as the most remarkable warship of her time when she first sailed down the James River powered by her eight nuclear reactors, the true benefits of nuclear propulsion were not proved until the 1964 around-the-world cruise of *Enterprise, Long Beach* (CGN-9), and *Bainbridge* (DLGN-25). Sailing from Gibraltar, the three nuclear-powered warships of Task Force One sailed south around Africa, crossed the Indian and Pacific oceans, rounded Cape Horn, and arrived in Norfolk sixty-five days and thirty-five thousand miles later without taking on fuel or provisions.

With both *Enterprise* and *Long Beach* homeported in Norfolk, the Norfolk Naval Shipyard placed a great priority on becoming nuclear certified. Capt. Art White was assigned as the shipyard's first Nuclear Power Superintendent in May 1962 to lead the Nuclear Power Division and to begin an intense program of training, recruiting new nuclear workers, certifying the yard's new nuclear welding facilities, and validating the yard's work procedures to handle stringent nuclear requirements. The first nuclear submarine docking, of ballistic missile submarine *Thomas A. Edison* (SSBN-610), occurred in June 1962 (although no repairs to the nuclear propulsion plant were made). The first scheduled availability of a nuclear vessel was the attack submarine *Scorpion* (SSN-589), in June 1964, and the first overhaul and nuclear refueling were conducted on attack submarine *Skate* (SSN-578) in April 1965.[33]

The yard's preeminence in nuclear repair went through a rocky period in 1973, when, at least in the opinion of Hyman Rickover, the yard's procedures had to be improved. Rickover took the unusual step of assigning a non-engineering duty officer, Rear Adm. Joe Williams Jr., to command the shipyard to "straighten that place out."

When Williams arrived in June 1973 for a tempestuous one-year tour, he found the yard already engaged in an intense period of work. During 1970 the yard had worked on eighty-one ships of twenty-five different types and, in 1971, performed 18 regular overhauls, 44 restricted availabilities, 4 fitting-out availabilities, and 1,487 technical availabilities. Williams set out to restructure processes, increase quality inspections, provide greater salaries and monetary bonuses for good work, and change shift hours (even cutting back on the operating hours of on-base banks and the officers club).

The ships of Task Force One—nuclear-powered carrier *Enterprise,* nuclear-powered cruiser *Long Beach*, and nuclear-powered destroyer *Bainbridge*—sailed around the world without refueling in 1964 in Exercise Sea Orbit to prove the viability of nuclear power for surface warships. *U.S. Naval Institute*

Williams inspected at all hours, frequently by riding his bicycle around the yard, and when he once found thirteen workers sleeping inside a steam condenser, he had them thrown off base. Williams's hard-nosed approach soon had the shipyard back in Rickover's good graces, and it has since evolved into one of the nation's top nuclear refueling sites, with a record since 1965 of more than 175 availabilities, overhauls, and refuelings aboard nuclear submarines, cruisers, carriers, and tenders.[34]

Just as it had celebrated the 300th anniversary of the first permanent English settlement in America with the Jamestown Exposition of 1907, Hampton Roads again took center stage with the celebration of the 350th anniversary in 1957. And just as the Navy had played a key role in 1907, so it would again fifty years later by hosting the Hampton Roads International Naval Review between 8 and 17 June 1957 as an integral part of the Jamestown Festival.

The centerpiece of the naval gathering was the review itself, which took place on 12 June, beginning with a naval aircraft flyover and Blue Angels aerobatics. Thirty-three ships from seventeen countries joined sixty U.S. Navy ships to form an imposing fourteen-mile double column of ships from Sewell's Point to Lynnhaven Bay. It was an impressive sight: ships were freshly painted, the brightwork shone, signal flags were on display, and crews proudly manned the rails. Battleships *Iowa* and *Wisconsin* and carriers *Saratoga,* HMS *Ark Royal,* and *Bois Belleau* (France) headed the extravaganza, which was reviewed by Secretary of Defense Charles E. Wilson from the decks of the Norfolk-based guided-missile cruiser *Canberra* (CAG-2). Among his guests was the revered Bull Halsey, who reminded everyone that he had taken part in the 1907 Jamestown Exposition as a junior officer.[35]

Canberra would be present for another intriguing ceremony on 26 May 1958. In gently rolling, slate-gray seas off the Virginia Capes, the cruiser solemnly rendezvoused with destroyer *Blandy* (DD-943), which carried a casket holding the remains of the Unknown Serviceman of the World War II European theater, and cruiser *Boston* (CAG-1), which carried the Unknowns of the Pacific theater and the Korean War. All

Norfolk Naval Air Station in 1964 showing the lengthening of runways. *Hampton Roads Naval Museum*

were transferred by high line aboard *Canberra* to the accompaniment of Chopin's "Funeral March," and a young Navy corpsman chose one of the two World War II caskets to represent all Americans who had lost their lives during the war. The selected casket and the Korean Unknown were returned to *Blandy* for transportation to Washington, DC, and burial with honors at the Tomb of the Unknowns in Arlington. The unselected Unknown was buried at sea with military honors.[36]

Within three months of the beginning of John F. Kennedy's administration in 1961, Tidewater's Navy would be squarely, and unhappily, on the front lines of a defining skirmish of the Cold War, the abortive invasion of Cuba by anti-Castro forces at the Bay of Pigs. Planning for the invasion had begun during the Eisenhower administration, led by a cell within the Central Intelligence Agency (CIA). With an amphibious landing in mind, the CIA asked for the help of Capt. Jacob "Jack" Scapa, an Amphibious Force assistant chief of staff in Little Creek. The Navy transferred two LCI landing craft to the operation, with strict orders to minimize the appearance of American involvement. Sailing from Central American training bases, the landing force of fifteen hundred Cuban exiles of Brigade 2506, escorted by American destroyers, rendezvoused with the Little Creek–based dock landing ship *San Marcos* (LSD-25) on the night of 16 April 1961. *San Marcos* transferred several LCU and LCVP landing craft to the exiles within five thousand yards of the beach while other American ships stood offshore in support. Norfolk-based destroyers *Murray* (DD-576) and *Eaton* (DD-510) helped escort the landing craft toward the beach at dawn but withdrew to sea at the opening of hostilities.

Although armed U.S. Navy A-1 and A-4 aircraft were ready to assist from carrier *Essex* (CVS-9) offshore, decision makers in Washington refused to give them permission to engage. Without American armed involvement, Brigade 2506 quickly faltered ashore. Within forty-eight hours, the exile force had been routed, and its remnants tried to escape by sea. Although she took scattered fire from shore (and did not fire back), *Eaton* intrepidly rushed back into the bay to pick up survivors with the ship's boats and rubber rafts. Naval officers in Hampton Roads were highly critical of the Bay of Pigs debacle, especially the bungling manner in which Washing-

The International Naval Review of 1957 put Hampton Roads on the worldwide map once again, provided a perfect venue for the United States to display its naval strength, and was even the subject of its own postage stamp. Ships from seventeen nations came for the celebration. Here the carriers *Saratoga* and *Valley Forge*, HMS *Ark Royal*, and a host of other ships are open for visitors. *National Archives*

ton conducted the operation.[37]

President Kennedy and Tidewater naval officers were on somewhat better terms a year later when the president presided over another notable Hampton Roads naval review on 13–14 April 1962. In an event that showcased the Navy at its best, Kennedy cruised aboard a Polaris missile submarine, took the salutes of forty-eight passing warships from the bridge of command ship *Northampton* (CLC-1), visited carrier *Enterprise,* witnessed a dramatic aircraft fire-power demonstration, and watched a Marine Corps amphibious assault at Camp Lejeune.

Tidewater's Navy, President Kennedy, and the island of Cuba would come together again in the fall of 1962 during the Cuban Missile Crisis. During August and September 1962, intelligence and photoreconnaissance increasingly pointed to an apparent Soviet buildup of offensive weapons on the island of Cuba. On 1 October, CINCLANT ordered an increase of readiness for forces in the Atlantic to conduct OPLAN 312 (air strikes on Cuba) and on 6 October ordered preparations to execute OPLANs 314 and 316 (the invasion of Cuba). Naval forces increased their surveillance of Cuban shipping, and an amphibious exercise was ordered for the Caribbean island of Vieques to mask the buildup of Little Creek–based ships.[38]

By mid-October U-2 photos for the first time showed Cuban preparations for the basing of SS-4 and SS-5 medium- and intermediate-range ballistic missiles. Kennedy reacted promptly and on 20 October ordered the Navy to establish a naval blockade around Cuba to prevent further transportation of Soviet offensive weapons to the island. To discourage rash Soviet behavior at sea, the Navy established Task Forces 135 and 136, consisting of carriers *Enterprise, Independence, Essex, Wasp, Shangri-La, Lake Champlain,* and *Randolph* and more than thirty smaller ships, and immediately deployed them into the Atlantic and the eastern Caribbean. Navy shore-based patrol planes kept a close watch over Soviet merchant shipping, and Navy attack and fighter aircraft, such as VF-41 from Oceana, were deployed to NAS Key West. On 22 Octo-

Douglas A3D Skywarrior aircraft line up for loading aboard *Forrestal* in April 1960, with *Independence* tied up across the pier. *U.S. Naval Institute*

ber, DEFCON 3, an increased military posture, was ordered, and more than two thousand Navy dependents from Guantanamo Naval Base were evacuated to Hampton Roads three days later.

By dawn on 24 October, American warships were reaching their assigned quarantine stations, and the first twelve destroyers formed an arc north of Puerto Rico five hundred miles from Cuba. A day later, six more destroyers had joined the patrol. Blockade units included Norfolk-based cruisers *Newport News* (CA-148) and *Canberra*, and Norfolk destroyers *Lawrence* (DDG-4), *Keith* (DD-775), *Soley* (DD-707), *Gearing* (DD-710), *Borie* (DD-704), *Dewey* (DLG-14), *Leary* (DDR-879), *Steinaker* (DDR-863), *J. R. Pierce* (DD-753), *John W. Weeks* (DD-701), and *Witek* (DD-848). Carrier *Essex* stood ahead of the arc in the mid-Atlantic, and *Randolph* stood behind. Command ship *Northhampton* left Norfolk to anchor near the mouth of the Potomac to await the possible embarkation of White House and Pentagon officials.[39]

Although they declared the blockade illegal, the Soviets ordered most of their ships to stop or reverse course; some continued on to test the American reaction. The opening intercept of the quarantine occurred at first light on 25 October, when *Gearing* sent a flashing light challenge to a Soviet tanker that replied, "My name is *Bucharest,* Russian ship from the Black Sea, bound for Cuba." After conversing with the master to confirm his manifest and with no evidence of military cargo on its decks, *Bucharest* was cleared for further transit.

Also on the twenty-fifth, carrier *Randolph* reported the first presence of a Soviet submarine in the quarantine area, and in the following days, two additional contacts were reported—a troubling escalation of tensions. On 26 October, the first quarantine boarding was conducted by a party of sailors from destroyers *John R. Pierce* and *Joseph P. Kennedy* (DD-850) aboard Lebanese-flagged merchantman *Marucla,* which carried Soviet goods destined for Cuba. An inspection produced no evidence of military cargo, and she was allowed to proceed.[40]

American naval forces now had to contend simultaneously with blockade duties, ASW searches, and preparations for an amphibious invasion. Tensions and activity increased by the hour, especially when the decision was made to aggressively harass every Soviet submarine that was contacted. Under constant pressure, several Soviet diesel submarines were forced to the surface, where they were asked, tongue in cheek,

The heyday of the battleship in Norfolk. *Missouri* pulls away from the pier in August 1954, leaving *Iowa* and escort carrier *Saipan. National Archives*

if they required assistance. Norfolk destroyers *Beale* (DD-471) and *Murray* dropped signaling hand grenades and dogged Soviet *Foxtrot*-class submarine *B-59* to the surface in mid-Atlantic on 27 October; tracking by Norfolk destroyers *Cony* (DD-508) and *Bache* (DD-470) continued the following day. Norfolk-based *Charles P. Cecil* (DD-835) forced Soviet *Foxtrot B-36* to the surface north of Puerto Rico on 31 October after thirty-five hours of contact. Chief of Naval Operations Adm. George W. Anderson, was later quoted as saying that "every Soviet submarine in the western Atlantic was made to surface at least once, or several times in some instances."[41]

Finally, on 28 October, Soviet Premier Nikita Khrushchev agreed to withdraw Soviet offensive weapons from Cuba if the United States would remove its own missiles from Turkey. Kennedy agreed, but the Navy remained vigilant, continuing to track Soviet merchants and submarines in the Atlantic and watching Soviet withdrawals closely. When the first reports arrived of Soviet ballistic missiles leaving Cuba on 9 November, the Navy moved to intercept and confirm the cargo. On 18 November, the Joint Chiefs of Staff stood down the blockade with the message: "Lift quarantine effective immediately. Return LANTFLT ships to home ports and normal operating areas." Within hours, the huge net of American naval power—sixty-three ships by that date—began to head back to port to be home by Thanksgiving.[42]

Despite its distance from Norfolk, the war in Southeast Asia during the 1960s and 1970s would call for the participation of many people from Tidewater. *Independence* was the first Atlantic Fleet carrier to "chop" to the Pacific for duty in Vietnam, arriving at Yankee Station in June 1965, with an air group that included Attack Squadron 75 from Oceana, equipped with new A-6 Intruders. She accomplished almost seven thousand combat sorties, including some of the first major strikes north of Hanoi-Haiphong. *America* arrived for a stint on 30 May 1968, and contributed a second deployment two years later and a third in July 1972, to receive a total of five battle stars.

In June 1967, *Forrestal* departed Norfolk for the Gulf of Tonkin, arriving there on 25 July. Over four days, planes of Carrier Air Wing 17 conducted about 150 sorties against tar-

During the opening years of the Cold War, seaplanes still held a key place in Navy planning for long-range patrol and ASW operations from austere forward sea bases without the need for foreign runways and supported by a fleet of seaplane tenders. At its height of operations, Breezy Point acted as a separate "airfield" at NAS Norfolk, with a square-shaped restricted seaplane operating area in Willoughby Bay for landings and takeoffs such as by these P5M Marlins over Willoughby Spit in 1952. *Hampton Roads Naval Museum*

gets in North Vietnam. At about 1050 on 29 July, the deck was crammed with aircraft readying for a major launch. The air was clear; the morning, which had begun cool, now surrendered to tropical heat, and most on deck appreciated the wind flowing down the deck. Plane crews had been hard at work spotting their squadron's aircraft in the best position for a synchronized launch. A-4 Skyhawks, armed and fueled, stood side-by-side on the port quarter of the flight deck, and F-4 Phantoms squatted along the starboard quarter. Suddenly, a Zuni rocket, triggered by stray voltage, accidentally fired from a F-4 fighter, striking the belly tank of a Skyhawk across the deck, with Lt. John McCain at the controls. Jet fuel spewed everywhere, and two of McCain's bombs were knocked to the deck. Aircraft across the flight deck were immediately engulfed in flaming jet fuel, and in the ensuing inferno, more than a dozen 1,000- and 500-pound bombs exploded, punching numerous holes in the carrier's three-inch-thick armored deck. McCain miracously escaped, but his plane captain and 131 *Forrestal* crewmen perished in the disaster; sixty-two more were injured before the ship's damage control parties could courageously gain control of the conflagration. *Forrestal* limped back to Norfolk under her own power to enter Norfolk Naval Shipyard for extensive repairs.[43]

During her first deployment to Vietnam in 1967–68, heavy cruiser *Newport News* was credited with firing more than 59,000 rounds of ammunition against enemy targets, a record

Atlantic Fleet units established an airtight naval quarantine around Cuba at the height of the Cuban Missile Crisis in 1962. Here sailors from destroyers *Joseph P. Kennedy* and *John R. Pierce* board the freighter *Marucla* carrying Soviet goods to Cuba. *U.S. Naval Institute*

that was extended during her second deployment in 1968–69, when she added 18,900 more rounds fired against the enemy. She also twice raided enemy positions around Haiphong harbor, once beating off the attack of several enemy PT boats as she retired. *Newport News* was well into her third deployment to Vietnam on 1 October 1972 and in action off the Demilitarized Zone when a defective detonating fuze within her center gun of No. Two turret caused a projectile to explode, killing twenty men and injuring another thirty-six. For the remaining years of her career, the ship sailed with an unusable turret locked in train and with the center muzzle removed—a grim memorial, easily recognizable in Hampton Roads, to the lives of her brave gun crew.

A host of other Norfolk-based units, such as heavy cruiser *Boston* (which provided intense shore bombardment during three Vietnam deployments) and destroyer *Vogelgesang* (DD-862) and other ships of Destroyer Squadron 32 (which paired combat duty with a round-the-world cruise in 1966), made the long cruise to see extended Seventh Fleet duty in Vietnam.

The war in Vietnam was felt in every corner of Tidewater's Navy. Operational tempo spiked, ships crammed the wharfs, and aircraft were lined up on the tarmac at Norfolk and Oceana. Training exercises intensified, and new types of ships, aircraft, and weaponry were brought into play. Normal routine for Navy men still included Cold War deployments to Europe, the Mediterranean, Latin America, and the Middle East. Destroyer *O'Hare* (DDR-889) was typical. Built in the last months of World War II, she served for thirty continuous years, homeported in Norfolk, first as a general-purpose destroyer. She was later converted for radar picket duties for fast carrier task forces and then "FRAM'ed" as an ASW destroyer. She logged a dozen Mediterranean, Red Sea, and Middle East deployments (including NATO exercises and patrols during times of crisis in Cyprus and Lebanon and along the Israeli-Egyptian border); sailed above the Arctic Circle; and was deployed twice to Vietnam (her final deployment found her on the gun line when the Vietnamese peace accords were finalized).[44]

The Cold War demanded a continuous overseas naval presence to match any Soviet incursions and to react to centers of crisis. Norfolk-based units responded to a host of emergencies, including the Suez Crisis (1956), Lebanon (1958), Congo

Disastrous explosions and fire swept the flight deck of Norfolk-based *Forrestal* on 29 July 1967 while she was conducting combat launches from Yankee Station off the coast of Vietnam. One hundred thirty-two *Forrestal* crewmen would die in the fiery ordeal that sent the ship into seven months of repairs. Films of the conflagration and the heroic response of the crew are still shown in Navy Damage Control classes. *U.S. Naval Institute*

(1960), the Dominican Republic (1965), the Six-Day War (1967), and the Yom Kipper War (1973).

Any deployment held its dangers, and any "routine" operation on the front lines of the Cold War could end in confrontation. Such was the case when the technical research ship *Liberty* (AGTR-5)—a World War II Victory ship converted for electronics intelligence collection—sailed from Norfolk on 2 May 1967 on a routine electronic intelligence-collecting deployment, first to the west coast of Africa and then into the Mediterranean. She was off the coast of Gaza on the morning of 8 June, intercepting communications from both Israel and Egypt, when the opening hours of the Six-Day War began. Clearly marked as American and steaming in international waters, she was attacked without warning by Israeli air and naval forces, which strafed her decks and attacked with rockets, napalm, and torpedoes. Cdr. William L. McGonagle (who would be awarded the Congressional Medal of Honor for his courage) ordered an immediate call for help: "Any station, this is ROCKSTAR [*Liberty*'s voice radio call sign]. We are under attack by unidentified jet aircraft and require immediate assistance." Four alert F-4 Phantoms were launched and vectored toward *Liberty* from carrier *America* but could not get to the ship before she had been heavily damaged and was listing dangerously to starboard. Although the governments of both the United States and Israel took the position that the attack was simply a tragic mistake, evidence has mounted through the years that Israel had attacked the vulnerable ship by design to mask an Israeli invasion of Syria. *Liberty* received voyage repairs in Malta and returned to Norfolk on 29 July with thirty-four of her crew dead and scores wounded.[45]

With Cold War headlines almost considered local news in Norfolk newspapers, it was not surprising (and not the least unnerving) that many in Tidewater thought of Hampton Roads as "Ground Zero" in any anticipated Soviet nuclear strike. Civil defense planning was a serious priority, and the Navy developed several contingency plans for harbor defense and unit deployments. One author described Hampton Roads in the atomic age as open to attack (even "inviting attack"), with the fleet vulnerable to being bottled up: "The Bay Bridge–Tunnel and the bridge portion of the Hampton Roads Tunnel are essentially walls . . . an enemy, if he had the desire, could block the limited number of channels into, and more importantly, out of Norfolk." Another pointed to Norfolk's vulner-

The 1967–68 deployment to Vietnam of heavy cruiser *Newport News* earned her earned her a Navy Unit Citation for a record fifty-nine thousand rounds expended in shore bombardment missions. *U.S. Navy*

ability to offensive mining: "It might be more cost-effective [for the U.S. Navy] to concentrate naval forces in just a few areas on either coast, but it is also making the job of any potential enemy much easier."[46]

The thought that the Navy was somehow bringing the threat of atomic attack to the Tidewater was not easy medicine to take, especially with the continued strained relations between Navy men and the surrounding communities. This relationship, frequently positive and economically successful, had been severely tested during the rapid military buildups of World Wars I and II. During each war, Tidewater had proved unable and largely unwilling to properly absorb the gigantic and unplanned influx of attention, dollars, and bluejackets. Although many benefited economically, the clear majority of the people of Tidewater felt that the suddenly increased Navy presence was a threat to both a treasured quality of life and day-to-day routine. Most in the Navy had an equally bad feeling for Norfolk, had difficulty finding convenient recreational alternatives, and were certainly influenced by generations of sour stories and scuttlebutt of lousy local liberty.

The 1950s were something of a low point in these relations. Although the good news was that the region had been spared severe postwar reductions in federal spending, the bad news was that the Navy had grown to enormous proportions, and the region had yet to find its comfort zone with its now dominant employer. Bluejackets ashore still largely congregated along the ten-block length of East Main Street, which many people disdainfully referred to as "sailor town," and among the dingy bars, locker clubs, and go-go clubs outside the naval base gates on Hampton Boulevard.

The nation's stormy battles with desegregation also affected the Tidewater-Navy association. The Navy was desegregated in word and increasingly in deed during the 1950s, and it frequently found itself at odds with policies and laws it faced in town. "Black sailors had a rough time in Norfolk in the 1950s," according to long-time Navy recreational services director Robert DeVary, "but the Navy also helped move Norfolk toward racial desegregation and made it more cosmopolitan." As much as it could, the Navy attempted to elevate the debate and frequently threatened certain actions to oppose segrega-

Friends and family welcome carrier *Independence* back to Norfolk on 4 March 1964 after a Sixth Fleet deployment. *Independence* would sail the following year as the first Atlantic Fleet carrier to deploy to the South China Sea in support of Vietnam operations. *Hampton Roads Naval Museum*

tion policies. When many public schools were closed in the late 1950s to prevent integration, for instance, the Navy pressed business leaders to help resolve the crisis by intimating that some of its operations might be sent elsewhere, since many Navy families could not afford the shift to private schools.[47]

The unrelenting threat of the Cold War and the Navy's continuing interest in Norfolk as its primary fleet concentration area began to materially improve the Tidewater-Navy relationship from the early 1960s onward. This slow improvement in how each party considered the other was driven by five primary factors: a steady Navy presence in Tidewater (with no dramatic changes in the Navy population or naval investment); the demographic effect of the Navy population (especially the great percentage of Navy personnel married with families and the increasing number of retiring service members settling in the area); the ready fit of Navy "industry" with Tidewater commercial industries (which stabilized and enhanced the entire Hampton Roads economy); an activist tenor taken by both Navy leaders and Tidewater communities in fostering an agreeable relationship; and a renewed sense of patriotism and commitment within the Navy community (generated by a series of events, including the end of the draft, the buildup of the Navy during President Ronald Reagan's terms, and Navy success in overseas campaigns).

Taken in aggregate, these factors reversed a deteriorating Tidewater-Navy relationship to mutual benefit. For the first time, the Navy and the region had a chance to strike a balance—the people of Hampton Roads could grasp the Navy's national and international perspective, and navy men realized they had a good thing in Tidewater. "Just say something bad about the Navy," commented Robert DeVary, "and the retired flags will roast you in the editorial sections the next day." Beginning in the 1950s, the Navy emphasized in both actions and words that it considered Norfolk a key to its long-range plans, and it intended to stay. According to the Norfolk Chamber of Commerce, Navy expenditures in Hampton Roads stabilized during the decade, varying little from $604.5 million in 1953 to $585.7 million in 1956. Military payrolls in 1956 added $74 million to the economy, and civilian payrolls provided an additional $157 million. Development at naval bases emphasized facility expansion, a fact not lost on the local community. By 1966, Naval District Commandant Rear Adm. Reynold D. Hogle listed ninety thousand active-duty personnel, fifty-two thousand retired people, fifty thousand dependents, and thirty-one thousand civilian employees within metropolitan Norfolk, "a total figure that makes one out of every three persons living in Tidewater connected in some way with the Navy."[48]

Both Navy and civic leadership helped spur the trend of improving relations. Beginning in 1954 the Navy helped build a firm foundation for the annual Azalea Festival beginning in 1954 by enthusiastically providing bands, color guards, and marching units in addition to an annual air show and sponsorship of NATO participation. Civic leaders sponsored the welcoming of returning ships. When an increasing number of naval personnel began to settle with their families in new housing developments from Virginia Beach to Ocean View, the Navy and the city cooperated in transit planning and other services, including providing recreational and child-care services in Navy housing areas. Navy leaders began to place a priority on on-base recreational alternatives to dilute the negativism of East Main and Hampton Boulevard, including construction of the McCormick Recreation Center at the Destroyer & Submarine Piers in 1955, improvement of on-base athletic facilities, and maintenance of well-policed Navy locker clubs.[49]

The most spectacular example of the benefits to be gained through close cooperation between Navy and Tidewater leaders occurred with the Navy's acquisition of the old Virginian Railroad right-of-way to the Sewell's Point coal piers. For years the Navy had lobbied for the land to expand Taussig and Hampton boulevards, extend piers, and extend the runway at NAS, but instead, negotiations had inevitably lagged, and the land was known much more infamously for its strip of dingy establishments.

Most of the coal facilities had been dismantled by 1967, and Congressman G. William "Bill" Whitehurst fought for $17.4 million in appropriations in 1971 to shift ownership of the 494.8-acre tract to the Navy. As Congressman Whitehurst tells the story, he had to personally persuade the pow-

A typical downtown scene in June 1953. *Sargeant Memorial Room, Norfolk Public Library*

erful chairman of the House Armed Services Committee, F. Edward Hebert, that the money "was critical to [the] district." Although he was unimpressed by Whitehurst's arguments, Hebert finally grumbled, "What's this going to do for you?" and asked whether the deal would make the *Ledger-Star* editor happy. After Hebert finally growled to his chief of staff to "give it to him," the funding was guaranteed, and Whitehurst later laughed that two statues should be placed at Wards Corner (with its notorious intersections, where the people of Norfolk had long suffered extended waits for endless lines of coal cars heading toward Sewell's Point), because if it weren't for the two men, the deal would never have happened.[50]

The Navy gained the property on 4 January 1974 and began to improve the site, to the delight of many. Whitehurst worked closely with Secretary of the Navy W. Graham Claytor to align additional funds for the demolition of the remaining seedy businesses on the tract.[51]

It was with submarine operations and undersea warfare that Hampton Roads made its greatest single contribution to the Cold War. Immediately after World War II, the submarine presence in Tidewater had been modest; Submarine Squadron Six and tender *Orion* (AS-18) moved to the Convoy Escort Piers (known later as the Destroyer & Submarine Piers, or simply D&S Piers) in June 1949. *Shark* (SSN-591), the squadron's first nuclear submarine, joined Squadron Six in June 1961, followed by *Scorpion* (SSN-589) three months later. The last diesel submarine of the squadron, *Sirago* (SS-485), was deactivated in June 1972. Submarine Squadron Eight joined Squadron Six in Norfolk in August 1979, and submarine tenders *L. Y. Spear* (AS-36) and *Emory S. Land*

Caroline Kennedy christens the aircraft carrier *John F. Kennedy* at Newport News Shipbuilding on 27 May 1967 with her mother, brother, John, and President Lyndon Johnson looking on. *Newport News Shipbuilding*

(AS-39) soon became regular sights at the piers.[52]

The valued submarine legacy in Hampton Roads was promoted considerably by the vibrancy of nuclear submarine construction at nearby Newport News Shipbuilding. The shipyard launched its first nuclear-powered submarine, Polaris submarine *Robert E. Lee* (SSBN-601), in 1959. Newport News's first nuclear-powered attack submarine, *Shark,* was commissioned on 9 February 1961. In all, the shipyard would build fourteen ballistic missile submarines; eight nuclear attack submarines of the *Sturgeon* class; twenty-nine attack submarines of the *Los Angeles* class; including the first and last members of the class—*Los Angeles* (SSN-688), commissioned on 13 November 1976, and *Cheyenne* (SSN-773), commissioned on 13 September 1996; and *Norfolk* (SSN-714), *Newport News* (SSN-750), and *Hampton* (SSN-767). Newport News's first two contributions of the new *Virginia*-class nuclear attack submarine included *Texas* (SSN-775) and *North Carolina* (SSN-777).

Cold War nuclear deterrent patrols began with Polaris submarines *George Washington* (SSBN-598) in November 1960 and *Patrick Henry* (SSBN-599) a month later, and the Atlantic Fleet Submarine Force commander moved from Groton, Connecticut, to Norfolk. "The Polaris chain of command went from the White House to JCS [Joint Chiefs of Staff] to CINCLANT, that's why SUBLANT moved from Groton to Norfolk in 60s," remembers Adm. Harold Shear. "[Adm. Robert L.] Dennison (CINCLANT) wanted to ensure that COMSUBLANT was at his beck and call beside him down in Norfolk . . . with offices on the CINCLANT compound and Polaris operations offices within the CINCLANT building."[53]

Almost overnight, Norfolk became one of the strategic centers of the Cold War, with its command of the sea-based leg of the nation's strategic deterrence triad. As important, the Atlantic campaign to counter Soviet submarine-launched missiles aimed at the United States also became centered in Hampton Roads, making Norfolk a focus for much of the little-advertised undersea skirmishes that would so color the Cold War.

It would be a yin-yang marriage for submarine staff officers in Norfolk. On one hand, they oversaw deployments of sophisticated Polaris deterrent submarines, while on the other hand, they planned missions for Atlantic attack submarines to potentially destroy the same submarines on the Soviet side. The two dimensions intersected in Norfolk. Bustling secret command

Submarine tender *Orion* was a long-term fixture in Norfolk. Here she tends Submarine Squadron Six diesel submarines *Burrfish, Tench, Tigrove, Sea Leopard,* and *Conger,* 13 April 1952. *National Archives*

centers, invisibly sitting within blocks of Tidewater parks and busy thoroughfares, now became the front lines in the no-nonsense battle for undersea dominance that would become one of the key determinants of ultimate victory in the Cold War. The positions of American, Allied, and Soviet submarines were carefully maintained first by magnetic "pucks" on large wall-sized charts in the controlled-access submarine operations center and later on large vertical computer displays. Ballistic missile submarine patrol areas were charted in an even more secure command center just a door away.

After the Soviet Union exploded its first atomic bomb, the prospect that it would field submarines with nuclear missiles that could attack the U.S. mainland abruptly elevated 1950s ASW from a mere tactical problem to a mission of national importance. This ASW imperative dominated underwater research, especially the effort to find ways to detect nuclear submarines amid the noise (low-frequency "tonals") that their machinery transmits through the water. Because sound travels well under water, "passive" receivers could detect these tonals at great range and generate "tippers" from which American units could pinpoint these submarines for attack.[54]

Five *Los Angeles*–class nuclear-powered attack submarines crowd berths at the Destroyer & Submarine Piers giving a subtle reminder of the importance of submarines in the history of Norfolk's waterfront. *U.S. Naval Institute*

The Navy's first line of defense in this energetic ASW battle quickly became the SOSUS (SOund SUrveillance System) detection system, a network of seabed listening hydrophone arrays deployed to listen for submarines approaching the United States. Beginning in 1954, a series of arrays was deployed from Nova Scotia to the Caribbean, and cables were brought ashore at "Naval Facilities" (or NavFacs), where the signals were processed. One NavFac of the SOSUS network was established at Cape Hatteras in 1956.

In 1958, the Atlantic SOSUS system was brought under the operational control of the Commander, Oceanographic System, Atlantic (COSL), in Norfolk, who oversaw an evaluation center that combined data from all Atlantic NavFacs for analysis. In an associated step, the Navy established Task Force Alfa in Hampton Roads in 1958. Task Force Alfa consisted of a Hunter-Killer (HUK) Group (an antisubmarine aircraft carrier, its air wing, and a destroyer squadron) and assigned submarines that experimented with advanced ASW tactics, including how best to use SOSUS for target "cueing." On 26 June 1962, NavFac Cape Hatteras made the first SOSUS detection of a Soviet diesel submarine.

The Navy's ASW priority drove improvements in passive acoustic detection, antisubmarine surface ships, and LAMPS I and LAMPS III helicopters to prosecute long-range contacts. Advances in acoustic sensors and in computing power—in what began to be referred to as the Integrated Undersea Surveillance System (IUSS)—also increased the capabilities of COSL. The Naval Ocean Processing Facility (NOPF) at Dam Neck, the main processing facility for newer undersea arrays and the primary SOSUS training facility, was established in 1979. Analysts on the watch floor poured over paper traces (later, electronic displays) of "grams" (acoustic printouts) to detect faint tonals at long ranges. Soon, the Surveillance Towed Array Sonar System (SURTASS) from T-AGOS ships (a kind of mobile SOSUS) augmented the SOSUS network. The first T-AGOS ship, *Stalwart* (TAGOS-1), arrived at Little Creek in 1984, supported by the IUSS Operational Support Center there. COSL (and then NOPF) collated acoustic findings with all-source intelligence and passed their data to other command centers.[55]

In October 1991, the mission of the IUSS was declassified,

and in August 1994 a single command in Dam Neck, Commander, Undersea Surveillance (CUS), assumed operational control and type commander duties of both Atlantic and Pacific IUSS activities. By 1996, the last NavFac had been decommissioned.

The stealth, acoustic advantage, and maneuverability of *Sturgeon*-class attack submarines made it possible, beginning in the 1960s, for Norfolk submariners to covertly trail and observe Soviet submarines. Attack submarine deployments to the Mediterranean tracked Soviet submarines to shield U.S. carrier battle groups; deployments to the North Atlantic trailed Soviet ballistic missile submarines operating in mid-ocean patrol areas (called "Yankee boxes") and patrolled deep into the Barents and Norwegian seas. As the IUSS improved, Norfolk submarines operated "barrier tactics" across the GIUK Gap.[56]

Cued by SOSUS and quieter than their adversaries, U.S. submarine trail operations became a mainstay of Norfolk submarine doctrine. Cdr. Kinnaird R. McKee set the pace in 1967–68 while in command of *Dace* (SSN-607) by slipping beneath Soviet submarines to record their noise levels and harmonics. In September 1969, Cdr. Chester M. "Whitey" Mack sailed from Norfolk in *Lapon* (SSN-661), intercepted a newly commissioned Soviet *Yankee*-class ballistic missile submarine south of Denmark Straits, and trailed her into the mid-Atlantic. Staying totally quiet, Mack established a close-in trail within the Soviet ship's baffles (astern, where sonar is blind) and tracked her for forty-seven days.[57]

Submarine trail operations gathered invaluable intelligence and gained a certain macho advantage for Norfolk submariners, but not all operations were incident free. There were reports of several collisions and near accidents in the close-quarters face-offs between opposing submarines. One of the worst occurred on 11 February 1992, when Norfolk-based attack submarine *Baton Rouge* (SSN-689) collided with a Soviet *Sierra*-class submarine while on patrol in the Barents Sea. The collision resulted in damage to both submarines; the Soviet ship was reported to never have returned to service, and *Baton Rouge* was inactivated less than a year later.[58]

Beginning in 1973, longer-range Soviet missiles and quieter submarines threatened the Navy's barrier strategy and shifted patrols closer to Soviet bases. This shift in tactics, directed predominantly from Norfolk, placed the Navy in an aggressive stance to neutralize Soviet submarines and evolved during the Cold War into an important national strategy to

A rare picture reflecting the emphasis the fleet placed on air defense of its carrier task forces during the Cold War. Here three eye-catching cruisers carrying Talos, Terrier, and Tartar missiles dominate the Norfolk waterfront in 1966: the guided-missile cruisers *Albany* and *Columbus* and nuclear-powered guided missile cruiser *Long Beach*. *U.S. Naval Institute*

counter the Soviet missile threat and maintain American dominance at sea, quietly and without great fanfare. "We always had the sense we would prevail," explained Capt. Mike Duncan. "We operated routinely in their backyard, watched their weapons exercises and tracked their best submarines. We had a lot of confidence; we operated with impunity."[59]

American submarines also secretly tapped Soviet undersea cables and deployed under the Arctic ice to hone tactics to find concealed Soviet submarines. Several times during the Cold War, the Atlantic Fleet submarine force deployed all available submarines to sea on forty-eight-hour notice in "Agile Player" exercises. Not only did this send an unnerving signal of American capability to Russian planners watching by satellite, it also underlined the importance of the submarine force to American strategic planners in Washington.[60]

Atlantic submarine tactics dovetailed nicely with the broad stratagem of the Reagan administration in the 1980s to spend heavily on military equipment and technology to force the Soviet Union into either a ruinous strategy of matching American improvements or an equally disastrous posture of falling behind militarily. It was a "bold offensive" run in "very slow motion," according to historian Norman Friedman, but it boosted the West's strength and confidence and destabilized the Soviet Union and the Warsaw Pact in equal proportions.[61] Navy Secretary John Lehman, an activist and in-your-face type of director, led the Navy's component of this broad strategy by emphasizing three elements that notably accelerated the U.S. Navy's relative superiority over the Soviets, each with a Norfolk focus.

First, Lehman orchestrated a widespread naval buildup toward a six-hundred-ship Navy through a revitalization of naval airpower, stealth attack aircraft, four large battleships, and modernization of the Navy's submarine force. Hampton Roads shipbuilding profited from this surge, and soon new ships began to choke Norfolk's piers. Second, the Navy published the remarkable Maritime Strategy, a highly public discussion of how the Navy was going to take the battle to the Soviets, especially with submarines and carrier battle forces operating right on the Soviet doorstep. The Maritime Strategy helped bolster the esprit de corps of Navy men across Hampton Roads while it clearly warned the Soviets that the U.S. Navy could not be countered. Third, Navy operational commanders started a carefully articulated process of demonstrating their resolve and strength with a series of exercises on the Soviet's oceanic flanks.

In 1985, Vice Adm. Henry "Hank" Mustin, commander of

The Naval Supply Depot was redesignated Naval Supply Center in December 1947. *U.S. Naval Institute*

the Norfolk-based Second Fleet, pressed for a highly visible demonstration of the Maritime Strategy, especially its stated objective of fighting into the Norwegian Sea to strike at Soviet military sites on the Kola Peninsula. The Atlantic Fleet had first shown this capability in 1981 (when Norfolk-based carriers *Eisenhower* and *Forrestal* had rounded Norway's North Cape), and now Mustin had in mind an even more eye-catching demonstration of U.S. naval capability.

Knowing that the Soviets would defend their northern flanks primarily with submarines and regimental-sized strikes of bombers armed with ship-killing missiles, Mustin devised an audacious scheme to operate aircraft carriers safely within the range of Soviet strategic targets. He would lock his carriers within narrow Norwegian fjords, where high surrounding peaks would protect them from antiship missiles and where mines could be sown in the fjords' narrow mouths to frustrate submarines. Mustin's ensuing NATO exercise, Ocean Safari, was principally concentrated in Norway's Vestfjord and successfully tested his plans with carriers *America* and HMS *Illustrious,* battleship *Iowa,* 166 other ships and more than 300 aircraft from eleven Allied nations.[62]

In many ways Ocean Safari was a crowning achievement of the Navy's Norfolk-led Cold War strategy, as it demonstrated the strength and resolve of a modern Atlantic Fleet that the Soviet Union could never hope to match. Norfolk commands did their part in the broad American strategy to "up" the military "ante" to put increasing pressure on Soviet leadership and to convince them that they could never win the Cold War.

A cornerstone of the Reagan doctrine called upon the United States to confront the Soviet Union in the Third World, and Norfolk-led naval forces responded in kind. During August 1981 carrier *Nimitz* countered Libyan efforts to limit the freedom of navigation in the Gulf of Sidra and, on 19 August, downed two Libyan fighters after they fired on two Oceana-based VF-41 Tomcats. The invasion of Grenada (Operation Urgent Fury) on 25 October 1983 helped thwart Cuban influence (and evacuated threatened Americans) and involved Little Creek–based helicopter landing ship *Guam* (LPH-9), Amphibious Squadron Four, the *Independence* task group, and other units of the Second Fleet led by Vice Adm. Joseph Metcalf III. Lebanon Multi-national Force operations

Norfolk-based nuclear attack submarine *Scorpion* was lost with all hands in May 1968 while returning from patrol in an accident probably the cause of either an explosion of a torpedo or the failure of internal piping. *U.S. Naval Institute*

from 1982 to 1984 included strikes on 4 December 1983 by carriers *Kennedy* and *Independence* against Syrian targets and shore bombardment from U.S. Sixth Fleet ships, including Norfolk-based cruiser *Virginia* (CGN-38) and battleship *New Jersey* (BB-62). Further actions against Libya in 1986 resulted in strikes from carriers *Coral Sea* and *America* during Operation El Dorado Canyon.

The tale of submarines in Hampton Roads during the Cold War was not without its tragedies, emphasized to all by the loss of attack submarine *Scorpion* in 1968. *Scorpion,* with a crew of ninety-nine, departed Norfolk on 15 February 1968 for a Mediterranean deployment as a last-minute replacement for another submarine. On her way home, she had been ordered to surveil a group of Soviet hydrographic ships (and possibly an *Echo-II* nuclear submarine) near the Canary Islands. On 21 May, after shadowing this group, *Scorpion* radioed her position and set a course toward Norfolk. Ordered to transit at eighteen knots, she was expected to arrive at 1300 on 27 May. Authorities began to worry when *Scorpion* failed to answer messages on 23 May, and in mid-afternoon of 27 May, with many families still standing forlornly on the Norfolk pier in a spring rain, the Navy launched a full search into her whereabouts with a "submarine missing" report.[63]

Acoustic tapes from underwater Atlantic hydrophones monitored in the Canary Islands and Newfoundland provided the first clues, recording a sharp explosion at about 1844 GMT on 22 May, followed, ninety-one seconds later, by several smaller noises stretching over three minutes that signaled hull implosions. On 5 June, the chief of naval operations formally announced that the ship was presumed lost and ordered the oceanographic survey vessel *Mizar* to sea. On 29 October, *Scorpion* was discovered to be split in two and buried in sand and silt at a depth of eleven thousand feet. Lying forlornly near the submarine on the ocean bottom was a navigator's sextant.[64]

A court of inquiry officially concluded that the *Scorpion*

Norfolk-based units also played a high-visibility role in American space efforts throughout the 1960s, primarily as recovery vessels at splashdown sites in the Atlantic for *Mercury* and *Gemini* capsules. Helicopters from Norfolk-based carrier *Randolph* (CVS-15) recovered astronaut Gus Grissom in the second suborbital Mercury mission on 21 July 1961 (shown here, although Liberty Bell-7 fell back into the water moments later and sank); destroyer *John R. Pierce* sprinted more than two hundred miles to recover astronaut Scott Carpenter's *Aurora 7* spacecraft when he overshot the planned landing zone; *Guadalcanal* (LPH-7) recovered astronauts Michael Collins and John Young in *Gemini 10;* and *Guam* recovered astronauts Pete Conrad and Dick Gordon in *Gemini 11. NASA*

disaster remained a mystery, that the cause could not be "ascertained from any evidence now available, " and that "no incontrovertible proof of the exact cause" could be found. However, the court listed several hypotheses, torpedo accidents being the most probable. One theory suggested that a hot running torpedo had exploded in the torpedo tube; another had the crew ejecting a torpedo that turned back toward them. To further investigate the cause, the Navy ordered deep submersible *Trieste II* to the site for a closer look. Again, evidence was inconclusive, with no specific proof found of an external torpedo explosion. Theories continue to be advanced, ranging from the (more likely) failure of the submarine's torpedo or piping to (highly unlikely) hypotheses that *Scorpion* had been a Soviet target after her surveillance of secret Russian underwater experiments.[65]

Because Norfolk stood at the center of the U.S. Navy's Atlantic planning, it surprised no one that it also had become a center of Cold War espionage and spawned the most notorious spy ring in American naval history, led by former Navy man John A. Walker Jr.

John Walker's espionage probably started as early as 1967, when he had access to a great cross section of American submarine message traffic while on duty at the SUBLANT communications center. Walker could read reports on submarine operations and trailing tactics and had access to technical manuals, submarine quieting technology, and daily "key lists" that were used to unscramble messages sent through the military's most widely used code machines.

When Walker retired from the Navy in 1976, he continued his espionage by drawing others into this scheme. First to be recruited was another Navy communications specialist, Jerry A. Whitworth, who continued Walker's access to crucial key lists. Then he enlisted his brother Arthur, who worked for a defense contractor, and then his son, Michael, an enlisted man assigned to Oceana's Fighter Squadron 102 and the Norfolk-based carrier *Nimitz*.

After years of clandestine activity, Walker's ex-wife finally tipped off the FBI, which launched a four-month surveillance of Walker, with more than a hundred agents assigned. On

Portsmouth Naval Hospital 26 August 1947. *National Archives*

20 May 1985, the FBI tailed Walker from Norfolk to Montgomery County, Maryland, where he dropped a shopping bag with 129 classified documents at the base of a utility pole near a prominent tree. Agents snatched the bag to discover that most of the documents were from Walker's son aboard the *Nimitz* and quickly arrested Walker at a nearby motel.

"The news shot through Norfolk like a lightning bolt," said one commentator. Newspaper reporters fanned out throughout the Tidewater, finding hundreds of acquaintances of John Walker who expressed a wide spectrum of reaction from shock to past suspicions.[66] Walker pled guilty in October, agreeing to help authorities assess the damage in exchange for leniency for his son. Everyone in the spy ring was given a life sentence except for Michael, who was sentenced to twenty-five years. When high-ranking Russian KGB officer Vitaly Yurchenko defected in 1985, he told the CIA that the Walker ring was viewed in the Soviet Union as the most important espionage victory in KGB history. During the Cold War, Hampton Roads was the American citadel the Soviets kept closest watch on. Norfolk was the manifestation of everything that worried them about the U.S. Navy. It was here that the drive toward a six-hundred-ship Navy could be monitored from daily satellite imagery. It was here that carrier battle groups and submarines would marshal before being thrown toward Russian flanks in the Barents Sea or the Mediterranean. It was here that each tenet of the Navy's Maritime Strategy was most in evidence.

Norfolk-led naval forces would blunt every Soviet Navy move of the Cold War. Every Russian advance in ships, technology, or global naval strategy would be bested by maritime capability or expertise emanating from the Virginia Tidewater. Every Russian leader knew the Maritime Strategy by heart, and every naval leader was reminded daily by fleet operational reports that the United States was fully capable of matching these careful words with action. Norfolk-based ships, submarines, and aircraft had the capability to put every Soviet ballistic missile submarine at risk and to neutralize the great majority of the Russian fleet. As the Cold War progressed, the capability gap between the Russian and American fleets widened as the dollars invested easily trumped the rubles spent. It was increasingly clear to all that the Soviet Navy could never have prevailed, and the Russians could sense that every bold move made by the American Navy somehow had its roots in the Virginia Tidewater. American nuclear submarines and carrier striking forces from Hampton Roads kept the Cold War cold, without ever firing a shot.

1991

Naval operations in the Middle East hold few mysteries for ships from Hampton Roads. With that region's prominence as a global crossroads and with its growing importance to American interests and the American economy, the Middle East had drawn the Navy to its shores with regularity since World War II. The small seaplane tender *Valcour* (AVP-55) served as the first flagship for the Navy's Middle East Force departing Norfolk in August 1949 for the first of sixteen deployments to the Middle East. For the next twenty years, three or four ships at a time were assigned to MIDEASTFOR, with *Valcour* rotating duties as command ship with *Duxbury Bay* (AVP 38) and *Greenwich Bay* (AVP 41), all of which were painted a distinctive white to counter the region's extreme heat.

Tempo was slow; the ships' missions were largely ceremonial. Newspaper headlines, what few there were, favored show-the-flag themes; wire photos caught ships' captains in formal whites, sitting stiffly next to sheiks in traditional garb. Enterprising Navy housewives in Virginia Beach and Ocean View soon broadened their eclectic international décor to include Persian rugs and brass samovars alongside Delft porcelain and Moroccan leather ottomans.

LaSalle (AGF-3) was converted for Persian Gulf duty in mid-1972 and sailed from Little Creek to relieve *Valcour* when the United States began to assume greater responsibility for the security of the region. As the 1970s stretched into the 1980s, Norfolk ship deployments began to include Persian Gulf and Indian Ocean destinations with increasing regularity.

Against the backdrop of the Iraq-Iran war of the 1980s, Norfolk ships and aircraft in the Middle East operated in a high-alert environment almost continuously. Gone were the halcyon days of exotic visits to bazaars and souks. Naval patrols in the Persian Gulf attempted to keep belligerents at bay during the so-called tanker war of the mid-1980s, which included efforts by the United States to "re-flag" and escort Kuwaiti tankers for their protection (Operation Earnest Will) and to sweep channels for mines with Navy helicopters. In response to the mining of an American frigate, Joint Task Force Middle East opened Operation Praying Mantis on 17 April 1988, which destroyed two Iranian oil platforms and sank three Iranian warships. Naval deployments took on an increasingly serious air, and crew training in Hampton Roads began to include machine gun marksmanship, ship boarding techniques, and mine watch procedures. The American presence intensified in the region during the1980s and was largely responsible for maintaining the flow of oil and keeping Iraq and Iran from expanding their conflict to their neighbors.[1]

When Iraq invaded Kuwait on 2 August 1990, the Navy had only six warships in the Persian Gulf. Carrier *Independence* and Norfolk-based carrier *Dwight D. Eisenhower* were rushed into immediate striking range, and the Navy backed them up with a general naval buildup that grew in momentum as fall turned to winter. Battleship *Wisconsin* departed Norfolk on 7 August, and the *John F. Kennedy* battle group was deployed from Norfolk on just four days' notice. Norfolk and Little Creek–based amphibious ready groups built around *Iwo*

There can be no greater aggregation of modern naval power than that described by this array of carrier air power gathered at the naval station's piers and captured in this high altitude photo in 1997. From left to right, nuclear-powered aircraft carriers *Dwight D. Eisenhower, John C. Stennis, Theodore Roosevelt, Enterprise,* and *George Washington. Hampton Roads Naval Museum*

Jima (LPH-2), *Guam* (LPH-9), and *Nassau* (LHA-4) also headed for the region. With Iraq regularly ignoring United Nations demands and sanctions, the Navy deployed twenty-four thousand Marines aboard Little Creek–based amphibious ships in early December. This was followed, three days after Christmas, by an event not seen in Hampton Roads in decades. On 28 December, in cold, drizzling rain, the ships of two complete battle groups, *America* (CV-66) and *Theodore Roosevelt* (CVN-71), slowly filed out of harbor, solemnly bound for war. It was a sight whose significance was not lost on Sharon Decker. In April 1972, she had stood in the rain at the Norfolk Naval Station with her young son A. J. resting on her hip and waved goodbye to her husband's ship as it was deployed to Vietnam. Now, she and her husband and son were back in the drizzle at the Naval Station, and twenty-year-old A. J. was the one who was leaving, this time for the Persian Gulf.[2] Ominously, as soon as *America* and *Theodore Roosevelt* were clear of the capes, carriers *Forrestal* and *Nimitz* were readied to be deployed if needed.

Others across Tidewater had also been tapped to support the formidable naval buildup in the Middle East. Naval Hospital, Portsmouth, had been placed on alert as early as 9 August for the mobilization and deployment of Fleet Hospital Five. Hospital equipment and supplies (much of them containerized and prepositioned at the island of Diego Garcia in the Indian Ocean), hospital personnel, and Tidewater Seabees all converged on Saudi Arabia to create what would become the largest field hospital in the region. During the war, about 1,350 Portsmouth medical personnel would operate the hospital, routinely providing a full range of hospital services, including medevac from a nearby airfield.[3] Portsmouth hospital personnel would also serve aboard hospital ship *Comfort* (TAH-20) and amphibious ships, and with Marines ashore.

Amphibious ships began to patrol the Persian Gulf in January 1991 and soon made up the largest amphibious task force the Navy had gathered since the Korean War. *Theodore Roosevelt* and her battle group rushed through the Suez Canal on 14 January, followed by *America* the next day. One day later, President George Bush announced the commencement of Operation Desert Storm.[4]

"The war started with a fireworks display in a distant land, a blurred day-for-night image of tracers streaking over Baghdad," reported the *Virginian-Pilot.* "As laser-guided bombs fell that January night, Iraq assumed the surreal glow of a pinball machine. . . . In Hampton Roads, war unfolded like an exotic, high-stakes, real-life, blood-and-guts miniseries, with friends and loved ones entwined in the plot."[5] More than 100 *Tomahawk* missiles streaked landward from cruisers, destroyers, and battleships in the Persian Gulf and Red Sea to start the air-war phase of hostilities (a second hundred would be fired the next day). Norfolk-based cruiser *San Jacinto* (CG-56) was said to have launched the first Tomahawk in combat, firing from the Red Sea, and each launch carefully meshed with U.S. Navy and Air Force air strikes. During the war, a total of 288 Tomahawk missiles were used, and Norfolk's *Wisconsin* (24 fired) and *Normandy* (CG-60) (26 fired) were major contributors to the effort.

Following on the heals of the devastating Tomahawk strikes, Navy pilots raced into the theater of operations, contributing to an efficient, modern air war that methodically decimated Iraqi air and naval forces, antiair defenses, ballistic missile launchers, communications networks, airfields, and electrical power sources during five punishing weeks. As the air war began, Norfolk carriers *John F. Kennedy* and *America*

Norfolk-based nuclear-powered guided missile cruiser *Mississippi* launches one of five Tomahawk missiles she contributed from her station in the Red Sea during Operation Desert Storm in 1991. *U.S. Naval Institute*

launched strikes from the Red Sea while *Theodore Roosevelt* took up station with two other carriers in the Persian Gulf. *America* showed the advantage of a carrier's mobility by shifting to the Persian Gulf on 14 February to be better positioned to support the ground-war phase of operations.

John F. Kennedy and Carrier Air Wing Three would launch 2,895 combat sorties during Desert Storm, delivering more than 3.5 million pounds of ordnance; the *America* and Carrier Air Wing One (the Navy's oldest air wing, first established at NAS Norfolk on 1 July 1938) would contribute 3,008 combat sorties, dropping an estimated 4 million pounds of ordnance; and *Theodore Roosevelt* and Carrier Air Wing Eight would fly 4,200 sorties (more than any other carrier) and drop more than 4.8 million pounds of ordnance.

Oceana-based aviators Lt. Robert Wetzel and Lt. Jeffrey Zaun, flying an Intruder, were listed as missing in action on 18 January during a nighttime strike. "News of the Oceana-based jet's downing ricocheted through the two neighborhoods a mile apart where the two fliers live," reported the *Virginian-Pilot.* "Reaction was tight-lipped, as the close-knit communities drew together, yielding only snippets of the aviators' lives." To the relief of many, Zaun appeared on Iraqi television several days later. "They took me to a TV studio and sat me next to the big guy who was asking the questions," he later recounted. "They told me what questions they were going to ask and they told me what my answers were going to be."[6] Wetzel's fate remained unknown until he was discovered in Iraqi custody, recovering from injuries.

Lt. Devon Jones and Lt. Lawrence Slade of Oceana-based Fighter Squadron 103 from *Saratoga* were shot down by what was believed to be a surface-to-air missile on 21 January. After ejecting, Slade was captured by Iraqi troops and held in Baghdad as a POW until the end of the war. Jones was able to evade capture for eight hours and was eventually rescued by special operations forces. Lt. Cdr. Barry T. Cooke and Lt. Patrick K. Connor, flying an A-6 Intruder of Attack Squadron 36 off *Theodore Roosevelt,* were shot down by enemy ground fire and killed on 2 February.

Norfolk ships at sea provided a forward screen for the carriers, attacked Iraqi minelayers, directed aircraft and helicopters over the gulf, and held Marines in waiting afloat. *Wisconsin* opened her first combat bombardment mission since 1952 on 6 February by lobbing eleven shells across a range of nineteen miles to destroy an Iraqi artillery battery in southern Kuwait. Using an unmanned aerial vehicle (UAV) to spot her fall of shot—a first in combat—*Wisconsin* continued bombardment missions to soften defenses along the Kuwait coastline for a possible amphibious assault. During Desert Storm, *Wisconsin* fired more than three hundred tons of high-explosive 16-inch projectiles in thirty-six different naval gunfire support missions.[7]

The Navy's sizable amphibious attack force sat in full readiness off the coast of Kuwait. With meticulous planning, an amphibious assault had been planned to augment the main Coalition ground attack from the south and west. When it became obvious, however, that the amphibious assault would require significant minesweeping and naval gunfire preparation, amphibious forces assumed the role of raiding offshore islands and holding Iraqi defense forces in place by the mere threat of attack.

Support for those deployed was high, and the people of Tidewater paid close attention to developments. "The nation is reawakening, as it does at the start of every war, to the necessity of Norfolk and Newport News and the rest of the seven cities of Hampton Roads," said Fred Ellis of the Navy League. "The Navy is the heart and soul of Norfolk."[8]

"[The war's] impact was felt in many ways," summarized a local newspaper, "in the toll brought by thousands of sudden deployments; in the anxieties of conflict abroad; in Christmases and honeymoons put on hold; in the images of local prisoners of war flickering on television screens the world over; but most of all, in lives lost in combat." It was also felt in the absence of so many. It was estimated that fifty thousand men and women from Tidewater deployed during the First Gulf War, and according to the Hampton Roads Chamber of Commerce, businessmen saw a dramatic downturn in commerce. Parking spots on base were easy to find; frigate *Elrod* (FFG-55) and carrier *Dwight D. Eisenhower* had their pick of normally scarce repair services at the Norfolk Naval Shipyard; and at Oceana, "when you walk out of the hangar, it's hard to miss your airplane. It's one of the few out there," one pilot said.[9]

The weight of the American attack ended the war a mere hundred hours after the ground attack had begun. With the rapid cessation of hostilities, talk across Tidewater quickly turned to expected homecomings. "In the summer it begins . . . with the autumn comes the buildup . . . winter brings the inevitability of war . . . now it is spring. America savors a military victory, swift and sure," editorialized the *Virginian-Pilot* as it helped to spur region-wide celebrations.[10]

As many turned homeward with the end of the war, the diminutive Little Creek–based minesweeper *Adroit* (MSO-509) was only hitting her stride. Originally sent to the Persian Gulf with three other minecraft in the fall of 1990 aboard a contract heavy-lift ship, she operated as part of a multinational mine-clearing force facing the threat of more than a thousand Iraqi mines strewn across the Kuwait approaches. The mine-clearing force had only barely dented the Iraqi minefields by war's end; as Middle East Force commander Rear Adm. Raynor A. K. Taylor commented, "the Iraqis might have agreed to a ceasefire, but their mines have not yet surrendered."[11] *Adroit* would not finish her mine-clearing operations until 10 September 1991.

John F. Kennedy was the first of the Norfolk battle groups to return, arriving on 28 March 1991. "The ship noses around the bend, a mere speck that gradually grows and at last halts, an immense mesa beside the multitude," wrote reporter Guy Friddell from the pier. "You can feel the tides of passion as those on deck and dock strain to pick loved ones out of the masses and break into smiles and dance and wave signs. Then the sailors come pounding down the gangplanks until, in a whirlpool of emotion, families are whole again, waltzing in each others arms, crying, laughing, exulting at being alive and together."[12] *America* reached Hampton Roads on 18 April, and *Theodore Roosevelt,* after flying patrols over northern Iraq in Operation Provide Comfort, finally returned on 28 June.

Hampton Roads has long served as the Atlantic Fleet home of Navy Special Warfare forces—units that were heavily involved in clandestine roles inside Iraq during the First Gulf War. Navy Special Warfare traces its history back to joint Army-Navy Scouts and Raiders reconnaissance units and Naval Combat Demolition Units (NDCUs) of World War II that brought some of the first underwater swimmer teams to Little Creek and Solomons Island for beach reconnaissance training. Led by salvage officers Lt. Mark W. Starkweather and Lt. James W. Darroch, a small detachment of sailors was picked to support Operation Torch landings in North Africa. They received training at Little Creek in demolition, cable cutting, and commando raid techniques during the summer and fall of 1942. At the same time, the Amphibious Scout and Raider School (Joint) was established at Little Creek to train both Army and Navy personnel in amphibious operations. Detachments from the Third and Ninth Infantry Divisions and scout boat crews from the ATB Solomons Boat Pool were among the first trained to support Torch operations; they included Lt. Phil H. Bucklew, who would later be called the "Father of Naval Special Warfare."[13]

Separate from the Scouts and Raiders, the chief of naval operations ordered the organization of new units to clear underwater obstacles and to mark landing beaches on 6 May 1943. The first NCDU started with thirteen volunteers who were sent to the Naval Amphibious Training Base at Solomons Island. Lt. Fred Wise from the Seabees was designated officer in charge, and Wise's first unit was sent to support Allied landings in Sicily in July 1943. Most of the unit stayed at the Amphibious Training Base at Fort Pierce, Florida, as instructors, joining Scouts and Raiders who also had shifted there for training. Lt. Cdr. Draper L. Kauffman established the training for follow-on units, teams that would be assigned to support landings in both the Atlantic and the Pacific.[14]

Some forty six-man NCDU teams were assigned to the "Omaha" and "Utah" landing beaches at Normandy to clear lanes for landing craft, armed with little more than knives, swim fins, rubberized canvas suits, and twenty 2-pound explosive charges. The NCDU teams were hit hard at Normandy: thirty-seven NCDU personnel were killed on D-Day, and another seventy were wounded. NCDU teams were later realigned into hundred-man underwater demolition teams (UDTs) and continued beach reconnaissance and demolition missions, primarily in the Pacific.

Following World War II, UDT was reduced to two skeleton teams on each coast; UDT-2 and UDT-4 were assigned to Little Creek. UDTs were again active during the Korean War in the clearing of amphibious landing areas, beach reconnaissance, guerrilla landings, and minesweeping support. In February 1954, the two Atlantic Fleet UDTs were redesignated as UDTs 21 and 22.

In January 1962, the first SEAL teams were established to conduct unconventional warfare, counter-guerrilla warfare, and clandestine operations in maritime and riverine environments; ten officers and fifty enlisted men (mostly from UDT-21) formed SEAL Team Two in Little Creek. Lt. Roy Boehm was named acting commanding officer of SEAL Team Two when Lt. John Callahan was delayed in reaching Little Creek. Boehm was so eager to get the team set up that he bought underwater breathing devices, parachutes, and 132 new AR-15 rifles off the open market instead of waiting for normal Navy supply channels, and it was said that he avoided court-martial only by unofficial input from President Kennedy.[15]

Team Two was barely formed when it was sent on its first mission in April 1962 to reconnoiter the Havana shoreline for a possible amphibious landing—months before the Cuban Missile Crisis. Six members of the team were delivered by submarine and surveyed two-plus miles of coastline before being extracted. During the missile crisis they repeated the mission, this time with more specific intent, while a second unit practiced for potential parachute insertions onto the island.[16]

Underwater Demolition Teams and Navy SEAL Teams have made Little Creek and Dam Neck their East Coast home since World War II. Here a combat swimmer from Little Creek–based UDT-22 awaits a high-speed pick up in 1965. *U.S. Navy*

For the next ten years, the focus of the UDT/SEAL teams was the war in Vietnam, and Seal Team Two sent its first units there in 1967. SEAL involvement in Vietnam was initially advisory in nature but soon included a host of small-unit and clandestine maritime operations in both North and South Vietnam.

In 1983, the teams reorganized, dropped the name "Underwater Demolition Team," and added two new SEAL and two SEAL delivery vehicle teams. SEAL Teams Two and Four were based in Little Creek; their areas of concentration were the traditional geographic regions of Europe and the Caribbean/Latin America, respectively. Training in Tidewater was conducted at various sites, including the beaches at Dam Neck and free-fall parachute practice at Fentress.[17]

SEAL Team Six, whose members were specially chosen, was also first based at Little Creek, with specialties in hostage rescue and antiterrorism. Team Six was established, it was said, in reaction to the failed Iranian hostage rescue operation of April 1980, for which military and Special Forces teams were roundly criticized. The Navy's first small antiterrorist unit was referred to as "Mob Six" (Mobility Six), possibly implying status as the sixth platoon of Team Two, and was led by the flamboyant but respected Cdr. Richard Marcinko. Team Six grew from this initial effort and was commissioned on 1 October 1980 and declared mission capable by 31 December. Correspondent Orr Kelly described its organization as "a new kind of SEAL team. Instead of operating in platoon-sized or smaller units, the members of Team Six were trained to work in much larger units. They practice operating in assault groups—called color teams—of thirty to forty men or, if the hostage rescue situation calls for it, multiple color teams." The training of Team Six was said to be intense, with significant international travel, liaison with other United States and Allied counterterrorist organizations, and, for a while, an additional mission to test the security of American military facilities. Much interest and controversy swirled around the team, especially when the unit's founder, Marcinko, was convicted and imprisoned for misuse of government funds. Seal Team Six was reconstituted as the Naval Special Warfare Development Group stationed at Dam Neck, with primary functions involving intelligence, counterterrorism, and national security work.[18]

As Naval Special Warfare has evolved and expanded, SEAL Teams Eight and Ten have been added to those stationed in Little Creek. Under new organizational concepts, SEAL teams and their support will periodically reorganize into "Naval Special Warfare Squadrons" for periodic and phased deployments and retraining.

SEAL operations in Grenada (with Teams Four and Six), Panama (Teams Two and Four), Desert Storm, the Balkans, Afghanistan, and the Second Gulf War point to their continuing viability. Efforts in Afghanistan, for instance, included small-unit operations, spotting for high precision guided bombs, advisory and security assistance with tribal forces, scouting and reconnaissance, and personnel security.

Frogmen have always operated their own boats and are organized, today, into Special Boat Units. The earliest dedicated Naval Special Warfare craft was the PTF (fast patrol boat), an outgrowth of the PT boats of World War II. Two PT boats were modernized and designated PTFs in December 1962 and moved to Little Creek to support UDT/SEAL operations, and in the summer of 1964, Boat Support Unit Two was established at Little Creek to orchestrate these efforts. Additional boats were built from Norwegian designs, and boat tactics and standard operating procedures between boats and SEALs were refined. Other small boat projects were also pursued, including the development of the landing craft swimmer recovery vessel (LCSR); coastal patrol and interdiction craft (CPIC); and swimmer delivery vehicles (SDVs). Mobile Support Teams were also established to deploy these boats where needed. During Vietnam, Mobile Support Teams provided combat craft support for SEAL operations, as did patrol boat, riverine (PBR), and swift boat sailors. As the Vietnam mission expanded into the riverine environment, additional craft, tactics, and training evolved for SEAL support. In 1971, Boat Support Unit Two was redesignated as Coastal River Squadron Two and, in 1983, as Special Boat Squadron Two to oversee Special Boat Units with specialty SEAL craft, Mobile Support Teams, and Patrol Coastal craft.

SDV teams have historical roots that reach back to Italian and British combat swimmers and wet submersibles of World War II. A free-flooding SDV, deliverable by submarine, was in operation during the 1960s, and SEALs now train with the Advanced SEAL Delivery System (ASDS), a dry submersible for advanced underwater mobility.

One of the most visible reflections of the military's changing mission in the post–Cold War era has been the realignment of many of the most senior commands in the nation to face new realities of warfare, international security, and joint force operations. Hampton Roads, again, is at the hub of these changes that affect America's Atlantic perspective.

Seeking to define a single, U.S.-based unified command with responsibility for training all services for joint operations, the Atlantic Command (under a new Unified Command Plan of 24 September 1993) assumed combatant command of the Army's Forces Command (FORSCOM), the Air Force's Air Combat Command (ACC), the Marine Corps' Forces Command Atlantic (MARFORLANT), and the Navy's Atlantic Fleet (CINCLANTFLT). A new mission, "to ensure all forces going into combat, anywhere in the world, would fight as integrated joint teams," was added to the command's existing Atlantic Ocean geographic mission. In October 1999, the name of Atlantic Command was changed to United States Joint Forces Command (USJFCOM) to emphasize an additional functional role of leading the transformation of U.S. military joint warfighting and, as such, is the only combatant unified command with both geographic area and functional responsibilities.

USJFCOM has several component efforts in Tidewater. The Joint Warfighting Center (JWFC) in Suffolk leads joint warfighter capability improvement through joint training with emphasis on counterterrorism and military transformation. The Joint C4ISR Battle Center (JBC), also in Suffolk, leads the transformation of joint force command, control, communications, computers, intelligence, surveillance, and reconnaissance (C4ISR) capabilities. The Norfolk-based Joint Forces Intelligence Command (JFIC) supports USJFCOM's intelligence needs. The Special Operations Command of USJFCOM helps integrate all Special Operations Forces.

A key priority of USJFCOM is "netting" the force. As such, it has helped Tidewater become a national leader in information technology and has orchestrated the testing of new concepts in joint battle management, knowledge management, and distributed information for the Navy and other services.

The Joint Forces Staff College, originally established as the Armed Forces Staff College on 13 August 1946, has shouldered similar joint and transformational objectives. From its founding on the fifty-five-acre site of a 1942 Navy receiving station, the college has evolved into a unique Tidewater institution. Its first class arrived on 26 January 1947, and the school's formal dedication was officiated a week later by the college's first commandant, Army Lt. Gen. Delos C. Emmons. From its outset, the college espoused an unofficial theme of housing officers' families on the same compound with the objective, as explained by Rear Adm. James Holloway, for "officers of the Navy, Army, and Marine Corps to work together and play together; your wives and children will live within the same compound and will come out of it as friends, with a mutual understanding and mutual customs."[19] The facilities have been improved over time, but the mission of the college, "to prepare selected mid-career officers for joint and combined staff duty and to immerse them in joint/combined operational planning, joint doctrine while developing cross-service teamwork," has remained consistent. The Joint Forces Staff College joined the National Defense University in 1981 as one of four collaborative institutions.

The Navy's Atlantic Fleet command has undergone similar transformation. Before 1985, the U.S. Atlantic Command, the Allied Command, Atlantic, and the U. S. Atlantic Fleet had been headed by a single command organization until a congressionally mandated reorganization of the U.S. Armed Force separated command of the U.S. Atlantic Fleet from the other two commands with its own four-star admiral. Adm. Wesley L. McDonald, the last to command all three organizations at the same time, relinquished command of the U.S. Atlantic Fleet to Adm. Carlisle A. H. Trost on 4 October 1985.

On 1 October 2001, the chief of naval operations designated CINCLANTFLT as concurrent commander for the new U.S. Fleet Forces Command (COMUSFLTFORCOM) with responsibility for overall coordination of the manning, equipping, and training of both Atlantic and Pacific fleet units during the interdeployment training cycle. The reorganized fleet command was also designed to fit better within the JFCOM structure and to act as Naval Component Commander to Strategic Command and Northern Command.

As these changes have jelled in recent years, so, too, has Norfolk's position as the primary center of naval operational planning, training, and execution. Fleet Forces Command centralizes many functions that were once executed in parallel Atlantic and Pacific fleet organizations. With this critical mass of naval operational command in Norfolk, other elements—including imaginative new efforts to enhance modern

Today, Norfolk Naval Shipyard encompasses eight hundred acres, seven dry docks, four miles of waterfront, nineteen miles of railroad tracks, and four hundred cranes. Dry Dock No.8, which opened in July 1942, is 1,092 feet 5 inches in length and can repair the Navy's largest aircraft carriers. *Norfolk Naval Shipyard*

naval capabilities—have tended to gravitate to Tidewater, sending a clear signal of the ascendancy of the region's importance in naval operational decision making, both today and tomorrow.

The Naval Network Warfare Command (NETWARCOM), established quietly in Little Creek in July 2002, provides a good example of this trend. Operating near a fleet concentration area and convenient to Fleet Forces Command and Navy leadership in Washington, this new organization can provide centralized authority for all network and information operations in the fleet.

The shift to Fleet Forces Command also caused an adjustment to the Navy's traditional Type Commander organization. Instead of separate surface, submarine, and air type commanders for the Atlantic and Pacific fleets, a single type commander within each warfare community was named; the commanders of Naval Surface Force Pacific and Naval Air Force Pacific became Commander, Naval Surface Forces, and Commander, Naval Air Forces, respectively, and the Commander, Submarine Force Atlantic, in Hampton Roads became Commander, Naval Submarine Forces.[20]

Following the model of senior American commanders in Norfolk, NATO also chose to realign and, in June 2003, disestablished the long-standing Allied Command, Atlantic, to form the new Allied Command Transformation (ACT) in Norfolk. In short order, a traditional dual-role command relationship was restored, in which the Commander, Joint Forces Command, assumed the concurrent role as Supreme Allied Commander Transformation. "ACT will shape the future of combined and joint operations," according to the NATO Secretary General, Lord Robertson. "It will identify new concepts, and bring them to maturity. It will then turn these transformational concepts into reality; a reality shared by the entire NATO Alliance. And it will do so in close cooperation with the US Joint Forces Command collocated here, to ensure that NATO's transformation stays in lock step with the changes taking place in the United States."[21]

The naval command structure of the bases and facilities in Hampton Roads has also been streamlined in recent years. From the end of World War II, COMNAVBASE and the Commander of the Fifth Naval District existed as a dual command, with separate staffs in which the naval district staff had the more wide-ranging responsibility. On 1 July 1962, the staffs were trimmed, and the COMNAVBASE staff was consolidated into naval district staff codes; but on 1 July 1975, with naval districts throughout the country heading for extinction, this condition was reversed, and the COMNAVBASE staff assumed naval district tasks. The Fifth Naval District was officially disestablished on 30 September 1980. This condition continued until 1999, when COMNAVBASE was disestablished for good in favor of a regional commander for Navy Region Mid-Atlantic with headquarters in Norfolk. To streamline shore installation management still further, the chief of naval operations directed that all management and oversight of shore installation support to the fleet be centralized in the Navy Installations command in Washington.[22] This initiative, part of an ongoing base management initiative known as "regionalization," reduced many of the traditional responsibilities of the base commander and, among other actions, saw the Naval Station and Naval Air Station merged into a single installation called Naval Station Norfolk on 5 February 1999.[23]

Norfolk Naval Shipyard, the nation's oldest, has also aimed at streamlining and efficiency. "We're trying to retool for the twenty-first century," said shipyard public affairs officer Steve Milner. "The shipyard's layout was originally designed to build ships, a mission we no longer do, and so we have reorganized around repair hubs, a carrier hub, submarine hub, all interconnected by rail systems to increase flexibility."[24] The yard has rearranged industrial processes, encouraged new relationships with nearby private yards, and emphasized its ability to respond to short-fused emergencies. Several of Norfolk Naval Shipyard's specialties are not performed in any other naval shipyard (such as boiler repair and work with propellers), and some of the most modern work done in any industrial facility (such as conversion of *Ohio*-class ballistic missile submarines to Tomahawk missile arsenals) is performed along the Elizabeth. Its vocational Apprentice School—one of the oldest in the nation, established in 1898—provides a firm foundation of master tradesmen to support future endeavors.

The danger and volatility of the Middle East throughout the 1990s and into the first decade of the twenty-first century continued to dominate the Navy's attention in Tidewater. Deployments to an area of near-constant threat can never be considered routine, and frequently Norfolk ships became the first responders to crisis, the most noticeable protectors of American interests, and the most visible targets for terrorism or retaliation. Units of Tidewater's Navy would respond to calls for action in 1992–93 (Somalia, Restore Hope), 1991–2003 (Iraq, Northern Watch, Southern Watch), 1995 (Somalia), 1996 (Iraq, Desert Strike), 1998 (Iraq, Desert Thunder), 1998 (Sudan/Afghanistan, Infinite Reach), 1998 (Iraq, Desert Fox),

Perhaps signaling a change in the look of naval warships in Hampton Roads, the experimental high-speed vessel *Swift* (HSV-2) operates from Little Creek in February 2004. *U.S. Navy*

and 2001 (Afghanistan, Enduring Freedom). Tidewater units participated in maritime interception operations in the Red Sea and Persian Gulf and in naval operations in support of allied operations in Kosovo, Bosnia, and Serbia.

Guided missile destroyer *Cole* (DDG-67), which had operated out of Hampton Roads since commissioning in June 1996, became a bull's-eye for a terrorist attack when she stopped in the port of Aden, Yemen, on 12 October 2000 for fuel. A small boat, crammed to the gunnels with explosives, detonated beside the ship, blasting a forty-foot hole in the destroyer's side. The crew reacted quickly to the unexpected catastrophe and slowly pulled the ship back from the verge of sinking. During a stress-filled ninety-six hours of sustained, intense damage control in conditions of extreme heat and tension, the crew isolated damaged electrical systems and contained fuel oil ruptures that could have erupted into even more catastrophic fires aboard a ship already on life support. Deprived of sleep, food, and shelter, the crew freed shipmates caught in the twisted wreckage and quietly and professionally restored a secure damage control perimeter that slowly restored ship stability and the viability of engineering systems that were vital to the ship's survival. Within twenty-four hours, a team of twenty-two Norfolk Naval Shipyard workers was on a plane, headed to *Cole* to help deal with the catastrophe. "One man even missed his wedding day to volunteer for the mission," said shipyard commander Capt. Mark Hugel. "On an average day we have folks scattered around the world to keep the Navy running."

Following the attack, in which seventeen sailors were killed and thirty-nine injured, *Cole* returned to the United States aboard the heavy lift ship *M/V Blue Marlin* for repairs. She rejoined the fleet in April 2002 after sixteen months and $250 million in repairs.

Bob Barfield of Portsmouth expressed a reaction that was typical in Hampton Roads: "The *Cole* incident hurt me," he said while looking at flags flying at half-mast. "I work around these sailors and I have so much respect for them. For anyone to attack them is an attack on me." A similarly somber President Clinton came to Norfolk on the dreary morning of 18 October to join fifteen thousand others gathered between carrier *Eisenhower* and destroyers *Ross* and *McFaul* at Pier 12 to honor the fallen.[25]

Those on board *Cole* and those in Hampton Roads who remember her legacy know that the ship still sails with reminders of her heroism and her encounter with terrorism. Seventeen brass stars have been inlaid in the ship's blue-tiled mess decks, and mounted on a nearby bulkhead is a small modest box containing crumbled remnants of metal, marble, and glass from the destroyed World Trade Center.[26]

Only a week after the September 11 terrorist attacks, the *Theodore Roosevelt* battle group left Norfolk in what would turn out to be a record-setting deployment to support attacks within Afghanistan during Operation Enduring Freedom. With aircraft of Carrier Air Wing One in constant combat over Afghanistan, *Roosevelt* logged 160 consecutive days at sea without a port call, breaking the previous record of 152 days set by *Dwight D. Eisenhower* in 1980. In sailor vernacular, this was known as the "Six Pack Cruise," as navy policy provides each crew member with two beers after every 45 consecutive days at sea.[27]

In the still-dark hours of 20 March 2003, fifty-eight ships and 29,500 personnel from the Virginia Tidewater stood on the front lines of war in the Mediterranean, Red Sea, and Persian Gulf. For over two months these ships had been practicing a complex military game plan, filled with coordinated missions, milestones, objectives, and contingency schemes. For many involved, the water, the watch routine, and the Iraqi target sets inside computer databases gave them an eerie feeling of déjà vu. There was little talk about the right or wrong of America's

The amphibious assault ships of Task Force 51 steam together in formation in the Persian Gulf during Operation Iraqi Freedom in 2003. The thirty-two ships of Task Force 51 comprised the largest amphibious force assembled since the Inchon landings of the Korean War. From left to right these ships include: *Tarawa, Kearsarge, Saipan, Bonhomme Richard, Bataan,* and *Boxer* (*Bataan, Kearsarge,* and *Saipan* are Norfolk based). *U.S. Navy*

objectives on this morning because that was not the priority among those who squinted at computer displays or snoozed in carrier ready rooms. Their thoughts, instead, were on the elements of modern war: way points, launch sequencing, ordnance loads, comm buttons, and blue force locators.

Leaning forward as they were, it surprised no one when Norfolk-based destroyer *Donald Cook* (DDG-75), attack submarine *Montpelier* (SSN-765), and four other ships received rushed orders to program the coordinates of what was thought to be President Saddam Hussein's hideout into forty Tomahawk missiles. In short order, the missiles shot skyward from *Donald Cook.* Stunning noise and glare from the rockets assaulted onlookers as the missiles tipped over in trajectory, steadied on course toward Baghdad, and rapidly disappeared to the northeast.

The missiles would crash into their intended target, signaling to an expectant world that the Navy was again a primary contributor in protecting American interests abroad. Norfolk-based carriers *Harry S. Truman* (CVN- 75) and *Theodore Roosevelt* stood in the Mediterranean, awaiting their turn to strike. Pilots traded their normal green flight suits for tan, for desert survival, with all of the normal identifying patches removed or replaced by makeshift name tags on silver duct tape.[28] Battle Group Commander Rear Adm. John D. Stufflebeem broke the news over the 1MC public address system: "For our part and in simple terms, we have been directed to conduct combat operations into Iraq."[29]

Around midnight on 22 March, nineteen fully armed strike aircraft were launched from *Truman* to join a similar number from *Roosevelt* streaking toward airfield and headquarters targets outside Baghdad. "Wearing night vision goggles, they saw anti-aircraft fire light up Iraq west of Baghdad, avoided surface-to-air missiles piercing the skies to their east and waited in line to be refueled in midair for the long trip home," wrote "embedded" reporter Matthew Dolan. "After a six-hour round trip, all returned safely to their Norfolk-based ships. 'It went textbook,' said F-14 pilot Commander Marcus Hitchcock, commanding officer of the Virginia Beach-based Fighter Squadron 32 and leader of the first Iraqi strike off the *Truman.*" Flying her "Give 'em Hell" battle flag, the *Truman* contributed a second wave of equal size immediately after recovering her first strike, concentrated on targets outside Mosul and Kirkuk in north-central Iraq.[30]

Over the next several days, each carrier fell into a steady routine of planning, arming, launching, recovering, sleeping, and eating as Coalition forces converged on Baghdad. In the eyes of correspondent Chris Tyree:

> The ship is illuminated by yellow-orange, sodium-vapor lights, and the smell of jet fuel is ever-present. Occasionally a sailor stops by the opening in the hangar bay to watch the moonlight flicker on the water below. The hangar is filled with Hornets and Tomcats and Prowlers and Dusty Dogs, all itching for action. Men and women crawl over the planes like ants attacking a picnic, testing this and replacing that. Two decks up, the various squadrons' ready rooms fill for the flight briefing. Pilots with names like "Speedy" Spedro and "Half" Nelson climb into their seats to hear the commander of the air wing give the final instructions for the night's bombing run: First they'll bomb an airfield, then they will look for a downed helicopter, and finally they'll drop the last of the ordnance onto a bunker filled with Iraqi fighters, all the while watching as surface-to-air missiles blaze by. The mission lasts six hours. The pilots, exhausted but safe, emerge from their planes rubbing the smalls of their backs, their jumpsuits soaked through with sweat.[31]

With the need for consistent naval aviation presence over Iraq, the twin Norfolk carriers asssumed a day-and-night rotation. Aboard *Roosevelt,* which took the nighttime half of the clock, "the days don't seem to blur together on this aircraft carrier, the nights do," reported Matthew Dolan. The traditional Reveille wake-up announcement trumpets throughout the ship just before the sun sets. Sailors chow down on breakfast at 5:30 p.m. The ship store opens at 10 at night. Dinner starts just before dawn and the barbers cut hair through the night until 10 a.m. Then it's lights out again. "It seems like every day is Monday," said Lt. (jg) Chad Trevett of Norfolk. "Well, Monday night."[32]

Truman had found her way to the eastern Mediterranean in early December 2002 as part of a regularly scheduled overseas deployment as tensions heightened and a buildup of Norfolk ships was in full swing. *Theodore Roosevelt* had been "surged" to join her with a rushed schedule of repairs and training. The *Roosevelt* battle group had slipped out of Hampton Roads after shortened holidays on 6 January, bound for what was first thought to be several weeks of training in the Caribbean. Rather than return to Norfolk, however, she rushed to the Mediterranean.[33] A dozen amphibious ships from Hampton Roads (headed by the large-deck *Iwo Jima, Nassau, Saipan, Kearsarge,* and *Bataan*) carried more than nine thousand Camp Lejeune Marines into battle, and the president's call for forces also included Hampton Roads medical personnel, SEALs, Seabees, Coast Guard ships, reservists, Oceana-

Amphibious assault ship *Kearsarge* receives a tumultuous welcome from friends and family as she returns from Operation Iraqi Freedom in 2003. *U.S. Navy*

based fighter squadrons VF-2 and VF-31 on Pacific Fleet carriers, and two of the smallest ships in the Navy, patrol craft *Chinook* (PC-9) and *Firebolt* (PC-10), which crossed the Atlantic in some of the worst weather of the year.[34]

At the Norfolk Naval Station, not a single carrier or large amphibious ship was to be seen. "I've never seen it this empty before," said Eric L. Smith, a lieutenant commander with more than twenty years' experience on the waterfront. The fleet was smaller in 2003 than during the 1991 Gulf War, but overseas commitments were just as high, meaning fewer ships remained behind when America mobilized.[35]

Nearly six hundred Tidewater-based Navy physicians, corpsmen, and medical specialists from the Naval Medical Center, Portsmouth, deployed to the Middle East to outfit Casualty Receiving and Treatment Ship teams operating from amphibious warships. Hospital personnel also helped staff hospital ship *Comfort* where treatment was extended to American servicemen, Iraqi civilians, and enemy prisoners of war.[36]

Primary hostilities of the Second Gulf War were completed by 14 April 2003, and the naval force assembled in Middle Eastern waters began to head for welcomes at home. Tomcat fighters from VF-31 were among the first aviation units to return to Tidewater, completing a ten-month deployment aboard carrier *Abraham Lincoln* (CVN-72). "Around 4 p.m., a familiar roar crescendoed from above," correspondent Matthew Jones reported. "High above, ten F-14's soared in tight formation, peeling off two by two before coming in to land. The planes taxied toward the hangar and, ever so slowly, lined up in two rows, their engines idling with a howl. The crowd held signs aloft: WELCOME HOME PAUL! And BACK SO SOON? Off went the jet's engines to cheers and applause. The men climbed out of their cockpits and the crowd swarmed them."[37]

Harry S Truman returned on 23 May to be greeted enthusiastically. "By 11 a.m., shivering sailors in their dress uniforms lined the rails on the *Truman's* flight deck. The image—a ring of sailors in white, almost shoulder-to-shoulder against the steel ship and gray sky—marked a dramatic last leg of the *Truman's* journey home. While the raindrops fell and the wind gusted, they stood at attention carrying only

In 2004, the Hampton Roads Naval Museum celebrated its twenty-fifth year with a mission to "encompass the role of the Navy in the Tidewater area from the days of the Revolution to the present day." Beginning with displays in Pennsylvania House on Norfolk Naval Base, this official U.S. Navy museum with its professional and dedicated staff now operates a world-class gallery at the downtown Nauticus National Maritime Center and is host to the display battleship *Wisconsin*. *BRL Pictures*

small American flags in their cold hands. But the sailors' enthusiasm won out over the foul conditions. As the packed pier came into view, sailors could hear "USA! USA!" being shouted by the crowd. They roared back with the same chant." *Truman* returned after dropping more bombs and missiles over Iraq than any other aircraft carrier—1,280 sorties, striking 588 targets.[38]

The *Theodore Roosevelt* added to the festivities across Tidewater with her return six days later, "a rousing return for sailors who missed a proper send off." The attack submarine *Montpelier* was one of the last to return in early July; she had the important distinction of having fired twenty Tomahawk missiles.[39]

When America goes to war, Tidewater's Navy is on the front lines. It has been that way since the birth of the republic, and the chronicle of the life and times of that region brings alive the mainstream history of a nation. Today and for years into the future, the full spectrum of American naval strength will reside in Hampton Roads—carriers, cruisers, destroyers, amphibious ships, submarines, supply and logistics ships, fighters, radar planes, and helicopters. If there is a single symbol of naval power today, it is the aircraft carrier; Tidewater is the birthplace of most of the Navy's carriers and home to almost half of them.

History is found along every inch of Hampton Roads shore—a living, reach-out-and-touch history that can tap the soul and stir the imagination. Within sight of the 1833 Dry Dock No. 1 at Norfolk Naval Shipyard, ninety-thousand-ton nuclear aircraft carriers berth; bricks from old Fort Nelson (dismantled in 1820) are part of the walls of the modern buildings of Portsmouth Naval Medical Center; and Jamestown Exposition houses still gaze out across Willoughby Bay.

The Navy and its treasured history touch the mainstream of Tidewater each day. The Navy stands as southeastern Virginia's largest single economic contributor, Oceana is the largest employer in Virginia Beach, and Newport News Shipbuilding is the largest private employer in the state. "Having relatives work at the shipyard is part of our culture," said Jennifer Dunn, a Newport News spokesperson whose father has worked for the company for more than thirty years. "Many of our employees are fourth- and fifth-generation shipbuilders."[40]

This comfortable feeling of historical perspective is everywhere in evidence, at times subtle and intuitive, and at other times bold and brash. Standing on the quarterdeck of carrier *Ronald Reagan* dockside in Newport News, you can feel the threads of history twisting tightly around you. To one side you can touch a life-size statue of the Gipper, one of the fleet's best friends, a president who sought a six-hundred-ship Navy to win the Cold War. To the other side you can look out across the James River to the exact spot where the *Monitor* and *Virginia* pirouetted at point-blank range in grim battle eight generations ago. Hearing *Reagan*'s ventilation blowers and seeing her crew members in action, you can sense the power of this largest of warships and imagine the excitement of generations of Navy men leaning into the wind across a carrier's deck to prepare a Hellcat, Spad, Phantom, or Tomcat for an alert-5 launch.

All strands of American naval history ultimately tie into Hampton Roads. Five days after the storied turret of the ironclad *Monitor* first broke the water's surface off Cape Hatteras from its watery grave, she was escorted in honor across Tidewater. The date was 10 August 2002, and the soul of the "glorious impregnable battery, the wonder of the age, the terror of rebels, and the pride of the North" was again crossing Hampton Roads, 140 years after she weighed anchor to be taken under tow seaward from Fortress Monroe.[41] Festooned with rust and sea growth, the nine-foot-tall turret still held a power all its own. "This is the ultimate icon of Civil War naval history," said the *Monitor* expedition's leader, John Broadwater. "This is the ultimate prize." Dents from a *Virginia* broadside can still be easily discerned in her thick iron plating, a symbol of the obvious: the Navy's roots in Tidewater are deep and unshakable.

GLOSSARY

AATC Antiaircraft Training Center
AC auxiliary collier
ACT Allied Command Transformation
AD destroyer tender
Adm. Admiral
AGF miscellaneous command ship
AK attack cargo ship
AR auxiliary repair ship
AS submarine tender
ASW antisubmarine warfare
ATB amphibious training base
AVP small seaplane tender
BB battleship
BRAC base realignment and closure process
CA heavy cruiser
CAG guided missile heavy cruiser
CG guided missile cruiser
CGN nuclear-powered guided missile cruiser
CINCLANT Commander in Chief, Atlantic Command
CINCLANTFLT Commander in Chief, U. S. Atlantic Fleet
CL light cruiser
CLG guided missile light cruiser
CNO Chief of Naval Operations
COMNAVAIRFOR Commander, Naval Air Forces
COMNAVAIRLANT Commander, Naval Air Forces, Atlantic Fleet
COMNAVBASE Commander, Naval Base, Norfolk
COMNAVSUBFOR Commander, Naval Submarine Forces
COMNAVSURFFOR Commander, Naval Surface Forces
COMSUBLANT Commander, Submarine Force, U.S. Atlantic Fleet
COSL Commander, Oceanographic System, Atlantic
COTCLANT Commander, Operational Training Command, Atlantic
CSS Confederate States Ship
CUS Commander, Undersea Surveillance
CV aircraft carrier
CVA attack aircraft carrier
CVAN nuclear-powered attack aircraft carrier
CVB large aircraft carrier
CVE escort aircraft carrier
CVN nuclear-powered aircraft carrier
CVS antisubmarine aircraft carrier
DD destroyer
DDG guided missile destroyer
DDGN nuclear-powered guided missile cruiser
DE destroyer escort
DL destroyer leader
ENS Ensign
FFG guided missile frigate
GIUK Greenland–Iceland–United Kingdom
HF/DF high-frequency direction finding
HMS His (or Her) Majesty's Ship
HUK hunter-killer group (ASW)
IUSS Integrated Undersea Surveillance System
JATO jet-assisted takeoff
LAMPS Light Airborne Multipurpose System (helicopter)
LCI landing craft, infantry
LCM landing craft, mechanized
LCSR landing craft, swimmer recovery vessel
LCU landing craft, utility
LCVP landing craft, vehicle-personnel
LHA amphibious assault ship (general purpose)
LHD amphibious assault ship (multipurpose)
LPD amphibious transport dock
LPH amphibious assault ship (helicopter)
LSD landing ship, dock
LSM landing ship, medium
LST landing ship, tank
LT Lieutenant
LT(jg) Lieutenant (junior grade)
MIDEASTFOR Middle East Force

NAAS	Naval Auxiliary Air Station
NAB	Naval Amphibious Base
NAOTS	Naval Aviation Ordnance Test Station
NARF	Naval Air Rework Facility
NAS	Naval Air Station
NATO	North Atlantic Treaty Organization
NATS	Naval Air Transport Service
NAVFAC	Naval Facility (SOSUS)
NDCU	Naval Combat Demolition Unit
NOB	Naval Operating Base
NOPF	Navy Ocean Processing Facility
NOTS	Naval Overseas Transportation Service
NSD	Naval Supply Depot
NTS	Naval Transportation Service
OLF	outlying landing field
PF	patrol frigate
PG	patrol gunboat
POW	prisoner of war
PTF	fast patrol boat
RADM	Rear Admiral
RDML	Rear Admiral (Lower Half)
SACLANT	Supreme Allied Commander, Atlantic
SACT	Supreme Allied Commander, Transformation
SDV	Seal Delivery Vehicle
SEAL	"Sea-Air-Land" (Navy Special Warfare Designation)
SOSUS	sound surveillance system
SS	submarine
SSBN	nuclear-powered ballistic missile submarine
SSN	nuclear-powered attack submarine
SUBLANT	Submarine Force, U.S. Atlantic Fleet
SURTASS	surveillance towed array sonar system
T-AGOS	auxiliary oceanographic survey ship
Tonal	a computer-processed representation of a discrete underwater sound frequency
UAV	unmanned air vehicle
UDT	underwater demolition team
USFLTFORCOM	U.S. Fleet Forces Command
USJFCOM	U.S. Joint Forces Command
USS	United States Ship
VADM	Vice Admiral
WPA	Works Progress Administration

CHRONOLOGY

1626 Capt. Thomas Willoughby establishes ownership of large tracts of land embracing the current Willoughby area of Hampton Roads and points along the Elizabeth River.

1633 Henry Seawell clears the land and establishes ownership on a point of land near the Willoughby property that would be called "Mr. Seawell's Pointe," later to be corrupted to "Sewell's Point."

1667 The Royal Navy assigns its first guardship to Hampton Roads, the frigate *Elizabeth* (46).

1680 A fort is built at Four Farthings Point (later Town Point) to the north of the confluence of the eastern and southern branches of the Elizabeth River near some of the first wharfs serving the tobacco trade, and ships begin to stop and refurbish in its protective shadow.

1682 The town site for "Norfolk Towne" is bought for the county court for ten thousand pounds of tobacco in cask from Nicolas Wise.

1767 Andrew Sprowle establishes a small shipyard on the Elizabeth River at Crab Creek, which he names "Gosport," in part to attract English shipowners and warship captains.

1775 The Continental Congress authorizes the first ships of the American Continental Navy.

1776 The Royal Governor of Virginia, Lord Dunmore, orders the bombardment of Norfolk, setting off a series of events that result in its complete destruction.

1776 The Virginia Convention authorizes the arming of private vessels, setting the stage for formation of the Virginia State Navy.

1779 British Adm. Sir George Collier captures Norfolk, Hampton, and Portsmouth and burns the Gosport yard.

1780 James Barron of Hampton is elevated to commodore of the Virginia State Navy.

1781 British and French battle lines fight to a draw at the Battle of Cape Henry, forty miles ENE of the cape.

1781 French Admiral Comte de Grasse bests British Rear Adm. Thomas Graves in the Battle of the Virginia Capes, isolating Lord Cornwallis at Yorktown and leading to his defeat by combined American and French armies.

1794 Congress passes an An Act to Provide a Naval Armament, formally founding the Navy of the United States and authorizing the construction of six frigates.

1794 William Pennock named as first Navy agent for Gosport.

1799 Frigate *Chesapeake* is launched at Gosport, Capt. Samuel Barron commanding.

1800 Hampton Roads shines as primary Navy support base for operations in the Quasi-war with France in the Caribbean.

1801 The Navy obtains title of the Gosport yard from the Commonwealth of Virginia.

1806 Capt. Stephen Decatur ordered to command Norfolk's gunboat flotilla.

1807 HMS *Leopard* fires on the *Chesapeake* (Capt. James Barron) off Cape Henry to force a search for British deserters. The *Chesapeake* is heavily damaged, with three killed.

1810 Capt. Samuel Barron named as the first commandant of the Gosport yard.

1811 David Glasgow Farragut first comes to Norfolk as a midshipman assigned to the frigate *Essex* to begin a fifty-year association with Norfolk.

1813 British impose a tight blockade on Hampton Roads and the Chesapeake, forcing the frigate *Constellation* into Norfolk harbor for safety.

1813 Americans defeat British amphibious assault at Craney Island, saving Norfolk and Portsmouth from capture.

1813 HMS *Victorious* and HMS *Plantagenet* in Hampton Roads and Lynnhaven Bay are the targets in some of the first attacks on ships by the torpedo (mine).

1816 Stephen Decatur persuades the Navy to retain the Gosport Navy Yard and solidify its presence in Hampton Roads.

1820 Stephen Decatur dies in a duel with Capt. James Barron of Hampton.

1820 Ship-of-the-line *Delaware* is launched from Gosport building ways.

1820 First formal midshipman training courses in the Navy are begun at Gosport by Chaplain David Adams.

1830 The naval hospital in Portsmouth (today the nation's oldest) admits its first patients.

1833 The largest dry dock in America is completed at Gosport, and ship-of-the-line *Delaware* becomes the first ship drydocked in North America.

1838 The U.S. Exploring Expedition sails from Hampton Roads under Lt. Charles Wilkes.

1852 Commo. Matthew Calbraith Perry sails from Norfolk to lead the "black ships" to open trade with Japan.

1861 Commo. Charles McCauley orders the burning of the Gosport yard and its ships in reserve, including the steam frigate *Merrimack*, to prevent it falling into insurgent hands during the opening days of the Civil War.

1861 Confederate forces under Capt. French Forrest assume control of the Gosport yard and restore it to service. The *Merrimack* is brought into dry dock for restoration.

1861 Commo. G. J. Pendergrast establishes a Union blockade of Hampton Roads.

1861 History's first waterborne ascent by an observation balloon is made by John La Mountain in an effort to map Confederate defenses at Sewell's Point.

1861 Ironclad ram *Virginia* is constructed at Gosport, utilizing the hull and engines of the *Merrimack*.

1861 A contract is made with inventor John Ericsson of New York City to build an innovative single-turret, low-freeboard ironclad to be called the *Monitor,* to be constructed in only three months.

1862 *Virginia* destroys the frigate *Congress* and the sloop-of-war *Cumberland* in her first sortie into Hampton Roads.

1862 *Monitor* and *Virginia* meet in the world's first ironclad battle in Hampton Roads. The battle is fought to a standstill.

1862 Navy ships and transports ferry Maj. Gen. George McClellan's Army of the Potomac to Fort Monroe and Hampton to begin its Peninsula Campaign to capture Richmond. Navy gunboats are assigned to guard McClellan's flanks along the James and York rivers.

1862 The *Virginia* is scuttled and burned with the fall of Norfolk and Portsmouth. The yard at Gosport is burned by the retreating Confederates.

1862 The Confederate Navy saves Richmond from attack by defeating a Union Navy squadron at Drewry's Bluff on the James River.

1862 *Monitor* founders off Cape Hatteras while in transit from Hampton Roads to Beaufort, North Carolina.

1866 Rear Adm. Stephen Rowan begins the tradition of the "Nine O'clock Gun" firing each evening at Norfolk Navy Yard.

1873 The "Virginius Affair" brings renewed focus to Hampton Roads as the best site to support U.S. Navy operations in the Caribbean and South Atlantic.

1889 The keel is laid for *Texas*, the first battleship and first ship of the New Steel Navy to be built at Norfolk Navy Yard.

1889 The repair yard that will become known as Newport News Shipbuilding & Dry Dock Company opens for business in Newport News.

1896 Newport News launches its first two Navy capital ships, the battleships *Kearsarge* and *Kentucky*.

1898 The "Flying Squadron" commanded by Commo. Winfield Scott Schley gathers in Hampton Roads in preparation for naval operations in the Spanish-American War.

1898 Simon Lake conducts trials and experiments of one of the world's first "modern" submarines, the *Argonaut*, in the Chesapeake Bay.

1902 Facilities across from the Navy yard at St. Helena are expanded for a new naval training station.

1903 The Fifth Naval District is established as the Navy's regional commander for Hampton Roads.

1905 Rear Adm. Robley Evans is named the first commander in chief of the Atlantic Fleet.

1907 The Jamestown Exposition opens at Sewell's Point to commemorate the three-hundredth anniversary of the Jamestown Settlement, with eye-catching Navy participation.

1907 With Theodore Roosevelt's enthusiastic send-off, sixteen battleships of the Great White Fleet set sail from Hampton Roads for a first-ever circumnavigation of the globe.

1910 In Hampton Roads, Eugene Fly becomes the first pilot to fly an aircraft from a ship. He flies from the deck of the cruiser *Birmingham* to nearby Willoughby Spit.

1917 Soon after World War I begins, Congress passes legislation to purchase the grounds of the former Jamestown Exposition for a training station, air station, supply station, and submarine station in what is referred to as Naval Operating Base (NOB), Hampton Roads. The naval training station at the NOB is the first to be put into operation.

1917 Naval aviation instruction and operations begin at the Curtiss Exhibition Company field in Newport News and are moved to the new field at Sewell's Point (to be called Chambers Field), where operations with both land planes and seaplanes can take place.

1917 Cdr. Joseph K. Taussig sails from Hampton Roads with Destroyer Division Eight, the first American military force sent to Europe for World War I.

1918 Naval Air Station, Hampton Roads, is commissioned, with Lt. Cdr. Patrick N. L. Bellinger in command.

1918 St. Julien's Creek Naval Ammunition Depot produces about 100,000 naval mines for the North Sea mine barrage to block U-boats from entering the Atlantic Ocean.

1918 A naval mine depot is first established at Yorktown, the precursor to later development of an extensive naval ammunition depot.

1919 The world flying endurance record of twenty hours, nineteen minutes and 1,250 miles is set by a F5L flying boat from Hampton Roads.

1919 The naval supply station at the NOB is commissioned, and two giant storehouses are completed, with rail access to nearby piers.

1921 Gen. Billy Mitchell of the Army conducts much-ballyhooed tests of the effectiveness of aerial bombing against ships and sinks the former German battleship *Ostfriesland* off Cape Charles.

1922 The *Langley*, the Navy's first aircraft carrier, is commissioned after conversion at the Norfolk Navy Yard, and the first U.S. Navy carrier takeoffs and landings are quickly recorded in experiments in the Chesapeake.

1938 Contracts for the twin battleships *Alabama* and *Indiana* are awarded to Norfolk Navy Yard and Newport News, helping to bring the region out of the Depression.

1941 Hampton Roads units are ordered to sea for extensive "neutrality" patrols to help combat U-boats months before Pearl Harbor and suffer the first naval losses of the war.

1942 In the opening months of the war, U-boats concentrate off the Chesapeake Bay and Cape Hatteras; the ensuing sinkings are easily observable from the shore.

1942 Coastal convoys begin along the Atlantic seaboard, with key assembly points in Hampton Roads and Lynnhaven Bay.

1942 Little Creek is established as the primary amphibious training base in the Atlantic and will train over 200,000 Navy and 160,000 Army personnel for the war.

1942 The Hampton Institute becomes the key training site in the country in advanced shipboard trades for African-American Navy recruits.

1942 Antiaircraft Training and Test Center, Dam Neck, is commissioned.

1942 Amphibious Scouts and Raiders and (a year later) Naval Combat Demolition Units (NCDUs), the precursors of UDTs and today's SEALs, begin training at Little Creek.

1943 Norfolk becomes the hub for the training of all carrier air groups for both Atlantic- and Pacific-based carriers.

1944 The Norfolk-based escort carrier *Guadalcanal* captures *U-505* in mid-Atlantic.

1944 Norfolk Navy Yard builds the carriers *Lake Champlain*, *Shangri-La*, and *Tarawa* and begins the battleship *Kentucky* of the *Iowa* class.

1945 During the war, Newport News builds eight carriers in twenty-seven months and is a major center for the construction of large amphibious ships.

1946 The Armed Forces Staff College is established in Norfolk to teach joint and combined operational planning and joint doctrine.

1948 Atlantic Fleet Headquarters is established in Norfolk.

1948 Long-range P-2 Neptune bombers help establish a credible heavy attack (atomic) capability for the Navy in tests from Hampton Roads.

1949 Headquarters for the Supreme Allied Commander, Atlantic, a NATO command, is established in Norfolk.

1949 The 68,000-ton flush-deck carrier *United States* is canceled while on the builder's ways at Newport News, igniting the "Revolt of the Admirals" and intense rivalry between the services.

1949 The Middle East Force is established, with Norfolk-based flagships and destroyers rotating into the force on deployment.

1950 The battleship *Missouri* strands near Old Point Comfort and is pulled free after two weeks' time in a monumental salvage operation.

1951 Naval Air Station Oceana reopens as a "Master Jet Complex" after its runways are lengthened and its facilities are improved for new carrier-based jet aircraft.

1952 Hampton Roads–based units begin to stream to the western Pacific to participate in Korean War naval operations.

1952 The first helicopter squadron to be based in Norfolk begins search-and-rescue and ASW operations with H-25 HUP and H-43 HUK helicopters.

1955 The first of the Navy's supercarriers, the *Forrestal*, is commissioned after delivery from Newport News.

1957 The Hampton Roads International Naval Review of the Jamestown Festival brings together ninety-three ships from eighteen countries.

1958 The Commander, Oceanographic System, Atlantic (COSL), is established in Norfolk to manage the expanding SOSUS underwater network in the Atlantic.

1960 The commander of the Atlantic Fleet submarine force moves from Groton to Norfolk in part to allow tighter management of Atlantic Fleet Polaris patrols.

1961 The Navy's first nuclear-powered aircraft carrier, the *Enterprise*, is commissioned at Newport News.

1961 Norfolk-based destroyers and amphibious ships participate in the ill-fated Bay of Pigs invasion of Cuba.

1962 DEFCOM-3 is ordered during the Cuban Missile Crisis, and Hampton Roads units are deployed as part of the naval quarantine.

1962 One of the first two SEAL teams, Team Two, is established at Little Creek.

1967 An ordnance accident in the Gulf of Tonkin heavily damages the carrier *Forrestal*, killing 131 crewmen and injuring many, including Lt. John McCain.

1967 Norfolk-based signals intelligence collection ship *Liberty* is attacked by Israeli planes and ships in waters off Gaza in the eastern Mediterranean, killing thirty-four.

1968 The heavy cruiser *Newport News* fires more than 59,000 rounds of ammunition against enemy targets in Vietnam on a single deployment.

1968 The Norfolk-based nuclear attack submarine *Scorpion* is lost at sea with all hands.

1980 The Fifth Naval District is disestablished; most of the staff responsibilities revert to Commander, Naval Base, Norfolk.

1983 SEAL Teams are reorganized, and Teams Two, Four, and Six are stationed in Hampton Roads. Team Six is formed as an antiterrorist and hostage rescue specialty unit.

1985 The Walker spy ring, with a Hampton Roads focus, is finally terminated by the FBI but not before causing extreme damage to naval operations.

1991 The *America*, *Theodore Roosevelt*, and *John F. Kennedy* battle groups, battleship *Wisconsin*, three amphibious ready groups, and other ships carrying approximately 50,000 men and women deploy for the first Gulf War, Operation Desert Storm.

1999 The Atlantic Command in Norfolk is redesignated as the U.S. Joint Forces Command (USJFCOM).

1999 Naval Station Norfolk and Naval Air Station Norfolk are merged into a single installation called Naval Station Norfolk.

1999 Commander, Naval Base, Norfolk, is disestablished in favor of a new Navy regional commander, Commander, Navy Region Mid-Atlantic, based in Norfolk.

2000 Norfolk-based destroyer *Cole* is attacked by a terrorist suicide boat in Aden with the loss of seventeen.

2001 Carrier *Theodore Roosevelt* logs 160 straight days at sea while supporting Operation Enduring Freedom in Afghanistan.

2002 The U.S. Fleet Forces Command is formed from the Atlantic Fleet to oversee the coordination and implementation of integrated manning, equipping, and training for units in both the Atlantic and Pacific.

2003 Carriers *Harry S Truman* and *Theodore Roosevelt*, the Atlantic Fleet amphibious force, and scores of other ships and squadrons from across Tidewater participate in the second Gulf War.

Appendix A
Tidewater Naval Commanders

Norfolk Navy Yard/Norfolk Naval Shipyard		
Capt. Samuel Barron	July 1810–November 1810	(1)
Lt. Robert Henley	November 1810–May 1811	*
Capt. Samuel Evans	May 1811–August 1812	
Capt. John Cassin	August 1812–June 1821	
Capt. Lewis Warrington	June 1821–December 1824	
Capt. James Renshaw	December 1824–May 1825	
Capt. James Barron	May 1825–May 1831	
Capt. Lewis Warrington	May 1831–October 1840	
Capt. William B. Shubrick	October 1840–October 1843	
Capt. Jesse Wilkinson	October 1843–October 1846	
Capt. Charles W. Skinner	October 1846–June 1847	
Capt. Lawrence Kearney	June 1847–January 1848	
Capt. John D. Sloat	January 1848–February 1851	
Capt. Silas H. Stringham	February 1851–April 1852	
Capt. Samuel L. Breese	April 1852–May 1855	
Capt. Issac McKeever	May 1855–May 1856	
Capt. Thomas A. Dornin	May 1856–April 1859	
Capt. Charles H. Bell	April 1859–August 1860	
Capt. Charles S. McCauley	August 1860–April 1861	
Flag Officer French Forrest, CSN	April 1861–May 1862	(2)
Capt. Sydney Smith Lee, CSN	May 1862	
Commo. John W. Livingston	May 1862–November 1864	
Capt. John M. Berrien	November 1864–October 1865	
Commo. Robert B. Hitchcock	October 1865–August 1866	
Rear Adm. Stephen C. Rowan	August 1866–August 1867	
Commo. Augustus H. Kilty	August 1867–October 1870	
Rear Adm. Charles H. Davis	October 1870–July 1873	
Commo. Thomas H. Stevens	July 1873–July 1876	
Commo. J. Blakeley Creighton	July 1876–July 1879	
Commo. Aaron K. Hughes	July 1879–July 1882	
Commo. William K. Mayo	July 1882–April 1885	
Commo. William T. Truxton	April 1885–March 1886	
Commo. George Brown	March 1886–January 1890	
Commo. Aaron W. Weaver	January 1890–January 1893	
Capt. Edward E. Potter	January 1893–July 1893	

* See Notes on page 279.

Norfolk Navy Yard/Norfolk Naval Shipyard (continued)

Rear Adm. George Brown	July 1893–June 1897	
Rear Adm. Norman H. Farquhar	June 1897–October 1899	
Rear Adm. Albert S. Barker	October 1899–July 1900	
Rear Adm. Charles S. Cotton	July 1900–April 1903	
Rear Adm. Purnell F. Harrington	April 1903–July 1906	@
Rear Adm. Robert H. Berry	July 1906–December 1907	@
Rear Adm. Edward D. Taussig	December 1907–November 1909	@
Rear Adm. William A. Marshall	November 1909–November 1911	@
Rear Adm. Robert M. Doyle	November 1911–December 1913	@
Rear Adm. Nathaniel R. Usher	December 1913–September 1914	@
Commo. Louis R. de Steiguer	September 1914–January 1915	* @
Rear Adm. Frank E. Beatty	January 1915–November 1915	@
Rear Adm. Walter McLean	November 1915–February 1918	@
Rear Adm. Augustus F. Fechteler	February 1918–April 1919	
Capt. Benjamin F. Hutchison	April 1919–November 1919	*
Rear Adm. Guy H. Burrage	November 1919–July 1921	
Rear Adm. Philip Andrews	July 1921–June 1923	
Rear Adm. Henry J. Ziegemeier	June 1923–January 1925	
Capt. Clarence S. Kempff	January 1925–May 1925	*
Capt. William T. Tarrant	May 1925–November 1925	*
Rear Adm. William C. Cole	November 1925–July 1928	
Rear Adm. Wat T. Cluverius	July 1928–May 1930	
Rear Adm. Frank H. Brumby	May 1930–Sept 1932	
Capt. William N. Jeffers	September 1932–February 1933	*
Rear Adm. A. St. Clair Smith	February 1933–July 1935	
Rear Adm. Charles S. Freeman	July 1935–October 1937	
Capt. Lawrence P. Treadwell	October 1937–November 1937	*
Rear Adm. Manley H. Simons	November 1937–June 1941	
Capt. Lawrence P. Treadwell	June 1941–August 1941	*
Rear Adm. Felix X. Gygax	August 1941–October 1944	
Rear Adm. Carl H. Jones	October 1944–December 1945	
Commo. Lisle F. Small	December 1945–November 1946	
Capt. Noah W. Gokey	November 1946–January 1949	
Rear Adm. Homer N. Wallin	February 1949–January 1951	
Capt. Robert L. Swart	January 1951–February 1951	*
Rear Adm. David H. Clark	February 1951–June 1953	
Capt. William H. Leahy	June 1953–August 1953	*
Rear Adm. Logan McKee	August 1953–September 1956	
Rear Adm. George A. Holderness Jr.	September 1956–June 1958	
Rear Adm. William H. Leahy	June 1958–June 1960	
Rear Adm. William E. Howard Jr.	June 1960–June 1963	
Rear Adm. James M. Farrin	June 1963–June 1965	
Rear Adm. James A. Brown	June 1965–June 1970	
Rear Adm. Jamie Adair	June 1970–June 1972	
Rear Adm. Randolph W. King	June 1972–June 1973	
Rear Adm. Joe Williams Jr.	June 1973–August 1974	
Rear Adm. Elmer T. Westfall	August 1974–June 1977	
Capt. Alfred Kurzenhauser	June 1977–July 1980	
Commo. David P. Donohue	July 1980–April 1983	
Capt. Michael R. Gluse	April 1983–June 1987	
Capt. Edward S. McGinley	June 1987–May 1990	
Rear Adm. James L. Taylor	May 1990–August 1994	
Capt. William R. Klemm	August 1994–August 1997	

Norfolk Navy Yard/Norfolk Naval Shipyard (continued)

Capt. Timothy E. Scheib	August 1997–August 2000
Capt. Mark A. Hugel	August 2000–November 2003
Capt. Joseph F. Campbell	November 2003–

Fifth Naval District/Naval Base, Norfolk/Navy Region Mid-Atlantic

Rear Adm. Purnell F. Harrington	April 1903–July 1906	@
Rear Adm. Robert H. Berry	July 1906–December 1907	@
Rear Adm. Edward D. Taussig	December 1907–November 1909	@
Rear Adm. William A. Marshall	November 1909–November 1911	@
Rear Adm. Robert M. Doyle	November 1911–December 1913	@
Rear Adm. Nathaniel R. Usher	December 1913–September 1914	@
Commo. Louis R. de Steiguer	September 1914–January 1915	* @
Rear Adm. Frank E. Beatty	January 1915–November 1915	@
Rear Adm. Walter McLean	November 1915–February 1918	@
Rear Adm. Walter McLean	February 1918–April 1919	#
Rear Adm. A. F. Fechteler	April 1919–May 1921	#
Rear Adm. Hugh Rodman	July 1921–January 1923	#
Rear Adm. Philip Andrews	January 1923–June 1923	* #
Rear Adm. H. J. Ziegemeier	June 1923–August 1923	* #
Rear Adm. Roger Welles	August 1923–September 1925	#
Rear Adm. Robert E. Coontz	November 1925–June 1928	#
Rear Adm. Guy H. Burrage	September 1928–June 1931	#
Rear Adm. William D. MacDougall	July 1931–June 1932	#
Rear Adm. Arthur L. Willard	July 1932–March 1934	#
Rear Adm. Frank H. Brumby	April 1935–September 1938	#
Rear Adm. Joseph K. Taussig	September 1938–June 1941	#
Rear Adm. Manley H. Simons	June 1941–May 1943	#
Rear Adm. H. Fairfax Leary	June 1943–October 1943	#
Rear Adm. David M. LeBreton	October 1943–August 1945	#
Rear Adm. Walden L. Ainsworth	August 1945–November 1948	&
Rear Adm. Ralph O. Davis	November 1948–January 1953	&
Rear Adm. Ingolf N. Kiland	January 1953–April 1957	&
Rear Adm. William O. Burch Jr.	December 1960–September 1961	&
Rear Adm. Wallis F. Petersen	September 1961–October 1963	&
Rear Adm. Edmund B. Taylor	November 1963–April 1966	&
Rear Adm. Reynold D. Hogle	June 1966–May 1968	&
Rear Adm. James C. Dempsey	June 1968–August 1970	&
Rear Adm. James O. Cobb	September 1970–January 1973	&
Rear Adm. Roy G. Anderson	January 1973–August 1974	&
Rear Adm. Richard E. Rumble	August 1974–April 1976	&
Rear Adm. William H. Ellis	April 1976–August 1978	&
Rear Adm. Richard E. Nicholson	August 1978–August 1979	&
Rear Adm. James H. Scott	August 1979–August 1980	&
Rear Adm. William B. Warwick	August 1980–October 1980	&
Rear Adm. Joseph F. Frick	October 1980–August 1983	+
Rear Adm. Jackson K. Parker	August 1983–September 1987	+
Rear Adm. Jimmy J. Pappas	September 1987–July 1989	+
Rear Adm. Wayne E. Rickman	July 1989–August 1989	+
Rear Adm. Kenneth L. Carlsen	August 1989–February 1991	+
Rear Adm. Byron E. Tobin Jr.	February 1991–November 1993	+
Rear Adm. Paul D. Moses	November 1993–September 1995	+
Rear Adm. Robert S. Cole	September 1995–September 1996	+
Rear Adm. R. Timothy Ziemer	September 1996–November 1999	+ %

Fifth Naval District/Naval Base, Norfolk/Navy Region Mid-Atlantic (continued)

Rear Adm. Christopher W. Cole	November 1999–August 2001	%
Rear Adm. David Architzel	August 2001–August 2003	%
Rear Adm. Stephen A. Turcotte	August 2003–	%

U.S. Atlantic Fleet/U.S. Fleet Forces Command

Rear Adm. Robley D. Evans	March 1905–May 1908	
Rear Adm. Charles S. Sperry	May 1908–March 1909	
Rear Adm. Seaton Schroeder	March 1909–June 1911	
Rear Adm. Hugo W. Osterhaus	June 1911–January 1913	
Rear Adm. Charles J. Badger	January 1913–September 1914	
Rear Adm. Frank F. Flechter	September 1914–June 1916	
Adm. Henry T. Mayo	June 1916–July 1919	
Adm. Henry B. Wilson	July 1919–June 1921	
Adm. Hilary P. Jones	June 1921–December 1922	
Adm. Ernest J. King	February 1941–December 1941	
Adm. Royal E. Ingersoll	December 1941–November 1944	
Adm. Jonas H. Ingram	November 1944–September 1946	
Adm. Marc A. Mitscher	September 1946–February 1947	
Adm. William H. P. Blandy	February 1947–February 1950	$
Adm. William M. Fechteler	February 1950–August 1951	$
Adm. Lynde D. McCormick	August 1951–April 1954	$
Adm. Jerauld Wright	April 1954–February 1960	$
Adm. Robert L. Dennison	February 1960–April 1963	$
Adm. Harold P. Smith	April 1963–April 1965	$
Adm. Thomas H. Moorer	April 1965–June 1967	$
Adm. Ephraim P. Holmes	June 1967–September 1970	$
Adm. Charles K. Duncan	September 1970–October 1972	$
Adm. Ralph W. Cousins	October 1972–May 1975	$
Adm. Isaac C. Kidd Jr.	May 1975–September 1978	$
Adm. Harry D. Train II	September 1978–September 1982	$
Adm. Wesley L. McDonald	September 1982–October 1985	$
Adm. Carlisle A. H. Trost	October 1985–June 1986	
Adm. Frank B. Kelso II	June 1986–November 1988	
Adm. Powell F. Carter Jr.	November 1988–January 1991	
Adm. Paul David Miller	January 1991–July 1992	
Adm. Henry H. Mauz Jr.	July 1992–October 1994	
Adm. William J. Flanagan Jr.	October1994–December 1996	
Adm. J. Paul Reason	December 1996–September 1999	
Adm. Vern Clark	September 1999–June 2000	
Adm. Robert J. Natter	June 2000–October 2003	\\
Adm. William J. Fallon	October 2003–February 2005	\\
Adm. John B. Nathman	February 2005–	\\

U.S. Atlantic Command/U.S. Joint Forces Command

Adm. William H. P. Blandy	February 1947–February 1950	$
Adm. William M. Fechteler	February 1950–August 1951	$
Adm. Lynde D. McCormick	August 1951–April 1954	$ ^
Adm. Jerauld Wright	April 1954–February 1960	$ ^
Adm. Robert L. Dennison	February 1960–April 1963	$ ^
Adm. Harold P. Smith	April 1963–April 1965	$ ^
Adm. Thomas H. Moorer	April 1965–June 1967	$ ^
Adm. Ephraim P. Holmes	June 1967–September 1970	$ ^
Adm. Charles K. Duncan	September 1970–October 1972	$ ^

U.S. Atlantic Command/U.S. Joint Forces Command (continued)

Adm. Ralph W. Cousins	October 1972–May 1975	$ ^
Adm. Isaac C. Kidd Jr.	May 1975–September 1978	$ ^
Adm. Harry D. Train II	September 1978–September 1982	$ ^
Adm. Wesley L. McDonald	September 1982–November 1985	$ ^
Adm. Lee Baggett Jr.	November 1985–November 1988	^
Adm. Frank B. Kelso II	November 1988–May 1990	^
Adm. Leon A. Edney	June 1990–July 1992	^
Adm. Paul David Miller	July 1992–October 1994	^
Adm. Harold W. Gehman	September 1997–September 2000	^ =
Adm. Edmund P. Giambastianni Jr.	October 2002–	^ =

Notes:

* Acting Commander.
@ Served as Commandant, Norfolk Navy Yard, and Commandant, Fifth Naval District.
# Served as Commandant, Fifth Naval District, and Commander, Naval Operating Base.
& Served as Commandant, Fifth Naval District, and Commander, Naval Base, Norfolk.
+ Served as Commander, Naval Base, Norfolk.
% Served as Commander, Navy Region Mid-Atlantic.
$ Served as Commander in Chief, Atlantic Command and Commander in Chief, Atlantic Fleet.
^ Served as Supreme Allied Commander, Atlantic/Supreme Allied Commander, Transformation.
= Served as Commander, U. S. Joint Forces Command.
\\ Served as Commander, U. S. Fleet Forces Command.
(1) Between 1794 and 1810, the Navy yard was managed on a day-to-day basis by an assigned Navy agent who reported directly to the secretary of the Navy, while the senior naval officer, either in the yard fitting out a ship or present in Hampton Roads, held some responsibility for the yard itself. Capt. Samuel Barron was the first to formally hold the title of Commandant for the Navy Yard.
(2) Capt. French Forrest of the Virginia State Navy, later Flag Officer of the Confederate States Navy.

Appendix B
Ships That Have Held Tidewater Names

Cape Henry **Cargo Ship 1918–1919**
(10,505 tons, 391′ length, 62 complement, armament: one 6″)
Cape Henry was launched 30 March 1918 and commissioned by the Navy on 25 October 1918. She delivered supplies to American forces in France during one transatlantic voyage and was decommissioned and returned to the Shipping Board on 3 March 1919.

Cape Henry **Vehicle Cargo Ship (AKR-5067) 1986–**
(21,747 tons, 750′ length)
Built in 1980 as *Barber Priam* by Mitsubishi Heavy Industries at Nagasaki, Japan. A roll-on/roll-off vessel with a stern ramp, she was purchased by the Military Sealift Command in 1986.

Chesapeake **Frigate 1800–1813**
(1,244 tons, 152′ length, complement 340, armament: thirty 18-pdr, twelve 32-pdr)
Chesapeake, rated a 36-gun frigate, was launched 2 December 1799 at Gosport Navy Yard and commissioned early the following year, Capt. Samuel Barron commanding. *Chesapeake* took the French privateer *La Jeune Creole* as a prize during the Quasi-war with France in 1800–1801 and participated in the blockade of Tripoli in 1803. In June 1807, near Hampton Roads, the British frigate HMS *Leopard* fired upon her after she initially refused demands to be boarded in a search for British deserters. The attack killed three men, wounded eighteen, and was a great blow to American prestige. With the outbreak of the War of 1812, the *Chesapeake* took several British merchantmen as prizes, but outside Boston on 20 May 1813 fell victim to the British frigate HMS *Shannon*. The *Chesapeake* was taken to Halifax for repairs and later was taken into the Royal Navy. She was sold at Plymouth, England, in 1820 and broken up.

Chesapeake **Salvage Vessel 1919**
(2,000 tons, 220′ length, complement 117, armament: one 3″)
The freighter *Chesapeake* was launched in 1900 by Harlan & Hollingsworth of Wilmington and purchased by the Navy on 31 August 1918 to be fitted out as a salvage ship. The *Chesapeake* sailed from New York on 12 May 1919 for Brest, France, where she joined the First Salvage Division supporting U.S. Naval Forces in European Waters. Decommissioned 25 October 1919.

Chesapeake **Sail Training Vessel 1899–1905**
(1,175 tons, 224′ length, complement 113, armament: six 4″, four 6-pdrs, two 1-pdrs)
A Naval Academy station ship and training vessel launched 30 June 1899. In 1905 her commander, Captain Schroeder, aware of the ignominious reputation of the namesake, petitioned the secretary of the Navy to have the ship's name changed. On 15 June 1905 she was renamed *Severn*.

Chesapeake **Transport Oiler (T-AOT-5084) 1991–**
(14,977 tons, 736′ length)
Chesapeake was a tanker of the Military Sealift Command and a Ready Reserve Force ship. She participated in Operation Iraqi Freedom after berthing at Diego Garcia.

Chincoteague **Seaplane Tender (AVP-24) 1943–1946**
(2,592 tons, 310′ length, complement 215, armament one 5″)
Chincoteague was launched 15 April 1942 by Lake Washington Shipyard, Houghton, Washington, and commissioned 12 April 1943. She first supported Allied operations in New Guinea but was hit by Japanese air attacks on 16 July 1943, which killed nine crewmen. She participated in the campaigns of Iwo Jima and Okinawa and tended seaplanes at Tsingtao, China, after the war. On 21 December 1946, the *Chincoteague* was decommissioned and placed in reserve. The *Chincoteague* received six battle stars for World War II service.

Elizabeth **Gunboat (iron protected) 1862**
(armament: two guns)
CSS *Elizabeth* was under construction when she was burned on the ways to avoid capture by Federal forces when Gosport Navy Yard was evacuated on 10 May 1862.

Elizabeth **Motor Patrol Boat (P-972) 1917–1919**

Elizabeth served in a noncommissioned status in the Fifth Naval District during World War I. On 12 December 1917, she was sunk in a collision with the American steamship *Northland* in the harbor of Norfolk; two lives were lost in the collision. *Elizabeth* was salvaged and resumed her former duties. On 10 November 1919, she was transferred to the War Department.

Epping Forest **Dock Landing Ship (LSD-4/MCS-7) 1943–1968**

(4,960 tons, 458′ length, complement 326, armament one 5″ gun)

Epping Forest was launched 2 April 1943 by Moore Dry Dock Co., Oakland, California, and commissioned on 11 October 1943. She participated in campaigns in the Marshall Islands, New Guinea, Guam, Peleliu, Leyte, Luzon, and Okinawa. In the Korean War she assisted with minesweeping operations in Wonsan harbor and was reclassified as a mine countermeasures support ship on 30 November 1962. She was stricken from the Navy List on 1 November 1968. The *Epping Forrest* earned eight battle stars for World War II and four for Korean War service.

Gloucester **Armed Galley 1776–1777**

Gloucester provided service on the James River during the American Revolution as a vessel of the Virginia State Navy and as a prison hulk. Destroyed 1781.

Note: The gunboat *Gloucester* (1891) and the patrol frigate *Gloucester* (PF-22) were named for a city in Massachusetts.

Gosport **Training Support Vessel 1965–2003**

R/V *Gosport* was used extensively by Norfolk Naval Shipyard to help train destroyers, frigates, and submarines for overseas operations by providing ASW support and by providing exercise torpedo support for sea trial operations.

Hampton **Gunboat 1862–1865**

(166 tons, 106′ length, armament: 9-inch gun forward and a 32-pounder aft)

CSS *Hampton* was a wooden gunboat built at Norfolk Navy Yard in 1862 and based there until May, when the yard was abandoned. *Hampton* moved up the James River and participated in significant river actions during the remainder of the war. The Confederates burned *Hampton* as they evacuated Richmond on 3 April 1865.

Hampton **Wooden Tug (SP-3049) 1918–1919**

(48 tons, 63′ length)

Hampton was built in 1905 by H. Turman of Turkey Point, Virginia, and chartered by the Navy in 1918. She was commissioned 21 April 1918 and served on general harbor duty in Hampton Roads under the jurisdiction of the Fifth Naval District until she was returned to her owner on 13 August 1919.

Hampton **Nuclear-Powered Attack Submarine (SSN-767) 1993–**

(6000 tons, 362′ length, 140 complement, armament: Tomahawk missiles, VLS tubes, Mk-48 torpedoes, four torpedo tubes)

Hampton was built by Newport News Shipbuilding, launched on 3 April 1992, and commissioned on 16 November 1993.

Note: Subchaser *Hampton* (PCS-1368) and attack transport *Hampton* (APA-115) were named after a city and county in South Carolina.

James River **Patrol Boat (SP-861) 1917–1918**

(58′ length, 5 complement, armament: two 1-pdrs.)

James River was a patrol boat acquired by the Navy in May 1917 from the Virginia State Fish and Oyster Commission. She served as a patrol boat in the Fifth Naval District during World War I. She was returned to her owners on 22 October 1918.

James River **Landing Ship Medium (Rocket) (LSMR–510) 1945–1947**

(790 tons, 206′ length, 138 complement, armament: 5″ rockets, one 5″, four 40 mm, eight 20 mm, four 4.2″)

James River was launched by Brown Shipbuilding Co., Houston, Texas, on 5 May 1945 and was commissioned 1 July 1945. She operated at Little Creek, in the Caribbean, and at San Diego. In her original configuration, she could fire 380 5-inch rockets a minute over a distance of up to ten thousand yards to support amphibious landings. Decommissioned 5 February 1947 and sold 12 April 1961.

Jamestown **Sloop-of-war 1844–1913**

(1,150 tons, 163′ length, 18 complement, armament: four 8″, eighteen 32-pdrs)

Jamestown was commissioned on 12 December 1844 by Gosport Navy Yard and for the next fifteen years served in various capacities with the Mediterranean, Brazil, and African squadrons. With the outbreak of the Civil War, *Jamestown* was assigned to the Atlantic Blockading Squadron, but then departed for the Pacific in October 1862 to protect American commerce from Confederate privateers. In later years she served in a variety of auxiliary roles as a transport and hospital ship at Panama, a guard ship in Alaska, and an apprentice training ship. *Jamestown* was destroyed by fire at Norfolk Navy Yard on 3 January 1913.

Jamestown **Armed Sidewheel Steamer 1861–1862**

(1,300 tons, 250′ length, armament: two guns)

CSS *Jamestown*, originally a passenger steamer, was built at New York in 1853 and seized at Richmond in 1861 for the Virginia Navy. She was commissioned into the Confederate Navy the following July (renamed *Thomas Jefferson* but was generally referred to as *Jamestown*). *Jamestown* participated in the Battle of Hampton Roads on 8–9 March 1862, during which she assisted CSS *Virginia* in attacking *Congress* and *Cumberland* and stood by during the battle between *Monitor* and *Virginia*. *Jamestown* captured three Union merchant ships in Hampton Roads on 11 April 1862. The Confederate Congress tendered special thanks to the officers and crew of *Jamestown* for their "gallant conduct and bearing" in combat. She joined the Confederate James River Squadron, where she was used to transport Army sick and wounded to Richmond and to support troops ashore. *Jamestown* was scuttled in the James River at Drewry's Bluff on 15 May 1862 to obstruct the channel.

Gunboat *Jamestown* (PG-55). *U.S. Naval Institute*

Jamestown **Gunboat (PG-55) 1941–1946**
(1,780 tons, 294′ length, 259 complement, armament: two 3″ guns)
Originally a yacht built as *Savarona* in 1928 and renamed *Alder* in 1929, she was said to be the largest and most luxurious yacht in the world. *Alder* was acquired by the Navy, converted into a gunboat, and commissioned as *Jamestown* on 26 May 1941. Subsequently she served as a motor torpedo boat tender in the South Pacific and was stationed at Espiritu Santo, Guadalcanal, Tulagi, New Guinea, Leyte, and Samar. She was redesignated AGP-3 on 13 January 1943 and decommissioned and sold on 6 March 1946. *Jamestown* was awarded a Presidential Unit Citation for actions at Guadalcanal.

Jamestown **Research Auxiliary Ship (AG-166/AGTR-3) 1963–1969**
(11,375 tons, 441′ length, 313 complement)
Jamestown, a converted Liberty ship, was launched as *J. Howland Gardner* on 10 July 1945, acquired by the Navy, renamed, and commissioned on 13 December 1963 at Norfolk Navy Yard. Her mission was "to conduct technical research operations in support of U.S. Navy electronic research projects," but she actually was a signals intelligence collection platform. *Jamestown* was redesignated AGTR-3 on 1 April 1964 and operated extensively off Vietnam. Scrapped in 1970.

Lynnhaven **Patrol Vessel 1863**
Lynnhaven was a small, ship-rigged vessel captured in the sounds of North Carolina and sunk as an obstruction at the outlet of the Chesapeake and Albemarle Canal. Later she was raised and purchased by the Navy on 19 May 1863.

Lynnhaven **Lighter (YF-328) 1942–1970?**
(650 tons, 133′ length, complement 11)
Since being placed in service in 1942, the covered lighter has shuttled various cargoes between ports and stations around Norfolk. YF-328 was named *Lynnhaven* on 8 June 1965.

Navy Yard **Steam Ferry (YFB-8)**
(80′ length)
Norfolk Navy Yard built YFB-8 as "Steam Cutter 291" in 1901 and used it as a ferry between Norfolk and various naval installations around Hampton Roads. Renamed *Navy Yard* in 1908, she operated there until she was sent to Dahlgren Proving Grounds in 1922. Towed back to Norfolk in 1929, she was struck from the Navy Register on 12 July and sold.

Nansemond **Steam Gunboat 1862–65**
(166 tons, 106′ length, armament two guns)
CSS *Nansemond* was built at Gosport and evacuated up the James River on 4 May 1862. The gunboat stayed in the James River until the war ended, fighting at Howlett's, Dutch Gap and Fort Harrison. When Richmond fell on 3 April 1865, *Nansemond* was destroyed to prevent capture by the Union.

Nansemond **Armed Sidewheel Steamer 1863–1865**
(340 tons, 146′ length, 63 complement, armament one 30-pdr, two 24-pdrs)
Nansemond, a side-wheel steamer built in 1862 as the *James F. Freeborn,* was purchased by the Navy on 18 August 1863 and renamed *Nansemond*. She joined the North Atlantic Blockading Squadron with

primary blockading assignments off Wilmington. After supporting the Union's final drive on Richmond, *Nansemond* was decommissioned on 8 August 1865. She saw later duty in the Revenue Cutter Service as *W. H. Crawford*. Sold 24 April 1897.

Nansemond **Passenger-Cargo Ship 1919**
(13,333 tons)
Nansemond was built in 1896 at Belfast, Ireland, as the German steamship *Pennsylvania*. She was interned and then seized when the United States entered World War I. She was renamed *Nansemond* and transferred to the Navy in January 1919 and made several voyages to and from Europe as a cargo carrier and troop transport. Decommissioned in September 1919 and scrapped in 1924.

Nansemond County **Tank Landing Ship (LST-1064) 1945–1946**
(1,625 tons, 232′ length, 266 complement, armament eight 40 mm, twelve 20 mm)
LST–1064 was launched on 14 February 1945 and commissioned 12 March 1945. Following shakedown in the Chesapeake Bay area, she sailed for the Pacific for cargo and ship supply transport and returned to the United States in January 1946. She was decommissioned on 21 August 1946. Named *Nansemond County* on 1 July 1955, she was transferred to Japan and renamed *Shiretoko.*

Newport News **Cargo Ship (AK-3) 1917–1924**
(10,000 tons, 371′ length, 150 complement, armament: four 3″)
Originally built as *Odenwald* in 1904 in Germany, *Newport News* was taken over by the Navy, renamed, and commissioned on 14 July 1917. She operated on transatlantic supply runs assigned to the Naval Overseas Transportation Service. Later *Newport News* operated on supply runs in the Pacific until she was decommissioned on 1 August 1924. She was later sold for scrapping.

Newport News **Heavy Cruiser (CA-148) 1949–1975**
(20,980 tons, 717′ length, 1,667 complement, armament: nine 8″, twelve 5″, twelve 3″)
Newport News was launched on 6 March 1948 by Newport News Shipbuilding and commissioned on 29 January 1949. She participated in frequent operations in the Mediterranean and northern Europe and in training cruises in the Caribbean and Western Atlantic. In 1962, she became the flagship of the Second Fleet and participated in the Cuban missile quarantine. In 1967, she deployed to Southeast Asia

Newport News, built at Newport News Shipbuilding, was destined to be the Navy's last conventional cruiser in service. This handsome heavy cruiser's design featured high-speed, balanced firepower, long cruising range, superior protection from air attack, and a rapid-firing and fully automatic main battery of 8-inch guns that made her a favored flagship. She also held the distinction as the first vessel in the fleet to have air-conditioning in virtually all living and working compartments. *National Archives*

and provided naval gunfire support against targets north of the Demilitarized Zone in Vietnam. On 1 October 1972, while in action off Vietnam, *Newport News* sustained an in-bore explosion in her center 8-inch gun of Number Two turret, killing twenty and injuring thirty-six. Decommissioned 27 June 1975.

Newport News **Nuclear-powered Attack Submarine (SSN-750) 1989–**

(5785 tons, 362′ length, 110 complement, armament: Tomahawk missiles, VLS tubes, Mk-48 torpedoes, four torpedo tubes)

Newport News was built at Newport News Shipbuilding, launched on 15 March 1986, and commissioned on 3 June 1989.

Norfolk **Brig 1798–1800**

(armament: eighteen guns)

Norfolk was built in 1798 by Nash and Herbert of Norfolk and was purchased for the Navy in 1798 for duty in the West Indies during the "Quasi-war" with France. She was noted as a "good sailer" and a fast ship. Sold at Baltimore in 1800.

Norfolk **Gunboat 1862**

(166 tons; 106′ length, armament: one 9″, one 32-pdr)

Norfolk was a sister to *Portsmouth, Hampton,* and other screw gunboats built for the Confederate Navy at the Gosport Navy Yard. *Norfolk* was burned on the ways to escape capture by Federal forces on 10 May 1862.

Norfolk **Heavy Cruiser (CA-137)**

The name *Norfolk* was assigned to hull CA-137, which was built in part from donations gathered from a subscription drive in the city between March and July 1943. CA-137 was laid down on 27 December 1944 at Philadelphia Naval Shipyard. Construction was canceled on 12 August 1945.

Norfolk **Destroyer Leader (DL-1) 1953–1970**

(5600 tons, 540′ length, armament: eight 3″, sixteen 20 mm, eight 21″ torpedo tubes)

Norfolk was an antisubmarine hunter-killer ship built on a large hull and designed to carry the latest radar, sonar, and other electronic devices. She was described by her skipper in the mid-1960s as "probably the most beautiful ship in the fleet with her clipper bow and sleek lines. She looked like the greyhound that she really was." *Norfolk* was launched on 29 December 1951 and commissioned on 4 March 1953. She participated in the International Fleet Review in Hampton Roads in June 1957 and during her career participated in numerous Atlantic Fleet operations. On one deployment she served as the flagship to the Middle East Force. *Norfolk* was decommissioned on 15 January 1970.

Variously described as a destroyer leader or hunter-killer ship, *Norfolk* was the first large ship built by the Navy following World War II. Her handsome lines were a regular sight on the Norfolk waterfront and she earned the honor of standing by Old Point Comfort during the International Naval Review of 1957 to receive the salute of all visiting foreign warships. *U.S. Naval Institute*

Norfolk **Nuclear-powered Attack Submarine (SSN-714) 1983–**
(5751 tons, 362′ length, 110 complement, armament: Tomahawk missiles, VLS tubes, Mk-48 torpedoes, four torpedo tubes)
Norfolk was built by Newport News Shipbuilding, launched on 31 October 1981, and commissioned on 21 May 1983.

Norfolk Revenge **Armed Galley 1776–1778**
(armament: two cannon)
Built and operated from Hampton during the American Revolution as a vessel of the Virginia State Navy.

Northampton **Patrol Boat (SP-670) 1917–1918**
(38′ length; armament: one 1-pdr gun)
Northampton, a wooden motorboat built by Wilson of Birdsnest, Virginia, was leased by the Navy from John A. Parsons of Norfolk on 5 May 1917. Assigned to the Fifth Naval District, *Northampton* operated on section patrol until she was returned to her owner on 19 December 1918.

Note: Cruisers CL-26 and CA-125/CLC-1, named *Northhampton,* were named for the city in Massachusetts.

Old Dominion **Coastal Collier 1917–1919**
(1,802 tons, 266′ length, complement 6)
Old Dominion, launched as a steamer by Harlan and Hollingsworth, Wilmington, Delaware, in 1872, was acquired by the Navy on 18 October 1917 and used as a barge and coastwise collier until she was sold on 2 October 1919.

Pocomoke **Patrol Boat (SP-571) 1917–1918**
(64′ length, armament: one 1-pdr)
Originally a freight boat built by Brewster Bros., Baltimore, Maryland, *Pocomoke* was commissioned 24 April 1917 for patrol duties on the Chesapeake and was returned to her owner 22 October 1918.

Pocomoke **Minesweeper/Patrol Boat (SP-265) 1917–1922**
(115′ length, armament: two 1-pdrs)
Pocomoke was built in Pocomoke City, Maryland, in 1902. She was purchased by the Navy and commissioned on 29 June 1917. She operated off the West Coast in 1919, was designated YT–43 on 17 July 1920, and was sold on 2 May 1922.

Pocomoke **Seaplane Tender (AV-9) 1941–1946**
(8,950 tons, 492′ length, 689 complement, armament: one 5″, 4 3″)
Pocomoke was laid down as S.S. *Exchequer* on 14 August 1939 by Ingalls Shipbuilding and Dry Dock Company, Pascagoula, Mississippi. She was acquired by the Navy on 16 October 1940 and commissioned on 18 July 1941. She was first stationed at Argentia, Newfoundland, tending patrol planes countering U-boats, but for most of World War II she supported aircraft in the Pacific theater. Decommissioned 10 July 1946. *Pocomoke* received two battle stars for World War II service.

Portsmouth **Gunboat 1862**
(166 tons, 106′ length, armament: one 9″, one 32-pdr)
CSS *Portsmouth* was one of the first of the hundred "Maury Gunboats" built to defend the Virginia–North Carolina coastline. *Portsmouth* was burned on the stocks at the Gosport Navy Yard on 10 May 1862 to prevent capture.

Portsmouth **Nuclear-powered Attack Submarine (SSN-707) 1983–2004**
(6129 tons, 362′ length, complement 110, armament: Mk 48 torpedoes, four torpedo tubes)
Portsmouth was commissioned on 1 October 1983 at Portsmouth, New Hampshire. She participated in operations in Grenada in 1983 and was assigned to the Pacific Fleet for most of her career. *Portsmouth* was decommissioned on 10 September 2004 in Norfolk.

Note: Armed ship *Portsmouth* (1789), sloop-of-war *Portsmouth* (1844), and cruiser *Portsmouth* (CL-102) were named after the city in New Hampshire.

Rappahannock **Steamer 1917–1924**
(17,000 tons, 471′ length, 155 complement, armament: one 5″, 1–3″)
Rappahannock was launched in 1913 as SS *Pommern* for the North German Lloyd Line and was interned and then seized when America entered World War I. She was renamed *Rappahannock* and commissioned in the Navy on 8 December 1917 and used as an animal transport, completing four transatlantic runs to France during the war. Decommissioned 10 December 1924 and sold.

Rappahannock **Fleet Oiler (T-AO-204) 1995–**
(9,500 tons, 677′ length)
Built by Avondale Shipyards, New Orleans, launched on 14 January 1995, and delivered to the Navy on 7 November 1995.

Note: Attack cargo ship *Suffolk* (AKA-69) and tank landing ship *Suffolk County* (LST-1173) were named after counties in Massachusetts and New York.

Tangier **Motor Yacht (SP-469) 1917–1918**
(62′ length, armament one 1-pdr)
Tangier, a motor yacht built by J. Woodtull at Orvington, Virginia, was acquired by the Navy from Mr. J. S. Parsons of Norfolk, Virginia, for patrolling the waters near Norfolk and was commissioned on 24 April 1917. She was returned to her owner on 22 October 1918.

Tangier **Seaplane Tender (AV-8) 1940–1947**
(11,760 tons, 492′ length, complement 1,075, armament: one 5″, four 3″, eight 40 mm)
Tangier was laid down as *Sea Arrow* on 18 March 1939 at Oakland, California, by Moore Dry Dock Co.; launched on 15 September 1939; renamed *Tangier* (AV-8) and commissioned on 8 July 1940 before undergoing conversion to a seaplane tender. *Tangier* was at Pearl Harbor during the Japanese attack, claiming three enemy planes and hits on a midget submarine in the harbor. She supported PBY flying boats in the South Pacific and served for a time as the flagship for Commander, Aircraft, Seventh Fleet. Decommissioned by January 1947. *Tangier* earned three battle stars during World War II.

Tappahannock **Oiler (A0-43) 1942–1970**
(7,004 tons, 530′ length, complement 213, armament: one 4″, four 3″, twelve 20 mm)

Tappahannock was launched on 18 April 1942 and commissioned on 22 June 1942. She saw service in the Pacific during World War II and later supported operations in Korea, the western Pacific, and Vietnam. Decommissioned on 6 March 1970. *Tappahannock* received nine battle stars for World War II and nine for Vietnam service.

Tidewater **Destroyer Tender (AD-31) 1946–1971**
(16,800 tons, 492′ length, 1,017 complement, armament: one 5″, eight 40 mm, twelve 20 mm)
Tidewater was launched on 30 June 1945 and commissioned at Charleston, South Carolina, on 19 February 1946. She remained active only long enough to complete sea trials and was decommissioned. On 2 October 1951, *Tidewater* was recommissioned and began a long association with the Atlantic destroyer force in her homeport of Norfolk; she also completed eleven overseas deployments. She was placed out of commission at Norfolk on 20 February 1971, was turned over to the Indonesian Navy, and was recommissioned as *Dumai*.

Virginia **Frigate 1777**
(681 tons, 126′ length, armament: twenty-four 12-pdrs, six 4-pdrs, six swivel guns)
Virginia was authorized by the Continental Congress on 13 December 1775, laid down in 1776 at Fells Point, Maryland, by George Wells, and commissioned in the spring of 1777. *Virginia* grounded on Middle Ground in Hampton Roads and was taken, uncontested, by British frigates *Emerald* and *Conqueror*. Renamed HMS *Virginia*, she was placed in service along the American coast. At the end of the war, she was condemned and sold.

Virginia **Frigate 1779**
(armament: thirty-two guns)
Virginia was under construction at Gosport for the Virginia State Navy when she was burned by the British in May 1779.

Virginia **Schooner 1797–1799**
(187 tons, 60′ length; armament: six 6-pdrs, eight 4-pdrs)
Built in 1797 for the United States Revenue Cutter Service at Portsmouth, Virginia, *Virginia* was transferred to the Navy for use in the undeclared naval war against France in the early summer of 1798 and was commissioned on 25 June, Capt. Francis Bright in command. *Virginia* participated in operations in the West Indies and Caribbean, helped capture the armed French schooner *Louis* on 26 April 1799, and was returned to the Revenue Cutter Service in June 1799.

Virginia **Ship-of-the-Line**
(2,633 tons, 197′ length, 820 complement, armament: seventy-four guns)
One of nine 74-gun warships authorized by Congress on 29 April 1816, *Virginia* was laid down at the Boston Navy Yard in May 1822,

Destroyer tender *Tidewater* (AD-31). *U.S. Naval Institute*

was finished about 1825, but was never commissioned. She was left on the stocks at Boston until she was broken up there, starting in 1874.

Virginia **Schooner/Gunboat 1862–1865**

(581 tons, 170′ length, armament: six 24-pdr howitzers, one 12-pdr rifle)

Built originally as the British merchantman *Pet* in 1861, she was acquired by a Havana merchant for use as a Confederate blockade runner and renamed *Virginia*. Captured by blockading forces off Mexico, *Virginia* was commissioned into the U.S. Navy in June 1862 and assigned duty with Rear Adm. David G. Farragut's West Gulf Blockading Squadron, primarily off the coast of Texas, where she amassed an impressive record of captures. *Virginia* was sold at public auction at New York City on 30 November 1865.

Virginia **Ironclad Ram 1862**

(3200 tons, 263′ length, 320 complement, armament: two 7″ rifles, two 6″ rifles, six 9″ rifles, two 12-pdr howitzers)

CSS *Virginia* was originally built at Boston Navy Yard as the steam frigate *Merrimack* and commissioned on 20 February 1856. On 20 April 1861, retiring Union forces burned *Merrimack* to the water line and sank her to preclude capture at Norfolk. Confederate forces raised *Merrimack,* rebuilt her as an ironclad ram, and commissioned her into the Confederate Navy on 17 February 1862. On 8 March 1862, with Flag Officer Franklin Buchanan, CSN, commanding, *Virginia* sortied into Hampton Roads, where she destroyed sloop-of-war *Cumberland* and frigate *Congress* and engaged frigate *Minnesota*. The next morning, now under the command of Lt. Catesby ap Roger Jones, *Virginia* dueled inconclusively with the new Union ironclad *Monitor* in the first naval battle ever fought between ironclad warships. When Confederate forces abandoned Norfolk, *Virginia* was scuttled, fired, and destroyed near Craney Island on 11 May 1862.

Virginia II **Ironclad Steamer 1864–1865**

(1600? tons, 197′ length; 150 complement, armament: one 11″ rifle, one 8″ rifle, two 6.4″ rifles)

CSS *Virginia II* was laid down at the Confederate Navy Yard at Richmond in 1863 and served with the Confederate James River Squadron in 1864 and 1865, participating in engagements at Trent's Reach, Dutch Gap, and Signal Hill. Destroyed by her crew in the James River before the evacuation of Richmond on 3 April 1865.

Virginia **Battleship (BB-13) 1906–1920**

(14,980 tons, 441′ length, complement 916, armament: four 12″, eight 8″, twelve 6″, four 21″ torpedo tubes)

Battleship *Virginia* was laid down on 21 May 1902 at Newport News Shipbuilding, launched on 6 April 1904, and commissioned on 7 May 1906. She participated in the opening ceremonies of the Jamestown Exposition in 1907, sailed with the Great White Fleet during its circumnavigation from 1907 to 1909, and participated in the American occupation of Vera Cruz in 1914. During World War I, she served with the 3rd Division, Battleship Force, Atlantic Fleet, as a gunnery

Battleship *Virginia* (BB-13). *U.S. Naval Institute*

training ship and convoy escort. Following the war, *Virginia* was decommissioned in 1920 and was sunk in an aerial bombing exercise on 5 September 1923.

***Virginia* Nuclear-Powered Guided Missile Cruiser (CGN-38) 1976–1994**

(9,473 tons, 585′ length, complement 473, armament: two 5″ guns; two antiaircraft guided missile launchers, ASROC, CIWS, Harpoon and Tomahawk launchers)

Virginia was launched on 14 December 1974 by Newport News Shipbuilding and commissioned on 11 September 1976. She conducted her first of nine deployments in 1979. In December 1990, she deployed in support of the first Gulf War, firing two Tomahawk missiles at targets in Iraq. *Virginia* was decommissioned and stricken on 10 November 1994.

***Virginia* Nuclear-Powered Attack Submarine (SSN-774) 2004–**

(7800 tons, 377′ length, complement 113, armament: Tomahawk missiles, twelve VLS tubes, four torpedo tubes)

Virginia is the lead ship in a new class of nuclear-powered attack submarines designed for battle-space dominance across a broad spectrum of regional and littoral missions as well as open-ocean, "blue water" missions. She was launched on 16 August 2003 at General Dynamics Electric Boat shipyard in Groton, Connecticut, and commissioned 23 October 2004.

***Virginian* Motor Tug 1918–1919**

(179 tons, 90′ length, complement 15)

Virginian was acquired by the Navy, commissioned in January 1918, and served as a tug in the Fifth Naval District—probably at Norfolk—throughout World War. I. On 12 May 1919, she was returned to her owner.

***Virginian* Troop Transport 1919**

(7,914 tons, 492′ length, complement 106)

Virginian was originally built as the steel-hulled, twin-screw steamship *Maine* in 1903 at Sparrows Point, Maryland, by the Maryland Steel Co. Renamed *Virginian* in 1908, she operated with the American-Hawaiian Steamship Co. until she was briefly acquired by the Navy in 1919 to help transport troops back from the European theater.

***Westover* Freighter 1918**

(12,205 tons, 423′ length, complement 92, armament: one 5″, one 6-pdr)

Virginia (SSN-774), lead ship of the latest class of attack submarines, was commissioned on 23 October 2004 at Naval Station Norfolk. The *Virginia*-class attack submarine was specifically designed to counter post–Cold War threats with improved stealth, sophisticated surveillance capabilities, and special warfare enhancements that enable it to meet the Navy's multimission requirements. With a modular design, the *Virginia* class will be able to accommodate technology upgrades throughout the life of the class. *U.S. Navy*

Westover, a steel-hulled, single-screw freighter built as *War Sun* at Seattle, Washington, by J. F. Duthie and Co. for the Cunard Steamship Line, was launched on 17 February 1918. She was taken over by the Navy, and renamed and commissioned at Newport News on 22 May 1918. While in a convoy for France, *Westover* was sunk by *U-92* on 11 July 1918 with the loss of eleven men.

White Marsh **Dock Landing Ship (LSD-8) 1944–1956**

(9,375 tons, 457′ length, 326 complement, armament: one 5″, twelve 40 mm, sixteen 20 mm)

White Marsh was launched on 19 July 1943 and commissioned on 29 January 1944. She participated in amphibious campaigns for Saipan, the Marianas, Palau, New Guinea, Leyte, Luzon, and Okinawa. She was decommissioned at Norfolk in March 1946 but was placed back in commission on 8 November 1950 and completed two deployments with the Seventh Fleet and two deployments with the Sixth Fleet before 1956. In September 1956, *White Marsh* was decommissioned and in November 1960 was transferred to the Taiwan Navy as *Chung Cheng*. *White Marsh* earned four battle stars for World War II service.

Williamsburg **Gunboat/Presidential Yacht (AGC-369) 1941–1953**

(1,805 tons, 243′ length, 81 complement, armament: two 3″, six .50-cal., two .30-cal.)

Originally named *Aras* and launched on 8 December 1930, *Williamsburg* was acquired by the Navy on 24 April 1941 and commissioned on 7 October. She served in the Icelandic theater of operations and also as flagship for Commander, Fleet Operational Training Command, Atlantic Fleet, in Norfolk during the war. After conversion in November 1945, *Williamsburg* relieved *Potomac* as the presidential yacht. *Williamsburg* served two presidents, Harry S Truman and Dwight D. Eisenhower, before being decommissioned at the Washington Navy Yard on 30 June 1953.

York County **Tank Landing Ship (LST-1175) 1957–1972**

(3,560 tons, 445′ length, 170 complement, armament: six 3″)

York County was launched on 5 March 1957 at Newport News Shipbuilding and was commissioned on 8 November 1957. *York County* participated in a host of amphibious operations in the Caribbean, Atlantic, and Mediterranean, including providing support to Marines

Yorktown represented a new type of ship for the New Steel Navy, a steel-hulled, twin-screw gunboat protected by a thin armored deck. After commissioning in 1889 she operated in the Squadron of Evolution and then in a thirty-year career primarily with the Pacific Fleet. *U.S. Naval Institute*

Yorktown was built at Newport News Shipbuilding and commissioned at NOB Norfolk on 30 September 1937. She reflected the first American carrier design to take advantage of lessons learned from large carrier operations by the *Lexington, Saratoga* and *Ranger. Yorktown's* highly successful design included a large and flexible flight deck, high speed, a large island, and improved defensive considerations. *Naval Historical Center*

during the 1965 crisis in the Dominican Republic. *York County* was decommissioned on 17 July 1972 and transferred to the Italian government as *Nave Caorle* (L-8991).

Yorktown **Sloop-of-war 1840–1850**

(566 tons, 117′ length, 150 complement, armament: sixteen 32-pdrs)

Yorktown was launched in 17 June 1839 by the Gosport Navy Yard and commissioned on 15 November 1840. *Yorktown* departed Hampton Roads almost immediately after commissioning for a three-year cruise of South America, the islands of the Pacific, and Mexican California. From 1844 to 1850, the sloop operated with the Africa Squadron, helping to curtail the slave trade, but on 6 September 1850 she broke up and sank after striking an uncharted reef at Isle de Mayo in the Cape Verde Islands, with no lives lost.

Yorktown **Gunboat (No.1) 1889–1919**

(1910 tons, 245′ length, 191 complement, armament: six 6″, four 3-pdrs, four 1-pdrs, two 30-cal mg)

Yorktown was launched on 28 April 1888 by the William Cramp and Sons shipyard of Philadelphia, Pennsylvania, and was commissioned on 23 April 1889. As one of the first ships of the new steel Navy, she was assigned to the "Squadron of Evolution" and served for many years in the Pacific, including actions during the Boxer Rebellion in China. She was placed out of commission at Mare Island on 12 June 1919 and sold.

Yorktown **Aircraft Carrier (CV-5) 1937–1942**

(19,800 tons, 809′ length, 2,919 complement, armament: eight 5″, twenty-two 50-cal mg, 80+ aircraft)

Yorktown was launched on 4 April 1936 at the Newport News Shipbuilding and commissioned on 30 September 1937. She was the first in a new class of aircraft carrier and was transferred to the Pacific in 1939 with the bulk of the U.S. Fleet, but returned to the Atlantic Fleet in April 1941 to conduct American neutrality patrols. *Yorktown* sailed for the Pacific shortly after Pearl Harbor and participated in an offensive sweep of the Gilbert Islands in January and the Battle of the Coral Sea in May 1942. *Yorktown* aircraft helped sink the Japanese light carrier *Shoho* and damage the carrier *Shokaku* while receiving damage from a bomb hit that penetrated the flight deck and exploded belowdecks, killing or seriously injuring sixty-six men. After only two days of repairs at Pearl Harbor, *Yorktown* sailed to rendezvous with carriers *Enterprise* and *Hornet* for the Battle of Midway on 4–6 June 1942. *Yorktown* aircraft helped sink the Japanese carriers *Soryu, Hiryu, Akagi,* and *Kaga* but absorbed three bomb hits and two torpedo hits. Later, Japanese submarine *I-158* fired two torpedoes at the carrier, and she sank on the morning of 7 June 1942. *Yorktown* earned three battle stars for her World War II service.

***Yorktown* Aircraft Carrier (CV-10) 1943–1970**

(27,100 tons, 872′ length, 3,448 complement, armament: twelve 5″, thirty-two 40 mm, forty-six 20 mm, 80+ aircraft)

Yorktown was launched on 21 January 1943 and commissioned on 15 April 1943 at Newport News Shipbuilding. *Yorktown* joined the fast carrier forces in the Pacific soon after commissioning and participated in campaigns at Tarawa, New Guinea, Truk, Saipan, Guam, Leyte, Luzon, Iwo Jima, Okinawa, and the Japanese home islands and in the battles of the Philippine Sea and Leyte Gulf. After being placed in reserve for a brief time, she was recommissioned on 20 February 1953 and later modified with an angled deck. In 1957 *Yorktown* was reclassified an antisubmarine warfare (ASW) aircraft carrier and during the Vietnam era conducted several deployments to the Far East and "Yankee Station" in the Gulf of Tonkin. On 27 June 1970, *Yorktown* was decommissioned. *Yorktown* earned eleven battle stars and a Presidential Unit Citation during World War II and five battle stars for Vietnam service.

***Yorktown* Guided Missile Cruiser (CG-48) 1984–**

(7592 tons, 567′ length, complement 374, armament: Tomahawk and Harpoon missiles, two antiaircraft missile launchers, two 5″ guns, CIWS)

Second ship of the *Ticonderoga*-class of guided missile cruisers carrying the Aegis weapons system, *Yorktown* was launched from Ingalls Shipbuilding in Pascagoula, Mississippi, on 17 January 1983 and commissioned on 4 July 1984. *Yorktown* completed five Mediterranean and five Caribbean deployments, including involvement with the *Achille Lauro* hijacking, two Black Sea excursions, three operations off the Libyan coast, and an intentional collision with a Soviet warship in what some observers called the "last incident of the Cold War."

Note: CSS *Patrick Henry*, a 1,300-ton side-wheel gunboat built in New York City in 1853 as the civilian steamer *Yorktown* and seized by the state of Virginia at the start of the Civil War, is frequently referred to by her original name in Civil War histories.

NOTES

Prologue

1. Philip D. Curtin, Grace S. Brush, and George W. Fisher, *Discovering the Chesapeake: The History of an Ecosystem* (Baltimore: Johns Hopkins University Press, 2001), 8.
2. David S. Powars, "The Effects of the Chesapeake Bay Impact Crater on the Geologic Framework and the Correlation of Hydrogeologic Units of Southwestern Virginia, South of the James River" (Reston, VA: U.S. Geological Survey, 2000), 8, 22.
3. Ibid., 26.
4. Curtin, Brush, and Fisher, *Discovering the Chesapeake*, 9.
5. Thomas C. Parramore, *Norfolk, The First Four Centuries* (Charlottesville: University Press of Virginia, 1994), 1, 3.; Samuel Eliot Morison, *The European Discovery of America: The Northern Voyages, A.D. 500–1600* (New York: Oxford University Press, 1971), 631.
6. David A. Clary, *Fortress America: The Corps of Engineers, Hampton Roads, and United States Coastal Defense* (Charlottesville: University Press of Virginia, 1990), 1.
7. Arthur Pierce Middleton, *Tobacco Coast* (Baltimore: Johns Hopkins University Press, 1953), 40, 337; Parramore, *Norfolk, The First Four Centuries*, 51.
8. George Holbert Tucker, *Norfolk Highlights 1584–1881* (Norfolk: Norfolk Historical Society, 1972), 6.
9. Alan Flanders, "Willoughby Left More Than a Spit in Hampton Roads," *Portsmouth Currents*, 2 March 2003, 3; Worley Levi Sewell, *History of the Sewell Families in America* (privately printed: Virginia Historical Society files, 1955), 35. Willoughby Spit dates from the mid-eighteenth century and was not a portion of Thomas Willoughby's lands during his life. A series of underwater shoals was formed over the years by the action of the waters of Hampton Roads and the Chesapeake Bay west of the Willoughby manor plantation. Quite suddenly in October 1749, the Norfolk area was visited by a tropical hurricane that destroyed Fort George (at the present site of Fort Monroe) and deposited sand on the Willoughby plantation shoals, which grew slowly over the years with further accumulations to become the Willoughby Spit that is known today. Captain Thomas Willoughby passed away on 15 April 1657 at age 57.
10. Tucker, *Norfolk Highlights*, 6; Sewell, *History of the Sewell Families in America*, 35.
11. Tucker, *Norfolk Highlights*, 4, 12.
12. Ibid., 16.
13. Middleton, *Tobacco Coast*, 384.

1776

1. Alf J. Mapp, Jr., *The Pirate Peer: Lord Dunmore's Operations in the Chesapeake Bay* (Centreville, Md.: Tidewater Publishers, 1981), 7, 63; John Frye, *Hampton Roads and Four Centuries as a World's Seaport* (Lewiston, N.Y.: Edwin Mellen Press, 1996), 49.
2. Ernest McNeill Eller, *Chesapeake Bay in the American Revolution* (Centreville, Md.: Tidewater Publishers, 1981), 17
3. Joe Law, *Norfolk Naval Shipyard: Its Remarkable History* (unpublished, Norfolk Naval Shipyard), 8.
4. Ibid.; Marshall W. Butt, *Norfolk Naval Shipyard, a Brief History* (Portsmouth, Va.: Public Information Office, NNSY, 1951), 2.
5. Marshall W. Butt, *Portsmouth Under Four Flags: 1752–1970* (Portsmouth: Portsmouth Historical Association, 1971), 10; Frye, *Hampton Roads and Four Centuries as a World's Seaport,* 48.
6. Law, *Norfolk Naval Shipyard: Its Remarkable History,* 7, 14.
7. Ibid., 19.
8. Frye, *Hampton Roads and Four Centuries as a World's Seaport,* 54; Mapp, *The Pirate Peer: Lord Dunmore's Operations in the Chesapeake Bay,* 81–85, 97; George Holbert Tucker, *Norfolk Highlights 1584–1881* (Norfolk: Norfolk Historical Society, 1972), 45; Thomas J. Wertenbaker, *Norfolk: Historic Southern Port* (Durham: Duke University Press, 1931), 57.

9. Wertenbaker, *Norfolk: Historic Southern Port,* 62.
10. Tucker, *Norfolk Highlights 1584–1881,* 45; Mapp, *The Pirate Peer: Lord Dunmore's Operations in the Chesapeake Bay,* 88. The effort to blame Dunmore for the destruction of Norfolk was mostly successful from a propaganda perspective. Both Virginia's constitution and Jefferson's Declaration of Independence cited Norfolk's destruction as a reason for breaking America's bonds with England.
11. Charles B. Cross, Jr., *The Chesapeake, A Biography of a Ship* (Chesapeake, Va.: Norfolk County Historical Society, 1968), 17; Mapp, *The Pirate Peer: Lord Dunmore's Operations in the Chesapeake Bay,* 97.
12. Joe Mosier, "To Protect the Several Rivers in This Colony: The Virginia State Navy of the Revolutionary War," *The Day Book* (November 1995): 5; Joseph A. Goldenberg and Marion West Stoer, *The Virginia State Navy* (Centreville, Md.: Tidewater Publishers, 1981), 174. Row galleys—the most common designs were about eighty feet in length with two masts, schooner rigged—were a popular addition, as they could carry small guns and could escape into shallow water if threatened by large British ships.
13. Goldenberg and Stoer, *The Virginia State Navy,* 175; Frye, *Hampton Roads and Four Centuries as a World's Seaport,* 39.
14. Brent Tarter, "The Barron Family," *Virginia Cavalcade* (Autumn 1998): 167; William Oliver Stevens, *An Affair of Honor: the Biography of Commodore James Barron, USN* (Chesapeake, Va.: Norfolk County Historical Society, 1969), 5.
15. Stevens, *An Affair of Honor*, 6; Tarter, "The Barron Family," 168; David McCullough, *John Adams* (New York: Simon & Schuster, 2001), 184.
16. Mapp, *The Pirate Peer*, 94.
17. Robert Armistead Stewart, *The History of Virginia's Navy of the Revolution* (Richmond: Mitchell & Hotchkiss, 1933), 69.
18. Stevens, *An Affair of Honor*, 12; Goldenberg and Stoer, *The Virginia State Navy,* 184.
19. Stewart, *The History of Virginia's Navy of the Revolution,* 18.
20. Eller, *Chesapeake Bay in the American Revolution,* 196.
21. Wade G. Dudley, *Splintering the Wooden Wall: The British Blockade of the United States, 1812–1815,* (Annapolis: Naval Institute Press, 2003), 20; Ernest McNeill Eller, *Washington's Maritime Strategy and the Campaign that Assured Independence* (Centreville, MD: Tidewater Publishers, 1981), 477.
22. Eller, *Chesapeake Bay in the American Revolution,* 21; J. A. Robinson, *British Invade the Chesapeake, 1777* (Centreville, MD: Tidewater Publishers, 1981), 358; Joseph A. Goldenberg, *Virginia Ports* (Centreville, MD: Tidewater Publishers, 1981), 323.
23. Stewart, *The History of Virginia's Navy of the Revolution,* 19.
24. Evan Thomas, *John Paul Jones: Sailor, Hero, Father of the American Navy* (New York: Simon & Schuster, 2003), 260; Eller, *Chesapeake Bay in the American Revolution,* 20.
25. Eller, *Chesapeake Bay in the American Revolution,* 39.
26. Marshall Booker, *Privateering from the Bay, Including Admiralty Courts and Tory as well as Patriot Operations* (Centreville, MD: Tidewater Publishers, 1981), 281.
27. Dudley, *Splintering the Wooden Wall*, 21.
28. Robert Fallaw and Marion West Stoer, *The Old Dominion Under Fire: The Chesapeake Invasions, 1779–1781* (Centreville, MD: Tidewater Publishers, 1981), 443.
29. William Laird Clowes, *The Royal Navy: A History from the Earliest Times to the Present* (London: Sampson, Low, Marston, and Company, 1899), Vol. IV, 26; Stewart, *The History of Virginia's Navy of the Revolution,* 73, published in the *Virginia Gazette* of 26 September 1779, quoted by Stewart.
30. David A. Clary, *Fortress America: The Corps of Engineers, Hampton Roads, and United States Coastal Defense* (Charlottesville: University Press of Virginia, 1990), 8. Fort Nelson was named after Brigadier General Thomas Nelson, signer of the Declaration of Independence, veteran of the Continental Army, then commander of Virginia's state militia, and, in 1781, Thomas Jefferson's successor as governor. During Collier's campaign, Major Thomas Matthews commanded the earthen parapet that measured fourteen feet high and fifteen feet thick but was manned by a mere 150 local militiamen.
31. Stewart, *The History of Virginia's Navy of the Revolution,* 75; Fallaw and Stoer, *The Old Dominion Under Fire*, 446.
32. Law, *Norfolk Naval Shipyard: Its Remarkable History,* 32; William M. E. Rachal, "When Virginia Owned a Shipyard," *Virginia Cavalcade* (Autumn 1952): 32; Howard I. Chapelle, *The History of the American Sailing Navy* (New York: Konecky & Konecky, 1949), 86. The Act of 20 November 1776 passed by the Continental Congress authorized the building of three 74-gun ships of the line, five 36-gun frigates, an 18-gun brig, and a packet.
33. Stewart, *The History of Virginia's Navy of the Revolution,* 75.
34. "Expedition to Portsmouth, Virginia, 1779," *William & Mary Quarterly* (1972); Collier to Clinton 16 May 1779, 184.
35. Fallaw and Stoer, *The Old Dominion Under Fire*, 446–50.
36. Stewart, *The History of Virginia's Navy of the Revolution,* 90.; Fallaw and Stoer, *The Old Dominion Under Fire*, 454.
37. Fallaw and Stoer, *The Old Dominion Under Fire*, 458.
38. Ibid., 463.
39. David J. Hepper, *British Warship Losses in the Age of Sail, 1650–1859* (East Sussex, England: Jean Bourdriot Publications, 1994), 61; Stewart, *The History of Virginia's Navy of the Revolution,* 96; Fallaw and Stoer, *The Old Dominion Under Fire*, 465.
40. W. M. James, *The British Navy in Adversity* (New York: Russell & Russell, 1926), 269.
41. Fallaw and Stoer, *The Old Dominion Under Fire*, 473.
42. James, *The British Navy in Adversity,* 274; Clowes, *The Royal Navy: A History from the Earliest Times to the Present,* Vol. III, 491.
43. Thomas, *John Paul Jones*, 106; Stewart, *The History of Virginia's Navy of the Revolution,* 91.

44. Fallaw and Stoer, *The Old Dominion Under Fire*, 467; Eller, *Chesapeake Bay in the American Revolution,* 195.
45. Stewart, *The History of Virginia's Navy of the Revolution,* 102.
46. Ibid.
47. James, *The British Navy in Adversity,* 282.
48. Harold A. Larrabee, *Decision at the Chesapeake* (New York: Bramhall House, 1964), 88.
49. Ibid., 157.
50. James, *The British Navy in Adversity,* 266.
51. Larrabee, *Decision at the Chesapeake,* 180.; James, *The British Navy in Adversity,* 286.
52. Larrabee, *Decision at the Chesapeake,* 139.
53. James, *The British Navy in Adversity,* 288; Larrabee, *Decision at the Chesapeake,* 159.
54. James, *The British Navy in Adversity,* 287.
55. Larrabee, *Decision at the Chesapeake,* 65. William B. Wilcox, as quoted in Larrabee, *Decision at the Chesapeake,* 66.
56. J. G. Shea, *The Operations of the French Fleet Under the Count de Grasse in 1781–1782* (New York: Da Capo Press, 1971), 69.
57. Larrabee, *Decision at the Chesapeake,* 188, 274.
58. Ibid., 190.
59. Ibid., 191.
60. Ibid., 199.
61. Ibid., 202.
62. James, *The British Navy in Adversity,* 292.
63. Shea, *The Operations of the French Fleet*, 73; Larrabee, *Decision at the Chesapeake,* 211.
64. Heather Burnett, "Bear Down and Engage: The Battle off the Virginia Capes, September 1781," *Day Book* (November 1995): 6.
65. James, *The British Navy in Adversity,* 296; Eller, *Washington's Maritime Strategy and the Campaign that Assured Independence,* 514.
66. James, *The British Navy in Adversity,* 296; Clary, *Fortress America*, 11; Clowes, *The Royal Navy: A History from the Earliest Times to the Present,* Vol. IV, 74. The *Fowey* witnessed both ends of the maritime struggle in the Chesapeake, serving as one of Dunmore's Loyalist vessels at the onset of the Revolution and meeting her end at Yorktown.
67. Clowes, *The Royal Navy: A History from the Earliest Times to the Present,* Vol. III, 47.; James, *The British Navy in Adversity,* 300.
68. Larrabee, *Decision at the Chesapeake,* 282.

1800

1. Board of Navy Commissioners, letter to the secretary of the Navy, 2 May 1815 (RG45, vol. 213, National Archives); Thomas C. Parramore, *Norfolk, The First Four Centuries* (Charlottesville: University Press of Virginia, 1994), 100; William L. Tazewell, *Norfolk's Waters: An Illustrated Maritime History of Hampton Roads* (Woodland Hills, CA: Windsor Publications, 1982), 49.
2. Parramore, *Norfolk, The First Four Centuries,* 106; Tazewell, *Norfolk's Waters*, 51.
3. David A. Clary, *Fortress America: The Corps of Engineers, Hampton Roads, and United States Coastal Defense* (Charlottesville: University Press of Virginia, 1990), 12.
4. Howard I. Chapelle, *The History of the American Sailing Navy* (New York: Konecky & Konecky, 1949), 121.
5. Ibid., 121–29; Marshall Smelser, *The Congress Founds the Navy 1787–1798* (South Bend, IN: University of Notre Dame Press, 1959), 71.
6. William H. Stewart, *History of Norfolk County, Virginia and Representative Citizens* (Chicago: Biographical Publishing Company, 1902), 489; Bryan Hannon, *Three American Commodores* (New York: Spinner Press, 1936), 42.
7. Hannon, *Three American Commodores,* 43–46; Charles B. Cross, Jr., *The Chesapeake, A Biography of a Ship,* (Chesapeake, VA: Norfolk County Historical Society, 1968), 19; Evan Thomas, *John Paul Jones: Sailor, Hero, Father of the American Navy* (New York: Simon & Schuster, 2003), 167. John Paul Jones's timeless quote, "I have not yet begun to fight," was contained in Dale's report of the battle, although Jones himself never claimed that passage, and the account is not supported by other officers aboard.
8. Hannon, *Three American Commodores,* 52.
9. Marshall W. Butt, *Norfolk Naval Shipyard, a Brief History* (Portsmouth, VA: Public Information Office, NNSY, 1951), 3; Dudley W. Knox, *Naval Documents Related to the Quasi-War between the United States and France* (Washington, DC: Government Printing Office, 1986), III, 545.
10. Chapelle, *The History of the American Sailing Navy,* 129; Smelser, *The Congress Founds the Navy 1787–1798,* 131.
11. Smelser, *The Congress Founds the Navy 1787–1798,* 181; Chapelle, *The History of the American Sailing Navy,* 142. When the bill to establish a Navy Department was passed on 25 April 1798, Virginia congressmen voted 4–11 opposed.
12. Chapelle, *The History of the American Sailing Navy,* 142.
13. Alan Flanders, "Old Ironsides Ran on Wind, and Good Gosport Rum," *Portsmouth Currents,* 3.
14. Eugene S. Ferguson, *Truxtun of the Constellation* (Baltimore: Johns Hopkins University Press, 2000), 43, 123.
15. Chapelle, *The History of the American Sailing Navy,* 143; Joe Law, *Norfolk Naval Shipyard: Its Remarkable History* (Norfolk Naval Shipyard, unpublised), 36. Interestingly, the brig *Norfolk* was originally offered for sale to the Navy by William Pennock, who then accepted her into the service.
16. *Norfolk Herald,* 30 June 1798, 1; Frederick C. Leiner, *Millions for Defense: The Subscription Warships of 1798* (Annapolis: Naval Institute Press, 2000), 129. The Navy would purchase a second brig from Myers in 1799, also named *Augusta,* of 175 tons with 14 guns and fit her out at Gosport.

17. Leiner, *Millions for Defense*, 130.
18. Knox, *Naval Documents Related to the Quasi-War*, II:127; Smelser, *The Congress Founds the Navy*, 180.
19. *Norfolk Herald,* 3 December 1799, 1.
20. Joe Mosier, "I Was Never at Sea in so Uneasy a Ship: The Trials, Misfortunes and Possible Curse of the United States Frigate Chesapeake," *Day Book,* January 1997, 6. The *Chesapeake* returned from her maiden deployment in January 1801 and was place in ordinary at Gosport as hostilities in the Quasi-war with France ended.
21. Knox, *Naval Documents Related to the Quasi-War*, V:105.
22. Ibid., V:488,V:535,VI:230; Butt, *Norfolk Naval Shipyard, a Brief History,* 4; William M. E. Rachal, "When Virginia Owned a Shipyard," *Virginia Cavalcade,* Autumn 1952, 35.
23. Paolo E. Coletta, *American Secretaries of the Navy* (Annapolis: Naval Institute Press, 1980), 71.
24. Document no. 27: "Expenditures of the Navy and Navy Yards 1798–1815," American State Papers, Naval Affairs, 85-6.
25. Ferguson, *Truxtun of the Constellation,* 215; William M. Jr. Fowler, *Jack Tars & Commodores: the American Navy 1783–1815* (Boston: Houghton Mifflin Company, 1984), 72. The 1801 Mediterranean Squadron would be Commodore Richard Dale's final Navy command. He retired in 1802 and spent the remainder of his days in Philadelphia, where he died in 1826. His son served as a midshipman during the *President's* (Captain Stephen Decatur) engagement with the *Endymion* in the last days of the War of 1812, losing a leg in the battle and dying two weeks later in Bermuda.
26. Knox, *Naval Documents Related to the Quasi-War*, III,505.; *Publick Ledger,* 9 May 1816, 2.
27. Mary-Jo Kline, *Political Correspondence and Public Papers of Aaron Burr* (Princeton, NJ: Princeton University Press, 1983), 552.
28. A. W. Ashbrook, *The History of Our Navy Yard* (Portsmouth: Retirement Federation of Civil Service Employees, 1927), 3. Lieutenant Robert Henley would later command a gunboat during the Battle of Craney Island and the brig *Eagle* in the Battle of Lake Champlain.
29. Law, *Norfolk Naval Shipyard: Its Remarkable History,* 43.
30. Spencer C. Tucker, *The Jeffersonian Gunboat Navy* (Columbia: University of South Carolina Press, 1993), 27.
31. Theodore Roosevelt, *The Naval War of 1812* (New York: Charles Scribner's Sons, 1906), 243; Tucker, *The Jeffersonian Gunboat Navy,* 28.
32. Fowler, *Jack Tars & Commodores*, 144; Chapelle, *The History of the American Sailing Navy,* 225; Tucker, *The Jeffersonian Gunboat Navy,* 58. Built in 1806: Gunboat Nos. 58–61 built in Hampton by George Hope, John Pool, and Richard Servant; Nos. 62–65 built in Mathews County by John Patterson and Hunley Gayle; Nos. 66–69 built in Portsmouth by John and Joseph Forster. Between 1806 and 1809 Nos. 146–155 were built at Norfolk by Theodore Armistead.
33. Arthur Sinclair, *Two Years on the Alabama* (Annapolis: Naval Institute Press, 1989), xi. Lieutenant Arthur Sinclair's father, Arthur, had emigrated from Scotland in 1745, settled in Surrey County, Virginia, and commanded a privateer in the French and Indian Wars. His son Arthur II was born in 1780 and entered the Navy in 1798.
34. Irvin Anthony, *Decatur* (New York: Charles Scribner's Sons, 1931), 159; Eleanore P. Gadsden, "Compilation of Wheeler Information" (Washington, DC: Stephen Decatur House Archives, 1997).
35. Isaac Chauncey, Letter to Stephen Decatur, 24 December 1805.
36. William Oliver Stevens, *An Affair of Honor: the Biography of Commodore James Barron, USN* (Chesapeake: Norfolk County Historical Society, 1969), 57; Leonard F. Guttridge and Jay D. Smith, *The Commodores* (New York: Harper & Row, 1969), 149. Joe Mosier, archivist of the Jean Outland Chrysler Library, ventures a different version of the Barron–Decatur meeting on the streets of Norfolk, saying that Barron knew of Susan Wheeler's disputed parentage and stung Decatur by declaring that he should not marry a "wood's colt" (a bastard).
37. *Gazette & Publick Ledger,* 10 March 1806, 3.
38. Dr. William Andrews, Oral family history; Gadsden, "Compilation of Wheeler Information." The citizens had wanted, at first, to name the street after Decatur, but he asked that his name not be used, and "Tripoli Street" ensued. Tripoli Street was later renamed Monticello Avenue and the Warren Street and Decatur's "Summer House" residence is, today, 517 Warren Street.
39. Stewart, *History of Norfolk County, Virginia and Representative Citizens,* 427; Stephen Decatur, letter to secretary of the Navy, 29 June 1807; Stephen Decatur, letter to secretary of the Navy, 4 January 1807; Guttridge and Smith, *The Commodores,* 110. National Archives RG45, M125, reel 8.
40. Fowler, *Jack Tars & Commodores*, 149.
41. Stevens, *An Affair of Honor*, 58.
42. William James, *The Naval History of Great Britain, From the Declaration of War by France in 1793 to the Accession of George IV* (London: Macmillan and Co., 1902), IV:250.
43. Stevens, *An Affair of Honor*, 58.
44. Guttridge and Smith, *The Commodores,* 124; Parramore, *Norfolk, The First Four Centuries,* 132–35.
45. Guttridge and Smith, *The Commodores,* 124.
46. James Barron, letter to secretary of the Navy, 6 June 1807 (RG45, M125, reel 8, National Archives); Jay D. Smith, "Commodore James Barron: Guilty as Charged?" *US Naval Institute Proceedings,* November 1967, 81; Guttridge and Smith, *The Commodores,* 115. Charles Gordon's rise in seniority was due, in part, to his connections—his uncles Samuel, James, and John Nicholson had all been captains in the Continental Navy, and his cousin Hannah had married Albert Gallatin, the secretary of the treasury.
47. Smith, "Commodore James Barron: Guilty as Charged?" 81.

48. Guttridge and Smith, *The Commodores,* 114; Smith, "Commodore James Barron: Guilty as Charged?" 81.
49. Charles Oscar Paullin, *Commodore John Rodgers; Captain, Commodore and Senior Officer of the American Navy, 1773–1838* (Annapolis: Naval Institute Press, 1909), 185.
50. *Proceedings of the Court Martial Covened for the Trial of Commodore James Barron et al of the United States Ship Chesapeake in the month of January 1808* (Washington, DC: Navy Department, 1822), 217.
51. Stevens, *An Affair of Honor*, 65.
52. *Proceedings of the Court Martial Covened for the Trial of Commodore James Barron et al.,* 138.
53. Ibid.
54. Guttridge and Smith, *The Commodores,* 126.
55. James, *The Naval History of Great Britain,* IV:251.
56. Ibid.
57. Guttridge and Smith, *The Commodores,* 129. Allen later served with Decatur as first lieutenant of the *United States* and was promoted to commander in July 1813, falling in action as captain of the brig *Argus* with HMS *Pelican* on 14 August 1813.
58. Stevens, *An Affair of Honor*, 72.
59. Guttridge and Smith, *The Commodores,* 131.
60. Ibid., 132; James, *The Naval History of Great Britain*, IV:252.
61. *Proceedings of the Court Martial Covened for the Trial of Commodore James Barron et al.,* 139; Guttridge and Smith, *The Commodores,* 133.
62. Guttridge and Smith, *The Commodores,* 133.
63. *Norfolk Gazette,* 24 June 1807, 1; Parramore, *Norfolk, The First Four Centuries,* 135.
64. George Holbert Tucker, *Norfolk Highlights 1584–1881* (Norfolk: Norfolk Historical Society, 1972), 61.
65. Stevens, *An Affair of Honor*, 73; Guttridge and Smith, *The Commodores,* 137; Tucker, *The Jeffersonian Gunboat Navy,* 59–60. Thomas Armistead contracted for all ten of the boats to be built in Tidewater in 1807. Three were built on Tanners Creed by Karden Talbott, two on Herbert's Nook by Alexander Herbert, one on the Eastern Branch by Henry Sparrow, two at Portsmouth by John Foster, and two at Herberts Point by James Herbert. They were all to be built to a modified Decatur plan with a 32-pounder bow gun and an aft-facing carronade as a "means of annoying the enemy while retreating . . . from a superior enemy."
66. Stephen Decatur, letter to secretary of the Navy, 29 June 1807 (RG45, M125, Reel 8, National Archives); Stephen Decatur, letter to secretary of the Navy, 19 July 1807.
67. Stevens, *An Affair of Honor*, 74; Parramore, *Norfolk, The First Four Centuries,* 135.
68. Stephen Decatur, letter to secretary of the Navy, 29 June 1807
69. Edwin M. Gaines, "The Chesapeake Affair: Virginians Mobilize to Defend National Honor," *The Virginia Magazine of History and Biography,* April 1956, 140.
70. Stephen Decatur, letter to secretary of the Navy, 4 July 1807 (RG45, M125, Reel 8, National Archives).
71. Thomas Jefferson, letter to Secretary of War Henry Dearborn, 7 July 1807 (Jefferson Mss., Reel 62, Library of Congress); Stephen Decatur, letter to secretary of the Navy, 8 July 1807 (RG45, M125, Reel 8, National Archives); Tucker, *The Jeffersonian Gunboat Navy,* 84–85.
72. Parramore, *Norfolk, The First Four Centuries,* 135; Guttridge and Smith, *The Commodores,* 140; James, *The Naval History of Great Britain,* IV:256.
73. Guttridge and Smith, *The Commodores,* 135.
74. Stephen Decatur, letter to secretary of the Navy, 4 July 1807 (RG45, M125, Reel 8, National Archives).
75. Stephen Decatur, letter to the secretary of the Navy, 17 July 1807 (RG45, M125, Reel 8, National Archives); "The Chesapeake Restored," *Norfolk Publick Ledger,* 27 July 1807, 1.
76. Guttridge and Smith, *The Commodores,* 143; Paullin, *Commodore John Rodgers*, 192. The distinguished Commodore Edward Preble had originally been tapped to chair the inquiry, but he died before the proceedings began. Barron's high standing in Tidewater attracted the services of Robert Barraud Taylor, a Norfolk attorney of considerable repute who later also served in the Virginia Assembly, in the General Court of Virginia, and as a brigadier general of militia.
77. Paullin, *Commodore John Rodgers*, 194; Stevens, *An Affair of Honor*, 80.
78. Paullin, *Commodore John Rodgers*, 194.
79. Stevens, *An Affair of Honor*, 81.
80. Paullin, *Commodore John Rodgers*, 196; *Proceedings of the Court Martial Covened for the Trial of Commodore James Barron et al.,* 350.; Stevens, *An Affair of Honor*, 92.
81. Parramore, *Norfolk, The First Four Centuries,* 37, 111; Paullin, *Commodore John Rodgers*, 199; Tucker, *The Jeffersonian Gunboat Navy,* 88.; Mosier, "I Was Never at Sea in so Uneasy a Ship," 8.
82. Paullin, *Commodore John Rodgers*, 4, 210.
83. Ibid., 240; Joe Mosier, "What Ship is That?" *The Day Book,* March 1998, 8.

1812

1. James Tertius DeKay, *A Rage for Glory: The Life of Commodore Stephen Decatur, USN* (New York: Free Press, 2004), 111.
2. Spencer C. Tucker, *The Jeffersonian Gunboat Navy* (Columbia: University of South Carolina Press, 1993), 103.
3. Thomas C. Parramore, *Norfolk, The First Four Centuries* (Charlottesville: University Press of Virginia, 1994), 144.
4. John M. Hallahan, *The Battle of Craney Island: A Matter of Credit* (Portsmouth, VA: Saint Michael's Press, 1986), 44; Christopher T. George, *Terror on the Chesapeake: the War of 1812 on the Bay* (Shippensburg, PA: White Mane Books, 2000), 3.
5. Lieutenant William Allen was promoted to master-commandant after action with the *Macedonian* and ordered to the com-

mand of the brig *Argus*. He died on 18 August 1813, four days after receiving a mortal wound during the engagement when *Argus* was taken by brig HMS *Pelican* (18) in English waters.

6. William S. Dudley, *The Naval War of 1812: A Documentary History* (Washington, DC: Naval Historical Center, 1985), I:633; Joseph C. Mosier, *The Battle of Craney Island: The Defense of Norfolk in the War of 1812,* 1997); Hallahan, *The Battle of Craney Island*, 29. Maritime History and Naval Heritage Index (http://www.cronab.demon.co.uk).
7. Wade G. Dudley, *Splintering the Wooden Wall: The British Blockade of the United States, 1812–1815* (Annapolis: Naval Institute Press, 2003), 73.
8. Geoffrey M. Footner, *USS Constellation: From Frigate to Sloop of War* (Annapolis: Naval Institute Press, 2003).
9. Charles Stewart, "Report to Secretary of the Navy," 5 February 1813; *Norfolk Ledger,* 5 February 1813, 1.
10. Theodore Roosevelt, *The Naval War of 1812* (New York: Charles Scribner's Sons, 1906), 215; *Norfolk Herald,* 8 February 1813, 1.
11. Parke Rouse Jr., "Low Tide at Hampton Roads," *U.S. Naval Institute Proceedings,* July 1969, 80.
12. David A. Clary, *Fortress America: The Corps of Engineers, Hampton Roads, and United States Coastal Defense* (Charlottesville: University Press of Virginia, 1990), 20. The land for Fort Norfolk was purchased from Edward and Sarah Poole for two hundred pounds sterling in 1795.
13. George, *Terror on the Chesapeake*, 3.
14. James Pack, *The Man Who Burned the White House* (Wiltshire, England: Redwood Burn Limited, 1987), 146.
15. Ibid., 140; Theodore Roosevelt, *The War with the United States 1812–1815* (London: Sampson, Low, Marston and Co., 1898), 68.
16. George, *Terror on the Chesapeake*, 8; Tucker, *The Jeffersonian Gunboat Navy,* 121. After leaving command of the Navy yard at Gosport, Samuel Evans was ordered to Boston to assume command of the frigate *Chesapeake.*
17. Pack, *The Man Who Burned the White House,* 148.
18. Ibid., 156.
19. William Jones, letter to Capt. Charles Stewart, 8 April 1813. in Dudley, *The Naval War of 1812,* II:347. Master Commandant Joseph Tarbell had served as a lieutenant in Preble's squadron during the Barbary Wars and, before being ordered to Norfolk, commanded the frigate *Adams* (28), which was bottled up in the Potomac by the blockade.
20. Dudley, *Splintering the Wooden Wall*, 96.
21. George, *Terror on the Chesapeake*, 42.
22. Pack, *The Man Who Burned the White House,* 158; Hallahan, *The Battle of Craney Island: A Matter of Credit,* 56.
23. George, *Terror on the Chesapeake*, 42.
24. Ibid., 45.
25. Ibid., 44; William James, *The Naval History of Great Britain, From the Declaration of War by France in 1793 to the Accession of George IV* (London: Macmillan and Co., 1902), IV:231.
26. George, *Terror on the Chesapeake*, 45.
27. Rouse, "Low Tide at Hampton Roads," 81. Lieutenant William B Shubrick would later command the Gosport Navy Yard beginning on 7 October 1840 and then the American Pacific Squadron during the war with Mexico and would retire a rear admiral.
28. George, *Terror on the Chesapeake*, 46.
29. Ibid., 45; Hallahan, *The Battle of Craney Island*, 102. Midshipman Charles S. McCauley, the nephew of the *Constellation's* former captain Charles Stewart, had been posted to the *Constellation* before the Battle of Craney Island.
30. William H. Gaines, "Craney Island, or Norfolk Delivered," *Virginia Cavalcade,* Winter, 1951, 35.
31. George, *Terror on the Chesapeake*, 47–48; Roosevelt, *The Naval War of 1812,* 246; Rouse, "Low Tide at Hampton Roads," 82.
32. Admiral Sir John Warren, letter to the First Secretary of the Admiralty John W. Croker, 24 June 1813 (found in Dudley II:361).
33. George Holbert Tucker, *Norfolk Highlights 1584–1881* (Norfolk: Norfolk Historical Society, 1972), 66.
34. Rouse, "Low Tide at Hampton Roads," 84; Pack, *The Man Who Burned the White House,* 158; George, *Terror on the Chesapeake*, 50. During their attack on Hampton, the British reported five killed, thirty-three wounded, and ten missing; Major Crutchfield listed seven killed, twelve wounded, eleven missing, and one man taken prisoner from the Hampton militia.
35. Tucker, *The Jeffersonian Gunboat Navy,* 125.
36. Henry Dearborn, letter to Secretary of State James Madison, 17 July 1807 (James Madison Mss. Reel 9, Library of Congress); Wallace Jr. Hutcheon, *Robert Fulton: Pioneer of Undersea Warfare* (Annapolis: Naval Institute Press, 1981), 99. Use of such weapons was already a well-known topic in naval circles. David Bushnell (inventor of the submersible "Turtle," which had attacked British warships during the American Revolution) had tried to use a floating mine against British warships in New London in December 1777.
37. Hutcheon, *Robert Fulton: Pioneer of Undersea Warfare,* 21, 110.
38. Sir George Cockburn, letter to Admiral Sir John Warren, 16 June 1813 (found in Dudley, II:355).
39. Kirkpatrick Sale, *The Fire of His Genius: Robert Fulton and the American Dream* (New York: Free Press, 2001), 156; Hutcheon, *Robert Fulton: Pioneer of Undersea Warfare.*
40. Charles Gordon, letter to secretary of the Navy, 20 September 1814 (found in Dudley, III: 308).
41. William L. Calderhead, "Naval Innovation in Crisis: War in the Chesapeake, 1813," *The American Neptune,* July 1976, 219.
42. Charles Gordon, letter to secretary of the Navy, 12 October 1813 (found in Dudley, II:388).
43. Dudley, *The Naval War of 1812*, III:14; Tucker, *The Jeffersonian Gunboat Navy,* 126.; Gordon, letter to secretary of the Navy, 12 October 1813 (found in Dudley II:388).

44. Dudley, *The Naval War of 1812*, III:15; Sir John Warren, orders to Captain Robert Barrie, 19 January 1814 (found in Dudley, III:16).
45. Gordon, letter to secretary of the Navy, 20 September 1814 (found in Dudley, III:308).
46. *Norfolk Publick Ledger,* 26 October 1814.
47. James, *The Naval History of Great Britain, From the Declaration of War by France in 1793 to the Accession of George IV,* VI:360.
48. Benjamin Crowinshield, letter to Captain John Cassin, 9 March 1815 (found in Dudley, III:366).
49. *Norfolk Publick Ledger,* 16 March 1815.
50. Charles Gordon, letter to the Secretary of the Navy, 15 February 1815 (found in Dudley, III:365).
51. Dudley, *Splintering the Wooden Wall*, 77.
52. Joe Mosier, "Prizes for Sale: Local Privateering in the War of 1812," *The Daybook,* July 2002, 6.
53. Charles Oscar Paullin, *Commodore John Rodgers; Captain, Commodore and Senior Officer of the American Navy, 1773–1838* (Annapolis: Naval Institute Press, 1909), 299.
54. Tucker, *Norfolk Highlights 1584–1881,* 58. Local newspapers reported the toast as: "Our Country! In her intercourse with foreign nations, may she always be in the right, and always successful, right or wrong."

1830

1. Littleton Tazewell, although chosen for the prestigious position of first secretary of the Navy Board, declined the appointment to continue with his law practice in Norfolk. It was during this time that he was rumored to be in line for appointment as secretary of the Navy.
2. Board of Navy Commissioners, letter to the secretary of the Navy, 2 May 1815 (RG45, vol. 213, National Archives).
3. Charles Oscar Paullin, *Commodore John Rodgers; Captain, Commodore and Senior Officer of the American Navy, 1773–1838* (Annapolis: Naval Institute Press, 1909), 311.
4. Board of Navy Commissioners, letter to the secretary of the Navy, 25 November 1815 (RG45, vol 213, National Archives). The Navy's studies in 1815–16, which would set the stage for locating a great naval base in Hampton Roads, were heavily influenced by a larger study demanded by Virginia's governor and congressional delegation of how best to defend the Chesapeake from future enemy attacks. That review would ultimately study the feasibility of building a string of forts between Cape Charles and Cape Henry, building fortifications along Lynnhaven Bay, or even building a fortification on the Middle Ground or Horseshoe Shoals.
5. John Rodgers, letter to the secretary of the Navy, 23 December 1816 (RG45, vol. 213, National Archives).
6. David Porter, letter to the secretary of the Navy, 27 December 1816 (RG45, vol. 213, National Archives).
7. Stephen Decatur, letter to secretary of the Navy, 2 January 1817 (RG45, vol. 213, National Archives).
8. Ibid.
9. Ibid.
10. Moses Myers, letter to P. Pederson, Danish Counsel General, 15 June 1818. Moses Myers Papers, Jean Outland Chrysler Library, Norfolk. James Monroe became the first president to visit Norfolk naval facilities on 8 June 1818, when he arrived to inspect Fortress Monroe, the defenses at Craney Island, and the two Gosport ships of the line.
11. Barron did not offer to return to the United States during the War of 1812, publicly citing monetary difficulties. Joe Mosier, archivist of the Jean Outland Chrysler Library, indicates that there is evidence in correspondence that a contributing factor to his tardiness in returning to America was that he had established a long-term relationship with a mistress in Copenhagen.
12. James Tertius DeKay, *A Rage for Glory: The Life of Commodore Stephen Decatur, USN* (New York: Free Press, 2004), 204.
13. J. D. Elliot, letter to John Myers, 26 March 1820 (Moses Myers Papers); Bill Eley, "With a Grateful Heart: Norfolk's Gift to the Man who Defended James Barron, The Rodney Urn," *The Day Book* (January 1997):10. The urn is now part of the Chrysler Museum collection.
14. William Oliver Stevens, *An Affair of Honor: the Biography of Commodore James Barron, USN* (Chesapeake, Va.: Norfolk County Historical Society, 1969), 164.
15. Ibid., 191.
16. Ibid., 179.
17. Charles Lee Lewis, *David Glasgow Farragut: Admiral in the Making* (Annapolis: U.S. Naval Institute, 1941), 316; Brent Tarter, "The Barron Family," *Virginia Cavalcade,* Autumn 1998, 171.
18. Lenoir Chambers and Joseph E. Shank, *Salt Water & Printers Ink* (Chapel Hill: University of North Carolina Press, 1967), 8; William H. Stewart, *History of Norfolk County, Virginia and Representative Citizens* (Chicago: Biographical Publishing Company, 1902), 498; Stevens, *An Affair of Honor,* 150. James Barron had two daughters from his second marriage, both of whom married naval officers—daughter Virginia to Lt. Jesse Pendergast and Mary to Lt. George Blake. Both Pendergast and Blake remained loyal to the Union Navy during the Civil War, the only portion of the Barron family not to identify with Virginia.
19. A. W. Ashbrook, *The History of Our Navy Yard* (Portsmouth, Va.: Retirement Federation of Civil Service Employees, 1927), 4. Shears were an early type of crane, usually composed of two upright spars fastened together at their upper ends and having tackle for hoisting masts or heavy objects such as guns into place aboard ship.
20. William James, *The Naval History of Great Britian, From the Declaration of War by France in 1793 to the Accession of George IV* (London: Macmillan and Co., 1902), 88; Christo-

pher Martin, *Damn the Torpedos: The Story of America's First Admiral, David Glasgow Farragut* (New York: Abelard-Schuman, 1970), 86; Joe Law, *Norfolk Naval Shipyard: Its Remarkable History* (Norfolk Naval Shipyard, unpublished), 459. A receiving ship was generally a hulk, roofed over and moored at a Navy yard or naval station, that served as a barracks, administrative center, and a place to "receive" and train new recruits. *Alert* served as the Norfolk yard's receiving ship from 1818 to 1829.

21. Law, *Norfolk Naval Shipyard: Its Remarkable History,* 366; Howard I. Chapelle, *The History of the American Sailing Navy* (New York: Konecky & Konecky, 1949), 315; Alan Flanders, *Bluejackets on the Elizabeth* (White Stone, Va.: Brandylane Publishers, 1998), 47. *Delaware* grounded in the mud at St. Helena when, at launch, restraining lines parted and she swept too far across the river. She featured a famous figurehead of the celebrated Delaware Indian Chief Tamanend that had been produced by noted woodcarver William Like and today is survived by a bronze replica prominently displayed at the U.S. Naval Academy. In 1817 it was intended that American ships-of-the-line be named for states, frigates for rivers, and sloops for cities or towns.
22. C. C. Lord, *Life and Times in Hopkinton, N. H.* (Concord, N.H.: Republican Press, 1890), IV; Law, *Norfolk Naval Shipyard: Its Remarkable History,* 53. About the same time that formal midshipman training was established aboard *Guerriere* at Gosport, a second school was established aboard the Navy receiving ship at New York.
23. Martin, *Damn the Torpedos,* 9.
24. Lewis, *David Glasgow Farragut: Admiral in the Making,* 25.
25. Martin, *Damn the Torpedos,* 17. After fitting out, the *Essex* sailed from Hampton Roads on 25 Oct. 1811. The *Essex* would later sail to the Pacific during the War of 1812 on a memorable cruise on which she decimated the English whaling industry, but would later be taken in a bloody battle against two British frigates, after which both Porter and Farragut would be repatriated.
26. Lewis, *David Glasgow Farragut: Admiral in the Making,* 295, 318; Martin, *Damn the Torpedos,* 86. Mrs. Farragut's sister, Jane Edna Marchant, was married on 15 Dec. 1832 to William D. Porter, Commodore David Porter's eldest son; Farragut signing the marriage bond in Norfolk.
27. Martin, *Damn the Torpedos,* 105.
28. Ibid., 112.; Lewis, *David Glasgow Farragut: Admiral in the Making,* 239. Ship-of-the-line *Pennsylvania* would serve as the receiving ship at Gosport from 1842 to 1861. She was the largest sailing warship ever built for the U.S. Navy, with four complete gundecks for her 120 guns.
29. Martin, *Damn the Torpedos,* 144.
30. "Fortifications MAD 206 ASP-MA" (Washington, DC: 1821), (New York: Arno Press), 2.
31. Law, *Norfolk Naval Shipyard: Its Remarkable History,* 450.
32. Thomas B. Buell, "Saga of Drydock One" *U.S. Naval Institute Proceedings,* July 1970, 62. Although the Navy Civil Engineer Corps was not founded until 1867, William P. S. Sanger was appointed civil engineer for the Navy on the staff of the Board of Navy Commissioners on 8 July 1836.
33. Ibid., 63–65; Richard D. Hepburn, *History of American Naval Dry Docks* (Arlington, Va.: Noesis, Inc., 2003), 23.
34. "Docking of the Delaware," *Norfolk & Portsmouth Herald,* 2. The huge gates that were originally planned for Dry Dock 1 were later replaced by a caisson as the method for keeping water out of the dock.
35. Joe Mosier, "Building a Naval Legacy: The Creation and Construction of Norfolk Naval Shipyard's Drydock No. 1," *The Day Book* (August 1995):6. Dry dock 1 was listed in the National Register during 1970, was recognized on 11 November 1971 as a National Historic Landmark, and was declared a National Historic Civil Engineering Landmark on 5 June 1978.
36. R. Christopher Goodwin and Associates Inc., "Architectural Inventory of Norfolk Naval Shipyard & Satellite Activities, Portsmouth, VA" (Norfolk, Va.: Navy Region Mid-Atlantic, 2003), 63.
37. John Cassin, letter to the secretary of the Navy, 25 August 1812 (found in William S. Dudley, *The Naval War of 1812: A Documentary History* (Washington, DC: Naval Historical Center, 1985), I:222); Law, *Norfolk Naval Shipyard: Its Remarkable History,* 391.
38. Ashbrook, *The History of Our Navy Yard,* 4.; *Norfolk & Portsmouth Herald,* 1.
39. Frigate *St Lawrence* spent much of her life in Norfolk. She exchanged gunfire with ironclad *Virginia* during the Battle of Hampton Roads and became a storeship in Norfolk in 1863 and then a marine barracks ship, also in Norfolk, until 1875.
40. Donald L. Canney, *Sailing Warships of the U.S. Navy* (Annapolis: Naval Institute Press, 2001), 84; Chapelle, *The History of the American Sailing Navy,* 360.
41. *Dictionary of American Naval Fighting Ships* (Washington, DC: Government Printing Office, 1959). Ultimately, "Hunter wheels" proved a failure, as the mechanical dynamics of the horizontal paddlewheels required too much coal in comparison with other, more efficient propulsion designs, such as the Ericcson screw propeller used in the *Monitor.*
42. Robert Erwin Johnson, *Thence Round Cape Horn: The Story of United States Naval Forces on Pacific Station 1818–1923* (Annapolis: Naval Institute Press, 1963), 25; Charles Lee Lewis, *Admiral Franklin Buchanan: Fearless Man of Action* (Baltimore: Norman, Remington Company, 1929), 47.
43. Nathaniel Philbrick, *Sea of Glory* (New York: Viking Penguin, 2003), 55.
44. Shayne Whiting, "Due South," *The Day Book* (August 1995):5.
45. James H. Ellis, *Mad Jack Percival: Legend of the Old Navy* (Annapolis: Naval Institute Press, 2002), 159.
46. Lewis, *Admiral Franklin Buchanan: Fearless Man of Action,* 80.; Samuel Eliot Morison, *Old Bruin: Commodore Matthew C. Perry 1794–1858* (Boston: Little, Brown and Co., 1967), 289.

47. "The Japanese Embassy, Arrival of the Roanoke at Hampton Roads," *New York Times,* 14 May 1860, 4. The Navy would also arrange to return the Japanese delegation to Japan in the screw frigate *Niagara,* completing the delegation's historic round-the-world trip in 1861.
48. Ashbrook, *The History of Our Navy Yard,* 6.; *Annual Report of the Secretary of the Navy* (Washington, DC: Government Printing Office, 1847); Law, *Norfolk Naval Shipyard: Its Remarkable History,* 63; Goodwin, "Architectural Inventory of Norfolk Naval Shipyard & Satellite Activities, Portsmouth, VA," 28; Edward P. Lull, *History of the United States Navy Yard at Gosport, Virginia (Near Norfolk)* (Washington, DC: Government Printing Office, 1874), 42.
49. Benjamin Franklin Cooling, *The New American State Papers, 1789–1860* (Wilmington, Del.: Scholarly Resources, 1979), 141; *Annual Report of the Secretary of the Navy* (Washington, DC: Government Printing Office, 1851); David A. Clary, *Fortress America: The Corps of Engineers, Hampton Roads, and United States Coastal Defense* (Charlottesville, Va.: University Press of Virginia, 1990), 52.
50. Jean A. Ponton, *Rear Admiral Louis M. Goldsborough, The Formation of a Nineteenth Century Naval Officer* (Washington, DC: Catholic University, 1996), 236.
51. Richmond C. Holcomb, *A Century with Norfolk Naval Hospital* (Portsmouth: Printcraft Publishing Co., 1930), 52.
52. Ibid., 68.
53. Ashbrook, *The History of Our Navy Yard,* 3; Law, *Norfolk Naval Shipyard: Its Remarkable History,* 404; Stewart, *History of Norfolk County, Virginia and Representative Citizens,* 429.
54. *United States Naval Hospital, Portsmouth, Virginia* (Philadelphia: Campus Publishing, 1944), 7.
55. Ibid.; William S. Forrest, *Historical and Descriptive Sketches of Norfolk and Vicinity* (Philadelphia: Lindsay and Blakiston, 1853), 190.; Holcomb, *A Century with Norfolk Naval Hospital,* 87.
56. Alan Flanders, "Yellow Jack's 1855 visit unforgettable," *Portsmouth Currents,* 7 September 2003, 3.
57. Holcomb, *A Century with Norfolk Naval Hospital,* 265; Ashbrook, *The History of Our Navy Yard,* 6.
58. Forrest, *Historical and Descriptive Sketches of Norfolk and Vicinity,* 322.
59. Ibid., 344.

1861

1. Christopher Martin, *Damn the Torpedos: The Story of America's First Admiral, David Glasgow Farragut* (New York: Abelard-Schuman, 1970), 153–54.
2. Charles Lee Lewis, *David Glasgow Farragut: Admiral in the Making* (Annapolis: U.S. Naval Institute, 1941), 290.
3. Ibid., 292; Martin, *Damn the Torpedos,* 154.
4. Lewis, *David Glasgow Farragut: Admiral in the Making,* 359.
5. Ibid. 289, 359; Brent Tarter, "The Barron Family," *Virginia Cavalcade,* Autumn 1998, 177.
6. Garrett J. Pendergast, *Letter Book of Flag Officer Garrett J. Pendergrast 1861.*
7. Gordon Calhoun, "A Classic American Warship," *The Daybook,* February 2004, 6.
8. A. W. Ashbrook, *The History of Our Navy Yard* (Portsmouth, Va.: Retirement Federation of Civil Service Employees, 1927), 7.
9. Joe Law, *Norfolk Naval Shipyard: Its Remarkable History* (Norfolk Naval Shipyard, unpublished), 69.
10. William H. Peters, "Inventory of Property Taken from the United States Government at the Navy Yard, Gosport and in and near Portsmouth, Virginia" (Portsmouth, Va.: 1861), 7.
11. Interestingly, Commodore McCauley's uncle and namesake, Charles Stewart, was still on the Navy List in 1861 as the Senior Flag Officer of the Navy. Commodore McCauley had been posted at the Gosport yard since 1 August 1860.
12. James Mason Hoppin, *Life of Andrew Hull Foote, Rear Admiral, United States Navy* (New York: Harper & Brothers, 1874), 147.
13. Gideon Welles, letter to Charles S. McCauley, 10 April 1861 (ORN I:4); Welles, letter to Charles S. McCauley, 11 April 1861 (ORN I:4); Welles, letter to Charles S. McCauley, 16 April 1861 (ORN I:4); Gideon Welles, ltr to Commander John Alden, 11 April 1861 (ORN I:4); Thomas O. Selfridge, Jr., *Memoirs of Thomas O. Selfridge, Jr.* (New York: Knickerbocker Press, 1924), 26; Joe Mosier, "The Man Who Lost Gosport: Commodore McCauley and the Burning of the Gosport Shipyard," *The Day Book,* March 1996, 8.
14. Welles, letter to Charles S. McCauley, 16 April 1861 (ORN I:4); Charles S. McCauley, letter to secretary of the navy, 16 April 1861 (ORN I:4).
15. John Marston, letter to G. J. Pendergrast, 17 April 1861 (ORN I:4); B. F. Isherwood, letter to secretary of the Navy, 18 April 1861 (ORN I:4); Mosier, "The Man Who Lost Gosport," 8.
16. John Niven, *Gideon Welles, Lincoln's Secretary of the Navy* (New York: Oxford University Press, 1973), 343.
17. Mosier, "The Man Who Lost Gosport," 9.
18. Eric Mills, *Chesapeake Bay in the Civil War* (Centreville, Md.: Tidewater Publishers, 1996), 16.
19. *Log of the USS Pawnee,* 19–20 April 1861; Robert Erwin Johnson, *Rear Admiral John Rodgers 1812–1882* (Annapolis: U.S. Naval Institute, 1967), 152; Selfridge, *Memoirs of Thomas O. Selfridge, Jr.,* 32.
20. Selfridge, *Memoirs of Thomas O. Selfridge, Jr.,* 34. Commander John Rodgers was the son of Commo. John Rodgers, the navy's first president of the Board of Navy Commissioners and War of 1812 hero.
21. Charles Wilkes, letter to Hiram Paulding, 22 April 1861 (ORN I:4); Mills, *Chesapeake Bay in the Civil War,* 28; H. G. Wright, letter to Lt. Col. E. D. Townsend, 26 April

1861 (Official Records Union and Confederate Armies I:2). After a Senate committee investigation of the loss of Gosport, the Navy quietly retired Flag Officer Charles S. McCauley on 21 December 1861. He died on 21 May 1869.

22. Thomas B. Buell, "Saga of Drydock One," *U.S. Naval Institute Proceedings,* July 1970, 65.
23. "The Burning of the Gosport Navy Yard," *Scientific American,* 11 May 1861, 304.
24. Selfridge, *Memoirs of Thomas O. Selfridge, Jr.,* 35.
25. Hiram Paulding, letter to the secretary of the Navy, 23 April 1861 (ORN I:4).
26. Niven, *Gideon Welles, Lincoln's Secretary of the Navy,* 345.
27. William H. Stewart, *History of Norfolk County, Virginia and Representative Citizens* (Chicago: Biographical Publishing Company, 1902), 446.
28. Peters, "Inventory of Property Taken from the United States Government at the Navy Yard, Gosport and in and near Portsmouth, Virginia," 8.
29. *Official Records of the Union and Confederate Navies in the War of the Rebellion* (Washington: Government Printing Office, 1894), II-2, 628; John Letcher, "Appointment Instructions," 16 April 1861 (ORN I:4). Lieutenant Pegram held a commission as a lieutenant in the Confederate Navy dated 10 June 1861 and during the next two years commanded batteries at Pig's Point and Sewell's Point. Later, as a commander, he commanded blockade-runner *Nashville* and ironclads *Richmond* and *Virginia II* in the James River Squadron.
30. Richard N. Current, *Encyclopedia of the Confederacy* (New York: Simon & Schuster, 1993), 606.
31. *Dictionary of American Naval Fighting Ships* (Washington, DC: Government Printing Office, 1959).
32. Niven, *Gideon Welles, Lincoln's Secretary of the Navy,* 346.
33. Ashbrook, *The History of Our Navy Yard,* 8.
34. Garrett J. Pendergast, *Letter Book of Flag Officer Garrett J. Pendergrast 1861.*
35. Robert M. Browning, Jr., *From Cape Charles to Cape Fear, the North Atlantic Blockading Squadron During the Civil War* (Tuscaloosa: University of Alabama Press, 1993), 143.
36. Ibid., 10; Virgil Carrington Jones, *The Civil War at Sea: The Blockaders* (New York: Holt, Rinehart, Winston, 1960), 111.
37. John W. H. Porter, *A Record of Events in Norfolk County, Virginia From April 19th, 1861 to May 10th 1862* (Portsmouth, VA: W. A. Fiske, 1892), 233; Richmond C. Holcomb, *A Century with Norfolk Naval Hospital* (Portsmouth: Printcraft Publishing Co., 1930), 281. Surgeon Samuel Barrington, the only medical officer at the Portsmouth Naval Hospital to stay loyal to the Union, surrendered the facility on 20 April 1861. Commander Charles F. McIntosh, who commanded the Confederate battery at Fort Nelson/Hospital Point in the opening days of the Civil War would later fall as the commanding officer of ironclad *Louisiana* during Farragut's attack on New Orleans.
38. Mills, *Chesapeake Bay in the Civil War,* 72; David A. Clary, *Fortress America: The Corps of Engineers, Hampton Roads, and United States Coastal Defense* (Charlottesville: University Press of Virginia, 1990), 101.
39. Walter Gwynn, letter to Robert E. Lee, 20 May 1861; Porter, *A Record of Events in Norfolk County, Virginia From April 19th, 1861 to May 10th 1862,* 230; Garrett J. Pendergrast, *Letter Book of Flag Officer Garrett J. Pendergast, 1861.*
40. Hunt Lewis, "Beyond the Monitor and the Virginia," *The Day Book,* March 1996, 1; Alan Flanders, "Military's Presence Overhead Has Its Roots in the Civil War," *Portsmouth Currents,* 3; James H. Rochelle, "The Confederate Steamship Patrick Henry," *Southern Historical Society Papers,* 1896, 128; Mills, *Chesapeake Bay in the Civil War,* 82.
41. Daniel Ammen, "DuPont and the Port Royal Expedition," *Battles and Leaders of the Civil War,* 671; Browning, *From Cape Charles to Cape Fear, the North Atlantic Blockading Squadron During the Civil War,* 10.
42. Jones, *The Civil War at Sea: The Blockaders,* 224.
43. Robert W. Daly, *Aboard the USS Monitor, The Letters of Acting Paymaster William Frederick Keeler, U. S. Navy, to his Wife, Anna* (Annapolis: U.S. Naval Institute, 1964), 155.
44. Browning, *From Cape Charles to Cape Fear, the North Atlantic Blockading Squadron During the Civil War,* 160. When Norfolk fell to the Union, the *Brandywine* was moored at Norfolk and Gosport for stores and naval repairs.
45. Jones, *The Civil War at Sea: The Blockaders,* 208.
46. Ammen, "DuPont and the Port Royal Expedition," 674; Johnson, *Rear Admiral John Rodgers 1812–1882,* 172; Robert Means Thompson and Richard Wainwright, *Confidential Correspondence of Gustavus Vasa Fox* (New York: De Vinne Press, 1920), I:205.
47. Jones, *The Civil War at Sea: The Blockaders,* 110.
48. Stephen R. Mallory, "Report of the Secretary of the Navy," (Richmond: 1862), 174; John L. Porter, "The Plan and Construction of the Merrimac," *Battles and Leaders of the Civil War,* 717.
49. Alan B. Flanders, *The Merrimac: The Story of the Conversion of the USS Merrimac into the Confederate Ironclad Warship CSS Virginia,* 1982), 40; John M. Brooke, "The Plan and Construction of the Merrimac," *Battles and Leaders of the Civil War,* 716; Jones, *The Civil War at Sea: The Blockaders,* 158.
50. Flanders, *The Merrimac: The Story of the Conversion of the USS Merrimac into the Confederate Ironclad Warship CSS Virginia,* 60.
51. William H. Roberts, *Civil War Ironclads* (Baltimore: Johns Hopkins University Press, 2002), 14.
52. Niven, *Gideon Welles, Lincoln's Secretary of the Navy,* 364.
53. *Galena* followed *Monitor;* it was commissioned on 21 April and arrived in Hampton Roads in May. Her ironclad career was short, however. She suffered from iron siding too light to resist enemy fire, and she finished the war re-rigged as an unarmored sloop-of-war. *New Ironsides* joined the Navy on

21 August 1862. She sailed first to Hampton Roads but then on to duty with the South Atlantic Blockading Squadron.

54. Thompson and Wainwright, *Confidential Correspondence of Gustavus Vasa Fox,* I:246.
55. A. A. Hoehling, *Thunder at Hampton Roads* (Englewood Cliffs, N.J.: Prentice-Hall, 1976), 85.
56. Arthur Sinclair, "How the Merrimac Fought the Monitor," *Heart's Magazine,* December 1913, 887. Captain Arthur Sinclair III would later command Confederate ironclad *Mississippi* and would be lost at sea in command of Confederate blockade runner *Lelia* in 1865. After the Battle of Hampton Roads, Arthur Sinclair IV served for two years aboard the Confederate raider *Alabama.*
57. Hoehling, *Thunder at Hampton Roads,* 75.
58. Ibid., 81, 6.; Charles Lee Lewis, *Admiral Franklin Buchanan: Fearless Man of Action* (Baltimore: Norman, Remington Company, 1929), 181.
59. Lewis, *Admiral Franklin Buchanan: Fearless Man of Action,* 183.
60. Ibid.
61. John V. Quarstein, *CSS Virginia: Mistress of Hampton Roads* (Appomattox: H. E. Howard, Inc., 2000), 74.
62. Hoehling, *Thunder at Hampton Roads,* 101.
63. E. V. White, *The First Iron-clad Naval Engagement in the World* (New York: J. S. Ogilvie Publishing Company, 1906), 14.
64. Selfridge, *Memoirs of Thomas O. Selfridge, Jr.,* 46.
65. Lewis, *Admiral Franklin Buchanan: Fearless Man of Action,* 185. There are several versions of Buchanan's final exhortation, all generally in agreement.
66. Quarstein, *CSS Virginia: Mistress of Hampton Roads,* 79.
67. Selfridge, *Memoirs of Thomas O. Selfridge, Jr.,* 48.
68. Ibid.
69. Ibid., 52. *Cumberland's* final broadsides probably caused *Virginia's* principal damage to her armor plating that was identified later in dry dock.
70. R. E. Colston, "Watching the Merrimac," *Battles and Leaders of the Civil War,* 712.
71. Lewis, *Admiral Franklin Buchanan: Fearless Man of Action,* 187. Inspired by both the Confederate conversion of *Merrimack* into an ironclad and by the turret design of *Monitor,* a Battle of Hampton Roads bystander, steam-frigate *Roanoke* was sent to the New York Navy Yard in March 1862 to be cut down and rebuilt as a triple-turret seagoing armored warship. She was sent to Hampton Roads in late June 1863 to rejoin the blockade and, although her deep draft restricted her to the main shipping channels, her six heavy guns provided a final barrier in case the Confederate ironclads on the James River should break out. Although probably envisioned as a formidable ironclad to deter foreign intervention in the war, her seagoing capabilities were found to be substandard, and she was restricted to traditional harbor defense roles for the duration.
72. Colston, "Watching the Merrimac," 713.
73. S. Dana Greene, "The Monitor at Sea and in Battle," *U.S. Naval Institute Proceedings,* November, 1923, 1842.
74. Hoehling, *Thunder at Hampton Roads,* 130.
75. Colston, "Watching the Merrimac," 714.
76. Ibid., 701; John Taylor Wood, "The First Fight of Iron-clads."
77. Rochelle, "The Confederate Steamship Patrick Henry," 131.
78. Dinwiddie B. Phillips, "Notes on the Monitor-Merrimac Fight," Battles and Leaders of the Civil War, 718; Hoehling, *Thunder at Hampton Roads,* 153. Captain Buchanan was advanced to admiral (flag officer) effective 26 August 1862, "for gallant and meritorious conduct in attacking the enemy's fleet in Hampton roads and destroying the frigate *Congress,* sloop of war *Cumberland* and three small steamers, whilst in command of the squadron in the waters of Virginia on the 8th of March 1862."
79. John Taylor Wood, "The First Fight of Iron-clads," *Battles and Leaders of the Civil War,* 703.
80. Hoehling, *Thunder at Hampton Roads,* 154.; Greene, "The Monitor at Sea and in Battle," 1843.
81. Hoehling, *Thunder at Hampton Roads,* 156.
82. J. L. Worden and H. Ashton Ramsay, *The Monitor and the Merrimac* (New York: Harper & Brothers Publishers, 1912), 50.
83. Hoehling, *Thunder at Hampton Roads,* 160.
84. Worden and Ramsay, *The Monitor and the Merrimac,* 52.
85. Greene, "The Monitor at Sea and in Battle," 1845.
86. Gustavus V. Fox, telegram to secretary of the Navy, 9 March 1862 (ORN I:7).
87. Porter, "The Plan and Construction of the Merrimac," 717; Wood, "The First Fight of Iron-clads," 706.
88. Louis M. Goldsborough, letter to Mrs. L. M. Goldsborough, 14 March 1862 (Goldsborough Papers); Thompson and Wainwright, *Confidential Correspondence of Gustavus Vasa Fox,* I:249.
89. Virgil Carrington Jones, *The Civil War at Sea: The River War* (New York: Holt, Rinehart, Winston, 1961), 8; *Official Records of the Union and Confederate Navies in the War of the Rebellion,* I-7, 83; Browning, *From Cape Charles to Cape Fear, the North Atlantic Blockading Squadron During the Civil War,* 48; Lieutenant Thomas Selfridge, late the executive officer of *Cumberland,* relieved Lieutenant Dana Greene on the evening of 9 March 1862 as temporary commander of *Monitor.* He was relieved by Lt. William Jeffers.
90. Louis M. Goldsborough, *Letter Book of Flag Officer L. M. Goldsborough,* 1861.
91. Ibid.
92. Ibid.
93. Goldsborough, letter to Mrs. L. M. Goldsborough, 6 April 1862 (Goldsborough Papers); Stephen W. Sears, *George B. McClellan: The Young Napoleon* (New York: Ticknor & Fields, 1988), 168.
94. Jones, *The Civil War at Sea: The River War,* 19.

95. Goldsborough, *Letter Book of Flag Officer L. M. Goldsborough.*
96. Goldsborough, letter to Mrs. L. M. Goldsborough, 14 March 1862 (Goldsborough Papers).
97. Jones, *The Civil War at Sea: The River War,* 23. Maury gunboats *Portsmouth, Norfolk, Nansemond* and *Hampton* would be completed at Gosport but only *Hampton* and *Nansemond* would see service in the James River Squadron, with the others burned on the stocks at Gosport in 1862.
98. *Dictionary of American Naval Fighting Ships,*
99. Browning, *From Cape Charles to Cape Fear, the North Atlantic Blockading Squadron During the Civil War,* 51; James Russell Soley, "The Navy in the Peninsular Campaign," Battles and Leaders of the Civil War, 266.
100. Porter, *A Record of Events in Norfolk County, Virginia From April 19th, 1861 to May 10th 1862,* 243; Stewart, *History of Norfolk County, Virginia and Representative Citizens,* 453. Captain Sydney Smith Lee, the brother of Robert E. Lee, had a distinguished naval career spanning over forty years. He had been at the siege of Vera Cruz during the Mexican War, served three years as the commandant of the Naval Academy, and had commanded Perry's flagship on the expedition to open Japan for trade. One son was Major General Fitzhugh Lee of Confederate cavalry fame, and a second son served as a midshipman aboard Confederate cruiser *Shenandoah.*
101. Flag Officer French Forrest would command the Confederate James River Squadron from March 1863 to May 1864 but was replaced by Secretary Mallory and was apparently dismissed from Confederate service.
102. J. E. Johnston, letter to Flag Officer Tattnall, 1 May 1862 (ORN II:1).
103. Thompson and Wainwright, *Confidential Correspondence of Gustavus Vasa Fox,* I:266; Jones, *The Civil War at Sea: The River War,* 24.; *Official Records of the Union and Confederate Navies in the War of the Rebellion,* I:7,331.
104. Goldsborough, letter to Mrs. L. M. Goldsborough, 7 May 1862 (Goldsborough Papers).
105. Wood, "The First Fight of Iron-clads," 709. In nautical usage, firing a gun to the disengaged side in these circumstances was tantamount to a call to defend one's honor. Tattnall was making the point that *Virginia* was fully ready to join in worthy combat and looked with disgust at *Monitor's* avoidance of a fight.
106. Thompson and Wainwright, *Confidential Correspondence of Gustavus Vasa Fox,* I:267.
107. Wood, "The First Fight of Iron-clads," 710.
108. Buell, "Saga of Drydock One," 66.
109. Jones, *The Civil War at Sea: The River War,* 28.
110. Wood, "The First Fight of Iron-clads," 710.
111. George Holbert Tucker, *Norfolk Highlights 1584–1881* (Norfolk: Norfolk Historical Society, 1972), 95.
112. Law, *Norfolk Naval Shipyard: Its Remarkable History,* 92; Ashbrook, *The History of Our Navy Yard,* 9.
113. Goldsborough, letter to Mrs. L. M. Goldsborough, 12 May 1862 (Goldsborough Papers).
114. Stephen Mallory, "Report of the Secretary of the Navy," 1862), 243.
115. Thompson and Wainwright, *Confidential Correspondence of Gustavus Vasa Fox,* I:276.
116. Ibid., I:277. Fort Norfolk was not handed back to the Navy until March 1863.
117. Holcomb, *A Century With Norfolk Naval Hospital,* 299.
118. Ibid., 376.
119. Goldsborough, *Letter Book of Flag Officer L. M. Goldsborough.*
120. Johnson, *Rear Admiral John Rodgers 1812–1882,* 206; Thompson and Wainwright, *Confidential Correspondence of Gustavus Vasa Fox,* I:288.
121. Lee to Jefferson Davis, 4 July 1862, quoted in Johnson, *Rear Admiral John Rodgers 1812–1882,* 213. On 4 July 1862, *Monitor* and the double-ender gunboat *Maratanza* captured the armed tug *Teaser* above City Point. *Teaser* had long been a thorn in the Union's side and was served as both a minelayer and tender for observation balloons.
122. John Rodgers, letter to Flag Officer Goldsborough, 29 June 1862 (ORN I:7).
123. Mark K. Ragan, *Union and Confederate Submarine Warfare in the Civil War,* Savas Publishing, 1999.
124. Thompson and Wainwright, *Confidential Correspondence of Gustavus Vasa Fox,* I:284.
125. Johnson, *Rear Admiral John Rodgers 1812–1882,* 217.
126. Gideon Welles, telegram to Charles Wilkes, 17 August 1862 (ORN I:7).
127. James Russell Soley, "The Union and Confederate Navies," Battles and Leaders of the Civil War, 630.
128. Frances Leigh Williams, *Matthew Fontaine Maury* (New Brunswick: Rutgers University Press, 1963), 378.
129. Browning, *From Cape Charles to Cape Fear, the North Atlantic Blockading Squadron During the Civil War,* 123. Spar torpedoes (explosive devices attached to the end of harpoon-like spar, rammed into the side of ship and then detonated by the attacking ship) were also designed that could be aimed below an ironclad's protective side armor, making the ironclad vulnerable to attack.
130. Ragan, *Union and Confederate Submarine Warfare in the Civil War.* After the failed submerged attack on Minnesota, other Confederate submersibles were also said to have been designed or built by the Tredeger Iron Works in Richmond.
131. R. Thomas Campbell, *Academy on the James* (Shippensburg, PA: Burd Street Press, 1998), 142. Benjamin Pollard Loyall of Norfolk, a U. S. Naval Academy graduate, served as a lieutenant in the Confederate Navy with duty at Gosport and during the Battle of Roanoke Island. He was a member of a secret expedition to release Confederates from a prison on Lake Erie and was meritoriously promoted to commander in February 1865 for actions in cutting out the Federal gunboat *Underwriter* at New Berne, North Carolina.

132. Browning, *From Cape Charles to Cape Fear, the North Atlantic Blockading Squadron During the Civil War,* 72, 80; William N. Jr. Still, *Iron Afloat: the Story of the Confederate Armorclads* (Indianapolis: Vanderbuilt University Press, 1971), 185.
133. John W. Grattan, *Under the Blue Pennant* (New York: John Wiley & Sons, 1999), 56. Commodore John W. Livingston assumed command of Norfolk Navy Yard on 20 May 1862 and was relieved by Captain John M. Berrien on 16 November 1864 who remained in command of the Yard for the duration of the war.
134. Ashbrook, *The History of Our Navy Yard,* 9; Thompson and Wainwright, *Confidential Correspondence of Gustavus Vasa Fox,* II:266.
135. An accidental fire destroyed *Brandywine* on 3 September 1864 while alongside the Norfolk Navy Yard.
136. *Dictionary of American Naval Fighting Ships*; Johnson, *Rear Admiral John Rodgers 1812–1882,* 273. The Confederate ironclad *Atlanta,* captured by Union forces, arrived at the Gosport shipyard for repairs before joining the Union James River Flotilla in 1864. The Confederate ironclad ram *Albemarle,* designed by Porter on an improved *Virginia* design, was likewise sent to the yard for repairs after her capture at the end of the war.
137. Niven, *Gideon Welles, Lincoln's Secretary of the Navy,* 460.
138. Grattan, *Under the Blue Pennant,* 145.
139. Martin, *Damn the Torpedos: The Story of America's First Admiral, David Glasgow Farragut,* 268.
140. Tarter, "The Barron Family," 173.
141. *Official Records of the Union and Confederate Navies in the War of the Rebellion,* I:2, 681; Tarter, "The Barron Family," 177. *Florida* was sailed to Hampton Roads after her disputed capture in a neutral Brazilian harbor. On 28 November 1864, *Florida* sank in Hampton Roads following a collision with a troop ferry under suspicious circumstances, possibly to remove the diplomatic embarrassment of her illegal capture by Union gunboat *Wachusett* in a neutral Brazilian port.
142. Dana Greene, "In the Monitor Turrett," *Battles and Leaders of the Civil War,* 729.
143. P. Drayton, report to Rear Admiral S. P. Lee, 1 January 1863 (ORN I:8).
144. Jones, *The Civil War at Sea: The River War,* 315.

1898

1. A. W. Ashbrook, *The History of Our Navy Yard* (Portsmouth, Va.: Retirement Federation of Civil Service Employees, 1927), 9.
2. Gordon Calhoun, "The Norfolk Navy Yard During the Navy's Dark Ages," *The Day Book* (March 2003): 6; Richmond C. Holcomb, *A Century with Norfolk Naval Hospital* (Portsmouth, Va.: Printcraft Publishing Co., 1930), 302.
3. Kenneth Wimmel, *Theodore Roosevelt and the Great White Fleet* (Dulles, Va.: Brassey's, 1998), 2; A. C. Cunningham, "The Development of the Norfolk Navy Yard," *U.S. Naval Institute Proceedings* (March 1910): 227.
4. Lenoir Chambers and Joseph E. Shank, *Salt Water & Printers Ink* (Chapel Hill: University of North Carolina Press, 1967), 94.
5. Calhoun, "The Norfolk Navy Yard During the Navy's Dark Ages," 15.
6. Ibid., 7.
7. John V. Quarstein, *CSS Virginia: Mistress of Hampton Roads* (Appomattox: H. E. Howard, Inc., 2000), 188.
8. *Annual Report of the Secretary of the Navy* (Washington, DC: Government Printing Office, 1881). Navy units attending the naval review on 12–13 October 1879 included the *Kearsarge, Minnesota, Portsmouth, Saratoga, Constitution, Tallaposa, Marion,* and *Powhatan.*
9. Secretary of the Navy, Report of the Commission on Navy Yards, 1 December 1883.
10. Joe Law, *Norfolk Naval Shipyard: Its Remarkable History* (Norfolk Naval Shipyard, unpublished), 119; Marshall W. Butt, *Norfolk Naval Shipyard, a Brief History* (Portsmouth, Va.: Public Information Office, NNSY, 1951), 8.
11. Fourteen of the most modern American warships attended the International Columbian Naval Rendezvous in Tidewater on 17–24 April 1893, headed by the new steel cruisers *Philadelphia* (C-4), *Atlanta, Baltimore* (C-3), *Chicago* (commanded by Capt. Alfred Thayer Mahan), *Newark* (C-1), *Vesuvius, Charleston* (C-2), and *San Francisco* (C-5); the steel dispatch boat *Dolphin;* the gunboats *Yorktown* (PG-1), *Bennington* (PG-4), and *Concord* (PG-3); the torpedo boat *Cushing* (TB-1); and the monitor *Miantonomoh.*
12. Joe Mosier, "The Steel Navy on Display," *The Day Book* (May 1997):6.
13. Ibid., 7.
14. William H. Stewart, *History of Norfolk County, Virginia and Representative Citizens* (Chicago: Biographical Publishing Company, 1902), 464.
15. John Frye, *Hampton Roads and Four Centuries as a World's Seaport* (Lewiston, N.Y.: Edwin Mellen Press, 1996), 86. Not all of Collis P. Huntington's business operations were as straightforward as those involving the establishment of Newport News Shipbuilding. He was accused, probably correctly, of both "buying" the California legislature and bribing congressman to promote his transcontinental railroad interests.
16. *Three Generations of Shipbuilding* (Newport News, Va.: Newport News Shipbuilding and Drydock Co., 1961), 4; Gordon Calhoun, "The Birth of a Giant," *The Day Book,* (May 1997):4.
17. Frye, *Hampton Roads and Four Centuries as a World's Seaport,* 87.
18. *Three Generations of Shipbuilding,* 10.; William E. Blewett, Jr., *Always Good Ships: A History of the Newport News*

Shipbuilding and Dry Dock Company (New York: Newcomen Society in North America, 1960), 10; Calhoun, "The Birth of a Giant," 8. The first naval boats built at Newport News for the Navy were the gunboats *Nashville, Wilmington,* and *Helena,* which were launched in 1895–1896.

19. Frye, *Hampton Roads and Four Centuries as a World's Seaport,* 89; John D. Alden, *The American Steel Navy* (Annapolis: Naval Institute Press, 1972), 121.
20. "Kentucky and Kearsarge," *Norfolk Dispatch,* 1; Chambers and Shank, *Salt Water & Printers Ink,* 207. *Kentucky* was scrapped in 1924, but *Kearsarge* survived until 1955 as the Navy's only crane ship.
21. *Three Generations of Shipbuilding,* 25.
22. Ira R. Hanna, *The Growth of Norfolk Naval Air Station and the Norfolk-Portsmouth Metropolitan Area Economy in the Twentieth Century* (Norfolk: Old Dominion, 1967), 6; Frye, *Hampton Roads and Four Centuries as a World's Seaport,* 99.
23. Alden, *The American Steel Navy,* 229.
24. Winfield Scott Schley, *Forty-Five Years Under the Flag* (New York: D. Appleton and Company, 1904), 259; Wimmel, *Theodore Roosevelt and the Great White Fleet,* 107. After establishing the Flying Squadron in Hampton Roads, Schley detached *Columbia* and *Minneapolis* to patrol the waters off New England and added protected cruiser *New Orleans,* yacht *Scorpion,* and collier *Sterling* to his force in Hampton Roads.
25. Schley, *Forty-Five Years Under the Flag,* 260.
26. Joe Mosier, "A Splendid Little Squadron," *The Day Book* (February 1995):6; David A. Clary, *Fortress America: The Corps of Engineers, Hampton Roads, and United States Coastal Defense* (Charlottesville: University Press of Virginia, 1990), 145; Stewart, *History of Norfolk County, Virginia and Representative Citizens,* 467; *United States Naval Hospital, Portsmouth, Virginia* (Philadelphia: Campus Publishing, 1944), 8.
27. Schley, *Forty-Five Years Under the Flag,* 261.
28. Holcomb, *A Century with Norfolk Naval Hospital,* 333.
29. R. Christopher Goodwin and Associates Inc., "Architectural Inventory of Norfolk Naval Shipyard & Satellite Activities, Portsmouth, VA" (Norfolk, Va.: Navy Region Mid-Atlantic, 2003), 41; Frederick S. Harrod, *Manning the New Navy, the Development of a Modern Naval Enlisted Force* (Westport, Conn.: Greenwood Press, 1978), 90; Cunningham, "The Development of the Norfolk Navy Yard," 236.
30. R. E. B. Stewart, "The Norfolk Navy Yard," *Jamestown Magazine,* 16. A torpedo flotilla station had been developed shortly after the turn of the century at the southern end of St. Helena but was removed to the Charleston, South Carolina Navy Yard by 1910.
31. Harrod, *Manning the New Navy,* 78.
32. A. C. Dillingham, "US Naval Training Service," *U.S. Naval Institute Proceedings* (June 1910):235.
33. Harrod, *Manning the New Navy,* 86.
34. Wimmel, *Theodore Roosevelt and the Great White Fleet,* 213.
35. *Final Report of the Jamestown Ter-Centennial Commission* (Washington, DC: Government Printing Office, 1909), 61.
36. Joseph Bucklin Bishop, *Theodore Roosevelt's Letters to his Children* (New York: C. Scribner's sons, 1919); Dan Smith, *From Here to There, Stories from a Mobile Virginia* (Richmond: Virginia Museum of Transportation, 1998).
37. *Final Report of the Jamestown Ter-Centennial Commission,* 58; Thomas J. Wertenbaker, *Norfolk: Historic Southern Port* (Durham: Duke University Press, 1931), 298.
38. "Naval Training Station Not Improbable," *Virginian-Pilot,* 9 November 1907, 1.
39. Ibid. Brownson was better known in the Navy for his resignation as a rear admiral and the director of the Bureau of Navigation in protest over Theodore Roosevelt's decision to give command of Navy hospital ships to doctors.
40. Chambers and Shank, *Salt Water & Printers Ink,* 268.
41. Wimmel, *Theodore Roosevelt and the Great White Fleet,* 202, 20.
42. Ibid., 221.
43. Ibid., 223.
44. Robert A. Hart, *The Great White Fleet: Its Voyage Around the World, 1907–1909* (Boston: Little, Brown and Company, 1965), 56.
45. Ibid., 49.
46. Wimmel, *Theodore Roosevelt and the Great White Fleet,* xiii.; Alden, *The American Steel Navy,* 333. Great White Fleet battleships *Kearsarge, Kentucky, Illinois, Missouri, Virginia, Louisiana,* and *Minnesota* were all products of Newport News Shipbuilding.
47. Robert D. Jones, *With the American Fleet from the Atlantic to the Pacific* (Seattle: Harrison Publishing Co., 1908), 218.
48. Hart, *The Great White Fleet: Its Voyage Around the World, 1907–1909,* 46.
49. Jones, *With the American Fleet from the Atlantic to the Pacific,* 21.
50. Ibid., 23.
51. Ibid., 25.
52. Edmund Morris, *Theodore Rex* (New York: Modern Library, 2001), 503.
53. Franklin Matthews, *With the Battle Fleet* (New York: B. W. Huebsch, 1908), 2.
54. Bruce Linder, *San Diego's Navy* (Annapolis: Naval Institute Press, 2001), 37.
55. Hart, *The Great White Fleet: Its Voyage Around the World, 1907–1909,* 293.
56. Wimmel, *Theodore Roosevelt and the Great White Fleet,* 243.

1914

1. Archibald D. Turnbull and Clifford L. Lord, *History of United States Naval Aviation* (New Haven: Yale University Press, 1949), 11; Vice Adm. Donald D. Engen, "Eugene

Ely—First from the Sea," *Foundation,* Spring 1995, 42; "Ely to Launch Biplane from Cruiser Birmingham," *Virginian-Pilot,* 13 November 1910, 1.

2. Alan Flanders, "Flying off Flattops Has Roots in Hampton Roads," *Portsmouth Currents,* 15 June 2003, 3; Charles M. Melhorn, *Two-Block Fox, the Rise of the Aircraft Carrier 1911–1929* (Annapolis: Naval Institute Press, 1974), 8.
3. *Log of USS Birmingham,* 14 November 1910.
4. "Ely Successfully Launches Biplane From Cruiser in Hampton Roads," *Virginian-Pilot,* 15 November 1910.
5. Engen, "Eugene Ely—First from the Sea," 46.
6. Simon Lake, *The Submarine in War and Peace* (Philadelphia: J. B. Lippincott Company, 1918), 182.
7. *Three Generations of Shipbuilding* (Newport News: Newport News Shipbuilding and Drydock Co., 1961), 108. After the U.S. Navy had rejected Simon Lake's *Protector* submarine design, five sisters of *Protector* were partially built at Newport News Shipbuilding by Simon Lake and sold to the Russian navy.
8. George Van Deurs, *Anchors in the Sky: Spuds Ellyson, the First Naval Aviator* (San Rafael, Calif.: Presidio Press, 1978), 170. Lieutenant Theodore Ellyson received his flying instruction from airplane inventor Glenn Curtiss in San Diego in 1911. When the Navy agreed to purchase two of Curtiss's "hydroaeroplanes" (sea planes) to form the Navy's first aviation squadron, Ellyson was designated as "Naval Aviator No. 1."
9. John J. Poluhowich, *Argonaut: The Submarine Legacy of Simon Lake* (College Station: Texas A&M University Press, 1999), 113; *Dictionary of American Naval Fighting Ships* (Washington, DC: Government Printing Office, 1959); Edward C. Whitman, "The Submarine Heritage of Simon Lake," *Undersea Warfare,* fourth quarter 2002,
10. "Destroyers Go to Capes," *New York Times,* 16 July 1916, 2; "Three Cruisers on Watch," *New York Times,* 19 July 1916, 1.
11. Ira R. Hanna, *The Growth of Norfolk Naval Air Station and the Norfolk-Portsmouth Metropolitan Area Economy in the Twentieth Century* (Norfolk: Old Dominion, 1967), 9–11.
12. Admiral Harrington had been a commandant of the Norfolk Navy Yard (1903–1906) and was called upon to periodically write the secretary of the navy and the chief of naval operations on Norfolk's behalf.
13. "Norfolk in By-Gone Days," *Ledger-Dispatch,* 11 November 1937, 14.
14. Ibid.
15. "Secretary Daniels Pays First Visit to the Norfolk Navy Yard," *Virginian-Pilot,* 4 April 1913, 1.
16. Gordon Calhoun and Joe Judge, "The Navy Builds a Home," *The Day Book,* November 1997, 7.
17. *Board of Directors Minutes, Norfolk Chamber of Commerce* (Norfolk: 1913), 11 November 1913; *Board of Directors Minutes, Norfolk Chamber of Commerce* (Norfolk: 1915), 20 July 1915.
18. *Board of Directors Minutes, Norfolk Chamber of Commerce,* 2 December 1915; *Board of Directors Minutes, Norfolk Chamber of Commerce* (Norfolk: 1916), 1 February 1916.
19. U.S. Atlantic Fleet Commander-in-Chief, "Permanent Rendezvous for the Atlantic Fleet," 1915 (RG 80 National Archives)
20. *Board of Directors Minutes, Norfolk Chamber of Commerce,* 3 April 1916; *Annual Report of the Secretary of the Navy* (Washington, DC: Government Printing Office, 1916), 198.
21. Frederick S. Harrod, *Manning the New Navy, the Development of a Modern Naval Enlisted Force* (Westport, CT: Greenwood Press, 1978), 81.
22. Bureau of Construction and Repair, Report of the Bureau of Construction and Repair to the Commissionon for Navy Yards and Naval Stations, 14 October 1916; *United States Naval Administration in World War II (DCNO-Air)* (Washington: 1945), 37–9; Turnbull and Lord, *History of United States Naval Aviation,* 75.
23. Josephus Daniels, letter to Senator Claude Swanson, 10 October 1916 (RG80, National Archives).
24. Theodore J. Wool, letter to secretary of the navy, 27 November 1916 (RG80, National Archives).
25. "Thinks Jamestown Site is Desirable," *Virginian-Pilot,* 7 January 1917, 1; Bruce E. Field, *Norfolk in Wartime: The Effect of the First World War on the Expansion of a Southern City* (East Carolina University, 1978), 32.
26. *Board of Directors Minutes, Norfolk Chamber of Commerce* (Norfolk: 1917), 7 April 1917, 3 July 1917; E. David Cronan, *The Cabinet Diaries of Josephus Daniels, 1913–1921* (Lincoln: University of Nebraska Press, 1963), 162.
27. Ray Stannard Baker, *Woodrow Wilson: Life and Letters* (New York: Doubleday, Doran and Company, 1939), 108.; Cronan, *The Cabinet Diaries of Josephus Daniels, 1913–1921,* 163; *United States Naval Administration in World War II (Fifth Naval District)* (Washington, DC: U.S. Navy, 1945), 72; Josephus Daniels, letter to the Speaker of the House of Representatives, 9 June 1917 (RG80, National Archives).
28. Thomas Shelton, letter to secretary of the navy, 17 February 1916 (RG80, National Archives); Stephen Paul Nasca, *Norfolk in the First World War,* (Norfolk: Old Dominion University, 1979), 18; *An Act to Supply the Military and Naval Establishment on Account of War,* 1917; "Naval Base Is Taken by US," *Ledger Dispatch,* 5 July 1917, 1.
29. "Report of Board Covering Valuation of Site For Naval Operating Base, Hampton Roads, VA" (Washington, DC: Government Printing Office, 1918), 6; Calhoun and Judge, "The Navy Builds a Home," 7; Thomas C. Parramore, *Norfolk, The First Four Centuries* (Charlottesville: University Press of Virginia, 1994), 287. Board on Compensation, "Report of the Board on Compensation for Site Naval Operating Base," 1917), Total land area = 473.9 acres with waterfront of 17,925 feet. Exposition site (374 acres): assessed $270, 347; asked $1,909,647; awarded $885,630.

Pine Beach (100 acres): assessed $91,769; asked 1,057,988; awarded $537,305. Total: assessed $362,117; asked 3,009,925; awarded 1,422,935. The total was 222,925 greater than that appropriated, and Congress later approved this amount in an additional appropriation on 5 March 1918.

30. "Building Greatest Base for the Navy," *Virginian-Pilot,* 29 July 1917, 21; "Great Naval Base on Roads Aim of Experts," *Virginian-Pilot,* 1 January 1917, 1.
31. *Annual Report of the Secretary of the Navy* (Washington, DC: Government Printing Office, 1917), 49.
32. A. C. Dillingham, "US Naval Training Service," *US Naval Institute Proceedings,* June 1910, 347.
33. *United States Naval Administration in World War II (Fifth Naval District),* 73.; *Board of Directors Minutes, Norfolk Chamber of Commerce,* 16 July 1917; Parramore, *Norfolk, The First Four Centuries,* 288; Nasca, *Norfolk in the First World War,* 20.
34. "Formal Opening of Naval Base," *Virginian-Pilot,* 13 October 1917, 3; *United States Naval Administration in World War II (Fifth Naval District),* Suppl. 27. Dayton would leave the training station and the naval station in June 1918 to assume command of the battleship *Michigan,* where he would earn a Navy Cross for heading battleship gunnery training in the last days of World War I. He would later rise to the rank of vice admiral as Commander, Naval Forces Europe, before his retirement in 1930.
35. R. Christopher Goodwin and Associates Inc., "Architectural Inventory of Norfolk Naval Shipyard & Satellite Activities, Portsmouth, VA" (Norfolk, VA: Navy Region Mid-Atlantic, 2003), 44; Harrod, *Manning the New Navy, the Development of a Modern Naval Enlisted Force,* 226. The steel sailing bark *Cumberland* also served as a receiving ship at the St. Helena training station from 1914 until ordered to similar duty at Annapolis on 7 April 1919.
36. Lenoir Chambers and Joseph E. Shank, *Salt Water & Printers Ink* (Chapel Hill: University of North Carolina Press, 1967), 287; *Annual Report of the Secretary of the Navy,* 22; *United States Naval Administration in World War II (Fifth Naval District),* Suppl. 27.
37. *United States Naval Administration in World War II (Fifth Naval District),* Suppl. 24; Thomas J. Wertenbaker, *Norfolk: Historic Southern Port* (Durham: Duke University Press, 1931), 305; Calhoun and Judge, "The Navy Builds a Home," 8.
38. *United States Naval Administration in World War II (Fifth Naval District),* Suppl. 24, Suppl. 7; Calhoun and Judge, "The Navy Builds a Home," 8; *United States Naval Administration in World War II (Fifth Naval District), Appendix I* (Washington, DC: U.S. Navy, 1945), 70.
39. "Pave Way to Assure Naval Base Extension; May Donate The Site," *Virginian-Pilot,* 22 August 1918; Cronan, *The Cabinet Diaries of Josephus Daniels, 1913–1921,* 326.
40. Nasca, *Norfolk in the First World War,* 23.
41. *Board of Directors Minutes, Norfolk Chamber of Commerce* (Norfolk: 1918), 13 August 1918; *United States Naval Administration in World War II (Fifth Naval District),* Suppl. 27.
42. "Dredging in River," *Ledger-Dispatch,* 6 July 1917; Calhoun and Judge, "The Navy Builds a Home," 8.
43. *Board of Directors Minutes, Norfolk Chamber of Commerce,* 14 March 1916.
44. *United States Naval Administration in World War II (DCNO-Air),* 46; Turnbull and Lord, *History of United States Naval Aviation,* 77, 126.
45. Parke Rouse Jr., *The Good Old Days in Hampton and Newport News* (Richmond: The Dietz Press, 1986), 95; *United States Naval Administration in World War II (DCNO-Air),* 54–58. The Curtiss Exhibition Company trained naval aviators under contract at the company's Atlantic Coast Aeronautical Station at Newport News, which extended from the tip of Jefferson Avenue at the ferry docks northward to Salter's Creek.
46. *United States Naval Administration in World War II (Fifth Naval District),* Suppl. 27. Lieutenant Cecil volunteered for aviation duty in 1915 and was designated Naval Aviator #42 in late 1916. He was placed in charge of officers and men of the Naval Reserve at Newport News from May to September 1917. He died in the crash of the airship *Akron* in April 1933.
47. Ralph D. Paine, *The First Yale Unit: A Story of Naval Aviation 1916–1919* (Cambridge, Mass.: Riverside Press, 1925), 212; Paolo E. Coletta, *United States Navy and Marine Corps Bases, Domestic* (Westport, Conn.: Greenwood Press, 1985), 150. Lieutenant McDonnell was a recipient of the Medal of Honor, awarded at Vera Cruz in 1914. He later rose to the rank of vice admiral.
48. Paolo E. Coletta, *Patrick N. L. Bellinger* (Lanham, MD: University Press of America, 1987), 111.
49. "Training the 'Eyes of the Fleet' at the Naval Base," *Virginian-Pilot,* 14 October 1917, 29.
50. Paul Stillwell, *Reminiscences of Admiral Alfred M. Pride, US Navy (ret)* (Annapolis: 1984), 87; *United States Naval Administration in World War II (Fifth Naval District),* Suppl. 27.
51. Coletta, *Patrick N. L. Bellinger,* 115.; Nasca, *Norfolk in the First World War,* 26; *United States Naval Administration in World War II (Fifth Naval District).*
52. *United States Naval Administration in World War II (DCNO-Air),* 74, 91.
53. Director of Naval Aviation, "Weekly Report," (Washington, DC: 1918), 4 November 1918; Paine, *The First Yale Unit: A Story of Naval Aviation 1916–1919,* 225.
54. Director of Naval Aviation, "Weekly Report," 20 November 1918.
55. Ibid., 12 February 1919.
56. *Naval Air Station, Norfolk VA* (Atlanta, GA: Albert Love Enterprises, 1952). AGA beacon derives its name from its manufacturer, American Gas Accumulator.

57. Coletta, *United States Navy and Marine Corps Bases, Domestic,* 383.
58. Coletta, *Patrick N. L. Bellinger,* 206.
59. *United States Naval Administration in World War II (Fifth Naval District),* 3, 66, 8.
60. Ibid., 70; Coletta, *United States Navy and Marine Corps Bases, Domestic,* 381.; Josephus Daniels, General Order No. 363, 29 January 1918.
61. *United States Naval Administration in World War II (Fifth Naval District).*
62. John T. Mason, *Reminiscences of Vice Admiral Bernhard H. Bieri, US Navy (ret)* (Annapolis: 1970), 36. Admiral Fechteler served as commander of the Sixth Division, Battleship Force, Atlantic Fleet, during World War I. One of his sons, Admiral William M. Fechteler, would serve as the chief of naval operations from 1951 to 1953. Another son, Lt. Frank C. Fechteler, a naval aviator, served in the first squadron assigned to *Langley* (CV-1) but perished in an airplane crash near Detroit on 18 September 1922. *Fechteler* (DE-157) was launched on 22 April 1943 by Norfolk Navy Yard and commissioned on 1 July 1943.
63. Joe Law, *Norfolk Naval Shipyard: Its Remarkable History* (Norfolk Naval Shipyard, unpublished), 399; Frank J. Allston, *Ready for Sea: The Bicentennial History of the US Navy Supply Corps* (Annapolis: Naval Institute Press, 1995), 47. Pursers had been named as commissioned officers in the Navy beginning in 1812.
64. *Building the Navy's Bases in World War II* (Washington, DC: Government Printing Office, 1947), 293; *United States Naval Administration in World War II (Fifth Naval District),* Suppl. 27.
65. *Activities of the Bureau of Yards and Docks 1917–18* (Washington, DC: Government Printing Office, 1921), 66; E. H. Van Patten, "Hier: Aujourd'hui, Demain," *PEP (Norfolk Supply Station Newspaper),* 1; *United States Naval Administration in World War II (Fifth Naval District),* 451. The responsibility for and use of Craney Island varied between the wars, but the Navy formally annexed the site in 1939. The tanks, at the time, contained molasses, and so were prepared to hold fuel, and the Navy replaced the pier.
66. Field, *Norfolk in Wartime: The Effect of the First World War on the Expansion of a Southern City,* 77–79; Reginald Wheeler, *The Road to Victory: A History of Hampton Roads Port of Embarkation in World War II* (New Haven: Yale University Press, 1946), 8. The Newport News port of embarkation was second only to New York City in the transport of troops to Europe during World War I.
67. Chambers and Shank, *Salt Water & Printers Ink,* 297.
68. Ibid., 298; Parramore, *Norfolk, The First Four Centuries,* 295; Marvin W. Schlegel, *Conscripted City, Norfolk in World War II* (Norfolk: Norfolk War History Commission, 1951), 3.
69. A. C. Dillingham, letter to the Chief of Naval Operations, 30 January 1918 (RG80, National Archives).
70. "Norfolk Swept by Greatest Fire in Its History," *Virginian-Pilot,* 2 January 1918, 1.
71. Chambers and Shank, *Salt Water & Printers Ink,* 298.
72. Theodore A. Curtin, *A Marriage of Convenience: Norfolk and the Navy, 1917–1967* (Old Dominion College, 1969), 30.
73. Robert K. Massie, *Castles of Steel* (New York: Random House, 2003), 704.
74. William N. Still Jr., *The Queenstown Patrol 1917: The Diary of Commander Joseph Knefler Taussig* (Newport: Naval War College Press, 1996), 5.
75. *United States Naval Administration in World War II (Fifth Naval District),* Suppl. 27.
76. Ibid., Suppl. 27, 501; Edward C. Whitman, "The School of War: US Submarines in World War I," *Undersea Warfare,* Spring 2004.
77. *United States Naval Administration in World War II (Fifth Naval District),* Suppl. 23.
78. Chambers and Shank, *Salt Water & Printers Ink,* 297.
79. *United States Naval Administration in World War II (Fifth Naval District),* 109.
80. Whitman, "The School of War: US Submarines in World War I"; Edwin P. Hoyt, *U-boats Offshore: When Hitler Struck America* (New York: Stein and Day Publishers, 1978), 146. There were no reported casualties near Hampton Roads from the German mine offensive of mid-1918, but cruiser *San Diego* fell victim to one of these mines off Fire Island, New York, the largest American warship lost in the war. *U-151* sank six merchant ships 80–120 miles off Cape Henry by torpedo and gunnery between 4 June and 10 June 1918.
81. Massie, *Castles of Steel,* 755.
82. Ibid., 754.; Winston S. Churchill, *The World Crisis* (New York: Scribner's Sons, 1931), 213. The American battleship division sent to join the Grand Fleet in November 1917, all coal-burners, did not represent the U.S. Navy's most modern ships, all oil-fired, as oil shipments to England had been drastically curtailed by U-boat sinkings.
83. Massie, *Castles of Steel,* 759.; *Dictionary of American Naval Fighting Ships.*
84. *Architectural Investigations of St Juliens Creek Annex* (Norfolk: Atlantic Division, Naval Facilities Engineering Command, 1997), 12. Before July 1918, the St. Julien's Creek naval ammunition depot was a subordinate command of the Norfolk Navy Yard.
85. *United States Naval Administration in World War II (Fifth Naval District),* 103; Joe Judge, "Hampton Roads' Hidden History: St. Julien's Creek Annex," *The Day Book,* July 1997, 3; *Architectural Investigations of St Juliens Creek Annex,* 12-3.
86. Reginald R. Belknap, "The Yankee Mining Squadron," *U.S. Naval Institute Proceedings,* December 1919, 1998; Joe Mosier, "Another Nail in the Kaiser's Coffin: The North Sea Mine Barrage of 1918," *The Day Book,* January 1996, 9. In addition to the *Baltimore* and *San Francisco,* eight former

merchant ships were converted into mine layers, including two ships, SS *Jefferson* and SS *Hamilton,* that had provided New York-Norfolk passenger service for the Old Dominion Steamship Line.

87. Mosier, "Another Nail in the Kaiser's Coffin," 8.; Belknap, "The Yankee Mining Squadron," 2008.
88. Goodwin, "Architectural Inventory of Norfolk Naval Shipyard & Satellite Activities, Portsmouth, VA," 42. The "Schmoele Tract" was 272 acres of land acquired in 1902 that had been the site of an abortive self-contained manufacturing community to be called Virginia City. During 1918, the Norfolk Navy Yard also created the position of industrial manager to efficiently manage the buildup in industrial operations, naming Naval Constructor Richard M. Watt as Norfolk's first industrial manager.
89. "Belgian Rules Depart for Home," *Virginian-Pilot,* 1 November 1919, 1; "Norfolk Naval Shipyard, Portsmouth, Virginia: 200 Years of Service," *Virginian Pilot,* 1967, 29. The Schmoele site lay largely undeveloped between 1902 and 1917, although in 1913 plans were drawn to develop it into a natural basin for moored ships. Dry Dock No. 5 was never built, its space utilized for other purposes. Dry Dock No. 4 once held ten submarines and four fleet targets at one time in October 1920.
90. Norfolk Navy Yard Commandant, *General Order Relating to Management of Norfolk Navy Yard,* 1914); Law, *Norfolk Naval Shipyard: Its Remarkable History,* 152; Marshall W. Butt, *Norfolk Naval Shipyard, a Brief History* (Portsmouth, VA: Public Information Office, NNSY, 1951), 9.
91. I. I. Yates, "A Navy Yard in War Time," *US Naval Institute Proceedings,* May 1920, 717; Kenneth J. Hagan, *This People's Navy: The Making of American Sea Power* (New York: The Free Press, 1991), 255; Law, *Norfolk Naval Shipyard: Its Remarkable History,* 154. The *Craven* (*DD-70*) was provided to the Royal Navy in 1940, becoming HMS *Lewes.*
92. Yates, "A Navy Yard in War Time," 714; Butt, *Norfolk Naval Shipyard, a Brief History,* 9.
93. *United States Naval Hospital, Portsmouth, Virginia* (Philadelphia: Campus Publishing, 1944), 8–9. During the naval hospital's renovation between 1907 and 1910, all operations were moved to a camp 750 feet from construction, where fifty-four tents were erected on raised floorboards for patients. The main building of the old hospital was renovated by leaving the outer walls and the front portico standing but replacing everything inside with a new fireproof structure.
94. Ibid., 8.; Richmond C. Holcomb, *A Century with Norfolk Naval Hospital* (Portsmouth: Printcraft Publishing Co., 1930), 454.
95. William N. Still, "Everybody Sick with the Flu," *U.S. Naval Institute Proceedings,* April 2002, 37; Holcomb, *A Century with Norfolk Naval Hospital,* 417.
96. *United States Naval Hospital, Portsmouth, Virginia,* 9.
97. Still, "Everybody Sick with the Flu," 39.
98. Ibid., 37.; Field, *Norfolk in Wartime: The Effect of the First World War on the Expansion of a Southern City,* 49; Holcomb, *A Century with Norfolk Naval Hospital,* 417.
99. *United States Naval Administration in World War II (Fifth Naval District),* Suppl. 24, 75; "Admiral A. C. Dillingham," *Virginian-Pilot,* 8 December 1925, 6; *Virginian-Pilot,* 2.; Chambers and Shank, *Salt Water & Printers Ink,* 288.
100. Parramore, *Norfolk, The First Four Centuries,* 289; Chambers and Shank, *Salt Water & Printers Ink,* 299.

1925

1. Lenoir Chambers and Joseph E. Shank, *Salt Water & Printers Ink* (Chapel Hill: University of North Carolina Press, 1967), 307.
2. Stephen Roskill, *Naval Policy Between the Wars: The Period of Anglo-American Antagonism, 1910–1929* (New York: Walker and Co., 1968), 331. Because of the Naval Limitation Treaty, the United States retained eighteen capital ships but scrapped fifteen others and canceled eleven uncompleted ships. At Norfolk Navy Yard, battleship *North Carolina* (BB52) was canceled at twenty-eight percent completion, and at Newport News battleship *Iowa* (BB53) met a similar fate, and was canceled at thirty-seven percent.
3. Ibid., 107; "Development of Naval Base Is to Go Forward," *Virginian-Pilot,* 21 March 1920, 1. In 1919, when the Atlantic and Pacific Fleets were reestablished, they were headed by Adm. Henry B. Wilson and Adm. Hugh Rodman respectively.
4. Gerald E. Wheeler, *Admiral William Veazie Pratt, USN* (Washington, DC: Department of the Navy, 1974), 142.
5. Roskill, *Naval Policy Between the Wars*, 107, 354; *United States Naval Administration in World War II (Commander, Atlantic Fleet)* (Washington DC: 1945), 5. In December 1930, the Battle Fleet was redesignated the Battle Force and the Scouting Fleet the Scouting Force. In January 1932, the Scouting Force was ordered to the Pacific for routine annual Fleet concentration but did not return to the Atlantic after the conclusion of exercises.
6. Marvin W. Schlegel, *Conscripted City, Norfolk in World War II* (Norfolk: Norfolk War History Commission, 1951), 3.
7. Burke Davis, *The Billy Mitchell Affair* (New York: Random House, 1967), 4, 52; Archibald D. Turnbull and Clifford L. Lord, *History of United States Naval Aviation* (New Haven: Yale University Press, 1949), 193.
8. Davis, *The Billy Mitchell Affair,* 67.
9. Ibid., 75.
10. Ibid., 77, 83; Turnbull and Lord, *History of United States Naval Aviation,* 194.
11. Turnbull and Lord, *History of United States Naval Aviation,* 198.
12. Davis, *The Billy Mitchell Affair,* 97.
13. Ibid., 98–99, 103; Turnbull and Lord, *History of United States Naval Aviation,* 197–98.

14. Davis, *The Billy Mitchell Affair,* 108; Turnbull and Lord, *History of United States Naval Aviation,* 199, 201–203. Mitchell's Army bombers were also active after the celebrated tests, sinking battleship *Alabama* at anchor off Tangier Island on 23–24 September in a night attack with blazing flares, gas bombs, and machine-gun fire, and later tests in September 1923 with old battleships *Virginia* and *New Jersey* and in November 1924 against the unfinished battleship *Washington* were similarly successful for airpower.
15. Davis, *The Billy Mitchell Affair,* 111, 7; Turnbull and Lord, *History of United States Naval Aviation,* 200–201.
16. Turnbull and Lord, *History of United States Naval Aviation,* 162; Norman Friedman, *U.S. Aircraft Carriers: An Illustrated Design History* (Annapolis: Naval Institute Press, 1983), 36; John Fass Morton, *Mustin: A Naval Family of the Twentieth Century* (Annapolis: Naval Institute Press, 2003), 132.
17. Whiting and Chevalier had both served as observers aboard British aircraft carriers during World War I.
18. Rear Adm. J. R. Tate, "Covered Wagon Days," *Naval Aviation News,* December 1970, 32.
19. Turnbull and Lord, *History of United States Naval Aviation,* 207; William F. Trimble, *Admiral William A. Moffett: Architect of Naval Aviation* (Washington, DC: Smithsonian Institution Press, 1994), 105; Charles M. Melhorn, *Two-Block Fox, the Rise of the Aircraft Carrier 1911–1929* (Annapolis: Naval Institute Press, 1974), 80. Although *Langley* went to sea with both types of arresting gear, the fore-and-aft gear was removed in 1929.
20. Melhorn, *Two-Block Fox,* 101; Paul Stillwell, *Reminiscences of Admiral Alfred M. Pride, US Navy (ret)* (Annapolis: 1984), 63.
21. Tate, "Covered Wagon Days," 33–34.; Trimble, *Admiral William A. Moffett,* 105.
22. Tate, "Covered Wagon Days," 30–32; Morton, *Mustin: A Naval Family of the Twentieth Century,* 135; Turnbull and Lord, *History of United States Naval Aviation,* 206; *Our Flying Navy* (New York: Macmillan, 1944), 17.
23. *United States Naval Administration in World War (DCNO-Air)* (Washington, DC: 1945), 240; Ira R. Hanna, *The Growth of Norfolk Naval Air Station and the Norfolk-Portsmouth Metropolitan Area Economy in the Twentieth Century* (Norfolk: Old Dominion, 1967), 27. Naval Air Station, Hampton Roads, was redesignated Naval Air Station, Norfolk, on 12 July 1921.
24. Turnbull and Lord, *History of United States Naval Aviation,* 151, 213.
25. Thomas Wildenberg, *Destined for Glory* (Annapolis: Naval Institute Press, 1998), 19, 33. *Putnam* was also used for the first tests of shipboard gunnery effectiveness with gun cameras installed at various locations on deck to simulate antiaircraft guns and garner statistics on the best means to shoot at attacking aircraft during its participation in dive-bombing tests by VF-5 off Cape Henry.
26. Director of Naval Aviation, *Weekly Report* (Washington, DC: 1918), 5 February 1919; Stillwell, *Reminiscences of Admiral Alfred M. Pride, US Navy (ret),* 57.
27. Stillwell, *Reminiscences of Admiral Alfred M. Pride, US Navy (ret),* 57.
28. Paul Stillwell, *The Reminiscences of Vice Admiral Gerald E. Miller* (Annapolis: US Naval Insitute, 1983), 21; John T. Mason, *Reminiscences of Vice Admiral Gerald E. Miller, U.S. Navy (ret)* (Annapolis: 1983), 18; Frederick S. Harrod, *Manning the New Navy, the Development of a Modern Naval Enlisted Force* (Westport, Conn.: Greenwood Press, 1978), 188.
29. George Van Deurs, *Anchors in the Sky: Spuds Ellyson, the First Naval Aviator* (San Rafael, Calif.: Presidio Press, 1978), 212.
30. John Fry, *USS Saratoga CV-3* (Atgien, Pa: Schiffer Publishing Ltd., 1996), 14.
31. Robert C. Stern, *The Lexington Class Carriers* (London: Arms and Armour Press, 1993), 60. On the last day of shakedown training, 27 January 1928, *Saratoga* operated with the dirigible *Los Angeles* off the Maryland Eastern Shore, securing it briefly to the deck, the only time such operations were ever conducted.
32. Van Deurs, *Anchors in the Sky,* 234.
33. "Crack Planes of Two Nations Race Today for Schneider Cup," *Virginian-Pilot,* 13 November 1926, 1; "Italian Flyer Wins Schneider Cup," *Virginian-Pilot,* 14 November 1926, 1; William O. Foss, *The United States Navy in Hampton Roads* (Norfolk: Donning Company, 1984), 81; Richard C. Knott, *A Heritage of Wings* (Annapolis: Naval Institute Press, 1997), 72.
34. Marshall W. Butt, *Norfolk Naval Shipyard, a Brief History* (Portsmouth, Va: Public Information Office, NNSY, 1951), 10.
35. Roger Welles, letter to Vice Adm. Philip Andrews, 16 November 1923 (Welles Papers); *'Shoving Off' in the U.S. Navy* (Norfolk: G. L. Optical Co., 1921), 9; "Admiral A. C. Dillingham," *Virginian-Pilot,* 8 December 1925; Harrod, *Manning the New Navy,* 82.
36. Welles, letter to Vice Adm. Philip Andrews, 16 November 1923 (Welles Papers).
37. *Cast Down Your Bucket Where You Are: An Ethnohistorical Study of the African-American Community on the Lands of the Yorktown Naval Weapons Station, 1865–1918* (Norfolk: 1992), 45. Oral histories indicate that as many as six hundred African-American families were displaced by the Navy when the Yorktown Naval Mine Depot was established in 1917–1918, yet deeds of sale can be found for only seventy-five parcels. Many efforts were made to resettle residents; however, none were government sponsored, but were made by congregations of local churches.
38. *United States Naval Administration in World War II (Fifth Naval District)* (Washington: US Navy, 1945), 461; Roger Welles, letter to Admiral Gherardi, 28 May 1924 (Welles Papers). The Naval Mine Depot at Yorktown came into its

own on 7 August 1918 when Presidential Executive Order 1472 seized a total area of 11,433 acres to allow the transfer of mining operations from St. Julien's Creek.

39. Paolo E. Coletta, *United States Navy and Marine Corps Bases, Domestic* (Westport, Conn.: Greenwood Press, 1985), 664.
40. Schlegel, *Conscripted City, Norfolk in World War II,* 3.
41. Paul Stillwell, *Battleship Arizona* (Annapolis: Naval Institute Press, 1991), 112.
42. Ibid., 113.; Richard Oulahan, "Hoover Sails South; Spends Day Resting," *New York Times,* 20 March 1931, 1.
43. Roger Welles, letter to Thomas H. Gilliam, Norfolk Chamber of Commerce, 13 May 1925 (Welles Papers).
44. S. Heath Tyler, letter to RADM Roger Welles, 22 June 1925 (Welles Papers).
45. Thomas J. Wertenbaker, *Norfolk: Historic Southern Port* (Durham: Duke University Press, 1931), 329.
46. Schlegel, *Conscripted City, Norfolk in World War II,* 6.
47. Ibid., 7.
48. Ibid.; Hanna, *The Growth of Norfolk Naval Air Station and the Norfolk-Portsmouth Metropolitan Area Economy in the Twentieth Century,* 21.
49. John T Mason, *Reminiscences of Admiral George W. Anderson, Jr., US Navy (ret)* (Annapolis: 1981), 48.
50. "Navy Department Emphasizes Necessity of Acquiring and Developing East Camp Field," *Virginian-Pilot,* 2 October 1932, 1.
51. *United States Naval Administration in World War II (DCNO-Air),* 264; Hanna, *The Growth of Norfolk Naval Air Station and the Norfolk-Portsmouth Metropolitan Area Economy in the Twentieth Century,* 32; Thomas C. Parramore, *Norfolk, The First Four Centuries* (Charlottesville: University Press of Virginia, 1994), 326.
52. *United States Naval Administration in World War II (DCNO-Air),* 294; Paolo E. Coletta, *Patrick N. L. Bellinger* (Lanham, MD: University Press of America, 1987), 203.
53. Schlegel, *Conscripted City, Norfolk in World War II,* 13; Hanna, *The Growth of Norfolk Naval Air Station and the Norfolk-Portsmouth Metropolitan Area Economy in the Twentieth Century,* 39.
54. Schlegel, *Conscripted City, Norfolk in World War II,* 40; *United States Naval Administration in World War II (Fifth Naval District) Appendix I* (Washington DC: US Navy, 1945), 56.
55. "Secrecy Shrouds Flight of Plane at Air Station Here," *Virginian-Pilot,* 22 March 1935, 3.
56. Amy Waters Yarsinske, "Without Us, They Don't Fly," *The Day Book,* July 1996, 6; Coletta, *United States Navy and Marine Corps Bases, Domestic,* 378; Hanna, *The Growth of Norfolk Naval Air Station and the Norfolk-Portsmouth Metropolitan Area Economy in the Twentieth Century,* 26.
57. Friedman, *U. S. Aircraft Carriers: An Illustrated Design History,* 412.
58. *United States Naval Administration in World War II (Fifth Naval District) Appendix I,* 48; *United States Naval Administration in World War II (Fifth Naval District),* 449; Frank J. Allston, *Ready for Sea: The Bicentennial History of the US Navy Supply Corps* (Annapolis: Naval Institute Press, 1995), 208. An Army Supply Base, also known as Norfolk Terminal and later Norfolk Army Base, was formally authorized on 21 December 1917 and construction began a month later on two piers, eight warehouses, and 30 miles of track and classification yards at a 912 acre site at Bush Bluff six miles north of the Lafayette River. In May 1918, four additional pieces of property totaling nearly 700 acres was added to the reservation and the Standard Oil Company opened a fuel depot with a capacity for 8 million gallons of fuel. When the terminal was completed it was the largest terminal of its kind in the country and was estimated to have cost over $30 million. In December 1940 the Navy negotiated an agreement with the War Department to take over the former Army Base Terminal (that had been transferred to the U. S. Shipping Board after World War I).
59. "Command History of Norfolk Naval Shipyard," (Portsmouth, VA: Norfolk Naval Shipyard, 1959), 11. Both destroyers in the Navy Yard's 1933 construction program were lost in the first year of the war, *Downes* destroyed by Japanese bombs as she lay in drydock at Pearl Harbor, *Tucker* sunk by a mine in the New Hebrides.
60. Ibid., 16; Norman Friedman, *U.S. Destroyers: An Illustrated Design History* (Annapolis: Naval Institute Press, 1982); Norman Friedman, *U.S. Cruisers: An Ilustrated Design History* (Annapolis: Naval Institute Press, 1984).
61. Wertenbaker, *Norfolk: Historic Southern Port,* 345.
62. Schlegel, *Conscripted City, Norfolk in World War II,* 4.
63. "Admiral Taussig Local Connections," *Virginian-Pilot,* 12 October 1938, 6.
64. Wertenbaker, *Norfolk: Historic Southern Port,* 344.
65. Ibid., 352; "Admiral Guest of Honor at Association of Commerce Dinner," *Virginian-Pilot,* 21 June 1941, 16; "Vice Admiral Taussig," *Virginian-Pilot,* 17 June 1941, 6. Not afraid to say what he believed in, Taussig occasionally would show up on the wrong side of officialdom, causing President Roosevelt to privately comment that he "had had enough of Joe." Such an occasion occurred when Taussig captured headlines before the Senate Naval Affairs Committee by accurately foretelling the threat of Japanese expansion warning: "When there are nations who believe only in the sword . . . peaceably inclined nations must go to war to defend themselves or accept domination." This highly visible splash by "our admiral" brought many complements from the Norfolk press with reminders of his "sterling record of service" and "friendliness and sympathy with local interests."
66. Two destroyers were named after the Norfolk Taussigs, DD-746 in honor of Rear Admiral Edward David Taussig and DE-1030 for Vice Admiral Joseph K. Taussig. Joseph K. Taussig's son, Joseph, Jr., continued the Taussig family contributions to the Navy when he graduated from the Naval

Academy in 1941 and received the Navy Cross for heroism as the officer of the deck of battleship *Nevada* during the Japanese attack on Pearl Harbor. He later served many years as the special assistant for safety and survivability for the secretary of the Navy.

67. Patrick Abbazia, *Mr. Roosevelt's Navy* (Annapolis: Naval Institute Press, 1975), 30.
68. E. B. Potter, *Bull Halsey* (Annapolis: Naval Institute Press, 1985), 83–86.
69. Ibid., 97–100. Halsey's best man at his wedding was David Bagley and the ushers were Tommy Hart, Husband Kimmel and Carl Ohnesorg, all young naval officers who would later rise to senior command.
70. Captain Patrick Bellinger served as King's chief of staff for Aircraft, Battle Force, before being transferred to command NAS Norfolk in June 1938.
71. Abbazia, *Mr. Roosevelt's Navy,* 50; Samuel Eliot Morison, *The Battle of the Atlantic; September 1939–May 1943* (Boston: Little, Brown and Company, 1984), 14.
72. Abbazia, *Mr. Roosevelt's Navy,* 65,79; "No Effect on Navy Operations," *Virginian-Pilot,* 2 September 1939, 6.
73. "Roosevelt Visits Navy Yard," *Portsmouth Star,* 29 July 1940, 1; Wertenbaker, *Norfolk: Historic Southern Port,* 347.
74. *Administrative History of the U.S. Atlantic Fleet in World War II* (Washington, DC: Department of the Navy, 1945), I:113; "Command History of Norfolk Naval Shipyard," 24; *United States Naval Administration in World War II (Fifth Naval District),* 479; Arthur Sydnor Barksdale, Jr., *History of the Norfolk Navy Yard in World War II* (n.p.: 1945), 24.; Morison, *The Battle of the Atlantic; September 1939–May 1943,* 15.
75. *Administrative History of the U. S. Atlantic Fleet in World War II,* I:128; Morison, *The Battle of the Atlantic; September 1939–May 1943,* 54; Abbazia, *Mr. Roosevelt's Navy,* 145.
76. Abbazia, *Mr. Roosevelt's Navy,* 173.
77. Ibid., 182.
78. Ibid., 230.
79. Schlegel, *Conscripted City, Norfolk in World War II,* 114.

1941

1. Theodore Taylor, *The Magnificent Mitscher* (Annapolis: Naval Institute Press, 1954), 105.
2. "Norfolk Stunned by News; Japanese Seized," *Virginian-Pilot,* 8 December 1941, 1; Marvin W. Schlegel, *Conscripted City, Norfolk in World War II* (Norfolk: Norfolk War History Commission, 1951), 126.
3. *United States Naval Administration in World War II (Fifth Naval District)* (Washington: U.S. Navy, 1945), Suppl. 23.
4. Ibid., 123.
5. "Norfolk's Male Japanese Held by City Police," *Virginian-Pilot,* 8 December 1941, 7; *United States Naval Administration in World War II (Fifth Naval District),* Suppl. 23.
6. "Air Raid Instructions," *Ledger-Dispatch,* 10 December 1941, 6; Schlegel, *Conscripted City,* 27, 118.
7. Carroll V. Glines, *The Doolittle Raid* (New York: Orion Books, 1988), 45; Lisle A. Rose, *The Ship that Held the Line* (Annapolis: Naval Institute Press, 1995), 19.
8. Schlegel, *Conscripted City,* 31, 35, 120.
9. Ibid., 116.; *United States Naval Administration in World War II (Fifth Naval District),* 546.
10. *United States Naval Administration in World War II (Fifth Naval District),* Suppl. 23.
11. Edwin P. Hoyt, *U-boats Offshore: When Hitler Struck America* (New York: Stein and Day Publishers, 1978), 19. At the commencement of hostilities with the United States, U-boat commander Dönitz began to plan what he called "einen kraftigen paukenschlag" or "a powerful blow on the kettledrum" and asked for a dozen long-range Type IX U-boats to conduct operations off the U.S. Atlantic coast.
12. Winston S. Churchill, *Memoirs of the Second World War* (Boston: Houghton Mifflin Company, 1959), 518.
13. Clay Blair, *Hitler's U-boat War: The Hunters 1939–1942* (New York: Random House, 1996), 454; Hoyt, *U-boats Offshore,* 21.
14. Blair, *Hitler's U-boat War,* 466.
15. "U-boats At Our Doors," *Virginian-Pilot,* 20 January 1942, 8.
16. *United States Naval Administration in World War II (Fifth Naval District),* Suppl. 23; Blair, *Hitler's U-boat War,* 503; Churchill, *Memoirs of the Second World War,* 531.
17. *United States Naval Administration in World War II (Convoy and Routing)* (Washington, DC: 1945), 101; Eastern Sea Frontier Commander, letter to Commander-in-chief, U.S. Fleet, 26 February 1942 (ltr A16, ser 979, War Diary, Eastern Sea Frontier Archives).
18. Hoyt, *U-boats Offshore,* 97; Blair, *Hitler's U-boat War,* 525, 47.
19. David A. Clary, *Fortress America: The Corps of Engineers, Hampton Roads, and United States Coastal Defense* (Charlottesville: University Press of Virginia, 1990), 160.
20. *United States Naval Administration in World War II (Fifth Naval District),* 532. The weather station at Cape Henry (the site of the Harbor Entrance Control Post for the Chesapeake approaches) had been reporting inbound and outbound ships from its start in 1873.
21. Ibid.; *United States Naval Administration in World War II (Fifth Naval District),* Suppl. 23. Although the Navy deployed the first underwater hydrophone array in the Chesapeake approaches in 1941, the Army also deployed a hydrophone array outside the outer line of its minefield in October 1943.
22. *United States Naval Administration in World War II (Fifth Naval District),* 515.
23. Ibid., Suppl. 23.
24. Ibid., 541.; *United States Naval Administration in World War II (Mine Warfare)* (Washington, DC: 1945), 117; Chief

of Naval Operations, letter to Commandant, Fifth Naval District, 23 December 1941 (RG80, National Archives).

25. *United States Naval Administration in World War II (Fifth Naval District),* 143, 544.
26. Ibid., 596, 649.; *United States Naval Administration in World War II (Fifth Naval District),* Suppl. 23.
27. *United States Naval Administration in World War II (Fifth Naval District),* 74, 668.
28. Ibid., 670. The bodies of twenty-nine German sailors from *U-85* were brought back to Norfolk and buried with full military honors under the magnolias at the Hampton National Cemetery.
29. Schlegel, *Conscripted City,* 216. Although many became concerned that the glow from brightly lit coastal cities silhouetted merchant shipping at night, German U-boat reports indicated that the real value of coastal lights to the enemy lay in helping U-boats safely navigate to patrol stations off American harbors.
30. *United States Naval Administration in World War II (Fifth Naval District),* 147; Blair, *Hitler's U-boat War,* 539.
31. Hoyt, *U-boats Offshore,* 132.
32. *United States Naval Administration in World War II (Convoy and Routing),* 101. The position of Fifth Naval District Port Director had been established in 1939.
33. *United States Naval Administration in World War II (Fifth Naval District),* Suppl. 20. The peak number of convoyed ships leaving Hampton Roads during World War II occurred during April 1944, with 310 ships sailing that month.
34. Blair, *Hitler's U-boat War,* 608.
35. "Battle of Atlantic Brushes Virginia Shores," *Virginian-Pilot,* 17 June 1942, 1; *United States Naval Administration in World War II (Fifth Naval District),* 603.; Hoyt, *U-boats Offshore,* 148. On hearing of the success of *U-701*'s mines in the Chesapeake shipping channel, Dönitz radioed *U-701* a "well done" and ordered the U-boat to a new patrol area off Cape Hatteras, where it was sunk on 7 July 1942 by an Army Hudson bomber, the only U-boat to be sunk exclusively by Army patrol aircraft, during the war
36. Clay Blair, *Hitler's U-boat War* (New York: Random House, 1998), 387; Blair, *Hitler's U-boat War,* 687; *United States Naval Administration in World War II (Fifth Naval District),* 15, 607. *U-6's* mines were discovered on 12 September and successfully swept, and the mines from *U-230* and *U-566* produced no sinkings.
37. Hoyt, *U-boats Offshore,* 181. *U-576* was sunk a day after her attack on convoy KS520 on 15 July 1942 near Cape Hatteras by depth charges from two Kingfisher aircraft and ramming by the *Unicoi.*
38. *United States Naval Administration in World War II (Fifth Naval District),* 729.
39. Joe Judge, "Museum Receives U-boat Artifact," *The Day Book,* Fall 2004, 4–6.
40. Blair, *Hitler's U-boat War,* 684.
41. Station Development Board Chairman, U.S. Naval Base, "Narrative History of Development of Naval Facilities in the Sewall Point Area to the Year 1951" (1952), 12.
42. Joe Mosier, "NAS Norfolk: Reflections of Victory," *Flagship,* Air Show Supplement, 15 July 1995.
43. *Building the Navy's Bases in World War II* (Washington, DC: Government Printing Office, 1947), 241; M. L. Shettle, Jr., *United States Naval Air Stations of World War II* (Bowersville, Ga: Schaertel Publishing Co., 1995), 165.
44. Hampton Roads, San Diego and Seattle were the first three naval air centers established, and Capt. J. M. Shoemaker, NAS Norfolk commanding officer, was named to head the Naval Air Center, Hampton Roads. Commander Naval Air Bases, Fifth Naval District, was disestablished on 1 January 1965, and NAS Norfolk was reassigned to the command of Commander, Fleet Air, Norfolk.
45. Ira R. Hanna, *The Growth of Norfolk Naval Air Station and the Norfolk-Portsmouth Metropolitan Area Economy in the Twentieth Century* (Norfolk: Old Dominion, 1967), 40.
46. Edwin P. Hoyt, *McCampbell's Heroes* (New York: Van Nostrand Reinhold Company, 1983), 3.
47. *United States Naval Administration in World War II (DCNO-Air)* (Washington, DC: 1945), 361.
48. Dave Parsons and Derek Nelson, *Fighter Country: The F-14 Tomcats of NAS Oceana* (Osceola, WI: Motorbooks International, 1992), 12.
49. Shettle, *United States Naval Air Stations of World War II,* 169; Paolo E. Coletta, *United States Navy and Marine Corps Bases, Domestic* (Westport, Conn.: Greenwood Press, 1985), 404; Parsons and Nelson, *Fighter Country,* 16.
50. Shettle, *United States Naval Air Stations of World War II,* 156; Hoyt, *McCampbell's Heroes,* 4.
51. Coletta, *United States Navy and Marine Corps Bases, Domestic,* 207.
52. Shettle, *United States Naval Air Stations of World War II,* 149; *Building the Navy's Bases in World War II,* 238.
53. Coletta, *United States Navy and Marine Corps Bases, Domestic,* 114.
54. *United States Naval Administration in World War II (DCNO-Air),* 420.
55. Schlegel, *Conscripted City,* 296; Hanna, *The Growth of Norfolk Naval Air Station and the Norfolk-Portsmouth Metropolitan Area Economy in the Twentieth Century,* 41; Mosier, "NAS Norfolk: Reflections of Victory."
56. "Command History of Norfolk Naval Shipyard" (Portsmouth, VA: Norfolk Naval Shipyard, 1959), 128; Lenoir Chambers and Joseph E. Shank, *Salt Water & Printers Ink* (Chapel Hill: University of North Carolina Press, 1967), 369; Philip Ziegler, *Mountbatten: A Biography* (New York: Alfred A. Knopf, 1985), 151. Mountbatten never did command *Illustrious* at sea. He was ordered back to Britain before the ship left the yard to serve as Commander, Combined Operations.
57. Thanks to Miriam Browning and Harold Freeman for this colorful Portsmouth World War II anecdote.
58. *Building the Navy's Bases in World War II,* 191.
59. R. Christopher Goodwin and Associates Inc., "Architectural Inventory of Norfolk Naval Shipyard & Satellite Activities, Portsmouth, VA" (Norfolk, Va: Navy Region Mid-Atlantic, 2003), 52.

60. Marshall W. Butt, *Norfolk Naval Shipyard, a Brief History* (Portsmouth, Va: Public Information Office, NNSY, 1951), 11; Joe Law, *Norfolk Naval Shipyard: Its Remarkable History* (Norfolk Naval Shipyard, unpublished), 401; Coletta, *United States Navy and Marine Corps Bases, Domestic,* 393.
61. Outside of Norfolk Navy Yard, Navy yard employees contributed to the repair of an additional 10,515 ships at private yards in Virginia and North Carolina and at the NOB's piers.
62. Arthur Sydnor Barksdale, Jr., *History of the Norfolk Navy Yard in World War II* (n.p.: 1945), 1; Coletta, *United States Navy and Marine Corps Bases, Domestic,* 392.
63. Law, *Norfolk Naval Shipyard: Its Remarkable History,* 225; Siegfried Breyer, *Battleships and Battle Cruisers, 1905–1970* (Garden City, NY: Doubleday & Company, 1970), 243. These *South Dakota*-class battleships saw the most service of any battleship class of the war; the *Alabama* served in the battles of Leyte Gulf, the Philippine Sea, and Okinawa; the *Indiana* at the Philippine Sea and Iwo Jima.
64. Law, *Norfolk Naval Shipyard: Its Remarkable History,* 225. There were several plans to convert the unfinished *Kentucky* into a guided missile battleship (BBG-1), but all were finally rejected in 1959, and she was scrapped. The *Kentucky's* turbines were transferred to the Fast Combat Support Ships *Sacramento* (AOE-1) and *Camden* (AOE-2).
65. Bob Ketenheim, *USS Shangri-La* (Paducah, Ky: Turner Publishing Company, 2002), 11. "Command History of Norfolk Naval Shipyard," 168. Interestingly, during her shakedown trials in the Chesapeake Bay in September 1944, the *Shangri-La* was used for experiments with Army B-25 and P-51 aircraft that operated from her deck before she sailed for the Pacific.
66. "Command History of Norfolk Naval Shipyard," 169; Norman Friedman, *U.S. Aircraft Carriers: An Illustrated Design History* (Annapolis: Naval Institute Press, 1983), 76.
67. Goodwin, "Architectural Inventory of Norfolk Naval Shipyard & Satellite Activities, Portsmouth, VA," 78.
68. Parke Jr. Rouse, *The Good Old Days in Hampton and Newport News* (Richmond: The Dietz Press, 1986), 214; Friedman, *U.S. Aircraft Carriers: An Illustrated Design History,* 390.
69. *United States Naval Administration in World War II (Fifth Naval District),* 119; Theodore A. Curtin, *A Marriage of Convenience: Norfolk and the Navy, 1917–1967* (Old Dominion College, 1969), 98.
70. "The History of Amphibious Training," *Bureau of Naval Personnel Training Bulletin,* 15 October 1944, 39; "Little Creek and 'Gator,' United States Atlantic Fleet," *Know Norfolk Virginia,* July 1945.
71. "The History of Amphibious Training," 45.; *Building the Navy's Bases in World War II,* 279. The beach party battalion and beachmaster units, the forerunner of the Naval Beach Group of today, was a group of personnel organized to ensure an crucial and orderly flow of personnel, materiel, and vehicles across a beach.
72. "Little Creek and 'Gator,' United States Atlantic Fleet," 67; Coletta, *United States Navy and Marine Corps Bases, Domestic,* 289.
73. *United States Naval Administration in World War II (Fifth Naval District),* 503.
74. *Dictionary of American Naval Fighting Ships* (Washington, DC: Government Printing Office, 1959), 570. The Navy's first LST (laid down at Newport News Shipbuilding on 16 June 1942) was, interestingly, numbered *LST-383* since lots for lowered-numbered ships had been awarded to a host of shipbuilders for rushed simultaneous construction.
75. "Little Creek and 'Gator,' United States Atlantic Fleet," 54, 68. Overseeing each facet of these complex amphibious operations and training was the Commander, Amphibious Force, Atlantic Fleet, from headquarters at the Nansemond Hotel at Ocean View (which were moved from the cramped quarters of Building 138 at the NOB in September 1942). The first commander of the Atlantic Fleet Amphibious Force was Rear Adm. Roland M. Brainard, who was relieved in April 1942 by Rear Adm. Henry K. Hewitt.
76. *United States Naval Amphibious Base Pictoral Review* (Atlanta, GA: Albert Love Enterprises, 1953).
77. *Unites States Naval Administration in World War II (Commander Fleet Operational Training)* (Washington, DC: 1945), 34. In 1940 Navy recruit training was conducted at Great Lakes, Illinois; Newport, Rhode Island; San Diego; and Norfolk.
78. Ibid., 3.
79. Paul Stillwell, *Reminiscences of Rear Admiral Jackson K. Parker, U.S. Navy (ret)* (Annapolis: 1987), 18.
80. *United States Naval Administration in World War II (Fifth Naval District) Appendix I* (Washington, DC: U.S. Navy, 1945), 77. The Radar Operator's School was moved to the Cavalier Hotel in Virginia Beach. The property was taken over on 12 October 1942 and the first classes began on 1 November. The hotel's famed Beach Club was an officer's recreation facility, where the entrance fees were ten cents, the price for towels was ten cents, and beach umbrellas were furnished without charge. A charge of fifty cents per hour was levied for the use of the club's badminton and paddle tennis courts.
81. United States Naval Administration in World War II (Fifth Naval District), Appendix I, 71. One example of the impact of transferring Fleet Service schools from Norfolk was the relocation of the school for Navy chaplains to the College of William & Mary campus.
82. *Unites States Naval Administration in World War II (Commander Fleet Operational Training),* 19.; U.S. Fleet Commander-in-chief, letter to Commander-in-chief, U.S. Atlantic Fleet, 9 January 1943 (RG80, COMINCH file, National Archives).
83. *Unites States Naval Administration in World War II (Commander Fleet Operational Training),* 31, 40, 91.
84. Ibid., 43, 77.
85. Ibid., 74; Commander-in-chief, U.S. Fleet, letter to Commander-in-chief, Atlantic Fleet, ser 112 of 9 January 1943.

86. *United States Naval Administration in World War II (Commander Fleet Operational Training),* 194, 276; *Administrative History of the U.S. Atlantic Fleet in World War II,* VIII:196.
87. *United States Naval Administration in World War II (Commander Fleet Operational Training),* 161.
88. Ibid., 227.; *Administrative History of the U. S. Atlantic Fleet in World War II* (Washington, DC: Department of the Navy, 1945), VIII:227; Chairman, "Narrative History of development of naval facilities in the Sewall Point Area to the year 1951," 7.
89. *United States Naval Administration in World War II (Fifth Naval District) Appendix I,* 36.
90. *Unites States Naval Administration in World War II (Commander Fleet Operational Training),* 20, 240–42.
91. *United States Naval Administration in World War II (Fifth Naval District),* Suppl. 27.
92. Ibid.; *United States Naval Administration in World War II (Fifth Naval District) Appendix I,* 71; *United States Naval Administration in World War II (Commander Fleet Operational Training),* 174.
93. Morris J. MacGregor Jr., *Integration of the Armed Forces, 1940–1965* (Washington, DC: Center of Military History, 1981), 67. At the same time that the Hampton Institute was established for the training of African Americans in naval technical subjects, a segregated Class "A" school for white machinist's mates was established in buildings of the former Norfolk Academy near Ward's Corner.
94. Paul Stillwell, *Reminiscences of Mr. Frank E. Sublett, Jr.* (Annapolis: 1989), 111.
95. Ibid., 114.
96. Ibid., 117.
97. Paul Stillwell, *The Golden Thirteen* (Annapolis: Naval Institute Press, 1993), 129.
98. Ibid., 89.
99. *United States Naval Administration in World War II (Fifth Naval District),* Suppl. 27; Schlegel, *Conscripted City,* 20.
100. *United States Naval Administration in World War II (Commander Fleet Operational Training),* 202; *Administrative History of the U.S. Atlantic Fleet in World War II,* VIII:202.
101. *United States Naval Administration in World War II (Commander Fleet Operational Training),* 204.
102. *Administrative History of the U. S. Atlantic Fleet in World War II,* VIII:204.; *United States Naval Administration in World War II (Commander Fleet Operational Training),* 174, 203. By 1944, Lieutenant Gallery was promoted to the rank of commander and was awarded the Legion of Merit for his initiative and service to the Anti-Aircraft Training and Test Center at Dam Neck. He went on to become commanding officer of the *Pittsburgh* during the Korean conflict and retired as rear admiral.
103. *Building the Navy's Bases in World War II,* 308.
104. Ibid., 294; Reginald Wheeler, *The Road to Victory: A History of Hampton Roads Port of Embarkation in World War II* (New Haven: Yale University Press, 1946), 17.
105. *United States Naval Administration in World War II (Fifth Naval District),* 450, 8; *Building the Navy's Bases in World War II,* 291. On 1 March 1944, the Naval Air Station's Aviation Supply Annex was redesignated as the Naval Aviation Supply Depot.
106. *Building the Navy's Bases in World War II,* 304.
107. *United States Naval Administration in World War II (Fifth Naval District),* 356. During the construction of Camp Peary, about a hundred families were displaced, and, with the lack of adequate housing, many took up residence at an abandoned Civilian Conservation Corps camp on property owned by the College of William and Mary. The Navy had refused to participate in their resettlement, and many thought they were tardy in making compensation. Seabees from naval construction battalions ultimately helped to build several houses for the displaced.
108. Ibid., Suppl. 26. During the war, various subordinate commands migrated to Camp Peary, including the Advance Base Supply Training Command, the Electrician's Mate Training School, the Naval Academy Preparatory School, and the Naval Training School for Ammunition Handling.
109. Ibid.; *United States Naval Administration in World War II (Fifth Naval District),* 466; "The Hampton Roads Port of Embarkation," *The Mariners Museum Journal,* Summer 1995, 27. The number of NTS ships operating from Hampton Roads steadily increased from 38 in 1943 to 121 by 1945. By war's end 3,294 ships had been dispatched from the port of embarkation, carrying 12.5 million tons of supplies and equipment and 1.6 million troops, and returning shipments included 134,293 prisoners of war and 32,688 convalescing troops.
110. Wheeler, *The Road to Victory,* 70; Schlegel, *Conscripted City,* 210.
111. Coletta, *United States Navy and Marine Corps Bases, Domestic,* 664.; *United States Naval Administration in World War II (Mine Warfare),* 50.
112. Coletta, *United States Navy and Marine Corps Bases, Domestic,* 665.
113. Ibid.
114. Ibid.; *Architectural Investigations of St Juliens Creek Annex* (Norfolk: Atlantic Division, Naval Facilities Engineering Command, 1997), 14; *Building the Navy's Bases in World War II,* 327.
115. Hospital staff at the naval hospital in Portsmouth on this day in August 1944 consisted of 113 medical officers, 359 nurses, 24 "cadet" nurses, 701 hospital corpsmen, 1,125 hospital corps students, 46 hospital corps instructors, 30 Marines, 374 civilians, 33 American Red Cross volunteers, 163 WAVES, 8 WAVE officers, and 79 other personnel.
116. *Building the Navy's Bases in World War II,* 358.
117. "The History of Naval Medical Center Portsmouth" (NMC Portsmouth, Virginia web page, unpublished, 2004).
118. Chambers and Shank, *Salt Water & Printers Ink,* 371.
119. Ibid., 372.; Charles F. Marsh, *The Hampton Roads Communities in World War II* (Chapel Hill: University of North

Carolina Press, 1951), 74, 8; Earl Lewis, *In Their Own Interests* (Berkeley: University of California Press, 1991), 168; Wheeler, *The Road to Victory,*

120. Lewis, *In Their Own Interests,* 169; Schlegel, *Conscripted City,* 61.
121. Marsh, *The Hampton Roads Communities in World War II,* 140.
122. Schlegel, *Conscripted City,* 250; Chambers and Shank, *Salt Water & Printers Ink,* 371.
123. Schlegel, *Conscripted City,* 103.
124. William O. Foss, *The United States Navy in Hampton Roads* (Norfolk: Donning Company, 1984), 88; Coletta, *United States Navy and Marine Corps Bases, Domestic,* 380.
125. Foss, *The United States Navy in Hampton Roads,* 88.; Schlegel, *Conscripted City,* 314.
126. Mary Ellen Newcomer, "There've Been Some Changes Made," *Our Navy,* Mid-July 1942, 16.
127. Lewis, *In Their Own Interests,* 171, 95.
128. Schlegel, *Conscripted City,* 315.
129. Ibid., 17, 153, 256.
130. Ibid., 308–309.
131. Ibid., 360–303.

1961

1. Paolo E. Coletta, *United States Navy and Marine Corps Bases, Domestic* (Westport, Conn.: Greenwood Press, 1985), 405.
2. Amy Waters Yarsinske, "Without Us, They Don't Fly," *The Day Book* (July 1996): 6. NAAS Monogram closed on 1 December 1945, NAAS Creeds was decommissioned on 15 October 1945, NAAS Pungo about the same time, and NAAS Fentress was placed on caretaker status on 1 January 1946, but a new, longer runway was constructed at the site by July 1952 to be used as an auxiliary landing field for NAS Oceana.
3. Coletta, *United States Navy and Marine Corps Bases, Domestic,* 379. The Assembly and Repair Department was redesignated as the Overhaul and Repair Department on 22 July 1948.
4. Ibid., 395. The Navy Yard's name had variously been referred to as Gosport, Norfolk Navy Yard, "U.S. Navy Yard, Norfolk" (its official designation dates to 10 May 1862). In 1929 the Navy Department confusingly anointed the yard with the title, "Norfolk Navy Yard, Portsmouth." The present name, Norfolk Naval Shipyard, was formalized in December 1945.
5. Secretary of the Navy, letter to COMNAVBASE Norfolk, ser 14PO2, 20 November 1945 (HRNM); Secretary of the Navy, General Order 223 (HRNM), 14 September 1945.; Secretary of the Navy Note 5450, "Establishment of Naval Station, Norfolk," 13 November 1952 (HRNM); Chief of Naval Operations, letter to the Commander, Naval Base Norfolk, 4 February 1952 (HRNM); Chief of Naval Operations, letter to Commandant, Fifth Naval District, 18 February 1948 (HRNM); Naval Base Norfolk Commander, letter to the Chief of Naval Operations, 26 February 1948 (HRNM); Fifth Naval District Commandant, letter to the Chief of Naval Operations, 27 February 1948 (HRNM).
6. Secretary of the Navy, SECNAVNOTE 5450 (HRNM); Secretary of the Navy, letter to COMNAVBASE Norfolk ser 595P24, "Designation of Naval Training Center, Norfolk," 15 March 1946 (HRNM); Chief of Naval Operations, letter ser 05PO8, "Designation of Naval Supply Centers," 1 January 1948 (HRNM); *United States Naval Administration in World War II (Fifth Naval District) Appendix I* (Washington, DC: U.S. Navy, 1945), 75; Operational Training Command Commander, Atlantic, message to Commander-in-chief, Atlantic Fleet, 25 September 1945. On 15 June 1948 the Naval Training Center was disestablished; the Service Schools were assigned to the Receiving Station. On 1 January 1953 all training was transferred to a new Naval Schools Command at the Norfolk Naval Station.
7. John T Mason and Paul Stillwell, *Reminiscences of Rear Admiral Odale D. Waters, Jr., USN (ret)* (Annapolis: 1994), 299.
8. Ibid., 298. On 1 April 1970, the Skiffes Creek Annex of the Yorktown Naval Weapons Station was disestablished and was designated the Special Weapons Department of the station. The Explosive Engineering and Research Department was redesignated the Naval Explosive Development Engineering Department. The Special Weapons, Missile Component Rework, and Production Department functions were combined into Yorktown's Ordnance Department in 1972.
9. Atlantic Fleet headquarters stayed afloat during World War II aboard four different flagships: the cruiser *Augusta* (CA 31) from April 1941 to January 1942; the historic sloop *Constellation* from January to August 1942; the patrol gunboat *Vixen* (PG 53) from August 1942 to May 1946; and the amphibious command ship *Pocono* (AGC 16) from May 1946 to April 1948. On 5 April 1948, Atlantic Fleet headquarters moved ashore in Norfolk.
10. Lenoir Chambers and Joseph E. Shank, *Salt Water & Printers Ink* (Chapel Hill: University of North Carolina Press, 1967), 395.
11. *Dictionary of American Naval Fighting Ships* (Washington, DC: Government Printing Office, 1959),
12. Ibid.
13. John A. Butler, *Strike Able-Peter; the Stranding and Salvage of the USS Missouri* (Annapolis: Naval Institute Press, 1995), 61.
14. Ibid., 62.
15. Ibid., 68, 80.
16. Ibid., 128; Allan E. Smith, "Refloating the USS Missouri," *US Naval Institute Proceedings* (February 1951):182.
17. Butler, *Strike Able-Peter,* 166, 74; Smith, "Refloating the USS Missouri," 185.
18. Coletta, *United States Navy and Marine Corps Bases, Domestic,* 404; Dave Parsons and Derek Nelson, *Fighter Country: The F-14 Tomcats of NAS Oceana* (Osceola, Wisc.: Motorbooks International, 1992), 17; Ira R. Hanna, *The Growth of Norfolk Naval Air Station and the Norfolk-Portsmouth Metro-*

politan Area Economy in the Twentieth Century (Norfolk: Old Dominion, 1967), 57.

19. Coletta, *United States Navy and Marine Corps Bases, Domestic,* 405.
20. "NAS Oceana: A Wasteland No More," *Naval Aviation News,* October 1971, 37, 9.
21. Yarsinske, "Without Us, They Don't Fly," 6. The Naval Air Rework Facility at NAS Norfolk, then known as Naval Aviation Depot, Norfolk closed in 1996, as part of the congressional "Base Realignment and Closure" (BRAC) process.
22. "Truculent Turtle" surrendered its position at the corner of Granby Street and Taussig Boulevard with the construction of Interstate 564 in 1967. The plane is now at the National Museum of Naval Aviation in Pensacola, Florida.
23. Norman Polmar, "The First Nuclear Bomber," *Naval History,* February 2003, 14.
24. "Directory of US Naval Air Stations and US Naval Air Facilities, Continental United States," 1954.
25. Capt E. Lee Duckworth, "Air Station Profile: NAS Norfolk," *Foundation,* Spring 1994, 93.
26. The WF-2 (E-1B) *Tracer,* with its pancake-like radar above an S-2 *Tracker* airframe, was affectionately called the "Willy Fudd" from its "WF" designation.
27. Ray Boucree, Interview, 18 July 2004.; "HC-6 Squadron History," 2004. Search and Rescue operations at NAS Norfolk would be supported continuously until the retirement of the Station's Search and Rescue Unit on 1 October 2004.
28. Duckworth, "Air Station Profile: NAS Norfolk," 95.
29. Richard C. Knott, *A Heritage of Wings* (Annapolis: Naval Institute Press, 1997), 206.
30. *Three Generations of Shipbuilding* (Newport News, Va.: Newport News Shipbuilding and Drydock Co., 1961), 106.
31. Jeffrey G. Barlow, *Revolt of the Admiral: The Fight for Naval Aviation 1945–1950* (Washington, DC: Naval Historical Center, 1994), 135.
32. Walter H. Waggoner, "Keel is Laid for Super-Carrier," *New York Times,* 19 April 1949, 1; Norman Friedman, *U. S. Aircraft Carriers: An Illustrated Design History* (Annapolis: Naval Institute Press, 1983), 252.
33. Joe Law, *Norfolk Naval Shipyard: Its Remarkable History* (Norfolk Naval Shipyard, unpublished), 362.
34. Paul Stillwell, *Reminiscences of Vice Admiral Joe Williams, Jr., US Navy (ret)* (Annapolis: 2002), 384, 400; Law, *Norfolk Naval Shipyard: Its Remarkable History,* 293, 363.
35. William O. Foss, *The United States Navy in Hampton Roads* (Norfolk: Donning Company, 1984), 115; *International Naval Review and Fleet Week, June 8–17 1957, Hampton Roads, Virginia* (Norfolk: 1957), 8. Thirty-three ships from seventeen countries, including Belgium, Canada, Columbia, Cuba, Denmark, Dominican Republic, France, Italy, the Netherlands, Norway, Peru, Portugal, Spain, Turkey, the United Kingdom, Uruguay, and Venezuela, joined sixty U.S. Navy ships during the Hampton Roads International Naval Review of 1957.
36. Jack Raymond, "Unknown Soldier of World War II is Selected at Sea," *New York Times,* 27 May 1958, 1; *Dictionary of American Naval Fighting Ships.*
37. Gordon Calhoun, "Task Force Alpha in the Bay of Pigs," *The Daybook* (Summer 2003): 15; "The Bay of Pigs Invasion: A Chronology of Events," George Washington University, 2001),
38. Laurence Chang and Kornbluh, "The Cuban Missile Crisis 1962" (New York: The New Press, 1998), 357. Interestingly, the exercise on the Caribbean island of Vieques just prior to the Cuban Missile Crisis was planned with a scenario that described the assault as a means to overthrow an imaginary tyrant named "Ortsac" ("Castro" spelled backwards).
39. Chief of Naval Operations, "Report on the Naval Quarantine of Cuba," 1962.
40. Ibid.
41. William Burr and Thomas S. Blanton, "The Submarines of October: US and Soviet Naval Encounters during the Cuban Missile Crisis" (2002); Knott, *A Heritage of Wings,* 237.
42. Chief of Naval Operations, "Report on the Naval Quarantine of Cuba."
43. John McCain, *Faith of My Fathers* (New York: Random House, 1999), 178.
44. FRAM = Fleet Rehabilitation and Modernization program. A broad upgrade program including humm and machinery, weapons, communications, and sensors for ships of middle age built during World War II, especially destroyers, to avoid obsolescence during the early 1960s.
45. James M. Ennes, Jr., *Assault on the Liberty: The True Story of the Israeli Attack on an American Intelligence Ship* (New York: Random House, 1979).
46. Michael R. Adams, "Norfolk: Lucrative Target?," *US Naval Institute Proceedings* (December 1974): 90; James C. Van Slyke, "Comment/Discussion," *US Naval Institute Proceedings* (April 1975): 87.
47. Robert DeVary, interview, 21 June 2003; Thomas C. Parramore, *Norfolk, The First Four Centuries* (Charlottesville: University Press of Virginia, 1994), 374.
48. DeVary, interview; Jack Kestner, "What the Navy Brings, Tidewater Keeps," *Ledger-Star,* 24 August 1966, 26.
49. DeVary, interview.
50. G. William Whitehurst, interview, 24 June 2003. G. William Whitehurst (R-Va.) served as the representative from the Second District from 1969 to 1987.
51. Ibid.; Steve Laabs, interview, 23 February 2003.
52. *Dictionary of American Naval Fighting Ships.*
53. Paul Stillwell, *Reminiscences of Admiral Harold Edson Shear, US Navy (ret.)* (Annapolis: 1997), 206; Paul Stillwell, *Reminiscences of Rear Admiral Norvell G. Ward, US Navy (ret.)* (Annapolis: 1996), 377. Vice Adm. Elton W. (Joe) Grenfell was given a third star with the shift of SUBLANT to Norfolk from Groton, commanding from 2 September 1960 to 1 September 1964. On 1 October 2001 Commander, Submarine Force, U.S. Atlantic Fleet, assumed additional

duties as Commander, Naval Submarine Force (COMNAV-SUBFOR).

54. Owen R. Cote, "The Third Battle: Innovation in the US Navy's Silent Cold War Struggle with Soviet Submarines," Naval War College Newport Papers.
55. Gerald Nifontoff, interview, 22 July 2004.
56. Michael Duncan, interview, 8 August 2004. The GIUK Gap is the oceanic chokepoint near Greenland, Iceland, and the United Kingdom, consisting of the Denmark and open ocean waters between Iceland and the British Isles.
57. Sherry Sontag and Christopher Drew, *Blind Man's Bluff: The Untold Story of American Submarine Espionage* (New York: Public Affairs, 1998), 127, 39. For his efforts, Cdr. Whitey Mack and the *Lapon* won the Presidential Unit Citation, the citation of which was typically "silent service": "presented for extraordinary heroism and outstanding performance of duty-during a period in 1969. Throughout this period, the USS *Lapon* successfully executed its unique mission. The results of the mission were of extreme significance to the United States. The outstanding courage, resourcefulness, persistence and aggressiveness of the officers and men of *Lapon* reflected great credit upon the Submarine Force and were in keeping with the highest traditions of the United States Naval Service."
58. Ibid., 284.
59. Duncan, interview.
60. Ibid.; Sontag and Drew, *Blind Man's Bluff,* 89.
61. Norman Friedman, *The Fifty-Year War* (Annapolis: Naval Institute Press, 2000), 486.
62. John Fass Morton, *Mustin: A Naval Family of the Twentieth Century* (Annapolis: Naval Institute Press, 2003), 379.
63. Sontag and Drew, *Blind Man's Bluff,* 3, 90.
64. Ibid., 97, 106.
65. Ibid., 19, 107.; Mark A. Bradley, "Why They Called the Scorpion "Scrapiron," *US Naval Institute Proceedings* (July 1998): 37.
66. Jack Kneece, *Family Treason: the Walker Spy Case* (Briarcliff, N.Y.: Stein and Day, 1986), 132. Michael Walker was paroled in February 2000, at age thirty-seven, having served fifteen years in prison.

1991

1. Chief of Naval Operations, "The United States Navy in 'Desert Shield'/'Desert Storm'" 1991.
2. *Virginian-Pilot/Ledger Star* Special Edition, *Virginian-Pilot,* 2 April 1991, E14.
3. Fleet Hospital Five also deployed to Croatia in 1995 with sixty-seven men and women from NMC Portsmouth, treating 10,000 U.N. patients, admitting 350 to the tent hospital, and performing 250 surgeries.
4. Chief of Naval Operations, "The United States Navy in 'Desert Shield'/'Desert Storm.'"
5. *Virginian-Pilot/Ledger Star* Special Edition, E3.
6. Ibid., F6, H30.
7. Chief of Naval Operations, "The United States Navy in 'Desert Shield'/'Desert Storm.'"
8. *Virginian-Pilot/Ledger Star* Special Edition, F8.
9. Ibid., E2, F14.
10. Ibid, E1.
11. Chief of Naval Operations, "The United States Navy in 'Desert Shield'/'Desert Storm.'"
12. *Virginian-Pilot/Ledger Star* Special Edition, F8.
13. Francis Douglas Fane and Don Moore, *The Naked Warriors* (Annapolis: Naval Institute Press, 1956), 10; Roger Clapp, Interview, 20 January 2004; John B. Dwyer, *Scouts and Raiders: The Navy's First Special Warfare Commandos* (Westport, CT: Praeger, 1993), 8. Beyond their beach commando duties, Scouts and Raiders also helped organize guerilla warfare against the Japanese in China.
14. Fane and Moore *The Naked Warriors,* 23.
15. Orr Kelly, *Brave Men Dark Waters* (Novato, CA: Presidio Press, 1995), 78.
16. Ibid., 97.
17. Ibid., 187.
18. Ibid., 187–88, 92.
19. *Command History, the Armed Forces Staff College 1946–1981* (1981), 7.
20. COMSUBLANT is an operational commander for the U. S. Strategic Command (STRATCOM) for strategic deterrent submarine operations. COMSUBLANT also has duties within NATO as the Commander, Allied Submarine Command (COMASC) and as principal advisor for undersea warfare to the Supreme Allied Commander, Europe (SACEUR).
21. Lord Robertson, "Remarks at the Commissioning Ceremony of the new Allied Command Transformation," 19 June 2003.
22. Chief of Naval Operations, OPNAV Notice 5040, 20 December 1961 (HRNM); Chief of Naval Operations, CNO letter ser 09B32/12653, 24 January 1975 (HRNM); Chief of Naval Operations, Streamlining Shore Installation Management, 27 March 2003 (Commander, Navy Region Mid-Atlantic Records). The Commander, Naval Installations, stood up on 1 October 2003 to manage and oversee all shore installation support to the fleet.
23. Although NAS Norfolk has merged with Naval Station Norfolk, Air Detachment-Norfolk of Naval Air Station Oceana manages the airfield and heliport facilities at Chambers Field. The Naval Aviation Depot (NADEP) closed its doors on 11 September 1996, a victim of the BRAC (Base Realignment and Closure) process of early 1993.
24. Steven Milner, Interview, 24 October 2003.
25. Claire Bushey, "Fleet Week Ceremony Pays Tribute to Cole's Sailors," *Virginian-Pilot,* 19 October 2000, A10; Jack Dorsey, "The Final Salute," *Virginian-Pilot,* 19 October 2000, 1.
26. Steve Vogel, "Bearing Reminders of Terror, USS Cole Returns to Action," *Virginian-Pilot,* 4 December 2003, 33.
27. "A Rousing Return for Sailors who Missed a Proper Send Off," *Virginian-Pilot,* 30 May 2003, 1.

28. "Norfolk-based Ships Joined in First Wave of Missile Launches against Iraq," *Virginian-Pilot,* 21 March 2003, 11.
29. Matthew Dolan, "Dispatches from the Front," 27 July 2003, s14.
30. Ibid., s19.
31. Chris Tyree, "Surreal Nature of War, and Its Realities, Linger Long after," *Virginian Pilot,* 27 July 2003, s18.
32. Matthew Dolan, "Dispatches from the Front," s22.
33. Ibid., s21.
34. Richard D. Butler, "A Big Navy Needs Little Ships," *U.S. Naval Institute Proceedings,* October 2003, 99; Matthew Dolan, "Patrol Boats Guard Passage to Southern Port in Iraq," *Virginian-Pilot,* 28 April 2003, 1. *Chinook* and *Firebolt* provided a host of port security support in the rivers of southern Iraq, including security patrols, maritime interception operations, ship escort, and searches for arms caches. Within the first week of the war they were working forty miles inside Iraq.
35. Matthew Dolan, "As War Looms, Norfolk Base Turns into Virtual Ghost Town," *Virginian-Pilot,* 3 March 2003, 1.
36. Matthew Dolan, "On Hospital Ship, War Brings Out Wide Ranging Skills of Personnel," *Virginian-Pilot,* 22 April 2003, 6. Naval Hospital, Portsmouth, was renamed Naval Medical Center, Portsmouth, in 1993.
37. Matthew Jones, "A Long-awaited Welcome," *Virginian-Pilot,* 3 May 2003, 1.
38. Jack Dorsey and Matthew Dolan, "Back on Home Ground," *Virginian-Pilot,* 24 May 2003, 1; Matthew Dolan, "Dispatches from the Front," *Virginian-Pilot,* 27 July 2003, 40.
39. "Newport News, Local Sub, about to Return," *Virginian-Pilot,* 29 April 2003, 14; "A Rousing Return for Sailors who Missed a Proper Send Off," 1; "Sub Montpelier is Due Home in Norfolk Thursday from Iraq," *Virginian-Pilot,* 9 July 2003, 19. Norfolk-based submarines *Newport News* and *Boise* also contributed to the Tomahawk barrage unleashed during the Second Gulf War.
40. Carolyn Shapiro, "Carrier Construction Is All in the Family," *Virginian-Pilot,* 11 July 2003, 7.
41. Sarah Emma E. Edmonds, *Nurse and Spy in the Union Army: The Adventures and Experiences of a Woman in Hospitals, Camps and Battle-Fields* (Hartford, CT: Williams, 1865); Matthew Jones, "Tough Turret Makes it Home," *Virginian-Pilot,* 10 August 2002, 1.

BIBLIOGRAPHY

Archival Sources and Government Documents

Armed Forces Staff College. *Command History 1946–1981*. 1981. Hampton Roads Naval Museum Archives.

Bureau of Aeronautics. *World War II Administrative History, vol. 11, Aviation Shore Establishments*. Washington, DC: Department of the Navy, 1947.

———. *Directory of U.S. Naval Air Stations and U.S. Naval Air Facilities, Continental United States*. 16 June 1954. Navy Department Library.

Bureau of Naval Personnel. The History of Amphibious Training. *Bureau of Naval Personnel Training Bulletin*. NAVPERS 14923. 15 October 1944. Navy Department Library.

Bureau of Yards and Docks. *Activities of the Bureau of Yards and Docks 1917–18*. Washington, DC: Government Printing Office, 1921.

Deck Logs of U.S. Naval Vessels. RG 24. Washington, DC: National Archives and Records Service.

Department of the Navy. *Administrative History of the U.S. Atlantic Fleet in World War II*. Washington, DC, 1945. Navy Department Library.

———. *Building the Navy's Bases in World War II*. Washington, DC: Government Printing Office. 1947. Navy Department Library.

———. *Directory of U.S. Naval Air Stations and US Naval Air Facilities, Continental United States*. H.O. Pub No. D-502. 16 June 1954. Navy Department Library.

———. *General Records, 1798–1947*. RG80., Washington, DC: National Archives and Records Service.

———. *Proceedings of the Court Martial Convened for the Trial of Commodore James Barron et al of the United States Ship Chesapeake in the month of January 1808*. Washington, DC. 1822. Navy Department Library.

———. *Report of Board Covering Valuation of Site for Naval Operating Base, Hampton Roads, VA*. Washington, DC: U.S. Government Printing Office, 1918.

———. *United States Naval Administration in World War II (Commander, Atlantic Fleet)*. Washington, DC, 1945. Navy Department Library.

———. *United States Naval Administration in World War II (Commander, Fleet Operational Training)*. Washington, DC, 1945. Navy Department Library.

———. *United States Naval Administration in World War II (Convoy and Routing)*. Washington, DC, 1945. Navy Department Library

———. *United States Naval Administration in World War II (DCNO-Air)*. Washington, DC, 1945. Navy Department Library.

———. *United States Naval Administration in World War II (Fifth Naval District)*. Washington, DC, 1945. Navy Department Library.

———. *United States Naval Administration in World War II (Fifth Naval District) Appendix I*. Washington, DC, 1945. Navy Department Library.

———. *United States Naval Administration in World War II (Mine Warfare)*. Washington, DC, 1945. Navy Department Library.

Director of Naval Aviation. Weekly Report. Washington, DC:, Department of the Navy. National Museum of Naval Aviation, Pensacola, FL.

"Expenditures of the Navy and Navy Yards, 1798–1815." Doc No. 27. *American State Papers, Naval Affairs*, vol. I. Washington, DC. Navy Department Library.

"Fortifications MAD 206 ASP-MA." Washington, DC. 15 February 1821. *American State Papers*, Class V, Military Affairs. Washington, DC. Navy Department Library.

Goldsborough, Louis M. *Louis Malesherbes Goldsborough Papers*. Manuscript Division. Library of Congress. Washington, DC.

Myers, Moses. *Moses Myers Papers*. Jean Outland Chrysler Library. Norfolk.

Naval Facilities Engineering Command. *Cast Down Your Bucket Where You Are: An Ethnohistorical Study of the African-American Community on the Lands of the Yorktown Naval Weapons Station, 1865–1918*. Norfolk, 1992. Navy Department Library.

———. *Architectural Investigations of St Julien's Creek Annex*. R. Christopher Goodwin & Associates. Norfolk. 1997. Norfolk Naval Shipyard Public Affairs Office.

Naval Operating Base, Norfolk. *Narrative History of Development of Naval Facilities in the Sewell's Point Area to the Year 1951*. Station

Development Board. 15 January 1952. Hampton Roads Naval Museum Archives.

Navy Region Mid-Atlantic. *Architectural Inventory of Norfolk Naval Shipyard & Satellite Activities, Portsmouth, VA*. Norfolk. July 2003. Norfolk Naval Shipyard Public Affairs Office.

Norfolk Naval Shipyard. *Command History*. Portsmouth, VA. August 1959. Portsmouth Naval Shipyard Museum.

Pendergrast, Garrett. J. *Letter Book of Flag Officer Garrett J. Pendergrast*. National Archives, RG45, entry 38. Washington, DC.

Peters, W. H. *Inventory of Property Taken from the United States Government at the Navy Yard, Gosport and in and near Portsmouth, Virginia. Portsmouth, VA*. 30 Nov 1861. Navy Department Library.

Office of the Chief of Naval Operations, RG 38, National Archives and Records Service, Washington, DC.

———. *Report on the Naval Quarantine of Cuba*. Naval Historical Center, Operational Archives Branch. Post 46 Command File, Box 10.

Register of Officers of the Confederate States Navy, 1861–65. Washington, DC: U.S. Government Printing Office. 1931. National Archives Research Library.

Secretary of the Navy. *Annual Reports*. Department of the Navy, Washington, DC.

———. RG80. Washington, DC: National Archives and Records Service.

U.S. Congress. *Preliminary Report of the Navy Yard Commission (Helm Report)*. 64th Cong., 2nd sess., 17 January 1917. H. Doc. 1946. Washington, DC: U.S. Government Printing Office. 1921.

———. "Report of the Commission on Navy Yards." 48th Cong., 1st sess. Ex Doc No. 55. Washington, DC, 1 December 1883.

———. "Report of Inspection of Navy Yard at Norfolk, VA." John R. Edwards. 63rd Cong., 1st sess. *General Condition at Navy Yards and Naval Stations on the Atlantic and Gulf Coast*. Washington, DC. 1913.

Welles, Roger. Welles Papers. Naval Historical Foundation Collection, Library of Congress, Washington, DC.

Books and Articles

Abbazia, Patrick. *Mr. Roosevelt's Navy*. Annapolis: Naval Institute Press, 1975.

Adams, Michael R. "Norfolk: Lucrative Target?" *U.S. Naval Institute Proceedings* (December 1974):90–91.

Alden, John D. *The American Steel Navy*. Annapolis: Naval Institute Press, 1972.

Allston, Frank J. *Ready for Sea: The Bicentennial History of the U.S. Navy Supply Corps*. Annapolis: Naval Institute Press, 1995.

Ammen, Daniel. "DuPont and the Port Royal Expedition." *Battles and Leaders of the Civil War I* (1887):671–91.

Anthony, Irvin. *Decatur*. New York: Charles Scribner's Sons, 1931.

Ashbrook, A. W. *The History of Our Navy Yard*. Portsmouth, Va.: Retirement Federation of Civil Service Employees, 1927.

Barlow, Jeffrey G. *Revolt of the Admirals: The Fight for Naval Aviation 1945–1950*. Washington, DC: Naval Historical Center, 1994.

Belknap, Reginald R. "The Yankee Mining Squadron." *U.S. Naval Institute Proceedings* (December 1919):1973–2011.

Bishop, Joseph B., Ed. *Theodore Roosevelt's Letters to his Children*. New York: C. Scribner's Sons, 1919.

Blair, Clay. *Hitler's U-boat War: The Hunted 1942–1945*. New York: Random House, 1998.

———. *Hitler's U-boat War: The Hunters 1939–1942*. New York: Random House, 1996.

Blewett, William E., Jr. *Always Good Ships: A History of the Newport News Shipbuilding and Dry Dock Company*. New York: Newcomen Society in North America, 1960.

Booker, Marshall. "Privateering from the Bay, Including Admiralty Courts and Tory as well as Patriot Operations." In *Chesapeake Bay in the American Revolution*. Edited by E. M. Eller. Centreville, Md: Tidewater Publishers, 1981, 261–81.

Bradley, Mark. A. "Why They Called the Scorpion 'Scrapiron.'" *U.S. Naval Institute Proceedings* (July 1998):52–55.

Brewington, M. V. *Chesapeake Bay, A Pictorial Maritime History*. New York: Bonanza Books, 1956.

Breyer, Siegfried. *Battleships and Battle Cruisers, 1905–1970*. Garden City: Doubleday & Company, 1970.

Brooke, John M. "The Plan and Construction of the Merrimac." *Battles and Leaders of the Civil War I* (1887):715–16.

Browning, Robert M., Jr. *From Cape Charles to Cape Fear, the North Atlantic Blockading Squadron During the Civil War*. Tuscaloosa: University of Alabama Press, 1993.

Buell, Thomas B. "Saga of Drydock One." *U.S. Naval Institute Proceedings* (July 1970):60–68.

Building the Navy's Bases in World War II. Washington, DC: Government Printing Office, 1947.

Burnett, Heather. "Bear Down and Engage: The Battle off the Virginia Capes, September 1781." *The Day Book,* November 1995, 1–7.

Butler, John A. *Strike Able-Peter; the Stranding and Salvage of the USS Missouri*. Annapolis: Naval Institute Press, 1995.

Butler, Richard D. "A Big Navy Needs Little Ships." *U.S. Naval Institute Proceedings* (October 2003):99–100.

Bushey, Claire. "Fleet Week Ceremony Pays Tribute to Cole's Sailors." *Virginian-Pilot,* 19 October 2000, A10.

Butt, Marshall W. *Norfolk Naval Shipyard, a Brief History*. Portsmouth, Va.: Public Information Office, NNSY, 1951.

———. *Portsmouth Under Four Flags: 1752–1970*. Portsmouth, Va.: Portsmouth Historical Association, 1971.

Calderhead, William L. "Naval Innovation in Crisis: War in the Chesapeake, 1813." *The American Neptune* (July 1976): 201–21.

Calhoun, Gordon. "A Classic American Warship." *The Daybook* (February 2004):6–18.

———. "Task Force Alpha in the Bay of Pigs." *The Daybook* (Summer 2003):6–8.

———. "The Birth of a Giant." *The Day Book* (May 1997):4–8.

———. "The Norfolk Navy Yard During the Navy's Dark Ages." *The Day Book* 8, no. 4(2003):6–15.

Calhoun, Gordon, and Joe Judge. "The Navy Builds a Home." *The Day Book* 4, no. 1(1997):1–8.

Callahan, Edward W. *List of Officers of the Navy of the United States and of the Marine Corps from 1775 to 1900*. New York: Haskell House Publishers, 1969.

Campbell, R. Thomas. *Academy on the James*. Shippensburg, Pa.: Burd Street Press, 1998.

Canney, Donald L. *Sailing Warships of the U.S. Navy*. Annapolis: Naval Institute Press, 2001.

Carrison, Daniel J. *The Navy from Wood to Steel, 1860–1890*. New York: Franklin Watts Inc. 1965.

Chambers, Lenoir, and Joseph E. Shank. *Salt Water & Printers Ink*. Chapel Hill: University of North Carolina Press, 1967.

Chapelle, Howard I. *The History of the American Sailing Navy*. New York: Konecky & Konecky, 1949.

Churchill, Winston S. *Memoirs of the Second World War*. Boston: Houghton Mifflin Company, 1959.

———. *The World Crisis*. New York: Scribner's Sons, 1931.

Clary, David A. *Fortress America: The Corps of Engineers, Hampton Roads, and United States Coastal Defense*. Charlottesville: University Press of Virginia, 1990.

Clowes, William L. *The Royal Navy: A History from the Earliest Times to the Present*. London: Sampson, Low, Marston and Company, 1899.

Coletta, Paolo E. Patrick N. L. Bellinger. Lanham, MD: University Press of America, 1987.

———. Ed. *American Secretaries of the Navy*. Annapolis: Naval Institute Press, 1980.

———. Ed. *United States Navy and Marine Corps Bases, Domestic*. Westport, Conn.: Greenwood Press, 1985.

Colston, R. E. "Watching the Merrimac." *Battles and Leaders of the Civil War* I (1887):712–14.

Cooling, Benjamin Franklin. *The New American State Papers, 1789–1860*. Wilmington, Del: Scholarly Resources, 1979.

Combe, Jack D. *Gunsmoke Over the Atlantic*. New York: Bantam Books, 2002.

Cote, Owen R. "The Third Battle: Innovation in the US Navy's Silent Cold War Struggle with Soviet Submarines." *Naval War College Newport Papers* 16(2003).

Cronan, E. David, Ed. *The Cabinet Diaries of Josephus Daniels, 1913–1921*. Lincoln: University of Nebraska Press, 1963.

Cross, Charles B. Jr. *The Chesapeake, A Biography of a Ship*. Chesapeake, Va.: Norfolk County Historical Society, 1968.

Cunningham, A. C. "The Development of the Norfolk Navy Yard." *U.S. Naval Institute Proceedings* (March 1910):221–38.

Current, Richard N., Ed. *Encyclopedia of the Confederacy*. New York: Simon & Schuster, 1993.

Curtin, Philip D., Grace S. Brush, et al. Eds. *Discovering the Chesapeake: The History of an Ecosystem*. Baltimore: Johns Hopkins University Press, 2001.

Curtin, Theodore A. *A Marriage of Convenience: Norfolk and the Navy, 1917–1967*. Thesis, Old Dominion College, 1969.

Daly, Robert W. Ed. *Aboard the USS Monitor, The Letters of Acting Paymaster William Frederick Keeler, U.S. Navy, to his Wife, Anna*. Annapolis: U.S. Naval Institute, 1964.

Davis, Burke. *The Billy Mitchell Affair*. New York: Random House, 1967.

DeKay, James T. *A Rage for Glory: The Life of Commodore Stephen Decatur, USN*. New York: Free Press, 2004.

Dictionary of American Naval Fighting Ships. Washington, DC: Government Printing Office, 1959.

Dillingham, A. C. "U.S. Naval Training Service." *U.S. Naval Institute Proceedings* (June 1910):343–74.

Dolan, Matthew. "As War Looms, Norfolk Base Turns into Virtual Ghost Town." *Virginian-Pilot,* 3 March 2003, 1.

———. "Dispatches from the Front." *Virginian-Pilot,* 27 July 2003.

———. "On Hospital Ship, War Brings Out Wide Ranging Skills of Personnel." *Virginian-Pilot,* 22 April 2003, 6.

———. "Patrol Boats Guard Passage to Southern Port in Iraq." *Virginian-Pilot,* 28 April 2003, 1.

Dorsey, Jack. "The Final Salute." *Virginian-Pilot,* 19 October 2000, 1.

Dorsey, Jack, and Matthew Dolan. "Back on Home Ground." *Virginian-Pilot,* 24 May 2003, 1.

Duckworth, E. Lee. "Air Station Profile: NAS Norfolk." *Foundation* (Spring 1994):92–97.

Dudley, Wade G. *Splintering the Wooden Wall: The British Blockade of the United States, 1812–1815*. Annapolis: Naval Institute Press, 2003.

Dudley, William S. Ed. *The Naval War of 1812: A Documentary History*. Washington, DC: Naval Historical Center, 1985.

Dwyer, John B. *Scouts and Raiders: the Navy's First Special Warfare Commandos*. Westport, Conn.: Praeger, 1993.

Edmonds, Sarah E. E. *Nurse and Spy in the Union Army: The Adventures and Experiences of a Woman in Hospitals, Camps and Battle-Fields*. Hartford: Williams, 1865.

Eley, Bill. "With a Grateful Heart: Norfolk's Gift to the Man who Defended James Barron, The Rodney Urn." *The Day Book* (January 1997):5–10.

Eller, Ernest M. Ed. *Chesapeake Bay in the American Revolution*. Centreville, Md: Tidewater Publishers, 1981.

Ellis, James H. *Mad Jack Percival: Legend of the Old Navy*. Annapolis: Naval Institute Press, 2002.

Engen, Donald D. "Eugene Ely—First from the Sea." *Foundation* (Spring 1995):42–47.

Ennes, James M., Jr. *Assault on the Liberty: The True Story of the Israeli Attack on an American Intelligence Ship*. New York: Random House, 1979.

Fallaw, Robert, and Marion W. Stoer. *The Old Dominion Under Fire: The Chesapeake Invasions, 1779–1781*. Centreville, Md: Tidewater Publishers, 1981.

Fane, Francis Douglas, and Don Moore. *The Naked Warriors*. Annapolis: Naval Institute Press, 1956.

Farago, Ladislas. *The Tenth Fleet*. New York: Ivan Obolensky. 1962.

Ferguson, Eugene S. *Truxtun of the Constellation*. Baltimore: Johns Hopkins University Press, 2000.

Field, Bruce E. *Norfolk in Wartime: The Effect of the First World War on the Expansion of a Southern City*. Thesis. East Carolina University, 1978.

Final Report of the Jamestown Ter-Centennial Commission. Washington: Government Printing Office, 1909.

Flanders, Alan. "Flying off flattops has roots in Hampton Roads." *Portsmouth Currents,* 15 June 2003, 3.

———."Old Ironsides ran on wind, and good Gosport rum." *Portsmouth Currents,* 13 April 2003, 3.

———. "Willoughby left more than a spit in Hampton Roads." *Portsmouth Currents,* 2 March 2003, 3.

———. "Yellow Jack's 1855 visit unforgettable." *Portsmouth Currents,* 7 September 2003, 3.

———. *Bluejackets on the Elizabeth.* White Stone, Va.: Brandylane Publishers, 1998.

Footner, Geoffrey M. *USS Constellation: from Frigate to Sloop of War.* Annapolis: Naval Institute Press, 2003.

Forrest, William S. *Historical and Descriptive Sketches of Norfolk and Vicinity.* Philadelphia: Lindsay and Blakiston, 1853.

Foss, William O. *The United States Navy in Hampton Roads.* Norfolk: Donning Company, 1984.

Fowler, William M. Jr. *Jack Tars & Commodores: The American Navy* 1783–1815. Boston: Houghton Mifflin Company, 1984.

Friedman, Norman. *The Fifty-Year War.* Annapolis: Naval Institute Press, 2000.

———. *U.S. Aircraft Carriers: An Illustrated Design His*tory. Annapolis: Naval Institute Press, 1983.

———. *U.S. Cruisers: An Illustrated Design History.* Annapolis: Naval Institute Press, 1984.

———. *U.S. Destroyers: An Illustrated Design History.* Annapolis: Naval Institute Press, 1982.

Fry, John. *USS Saratoga CV-3.* Atgien, Pa.: Schiffer Publishing Ltd., 1996.

———. *Hampton Roads and Four Centuries as a World's Seaport.* Lewiston, N.Y.: Edwin Mellen Press, 1996.

Gaines, Edwin M. "The Chesapeake Affair: Virginians Mobilize to Defend National Honor." *The Virginia Magazine of History and Biography* 64, no. 2(1956):130–42.

Gaines, William H. "Craney Island, or Norfolk Delivered." *Virginia Cavalcade* I(3)(1951):32–35.

George, Christopher T. *Terror on the Chesapeake: the War of 1812 on the Bay.* Shippensburg, Pa.: White Mane Books, 2000.

Glines, Carroll V. *The Doolittle Raid.* New York: Orion Books, 1988.

Goldenberg, Joseph A. "Virginia Ports." In *Chesapeake Bay in the American Revolution,* 310–40. Edited by E. M. Eller. Centreville, Md: Tidewater Publishers, 1981.

Goldenberg, Joseph A., and M. W. Stoer. "The Virginia State Navy." In *Chesapeake Bay in the American Revolution,* 170–203. Edited by E. M. Eller. Centreville, Md: Tidewater Publishers, 1981.

Grattan, John W. *Under the Blue Pennant.* New York: John Wiley & Sons, 1999.

Greene, Dana. "In the Monitor Turret." *Battles and Leaders of the Civil War.* I(1887):719–29.

Greene, S. Dana. "The Monitor at Sea and in Battle." *U.S. Naval Institute Proceedings* (November 1923):1839–47.

Griffin, Alexander R. *A Ship to Remember, the Saga of the Hornet.* New York: Howell Soskin Publishers, 1943.

Guttridge, Leonard F., and Jay D. Smith. *The Commodores.* New York: Harper & Row, 1969.

Hagan, Kenneth J. *This People's Navy: The Making of American Sea Power.* New York: Free Press, 1991.

Hallahan, John M. *The Battle of Craney Island: A Matter of Credit.* Portsmouth, Va.: Saint Michael's Press, 1986.

Hanna, Ira R. *The Growth of Norfolk Naval Air Station and the Norfolk-Portsmouth Metropolitan Area Economy in the Twentieth Century.* Thesis. Old Dominion University, 1967.

Hannon, Bryan. *Three American Commodores.* New York: Spinner Press, 1936.

Harrod, Frederick S. *Manning the New Navy, the Development of a Modern Naval Enlisted Force.* Westport, Conn.: Greenwood Press, 1978.

Hart, Robert A. *The Great White Fleet: Its Voyage Around the World, 1907–1909.* Boston: Little, Brown and Company, 1965.

Headley, Joel T. *Farragut and Our Naval Commanders.* New York: E. B. Treat & Co., 1867.

Hepburn, Richard D. *History of American Naval Dry Docks.* Arlington: Noesis, Inc., 2003.

Hepper, David J. *British Warship Losses in the Age of Sail, 1650–1859.* East Sussex, England: Jean Bourdriot Publications, 1994.

Hoehling, A. A. *Thunder at Hampton Roads.* Englewood Cliffs, N.J.: Prentice-Hall, 1976.

Holcomb, Richard C. *A Century with Norfolk Naval Hospital.* Portsmouth, Va.: Printcraft Publishing Co., 1930.

Hoppin, James M. *Life of Andrew Hull Foote, Rear Admiral, United States Navy.* New York: Harper & Brothers, 1874.

Hoyt, Edwin P. *McCampbell's Heroes.* New York: Van Nostrand Reinhold Company, 1983.

———. *U-boats Offshore: When Hitler Struck America. New* York: Stein and Day Publishers, 1978.

Hutcheon, Wallace, Jr. *Robert Fulton: Pioneer of Undersea Warfare.* Annapolis: Naval Institute Press. 1981.

International Naval Review and Fleet Week, June 8–17, 1957, Hampton Roads, Virginia. Pamphlet. Norfolk. 1957. Hampton Roads Naval Museum Archives.

James, William. *The British Navy in Adversity.* New York: Russell & Russell, 1926.

———. *The Naval History of Great Britain, From the Declaration of War by France in 1793 to the Accession of George IV.* London: Macmillan and Co., 1902.

Johnson, Robert Edwin. *Rear Admiral John Rodgers 1812–1882.* Annapolis: U.S. Naval Institute, 1967.

———. *Thence Round Cape Horn: The Story of United States Naval Forces on Pacific Station 1818–1923.* Annapolis: Naval Institute Press, 1963.

Jones, Matthew. "A Long-awaited Welcome." *Virginian-Pilot,* 3 May 2003, 1.

———. "Tough Turret Makes it Home." *Virginian-Pilot,* 10 August 2002, 1.

Jones, Robert D. *With the American Fleet from the Atlantic to the Pacific.* Seattle: Harrison Publishing Co., 1908.

Jones, Virgil C. *The Civil War at Sea: The Blockaders*. New York: Holt, Rinehart, Winston, 1960.

———. *The Civil War at Sea: The River War*. New York: Holt, Rinehart, Winston, 1961.

Judge, Joe "Hampton Roads' Hidden History: St. Julien's Creek Annex." *The Day Book* 3, no. 5(1997):3.

Kelly, Orr. *Brave Men Dark Waters*. Novato, Calif.: Presidio Press, 1995.

Kestner, Jack. "What the Navy Brings, Tidewater Keeps." *Ledger-Star,* 24 August 1966, 26.

Ketenheim, Bob. *USS Shangri-La*. Paducah, Ky.: Turner Publishing Company, 2002.

Kline, Mary-Jo. Ed. *Political Correspondence and Public Papers of Aaron Burr*. Princeton: Princeton University Press, 1983.

Kneece, Jack. *Family Treason: the Walker Spy Case*. Briarcliff, N.Y.: Stein and Day, 1986.

Knott, Richard. C. *A Heritage of Wings*. Annapolis: Naval Institute Press, 1997.

Knox, Dudley W., Ed. *Naval Documents Related to the Quasi-War between the United States and France*. Washington, DC: Government Printing Office, 1986.

Lake, Simon. *The Submarine in War and Peace*. Philadelphia: J.B. Lippincott Company, 1918.

Larrabee, Harold. A. *Decision at the Chesapeake*. New York: Bramhall House, 1964.

Leiner, Frederick. C. *Millions for Defense: The Subscription Warships of 1798*. Annapolis: Naval Institute Press, 2000.

———. "The Norfolk War Scare." *Naval History* (Summer 1993) 36–38.

Lewis, Charles Lee. *Admiral Franklin Buchanan: Fearless Man of Action*. Baltimore: Norman, Remington Company, 1929.

———. *David Glasgow Farragut: Admiral in the Making*. Annapolis: U.S. Naval Institute, 1941.

Lewis, Earl. *In Their Own Interests*. Berkeley: University of California Press, 1991.

Lewis, Hunt. "Beyond the Monitor and the Virginia." *The Day Book* (March 1996):1–6.

Linder, Bruce. *San Diego's Navy*. Annapolis: Naval Institute Press, 2001.

"Little Creek and 'Gator.'" *Know Norfolk Virginia,* July 1945, 68. Kirn Memorial Library.

Lord, C. C. *Life and Times in Hopkinton*. Concord, N.H.: Republican Press, 1890.

Lull, Edward P. *History of the United States Navy Yard at Gosport, Virginia (Near Norfolk)*. Washington, DC: Government Printing Office, 1874.

MacGregor, Morris J., Jr. *Integration of the Armed Forces, 1940–1965*. Washington, DC: Center of Military History, 1981.

Mapp, Alf J., Jr. "The Pirate Peer: Lord Dunmore's Operations in the Chesapeake Bay." In *Chesapeake Bay in the American Revolution, 55–97*. Edited by E. M. Eller. Centreville, Md: Tidewater Publishers, 1981.

Marsh, Charles F. Ed. *The Hampton Roads Communities in World War II*. Chapel Hill: University of North Carolina Press, 1951.

Martin, Christopher. *Damn the Torpedoes: The Story of America's First Admiral, David Glasgow Farragut*. New York: Abelard-Schuman, 1970.

Mason, John T., and P. Stillwell. *Reminiscences of Rear Admiral Odale D. Waters, Jr., USN* (ret.), 424. U.S. Naval Institute Oral History Collection. Annapolis, 1994.

Mason, John T. *Reminiscences of Admiral George W. Anderson, Jr., U.S. Navy* (ret.), 353. U.S. Naval Institute Oral History Collection. Annapolis, 1981.

———. *Reminiscences of Vice Admiral Bernhard H. Bieri, U.S. Navy* (ret.), 255. U. S. Naval Institute Oral History Collection. Annapolis, 1970.

———. *Reminiscences of Vice Admiral Gerald E. Miller, US Navy* (ret.), 398. U.S. Naval Institute Oral History Collection. Annapolis, 1983.

Massie, Robert K. *Castles of Steel*. New York: Random House, 2003.

Matthews, Franklin. *With the Battle Fleet*. New York: B. W. Huebsch, 1908.

McCain, John. *Faith of My Fathers*. New York: Random House, 1999.

McCullough, David. *John Adams*. New York: Simon & Schuster, 2001.

Melhorn, Charles M. *Two-Block Fox, the Rise of the Aircraft Carrier 1911–1929*. Annapolis: Naval Institute Press, 1974.

Middleton, Arthur Pierce. *Tobacco Coast*. Baltimore: Johns Hopkins University Press, 1953.

Mills, Eric. *Chesapeake Bay in the Civil War*. Centreville, Md: Tidewater Publishers, 1996.

Morison, Samuel. E. *Old Bruin: Commodore Matthew C. Perry 1794–1858*. Boston: Little, Brown and Co., 1967.

———. *The Battle of the Atlantic; September 1939–May 1943*. Boston: Little, Brown and Company, 1984.

———. *The European Discovery of America: The Northern Voyages, A.D. 500–1600*. New York: Oxford University Press, 1971.

Morris, Edmund. *Theodore Rex*. New York: Modern Library, 2001.

Morton, John F. *Mustin: A Naval Family of the Twentieth Century*. Annapolis: Naval Institute Press, 2003.

Mosier, Joe. "Another Nail in the Kaiser's Coffin: The North Sea Mine Barrage of 1918." *The Day Book* (January 1996):8–9.

———. "Building a Naval Legacy: the creation and construction of Norfolk Naval Shipyard's Drydock No. 1." *The Day Book* I, no. 5(1995):1–7.

———. "I Was Never at Sea in so Uneasy a Ship: The Trials, Misfortunes and Possible Curse of the United States Frigate Chesapeake." *The Day Book* (January 1997):1–8.

———. "NAS Norfolk: Reflections of Victory." *Flagship* 1.

———. "Prizes for Sale: Local Privateering in the War of 1812." *The Daybook* (July 2002):6–13.

———. "The Man Who Lost Gosport: Commodore McCauley and the Burning of the Gosport Shipyard." *The Day Book* (March 1996):8–11.

———. "The Steel Navy on Display." *The Day Book* (May 1997):1–7.

———. "To Protect the Several Rivers in This Colony: The Virginia State Navy of the Revolutionary War." *The Day Book* (Nov 1995):4–11.

———. "What Ship is That?" *The Day Book* 4(3):1–7, 1998.

Napier, Arthur. *Naval Review Held at Hampton Roads October 12–13, 1879*. Pamphlet. Norfolk: Landmark Books. Hampton Roads Naval Museum Archives.

Nasca, Stephen P. *Norfolk in the First World War*. Thesis. Old Dominion University, 1979.

Naval Air Station, Norfolk, VA. Yearbook. Atlanta, Ga.: Albert Love Enterprises. 1952. Navy Department Library.

Newcomer, Mary E. "There've Been Some Changes Made." *Our Navy* (Mid-July 1942):16.

Norfolk At War. Norfolk: The Norfolk Advertising Board, 1943. Kirn Memorial Library.

Norfolk Naval Shipyard, Portsmouth, Virginia: 200 Years of Service. Pamphlet. Portsmouth, Va. February 1967. Portsmouth Naval Shipyard Museum.

Niven, John. *Gideon Welles, Lincoln's Secretary of the Navy*. New York: Oxford University Press, 1973.

Official Records of the Union and Confederate Navies in the War of the Rebellion. Washington, DC: Government Printing Office, 1894.

Official Records of the Union and Confederate Armies in the War of the Rebellion. Washington, DC: Government Printing Office, 1893.

Oulahan, Richard. "Hoover Sails South; Spends Day Resting." *New York Times,* 20 March 1931, 1.

Our Flying Navy. New York: Macmillan Company, 1944.

Pack, James. *The Man Who Burned the White House*. Wiltshire, England: Redwood Burn Limited, 1987.

Paine, Ralph D. *The First Yale Unit: A Story of Naval Aviation 1916–1919*. Cambridge, Massachusetts: Riverside Press, 1925.

Parramore, Thomas C. *Norfolk, The First Four Centuries*. Charlottesville: University Press of Virginia, 1994.

Parsons, Dave and Derek Nelson. *Fighter Country: The F-14 Tomcats of NAS Oceana*. Osceola, Wis.: Motorbooks International, 1992.

Paullin, Charles Oscar. *Commodore John Rodgers; Captain, Commodore and Senior Officer of the American Navy, 1773–1838*. Annapolis: Naval Institute Press, 1909.

Philbrick, Nathaniel. *Sea of Glory: America's Voyage of Discovery. The U.S. Exploring Expedition 1838–1842*. New York: Viking Penguin, 2003.

Phillips, Dinwiddie B. "Notes on the Monitor-Merrimac Fight." *Battles and Leaders of the Civil War* I(1887):718.

Polmar, Norman. "The First Nuclear Bomber." *Naval History* (February 2003):14–16.

Poluhowich, John J. *Argonaut: The Submarine Legacy of Simon Lake*. College Station, Tex.: Texas A&M University Press, 1999.

Ponton, Jean A. *Rear Admiral Louis M. Goldsborough, The Formation of a Nineteenth Century Naval Officer*. Thesis. Washington, DC, Catholic University, 1996.

Porter, John L. "The Plan and Construction of the Merrimac." *Battles and Leaders of the Civil War* I(1887):716–17.

Porter, John W. H. *A Record of Events in Norfolk County, Virginia From April 19th, 1861 to May 10th 1862*. Portsmouth, Va.: W. A. Fiske, 1892.

Potter, E. B. *Bull Halsey*. Annapolis: Naval Institute Press, 1985.

Powars, David S. "The Effects of the Chesapeake Bay Impact Crater on the Geologic Framework and the Correlation of Hydrogeologic Units of Southwestern Virginia, South of the James River." Reston, Va.: U.S. Geological Survey, 2000.

Quarstein, John V. *CSS Virginia: Mistress of Hampton Roads*. Appomattox: H. E. Howard, Inc., 2000.

Rachal, William M. E. "When Virginia Owned a Shipyard." *Virginia Cavalcade* (Autumn 1952):31–35.

Ragan, Mark K. *Union and Confederate Submarine Warfare in the Civil War*. Cambridge, Mass.: Da Capo Press, 2002.

Raymond, Jack "Unknown Soldier of World War II is Selected at Sea." *New York Times,* 27 May 1958, 1.

Roberts, William H. *Civil War Ironclads*. Baltimore: Johns Hopkins University Press, 2002.

Robinson, J. A. "British Invade the Chesapeake, 1777." In *Chesapeake Bay in the American Revolution,* 341–77. Edited by E. M. Eller. Centreville, Md: Tidewater Publishers, 1981.

Rochelle, James. H. "The Confederate Steamship Patrick Henry." *Southern Historical Society Papers* 14(1896):127–36.

Roosevelt, Theodore. "The War with the United States 1812–1815". In *The Royal Navy, Vol. VI*. Edited by W. L. Clowes. London: Sampson, Low, Marston and Co., 1898.

———. *The Naval War of 1812*. New York: Charles Scribner's Sons, 1906.

Rose, Lisle A. *The Ship that Held the Line*. Annapolis: Naval Institute Press, 1995.

Roskill, Stephen. *Naval Policy Between the Wars: The Period of Anglo-American Antagonism, 1910–1929*. New York: Walker and Co., 1968.

Rouse, Parke Jr. "Low Tide at Hampton Roads." *U.S. Naval Institute Proceedings* (July 1969):79–86.

———. *The Good Old Days in Hampton and Newport News*. Richmond, Va.: The Dietz Press, 1986.

Sale, Kirkpatrick. *The Fire of His Genius: Robert Fulton and the American Dream*. New York: Free Press, 2001.

Schlegel, Marvin W. *Conscripted City, Norfolk in World War II*. Norfolk: Norfolk War History Commission, 1951.

Schley, Winfield Scott. *Forty-Five Years Under the Flag*. New York: D. Appleton and Company, 1904.

Sears, Stephen W. *George B. McClellan: The Young Napoleon*. New York: Ticknor & Fields, 1988.

Selfridge, Thomas O., Jr. *Memoirs of Thomas O. Selfridge, Jr.* New York: Knickerbocker Press, 1924.

Sewell, Worley L. *History of the Sewell Families in America*. Privately printed. Files of the Virginia Historical Society, 1955.

Shapiro, Carolyn. "Carrier Construction is All in the Family." *Virginian-Pilot,* 11 July 2003, 43.

Shea, J. G. Ed. *The Operations of the French Fleet Under the Count de Grasse in 1781–1782*. New York: Da Capo Press, 1971.

Shettle, M. L., Jr. *United States Naval Air Stations of World War II*. Bowersville, Ga.: Schaertel Publishing Co., 1995.

"Shoving Off" in the U.S. Navy. Norfolk: G. L. Optical Co., 1921.

Simanton, John. "Wolves at the Gates of Norfolk: Operation Paukenschlag Gives America a Wake-up Call." *The Day Book* (January 1996):4–5.

Sinclair, Arthur. "How the Merrimac Fought the Monitor." *Hearst's Magazine,* December 1913, 884–94.

———. *Two Years on the Alabama.* Annapolis: Naval Institute Press, 1989.

Smelser, Marshall. *The Congress Founds the Navy 1787–1798.* South Bend: University of Notre Dame Press, 1959.

Smith, Alan E. "Refloating the USS Missouri." *U.S. Naval Institute Proceedings* (February 1951):181–95.

Smith, Dan. Ed. *From Here to There, Stories from a Mobile Virginia.* Richmond: Virginia Museum of Transportation, 1998.

Smith, Jay D. "Commodore James Barron: Guilty as Charged?" *U.S. Naval Institute Proceedings* (November 1967):79–85.

Soley, James R. "The Navy in the Peninsular Campaign." *Battles and Leaders of the Civil War* II (1887):264–70.

———. "The Union and Confederate Navies." *Battles and Leaders of the Civil War I* (1887):611–31.

Sontag, Sherry, and Christopher Drew. *Blind Man's Bluff: The Untold Story of American Submarine Espionage.* New York: Public Affairs, 1998.

Stern, Robert C. *The Lexington Class Carriers.* London: Arms and Armour Press, 1993.

Stevens, William O. *An Affair of Honor: the Biography of Commodore James Barron, USN.* Chesapeake, Va.: Norfolk County Historical Society, 1969.

Stewart, Robert A. *The History of Virginia's Navy of the Revolution.* Richmond, Va.: Mitchell & Hotchkiss, 1933.

Stewart, R. E. B. "The Norfolk Navy Yard." *Jamestown Magazine,* 14–18.

Stewart, William H. *History of Norfolk County, Virginia and Representative Citizens.* Chicago: Biographical Publishing Company, 1902.

Still, William N. "Everybody Sick with the Flu." *U.S. Naval Institute Proceedings* (April 2002):36–40.

———. *Iron Afloat: the story of the Confederate Armorclads.* Indianapolis: Vanderbuilt University Press, 1971.

———. Ed. *The Queenstown Patrol 1917: The Diary of Commander Joseph Knefler Taussig.* Newport: Naval War College Press, 1996.

Stillwell, Paul. *Battleship Arizona.* Annapolis: Naval Institute Press, 1991.

———. *Reminiscences of Admiral Alfred M. Pride, US Navy* (ret.), 234. U.S. Naval Institute Oral History Collection. Annapolis, 1984.

———. *Reminiscences of Admiral Harold Edson Shear, U.S. Navy* (ret.), 390. U.S. Naval Institute Oral History Collection. Annapolis, 1997.

———. *Reminiscences of Mr. Frank E. Sublett, Jr.*, 200. U.S. Naval Institute Oral History Collection. Annapolis, 1989.

———. *Reminiscences of Rear Admiral Jackson K. Parker, U.S. Navy* (ret), 500. U.S. Naval Institute Oral History Collection. Annapolis, 1987.

———. *Reminiscences of Rear Admiral Norvell G. Ward, U.S. Navy* (ret.), 398. U.S. Naval Institute Oral History Collection. Annapolis, 1996.

———. *Reminiscences of Vice Admiral Joe Williams, Jr., U.S. Navy* (ret.), 449. U.S. Naval Institute Oral History Collection. Annapolis, 2002.

———. *The Reminiscences of Vice Admiral Gerald E. Miller.* Annapolis: U.S. Naval Institute, 1983.

———. Ed. *The Golden Thirteen.* Annapolis: Naval Institute Press, 1993.

Tarter, Brent. "The Barron Family." *Virginia Cavalcade* (Autumn 1998):166–77.

Tate, J. R. "Covered Wagon Days." *Naval Aviation News* (December 1970):28–36.

Taylor, Theodore. *The Magnificent Mitscher.* Annapolis: Naval Institute Press, 1954.

Tazewell, William L. *Norfolk's Waters: An Illustrated Maritime History of Hampton Roads.* Woodland Hills, Calif.: Windsor Publications, 1982.

Thomas, Evan. *John Paul Jones: Sailor, Hero, Father of the American Navy.* New York: Simon & Schuster, 2003.

Thompson, Robert Means, and Richard Wainwright. Eds. *Confidential Correspondence of Gustavus Vasa Fox.* New York: De Vinne Press, 1920.

Trimble, William F. *Admiral William A. Moffett: Architect of Naval Aviation.* Washington, DC: Smithsonian Institution Press, 1994.

Tucker, George H. *Norfolk Highlights 1584–1881.* Norfolk: Norfolk Historical Society, 1972.

Tucker, Spencer C. *The Jeffersonian Gunboat Navy.* Columbia: University of South Carolina Press, 1993

Turnbull, Archibald D., and Clifford L. Lord. *History of United States Naval Aviation.* New Haven: Yale University Press, 1949.

Tyree, Chris "Surreal Nature of War, and Its Realities, Linger Long After." *Virginian-Pilot,* 27 July 2003.

United States Naval Amphibious Base Pictorial Review. Yearbook. Atlanta, Ga.: Albert Love Enterprises. 1953. Navy Department Library.

United States Naval Hospital, Portsmouth, Virginia. Yearbook. Philadelphia: Campus Publishing, 1944. Navy Department Library.

Van Deurs, George. *Anchors in the Sky: Spuds Ellyson, the First Naval Aviator.* San Rafael: Presidio Press, 1978.

VanPatten, E. H. "Hier: Aujourd'hui, Demain." *PEP* (Norfolk Supply Station Newspaper), 1.

VanSlyke, James C. "Comment/Discussion." *U.S. Naval Institute Proceedings* (April 1975):87.

Vogel, Steve "Bearing Reminders of Terror, USS Cole Returns to Action." *Virginian-Pilot,* 4 December 2003, 33

Waggoner, Walter H. "Keel is Laid for Super-Carrier." *New York Times,* 19 April 1949, 1.

Watson, Paul Barron. *The Tragic Career of Commodore James Barron.* New York: Coward-McCann. 1942.

Wertenbaker, Thomas J. *Norfolk: Historic Southern Port.* Durham: Duke University Press, 1931.

Wheeler, Gerald E. *Admiral William Veazie Pratt, USN*. Washington, DC: Department of the Navy, 1974.

Wheeler, Reginald. Ed. *The Road to Victory: A History of Hampton Roads Port of Embarkation in World War II*. New Haven: Yale University Press, 1946.

White, E. V. *The First Iron-clad Naval Engagement in the World*. New York: J. S. Ogilvie Publishing Company, 1906.

Whiting, Shayne "Due South." *The Day Book* I, no. 5(1995):5.

Whitman, Edmund C. "The School of War: U.S. Submarines in World War I." *Undersea Warfare* (Spring 2004).

———. "The Submarine Heritage of Simon Lake." *Undersea Warfare* (Fourth quarter 2002).

Wildenberg, Thomas. *Destined for Glory*. Annapolis: Naval Institute Press, 1998.

Williams, Francis L. *Matthew Fontaine Maury*. New Brunswick, N.J.: Rutgers University Press, 1963.

Wimmel, Kenneth. *Theodore Roosevelt and the Great White Fleet*. Dulles, Va.: Brassey's, 1998.

Wood, John T. "The First Fight of Iron-clads." *Battles and Leaders of the Civil War* I(1887):692–711.

Worden, J. L., and H. Aston Ramsay. *The Monitor and the Merrimac*. New York: Harper & Brothers Publishers, 1912.

Yarsinske, Amy W. "Without Us, They Don't Fly." *The Day Book* 2, no. 5(1996):1–7.

Yates, I. I. "A Navy Yard in War Time." *U.S. Naval Institute Proceedings* (May 1920):713–18.

Ziegler, Philip. *Mountbatten: A Biography*. New York: Alfred A. Knopf, 1985

Unpublished Sources

Barksdale, Arthur S., Jr. *History of the Norfolk Navy Yard in World War II*. 1945. Portsmouth Naval Shipyard Museum.

Burr, William, and Thomas S. Blanton. "The Submarines of October: US and Soviet Naval Encounters during the Cuban Missile Crisis." George Washington University National Security Archive (online). 31 October 2002.

Board of Directors Minutes. Norfolk Chamber of Commerce. Norfolk, 1913–1918.

Chang, Laurence, and E. Kornbluh. "The Cuban Missile Crisis 1962." George Washington University National Security Archives (online).

Chief of Naval Operations. *The United States Navy in Desert Shield/Desert Storm*. 15 May 1991. U.S. Navy Historical Center (online).

Gadsden, Eleanore P. "Compilation of Wheeler Information." Report. Stephen Decatur House Archives, Washington, DC, 1997.

Law, Joe M. *Norfolk Naval Shipyard: Its Remarkable History*. Norfolk Naval Shipyard Public Affairs Office, 2004.

Mosier, Joe. *The Battle of Craney Island: The Defense of Norfolk in the War of 1812*. Available at http://www.cronab.demon.co.uk. 1997.

Robertson, Lord. "Remarks at the Commissioning Ceremony of the New Allied Command Transformation." 19 June 2003. Available at http://www.nato.int.

Three Generations of Shipbuilding. Newport News, Va.: Newport News Shipbuilding and Drydock Co. Newport News, 1961.

Interviews and Correspondence with the Author

Dr. William Andrews
Capt. Ray Boucree, USN (ret.)
Ms. Miriam Browning
Mr. Gordon Calhoun
Mr. Roger Clapp
Rear Adm. Christopher W. Cole, USN (ret.)
Mr. Robert E. DeVary
Capt. Mike Duncan, USN (ret.)
Ms. Alice Hanes
Lt. Commander Ron Hill, USN
Mr. Jack Hornbeck
Capt. Mark A. Hugel, USN
Mr. Joe Judge
Mr. Jeff Kibben
Capt. Steve Laabs, USN (ret.)
Mr. Joe M. Law
Ms. Cynthia Malinick
Mr. Steve Milner
Mr. Joe Mosier
Capt. Gerry Nifontoff, USN (ret.)
Ms. Becky Poulliot
Capt. Milton L. Reynolds, USN (ret.)
Capt. Dana Roberts, USN (ret.)
Lt. (jg) Courtenay Smith, USN
Rear Adm. James L. Taylor, USN (ret.)
Rear Adm. Steve Turcotte, USN
Congressman G. William Whitehurst

INDEX

Numbers in *italics* indicate pages with figures.

ABOUT THE AUTHOR

Bruce Linder, a retired captain in the U.S. Navy, lived in Norfolk while growing up and commanded a Navy guided missile frigate there. A past winner of the Naval Institute's Arleigh Burke Essay Contest, Linder is the author of more than forty magazine and journal articles on naval history and naval policy. His first book published by the Naval Institute Press, *San Diego's Navy*, won the San Diego Book Award for best nonfiction book of 2001 in San Diego. He lives in Coronado, California, where he is employed as a defense and technology consultant.

The Naval Institute Press is the book-publishing arm of the U.S. Naval Institute, a private, nonprofit membership society for sea service professionals and others who share an interest in naval and maritime affairs. Established in 1873 at the U.S. Naval Academy in Annapolis, Maryland, where its offices remain today, the Naval Institute has members worldwide.

Members of the Naval Institute support the education programs of the society and receive the influential monthly magazine *Proceedings* and discounts on fine nautical prints and on ship and aircraft photos. They also have access to the transcripts of the Institute's Oral History Program and get discounted admission to any of the Institute-sponsored seminars offered around the country. Discounts are also available to the colorful bimonthly magazine *Naval History.*

The Naval Institute's book-publishing program, begun in 1898 with basic guides to naval practices, has broadened its scope to include books of more general interest. Now the Naval Institute Press publishes about one hundred titles each year, ranging from how-to books on boating and navigation to battle histories, biographies, ship and aircraft guides, and novels. Institute members receive significant discounts on the Press's more than eight hundred books in print.

Full-time students are eligible for special half-price membership rates. Life memberships are also available.

For a free catalog describing Naval Institute Press books currently available, and for further information about joining the U.S. Naval Institute, please write to:

Customer Service
U.S. Naval Institute
291 Wood Road
Annapolis, MD 21402-5034
Telephone: (800) 233-8764
Fax: (410) 269-7940
Web address: www.navalinstitute.org